RAMAKRISHNA
As We Saw Him

Sri Ramakrishna in samadhi during a kirtan at Keshab Sen's house in Calcutta. He is surrounded by Brahmo devotees, with Hriday, his nephew, supporting him.

(Photo taken on September 21, 1879)

RAMAKRISHNA
As We Saw Him

EDITED, TRANSLATED,
AND WITH A
BIOGRAPHICAL INTRODUCTION BY

Swami Chetanananda

VEDANTA SOCIETY OF ST. LOUIS

© VEDANTA SOCIETY OF ST. LOUIS, 1990
Second printing 1991

Printed and bound in the United States of America.

Library of Congress Cataloging-in-Publication Data

Chetanananda, Swami.
   Ramakrishna as we saw him / edited, translated, and with a
biographical introduction by Swami Chetanananda. — 1st ed.
      p.   cm.
   Includes bibliographical references.
   ISBN 0-916356-64-7 (alk. paper). — ISBN 0-916356-65-5 (pbk. :
alk. paper)
   1. Ramakrishna, 1836-1886. 2. Ramakrishna Mission—Biography.
3. Hindus—India—Biography. I. Title.
BL1280.292.R36C44 1990
294.5'55'092—dc20
[B]   90-32015

   Those who wish to learn in greater detail about the teachings contained
in this book may write to: Secretary, Vedanta Society of St. Louis, 205 South
Skinker Boulevard, St. Louis, Missouri 63105, U.S.A.

Contents

III. Brahmo Devotees and Admirers

IV. Appendix

Illustrations

Preface

Once a Catholic woman said to me that she had been regularly attending Mass for the last twenty-five years but was not experiencing any joy. She expressed a desire to learn the technique of Vedantic meditation without changing her religious faith. Observing her sincerity I told her: "Please practise meditation twice a day. There are various kinds of meditation, such as meditation on the form of God, on his divine qualities, on his message, or on his divine play. The infinite God takes a finite human form and plays in this world like one of us so that we can feel his presence and get a glimpse of his infinite nature. This is not a myth. It is a fact. The lives of Buddha, Christ, and Ramakrishna prove it. Human beings see these God-men or avatars with their eyes, hear their voices with their ears, touch their physical forms with their hands.

"If you want to feel the presence of God quickly," I told her, "practise meditation on the lila, or divine play, of God-men. Please close your eyes and mentally visualize Christ walking through the street. The multitude is following him. He enters the house of Simon. Mary Magdalene, a fallen woman, washes the feet of Jesus with her tears and then wipes them dry with her long hair. She opens an alabaster box and anoints his feet with scented ointment. The compassionate Christ blesses Mary, putting his hands on her head. It is a small episode in Christ's life. Try to visualize these scenes, one after another. Go slowly. Until the first scene has taken a luminous form in your mind, don't go to the next scene. After visualizing the entire episode, look at your clock. You will see that you have lived with Christ for twenty minutes, forgetting space, time, and causation. This is called meditation on the lila, or the divine play, of the Lord."

Truly we know very little about the personal or public life of Christ or Buddha. We read their messages in the Bible and the Tripitakas, but the message is not enough. When people get interested in the message, they want to know more about the messenger, and this is how they establish a relationship with him. So we try to get firsthand detailed information about him. We want to know about his surroundings, his relatives and friends, his daily routine, what kind of food he eats, how he acts with people. We want all the details, from his sense of humour to his method of teaching.

But God-men do not write about themselves. They are content to live their great lives and let others explain how their lives were led. Sri Ramakrishna did not like publicity at all. He specifically forbade one of his disciples to write his biography during his lifetime, saying that if it were published, his body would not last. Once Keshab Chandra Sen said to Sri Ramakrishna: "Sir, if you permit, I want to make your message known to the public. It will definitely do good to the people and bring peace to the world." Sri Ramakrishna replied in an ecstatic mood: "It is not the right time to spread the message of this place [meaning, his message] through lecturing and newspapers. The power and ideas which are within this body will automatically spread all over in the course of time. Hundreds of Himalayas will not be able to suppress that power." He then went into samadhi.

Romain Rolland, the great French writer, wrote in the beginning of his book The Life of Ramakrishna: "I am bringing to Europe, as yet unaware of it, the fruit of a new autumn, a new message of the Soul, the symphony of India, bearing the name of Ramakrishna. . . . The man whose image I here evoke was the consummation of two thousand years of the spiritual life of three hundred million people."

Once Swami Vivekananda, the foremost disciple of Sri Ramakrishna, said, "It was not the words of Sri Ramakrishna but the life he lived that was wanted, and that is yet to be written." I have tried to uncover that hidden personal life by translating and editing these precious reminiscences, which were either written or told by the Master's relatives, disciples, and admirers. Some of these people lived with him twenty-four hours a day and others stayed with him occasionally. These people actually witnessed the Master's divine play, and they left these wonderful reminiscences for future generations so that every detail of his God-intoxicated life would be available to us. Readers will find much information about Sri Ramakrishna in this book, and it could be considered a sequel to The Gospel of Sri Ramakrishna and Sri Ramakrishna, The Great Master.

For the last several years I have done extensive research and collected these spiritual treasures for my personal meditation and also because I strongly believe they will help many people. At the end of each section the sources are given. Also, for the sake of readability and uniformity, I have edited some of the materials from Sri Ramakrishna, The Great Master and other books and magazines. In a few places the same story was told by different people, but I did not eliminate the repetition because it would have disrupted the continuity of thought.

Materials were collected from so many sources that it is difficult to mention each publisher's name. However, I thankfully acknowledge these important ones: Advaita Ashrama (Calcutta), Ramakrishna Math (Madras), Udbodhan (Calcutta), Ramakrishna Vedanta Math (Calcutta), Vedanta Press (Hollywood), Ramakrishna-Vivekananda Center (New York), Ananda Ashrama (Cohasset), Srima Trust (Chandigarh), General Printers and Publishers (Calcutta), and Karuna Prakashani (Calcutta).

I am grateful to the Vedanta students who helped edit and type the manuscript.

Finally, I must mention one thing: While working on this project, this verse of the Gita (12.8) arose in my mind again and again: "Fix your mind on me alone, rest your thought on me alone, and in me alone you will live hereafter. Of this there is no doubt." What a wonderful reassurance! To me it is God's promise to all of us.

Chetanananda
St. Louis, U.S.A.

Sri Ramakrishna in samadhi

(Photo taken at the studio of the Bengal Photographers,
Calcutta, on December 10, 1881)

Sri Ramakrishna

Blessed is the country where Sri Ramakrishna was born, blessed are the parents who took care of the Divine Child, blessed are the people who, without seeing him, have inherited his invaluable spiritual legacy, and thrice blessed are the few who saw him, heard his words, touched him, talked with him, and lived with him. "In the life of Ramakrishna, the Man-God," wrote Romain Rolland, "I am about to relate the life of this Jacob's ladder, whereon the twofold unbroken life of the Divine in man ascends and descends between heaven and earth."

Sri Ramakrishna was born on February 18, 1836, in Kamarpukur, a small village sixty miles northwest of Calcutta. His father, Khudiram Chattopadhyay, and mother, Chandramani, were very devoted to God, and both had visions about their son before he was born. Sri Ramakrishna grew up in Kamarpukur and was sent to the village school where he learned to read and write, but he soon lost interest in this "bread-earning education."

When he was six or seven years old he had his first superconscious experience. "One morning," he recalled in later life, "I took some puffed rice in a small basket and was eating it while I walked along the narrow ridges of the rice fields. In one part of the sky a beautiful black cloud appeared, heavy with rain. I was watching it and eating the rice. Very soon the cloud covered almost the whole sky. And then a flock of cranes came flying. They were as white as milk against that black cloud. It was so beautiful that I became absorbed in the sight. Then I lost consciousness of everything outward. I fell down and the rice was scattered over the ground. Some people saw this and came and carried me home."

Khudiram died in 1843. Sri Ramakrishna keenly felt the loss of his father and became more indrawn and meditative. Sometimes he used to go to the nearby cremation ground alone and practise spiritual disciplines there. He also visited the rest house in the village where pilgrims, especially monks, would stop on their way to Puri. He learned from them many songs and prayers. There were, moreover, some friends with whom he played, and together they often sang and acted out religious dramas. When he was nine years old, following the brahminical tradition, he was invested with the sacred thread, which allowed him to perform ritualistic worship. Gradually he began to help the household by conducting the worship of the family deities.

Sri Ramakrishna moved to Calcutta in 1852 to assist his elder brother, Ramkumar, who was conducting a school and performing ritualistic worship in private homes for a living. On May 31, 1855, Ramkumar officiated at the dedication ceremony of the Kali temple of Dakshineswar, which had been founded by Rani Rasmani, a wealthy woman of Calcutta. Sri Ramakrishna was present on that occasion. Soon after this he moved to Dakshineswar, which was just a few miles north of Calcutta, and in time he became a priest in the temple.

Sri Ramakrishna now began his spiritual journey in earnest. While performing the worship of the Divine Mother, he questioned: "Are you true, Mother, or is it all a fabrication of my mind – mere poetry without reality? If you do exist, why can't I see you?" As days passed, Sri Ramakrishna's yearning for God became more and more intense, and he prayed and meditated almost twenty-four hours a day. One day he became desperate. As he later described it: "In my agony I said to myself, 'What is the use of this life?' Suddenly my eyes fell on the sword that hangs in the temple. I decided to end my life with it then and there. Like a madman I ran to it and seized it. And then – I had a marvellous vision of the Mother and fell down unconscious."

After this it was not possible for Sri Ramakrishna to continue the worship in the temple. His relatives thought that he had become mad, so they brought him back to Kamarpukur and arranged his marriage. In 1859 he was married to Sarada Mukhopadhyay, a young girl from the neighbouring village of Jayrambati. Sri Ramakrishna returned to Dakshineswar in 1860 and was again caught up in a spiritual tempest. He forgot his home, wife, family, body, and surroundings. He once described his experiences of that period:

No sooner had I passed through one spiritual crisis than another took its place. It was like being in the midst of a whirlwind – even my sacred thread was blown away. I could seldom keep hold of my dhoti [cloth]. Sometimes I would open my mouth, and it would be as if my jaws reached from heaven to the underworld. "Mother!" I would cry desperately. I felt I had to pull her in, as a fisherman pulls in fish with his dragnet. A prostitute walking the street would appear to me to be Sita, going to meet her victorious husband. An English boy standing cross-legged against a tree reminded me of the boy Krishna, and I lost consciousness. Sometimes I would share my food with a dog. My hair became matted. Birds would perch on my head and peck at the grains of rice which had lodged there during the worship. Snakes would crawl over my motionless body.

An ordinary man couldn't have borne a quarter of that tremendous fervour; it would have burnt him up. I had no sleep at all for six long years. My eyes lost the power of winking. I stood in front of a mirror and tried to close my eyelids with my finger — and I couldn't! I got frightened and said to Mother: "Mother, is this what happens to those who call on you? I surrendered myself to you, and you gave me this terrible disease!" I used to shed tears — but then, suddenly, I'd be filled with ecstasy. I saw that my body didn't matter — it was of no importance, a mere trifle. Mother appeared to me and comforted me and freed me from my fear.

Bhairavi Brahmani, a Tantric nun, came to Dakeshineswar in 1861 and initiated Sri Ramakrishna into tantra sadhana [disciplines]. Later he practised vatsalya bhava [the attitude of a parent towards the Divine Child] under Jatadhari, a Vaishnava monk, and after that, madhura bhava [the attitude of a lover towards the Divine Beloved]. Again, in 1864 he was initiated into sannyasa [monastic vows] by Tota Puri, a Vedanta monk, and he attained nirvikalpa samadhi, the culmination of spiritual practices. In that state the aspirant realizes his oneness with Brahman, the Ultimate Reality.

In 1866 Sri Ramakrishna practised Islam under the guidance of a Sufi named Govinda Roy. He later told his disciples: "I devoutly repeated the name of Allah, and I said their prayers five times a day. I spent three days in that mood, and I had the full realization of the sadhana of their faith." Furthermore, in 1874 he had a vision of the Madonna and the Child Jesus in the parlour of Jadu Mallik's garden house in Dakshineswar. A few days later, while walking in the Panchavati, he saw a foreign-looking person coming towards him. The man had a beautiful face with large, brilliant eyes. As Sri Ramakrishna pondered who this stranger could be, a voice within said: "This is Jesus Christ, the great yogi, the loving son of God, who was one with his Father, and who shed his heart's blood and suffered tortures for the salvation of mankind." Jesus then embraced Sri Ramakrishna and merged into his body. Thus, after realizing God in different religions, Sri Ramakrishna proclaimed, "As many faiths, so many paths."

Sri Ramakrishna met many well-known people of his time, such as Michael Madhusudan Datta, Devendra Nath Tagore, Dayananda Saraswati, Ishwar Chandra Vidyasagar, Dr. Mahendralal Sarkar , Bankim Chatterjee, Joseph Cook, Mr. Williams, Mr. Missir, and others. In 1875

Sri Ramakrishna met Keshab Chandra Sen, a leader of the Brahmo Samaj. Many people learned about the saint of Dakshineswar through Keshab's writings in the Brahmo journals. Between 1879 and 1885 the monastic and lay disciples came to Sri Ramakrishna. He trained them so that they could carry on his mission, and he made Swami Vivekananda their leader.

Sri Ramakrishna's message to the modern world was: "Do not care for doctrines; do not care for dogmas or sects or churches or temples. They count for little compared with the essence of existence in each man, which is spirituality; and the more a man develops it, the more power he has for good. Earn that first, acquire that, and criticize no one; for all the doctrines and creeds have some good in them. Show by your lives that religion does not mean words or names or sects, but that it means spiritual realization."

When the flower blooms, bees come of their own accord. People from all over came to Sri Ramakrishna, and he sometimes would talk about God as much as twenty hours a day. This continued for years. His intense love for humanity would not allow him to refuse to help anyone. In the middle of 1885 this tremendous physical strain resulted in throat cancer. When his disciples tried to stop him from teaching, he said: "I do not care. I will give up twenty thousand such bodies to help one man."

Sri Ramakrishna passed away on August 16, 1886, at a garden house in Cossipore, a suburb of Calcutta. Romain Rolland stated: "The man himself was no more. His spirit had departed to travel along the path of collective life in the veins of humanity."

I
Relatives and Monastic Disciples

Sri Sarada Devi at the age of forty-five
(Photo taken at Calcutta in 1898)

1

Sri Sarada Devi

Sri Sarada Devi (1853-1920), also called Holy Mother, was the spiritual consort of Sri Ramakrishna. She was married to him at an early age, and when she was eighteen years old she came to the temple garden of Dakshineswar to live near him and serve him. Because of her long and close association with the Master, her reminiscences are especially valuable. After his passing away she continued the spiritual ministry which he began.

The Source

The Master used to say that his body had come from Gaya. When his mother passed away he asked me to offer *pindam* [funeral cakes] at Gaya. I replied that I was not entitled to perform those rites when the son himself was alive. The Master replied: "No, no, you are entitled to do it. Under no circumstances can I go to Gaya. If I go, do you think it will be possible for me to return?"[1] So I did not want him to go there. And later on I performed the rites at Gaya.

The Master, a Perfectionist

When the Master came to Kamarpukur with indigestion I was only a child-wife. He would get up while it was still rather dark and say to me, "Prepare such-and-such dishes for me tomorrow," and we used to cook them for him. One day we ran out of a particular kind of spice and Lakshmi's mother [Sri Ramakrishna's sister-in-law] said: "Well then, carry on without it. Since we haven't got it, what else can we do?" The Master overheard this conversation and said: "What do you mean? If

---

[1] Tradition has it that Sri Ramakrishna's birth was preceded by a vision his father had at Gaya of Vishnu, who announced that he would be born as his son. Hence, the spiritual association Sri Ramakrishna had with Gaya was likely to overwhelm him if he went there. Gaya is also associated with Buddha and Chaitanya as the turning point in their lives.

you are out of that spice, why do you not send somebody to buy a pice worth? One should not omit things that are necessary. Don't you know that it is for this particular flavouring in your curries that I left the delicious dishes and the thickened milk of Dakshineswar and came here? And now you want to leave out the flavouring!" Lakshmi's mother felt ashamed and immediately sent for the spices.

Cooking for the Master

One day the Master and Hriday [Ramakrishna's nephew] were eating together. Lakshmi's mother and I would cook at Kamarpukur. She was an excellent cook. The Master tasted something she had prepared and remarked, "Hridu, the person who cooked this is a specialist." Then he ate something that I had cooked and said, "And this one is a quack." At this Hriday replied: "True, but the quack is at hand and you have only to call her, whereas the specialist is very expensive and not always available. The quack is at your beck and call at all times." The Master said: "Quite right. She is always there."

One day at Dakshineswar the Master asked me to cook something nice for Naren. I prepared moog dal [a type of lentil] and chapatis [unleavened bread]. After the meal he asked Naren, "How did you like it?" Naren replied, "Quite nice, just like invalid's food." Then the Master said to me: "What was that you cooked for him? Next time prepare chana dal and thicker chapatis for him." And I did so. Naren ate it and was highly pleased.

An Ideal Husband

The Master said about me: "Her name is Sarada. She is Saraswati [the goddess of learning]. That is why she loves to adorn herself." He said to Hriday: "Go and see how much money there is in your chest. Have a pair of beautiful armlets made for her." The Master was ill at that time, and yet he had those armlets made at a cost of three hundred rupees. But he would not touch money himself.

My mother would grieve, "I have married my Sarada to such a crazy husband that she can't enjoy ordinary married life or have any children and hear them call her mother." One day the Master heard her and said: "Don't grieve over that, Mother. Your daughter will have so many children, you will see, that her ears will ache at hearing the cry of 'Mother.'" He was quite right. Whatever he said has come to pass.

*   *   *

The Master was interested in nothing but God. When I asked him what I should do with the saris, conchshell bangles, and other things with which he had worshipped me when he performed the *Shodashi*

Puja,[2] he said after a little thought, "Well, you can give them to your own mother" — my father was still living — "but be careful that when making the gifts, you don't look upon her as your personal mother but as the Mother of the Universe." I did so. Such was his teaching.

The Master's Manners and Thoughtfulness

How kind was the Master's behaviour to me! He never spoke a single word that could hurt me. One day at Dakshineswar I carried his food to his room and, thinking it was Lakshmi [his niece], he said, "Shut the door as you go out," addressing me familiarly as *tui.*[3] I replied, "All right." Hearing my voice, he was startled and cried: "Oh, it is you! I thought it was Lakshmi. Please don't mind." I answered, "What does it matter?" He never showed any disrespect towards me, and he was always most considerate of my welfare.

One day he brought me some strands of jute and said: "Twist these into hangers for me, please. I want to keep sweets and luchis [fried bread] in them for the boys." I made the hangers for him and used the leftover rough fibres as stuffing for a pillow. I placed a mat over some sackcloth and slept with this jute pillow under my head. I slept no worse then than I do now with these fine mattresses and pillows. There is no difference.

Sri Ramakrishna's Childlike Nature

When the Master was staying at Dakshineswar, Rakhal [Swami Brahmananda] and other devotees were very young. One day Rakhal came to the Master and said that he was very hungry. The Master went to the Ganga and cried out: "Oh Gaurdasi, come here! My Rakhal is hungry." At that time there was no refreshment stall at Dakshineswar. A little later a boat was seen coming up the Ganga. It anchored at the temple ghat. Balaram Babu, Gaurdasi, and some other devotees came out of the boat with some rasagollas [sweet cheese balls]. The Master was very happy and shouted for Rakhal. He said: "Come here. Here are sweets. You said you were hungry." Rakhal became angry and remarked, "Why are you broadcasting my hunger?" The Master said: "What is the harm? You are hungry. You want something to eat. What is wrong in speaking about it?" The Master had a childlike nature.

---

[2] This refers to the occasion when the Master worshipped Holy Mother as a manifestation of the Divine Mother.

[3] In the Bengali language there are three forms of the second personal pronoun. When addressing a revered elder, *apani* is used. To a person of equal rank and age, one says *tumi*. But the familiar form, *tui*, is used only when speaking to juniors or servants. Thus it would have been considered disrespectful had the Master knowingly addressed Holy Mother in this manner.

Rakhal's Parents

The Master said to Rakhal's father, "A good apple tree begets only good apples." In this way he would satisfy him. When Rakhal's father would come to Dakshineswar the Master would carefully feed him delicious things. The Master was afraid that he would take the boy away. Rakhal had a stepmother. When she would come to Dakshineswar the Master used to tell Rakhal: "Show her everything. Take good care of her so that she will think her son loves her dearly."

Vrinda, the Maidservant

Vrinda was by no means an easy woman. A fixed number of luchis [fried bread] was set aside for her refreshment. She would be extremely abusive if that was found wanting. She would say: "Look at these sons of gentlemen! They have eaten my share also. I do not get even a few sweets."

The Master was afraid lest those words should reach the ears of the young devotees. One day, early in the morning, he came to the nahabat [the concert tower, where Holy Mother lived] and said: "Well, I have given Vrinda's luchis to others. Please prepare some for her. Otherwise she will become abusive. One must avoid wicked persons."

As soon as Vrinda came I said to her: "Well, Vrinda, there is no refreshment for you today. I am just preparing luchis." She said: "That's all right. Please do not take the trouble. You may give me raw food-stuffs." I gave her flour, butter, potatoes, and other vegetables.

The Red Flower

Once at Dakshineswar a girl named Asha picked a beautiful red flower from a bush which had very dark leaves. Holding the flower she wept and kept saying: "What is this! Why should such a lovely red flower have such dark leaves? O Lord, how wonderful is your creation!" Seeing her tears, the Master asked: "What is the matter? Why are you weeping?" She was quite unable to explain but continued to cry until the Master comforted her with many words.

An Appreciation

One day while living at Dakshineswar I made a big garland of seven strands with some jasmine and red flowers [rangan or ixora]. I soaked the garland in water in a stone bowl and the buds quickly turned into full blossoms. I then sent the garland to the Kali temple to adorn the image of the Divine Mother. The ornaments were taken off Kali's body and she was decorated with the garland.

The Master came to the temple. He at once fell into an ecstatic mood seeing the beauty of Kali so much enhanced by the flowers. Again and again he said: "Ah! These flowers are nicely set off against the dark complexion of the Divine Mother! Who made the garland?" Someone mentioned me. He said, "Go and bring her to the temple." As I came near the steps I found some of the men devotees there — Balaram Babu, Suren Babu, and others. I felt extremely bashful and became anxious to hide myself. I took shelter behind the maid Vrinda, and was about to go up to the temple by the back steps. The Master immediately noticed this and called out: "Don't use those steps. The other day a fisherwoman was climbing those steps and slipped. She had a terrible accident and fractured her bones. Come by these front steps." The devotees heard those words and made room for me. I entered the temple and found the Master singing, his voice trembling with love and devotion.

The Master's Compassion

A man had a mistress. One day the woman came to the Master and said with repentance: "That man ruined me. Then he robbed me of my money and jewellery." The Master was aware of the innermost contents of people's minds, but still he wanted to hear everything from their own lips. He said to the woman: "Is it true? But he used to give us grand talks about devotion." In the end the woman confessed to him all her sins and was thus released from their evil effects.

God and Mammon

What is there in money, my child? The Master could not touch it. His hand would recoil at the touch of money. He said to Ramlal [Sri Ramakrishna's nephew]: "This world is illusory. Had I known it to be otherwise, I would have covered your Kamarpukur village with leaves of gold. But I know the world is impermanent. God alone is real."

Divine Help

Blood dysentery is not a trifling disease. The Master would often be down with it, especially during the rainy season. At one time he was rather seriously ill. I was attending on him. A woman from Varanasi had recently come to Dakshineswar, and she suggested a remedy. I followed her directions and the Master was soon cured. After this the woman could not be found. I never met her again. She had really helped me a great deal. I inquired about her at Varanasi but could not find her. We often saw that whenever the Master required something, people would come of themselves to Dakshineswar and then disappear just as suddenly.

A Ghost Story

One day the Master went to Beni Pal's garden house [in Sinthi] with Rakhal. He was strolling in the garden when a spirit came to him and said: "Why did you come here? We are being scorched. We cannot endure your presence. Leave this place at once." How could it stand his purity and blazing holiness? The Master walked away with a smile and did not disclose it to anybody.

Immediately after supper he asked someone to call for a carriage, though it had been previously arranged that he would spend the night there. A carriage was brought and he returned to Dakshineswar that very night. Hearing the sound of the carriage near the gate, I strained my ears and heard the Master speaking with Rakhal. I was startled. I thought: "I do not know if he has taken his supper. If not, where can I get food at this late hour?" I always kept something in store for him, at least farina. He sometimes asked for food at odd hours. But I was quite sure of his not coming back that night and so my store was empty. All the gates of the temple garden were barred and locked. It was one o'clock in the morning. He clapped his hands and began to repeat the names of God, and after a while someone opened the gate. Meanwhile I was anxiously thinking about what to do in case he was hungry. As he came in he shouted to me: "Don't be anxious about my food. I have finished my supper." Then he narrated to Rakhal the story of the ghost. Rakhal was startled and said: "Dear me! It was really wise of you not to have told me about it at that time. Otherwise my teeth would have been set on edge through fear. Even now I am seized with fear."

The Picture of Sri Ramakrishna

Several prints were made of the Master's first photograph. The brahmin cook took one of them. The picture was at first very dark, just like the image of Kali, and therefore it was given to the brahmin. When he left Dakshineswar for some place — I do not remember where — he gave it to me. I kept the photograph with the pictures of other gods and goddesses and worshipped it. At that time I lived on the ground floor of the nahabat. One day the Master came there, and at the sight of the picture he said, "Hello, what is all this?" Lakshmi and I had been cooking under the staircase. Then I saw the Master take in his hand the bel leaves and flowers kept there for worship and offer them to the photograph. He worshipped the picture. This is the same picture. That brahmin never returned, so the picture remained with me.[4]

---

[4] This picture is now in the shrine of Holy Mother's house, Udbodhan, Calcutta.

What Did the Master Look Like?

His complexion was like the colour of gold — like that of *harital* [a yellow orpiment]. It blended with the colour of the gold amulet which he wore on his arm. When I rubbed him with oil I could clearly see a lustre coming out of his entire body. People looked at him wonderstruck when he went with slow, steady steps to the Ganga to take his bath. And when he came out of his room at the temple, people stood in line and said to one another, "Ah, there he goes!" It also happened at Kamarpukur. Men and women looked at him with mouths agape whenever he chanced to come out of his house. One day he went for a walk in the direction of the canal known as Bhutir Khal. The women who had gone there to fetch water stared at him and said, "There goes the Master!" The Master was annoyed at this and said to Hriday, "Well, Hridu, please put a veil over my head at once."

The Master was fairly stout. Mathur Babu had given him a low stool on which to sit. It was rather wide, but it was not quite big enough to hold him comfortably when he sat cross-legged on it to eat his meals.

I never saw the Master sad. He was joyous in the company of everyone, whether a boy of five or an old man. I never saw him morose, my child. Ah, what happy days those were! At Kamarpukur he would get up early in the morning and tell me: "Today I shall eat this particular dish. Please cook it for me." With the other women of the family I would arrange his meal accordingly. After a few days he said: "What has come over me? The moment I get up from sleep I say: 'What shall I eat? What shall I eat?'" Then he said to me: "I have no desire for any particular food. I shall eat whatever you cook for me."

What a Detached Mind!

One day Hazra said to the Master: "Why do you constantly long for Narendra and the other youngsters? They are quite happy by themselves, eating, drinking, and playing. You had better fix your mind on God. Why should you be attached to them?" At these words the Master took his mind away from the young disciples completely and merged it in the thought of God. Instantly he entered into samadhi. His beard and hair stood straight on end like the kadamba flower. Just imagine what kind of a man the Master was! His body became hard like a wooden statue. Ramlal, who was attending on him, said repeatedly, "Please be your former self again." At last his mind came down to the normal plane. It was only out of compassion for people that he kept his mind on the material plane.

Sri Ramakrishna's Renunciation

Once there was a mistake in the accounts relating to the Master's salary. I asked him to talk to the manager of the temple about it, but he said: "What a shame! Shall I bother myself about accounts?" Once he said to me: "He who utters the name of God never suffers from any misery. No need to speak about you!" These are his very words. Renunciation was his ornament.

*   *   *

You will gain everything if you but take refuge in the Master. Renunciation alone was his splendour. We utter his name and eat and enjoy things because he renounced all. People think that his devotees also must be very great, as he was a man of such complete renunciation.

Ah, me! One day he came to my room in the nahabat. He had no spices in his small bag. He used to chew them now and then. I gave him some to chew there and also handed over to him a few packed in paper to take to his room. He then left, but instead of going to his room, he went straight to the embankment of the Ganga. He did not see the way, nor was he conscious of it. He was repeating, "Mother, shall I drown myself?" I became restless with agony. The river was full to the brim. I was then a young woman and would not go out of my room, and I could not see anyone around. Whom could I send to him? At last I found a brahmin belonging to the Kali temple coming in the direction of my room. Through him I called Hriday, who was then taking his meal. He left his plate, ran to the Master, caught hold of him, and brought him back to his room. A moment more and he would have dropped into the Ganga.

Because I put a few spices in his hand he could not find his way. A holy man must not lay things by. His renunciation was one hundred percent.

*   *   *

Once a Vaishnava monk came to the Panchavati. At first he showed a great deal of renunciation. But, alas, finally like a rat, he began to pull and gather various things — pots, cups, jar, grain, rice, pulses, and so forth. The Master noticed it and said one day: "Poor thing! This time he is going to be ruined!" He was about to be entangled in the snare of maya. The Master advised him strongly about renunciation, and further, asked him to leave the place. Then he went away.

The Master's Love for the Devotees

Once Balaram's wife was ill. The Master said to me, "Go to Calcutta and visit her." "How can I go?" I said. "I don't see any carriage or other conveyance here." The Master replied in an excited voice: "What!

Balaram's family is in such trouble and you hesitate to go! You will walk to Calcutta. Go on foot." At last a palanquin was brought and I set out from Dakshineswar. Twice I visited her during her illness. On another occasion I went on foot at night from Shyampukur.

*   *   *

The younger Naren used to come to the Master. He was thin and dark, with pockmarks on his face, and the Master was very fond of him. When Patu and Manindra came to see the Master, they were very young, about ten or eleven years old. Once at the Cossipore garden during the Holi festival [a spring festival associated with Krishna] everybody had gone out to play with abir [red powder], but these two would not go. They began to fan the Master, changing hands frequently. They were so young that they could not manage it. They also massaged the Master's legs. The Master had a cough, so his head ached and he needed constant fanning. He kept saying to them: "Go away now. Go downstairs and play with abir. Everybody has gone." But Patu said: "No, sir, we are not going. We are staying here. How can we go away and leave you?"

They refused to go. The Master could not check his tears. He said: "Oh, my dear, they are my Ramlala [the child Ramachandra], here to take care of me. They are mere children, but they will not leave me, even to enjoy themselves!"

The Meaning of the Master's Suffering

At the time of his illness, the Master expressed a desire to eat an amlaki fruit. Durga Charan procured some after searching for three days without any food or sleep. The Master then asked him to take his meal, and he himself took some rice in order that the food would be prasad. I said to the Master: "You are taking rice quite well. Why, then, should your meal consist only of farina pudding? You should take rice rather than pudding." "No, no," he said. "I would rather take farina during these last days of my life." It was such unbearable suffering for him to eat even the farina! Every now and then he would throw it out through his nose.

The Master used to say: "I have been suffering for all of you. I have taken upon myself the miseries of the whole world." The Master suffered as he had taken on himself the sins of Girish.

The Effect of Karma

Karma [action] alone is responsible for our misery and happiness. Even the Master had to suffer from the effect of karma. Once his elder brother was drinking water while delirious. The Master snatched the glass out of his hand after he had drunk just a little. The brother became angry and said: "You have stopped me from drinking water. You will also suffer likewise. You will also feel such pain in your throat." The Master said: "Brother, I did not mean to injure you. You are ill. Water will harm you. That is why I have taken the glass away. Why have you, then, cursed me in this manner?" The brother said, weeping: "I do not know, Brother. Those words have come from my mouth. They cannot but bear fruit." At the time of his illness the Master told me, "I have got this ulcer in my throat because of that curse." I said to him in reply, "How can a person possibly live if such a thing as this can happen to you?" The Master remarked: "My brother was a righteous man. His words must come true. Can the words of anyone and everyone be thus fulfilled?"

The result of karma is inevitable. But by repeating the name of God you can lessen its intensity. If you were destined to have a wound as wide as a ploughshare, you will get a pinprick at least. The effect of karma can be counteracted to a great extent by japam and austerities.

An Accident

The Master used to have great fun with the boys. Naren [Swami Vivekananda] and Baburam [Swami Premananda] would roll on the ground with sidesplitting laughter. Once while living in the Cossipore garden I was climbing the steps, carrying a bowl of milk, when I felt giddy and fell. All the milk was spilled and my heel was dislocated. Naren and Baburam came running and took care of me. There was a great inflammation of the foot. The Master heard of the accident and said to Baburam: "Well, Baburam, it is a nice mess I am in now. Who will cook my food? Who will feed me now?" He was then ill with cancer of the throat and lived only on farina pudding. I used to make it and feed him in his room in the upper story of the house. I had a ring in my nose then. The Master touched his nose and made a sign of a ring by making a circle with his finger in order to indicate me. He then said, "Baburam, can you put her [*making the sign*] in a basket and carry her on your shoulder to this room?" Naren and Baburam were convulsed with sidesplitting laughter. Thus he used to cut jokes with them. After three days the swelling subsided. Then they helped me to go upstairs with his meals. Golap-ma made the pudding during those three days and Naren fed him.

Body and Soul

Everything — husband, wife, or even the body — is only illusory. These are all shackles of illusion. Unless you can free yourself from these bondages you will never be able to go to the other shore of the world. Even this attachment to the body, the identification of the self with the body, must go. What is this body, my child? It is nothing but three pounds of ashes when it is cremated. Why so much vanity about it? However strong or beautiful this body may be, its culmination is in those three pounds of ashes. And still people are so attached to it. Glory to God!

The Master would say: "Musk forms in the navel of the deer. Being fascinated with its smell, the deer run here and there. They do not know where the fragrance comes from. Likewise, God resides in the human body and man does not know it. Therefore he searches everywhere for bliss, not knowing that it is already within him. God alone is real. All else is false."

Practise, Practise, Practise!

Can one have the vision of God every day? The Master used to say: "Does an angler catch a big carp every day the moment he sits with his rod? Arranging everything about him, he sits with the rod and concentrates. Once in a while a big carp swallows the hook, but many times he is disappointed. Don't relax the practices for that reason." Do more japam.

Why are you so restless, my child? Why don't you stick onto what you have? Always remember, "I have at least a Mother, if none else." Do you remember those words of the Master? He said he would reveal himself to all that take refuge in him — reveal himself at least on their last day. He will draw all to himself.

"I Will Be Worshipped in Every House"

Once when the Master was lying ill at Cossipore a few devotees brought some offerings for Mother Kali at the Dakshineswar temple. On hearing that the Master was at Cossipore they offered everything they had brought before a picture of the Master, and then partook of the prasad. When the Master heard this, he remarked, "All these things were brought for the great Mother of the Universe, and they have offered them here [*meaning himself*]!" I was frightened very much at this and thought: "He is suffering from this dangerous disease. Who knows what might happen? What a calamity! Why did they do it?"[5]

The Master too referred to this incident again and again. Afterwards, at a late hour in the night, he said to me: "You will see how in the course of time I will be worshipped in every house. You will see everyone accepting this [*meaning himself*]. This is surely going to happen." That was the only day I heard him using the first person pronoun with

---

[5] It is sacrilegious to offer a man the gifts that are meant for a deity, and hence this fear that it may cause some misfortune.

reference to himself. Usually he would speak of himself not as "I" or "me," but as "this case" or as "belonging to this," pointing to his body.

Longing and Vision

He who eagerly prays to God will see him. One of our devotees, Tejachandra Mittra, passed away. What a sincere soul he was! The Master used to frequent his house. Someone had deposited two hundred rupees with Tejachandra. One day he was robbed of that amount by a pickpocket in the tram car. He discovered the loss after some time and suffered terrible mental agony. He came to the bank of the Ganga and prayed to the Master with tears in his eyes, "O Lord, what have you done to me?" He was not rich enough to make up that amount from his own pocket. As he was thus weeping he saw the Master appear before him and say: "Why do you weep so bitterly? The money is there under a brick on the bank of the Ganga." Tejachandra quickly removed the brick and really found there a bundle of banknotes. He narrated the incident to Sharat [Swami Saradananda]. Sharat said: "You are lucky to get the vision of the Master even now. But we do not see him." Why should Sharat and others like him see him anymore? They have seen him enough, and all their desires have been fulfilled.

Visions of the Master

When the Master passed away I also wanted to leave my body. He appeared before me and said: "No, you must remain here. There are many things to be done." I myself realized later on that this was true. I had so many things to do. The Master used to say: "The people of Calcutta live like worms crawling in darkness. You will guide them." He said that he would live for another hundred years in a subtle body, in the hearts of the devotees. He further said that he would have many devotees among white people.

After the passing away of the Master I was at first greatly frightened, for I wore a sari with thin red borders and had gold bangles on my wrist, which made me afraid of people's criticism.[6] One day the Master appeared before me and asked me to feed him khichuri [rice and lentils cooked together]. I cooked the dish and offered it to Raghuvir[7] in the temple. Then I mentally fed the Master with it.

---

[6] Hindu widows, according to traditional custom, are required to wear a white sari without any border and to give up all ornaments. Holy Mother at first wanted to follow this custom, but Sri Ramakrishna appeared in a vision and told her not to do so as he was not really dead.

[7] The tutelary deity of Sri Ramakrishna's family at Kamarpukur.

On my way to Vrindaban I saw the Master at the window of my train compartment and he said to me, "Take special care of the amulet lest you lose it." He had given me his own amulet, and I was wearing it on my arm. I used to worship it. Later I gave it to the Belur Math, and now they worship it there.

"In Every Age I Come Back"

The Master said he would come again after a hundred years. Meanwhile, for those hundred years he would live in the hearts of those who love him. Standing on the semicircular verandah of Dakshineswar, the Master said this, pointing towards the northwest. I told him I could not come again. Lakshmi also said she would not come again, even if she were chopped into shreds like tobacco leaves! The Master laughed and said: "How can you avoid coming? Our roots are twined together like the kalmi plant [a creeper that grows on the surface of a pond]. Pull one stem and the whole clump will come forward."

The Master used to say: "You have come to the garden to eat mangoes. Very well, eat them, enjoy them, and go. What does it matter to you how many branches and leaves there are?"

[From: *In the Company of Holy Mother*, by Her Direct Disciples (Calcutta: Advaita Ashrama), 1980; *Sri Sarada Devi, The Holy Mother*, by Swami Tapasyananda & Swami Nikhilananda (Madras: Sri Ramakrishna Math), 1958]

Lakshmi Devi, Sri Ramakrishna's niece

2

Lakshmi Devi

Lakshmi Devi (1864-1926) was the daughter of Sri Ramakrishna's brother Rameshwar. Soon after her marriage she became a widow and went to live at Dakshineswar with Sri Ramakrishna and Holy Mother. In the later part of her life she drew many disciples around her and inspired them with stories and teachings of the Master.

At Dakshineswar we [Holy Mother and Lakshmi] used to live in the nahabat [a small concert tower at the temple garden]. When the Master wished to indicate to his visitors about the Mother, he would make a circle with his finger at the tip of the nose. This was because the Mother wore a nose ring. He used to refer to the nahabat as a cage and to us as *Shuk-Sari* [two birds in Indian folklore who were adept in talking about Krishna's glories]. When fruits and sweets that had been offered to the Divine Mother were brought to the Master, he would remind Brother Ramlal: "Don't forget that there are two birds in that cage. Give them some fruits and peas." Newcomers would take the Master's words literally. Even Master Mahashay [the recorder of *The Gospel of Sri Ramakrishna*] did so at first.

Village women would come to visit the Mother, and sometimes the Master could overhear their conversation. Once he said to the Mother: "These women come and stroll by the goose pond. Seeing me they talk among themselves and I hear what they are saying. They say: 'This man is good, but one thing is strange! He does not sleep with his wife at night.' Please don't pay any heed to their talk. They are worldly women. They may teach you how to divert my mind towards the world through tricks or medicine. Please don't follow their advice. I have given myself completely to God." The Mother was embarrassed and reassured the Master: "Oh, no, no. I won't pay any attention to them."

How we managed in that tiny room of the nahabat, I sometimes wonder. It was the Master's divine play! Usually it was shared by Holy

Mother, another girl, and me. Sometimes Gopaler-ma, who was a large woman, or other women devotees from Calcutta would stay with us. Moreover, we had to store our groceries, cooking vessels, dishes, and even the water jar in that room. Since the Master had a weak stomach we also had to store the food for his special diet.

The Master did not sleep much at night. When it was still dark outside he would move around the temple garden, and while passing near the nahabat he would call: "O Lakshmi, O Lakshmi. Get up. Ask your aunt to get up also. How long will you sleep? It is almost dawn. The crows and cuckoos are about to sing. [*This is a sign of daybreak in tropical countries.*] Chant the name of the Divine Mother."

Sometimes in winter, when the Master would call me, Mother, while lying under her quilt, would whisper to me: "Keep quiet. He has no sleep in his eyes. It is not the right time to get up, and the birds have not yet started singing. Don't respond." But if the Master did not get any response, he would pour water under the doorsill, and since we slept on the floor we had to get up without delay. Even so, sometimes our beds got wet.

The Master lost some hair from the front of his head because of excessive heat in his body, and some of his hair and beard turned grey. He did not care to live long, to be an old man. He would say, "I don't want to hear people saying that there is an 'old monk' in Rasmani's temple garden." "Don't say that," the Mother replied. "You are not old. Do you think you are old enough to leave this world? Moreover, if you live here as an old monk, people will say a 'wise monk' lives in Rasmani's Kali temple." The Master replied: "Pooh! Who is going to call me a wise monk? Anyhow, I can't bear it if anybody calls me 'old fellow.'"

After a short period of marriage I became a widow and went back to my father's home. I was then a beautiful young girl. One day the Master told me: "Do your duties and practise religion at home. Do not travel to the holy places by yourself. Who knows who might harm you? Live with your aunt. Life in the world is not safe."

When the Master was in his village, every evening he sat by the door of his parental home, watching the people as they passed along the street. All the women had to go that way to bring water from the tank. They would come with their jugs and seeing him at the door, they would sit down in the little yard in front, with their water jugs beside them, and forget everything in the joy of hearing him talk or sing of God. Fearing lest they might be neglecting their duties, he asked about them. One girl said: "I have a cow. When I heard that you were coming, I cut straw enough to last a month and filled my room with it." To another he said,

"How is your baby?" "Oh! I forgot," she exclaimed. "I left it with a neighbour." She had walked more than a mile to come and see him.

One day the Master said to the women, "Now, today you must sing and I will listen." They all remained silent. Not one dared utter a sound. But there was one girl whom the Master loved very much, so much that whenever she did not come he would send for her. As soon as she saw that no one else would sing, she sang a song in a weak high-pitched, quavering voice. All the other girls began to laugh at her, but when she had finished, the Master was delighted. "See how great is her devotion," he exclaimed. "Just because I asked her, she has sung so frankly and simply. She alone among you has true devotion."

The Master could not stand to see women who were shameless and wanton. He said to the Mother: "Don't be like them. They have one leg under a bel tree and the other under a banyan tree. Their behaviour is shameless. Women must be unassuming. Modesty is the ornament of women."

Chinu Shankhari, who was well known in Kamarpukur, was a boy-hood friend of the Master. He was a devout Vaishnava and had acquired some supernatural powers through spiritual discipline. Holding the Master he would say, "Gadai, when I see you I think of Gauranga." Some of our Kamarpukur neighbours went to Dakshineswar for a holy bath in the Ganga, and they told the Master a story about Chinu's supernatural powers. They said that one day some guests came to Chinu's house and asked for food, expressing a desire to eat a sour preparation of fish with mango. Since it was not the season for mangoes, Chinu was very worried and prayed to the Lord that he might be able to fulfill the desire of his guests. At the last moment, unexpectedly and inexplicably, he obtained some mangoes and fed his guests with great joy.

The Master listened to the story, and when he went to Kamarpukur he said to Chinu: "Shame! Shame! Fie on your supernatural powers. Do not use them again. People will exploit you and disturb your spiritual life. Please don't pay any heed to those powers. Otherwise your mind will fall to a lower state."

The Master never visited Puri. One day Balaram Babu brought some prasad of Lord Jagannath. The Master touched it with his head and saluted the Lord. He was then in an ecstatic mood. After a while he said: "I went to the place of Jagannath. There everything is great and vast — the vast ocean and long, wide roads. If this body goes there, it will not come back."

When I was at Dakshineswar with the Mother, she told me that the Master had written a mantram on her tongue, and she suggested that I ask him to do the same for me. I said: "I am too shy to ask him. There are so many visitors in his room."

Then another day I went to salute the Master. I didn't say anything, but he asked me of his own accord, "What deity do you love most?" Delighted at his question, I replied, "Radha-Krishna." He then wrote the mantram on my tongue. I had a rosary of tulsi beads around my neck which Sister Prasanna of Kamarpukur's Laha family had given me with the comment that they were very becoming to me.

Sometime earlier the Mother and I had received some instructions about the worship of the Divine Mother from an old monk whose name was Swami Purnananda. He was a very handsome person, very calm and quiet. When the Mother told the Master about it, he said: "It is all right. I have given the right mantram to Lakshmi."

While I was in Dakshineswar I would sometimes remember Mother Shitala, who is another form of the Divine Mother and one of our family deities. At that time if sweets were presented to the Master he would say: "Feed these sweets to Lakshmi. It will be a grand offering to Mother Shitala, because Lakshmi is part of her." Once he asked Girish Babu to do this.

Whenever there was kirtan [devotional singing] in his room, the Master would ask Brother Ramlal to open the door facing the nahabat. He would say: "A current of devotion and bliss will flow here. If they do not see or hear, how will they learn?" The Mother used to watch through a tiny hole in the bamboo screen, and that made her happy. Sometimes the Master would comment with a laugh, "O Ramlal, the opening in your aunt's screen is getting bigger and bigger."

The Master used to tell the Mother and me stories from the Ramayana and the Mahabharata, such as the story of King Nala, and he would then question us to see if we had understood them. He would also make me repeat them, and afterwards he would remark with satisfaction, "That is why I call you a shuk [parrot]."

The Master always encouraged us to practise spiritual disciplines. He would tell us: "Pray unceasingly. Be sincere. Don't show your spiritual disciplines to others. If the character is not good, what good will japam do? Young women should be very careful. Be pure. The trees suck water from the earth through their roots, unperceived. Likewise, some people show a religious nature outwardly but secretly enjoy lustful things. Don't be a hypocrite."

One time he said to me: "If you cannot remember God, think of me. That will do."

All through his life the Master had stomach trouble. When Grandma [Sri Ramakrishna's mother] was living in Dakshineswar, the Master would salute her every morning. Grandma was a large woman and very beautiful, but she was also old-fashioned and very shy. Even before her youngest son [Sri Ramakrishna] she would cover her face with a veil. When he came she would ask him, "How is your stomach?" The Master would reply, "Not very good." Grandma would then advise: "Don't take the prasad of Mother Kali. [*It was very spicy food.*] As long as your stomach is not all right your wife will cook plain soup and rice for you. Please eat only that."

Sometimes the Master would get tired of eating invalid's food every day and would ask his mother to cook one or two dishes and season them as she used to do in Kamarpukur. So occasionally Grandma cooked for him and the Master enjoyed it.

The Master used to encourage women to cook. "It is a good occupation for the mind," he would say. "Sita was a good cook, and so were Draupadi and Parvati. Mother Lakshmi [the goddess of fortune] would herself cook and feed others."

After the death of her two older sons, Grandma became somewhat passive and withdrawn. Furthermore, she would not take her lunch until she had heard the noon whistle of the Alambazar Jute Mill. As soon as it sounded she would exclaim: "Oh! There is the whistle of heaven. That is the signal for offering food to Lakshmi and Narayana." A problem would arise on Sundays, however, when the jute mill was closed. No whistle was blown at noon, and consequently she would not eat. This worried the Master very much, and he would lament: "Oh dear! My old mother will refuse her food today and she will be weak." Brother Hriday would say to the Master: "Don't be anxious, Uncle. When Grandma is hungry she will eat of her own accord." But the Master would reply: "Oh no. I am her son. It is my duty to look after my old mother." With much coaxing the Master would persuade his mother to eat the prasad of Krishna.

One day Brother Hriday made a high-pitched sound by blowing through a pipe. He then said to Grandma: "There, Grandma, did you hear the whistle of heaven? Now please eat your food." But Grandma laughed and said: "Oh no. You made the sound with your pipe." Everyone laughed.

When Grandma passed away the Master wept.

The Mother used to carry the Master's meals to his room. Pointing to her, sometimes the Master would say in a joking manner: "Luckily, I have the shade of this tree. Otherwise, who would prepare food for me? Such a man who cannot manage his own cloth and he has married!"

One day I went with the Mother to carry the Master his food. Rakhal and others who were with him immediately left the room, leaving us alone there. The Master was lying on his bed in samadhi, but he looked so devoid of life that the Mother, having long been anxious for his health, began to weep, thinking he had left the body. Then she remembered that he had once said to her that if she ever found him in this state, she was just to touch his feet and that would bring him back. So she began to rub his feet. Rakhal and the others, hearing the weeping, hurried back into the room, and they too began to rub him vigourously.

This brought him back to consciousness and, opening his eyes, he asked with surprise what the matter was. Then, realizing their fears, he smiled and said: "I was in the land of the white people. Their skin is white, their hearts are white, and they are simple and sincere. It is a very beautiful country. I think I shall go there." "But you will get very hungry if you go there," the Mother replied with anxious solicitude. Then the Master struck his forehead with his hand two or three times and said to the Mother: "Oh! You are so foolish! You do not know anything."

One night the Master was filled with the spiritual mood of Radha and had so identified himself with her that he decided to go to the arbour to meet Krishna. Coming out of his room, he entered the rose garden. He had no outward consciousness. He soon got caught in the rose bushes and was scratched all over from the thorns, and there he stood. The night watchman found him and woke us. At once I went to the temple manager and brought him there. Many others, awakened by the noise, crowded around. The Mother also came there and burst into tears. This was the first time that she was seen in public. When the Master was carried to his room he said: "I am going to the arbour. Why are you troubling me? Let me go." After this, the Mother and I began to sleep in his room. A couple of days later, however, he said to us: "Why are you suffering this way? It is so hot now. You had better sleep in the nahabat." We obeyed.

Once the Master asked me to eat some of Mother Kali's prasad. I was reluctant to eat a piece of fish [because a Hindu widow is a strict vegetarian], but the Master insisted [knowing that Lakshmi was the goddess Shitala]. He said to me: "It is prasad. Don't hesitate. Eat. If you don't listen to me you will have to be born again. You may get an ugly, fat husband who will force you to lead a worldly life against your will." "Well," I said, "I certainly don't want to be involved in maya again. Perhaps it is better to eat this nonvegetarian prasad."

What love the Master had for the devotees! Once Balaram Babu came to Dakshineswar by boat with his wife and children. They visited with the Master for a while, and they all left for Calcutta in the afternoon. The Master himself went to the chandni ghat to see them off. Smiling at them, he said, "Come again."

Their boat pulled out into the river, and the Master stood there watching until they had gone quite a distance. In the meantime a storm began to blow and the sky quickly became dark with clouds. I noticed that the Master was quite worried. He started pacing back and forth like a restless boy, his anxiety increasing as he watched the progress of the violently rocking boat.

Impatiently he was asking everyone: "What will happen? Will Balaram and his family survive this storm? Alas! What will happen? People will say that Balaram went to see that worthless, unfortunate holy man in Dakshineswar and lost his life coming back. Tell me, what will happen?" Gradually the boat disappeared from sight. The Master returned to his room, his face gloomy, his mind very much disturbed, and he resumed his restless pacing, lamenting: "Mother, will you tarnish my face? Won't you hear my prayer? Mother, what will happen?"

Seeing the Master's state of mind, Yogin, without saying anything, set out for Calcutta in the midst of the storm to get news of Balaram Babu. He took a share-carriage from Alambazar, and within a few hours he was back [by then night had fallen] and was able to report to the Master that Balaram Babu and his family had arrived home safely.

Yogin said to him: "It is by your grace that they had no mishap on the river and reached home safely. Seeing your anxiety, I went myself for news of them. They said the boat was rolling heavily in the storm and at one point almost overturned, but it somehow regained its balance."

The Master was overjoyed to hear the news. Then he said to Yogin slowly: "What did you say? By my grace? Don't repeat to anyone what you have said. Keep it in your mind. Remember! By the grace of the Mother they reached home safely."

I still remember the day he passed away at the Cossipore garden house. He was seated on his bed, reclining against a pillow. It was noon. All were silent. Everyone thought that his voice was completely gone. But as soon as the Mother and I entered his room he slowly whispered: "You have come. Listen, I am going somewhere across the water, a long distance." The Mother burst into tears.

Again he whispered: "Don't worry. They [*pointing to the disciples*] will look after you just as they are taking care of me. Keep watch over Lakshmi. She will be your companion."

Even now I remember his face on that last day, seated on his bed, merged in samadhi, with tears rolling down his cheeks.

[From: *Ramakrishna-Saradamrita*, by Swami Nirlepananda (Calcutta: Karuna Prakashani), 1968; *Days In An Indian Monastery*, by Sister Devamata (La Crescenta: Ananda Ashrama), 1927; *Prabuddha Bharata* (Mayavati: Advaita Ashrama) vol. 34, no. 9, 1929]

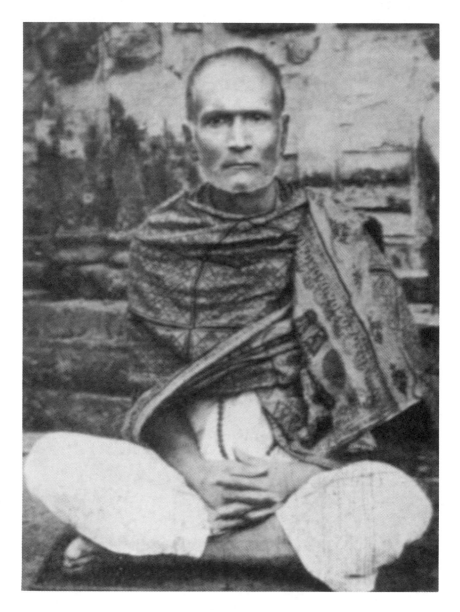

Ramlal Chattopadhyay, Sri Ramakrishna's nephew

3

Ramlal Chattopadhyay

Ramlal Chattopadhyay (1858-1933) was a son of Sri Ramakrishna's elder brother Rameshwar. When he was in his early twenties he came to Dakshineswar and became a priest of the Kali temple as well as an attendant of Sri Ramakrishna. He was known among the disciples and devotees of the Master as Ramlal Dada. Ramlal's reminiscences were recorded by Kamal Krishna Mittra in his diary and the dates are given at the end of each entry.

See God with Open Eyes

If anyone would meditate or close his eyes while repeating his mantram inside the Kali temple, the Master would tell him: "What are you doing? You are seated here in front of the living Mother. See her to your heart's content. Practise those spiritual disciplines elsewhere, where you cannot get this direct experience. Suppose you have gone home to visit your mother. Would you sit before her with closed eyes and repeat her name?" (1 October 1931)

Chanting the Name of the Lord

In the mornings and evenings Sri Ramakrishna used to dance, chanting the names of the Lord:

"Jaya Govinda, Jaya Gopala"
   [Victory to Govinda, Victory to Gopala]
"Keshava Madhava Dina Dayala"
   [O Keshava, Madhava, the compassionate friend of the lowly]
"Hare Murare Govinda, Basu-Daivaki Nandana Govinda"
   [O Hari, Murari, Govinda, O son of Vasudeva and Devaki]
"Hare Narayana Govinda He"
   [O Hari, Narayana, Govinda]
"Hare Krishna Basudeva"
   [O Hari, Krishna, son of Vasudeva] (3 January 1932)

The Meaning and Method of Japam

Sri Ramakrishna once explained the meaning of the name *Rama*: "*Ra* means the universe; *Ma* means God, or the ruler. He who is the ruler of the universe is Rama." He also showed how to repeat the mantram on one's fingers: "While repeating the mantram one should not touch the joints of the fingers, nor should the thumbnail touch the fingers. Furthermore, if there is any gap between the fingers, the results of the japam will go through it." He used to say, "Relax after finishing your duties, and smile after conquering your enemy." (4 December 1931)

The Power of the Name

Sri Ramakrishna used to say: "The human mind cannot comprehend the divine sport [lila] of God. By a mere wish he makes the impossible possible and the possible impossible." Concerning the power of the name, Sri Ramakrishna once said to Ishan Mukherjee: "Well, if there is a collision between two trains, some people will die and some will survive. Those who started their journey chanting the name of Mother Durga survived, and those who did not, died. According to somebody's karma, his foot is supposed to be pierced by a plough, but as he started his journey chanting the name of Mother Durga, a blade of kusha grass entered his foot instead. This shows that he escaped major injury through the power of the Mother's name. What do you think about it?" Ishan: "Yes, sir. It is possible." (31 May 1931)

On Fasting

About fasting, the Master used to say: "After eating a little prasad [offered food] of the Divine Mother, if you eat your regular food, it will not harm you. One gets the benefit of fasting — that is, purity of the mind — when one observes it wholeheartedly. But if fasting causes stomach pains, it is almost impossible to practise spiritual disciplines or to perform any work. In the kali yuga [the iron age] the span of life is short and the human body is weak and cannot survive long without food. It is difficult to concentrate on God while fasting. Therefore, eat something first and then practise spiritual disciplines." (1 November 1931)

Days in Dakshineswar

The barber came to the temple garden on Mondays to cut the Master's hair. [*Sri Ramakrishna could not be shaved with an open razor because his skin was very soft, so the barber would just trim his beard.*]

Hriday served the Master wholeheartedly. The Master used to say that that type of service was rare and that even parents could not serve their children so well. But later Hriday gave the Master a lot of trouble. It was interesting to watch a quarrel between them. When the Master got angry with Hriday he would scold him using very strong words. Hriday usually kept quiet, but occasionally he would say: "Uncle, what are you saying? I am your nephew." And again when Hriday became angry, the Master would keep quiet. After such quarrelling I would think they would never speak to each other again. But after a short while they would smile and talk and tease each other.

This is the room [Sri Ramakrishna's room at Dakshineswar] where the Master sang, danced, talked, and joked with people. He was full of fun. Sometimes he made us laugh so hard that our stomachs would ache. Like a child, he would ask the devotees: "Well, I have actually seen and heard all these funny things. Is it wrong for me to tell you?" The devotees would say: "No, sir. It is not wrong. Please tell us more. We love it." (9 and 13 November 1931)

Devotion of the Worldly Calcutta People

The Master would sometimes ask me to sing some of his favourite songs, such as, "O Mother, save my soul," "Mother, how you have deluded this world!" or "When shall I attain samadhi?" If I felt shy about singing in front of people, he would scold me, saying: "Why are you afraid? As long as you have shame, hatred, and fear, you won't attain perfection. Worldly people are like worms." He further told me: "When you sing any song about a particular god or goddess, first visualize that the deity is in front of you, and then think that you are singing for him or her and forget yourself. Never think that you are singing for any human being. Thus, you won't feel any shyness."

The Master said: "Most of the people of Calcutta are worldly. They are respectful one moment and disrespectful the next. Some people criticize me because I wear a red-bordered cloth, black polished slippers, and recline on a bolster. I consider such comments of worldly people to be like the ebb and flood tides of the Ganga. I have seen how the water level of the Ganga may be full in the morning, but later it subsides. People say so many things. I spit on their good comments as well as their bad comments. But there are some people in Calcutta who are endowed with faith and devotion, and they do not forget to pay their respects to a holy man." (8 May 1929 and 4 January 1931)

Sri Ramakrishna's Dancing

[*Ramlal demonstrated how the Master would sing and dance in ecstasy.*] When the Master would sing this song, "O Mother, this world is a marketplace of crazy people," he would dance this way: He would raise his left hand up, and his right hand would be parallel to his left shoulder. Then he would bend and twist his right knee, stamp his right foot on the floor, and turn at the waist. When the Master was in a great mood, he would dance back and forth and also in a circle. When he would sing, "O Mother, you live in various moods," he would dance, clapping his hands, moving his waist, and keeping the rhythm with his feet.

Nowadays the songs the Master used to sing are sung in different tunes, and it is jarring to my ears. (8 May 1929 and 26 May 1931)

Sri Ramakrishna's Singing

If someone broke the rhythm while singing, the Master would cry out "Oohu, oohu." But if the person sang with devotion and deep absorption, such irregularity would not disturb him. He was not interested in ragas, raginis [metres], or the science of music. The Master sang in ecstasy, and his voice was soft, sweet, and melodious. Sometimes when he was singing, he would improvise some joyous phrase. I saw the Master enter into samadhi many times while singing. Sometimes he would ask me or Swamiji to sing, and while listening he would again enter into samadhi.

When I sing accompanied by drums, my mind dwells on the rhythm of the drums, and for that reason it is hard for me to sing wholeheartedly for God. Noticing this the Master used to say: "Suppose a man is singing kirtan rhythmically, repeating, 'Nitai amar mata hati [My Nitai is a mad elephant].' Gradually when his emotion deepens, he repeats, 'Hati.' And at last he goes into samadhi, saying only 'Ha.'" (20 May 1929)

Sri Ramakrishna's Daily Routine

The Master usually got up at three or three-thirty in the morning, and as soon as he got out of bed I would wake up. When he went to the pine grove I would either lead the way or follow him with a jug and towel. He would then go to the pond, throw off his cloth, and sit on the ghat, dangling his legs. I would bring him water and he would wash his face, hands, and feet. After covering himself with his towel, he would return to his room. Meanwhile I would quickly scour the jug, wash his cloth, and then hurry after him. In his room he would put on a fresh cloth and go to the southern verandah to brush his teeth. . . . After that he would take a little Ganga water on his palm and sprinkle it on his head, saying, "Brahma-Vari, Brahma-Vari! Ganga, Ganga! Hari Om Tat Sat! [The water of the Ganga is as pure as Brahman. God is the only Reality.]" Then he would take some prasad of Jagannath and Kali and also a few bits of dried bel leaves that had been offered at the shrine of Tarakeshwar Shiva, which he kept in a small bag. With joined palms he would salute all the holy pictures in his room and then sit down on the small cot.

The Master was usually in one of two moods. On some days he would observe all the traditional methods of purification; on other days he would completely ignore them. When he was in this second mood, he would not even wash himself properly. He would ask for food as soon as he returned from the pond in the morning and reluctantly wash his hands with water after eating. One day he explained: "You see, Mother keeps me sometimes in the mood of a child, sometimes in the mood of a madman, and sometimes in the mood of a carefree soul."

At about nine or ten in the morning, after he had finished talking with the devotees, I would rub oil on his body. But I would put oil on his head only with his permission. One day, without asking first, I put my hand on his head in order to rub oil on his hair. He became angry and scolded me, and then he suddenly went into samadhi. I was struck dumb with wonder, and my heart began to pound in fear. After a long time he gave a deep sigh and came back to the normal conscious plane. Then he told me: "Do not put your hand on my head that way. There is no telling what spiritual condition I may be in. Ask for permission before you touch my head."

On another day, seeing a thread on his hair, I automatically reached out my hand to remove it. Again he got very angry and said: "What! You are touching my head again?" I had forgotten his warning. . . . After oil had been rubbed on him, he would go to the chandni ghat on the Ganga for a bath and then go to the Kali temple. There he would decorate the Mother with flowers or offer flowers and bel leaves at her feet. Sometimes he would put flowers on his own head and then merge into samadhi. (*Prabuddha Bharata*, 1930, pp. 13-14)

The Master's Frugality

The Master suffered from stomach trouble during the rainy season, and he would then eat only rice, bitter squash curry, and soup. Hriday and I slept on the floor of the Master's room. Once at midnight we woke up to find him cutting vegetables and gathering rice and spices. Hriday said to the Master: "Uncle, what are you doing? Can't you do that in the morning? Both of us are here. We will do everything for you. Why don't you go to bed and sleep? Besides, Uncle, your household work makes me laugh. That quantity of vegetables and rice is hardly enough for one person. You are so miserly!" The Master replied: "Look, when I woke up, at first I sat quietly. Then I thought that it was not good to sit idle, so I should do some household work. Some people do not know how much food I eat, so they cook too much and waste it. Do you know why I was preparing those things? I have seen the temple officials waste so much food on their plates.

"Look, Hriday, you are a son of a high class brahmin, and for a morsel of food and some money you are now working at this Kali temple. If you had land and money in Sihar, would you come here for a job? Learn how to be frugal. Otherwise the goddess of fortune will leave you." "You are right, Uncle," said Hriday.

One morning the Master asked someone to cut a twig for him so that he could clean his teeth. The person brought three twigs. The Master took one and said to him: "Rascal! I asked you to bring one twig. Why did you bring three? However, save those two." The next morning the Master asked the same person for another twig. When he was about to go to the garden, the Master said: "Where are you going? Why don't you give me one of those that you brought yesterday?" Then the Master continued: "Without checking the stock, why are you running to get a new one? Have you created that tree? You are about to break its branches at your own whim! Only the Creator knows how difficult it is to create. You are dullheaded. Learn how to work methodically. Do not waste anything." (8 October 1931)

Five Pictures

One day the Master asked Beni Madhav of Sinthi: "Could you bring me some good holy pictures for my room?" Some time later Beni Madhav asked me to collect them from him. I brought the Master five pictures — Dhruva, Prahlad, Gauranga, Jagannath, and Kamale Kamini [a goddess standing on a lotus]. Now the last two pictures are in Kamarpukur. (9 November 1930)

A Ghost

Formerly the Master and Hriday lived in a large room of the kuthi [the owner's bungalow] at the Dakshineswar temple garden, and the Master's mother slept in an adjoining small room. Often at night they heard a man wearing shoes go up and down the stairs, opening doors and windows. It was a ghost, possibly a European. The kuthi had been a European residence before the temple was built. The Master used to say: "We cannot say that this world is entirely false because we actually see it with our own eyes. Nor can we say that it is real. For example, just see how this garden has changed. Previously it was a graveyard and this kuthi the house of a European. But now the temple and so many other things are here! Later this temple also will vanish, and then who knows what will come next?" (*Spiritual Talks*, 4th edition, 1968, pp. 66-67)

Captain

The Master used to say: "Even the dogs and cats of the Dakshineswar temple garden are blessed. Look, they are eating Mother's prasad, seeing the Ganga and drinking its water, and roaming around the temples." There was a dog in the temple garden that the Master called Captain. Captain quite often sat on the front terrace of the Mother's temple. Whenever the Master would call him, the dog would come and roll at his feet. Then the Master would feed him luchis [fried bread] and sandesh [a sweet]. The Master once said: "Look, there are so many dogs here but none of them sits in front of the Mother except Captain. I have not seen any other dog that sits on the steps near the Ganga and drinks Ganga water. Captain has been born as a dog as the result of a curse. He had some good samskaras [tendencies] in his previous life, so he is here. He is a blessed soul." (16 October 1931)

The Master's Vision about His Suppliers

One day the Master put a rupee in one hand and some clay in the other and then threw them both into the Ganga, saying, "Rupee is clay and clay is rupee." After a while he began to worry that his action might have offended the goddess of fortune, so he went to the Mother's temple. Later he said to me: "Ramlal, I told the Mother everything, and she replied: 'No, Lakshmi, the goddess of fortune, will not be angry with you. Don't be afraid. Look, these are your suppliers. They will feed you.' The Mother then showed me a vision: I saw many bubbles rising around the Divine Mother. Gradually those bubbles took the forms of Mathur, Balaram, Surendra, and many others. They were clapping their hands around the Mother and saying, 'Victory to Kali! Victory to Shiva!' After that they merged with the Mother, one by one. Then I saw some people with white complexion. I shall not be able to meet them, but you will see them." Nowadays I find that many Westerners have become devotees of the Master. Swamiji went to the West and lectured, and as a result, many rich people became his devotees and helped his work. (8 October 1931)

Man's Will or God's Will

A person once asked the Master, "How can we ascertain whether something is man's will or God's will?" Sri Ramakrishna replied: "Suppose a man has made arrangements to go to Varanasi and is ready to leave. In the meantime a cable comes from his country home that his brother is about to die and if he wants to see him, he should come immediately. He cancels his trip to Varanasi and hurriedly returns home. Now you decide whose will it is." (21 October 1930)

Sri Ramakrishna Was All-Knowing

I was an attendant of the Master. Gradually the disciples of the Master began to come to Dakshineswar, so one day I said to the Master: "I haven't visited Kamarpukur for a long time. I think I should go there and clear the taxes on our property." The Master said, "If you go, then who will look after me?" I replied: "Well, these devotees are coming regularly and they often stay here at night. They can look after you. Besides, I won't be gone long. As soon as I finish my work, I shall return." The Master then said: "Yes, they are coming, but they do not know my way of life. They cannot serve me like you."

The next morning when I asked the Master's permission again, he thought for a while and then said: "No, you won't be able to go to Kamarpukur. It is not the will of the Mother that you should leave me and go there." I told him: "But I am ready to go. I only need the temple manager's permission." Hearing this, the Master made a circle in the air with his finger and wrote something there. Then he said: "Ramlal, you won't be able to go to Kamarpukur. Go to the manager and see what he says." When I approached the manager, he said: "No, it's not possible for you to leave now because the staff needed to carry on the day-to-day work of the temples is short-handed." Thus, my visit to Kamarpukur was cancelled.

Once the Master told me: "Offer whoever comes here, whether known or unknown, a little prasad and a glass of Ganga water. You will not have to do anything else. This service to the devotees will give you the result of japam, austerity, and sacrifice." So I follow what the Master said to me and it gives me joy. (13 November 1931 and 23 October 1931)

The Christian Doctrine of Sin

One day the Master said to me, "Ramlal, go to the Alambazar market and buy some tobacco, fennel seed, and cubeb." I went to the market and came across a Christian missionary who was preaching Christianity on the street and distributing a pamphlet, "The Gospel According to Matthew," in Bengali. I took a copy and returned to the Master. He asked: "What is that book? Please read to me." After listening for some time, the Master said: "Stop. You need not read anymore. This book only talks about sin and sin. There is a saying, 'As one thinks, so one becomes.'" He further said: "God is the ruler of this universe and all beings are his children. O my mind, know it for certain, you are a child of God." (28 October 1931)

At the Star Theatre

One day Girish Ghosh came to the Master and asked: "Sir, we are presenting the play *Daksha Yajna* [The Sacrifice of King Daksha] at the Star Theatre tonight. Would you like to see it?" The Master replied, "Yes, Ramlal and I will go." Then the Master and I hired a carriage and left for the theatre. By mistake we entered through the back way, which was dirty, and found that no one was there. Seeing an actress nearby, the Master said, "Hello, could you inform Girish that some visitors have come from Dakshineswar?" Girish immediately came and fell at the Master's feet and remained on the ground for a few minutes. The Master asked Girish to get up, and when he did his shirt was dirty. The Master began to brush his shirt with his hand and said, "Ah, you have spoiled this clean shirt!"

Girish took us upstairs and arranged for box seats, and then he called the actresses, who at that time were putting on their makeup. They came immediately. Girish told them: "Bow down at the Master's feet. You won't get another chance such as this to purify yourselves." Then the Master said to them: "Enough! O blissful mothers, please get up. You are giving joy to people by your singing and dancing. Now go back to your dressing room for your makeup."

During the first scene Girish appeared on stage in the role of King Daksha and announced, "Today I shall remove the name of Shiva from this world." At this, the Master said to me, "O Ramlal, what is this rascal saying?" When that scene was over, Girish came to the Master and asked with folded hands, "Sir, how did you enjoy the part of King Daksha?" The Master said: "Look Girish, you were saying, 'I shall remove Shiva's name from this world.' Such words should not come from your lips." Girish replied: "Sir, what can I do? I had to say all these things just for the sake of my stomach." Then the Master said, "Yes, I understand."

Girish left, and the next scene began. When Sati [the wife of Shiva and the daughter of King Daksha] came on stage, the Master went into samadhi. He remained in samadhi till the end of the play, except for a few moments when he exclaimed, "Ah! Ah!" After the play was over I escorted the Master to the carriage, but he was in an intoxicated mood. Girish again came, bowed down to the Master, and asked, "Sir, how did you enjoy the play?" The Master could not talk. We left for Dakshineswar. After regaining normal consciousness, the Master asked me, "Ramlal, tell me about the last part of the play." I told him the story. He said: "Ah, I could not see the whole play. However, after listening to you I am satisfied." (8 October 1931)

The Master's Ecstasy on the Street

One day Sri Ramakrishna and I were returning from Calcutta by horse carriage. When the carriage reached the crossroad at Baranagore, he asked, "Is it Baranagore?" "Yes," I replied. He said: "I am extremely hungry. Do you have any money in your pocket?" "Yes, I have." I always took some money with me whenever I went anywhere with the Master, since occasionally he would ask me to give coins to the beggars on the street. Then he asked, "Could you buy some *kachuri* [fried bread] from Fagu's shop?" I replied: "Of course. Please wait. I shall bring it very quickly."

When I came back with the food, I found the Master was not in the carriage. I asked the coachman, "Where has the Master gone?" He replied, "The Master left the carriage some time ago and went in that direction." Leaving the food in the carriage, I ran and found the Master walking rapidly. I called: "Master, where are you going? I have brought the food for you." But he did not listen to me at all. I then grabbed his hand and said: "Where are you going alone? Let us return to our carriage." The Master exclaimed: "What! What! Who are you?" Then he took a couple of deep breaths and rubbed his head. Gradually he became normal. Then he told me: "Look. Let me tell you something: Before you go somewhere leaving me alone, say to me: 'I am going. Please sit here. Don't go anywhere until I return.' If I agree, then this kind of thing will not happen."

When the Master was in samadhi his gaze was fixed, as is seen in his photograph. Tears of joy would flow from the outer corners of his eyes and roll down his moustache, beard, and chest. Sometimes after samadhi he would talk in a mysterious language that no one could understand. (21 April 1931)

A Boat Trip with Keshab Sen

One day Keshab Sen came to Dakshineswar with his followers and asked the Master: "Sir, Mr. Cook is a pandit and devotee, and he is waiting in the boat. Would you like to go on a boat ride with us?" The Master agreed and said to me, "O Ramlal, you come with me." When we reached the boat, Keshab introduced the Master to Mr. Cook, who was very happy.

After a while the steamboat came near the Barabazar bridge, and the Master said to Keshab: "Keshab, I am hungry. Could you give me something to eat?" Keshab: "Tell me, sir, whatever you would like to eat, I shall get for you." The Master: "Let Ramlal go and get some jilipi [a sweet]." I came back with jilipi, betel roll, and tobacco for the Master.

Then the Master asked me to clean a place on the steamer with Ganga water, and he ate the refreshments there. After he had finished eating, he smoked tobacco. It was evening and he was in an ecstatic mood. We helped him get down from the steamer, and he was staggering as we put him in the carriage. The Europeans laughed and whispered to Keshab. I asked Keshab why they were laughing, and he replied: "They said that the Master has drunk too much wine, so he is staggering. I told them that he did not drink any wine. He is in a divine mood, and that is why he is intoxicated." Those people were amazed, seeing the Master in samadhi.

After arriving at Dakshineswar the Master became normal. I told him that the Europeans had laughed when they saw him staggering like a drunkard. "Is that so?" the Master said with a smile. (11 December 1931)

Keshab's Lecture at Dakshineswar

It was the full moon night of Lakshmi puja. In the evening Keshab Sen and his followers along with the Master and his devotees assembled at the chandni ghat of Dakshineswar. I prepared three large baskets of puffed rice with coconut and other spices, which they all enjoyed. After some time the Master said to Keshab: "Keshab, we want to hear you lecture. Look, what a beautiful evening! The full moon is smiling and the Ganga is flowing nearby. Now a desire has come to hear something from your lips."

Keshab was a little hesitant and felt shy to lecture in front of the Master. But he could not refuse the Master's request, so he stood on the pavement of the chandni and gave a talk. (11 December 1931)

The Master's Anxiety for Swamiji

Seeing the Master's anxiety for Swamiji, I asked him, "Why are you so anxious about him?" The Master replied: "As Rasik [Rasiklal Sarkar, a worker at the Kali temple] is your friend and Hazra is Naren's friend, so Naren is my friend. Naren told me that he would come on Wednesday, and now another Wednesday is approaching and still he has not come. Please go to his house and bring me news of him." Then he told me: "Look, Ramlal. The Marwari devotees gave me sweets, nuts, and raisins. I shall not eat these things. Give them to Naren and bring me news about his health."

The Master put the food in a bundle and handed it to me, and I left for Calcutta. In those days one could go to Calcutta by share carriage from Baranagore. There was no other passenger for the carriage, however. And as it would not leave until another passenger came, I decided to walk all the way to Swamiji's house. Swamiji reprimanded me, saying, "Brother, didn't you have any money?" I replied: "Yes, I have money.

But I realized that the carriage would be leaving late, so I walked."
Swamiji washed my feet and fanned me. I said to him: "You told the
Master that you would visit him on Wednesday, but you didn't. He was
worried about you and has sent me with all these things." Swamiji said:
"Yes, Brother, I always plan to visit the Master, but the pressure of my
family does not allow me to go anywhere. I shall go with you right now."
Swamiji changed his clothes and nicely combed his curly hair. When we
reached Dakshineswar Swamiji bowed down to the Master. The Master
wiped the dust from Swamiji's forehead. Then he ruffled Swamiji's hair
with his fingers and said: "This foppishness does not befit you. Will you
stay here today?" "Yes, Master," replied Swamiji. Then the Master told
me, "Ramlal, please arrange some nice food for him." (21 October 1931)

Swamiji's Truthfulness

When Swamiji was leaving Dakshineswar, he said to the Master that
he would visit him again the next Wednesday. The Master asked, "What
time?" and Swamiji replied, "At three o'clock." The following Wednesday Swamiji arrived at Dakshineswar at two o'clock and waited
outside the gate. He did not come to the Master then, as he had promised
to see him at three o'clock.

The Master was talking to the devotees in his room. When he was
informed that Swamiji was waiting outside the gate, he asked the
devotees to wait, and he walked towards the gate. Seeing Swamiji, the
Master asked: "Hello, Naren. When did you come? Why are you standing here? What happened?" Swamiji replied: "Sir, I promised you that I
would come at three o'clock, but I left home earlier and when I arrived
here I found that it was two o'clock. For the sake of truth I am waiting
here." The Master was very pleased to hear that. They remained there
talking for some time, and then at three o'clock Swamiji went with the
Master to his room. (21 October 1931)

Shiva Acharya and Brahmavrata Samadhyayi

One day I went to hear Shiva Acharya sing kirtan at Alambazar. Later
I reported to the Master about a song that I had heard there, "Who has
sung the precious name of Sri Rama in my ear?" The Master said, "Oh,
I missed this wonderful kirtan!" A few days later Shiva Acharya came
to visit the Dakshineswar temple, and I asked him to meet the Master.
He agreed. The Master said to him: "Ramlal heard your kirtan and told
me about it. Why don't you sing that song for me?" Shiva Acharya sang,
and tears began to flow from the Master's eyes. Gradually he went into
samadhi. The Master later asked me to copy that song. He told Shiva
Acharya: "Your singing brings joy to so many people. It is wonderful

that you can sing for four or five hours at a stretch without your voice giving out. God's power dwells in the heart of one who attracts many people and gives joy to them."

Shiva Acharya invited the Master to visit Bhadrakali [a village on the western side of the Ganga], and the Master agreed. One day Shiva Acharya came with four boats decorated with flags, and the Master, along with some devotees, went to his place. We sang kirtan on the way. The Master was received at the village with garlands, and people chanted the Lord's name while distributing candy. The Master was in ecstasy.

They had a debate at that meeting. Brahmavrata Samadhyayi was a great scholar and logician. The Master listened to what he said and observed how he was refuting others' arguments. All of a sudden the Master said: "Mother, this fellow is arguing too much. He is a dry scholar." Then the Master rushed to the scholar, touched his right knee, and said, "What did you say?" "I didn't say anything," Samadhyayi replied in bewilderment. The Master's touch had changed Samadhyayi's mind. The Master then said, "Just now you were talking about so many things and arguing with people." "I was joking with them. Please don't take me seriously," replied the pandit. Afterwards we brought the Master back to Dakshineswar. (24 September 1931)

Digambar Banerjee

Digambar Banerjee was a poor man from the village of Sihar. One day he brought a rosary of one hundred and eight beads and after sanctifying it with Ganga water and sandal paste, offered it to the Master for his blessing. The Master returned the rosary to him and said; "Repeat the mantram on this rosary, and every day chant God's name with drum and cymbals. It will do you good. In this kali yuga God's name is the essential thing. Chanting God's name will bring the results of meditation, worship, and sacrifice."

By the grace of the Master, Digambar Banerjee became a rich landlord. He used to chant God's name every day according to the Master's instructions and would feed those who joined the kirtan. What love and faith he had for the Master! (8 October 1931)

Vijay Krishna Goswami

Vijay Krishna Goswami used to visit the Master, but he was closely connected with the Brahmo Samaj. One day the Master said to him, "Vijay, please come alone one day to see me. I shall tell you something." After some days Vijay came by himself to Dakshineswar, and the Master told him: "Look, Vijay. Your involvement with the Brahmo Samaj does not suit your nature. You are a descendant of Advaita Acharya, a great devotee of Chaitanya. A fountain of devotion is hidden within. You should be wearing a rosary around your neck, putting marks on your forehead, and chanting the Lord's name, but instead you are involved with this socio-religious organization. Seeing you in this condition I feel bad, so I am telling you what is good for you." Vijay then fell at the Master's feet and asked, "Sir, is there any hope for me?" "Of course," said the Master. "Be intoxicated with the name of the Lord, and then his grace will well up within you."

Vijay followed the Master's advice and a great change came over him. He spent most of his time repeating his mantram with a rosary, and he practised sadhana in many holy places.

One day Vijay visited the Master dressed like a Vaishnava [i.e., with rosaries around his upper arms and neck and marks on his forehead and nose]. Seeing him the Master said: "Very good! Your dress suits your nature. You are on the right track. It seems that the Lord's name is bubbling up from within. It has been suppressed for a long time, but now it will manifest itself." Vijay bowed down to the Master and said: "Sir, bless me. Don't push me away. I know you are God himself acting like a human being." The Master replied: "The Mother knows everything. I don't know anything. It is the Mother who speaks and does everything through me." (13 November 1931)

I Doubted the Master

I used to address the Master as *apani* [a respectful term used for seniors or revered persons] because I did not feel that he was my own uncle. As I could not understand his behaviour, moods, or samadhi, a doubt arose in my mind. I thought: "The Master is an unlettered person, but still all great scholars are defeated by him. Is he truly an Incarnation of God?" One day I said to the Master: "A doubt has arisen in my mind about you. I am confused." The Master replied: "Look, Ramlal. One cannot understand this mystery through the intellect. You have seen jilipis [a sweet]. From the outside they look dry, so how would one know that they are full of sweet syrup inside? If you think of me as an avatar [a Divine Incarnation], then you are blessed that you have the opportunity to serve me. Besides, you are my blood relative. What else do you want?"

In those days I did not recognize the Master's greatness. Although we were his blood relatives, we did not realize who he was. But through his grace, I have this much faith: that since we were born into his family, we have found refuge at his lotus feet. From his own lips I heard that when a man attains illumination, seven generations of his family before and after him become liberated. And to think that the Lord himself was born in our family as a human being! Through his grace and his holy company we too have had many visions and spiritual experiences. Thus he gave us faith and devotion for him. (23 October 1931; *The Eternal Companion*, 3rd ed., 1970, p. 132)

Sri Ramakrishna as the Kalpataru

On the afternoon of 1 January 1886, at the Cossipore garden house, the Master said to me: "Ramlal, today I feel better. Let us go for a walk in the courtyard." I said: "Yes, you look better. Let us go." The Master put on his cap that covered his ears and carried a cane in his hand. I put on a shawl and carefully helped him down the stairs. After strolling along the garden path, the Master stood on the lawn and went into ecstasy. He was surrounded by the devotees, who began showering flowers on him and chanting hymns. He told them: "What more shall I say to you? Be illumined!" Then he blessed some devotees by touching their chests. To others he said that they would have to wait for a while.

I was then standing behind the Master and thinking: "All these devotees have got some spiritual experiences, but what have I achieved? I only carried the Master's waterpot and towel." As soon as this thought crossed my mind, he looked at me and said: "Ramlal, what are you thinking? Come here." He pushed aside my shawl and touched my chest, saying, "Now see." It is hard for me to describe that wonderful, luminous form. Before that, during my meditation I could see with my mind's eye only a part of my Chosen Deity. When I saw his feet I could not see his face; and again, when I saw his form from the face to the waist, I could not see his feet. Moreover, whatever I saw never seemed to be alive. But no sooner had the Master touched me that day than the whole form of my Chosen Deity appeared in my heart as a living presence, looking benign and effulgent. (1 January 1930; *Sri Ramakrishna, The Great Master*, 5th edition, 1979, p. 1025)

"My Hands and Feet Are Burning"

At the Cossipore garden house during the Master's last illness, Swami Niranjanananda would sit on the staircase to prevent anyone from entering the Master's room. But the Master told his disciples to allow me to visit him at any time. One day when I went to see him he got up and told me: "Ramlal, my hands and feet are burning. Please bring some Ganga water and sprinkle it on me." He was extremely restless. I asked, "What happened?" He replied: "I came into this world secretly with a few close devotees, and now Ram [Ram Chandra Datta] is spreading my name. He brings all sorts of people here and asks me to touch and bless them. How much burden can I carry? I got this disease by taking the sins of these people upon myself. Look, I shall not stay in this world any longer." I consoled him: "No, no. You will not have to receive any visitors or touch anybody." Then I brought the Ganga water and washed his hands and feet, and gradually he calmed down.

The Master's body was very pure, and he was all-compassionate and a saviour of souls. While touching his feet, people prayed for so many things. Many people even criticized him, but the Master carried their spiritual responsibilities as well. When the doctor saw the bleeding in the Master's throat, he forbade him to talk. But the Master talked till the last for the good of the devotees. (1 January 1930)

Sri Ramakrishna's Last Day

I was not present on the last day of the Master's life. I was sleeping in his room at Dakshineswar. At two in the morning Senior Gopal and somebody else [Latu] came from Cossipore and knocked on my door. They told me: "Swamiji has asked us to bring you to Cossipore immediately. No one present there can ascertain whether the Master is in deep samadhi or has actually given up his body. Swamiji said that since you lived constantly with the Master for so many years, you would be able to judge his condition correctly." I burst into tears and rushed to Cossipore with them. I saw the Master lying flat on his back. His look was steady, and he seemed to be smiling. I said: "I see signs of samadhi. But I suggest that we call Captain [Vishwanath Upadhyay] who is also very knowledgeable." Swamiji immediately sent somebody to call him. When Captain came he also noticed signs of samadhi. He suggested that ghee [clarified butter] be rubbed on the Master's backbone. At first the backbone felt slightly warm but gradually it turned cold. Captain realized then that it was *mahasamadhi* and that the Master had passed away. The Master went into samadhi at one o'clock in the morning. By noon his face was starting to dry out and his eyes gradually closed. I heard that at the last moment the Master had said only "Ma." (26 October 1931)

After Sri Ramakrishna's Passing Away

A young Ramait monk [a worshiper of Ramachandra] in Ayodhya had a vision that God had again incarnated on earth, somewhere in the east. In order to see him, the monk started on foot eastward from Ayodhya. When he reached Bengal he heard that there was a great saint named Sri Ramakrishna near Calcutta. He finally found Dakshineswar after a long search and asked someone, "Where is Ramakrishna Paramahamsa?" The people of the Kali temple told him that the Master had just passed away a few days before. Hearing this heartbreaking news, the monk exclaimed: "What! He passed away? I have come from Ayodhya on foot [nearly a thousand miles] just to see him. I went through so much hardship to get here and he has left the body!" The young monk began to sob.

The manager of the Kali temple offered him some food from the temple store but he refused it. He went to the Panchavati and stayed there for two or three days without eating. One night Sri Ramakrishna appeared before him and said: "You have not eaten anything for several days. I have brought this pudding for you. Please eat it." He fed the monk and disappeared.

The next morning I went to the Panchavati and found the monk full of joy. I asked: "What happened? You were so unhappy yesterday. Why are you so cheerful today?" Then he told me everything. He even showed me the earthen bowl in which the Master had brought the pudding. [*Ramlal preserved that bowl for a long time, but somehow it was destroyed.*] (*Udbodhan*, vol. 49, no. 10)

[From: *Sri Ramakrishna O Antaranga Prasanga,* by Kamal Krishna Mittra (Dakshineswar: K. K. Mittra), 1932; *Udbodhan* (Calcutta: Udbodhan Office), vol. 49, no. 10, 1947]

Swami Vivekananda in London, 1896

4

Swami Vivekananda

Swami Vivekananda (1863-1902) met Sri Ramakrishna in 1881 when he was a college student, and he associated closely with the Master for the next five years. As the foremost disciple of the Master, his life was closely linked with the later part of the Master's life. Swami Vivekananda's reminiscences are thus scattered all over his biography. In 1893 he brought the message of Vedanta to the West, and in 1897 he founded the Ramakrishna Mission.

First Meeting with Sri Ramakrishna

My first visit to Sri Ramakrishna was at the temple garden at Dakshineswar, in his own room. That day I sang two songs.

As soon as I had finished the first song,[1] the Master stood up, took me by the hand, and led me onto the northern verandah. It was winter, so the open spaces between the pillars were covered with screens of mat-

---

[1] Let us go back once more, O mind, to our own abode!
Here in this foreign land of earth
Why should we wander aimlessly in stranger's guise?
These living beings round about, and the five elements,
Are strangers to you, all of them; none is your own.
Why do you thus forget yourself,
In love with strangers, O my mind?
Why do you thus forget your own?
　Ascend the path of truth, O mind! Unflaggingly climb,
With Love as the lamp to light your way.
As your provision for the journey, bring with you
The virtues, carefully concealed; for, like two highwaymen,
Greed and delusion wait to rob you of your wealth.
And keep beside you constantly,
As guards to shelter you from harm,
Calmness of mind and self-control.

　(*continued on next page*)

ting to keep out the north wind; and this meant that, when the door of the room was closed, anyone standing on the verandah was hidden from both inside and outside. As soon as we were on the verandah, the Master closed the door. I thought he must be going to give me some instruction in private. But what he said and did next was something I could never have believed possible. He suddenly caught hold of my hand and began shedding tears of joy. He said to me, affectionately as if to a familiar friend: "You've come so late! Was that right? Couldn't you have guessed how I've been waiting for you? My ears are nearly burned off, listening to the talk of these worldly people. I thought I would burst, not having anyone to tell how I really felt!" He went on like that — raving and weeping. And then suddenly he folded his palms together and began addressing me as if I were some divine being: "I know who you are, My Lord. You are Nara, the ancient sage, the incarnation of Narayana. You have come back to earth to take away the sufferings and sorrows of mankind."

I was absolutely dumbfounded. I said to myself: "What kind of a man is this? He must be raving mad! How can he talk like this to me, who am nobody — the son of Vishwanath Datta?" But I didn't answer him, and I let this wonderful madman go on talking as he chose. Presently he asked me to stay there on the verandah, and he went back into the room and came out again bringing butter, rock candy, and a few pieces of sandesh; and then he began feeding me with his own hands. I kept asking him to give me the sweetmeats, so I could share them with my friends, but he wouldn't. "They'll get some later," he said. "You take these for yourself." And he wouldn't be satisfied until I'd eaten all of them. Then he took my hand and said, "Promise me — you'll come back here soon, alone." I couldn't refuse his request; it was made so earnestly. So I had to say, "I will." Then I went back into the room with him and sat down beside my friends.

I sat and watched him. There was nothing wrong in his words, movements, or behaviour towards others. Rather, from his spiritual words and ecstatic states he seemed to be a man of genuine renunciation. And there was a marked consistency between his words and life. He

---

(continued)
  Companionship with holy men will be for you
A welcome rest-house by the road;
There rest your weary limbs awhile, asking your way,
If ever you should be in doubt, of him who watches there.
If anything along the path should frighten you,
Then loudly shout the name of the Lord;
For He is Ruler of that road,
And even Death must bow to Him.

used the most simple language, and I thought, "Can this man be a great teacher?" I crept near him and asked him the question which I had asked so often, "Sir, have you seen God?" "Yes, I see him just as I see you here, only in a much more intense sense." "God can be realized," he went on. "One can see and talk to him as I am seeing and talking to you. But who cares? People shed torrents of tears for their wife and children, for wealth or property, but who does so for the sake of God? If one weeps sincerely for him, he surely manifests himself." That impressed me at once. For the first time I found a man who dared to say that he had seen God, that religion was a reality to be felt, to be sensed in an infinitely more intense way than we can sense the world. As I heard these things from his lips, I could not but believe that he was saying them not like an ordinary preacher, but from the depths of his own realizations. But I could not reconcile his words with his strange conduct with me. So I concluded that he must be a monomaniac. Yet I could not help acknowledging the magnitude of his renunciation. "He may be a madman," I thought, "but only the fortunate few can have such renunciation. Even if insane, this man is the holiest of the holy, a true saint, and for that alone he deserves the reverent homage of mankind!" With such conflicting thoughts I bowed before him and begged leave to return to Calcutta.

Second Visit

I had no idea that the Dakshineswar temple was so far from Calcutta, because I had been there only once before and that was in a carriage. This time, it seemed as if the journey would never end, however far I walked. But, after asking many people the way, I arrived at Dakshineswar at last and went straight to the Master's room. I found him sitting, deep in his own meditations, on the smaller bed which stands beside the bigger one. There was no one with him. As soon as he saw me, he called me joyfully to him and made me sit down on one end of the bed. He was in a strange mood. He muttered something to himself which I couldn't understand, looked hard at me, then rose and approached me. I thought we were about to have another crazy scene. Scarcely had that thought passed through my mind before he placed his right foot on my body. Immediately I had a wonderful experience. My eyes were wide open, and I saw that everything in the room, including the walls themselves, was whirling rapidly around and receding, and at the same time, it seemed to me that my consciousness of self, together with the entire universe, was about to vanish into a vast, all-devouring void. This destruction of my consciousness of self seemed to me to be the same thing as death. I felt that death was right before me, very close. Unable to control myself, I cried out loudly, "Ah, what are you doing to me? Don't you know I have my parents at home?" When the Master heard this, he gave a loud laugh. Then, touching my chest with his hand, he said: "All right — let it stop now. It needn't be done all at once. It will happen in its own good time." To my amazement, this extraordinary vision of mine vanished as suddenly as it had come. I returned to my normal state and saw things inside and outside the room standing stationary, as before.

Although it has taken so much time to describe all this, it actually happened in only a few moments. And yet it changed my whole way of thinking. I was bewildered and kept trying to analyze what had happened. I had seen how this experience had begun and ended in obedience to the will of this extraordinary man. I had read about hypnotism in books and I wondered if this was something of the same kind. But my heart refused to believe that it was. For even people of great willpower can only create such conditions when they are working on weak minds. And my mind was by no means weak. Up to then, in fact, I had been proud of my intelligence and willpower. This man did not bewitch me or reduce me to his puppet. On the contrary, when I first met him, I had decided that he was mad. Why then should I have suddenly found myself in this state? It seemed an utter mystery to me. But I determined to be on my guard, lest he should get further influence over me in the future.

The next moment I thought, "How can a man who shatters to pieces a resolute and strong mind like mine be dismissed as a lunatic?" Yet that was just the conclusion at which one would arrive from his effusiveness on our first meeting — unless he were an Incarnation of God, which was indeed a far cry. So I was in a dilemma about the real nature of my experience as well as about the truth of this wonderful man, who was obviously as pure and simple as a child. My rationalistic mind received an unpleasant rebuff at this failure in judging the true state of things. But I was determined to fathom the mystery somehow.

Thoughts like these occupied my mind during the whole of that day. But he became quite another man after that incident and, as on the previous occasion, treated me with great kindness and cordiality. His behaviour towards me was like that of a man who meets an old friend or relative after a long separation. He seemed not to be satisfied with entertaining and taking all possible care of me. This remarkably loving treatment drew me all the more to him. At last, finding that the day was coming to a close, I asked leave to go. He seemed very dejected at this and gave me permission only after I had promised to come again at my earliest convenience.

Experience of Cosmic Consciousness

Knowing Naren's inherent nature, Sri Ramakrishna instructed him in monistic Vedanta, which teaches that the individual soul and Brahman are identical. One day Naren was telling Hazra about Vedantic nondualism and his unwillingness to accept it. "Can it be," he said, "that the water pot is God, that the drinking vessel is God, that everything we see and all of us are God?" Naren laughed scornfully at the idea and Hazra joined in. While they were laughing, Ramakrishna came up to them. "What are you two talking about?" he asked Naren affectionately; then, without waiting for an answer, he touched Naren and went into samadhi. Naren related the effect of the touch:

At the marvellous touch of the Master, my mind underwent a complete revolution. I was aghast to realize that there really was nothing whatever in the entire universe but God. I remained silent, wondering how long this state of mind would continue. It didn't pass off all day. I got back home, and I felt just the same there; everything I saw was God. I sat down to eat, and I saw that everything — the plate, the food, my mother who was serving it, and I myself — everything was God and nothing else but God. I swallowed a couple of mouthfuls and then sat still without speaking. My mother asked me lovingly: "Why are you so quiet? Why don't you eat?" That brought me back to everyday consciousness, and I began eating again. But, from then on, I kept having the same experience, no matter what I was doing — eating, drinking, sitting, lying down, going to college, strolling along the street. It was a kind of intoxication; I can't describe it. If I was crossing a street and saw a carriage coming towards me I didn't have the urge, as I would ordinarily, to get out of its way for fear of being run over. For I said to myself: "I am that carriage. There's no difference between it and me." During that time, I had no sensation in my hands or my feet. When I ate food, I felt no satisfaction from it; it was as if someone else was eating. Sometimes I would lie down in the middle of a meal, and then get up again after a few minutes and go on eating. Thus it happened that on those days I would eat far more than usual, but this never upset me. My mother became alarmed; she thought I was suffering from some terrible disease. "He won't live long," she'd say.

When that first intoxication lost part of its power, I began to see the world as though it were in a dream. When I went for a walk around Cornwallis Square [now Azadhind Bag], I used to knock my head against the iron railings to find out if they were only dream-railings or real ones. The loss of feeling in my hands and feet made me afraid that I was going to be paralyzed. When I did at last return to normal consciousness I felt convinced that the state I had been in was a revelation of nondualistic experience. So then I knew that what is written in the scriptures about this experience is all true.

Days of Ecstasy at Dakshineswar

It is impossible to give others any idea of the ineffable joy we derived from the presence of the Master. It is really beyond our understanding how he could train us, without our knowing it, through fun and play, and thus mould our spiritual life. As the master wrestler proceeds with great caution and restraint with the beginner — now overpowering him in the struggle with great difficulty, as it were, and again allowing himself to be defeated to strengthen the pupil's self-confidence — in exactly the same manner did Sri Ramakrishna handle us. Realizing that the Atman [Self], the source of infinite strength, exists in every individual, pigmy though he might be, he was able to see the potential giant in all. He could clearly discern the latent spiritual power which would in the fullness of time manifest itself. Holding up that bright picture to view, he would speak highly of us and encourage us. Again he would warn us lest we should obstruct this future consummation by becoming entangled in worldly desires, and moreover he would keep us under control by carefully observing even the minute details of our life. All this was done silently and unobtrusively. That was the secret of his training of the disciples and of his moulding of their lives.

Once I felt that I could not practise deep concentration during meditation. I told him of it and sought his advice and direction. He told me his personal experiences in the matter and gave me instructions. I remember that as I sat down to meditate during the early hours of the morning, my mind would be disturbed and diverted by the shrill note of the whistle of a neighbouring jute mill. I told him about it, and he advised me to concentrate my mind on the sound of the whistle itself. I followed his advice and derived much benefit from it.

On another occasion I felt difficulty in totally forgetting my body during meditation and concentrating the mind wholly on the ideal. I went to him for counsel, and he gave me the very instruction which he himself had received from Tota Puri [his guru] while practising samadhi according to Vedantic disciplines. He sharply pressed between my eyebrows with his fingernail and said, "Now concentrate your mind on this painful sensation!" I found I could concentrate easily on that sensation as long as I liked, and during that period I completely let go the consciousness of the other parts of my body, not to speak of their causing any distraction hindering my meditation. The solitude of the Panchavati, associated with the various spiritual realizations of the Master, was also the most suitable place for our meditation.

Besides meditation and spiritual exercises, we used to spend a good deal of time there in sheer fun and merrymaking. Sri Ramakrishna also joined in with us, and by taking part, enhanced our innocent pleasure. We used to run and skip about, climb on the trees, swing from the creepers, and at times hold merry picnics. On the first day that we picnicked the Master noticed that I had cooked the food myself, and he partook of it. I knew that he could not take food unless it was cooked by brahmins, and therefore I had arranged for his meal at the Kali temple. But he said, "It won't be wrong for me to take food from such a pure soul as you." In spite of my repeated remonstrations, he enjoyed the food I had cooked that day.

"Ramakrishna Dedicated Me"

Early in 1884 Naren's father Vishwanath died of a heart attack; he had been ailing for some time. When the time came to look into Vishwanath's financial affairs, it was found that he had been spending more than he earned and had left nothing but debts. Some relatives even tried to get a share in the family home by means of a lawsuit. They lost the suit, but Naren was still faced by his duty, as the oldest male member of the family, to support his mother and brothers. He had never known adversity of any kind before. He narrated his struggles:

Even before the prescribed period of mourning was over, I was running hither and thither in search of a job. Dizzy from lack of food, I had to go from office to office barefoot in the blazing sun, carrying my application papers. Everywhere I met with a refusal. From that first experience I learned that unselfish sympathy is very rare in this world; there is no place here for the poor and the weak. Even those who, only a few weeks previously, would have regarded it as a piece of luck if they could do me a favour, now made wry reluctant faces, though they could easily have helped me if they had wished. One day, during that time, when I was walking around in the sun, the soles of my feet became blistered. I was completely exhausted and had to sit down in the shade of the Ochterloney Monument on the Maidan. A friend who happened to be with me wanted to console me, so he sang:

> Here blows the wind, the breath of Brahman —
> It is his grace we feel —

But when I heard that song, I felt as if he were beating me violently on the head. Thinking of the helplessness of my mother and my brothers, I was filled with resentment and despair. "Be quiet!" I told him. "That fanciful nonsense is all right for people living in the lap of luxury — people who have no idea what hunger is — people whose nearest and dearest aren't going in rags and starving. No doubt it sounds true and beautiful to them — as it did to me, in the old days. But now I've seen what life is really like. That song is just a pack of lies."

I dare say my friend was terribly hurt by my words. How could he understand the grinding poverty which had made me utter them? Some mornings, when I got up, I would find that there wasn't enough food for all of us, so I'd tell my mother, "A friend has invited me to lunch." On such days I had nothing to eat, for I had no money in my pocket. I was too proud to say anything about this to anyone outside my family. Sometimes rich men would invite me into their houses to sing and play at their parties, and I went, just as I had always done. Most of them never concerned themselves about how I was getting along. A very few used to ask, "Why do you look so pale and sad today?" But only one of them ever found out — and that wasn't through me — how things really were. He used to send money to my mother from time to time, anonymously. I am under an eternal debt to him.

In spite of all these trials and tribulations, I did not lose my faith in the existence of God, nor did I doubt that "God is good." I used to wake up from sleep in the morning, remember the Lord, and leave my bed taking his name. Then with firm determination and hope I went from place to place in search of some means of earning money. I was leaving my bed as usual, calling on the Lord, when one day my mother heard my words from the adjacent room and said bitterly: "Stop, lad. You have been constantly repeating the name of the Lord since your childhood — and what has he done for you?" The words hurt me terribly. Cut to the quick, I pondered: "Does God actually exist? If so, does he hear the plaintive prayer of man? Why then is there no response to my many prayers to him? Whence is so much evil in the creation of a benign Creator? Why is there so much calamity in the kingdom of one who is all Bliss?" . . . My heart was pierced through by a feeling of wounded love, and doubt in the existence of God assailed me.

It was against my nature to do anything and conceal it from others. Even as a child, I had never been able to conceal my least thought or action, either from fear or any other motive. So it wasn't surprising that I now began to tell people aggressively that God did not exist; and that, even if he did exist, it was no use calling on him because it produced no results. Of course, the rumour soon spread around that I had become an atheist, and furthermore that I was mixing with people of bad character and visiting houses of ill repute.

Such news travels fast. It didn't take long for these words of mine, in a completely distorted version, to reach the ears of the Master, not to mention those of his devotees in Calcutta. Some of them came to visit me, to find out the truth, and they made it obvious that they believed at least part of what they had heard, if not all. I was bitterly wounded to realize that they could think so little of me. I told them that it was cowardice to believe in God merely from fear of hell. Quoting Hume, Mill, Bain, Comte, and other Western philosophers, I argued fiercely that there is no evidence of the existence of God. And so they went away, more than ever convinced, as I afterwards learned, of my downfall. In my defiant mood, this actually made me happy. Then the thought came to me that perhaps the Master now believed the same thing. As soon as I thought that, I felt terrible pain. But I said to myself, "Let him believe it, then. If he does, I can't help it. People's good or bad opinions are worth nothing anyhow." Later, I discovered that the Master *had* heard all of these lies about me. At first he had made no comment. Then, when one of the devotees wept and said, "Sir, we never dreamed Naren would sink so low!" the Master cried out excitedly, "Silence, you scoundrels! Mother has told me that he could never do such things. If you talk about this anymore, I won't have you in the room!"

I now became absolutely indifferent to the praise or blame of the world. I was firmly convinced that I wasn't born to earn money, support a family, or seek worldly enjoyments. Secretly, I was preparing to renounce the world, as my grandfather had done. The day arrived on which I had decided to start life as a wandering monk — and then I heard that, on that very day, the Master was coming to the house of a devotee in Calcutta. I thought this was very fortunate: I should see my guru before I left home forever. But, as soon as I met the Master, he told me imperiously, "You must come with me to Dakshinewar today." I offered various excuses, but he wouldn't take no for an answer. I had to ride back with him. In the carriage we didn't speak much. When we got to Dakshineswar I sat in his room for some time. Others were present. Then the Master went into a state of ecstasy. He came over to me suddenly, took my hand in his, and sang, with tears pouring down his face:

We are afraid to speak, and yet we are afraid to keep still;
Our minds, O Radha, half believe that we are about to lose you!

All this time I had fought back the strong emotion I was feeling. Now I couldn't do so any longer, and my tears poured down like his. I felt sure that the Master knew all about my plans. The others were astonished to see us behave in this way. After the Master had returned to normal consciousness, one of them asked him what was the matter. He smiled and answered, "It's just something between the two of us." That night he sent the others away and called me to him and said: "I know you have come to the world to do Mother's work. You can never lead a worldly life. But, for my sake, stay with your family as long as I'm alive."

I bade good-bye to the Master and returned home the next day. And immediately a hundred thoughts about the family occupied my mind. I began going from place to place now as before and made various kinds of efforts. I worked in the office of an attorney and translated a few books, as a result of which I earned a little money and the household was managed somehow. But these were all temporary jobs, and in the absence of any permanent work no smooth arrangement for the maintenance of my mother and brothers could be made. I remembered a little later: "God grants the Master's prayers. I shall make him pray for me so that the suffering of my mother and brothers for want of food and clothing might be removed. He will never refuse to do so for my sake."

I hurried to Dakshineswar and persistently asked him to pray to Mother that the pecuniary difficulty of my mother and brothers might be removed. The Master said to me affectionately: "My child, I cannot say such words, you know. Why don't you yourself pray? You don't accept Mother. That is why you suffer so much." I replied: "I have no knowledge of Mother. Please pray to Mother yourself for my sake. You must pray. I will not leave you unless you do so." The Master said with affection: "I prayed to Mother many times indeed to remove your sufferings. But as you do not accept Mother, she does not grant the prayer. Well, today is Tuesday, a day especially sacred to Mother. Mother will, I say, grant you whatever you ask for. Go to the temple tonight, bow down to her, and pray for a boon. My affectionate Mother is the Power of Brahman. She is pure Consciousness embodied. She has given birth to the universe according to her will. What can she not do, if she wills?"

A firm faith arose in my mind that all the sufferings would certainly come to an end as soon as I prayed to Mother, inasmuch as the Master had said so. I waited for the night in great expectancy. The night arrived at last. Three hours of the night had elapsed when the Master asked me to go to the holy temple. As I was going, a sort of profound inebriation possessed me. I was reeling. A firm conviction gripped me that I would actually see Mother and hear her words. I forgot everything else and became completely merged in that thought alone. Coming into the temple, I saw that Mother was actually pure Consciousness, was actually living, and was really the fountainhead of infinite love and beauty. My heart swelled with loving devotion, and, beside myself with bliss, I made repeated salutations to her, praying: "Mother, grant me discrimination, grant me detachment, grant me divine knowledge and devotion. Ordain that I may always have an unobstructed vision of you." My heart was flooded with peace. The whole universe completely disappeared and Mother alone remained filling my heart.

No sooner had I returned to the Master than he asked, "Did you pray to Mother for the removal of your worldly wants?" Startled at his question, I said: "No, sir, I forgot to do so. So what should I do now?" He said, "Go quickly again and pray to her." I started for the temple once more, and coming to Mother's presence, became inebriated again. I forgot everything, bowed down to her repeatedly, and prayed for divine knowledge and devotion before I came back. The Master smiled and said, "Well, did you tell her this time?" I was startled again and said: "No, sir. Hardly had I seen Mother when I forgot everything on account of the influence of an indescribable Divine Power and prayed for knowledge and devotion only. What's to be done now?" The Master said: "Silly boy, could you not control yourself a little and make that prayer? Go once more, if you can, and tell her those words. Quick!"

I started a third time, but as soon as I entered the temple a formidable sense of shame occupied my heart. I thought what a trifling thing have I come to ask of Mother! It is, as the Master says, just like the folly of asking a king, having received his grace, for gourds and pumpkins. Ah! How low is my intellect! Overpowered with shame and aversion I bowed down to her over and over again, saying: "I don't want anything else, Mother. Do grant me divine knowledge and devotion only." When I came out from the temple, it occurred to me that it was certainly the play of the Master. Otherwise, how was it that I could not speak the words though I came to pray to her as many as three times? Afterwards I insisted that he ensure my mother's and brothers' freedom from lack of food and clothing, saying, "It is certainly you who made me intoxicated that way." He said affectionately to me: "My child, I can never offer such a prayer for anyone. It does not indeed come out of my mouth. You would, I told you, get from Mother whatever you wanted. But you could not ask her for it. You are not meant for worldly happiness. What can I do?" I said: "That won't do, sir. You must utter the prayer for my sake. It is my firm conviction that they will be free from all sufferings if you only say so." As I kept on persisting, he said, "All right — they will never lack plain food and clothing."

*   *   *

Ramakrishna dedicated me to her [Divine Mother]. And I believe that she guides me in every little thing I do and just does what she likes with me. Yet I fought so long. I loved the man [Sri Ramakrishna], and that held me. I thought him the purest man I had ever seen, and I know that he loved me as my own father and mother had not the power to do.

Experience of Nirvikalpa Samadhi

One day in the Cossipore garden, I expressed my prayer [for nirvikalpa samadhi] to Sri Ramakrishna with great earnestness. Then in the evening, at the hour of meditation, I lost consciousness of the body and felt that it was absolutely nonexistent. I felt that the sun, moon, space, time, ether, and all had been reduced to a homogeneous mass and then melted far away into the unknown. Body-consciousness almost vanished, and I nearly merged in the Supreme. But I had just a trace of the feeling of ego so I could again return to the world of relativity from samadhi. In this state of samadhi all difference between "I" and "Brahman" goes away, everything is reduced to unity, like the water of the Infinite Ocean — water everywhere, nothing else exists. Language and thought, all fail there. Then only is the state "beyond mind and speech" realized in its actuality. Otherwise, as long as the religious aspirant thinks or says, "I am Brahman" — "I" and "Brahman," these two entities persist — there is the involved semblance of duality. After that experience, even after trying repeatedly, I failed to bring back the state of samadhi. On informing Sri Ramakrishna about it, he said: "If you remain day and night in that state, the work of the Divine Mother will not be accomplished. Therefore you won't be able to induce that state again. When your work is finished, it will come again."

Sri Ramakrishna Transmitted Power

Two or three days before Sri Ramakrishna's passing away, she whom he used to call "Kali" entered this body. It is she who takes me here and there and makes me work, without letting me remain quiet or allowing me to look to my personal comforts.

Before his leaving the body, he called me to his side one day, and asking me to sit before him, looked steadily at me and went into samadhi. Then I felt that a subtle force like an electric shock was entering my body! In a little while I also lost outward consciousness and sat motionless. How long I stayed in that condition I do not remember. When consciousness returned I found Sri Ramakrishna shedding tears. On questioning him, he answered me affectionately: "Today, giving you my all, I have become a beggar. With this power you are to do much work for the good of the world before you return." I feel that that power is constantly directing me to this or that work. This body has not been made for remaining idle.

Sri Ramakrishna Revealed Himself

One day while Sri Ramakrishna was staying at the Cossipore garden, his body in imminent danger of falling off forever, I was sitting by the side of his bed and saying in my mind, "Well, now if you can declare that you are God, then only will I believe you are really God himself." It was only two days before he passed away. Immediately he looked up towards me and said, "He who was Rama, he who was Krishna, verily is he now Ramakrishna in this body, and not in your Vedantic sense."[2] At this I was struck dumb.

[From: *Sri Ramakrishna, The Great Master*, by Swami Saradananda (Madras: Sri Ramakrishna Math), vol. 2, 1979; *Ramakrishna and His Disciples*, by Christopher Isherwood (London: Methuen & Co., Ltd.), 1965; *Life of Swami Vivekananda*, by His Eastern & Western Disciples (Calcutta: Advaita Ashrama), vol. 1, 1979; *The Complete Works of Swami Vivekananda* (Mayavati: Advaita Ashrama), vols. VI & VII, 1968-69]

---

[2] A few words may be said here about the meaning of the Incarnation in the Hindu religious tradition. One of the main doctrines of Vedanta is the divinity of the soul: every soul, in reality, is Brahman. Thus it may be presumed that there is no difference between an Incarnation and an ordinary man. To be sure, from the standpoint of the Absolute, or Brahman, no such difference exists. But from the relative standpoint, where multiplicity is perceived, a difference must be admitted. Embodied human beings reflect godliness in varying measure. In an Incarnation this godliness is fully manifest. Therefore an Incarnation is unlike an ordinary mortal or even an illumined saint.

To give an illustration: There is no difference between a clay lion and a clay mouse, from the standpoint of the clay. Both become the same substance when dissolved into clay. But the difference between the lion and the mouse, from the standpoint of form, is clearly seen. Likewise, as Brahman, an ordinary man is identical with an Incarnation. Both become the same Brahman when they attain final illumination. But in the relative state of name and form, which is admitted by Vedanta, the difference between them is accepted. According to the Bhagavad Gita (IV. 6-8), Brahman in times of spiritual crisis assumes a human body through Its own inscrutable power, called maya. Though birthless, immutable, and the Lord of all beings, yet in every age Brahman appears to be incarnated in a human body for the protection of the good and the punishment of the wicked.

Swami Brahmananda

5

Swami Brahmananda

Swami Brahmananda (1863-1922) met Sri Ramakrishna in the middle of 1881 and lived with him almost constantly until the Master's passing away. The Master had a vision about him prior to their first meeting, and as soon as he saw Brahmananda, recognized him as his spiritual son. The swami later became the first president of the Ramakrishna Order.

Living with Sri Ramakrishna

Some devotees would tell Sri Ramakrishna about their spiritual experiences. Hearing them, one young disciple[1] asked the Master to grant him some spiritual experiences. The Master told him: "Look. That kind of experience comes when one practises meditation and prayer regularly and systematically. Wait. You will get it eventually."

A couple of days later, in the evening, the young disciple saw the Master walking towards the Divine Mother's temple, and he followed him. Sri Ramakrishna entered the temple, but the disciple did not dare go inside, so he sat in the natmandir [the hall in front of the Mother's temple] and began to meditate. After a while he suddenly saw a brilliant light, like that of a million suns, rushing towards him from the shrine of the Divine Mother. He was frightened and ran to the Master's room.

A little later Sri Ramakrishna returned from the shrine. Seeing the young disciple in his room, he said: "Hello! Did you sit for meditation this evening?" "Yes, I did," answered the young disciple, and he related to the Master what had happened. Then the Master told him: "You complain that you don't experience anything. You ask, 'What is the use of practising meditation?' So why did you run away when you had an experience?"

It is natural to experience depression now and then. I also felt like that once while I was in Dakshineswar. I was then quite young and the

---

[1] This young disciple was Swami Brahmananda himself.

Master was about fifty years old, so I was shy about speaking openly with him. One day I was meditating in the Kali temple. I could not concentrate my mind. This made me very sad. I said to myself: "I have been living here so long, yet I have not achieved anything. What is the use of staying here then? Forget it! I am not going to say anything about it to the Master. If this depressed condition continues another two or three days, I shall return home. There my mind will be occupied with different things." Having decided this in the shrine, I returned to the Master's room. The Master was then walking on the verandah. Seeing me, he also entered the room. It was customary after returning from the shrine to salute the Master and then eat a light breakfast. As soon as I saluted the Master, he said, "Look. When you returned from the shrine, I saw that your mind seemed to be covered with a thick net." I realized that he knew everything, so I said, "Sir, you know the bad condition of my mind." He then wrote something on my tongue. Immediately I forgot all my painful depression and was overwhelmed with an inexpressible joy.

As long as I lived with him I had spontaneous recollection and contemplation of God. An ecstatic joy filled me all the time. That is why one requires a powerful guru — one who has realized God. Before initiation the guru and the disciple should test each other for a long time. Otherwise there may be regrets afterwards. This is no passing relationship.

Ah, how joyfully we lived with the Master at Dakshineswar! Sometimes we would be convulsed with side-splitting laughter by his humour and wit. What we now cannot experience by meditation, we then attained automatically. If my mind went astray even a little, he would understand it from my appearance and would pass his hand over my chest, setting my mind right. And how free I was with him! One day, on the semicircular west porch, I was rubbing oil on his body. For some reason I got angry with him. I threw away the bottle of oil and strode off with the intention of never returning. I got as far as Jadu Mallik's garden house but could not move further. I sat down. In the meantime he had sent Ramlal to call me back. When I returned he said: "Look. Could you go? I drew a boundary line there."

On another occasion I did something wrong and became extremely penitent. I went to confess it to him. As soon as I arrived he asked me to follow him with his water jug. While returning he said: "You did this certain thing yesterday. Never do it again." I was surprised. I wondered how he had known.

Another day when I returned from Calcutta he said: "Why can't I look at you? Have you done anything wrong?" "No," I replied, because I understood "wrong action" to mean stealing, robbery, adultery, and so on. The Master again asked me, "Did you tell any lie?" Then I remembered that the day before, while chatting and joking, I had told an untruth.

There is nothing outside. Everything is inside. People are fond of music, but they do not realize that the music we hear with our ears is trivial compared to the music within. How sweet and soothing it is! During his meditation in the Panchavati, Sri Ramakrishna used to listen to the melody of the vina [a stringed instrument] within.

Once I was meditating in the Panchavati at noon while the Master was talking about the manifestation of Brahman as sound [*Shabda-Brahman*]. Listening to that discussion, even the birds in the Panchavati began to sing Vedic songs and I heard them.

The Master's Spiritual States

Holy company is necessary. When one sees and hears holy people, spiritual feelings arise in the mind and doubts go away. One imbibes deeper impressions by observing a pure, God-intoxicated life than by reading hundreds of books. Adhar Sen [a devotee of Sri Ramakrishna] used to visit the Master quite often accompanied by a school subinspector, who sometimes experienced ecstasy. One day when they arrived at Dakshineswar the Master was in samadhi. There was such a smile on his face, as if it could not contain so much joy. Then Adhar said to his friend: "Seeing your trance, I conceived a disgust for it. It seemed to suggest great suffering within you. Can divine ecstasy ever cause pain? The blissful ecstasy of the Master has opened my eyes. I would have found it impossible to come here anymore if his ecstasy had been like yours." Doubt would have remained in Adhar's mind had he not gone to the Master and seen his samadhi. This is the result of holy company.

Usually Sri Ramakrishna never slept for more than an hour or so at night. He would pass the night sometimes in samadhi, sometimes singing devotional songs, and sometimes chanting the Lord's name. I often saw him in samadhi for an hour or more. In that state he could not talk in spite of repeated efforts. Regaining outer consciousness, he would say: "Look. When I am in samadhi I want to tell you my experiences, but at that time I lose my power of speech." After samadhi, he used to mutter something. It seemed to me that he was talking with somebody. I heard that in earlier years the Master stayed in samadhi most of the time.

The Master would go into different kinds of samadhi at different times. Sometimes his whole body would become stiff like a log. Coming down from this state, he could easily regain normal consciousness. At other times, however, when he was absorbed in deep samadhi, it would take a longer period for him to return to consciousness of the outer world. On such occasions he would take a deep breath after gasping for a while, like a drowning man coming up out of water. Even after he had composed himself, he would talk like a drunkard for some time, and not all of his speech was intelligible. At that time he would often express some small desire: "I shall eat sukta [a bitter squash curry]," "I shall smoke tobacco," and so on. And sometimes he would rub his face, moving his hands up and down.

[*Swami Brahmananda then raised a question himself and continued the conversation.*] Can you tell me why the Master made rapid spiritual progress without having any particular external help? It is hard to discern any cause other than a few inborn *samskaras* [tendencies]. Is it not a miracle? There are many more wonders in his life. Once a monk gave the Master a metal image of Ramlala [the child Rama]. When the Master carried that image to the Ganga for a bath, it would swim in the river. The Master himself told us this. Under such circumstances how does one differentiate between matter and consciousness?

The Master said that in the beginning he did not feel any strong desire to renounce the world, but a spiritual tempest blew over him which changed his whole life.

Before the Master passed away at the Cossipore garden house, he would tell us about his visions of the Infinite. One day Girish and Swamis Vivekananda, Ramakrishnananda, Niranjanananda, and I were present in his room. We were then young boys, but Girish was elderly and extremely intelligent. Hearing a few words about the Infinite from the Master, Girish exclaimed: "Sir, don't talk anymore. I get dizzy." Oh, what a conversation! The Master used to say: "Shukadeva is like an ant that is satisfied with a small particle of sugar. Rama, Krishna, and other Incarnations are like bunches of grapes hanging on the tree of Satchidananda." These are mere thoughts about the Infinite. It is hard to comprehend.

On one occasion Sri Ramakrishna said: "One day as I was meditating in the Kali temple, I saw in a vision the veils of maya disappearing one after another. In another vision the Divine Mother showed me the light of Brahman, which surpassed the light of even millions of suns together. I then saw that a luminous form emerged from that infinite light and again merged back into its source. I experienced that the formless Brahman took a form and again became formless."

Oh, what superhuman power the Master had! At that time we thought it was merely a peculiar power with him, but we could not understand the nature of it. Now we realize what a wonderful power it was! One day I said to him: "Sir, I cannot get rid of lust. What shall I do?"

He touched me in the region of the heart, muttering some indistinct words. All lust vanished from me forever! I have never felt its existence since then. Do you see the wonder of it?

I never saw him manifest any powers such as *anima* [the power to assume minute forms] or others, but he had a very clear insight into human character. I witnessed a number of supernatural things in his life.

The Master's Spiritual Instructions

It would have been wonderful if the Master's sayings, especially those about his devotional practices, spiritual unfoldment, and experiences, could have been recorded exactly and correctly — that is to say, immediately after hearing them from him. When he talked about knowledge [jnana], he did not talk about anything else. Again, when he talked about devotion [bhakti], he spoke of nothing but devotion. He repeatedly imprinted in our minds that worldly knowledge is insignificant and futile, that one must exert oneself to attain spiritual knowledge, devotion, and love alone.

The Master could seldom sleep at night. He did not allow the boys who lived with him to sleep either. When others had gone to bed he would wake up his disciples, saying: "What is this? Have you come here to sleep?" Then he would instruct each disciple and send him for meditation to the Panchavati, Kali temple, or Shiva temple, according to his inclination. After practising japam and meditation as directed, each would return to the room and sleep. Thus the Master made his disciples work hard. Often he would say: "Three classes of people stay awake at night: the yogi, the enjoyer, and the sick person. You are all yogis, so sleeping at night is not meant for you."

Sri Ramakrishna used to say, "Eat as much as you like during the day but eat sparingly at night." The idea is that the full meal taken at noon will be easily digested, and if you eat lightly at night, your body will remain light and you can easily concentrate the mind. A heavy meal at night produces laziness and sleep.

Sri Ramakrishna used to encourage everybody to practise meditation. A person falls from spiritual life if he does not practise meditation regularly. The Master asked his guru Tota Puri, "You have attained perfection, so why do you still practise meditation?" Pointing to his shining brass pot, Tota Puri replied, "If you do not clean brass every day, it will be covered with stains." The Master used to say: "The sign of true meditation is that one forgets one's surroundings and body. One will not feel even a crow sitting on one's head." Sri Ramakrishna attained that state. Once while he was meditating in the natmandir, a crow sat on his head.

The temple garden of Dakshineswar, which Rani Rasmani had built, provided everything Sri Ramakrishna needed for practising sadhana. If you have true faith, love, and devotion, God will provide everything you need.

A monk saved ten thousand rupees in a bank. Hearing this, the Master said, "He who calculates pros and cons and plans for the future will ruin his spiritual life."

Usually the Master would not allow anyone to stay with him for more than two or three days, but once a young man stayed with him for several days. This annoyed some devotees, and they complained to the Master that he was teaching the young man the path of renunciation. The Master answered: "Let him take up a worldly life. Am I dissuading him from it? Let him first attain knowledge and then enter the world. Do I teach everybody to renounce lust and gold? I talk about renunciation to the ones who need only a little encouragement." He used to say to the rest, "Go and enjoy hog-plum pickle, and come here for medicine when you have colic."

Sometimes the Master would ask people: "Can you tell me what kind of state I am passing through? What makes me go so often to those who cannot buy me a penny's worth of puffed sugar cakes and who have not even the means to offer me a torn mat to sit on?" He used to explain afterwards: "I find that certain people will easily attain success. It will be very difficult for the rest, for they are, as it were, pots for curd. One cannot keep milk in them." He would tell them, "I pray for you so that you may realize God quickly."

One day when the topic of the *Kartabhajas*[2] came up in the course of conversation, Girish Ghosh [a devotee of the Master] sarcastically remarked that he would write a drama about them. Hearing this, the Master gravely said: "You see, some people in that sect also have attained perfection. It too is a path."

One day Swami Turiyananda asked the Master, "How can I get rid of lust?" The Master replied: "Why should it be gotten rid of? Turn it in another direction." He said the same thing about anger, greed, infatuation, and other passions. These words of the Master inspired the young disciple.

The Master used to say, "Wherever there is extreme longing, God reveals himself more." He also said to some people, while pointing to himself: "Have love for this. That will do." Oh! Such a wonderful play is over!

---

[2] Kartabhajas — a minor sect of Vaishnavas (worshippers of Vishnu).

Again, he used to say, "One needs intense longing to realize God." In this connection the Master often told a story: Once an aspirant asked his teacher how to realize God. The teacher, without answering, took the disciple to the nearest pond and held him under the water. After a while, when the student was extremely restless and about to collapse, the teacher pulled him out of the water and asked, "How did you feel under the water?" "I was dying for a breath of air," he answered. "When you feel like that for God," said the teacher, "you will realize him."

Another time he said: "Do you know what type of love is necessary for God-realization? As a dog with a wound in its head becomes frantic and jumps around, so one should desperately seek God."

The Master used to say that there should not be any theft [i.e., hypocrisy] in the inner chamber of the heart. He had great affection for the simple-hearted. He used to say: "I don't care for flattery. I love the person who calls on God sincerely." The Master also said that all impurities of the mind disappear by calling on God with a sincere heart.

Sri Ramakrishna and Swami Vivekananda

Sri Ramakrishna looked upon all as God. Once Swami Vivekananda said to him, "Sir, since you love us so much, will you finally turn out to be another Jada Bharata?"[3] The Master replied: "One becomes a Jada Bharata by thinking about inert objects, but I think only of consciousness. The day I feel attached to you, I shall drive you all away."

One day the Master did not speak to Swamiji [Swami Vivekananda] for some reason, but Swamiji was unperturbed and remained cheerful. Observing this, the Master said, "He is a great soul." On another day when Keshab Sen [a devotee of the Master] eulogized Swamiji, the Master told him: "Do not praise him so much. He has yet to blossom out."

*   *   *

At first Swami Vivekananda [then known as Narendra] indulged in a lot of dry discussion with the Master. At that time he believed that God was only formless. He even told the Master, "Sir, these visions of yours are all hallucinations." He used to ridicule those who bowed down to the gods and goddesses in the temples. Some devotees were annoyed

---

[3] In ancient times there was a king named Jada Bharata, who spent the last years of his life as a recluse in the forest. One day he saw a pregnant deer being attacked by a lion. She jumped into the river and while trying to get back up on shore, gave birth to a fawn and died. Jada Bharata saved the fawn, raised it, and became very attached to it. At the time of his death he was thinking of the deer and as a result was reborn as a deer. When that deer-life ended he was again reborn as a brahmin and attained illumination. See: *Vishnu Purana*

with Swamiji for this, but the Master was never irritated with him. The Master said, "Nowadays it is hard to find a soul like Naren." Later, when the Master showed Swamiji forms of gods and goddesses, he began to believe in them. From then on Swamiji would say, "If one has steadfast devotion for God, whether with form or without form, one attains perfection."

Other Reminiscences

Oh, how deep was the Master's devotion to truth! If he happened to say that he would not eat any more food, he could not eat more, even if he was hungry. Once he said that he would go to visit Jadu Mallik [whose garden house was adjacent to the Dakshineswar temple garden] but later forgot all about it. I also did not remind him. After supper he suddenly remembered the appointment. It was quite late at night, but he had to go. I accompanied him with a lantern in my hand. When we reached the house we found it closed and all apparently asleep. The Master pushed back the doors of the living room a little, placed his foot inside the room, and then left.

He could see the inside of a man by merely looking at his face, as though he were looking through a glass pane. Whenever a visitor came he would look him over from head to foot, and he would understand everything. Then he would answer that person's questions.

Even great saints cannot always give up egotism. Swami Bhaskara-nanda [of Varanasi] showed me his own photograph and said, "See, my picture is being sold!" But the Master! When Keshab Sen wrote about him in his paper, the Master forbade him to do so again.

One day the son of a public woman came to Dakshineswar. The Master was sleeping in his room. The man entered and touched his feet. The Master at once jumped up, as if someone had thrown fire on him. He said: "Tell me frankly all the sins you have committed. If you cannot, then go to the Ganga and say them loudly. You will be freed from them." But the man was ill-fated and could not do so.

[From: *A Guide to Spiritual Life: Spiritual Teachings of Swami Brahmananda* by Swami Chetanananda (St. Louis: Vedanta Society), 1988]

6

Swami Adbhutananda

Swami Adbhutananda (?-1920), or Latu Maharaj, was an uneducated, unsophisticated shepherd boy. From the time he joined the Master at Dakshineswar until the Master's death, Latu was almost constantly in attendance on him. Latu's reminiscences of Sri Ramakrishna therefore have a special value in their wealth of detail and insight.

It was 11 March 1883, Sri Ramakrishna's birthday. The Master asked me to bring him some water from the Ganga for his bath. He took his bath with one pitcher of water and afterwards went to the Kali temple. Some of us had to work in the kitchen. Between one hundred and one hundred and fifty people had their meal at Dakshineswar on that occasion, and whatever was left from the meal was distributed to the poor. Manomohan Babu brought a kirtan party from Konnagar, and the Master sang with them. Later he asked us to join him in the Panchavati. The Master told us that day that he was not only a sannyasin [monk], but king among the sannyasins.

Once while staying at Dakshineswar, Rakhal [Swami Brahmananda] became sick. The Master told him: "Take this prasad of Lord Jagannath. Then you will be all right." Such is the effect of the prasad of Jagannath! You people don't believe that. The Master used to say, "Before you take your food, eat one or two particles of Jagannath prasad."

On Dashahara day [a special celebration in honour of the Ganga] the Master asked us to offer worship to the Mother Ganga. He told Rakhal, "Mother Ganga is a living goddess, and today one should worship her." At that time Rakhal did not regard the Ganga as a goddess, and as the Master knew this, he told him: "One day while I was walking near the embankment of the Ganga, I had a doubt: Is Mother Ganga truly a goddess? At that moment I heard the distinct sound of a conch coming from the middle of the river. Gradually the sound came nearer, and I saw a boy travelling across the water, blowing a conch, and a goddess

Swami Adbhutananada at Alambazar monastery in 1896

was following him. That vision dispelled all my doubts."[1] Rakhal was amazed to hear this and said: "We don't know about such things. We only know the Ganga as a river of water, befouled by the boatmen." The Master replied sharply: "Take care! Don't you befoul the Mother Ganga!" From that day on Rakhal had great respect for the Ganga.

That was also the first year [1883] that I attended the festival at Panihati with the Master. Rakhal, Bhavanath, and others went in Ram Babu's carriage. Many other devotees of the Master also attended. Navadwip Goswami was there, and the Master suddenly began to sing with him. All of us were startled to see the Master go into *bhava samadhi*. His breathing stopped; his face, eyes, even the palms of his hands, reddened. Seeing him in this ecstatic mood, many people rushed to take the dust of his feet. We were in a dilemma. Everybody wanted to touch the Master, and though we forbade them, they ignored us. So there was an uproar.

Ram Babu said to me: "Leto, don't try to stop them. Let the people touch him and be blessed." But I didn't obey him, for I knew that if just anybody touched the Master while he was in samadhi, he would experience terrible pain.

At last, three of us — Rakhal, Bhavanath, and I — escorted him from the grounds to the parlour. But how difficult it was to resist those devotees! Even as we headed for the parlour, people continued to touch his feet. Then do you know what Ram Babu did? He took a handful of dust from the ground and touched it to the Master's feet and then started to distribute it among the people. Thus the Master was released from the crowd.

The following year [*actually this visit was in 1885*] I also went to Panihati with him. This time we went by boat. Someone asked Holy Mother [Sri Sarada Devi] to accompany us, but she refused. The Master praised her for this: "See her wisdom. She refused to go with us so that no one would make critical comments about us." That year the Master took prasad with all and danced in ecstasy with both hands raised.

At this same festival the Master was offered five rupees — other holy men received only one or two rupees. [*It is an Indian custom to honour a holy man with gifts.*] The Master would not accept the money. The manager of the festival insisted, however, and secretly gave the money to Rakhal. With the money Rakhal bought a basket of mangoes and a package of sweets for the Master. When the Master came to know of it, he was angry with Rakhal and warned him: "Never do anything like

---

[1] This vision of Sri Ramakrishna's corroborates the mythological story of how Bhagirath brought the Ganga from heaven to earth in order to save his departed ancestors.

that again. Your acceptance means my acceptance. A monk must be like the birds and not lay things up for the future."

About two months before Durga Puja [the autumn festival of the goddess Durga] we accompanied the Master to Jadu Mallik's house at Pathuriaghat [in Calcutta]. Although I had seen Jadu Mallik before in his garden house [adjacent to the Dakshineswar temple], I had never been to his home. The Master came to see the new image of the goddess Simhavahini, who was the presiding deity at Jadu Mallik's house. After visiting the shrine, the Master asked about Jadu Babu.

Jadu Babu was lying on a marble bench. He greeted the Master: "Welcome, welcome, young priest. You don't come this way very often anymore. But since Mother is here now, you have remembered us."

In reply the Master said: "What type of man are you? Mother has come here and you didn't let me know!"

"Young priest, I have never met a man so well informed about the Mother as you," replied Jadu Babu. "She arrived just yesterday, and you have come already. When have I had the time to send the news to you?"

"All right," said the Master, smiling. "Now please ask for some of the Mother's prasad to be brought. It would not be auspicious if we returned home without having taken anything." [It is considered inauspicious for a householder not to offer anything to a holy man who visits his home.]

Still lying on the bench, Jadu Babu ordered someone to bring some prasad, and that was done instantly. When the Master was ready to leave, Jadu Babu said, "Won't you say hello to my own mother?"

So the Master shouted: "Hello, Jadu's mother! Will you give me a glass of water?" Jadu's mother came downstairs with a glass. The Master took it and sipped from it once.

When the Master returned to the carriage, the devotees said: "Sir, please don't go to such a rich man's house again. Why should you visit him? He did not even ask you to be seated. Why should you be subjected to such insults?"

The Master answered: "These are worldly people, and they are always desiring worldly things. Yet in between their worldly thoughts they worship the Mother. You don't even do that much. Why should your heads ache over whether he did or didn't ask me to sit down? You came to visit the Mother, and as a bonus you received prasad. Isn't that enough for you? Who else would have given you prasad at such an unusual hour? Did you come only to visit Jadu and to be offended because he did not ask you to be seated?"

The devotees who had spoken against Jadu Babu became silent. Thus the Master would test us. "If you want to be a sadhu [holy man]," he would say, "give up the idea of self-importance. Pay no attention to whether you are respected or not."

One day the Master told Jadu Babu: "You have saved so much for this world. What have you acquired for the next?"

Jadu Babu replied: "Young priest, you are the one who will take care of the other world for me. You will save me at the moment of death, and I am waiting until then. If you don't grant me liberation, your name 'deliverer of the fallen,' will be marred, so you cannot forget me at my death."

You see, although Jadu Mallik had plenty of money, he couldn't give up the desire for more. Another time the Master told him, "Jadu, you have saved so much money, yet still you want more."

Jadu Babu replied: "That desire will not go. You cannot give up the desire for God. In the same way, we worldly people cannot give up our desire for money. Why should I renounce money? You renounce all the things of the world and yearn for God, while I am a beggar asking for more and more of his riches. Doesn't worldly wealth also belong to him?"

The Master was very pleased to hear this line of argument. "If you maintain this attitude, you have no need to worry. But tell me, Jadu, are you saying this sincerely?"

Then Jadu Babu replied, "Young priest, you know that I cannot hide anything from you."

On another occasion the Master said to Jadu Babu: "You used to chant the name of God, but now you do not think of him. Why is this?"

Jadu Babu said: "Since I have known you, I don't feel the need to call on God. And I have found that if I chant the name of the Lord, my mind cannot concentrate on worldly affairs. So I neglect the Lord in order to look after my fortune."

"Don't go so far, Jadu," said the Master. "Why must you be like an ox yoked to a grinding mill?"

"That is the result of my past actions," said Jadu Babu.

The Master taught me a great deal. Sometimes he would purposely send me to Loren [Swami Vivekananda], so that I would hear about many things from him. Often the Master would arrange a debate between Girish Babu [Girish Ghosh] and Loren, but Loren was powerful and not afraid to challenge anyone. He would argue a lot, and I would report it all to the Master. Now and then the Master would test me. Once he asked, "Naren said all this and you kept quiet?"

"What do I know?" was my answer. "How can I compete with Loren?"

The Master said: "You have heard so many things here [*meaning himself*] and you said nothing? You should have told him that if God did not create this world, then who did?"

"Loren says that this creation is a natural process," I replied.

"Is it possible for nature to create?" the Master said. "If there is an effect, there must be a cause that preceded it. There is a powerful Being behind this creation."

Did you know that the Master snatched me from the snares of the world? I was an orphan. He flooded me with love and affection. If he had not accepted me, I would have been like an animal, spending all my days working like a slave. My life would have been worth nothing. I am an unlettered man. He used to tell me: "Always keep your mind spotless. Don't allow impure thoughts to enter it. If you find such desires tormenting you, pray to God and chant his name. He will protect you. If the mind still will not remain calm, then go to the temple of the Mother and sit before her. Or else come here [*pointing to himself*]."

Once a devotee at Dakshineswar was behaving badly, and I found it impossible to check my irritation. I scolded him and he felt very hurt. The Master knew how the devotee had suffered, and when the devotee had gone he said to me: "It is not good to speak harshly to those who come here. They are tormented with worldly problems. If they come here and then are scolded for their shortcomings, where will they go? In the presence of holy company never use harsh words to anyone, and never say anything to cause pain to another."

Do you know what he told me next? "Tomorrow, visit this man and speak to him in such a way that he will forget what you said to him today." So the next day I visited him. My pride was humbled. I spoke to him very sweetly. When I returned, however, the Master asked, "Did you offer him salutations from me?"

Amazed at his words, I said that I had not. Then he said, "Go to him again and offer him my salutations."

So again I went to that man and conveyed the Master's salutations. At this the devotee burst into tears. I was moved to see him weeping. When I returned this time the Master said, "Now your misdeed is pardoned."

One day Girish Ghosh saluted the Master by raising his folded hands to his forehead. The Master immediately returned the salutation by bowing from the waist. Girish saluted the Master again. The Master saluted Girish Babu with an even deeper bow. At last, when Girish Babu prostrated flat on the ground before him, the Master blessed him. Later Girish Babu would say: "This time the Lord has come to conquer the world through prostrations. In his incarnation as Krishna it was the flute;

as Chaitanya, the Name. But the weapon of his powerful Incarnation this time is the salutation." The Master used to say: "Learn to be humble. The ego will be thus removed."

One day Hazra said to the Master: "Gadadhar [*another name of Sri Ramakrishna*], you are not proceeding along the right lines. If you continue like this, people won't respect you for long. At least show them a little something! Why not count beads as I do?"

This made the Master laugh. He called Harish, Gopal, and Rakhal and said to them: "Do you know what advice Hazra is giving me? He is telling me to start counting beads. But you see, I can't do those things now. Still, he says that people won't respect me if I don't tell beads. Is this true?"

"Pay no attention to his words," said Harish. "He is just a fool."

"Don't say that," said the Master. "The Divine Mother is speaking through him."

Harish was surprised. "What? The Divine Mother speaking through Hazra?"

"Yes," answered the Master. "Mother conveys her messages like this."

Nevertheless, Hazra's mind was a bit twisted. While practising japam he would meditate on worldly things, so he didn't make any progress. But he escaped the snares of the world by holding onto Loren. It was due to Loren's insistence that the Master blessed Hazra. After the Master passed away, Hazra began to think of himself as an avatar — even greater than the Master.

One day Hazra had a desire to massage the Master's feet, but the Master wouldn't let him. Hazra felt hurt. He left the room and sat outside and was very morose. At last the Master called him back, and that day only he served the Master.

On another occasion Hazra wanted to lecture to those who came to the temple. When they arrived to see the Master, he told them: "Today Sri Ramakrishna is not here. What will you gain by merely sitting in his room? Come and listen to what I have to say." But nobody went to him.

Loren was Hazra's bosom friend. He would prepare tobacco for Loren and have long discussions with him. Loren used to tease him: "Really, you are a wonderful *siddha-purusha* [perfect soul]. At last I have found a rare soul who is constantly telling his beads. Your rosary is very nice — such big, bright beads. There is none like you."

Then Hazra would swell with pride and tell us: "You people cannot understand me — not even Sri Ramakrishna. Only Naren knows me." Just see his pride. Man falls in this way. He used to chant, "Soham, soham [I am Brahman]." The Master would tell us: "Don't associate with Hazra.

Yours is the path of devotion. What will you do with that dry knowledge?"

When I first saw Balaram Babu, I did not recognize him to be a
Bengali. He wore a turban [*as is customary with Punjabi Sikhs*] and carried
a staff, and he wore a long robe with another cloth over that. He also had
a long beard. Now and then we went to his house. The Master used to
say, "Balaram's house is my Calcutta fort, my parlour."

Balaram Babu arranged for the daily worship of Lord Jagannath in
his home. The Master said that the food there was very pure. I have heard
that the Master visited his home a hundred times and that Balaram Babu
maintained a record of these visits. Balaram Babu also visited Dakshineswar very often. The Master once saw him in a vision as a member
of a kirtan party led by Sri Chaitanya.

Balaram Babu would escort the Master to the inner apartments [the
women's quarters] of his home. However, his cousin, Harivallabh Babu,
did not approve. Girish Babu and Harivallabh Babu were close friends,
so Girish Babu heard about it. One day when the Master had come to
Balaram Babu's home [*actually, the Shyampukur house*], Girish Babu called
Harivallabh Babu to come and see the Master. Both of them [*the Master
and Harivallabh Babu*] started to weep. I could not understand why.
Afterwards I went to see Harivallabh Babu in Cuttack in order to learn
the reason, but he did not disclose it.

Balaram Babu would save money from his household budget and use
it to serve the monks. His relatives thought he was a miser. I never knew
how rich he was! One day, seeing him lying on a narrow bed, I said:
"Why don't you get yourself a larger bed? This one is too narrow for
you." Do you know what he said? "This earthly body will one day return
to the earth. Why should money be spent for my bed when it can be
much better spent in service to holy people?"

One day Balaram Babu hired a horse carriage for the Master. The fare
from Calcutta to Dakshineswar was only twelve annas [three-fourths of
a rupee], and such a cheap carriage greatly inconvenienced the Master.
One wheel of the carriage came off along the way. The horses did not
behave either. If they were whipped, they ran; otherwise they would not
move. The Master did not reach Dakshineswar until midnight. Later he
would often joke about this incident.

On Kali Puja day the Mother's temple and the chandni [the covered
portico at the temple garden entrance on the river] would be decorated
with lights. Ramlal Dada would come to ask for the Master's blessing
before beginning the worship in the temple. During the day the Master
would stay in his room, visiting the Mother only at night. Music would
be played in the concert tower all night long.

One year Kali Puja fell on a Saturday [an auspicious day for worshipping the Divine Mother]. The Master told us: "Practise japam tonight. Anyone who practises japam on very auspicious nights like this will soon reach perfection." The Master did not allow us to sleep that night. He sang until the late hours.

On Jagaddhatri Puja we would go with him to Manomohan Babu's house. Once a musician there played the drum so beautifully that the Master went into samadhi.

The Master went to see a yatra [an open-air theatrical performance] at a devotee's home in the village of Dakshineswar. Baburam, Ramlal Dada, and I went with him. The main actor was a good person, and he greeted the Master warmly. The next day the actor came to the Kali temple and sang many beautiful songs for the Master. Afterwards the Master told him, "Your life's purpose will be fulfilled through the writing of such songs." He asked Ramlal Dada to copy the songs.

Another time a yatra party came to the Dakshineswar temple. I watched the performance all night long. The Master was also there. The story was of a man who loved a woman so much that he dug a tunnel under the ground so that he could meet with her. Just see the power of love! The Master used to say that when three attachments become one, then God is realized. [That is, when one loves God with the combined force of the attachment of the chaste wife for her husband, that of a mother for her child, and that of a rich miser for his wealth, then one is sure to realize him.]

Once when the Master was sick, Doctor Mahendranath Paul came to see him. Before leaving, he gave five rupees to Ramlal Dada for the Master. The Master did not know this. That night he tossed and turned in bed. I fanned him for a long time, but still he was restless. Finally he said to me: "Please call Ramlal. That rascal must have done something — otherwise, why am I not able to sleep?" It was then one or two o'clock in the morning. As soon as Ramlal Dada arrived, the Master said: "You rascal. Go and return that money to the man who gave it to you in my name." Then Ramlal Dada told the Master the whole story. That very night I accompanied him to Mahendranath Paul's house, where he roused the doctor from his sleep and returned the money.

Ram Babu brought a basket of *jilipis* [an Indian sweet] for the Master one day, but on his way to Dakshineswar he gave one sweet from the basket to a young boy. The Master could not eat the jilipis and he told him, "Never give away a part of anything you bring for me, for then it cannot be offered to the Divine Mother; and you know that I cannot eat anything without offering it to the Mother first."

Some time after the Master hurt his arm, Tarak [Swami Shivananda] came to Dakshineswar. He brought prasad, holy clay, some holy dust, and a rosary from Vrindaban for the Master. When he noticed the bandage on the Master's arm, he asked, "What happened to your arm?"

The Master replied: "I was going to take a look at the moon, when my feet tripped over a low railing and my arm was broken. The suffering has not stopped."

"Is it a dislocation or a fracture?" Tarak asked.

"I don't know," said the Master. "These people have simply bandaged my hand. I like to chant the Mother's name with my mind at ease — but just see the trouble now. They won't even let me undo the bandage. Is it possible to call on the Mother in such a painful state? Sometimes I think, what nonsense this bandage is! Let me break all these bonds and merge in the Divine. Then again I think, no, this is just another aspect of the divine play. There is also some joy in this."

Tarak told the Master, "By your mere wish you can be cured."

"What!" exclaimed the Master. "Can I cure myself by only a wish?" Then he paused a moment and added: "No. Suffering from this affliction is good, for those who come here with desires will see the condition I am in and will go away. They won't bother me." Then he said, "Mother, you played a clever trick." At that he started to sing. Soon he merged into samadhi.

When Brother Niranjan [Swami Niranjanananda] came to the Master for the first time, the Master told him: "Look here, my boy. If one does ninety-nine good turns to a person and one bad, the person remembers the bad one and forgets the others. But if he does ninety-nine bad turns to God and one good, the Lord remembers the good one and forgets all the rest. This is the difference between human love and divine love. Remember this."

One day the Master touched Brother Niranjan in ecstasy. Then Niranjan could not close his eyes for three days and nights. He had the continuous vision of light, and he kept chanting the Lord's name. Before coming to the Master he had been interested in spiritualism and would act as a medium. The Master teased him: "This time it is not an ordinary spirit who has possessed you, my boy. The real Divine Spirit has jumped on your shoulders. Try as you may, you won't be able to get rid of him."

A man came into the Master's room one day and started to talk about worldly things. The Master said: "This is not the place to talk of such matters. Please go to the temple manager's office." The man left the room. Then the Master told me: "Sprinkle the room with water from the Ganga. That man is a slave to lust and gold. Seven cubits below the spot where he sat is polluted. Sprinkle the water well."

One day we went with the Master to Bhadrakali [across the Ganga from Dakshineswar] to hear a scholar speak. The man said such foolish things, however, that the audience became confused. The Master told him: "After much *tapasya* [austerity] a person achieves faith in God; yet you, a scholar, are creating doubt about him. What type of learning do you have?"

The scholar replied nervously: "Oh, no, no, sir. I wasn't serious." The Master understood that the man was merely posing as a great scholar. He touched the man's body and said: "Your mind has become dry, like a weather-beaten piece of wood. After reading so many scriptures, have you learned only to speak hypocrisy?" The scholar was embarrassed and finally left. The Master used to deal in this way with dry intellectuals.

One day Girish Babu came to Dakshineswar quite drunk. The Master asked me: "Go and see if he left anything in his carriage. If you find something, bring it here."

I did as I was told and found a bottle of wine and a glass. I brought both to the Master. When the devotees saw the wine bottle, they began to laugh, but the Master said to me: "Keep the bottle for him. He will want it for a final drink." Just see how liberal the Master was towards his devotees!

Girish Babu arrived one night with Kalipada Ghosh. Kalipada was a terrible drunkard. He refused to give money to his family, spending it for wine instead. But his wife was very pure. I heard that many years earlier she had come to the Master, seeking some kind of medicine that would change her husband's tendencies. The Master sent her to Holy Mother. Holy Mother sent her back to the Master. He again sent her to Holy Mother, and this exchange went on three times. At last, Holy Mother wrote the Master's name on a bel leaf that had been offered to the Lord and gave it to Kalipada's wife, telling her to chant the Lord's name.

Kalipada's wife chanted the Lord's name for twelve years. When the Master first met Kalipada, he said, "This man has come here after tormenting his wife for twelve years." Kalipada was startled, but said nothing.

Then the Master asked him, "What do you want?"

Kalipada asked shamelessly, "Can you give me a little wine?"

The Master smiled. "Yes, I can. But the wine I have is so intoxicating that you will not be able to bear it."

Kalipada took him literally and said: "Is it real British wine? Please give me a little to soak my throat."

"No, it is not British wine," said the Master, still smiling. "It is completely homemade. This wine cannot be given to just anyone, for not everyone can stand it. If a person tastes this wine even once, British wine will seem insipid to him ever after. Are you ready to drink my wine instead of the other?"

For a moment Kalipada was thoughtful, and then I heard him say, "Please give me that wine which will make me intoxicated my entire life." The Master touched him, and Kalipada started to weep. We tried to calm him, but he went on weeping in spite of our attempts.

Once the Master was going somewhere by boat with Kalipada. While they were on the boat, he wrote a mantram on Kalipada's tongue. Later Kalipada became a great devotee and did much to serve the Master. Just see! If the wife is pure and loving, she will even practise austerities for the welfare of her husband. It was because of his wife that Kalipada was saved.

I used to accompany the Master to the theatre, where Girish Babu would show him much respect. He used to arrange for a high box seat for the Master and appoint a man to fan him as well. He himself would often come to see the Master on the upper level. On one occasion Girish Babu approached the Master quite drunk and addressed him affectionately: "You must become my son. I have not been able to serve you in this life, but if you are born again as my son, I can do so. Please promise me that you will be my son."

"What are you saying?" asked the Master. "Why should I be born as your son?" Then Girish Babu became very angry and scolded the Master severely. Hearing him abusing the Master so, I could not hold back my anger. I had a stick in my hand and was ready to hit Girish Babu, but Deven Babu said, "Since the Master is bearing all of this, why should you raise your stick?" I am sure that if Deven Babu had not told me that, I would have given Girish Babu a good blow. I was that angry.

On our way back to Dakshineswar, Deven Babu told the Master what I had almost done. The Master exclaimed: "Wouldn't it have been awful if you had hit Girish? Didn't you notice? After abusing me, he fell to the ground when I got into the carriage and took the dust of my feet. Didn't you see his faith?" And during the trip the Master repeatedly prayed: "O Mother, Girish is an actor. How can he understand your glory? Mother, please forgive him.

"The devotees came to know of the incident at the theatre, and many of them told the Master that he shouldn't visit Girish. Ram Babu also heard about it, and he came to Dakshineswar the following day. As soon as he entered the room, the Master asked him, "Ram, what do you have to say about Girish?" "Sir," Ram Babu told him, "the serpent Kaliya told Krishna: 'Lord, you have given me only poison. Where can I get nectar to offer you?'[2] It is the same with Girish. Where will he get nectar? Why, sir, should you be displeased with him?"

The Master responded, "Then take us in your carriage to Girish's." And the Master, accompanied by Ram Babu, me, and two others, started for Girish Babu's home in Calcutta.

Meanwhile, Girish Babu had been very repentant. He had refused food and was weeping a great deal. We reached his house a little before evening. Hearing that the Master had come, Girish Babu approached him with tears in his eyes and fell at his feet. Only when the Master said, "All right, all right," did he finally get up.

A long conversation followed. I remember Girish Babu saying: "Master, if you had not come today, I would have concluded that you still had not attained that supreme state of knowledge where praise and blame are equal, and, moreover, that you could not be called a paramahamsa [an illumined soul of the highest order]. I would have considered you to be an ordinary man like us. But today I have understood that you are that Supreme One. You will not be able to hide this from me anymore. I shall never desert you. My welfare is now in your hands. Please tell me that you will be responsible for me and that you will save me."

When Keshab Babu [a Brahmo leader] was very sick, the Master went to see him. Keshab came down from the upper story when he heard that the Master had arrived. After seeing how ill Keshab Babu was, the Master said, "This time I can't understand the will of the Mother." Within three or four months Keshab Babu passed away.

An earlier time when Keshab Babu was sick, the Master promised to offer green coconut and sugar to the goddess Siddheshwari after his recovery. Keshab Babu got well, and the Master sent Mother Siddheshwari the promised offerings.

Keshab's followers invited the Master to join them at a garden house in Sinthi at the time of their annual festival. Many famous people came. It was there that I first met Shivanath Shastri, who was much loved by the Master. The Master would say about him: "When one hemp smoker meets another hemp smoker, he feels happy. In that way I am happy." But Shivanath would avoid the Master. One day he said he would come to Dakshineswar, but he did not keep his word. The Master commented:

---

[2] As the story is told in the Bhagavatam, Kaliya was a venomous snake who polluted the sacred waters of the Yamuna river and preyed upon the cows and cowherd boys of Vrindaban. Krishna, the friend of the cowherd boys, came to slay Kaliya. The snake attacked him, but Krishna jumped onto the snake's hood. Then Kaliya began to spew out poison in great quantities. When Krishna asked him why he was emitting poison, Kaliya replied: "Lord, it is you who have given me poison. It is all I have with which to worship you. Where shall I get nectar?"

"He promised me that he would come, but he did not. That is not good. One should not break one's word. Truthfulness is the tapasya [austerity] of the kali yuga [the present age]. He who does not adhere to truth cannot realize God."

Once he said to Shivanath: "Is it true that you have said that my brain is unbalanced? Day and night you think of worldly things and consider your head to be all right, while day and night I think of God, and you think my head is unbalanced!"

The Master told Mani Mallik one day: "Why do you calculate so much? A devotee should spend all that he earns." When Mani Mallik would visit Dakshineswar, the Master would ask him, "How did you come here?" In order to save money, Mani Mallik used to walk from his home to Garanhata, from there take a share-carriage to Baranagore, and would then proceed to Dakshineswar on foot. On some days his face would be sunburned. The Master asked him: "Why do you come here under such hardship? Can't you come all the way by carriage?"

Mani Mallik replied: "If I ride a one-horse carriage, my children will think it necessary to ride in one with two horses. Also, you have said that a virtuous householder should save money for his children and for charity."

Once Mani Mallik returned from a pilgrimage and told the Master, "I found that in the holy places some sadhus [monks] constantly ask for money."

The Master replied: "You are irritated because sadhus ask you for one or two pice? One should not go on a pilgrimage with this sort of attitude. While on pilgrimage one should be charitable. Sadhus earn no money, so one should give a few pice to them. You people want to enjoy all the good things of this world and let the sadhus renounce. You expect them to live on air."

Once there was a scarcity of water in the village where Rakhal was born, so the Master asked Mani Mallik to have a reservoir dug there. Mani Mallik also donated money for the education of poor children.

One day the Master told him: "Now that you are old, forget this world and meditate on God. One should meditate on God in the heart. Thus love grows."

When his son passed away, Mani Mallik came to the Master to unburden his grief. The Master listened to everything. Then he began to sing. When the singing was over, Mani Mallik's grief had melted away.

We often went with the Master to Adhar Babu's house in Shobha-bazar. He looked upon Adhar Babu's house as one of his Calcutta "parlours." Sometimes Adhar Babu would arrange a festival at his house and would feed us well. His mother was a great devotee. She would buy costly mangoes in the off-season and send them to the Master, together with bananas and sweets. The Master took great delight in these things. On one occasion at Adhar Babu's house the Master told him, "Please be sure not to give me a sour mango." So Adhar Babu brought him the best mango he could find. The Master relished it greatly and said, "Most likely this one was selected by your mother!"

One day we were invited to Adhar Babu's house, but Adhar Babu had forgotten to invite Ram Babu, who was greatly offended. Ram Babu complained to the Master, "What wrong have I done to have been left out like this?" The Master tried to console him and said: "Look, Ram, Rakhal was asked to arrange this, and he simply forgot to invite you. Should you be angry with Rakhal? He is just a boy." Later Adhar Babu himself went to Ram Babu's house and invited him to the gathering.

It was also at Adhar Babu's that I first saw Bankim Chandra Chatterjee [a celebrated Bengali writer]. Bankim was extremely intelligent. He tried to test the Master, but he came away outdone. When he was about to leave, he asked the Master to visit him. But since he never sent an invitation, the Master did not go to his house.

Many famous kirtan singers would come to Adhar Babu's house. I remember once hearing a song based on the Chandi [a scripture on the glory of the Divine Mother] that impressed me very much.

Adhar Babu used to come to Dakshineswar every day, even bringing his food with him. Often he would fall asleep once he had arrived. Some people criticized him for this, but do you know what the Master told them? "What do you people know? This is the Divine Mother's place. It is the abode of peace. Instead of engaging in worldly talk, he sleeps. That is all right. A little peace still comes to such people."

One day Adhar Babu asked the Master, "What powers do you have?" The Master laughed and said, "By the grace of the Mother, I lull to sleep those very deputy magistrates who are feared and respected by many others." [*Adhar was a deputy magistrate.*]

The Master visited Kalighat [the famous Kali temple in South Calcutta] now and then and would rejoice there with the devotees. Adhar Babu would provide his carriage for the Master on those occasions.

The Master warned Adhar Babu not to ride on horseback, but he did not listen, and he was killed by being thrown from a horse. On hearing the news of his death, the Master said: "One by one my parlours are closing. I see an end coming to my gatherings."

Some days the mind is in a state in which something one sees makes a particularly deep impression. I saw the Master in samadhi many times, but there is one time I especially remember. He was showing us that day how to yearn for God. He merged into samadhi and remained so for ten or fifteen minutes. His whole body complexion changed. His face radi-ated fearlessness and compassion. It is impossible for me to describe that sight, and even now I cannot forget it.

The Passing Away of the Master

Every night, just before going to bed, the Master would say, "Hari Om Tat Sat [Verily, the Lord is the only Reality]." That last night [at Cossipore garden house] he uttered this as I was fanning him. It was nearly eleven o'clock at night. Then he heaved a sigh and seemed to go into samadhi. Brother Loren asked us to chant "Hari Om Tat Sat." We continued to chant until one o'clock, when the Master came down from samadhi. Then he ate a little farina pudding which Shashi [Swami Ramakrishnananda] fed him. Suddenly he went into samadhi again. Seeing this, Loren grew worried. He called Gopal Dada [Swami Advai-tananda] and asked him to get Ramlal Dada.

Gopal Dada and I left immediately for Dakshineswar, and Ramlal Dada came back with us. He examined the Master and said: "The crown of his head is still warm. Please call Captain [Vishwanath Upadhyay]."

Shortly after that Captain arrived. He asked us to rub the Master's body with ghee [clarified butter]. Shashi rubbed his body and Vaikuntha massaged his feet, but it was to no avail. Later that morning Doctor Mahendra [*Doctor Mahendralal Sarkar*] came to examine the Master and said, "He has given up the body."

Holy Mother was unable to restrain herself. When she came to the Master's room, she cried, "O Mother Kali, what have I done that you have left me?" Seeing the Mother weeping, Baburam [Swami Prema-nanda] and Yogin [Swami Yogananda] went up to her, and Golap-ma [a woman disciple of Sri Ramakrishna and companion of Holy Mother] took her to her room.

In the meantime the Calcutta devotees had received the news, and one after another they began to arrive. A photograph [*actually two*] was taken of the Master with the devotees. By that time it was afternoon.

The Master's body remained on a cot, beautifully decorated, until it was carried to the cremation ground at Cossipore. Ram Babu told me to stay at the garden house until Akshay Babu returned from the cremation ground. So I stayed there while the others went. Only once did I hear Holy Mother weeping. After that she was silent. Never have I seen a woman with such strength.

That night I went to the cremation ground. I saw many people sitting quietly on the bank of the Ganga. Shashi was near the funeral pyre with a fan in his hand, and Sharat [Swami Saradananda] was with him. Both Sharat and Loren sought to console Shashi. I took him by the hand and tried to lift his spirits a little, but he remained motionless with grief. Then Shashi collected the ashes and bones of the Master and put them in an urn. He placed the urn on his head and carried it to the garden house, where it was kept on the Master's bed.

The following day Golap-ma told us that the Master had appeared to Holy Mother in a vision and had forbidden her to remove her bracelets. He said: "Have I gone to another place? Here I am. I have just passed from one room to another." When those who were mourning heard this from Golap-ma, they cast away their doubts. "Service to the Master is to be continued as before," they said.

Niranjan, Shashi, Gopal Dada, and Tarak stayed at Cossipore that day. Holy Mother asked Yogin and me to go to Calcutta to collect food and materials for the worship of the Master. That noon, cooked food was offered to the Master and afterwards the Ram Nam was sung. Then everyone except Gopal Dada, Tarak, and me left for their homes.

Three or four days later, Holy Mother went to Dakshineswar with Golap-ma, Lakshmi Didi [Sri Ramakrishna's niece], and me, but we returned before nightfall. I heard later that at noon that day Shashi, Niranjan, Loren, Rakhal, and Baburam had come to Cossipore, and Ram Babu had visited in the afternoon. Ram Babu wanted to vacate the garden house, so he asked the disciples to return to their homes. Both Niranjan and Shashi were shocked to hear this, for they wanted the worship of the Master to continue. That very night Niranjan left for Balaram Babu's house.

The next day Balaram Babu arrived at Cossipore to escort Holy Mother to his home. They took various articles of the Master's with them. I stayed on at Cossipore with Gopal Dada and Tarak. During those days everyone would come to the garden house at noon and stay until some time during the evening.

Ram Babu wanted to enshrine the relics of the Master at his garden house at Kankurgachi and establish a monastery there, but Shashi and Niranjan refused to accept this idea. They told him that they would not give him the relics. Loren tried to pacify them and said: "Brothers, it is not good to quarrel over this urn. We have no monastery ourselves, and Ram Babu is willing to give the title of his garden house in the name of the Master. It is a good proposition. We should begin his worship there. If we can build our characters according to the Master's ideal, we will have achieved the purpose of our lives."

I went to Ram Babu's house the day before Janmashtami [Krishna's birthday], and the next morning we formed a procession and walked from there to Kankurgachi, singing kirtan the entire way. Shashi carried the urn with the Master's ashes on his head.[3] During the consecration ceremony, as they were covering the urn with earth, Shashi cried out, "Oh, the Master is in pain!" The others there wept to hear his words.

On the day of the Master's passing away, while returning from the Cossipore cremation ground, Upen Babu had been bitten by a snake. Nityagopal had used a red-hot iron to cauterize the wound. Although his injury had not yet healed, Upen Babu still joined in the kirtan. He liked holy company very much.

After the Kankurgachi ceremony, Ramlal Dada made arrangements for a feast at Dakshineswar. There was also a kirtan that day. Ramlal Dada went to Balaram Babu's house to invite Holy Mother to come to Dakshineswar, but she refused. However, I attended the feast.

After the Master passed away, I could not stay at Cossipore much longer because of the grief I felt. Now and then I would go to Ram Babu's house and from there I would go to Loren's. Loren would recount many things about the Master. I told him, "Brother Loren, I am telling you frankly — the Master loved you so much that he could not live without you." Loren laughed and said: "Brother, never mind. He loved you, Shashi, and Rakhal so much that he will always be *with* you. How little I served him compared to all of you." Just see how humble Brother Loren was!

One day one of the disciples was lamenting, "So the Master has left us." I was shocked to hear this remark and said: "He is dead to sceptics, but alive to those who believe in him. Don't you remember that he appeared to Holy Mother? When you have that kind of faith, he will appear to you also."

[From: *Swami Adbhutananda: Teachings and Reminiscences*, by Swami Chetanananda (St. Louis: Vedanta Society), 1980]

---

[3] Actually, unknown to Ram Chandra and other householder disciples, Shashi and Niranjan quietly divided Sri Ramakrishna's relics into two parts. The larger portion was taken to Balaram Basu's house and later worshipped by the young monastic disciples in their monastery. Eventually, when the headquarters of the Ramakrishna Order was established at Belur some years later, these relics were enshrined there. The smaller portion was taken to the Kankurgachi garden house as Ram Chandra wished.

7

Swami Premananda

Swami Premananda (1861-1918) met Sri Ramakrishna in 1882 and became his monastic disciple, living with the Master and serving him. His sister was married to Balaram Basu, a great householder disciple of the Master. The Master regarded Swami Premananda as one belonging to the class of Ishwarakotis (great souls) and said that he was pure to his very marrow. In later days the swami was one of the trustees of the Ramakrishna Math and Mission and was the manager of the Rama-krishna Monastery at Belur.

Days with Sri Ramakrishna

Swami Brahmananda and I went to Hathkhola ghat [in West Calcutta] to take a boat for Dakshineswar, and there we met Ramdayal Babu. Learning that he was also going to see Sri Ramakrishna, we got in a boat together. It was almost dusk when we reached Rani Rasmani's Kali temple. We went to the Master's room and were told that he had gone to the temple to pay obeisance to the Mother of the Universe. Asking us to stay there, Swami Brahmananda went towards the Mother's temple to find the Master. Soon I saw him holding onto the Master very carefully and guiding him, saying: "Steps. Go up here, down here." I had already heard that the Master would often become overwhelmed with ecstasy and lose outer consciousness. Therefore I knew that he was in an ecstatic mood when I saw him coming, reeling like a drunken man. He entered the room in that state and sat on a small bedstead. Shortly afterwards he came back to normal consciousness and asked me a few questions about myself and my relations. He then began to examine the features of my face, hands, feet, and so on. For some time he held my forearm in his hand to feel its weight, and then he said, "Good." He alone knew what he meant by that. Afterwards he asked Ramdayal Babu about Narendra's health. Hearing that he was all right, the Master said: "It has

Swami Premananda

been a long time since he came here. I want to see him. Please ask him to come sometime."

A few hours were spent delightfully in religious talk. We took our supper at 10:00 P.M. and lay down on the southeast verandah of the Master's room. Beds were arranged for the Master and Swami Brahmananda in the room. But scarcely had an hour passed when the Master came out of his room with his cloth under one arm and came to our bedside. Addressing Ramdayal Babu, he asked affectionately, "Are you sleeping?" Both of us quickly sat up in our beds and replied, "No, sir." The Master said: "Look. I have not seen Narendra for a long time, and I feel as if my whole soul were being forcibly wrung like a wet towel. Please ask him to come once and see me. He is a person of pure sattva qualities. He is Narayana himself. I cannot have peace of mind if I don't see him now and then."

Ramdayal Babu had been visiting Dakshineswar for some time, so the boylike nature of the Master was not unknown to him. Seeing that childlike behaviour, he knew that the Master was in ecstasy. He tried to console the Master by promising that he would see Narendra first thing in the morning and ask him to come, and similar other things. But the Master's mood was not at all alleviated that night. Knowing that we were getting no rest, he would return to his room now and then for some time. But after a while he would forget and again come back to us and begin speaking of Narendra's good qualities, expressing pathetically the terrible anguish of his mind on account of Narendra's long absence.

Observing that terrible pang of separation of his, I was astonished and thought: "How wonderful is his love! And how hardhearted must be that person for whom his longing is so devastating and his behaviour so pathetic!" The night passed in this way. In the morning we went to the temple and paid our obeisance to the Divine Mother. Then, bowing down to the Master, we took leave of him and returned to Calcutta.

Three or four days after my first visit to the Master, I happened to see Ramdayal Babu at Baghbazar [in North Calcutta], and he told me: "The Master wants to see you. Please visit him." Amazed, I asked, "Why has he called for me?" I didn't realize then how compassionate the Master was.

I again went to Dakshineswar, and as soon as I arrived the Master affectionately asked me to carry some firewood to the Panchavati grove. That day the Master arranged a picnic there. Thus the Master trained us by giving us some responsibilities.

My mother would not allow me to stay very long at our village home [Antpur] even during holidays for fear that I might mix with bad boys and be ruined. But she would cry whenever I left home to return to

Calcutta. The Master also used to cry whenever I left Dakshineswar to return to Calcutta. Oh, how can I explain to you how much he loved us! He would go to Calcutta in a carriage just so he could feed Purna [a young devotee]. He would wait near the school where Purna went, send someone to bring the boy, and then feed him delicacies. He would say: "What has happened to me? You do not even have a mat[1] with which to receive me, yet I am restless to see you!"

One day he was found waiting outside Balaram Babu's house where I was staying. Balaram Babu was not at home, and the Master hesitated to go inside, thinking he might be humiliated. He had come to see me. Someone finally called him in. His love knew no bounds, and one drop of it completely filled us. Each one thus thought himself to be the most beloved of the Master.

He used to tell us, "I can stand everything except egotism." That is why when he wanted to meet someone, he would send Hriday beforehand to see if that person was proud. He has left a mould for us. We now have to knead the clay of the mind, eliminating all stones and rubbish from it, and cast it in the mould. A beautiful form will then emerge. The Master came for the whole world.

One night I was sleeping in the Master's room. At dead of night I woke up and found him pacing from one end of his room to the other, saying: "Mother, I do not want this. Do not bring me honour from men. Don't, Mother, don't. I spit on it!" Saying this, he paced back and forth like a madman. I was filled with wonder. I thought: "How strange! People are so eager for name and fame, and he is pleading with the Mother not to give it to him! Why is this happening before me? Is it to instruct me?"

The Master could not bear any kind of bondage. If the edge of his mosquito curtain was tucked under the mattress, he would feel suffocated. It was instead dropped around the edge of his bed. He could not even button his shirt. We had to do that for him. And neither could he bolt his door. He saw God in everything. One day someone tore a piece of new cloth in front of him and he cried out, "Oh, pain!"

Be pure. Purity is religion. Unite your speech and mind. Sri Ramakrishna was the embodiment of purity. A man earned a lot of money by taking bribes. One day this person touched the Master's feet while he was in samadhi and he cried out in pain. During the Master's samadhi we had to hold him so he would not fall, but we were afraid. We thought that if we were not pure enough, then, when we touched him during samadhi, he would publicly cry out in pain. So we prayed for purity.

---

[1] People in India generally sit cross-legged on the floor, so they use carpets or mats in their drawing rooms instead of chairs to receive guests.

No impure person could live with the Master and give him personal service. It was the Master's grace that I was allowed to live with him. Once I saw a person secretly put money under the Master's mattress when he was not in his room. Later when the Master came back, he could not go near the bed. His renunciation was phenomenal. Can an ordinary person conceive of such things? We have seen his ideal life, so we speak with conviction.

One day the Master went to see the play *Chaitanya Lila* [The Divine Play of Chaitanya] at the Star Theatre. Before we left Dakshineswar, he said to me: "Look. If I go into samadhi there, people will turn towards me and there will be a commotion. If you see me on the verge of samadhi, talk to me about various other things." But when he went to the theatre he could not stop going into samadhi, even though he tried. I began to repeat the name of God, and slowly he came round. Such experiences of *bhava* [ecstasy], *mahabhava* [great ecstasy], and samadhi were natural with him. He had to struggle hard in order to hold his mind down to the normal plane. Compared to him we are very small receptacles, so we work hard, practising various kinds of spiritual disciplines, to try to attain a little ecstasy. For us it is so difficult.

Knowing that the Master greatly liked lemons, Yogin [Swami Yogananda] used to bring him a lemon every day. One day the Master said to him: "Where did you get the lemon yesterday? I could not eat it." Yogin was aware that the Master could not take things brought from evil or impure persons, but this lemon was from the same tree as the previous lemons. Why was it then that the Master could not take this one? Yogin was very disturbed and began to look for the cause. After careful inquiry he learned that the orchard from which he had been bringing the fruits had changed hands on the day prior to the incident, because the lease had expired. Yogin had received permission to get the lemons from the former lessee. On that particular day, therefore, the permission no longer held, and his taking of the lemon was really a theft, though unconscious.

The Master could see the mind of the donor in the things given to him. He could not take any food that had been contaminated by the least sin. How wonderful was his purity! He could not tolerate the approach or touch of any impurity.

One day Vijay Krishna Goswami came and begged the Master to free him from lust. The Master touched him, and that touch produced wonderful results. On another occasion a person came and requested help from Sri Ramakrishna, saying: "Sir, I feel so attracted to my wife that I cannot devote my mind to anything else. All my business is going to rack and ruin. Please change my mental condition." "Very well," said the Master. "Bring some fruits one day. I shall eat up your maya [delusion]." When the fruits were brought, however, the Master could not eat them. He tried but could not raise them to his lips. I was told the man suffered a great deal afterwards on account of his wife.

The Master showered his grace on Girish Chandra Ghosh and even on many prostitutes. One day the ladies of Balaram Babu's family were sitting before the Master in his room when a prostitute named Ramani passed along the road nearby. The Master called to her and asked, "Why don't you come nowadays?" The ladies were scandalized to hear the Master talking with a prostitute.

Shortly afterwards the Master took them to visit the shrines. When they reached the Kali temple the Master said to the Mother: "Mother, thou indeed hast become the prostitute Ramani. Thou hast become both the prostitute and the chaste woman!" The ladies understood that they were wrong in hating Ramani, that the Master spoke with her, knowing her to be the Mother herself, and that they should not be so proud of their chastity, for it was all due to the Mother's will.

In the beginning we did not understand what true religion was. The Master loved us more than our own parents did. His magnetic love drew us to Dakshineswar. What an attraction! What unconditional love! It was unparalleled. He used to cry for Narendra loudly, and again he would laugh and tease him like a friend.

He explained to us the theory of creation according to the Sankhya philosophy as well as the doctrine of Purusha and Prakriti through humorous stories. Watching his gestures and listening to his stories, we laughed and laughed. He also told us about the cause of creation: "This manifested universe is real, and again, the unmanifest is also real. Purusha [the conscious principle] is true, and again, Prakriti [the unconscious principle] is also true." [*What Sri Ramakrishna meant was that Brahman and Shakti (power) are identical, like fire and its burning power.*]

Sometimes the Master would entertain us by imitating a dancing girl, placing one hand on his waist and moving his other hand about. Again, through humour, tales, and parables, he would explain to us the most intricate philosophies, which were confusing even to scholars. His wonderful skill in teaching left a deep impression on our hearts forever. The Master was adept in explaining the supreme spiritual truths in simple, sweet language.

We saw how lovingly the Master used to receive the devotees at Dakshineswar! He would ask, "Do you want to chew a betel roll?" If the devotee said, "No," he would then ask, "Would you like to smoke tobacco?" Thus, in so many ways he would take care of the devotees.

Sri Ramakrishna was selective in accepting disciples. Once he told Keshab Chandra Sen, "You are having troubles in your organization because through lack of discrimination you allowed black sheep in your fold." The Master accepted disciples after testing them in various ways. He did not even spare Swamiji. He was versed in physiognomy, and so he used to examine the shape of a disciple's eyes, hands, feet, and so forth. He knew different ways to judge whether a person was truly a spiritual aspirant or not. He could not bear the atmosphere of worldly people.

The Master wanted to test Naren's love for him, so he stopped talking to him for some days. But Naren was not hurt, and he remained jolly as usual. He did not stop visiting the Master. Then one day the Master said to him, "I don't talk to you, but still you visit me." "Sir, I love you," said Naren, "so I come to see you." For this the Master eulogized Naren.

The Master could not bear it if anybody criticized Naren. Once Prankrishna Mukhopadhyay, whom the Master called "the fat brahmin," criticized Naren. The Master was very displeased with him because Naren to him was Lord Shiva himself, one of the seven sages, the jewel in his crown. And this fat brahmin had criticized his Naren! According to Vaishnava tradition it is a sin to criticize a devotee of God. After some days Prankrishna sent some fruits to the Master at Dakshineswar. The Master immediately returned those fruits to him because he had criticized Naren. The fat brahmin rushed to Dakshineswar, panting all the way, fell at the feet of the Master, and apologized. The Master then forgave him.

Only a jeweller knows the value of a jewel. Only the Master knew the greatness of Swamiji. After his father died Swamiji had to struggle to get a morsel of food for his mother and younger brothers and sisters. In addition, there was a legal battle with his relatives. Hearing about Swamiji's suffering, the Master said: "Naren was born with great power. But the Divine Mother is preparing him through these trials and tribulations. If he gets regular meals every day, he will overturn the world. He has enough power to institute thirty-six kinds of religious ideas."

One day Girish Ghosh said to the Master that he would write a book denouncing the left-handed practices of the Kartabhaja sect of Vaishnavism. The Master gravely replied: "It is also a path. Some people have made progress in spiritual life through that path." He forbade criticism of anybody, even a worm.

"Never see faults in others. Rather see your own faults," said the Master. Once, in front of the Master, some visitors were criticizing the character of Satish Giri, the abbot of the Tarakeshwar monastery. Immediately Sri Ramakrishna diverted their attention to the abbot's good qualities. The Master did not like his devotees to gossip.

On another occasion a brahmin scholar was arguing with the Master. Sri Ramakrishna tried to convince the scholar of his views, but the latter was adamant and continued arguing. The Master went out for a while and then came back to his room in an ecstatic mood. Touching the body of the scholar with his hand, he said, "Hello, I am telling the truth and you are not accepting my words!" That magic touch immediately changed the mind of the scholar, and he said: "Sir, I agree with what you have said. I was arguing with you just for the sake of argument."

Once the Master assured a devotee: "Have you committed a sin? Don't be afraid. Take a vow, 'I will not sin anymore.' I shall swallow all of your sins."

Happiness and misery come from God. I think there is a reason behind life's experiences which human beings do not know. They are shortsighted. Sri Ramakrishna told us this story: "Once a king went hunting in a forest with his minister. The king's finger was accidentally cut and he asked the minister, 'Why did I get this cut?' The minister replied, 'O king, there must be a deep meaning behind this accident.' The king was not satisfied with this answer, so he pushed the minister into a deep well. Fortunately there was not much water in the well. Then the king asked the minister, 'Is there any hidden cause behind my cruel action?' 'Of course,' replied the minister from the well.

"In the meantime some robbers were passing through that forest, and they came upon the king alone and decided to chop off his head in front of their deity, Mother Kali. After performing a ritual they took the king to the sacrificial place, and then noticed the cut on his finger. Now according to their custom, a defective body cannot be offered to the deity, so they verbally abused the king and set him free. The king thanked God, and remembering the wisdom of his minister, rushed back to the well and rescued him. Then the king narrated what had happened and apologized to the minister for his rude behaviour. The latter said, 'O king, what God does is good for us. If we had both been caught by those robbers, I would have been beheaded. You saved my life by pushing me into the well.'"

No action is meaningless. We are human beings with very little intellect. We get depressed over trifles and again we become easily pleased. This is human nature.

One day Dr. Mahendralal Sarkar came to the Master at Shyampukur at about ten o'clock in the morning and left at about three or four o'clock that afternoon. On seeing this, Mani Mallik said: "Sir, one day there was music at Kristodas Pal's. All the important people of Calcutta came to the party. Dr. Sarkar also came but rose to leave after about five minutes.

On being requested to stay a little longer, he said: 'No, I cannot. I have much work to do.' That same Mahendralal Sarkar today spent five or six hours here apparently for nothing. This is certainly strange!"

Though the Master did not know how to read or write well, many books were read to him, and he remembered everything he heard. Once at the Cossipore garden house Swami Ramakrishnananda was reading to him the Adhyatma Ramayana [the story of Rama] in the original Sanskrit. Swamiji asked the Master: "Sir, you do not know how to read or write. Do you understand anything of this Sanskrit reading?" The Master replied: "Though I have not read it myself, I have heard many things. And I know the meaning of every word." Everything about him was unique. The Master encouraged us to read *Chaitanya Charitamrita*, *Chaitanya Chandrodaya*, and other devotional scriptures. Yet he would occasionally comment, "Those books are one-sided."

The Master's life was a living, blazing Upanishad. None could have understood the meaning of the Radha-Krishna cult if Sri Chaitanya had not been born and demonstrated it in his life. In the same way, the Master was the living demonstration of the truths of the Upanishads. The Upanishads have been available for many centuries and many people have read them. Yet people bowed down to our uneducated Master and accepted his words as sacred truths. He never read the Upanishads or other books. How is it that he could explain those subtle and complex truths in such a simple and direct manner?

If you want to read the Vedas, you must first commit the grammar to memory and then read various commentaries in which each commentator has sought to explain the texts in his own way. Innumerable scholars have been arguing over the texts without coming to any conclusion. Our Master, however, explained all those truths in very simple language, and his words are extant. With such a living fountain before you, why dig a well for water?

When Sri Ramakrishna was bedridden at Cossipore garden house, Naren one day told him, "Sir, you have poured out your affection and grace on me, but I don't understand what I have achieved!" The Master answered: "Wait a little. Gradually you will understand what you have attained." Then Naren said: "Sir, you say I shall be able to know in the course of time. But if I die tomorrow?" The Master immediately replied: "All right. You will get it [the highest spiritual experience] tomorrow."

One day the Master asked me to cook food for him and he ate from my hand. He was so gracious to me! A day or two before his passing away he asked all of us to feed him pudding, and thus he withdrew all his restrictions.

Some Characteristics of Sri Ramakrishna

The keynote of the Master's life in this Incarnation was the complete absence of expression of supernatural powers or lordly qualities. In the life of all previous Divine Incarnations we find, more or less, the manifestation of supernatural powers. For example: Krishna held up the Govardhan mountain with one finger, Jesus fed five thousand people with only five loaves of bread, Shankara made the river obey him, Buddha walked in the air, and so on. But in Sri Ramakrishna's life we don't find such miraculous feats. It is a very interesting feature of this Incarnation.

Again, we find that other Divine Incarnations charmed the world with the brilliance of their physical beauty. But Sri Ramakrishna's physical beauty was inconspicuous. Once Girish Ghosh asked, "Why, sir, is there no physical beauty this time?" During his sadhana [spiritual practices] a lustre began to emanate from his body. So the Master prayed to the Divine Mother: "What need have I of physical beauty, Mother? Give me spiritual beauty."

Most of the Divine Incarnations were well versed in the scriptures and some were great scholars, but Sri Ramakrishna was different. Chaitanya defeated the all-conquering pandits of his day and became a very famous scholar. What to speak of Shankaracharya, the great philosopher! Buddha studied the scriptures and realized that it would not bring liberation. Needless to say, Krishna, the interpreter of the Upanishads, was a great scholar.

But our Master? He could hardly read or write. It was a sight to see how great scholars were struck dumb while discussing philosophical matters with the Master. Do you know why? There is a world of difference between understanding through discussion and knowing through realization. How much can one explain about Varanasi after studying a map? People listen to that person who has recently been to Varanasi. The Master knew all planes of consciousness. Once Swamiji was highly praising a man. The Master then listened to that man for a while and afterwards passed a very different judgement on him, which, to the surprise of Swamiji, was found to be true. Our Master had a unique insight into things and persons.

Other avatars, or Incarnations, have preached their philosophies and doctrines. Each one glorified his own particular path. But Sri Ramakrishna said, "As many faiths, so many paths." The Master never preached his own doctrine. He would talk about God to those who loved him and would go to him for that purpose. Keshab wrote about the Master in his paper. Hearing of it, the Master said to him, "If you do that, don't come to me." He did not care for name and fame. He used to say: "When the flower blooms the bees come of their own accord. Let character be formed, and the world will be attracted by its beauty."

Generally, people think that their own religious beliefs are the best, and some have gone so far as to say that there is no salvation except through their religion. But our Master used to say: "There are infinite ways of reaching the Infinite, and the doctrines are but ways and not the goal. A blind man touched a leg of an elephant and at once jumped to the conclusion that an elephant is like a pillar. Another touched its ear and concluded that it is like a winnowing fan. Both were right, and again both were wrong. All quarrels are due to this partial experience. None saw the whole elephant." The Master demonstrated by his life that Truth can be reached through all religions. There is no reason to quarrel about religious views. All religions are true.

Sri Ramakrishna used to say, "The goal of human life is to realize God." Without God, life is full of misery. So at any cost we must realize him. What is the use of being conversant in all religions and doctrines? The Master would say: "You have come to eat mangoes in the garden. What is the use of counting leaves and branches?" What will it avail you except loss of energy if you go on discussing whether God has a form or not, whether reincarnation is true or not. If you want to know what road leads to Varanasi, you must have faith in the words of those who have gone there. Then you will have to go there yourself and see things with your own eyes. But instead of that, if you shut yourself up in a room and make your brain dizzy, imagining things about Varanasi, you will have no real conception of that holy city. And what is it to me if there is such a thing as rebirth or not? My goal is to realize God in this very life.

The Master would say: "What is required is heart, intense hankering, sincere longing for God. When, to a person, life without God is unbearable, then alone God reveals himself to that soul." This is the essence of the Master's teachings. During his sadhana, when the day was drawing to its close and the sun was sinking on the western horizon, he used to burst into tears out of agony, crying: "Oh, thou art going away! What hast thou done for me? I remain the same unaltered man." And in this intense agony, he would rub his face on the ground. Life became meaningless to him because he could not realize God. Due to the absence of the Lord, he experienced the burning pain of a venomous snakebite. Just imagine the intensity of his dispassion! Once some grains of rice somehow got into his long matted hair and germinated, so oblivious was he of his body.

Each avatar represented a particular ideal. It is not that other ideals were absent in them. They were the embodiments of all ideals, but they publicly gave expression to a particular one, according to the need of the people of their time. Chaitanya was an Incarnation of divine love. He was love crystallized. So also Shankara was the embodiment of knowledge, and Buddha of renunciation. Krishna was the embodiment of selfless work, and he synthesized all religions and philosophies. He demonstrated that karma, jnana, bhakti, and yoga are all components of the great sadhana. To prove this, he formed his life on the basis of selfless action. Selfless action purifies the heart, and in the pure heart comes renunciation. Buddha came with this renunciation. He did nothing for himself, not even for his own salvation. Everything he did was for the good of others, for suffering humanity. After renunciation comes knowledge. Shankara brought this knowledge. And after knowledge comes love, so Chaitanya came to distribute this love to all. People thought that all these paths were contradictory. In this present age Sri Ramakrishna removed all these contradictions and brought a harmony of all paths of yoga and of all religions.

Sri Ramakrishna was the embodiment of compassion. There was no limit to his mercy. Once he went on a pilgrimage with Mathur to Varanasi, and on their way they stopped at Deoghar to visit Lord Shiva. Seeing the poverty and distress of the people of that region, the Master told Mathur: "Feed and clothe these people well or else my pilgrimage ends here. I am not going to leave these poor people."

In spite of being criticized, the Master helped people. When he was suffering from the excruciating pain of cancer, every day he would wait for seekers of God to come. Sometimes he would look out at the street and say: "What has happened? Nobody has come today." Once Hazra said to the Master: "Why are you so anxious to see Naren? Put your mind in God. There is no reason to think about those boys." Like a simple child the Master believed what Hazra said, and he went to the Panchavati, where he had most of his visions. There the Divine Mother told him: "What a fool you are! Have you come to this world for your own enjoyment? Shame!" Then the Master said: "Mother, if for the good of humanity I am to suffer a million times, I shall bear it gladly." Hardly six months passed before he contracted cancer. He could not talk but only whisper. He was hungry but could not eat. He found no relief either in sitting or in lying down. Day and night he felt a burning sensation all over his body. In spite of all this terrible suffering, he never desisted from showering grace on people and helping them realize God. This went on for a year and a half. If this is not crucifixion, I don't know what it is.

We sometimes find people wasting time by sitting idle in the name of japam and meditation. This is a sign of tamas [inertia]. The Master did much work. We saw him working in the garden, and he also swept his room. He could not tolerate work done in a slipshod manner. He himself did everything precisely and gracefully, and he taught us to do the same. He would scold us if we did not put tools and other things back in their proper places. Once he taught me how to prepare betel rolls. He did all these things, and yet how inward he was all the time! If any of us were cheated when buying something, he would ridicule us, saying, "I have asked you to be pious but not to be fools." We heard him say many times, "Yoga is skill in action."

Sri Ramakrishna practised various kinds of sadhana and was blessed by realizing God through other religions as well. As a result of seeing God in every being, he had neither enemy nor friend. In other words, he had transcended the pairs of opposites. He was always intoxicated with divine love. He had not the slightest desire to form a sect or the like. It was not possible for him to do this because he was a knower of Brahman and all-loving. His unitive experience removed the differences between religions. People create sects when their hearts are full of weakness, fear, and hatred. Know for certain that our Order will fall if ever the idea of groupism enters into it. Many times conflicts among sects have ruined India's religious culture. The stagnant water of a little pond becomes dirty and foul, but the flowing water of a river is never polluted. Be careful! Let there be no fanaticism in our Order. Never disturb others' faiths.

Sri Ramakrishna did not have an iota of egotism in him. The Divine Mother kept in him the 'I' of the jnani [man of knowledge] for the sake of maintaining his body. We saw with our own eyes the incarnation of perfect humility. When the beggars finished their meals at the Dakshineswar temple garden, the Master carried their dirty leaf-plates on his head. And in order to eradicate any sense of superiority over the untouchable sweepers, he cleaned the toilets of the temple garden with his long hair. Regarding humility, the Master told this story: "Once a guru said to his disciple, 'Please bring me something which you think is inferior to you.' The disciple could not find anything inferior to him, and at last decided that filth must be worse than him. When he was about to pick up some filth, it said: 'Don't touch me! Don't touch me! I have come to this degraded state because of human contact. When I was delicious food people loved me, and now I am a despicable object.' Hearing this from the filth, the disciple's ego was crushed. He realized that nothing was inferior to him."

The Master acted as if he were an ignorant person, but how much of the sciences he knew! He knew the language of birds and how to read a person's nature and character from the shape of his body, and he also knew the Vedas, the Vedanta, the Puranas, and the Tantras. Almost everything was known to him, as a person knows an amlaki fruit held in the palm of his hand. He used to say, "I can see the inside of a man by looking at his eyes and face." The Master used to examine every limb of his disciples when they went to him for the first time. He did it with me also. Heaven knows from where he attained all his knowledge and skills!

The scriptures speak of *urdhva sauratam*, or absolute conquest of the sex impulse. We could never have believed in such a thing had we not known the Master. What wonderful control he had over every nerve and muscle of the body! At the time of washing the cancerous tumour in his throat, which caused such terrible suffering, he would ask us to wait for a moment and then he would say, "Now wash." Then he would feel no pain or suffering.

Do you know the reason for this? The yogis acquire mastery over all parts of the body. They can even stop the heartbeat and withdraw or deflect at will nerve-currents from a particular part of the body. That part of the body then becomes inert, like lifeless matter. It becomes dead to all sensations. It does not respond even if you stick a knife into it. Don't think these are just stories. We saw all these things with our own eyes. Sri Krishna sported with the gopis after withdrawing the prana [vital force] from his physical body. Now try to understand what urdhva sauratam means.

You should also know that though the avatars remain established in the Atman, there is still some identification with the psycho-physical instrument, however tenuous that may be. But they can, whenever they desire, withdraw even that. A bit of it is necessary; otherwise the body cannot survive. As the Master used to say, "Though the kernel of a dry coconut becomes separated from the shell, it nevertheless remains in contact with the shell at some point or other."

As regards caste, the Master used to say that the devotees formed a class by themselves. They did not need to observe caste rules with each other. But he could not eat from the hands of a person of evil character, though the latter might have been born into a high caste. He could not even sit on a seat spread on the floor by such a person. On the other hand, he was once going to touch the leaf-plate from which someone had eaten. That person at once cried out: "Sir, what are you doing? I have eaten forbidden food. Please don't touch my used leaf-plate." The Master replied: "There is no harm in it. Your mind is pure."

About food, the Master used to say: "Though a person takes the purest food sanctioned by the scriptures yet has no love for God and is very worldly, his food is as good as pork and beef. [*Pork and beef are prohibited for Hindus.*] But if one who is endowed with devotion and faith takes 'forbidden food,' it is not to be regarded as forbidden. It is pure and sacred."

The Master often poked fun at persons with a mania for physical purity. He used to say that such persons, in their very attempts to keep themselves from all impurity, live in constant fear of being contaminated and thus immerse their minds in impurity. It is therefore very difficult for them to think of God. From this, one should not jump to the conclusion that by flinging all rules of cleanliness to the winds one becomes an illumined soul.

Sri Ramakrishna lived in this world by giving the power of attorney to the Divine Mother, and Girish Ghosh gave the power of attorney to the Master. Giving the power of attorney means completely surrendering oneself to another. Girish saw his own shortcomings, so he surrendered to the Master for his spiritual welfare. It is an extremely difficult thing to do. As long as a person has an iota of ego, he cannot give the power of attorney to another. The Master used to say, "After giving the power of attorney, one should live like a dry leaf at the mercy of the wind, or like a kitten who remains wherever its mother is pleased to keep it — sometimes on a fancy bed and sometimes on the ashes of the hearth." That person has truly given the power of attorney who can fix his mind on God without being perturbed by happiness and misery, and who, like Arjuna in the midst of cruel duties, can calmly say, "O Krishna, sit in my heart, and whatever you want me to do I will do." For one who has renounced all duties and taken complete refuge in God, God takes on the responsibility of that person and frees him from all sins.

The Master encouraged us to read the scriptures and holy books. He kept some books such as *Mukti O Tahar Sadhan* [Liberation and Its Practice] in his room and sometimes asked us to read them to him. When a person is reading about God, his mind is absorbed in him. It is not possible for a person to practise japam and meditation all the time, so studying the scriptures is another discipline. But until God's grace dawns, everything is futile. The Upanishad says: "This Atman cannot be attained through discussion, or through hearing and memorizing the Vedas. It is realized by him whom the Atman chooses. To such a one It reveals Its real nature." When God's grace comes, a person attains infinite knowledge. Then he does not care to read books. There is a great difference between direct realization and mere book learning. The Master used to say, "As long as the southern breeze does not blow, a fan is needed."

Visiting holy places awakens one's God-consciousness. But the Master used to say: "Whoever does not have it here [i.e., in the heart], does not have it there [i.e., in holy places]. Whoever has it here, has it there too." Pilgrims make places holy. Suffering people get peace in a holy place because holy people purify it with their good thoughts and spiritual vibrations. And again, a holy place loses its greatness and purity if worldly people pollute it with evil thoughts and actions. In the old days the real devotees would go through much hardship for a pilgrimage, but now rich people visit holy places either for a change of air or for some other trivial reason.

May Sri Ramakrishna bless you so that you can be absorbed in thoughts of him alone. God is not a matter of talk, but an object of realization. We must find him at any cost in this very life. There is no way for suffering humanity to find permanent peace except through God-realization. He alone can assuage our burning hearts.

[From: *Sri Ramakrishna, The Great Master*, by Swami Saradananda (Madras: Sri Ramakrishna Math), vol. 2, 1979; *Premananda*, by Swami Omkareswarananda (Deoghar: Ramakrishna Sadhan Mandir), vols. I & II, 1935 & 1946; *Swami Premanander Patravali* (Bombay: Ramakrishna Math), 1963; *Swami Premananda* (Antpur: Ramakrishna-Premananda Ashrama), 1965; *Spiritual Talks*, by The First Disciples of Sri Ramakrishna (Calcutta: Advaita Ashrama), 1968; *Swami Premananda: Teachings and Reminiscences*, by Swami Prabhavananda (Hollywood: Vedanta Press), 1968; *Prabuddha Bharata* (Mayavati: Advaita Ashrama), December 1937 & August 1948]

8

Swami Shivananda

Swami Shivananda (1854-1934) first met Sri Ramakrishna in 1880 in Calcutta. His father was a legal adviser to Rani Rasmani and had met the Master at Dakshineswar a number of times in the late 1850s. Swami Shivananda lived with and served the Master and later practised hard austerities in various holy places of India. The purity of his life earned him his popular name, Mahapurusha (great soul), given to him by Swami Vivekananda. After the death of Swami Brahmananda, Swami Shivananda became the second president of the Ramakrishna Order.

First Meetings with Sri Ramakrishna

When I was a boy I had a deep longing to know God and realize him, and that longing intensified with the years. Driven by that urge I would go to the Brahmo Samaj and visit holy men, who I thought would be able to help me. What they advised me to do I practised. Family life had no attraction for me, even when I was young. My education came to an end early on account of the straitened circumstances of the family. Since I was the only male child and had two dependent sisters, I had to come to Calcutta to seek a job. This made my heart very heavy, and I often wept and prayed to God, asking him to free me from all these ties.

I first met Sri Ramakrishna in Calcutta at the house of Ram Chandra Datta. A relative of Ram Babu worked in the same office with me. He would visit Sri Ramakrishna and often speak to me about him. In those days I read about the Master in Keshab Chandra Sen's paper, *Dharmatattva*. I did not, however, know where Dakshineswar was or how to get there. I was later told by Ram Babu's relative that it was located opposite Bally Khal.

One Saturday that gentleman informed me that the Master would be visiting Ram Babu's house that day and I could see him if I went there. I said: "The place is very close to where I live. I shall surely go."

Swami Shivananda in Calcutta, 1927

For many years I had been eager to explore and understand the nature of samadhi. I sincerely wanted to know exactly what it was. I had questioned many people, but no one had been able to explain it to me. One person, however, had said: "None can realize samadhi in this age. I have seen only one man who has, and that is Ramakrishna Paramahamsa of Dakshineswar."

That evening I went to Ram Babu's house. I found the Master sitting in a room crowded with people. The Master was in an ecstatic mood. I saluted him and sat nearby. One can well imagine my surprise when I heard him talking eloquently on a subject which I had been so eager to know about — samadhi! I remember that he elaborated on nirvikalpa samadhi. He said that very few can attain it and that if one attained it, one's body dropped off in twenty-one days.

I did not talk to the Master on that occasion. A month later I went to Dakshineswar and became acquainted with him. In the dim light of an oil lamp I saw the Master seated cross-legged in his room, with three or four others on the floor in front of him. The small audience suited me. At once I felt a deep attachment for the Master. I felt as if I had known him a long time. My heart became filled with joy. I saw in him my tender, loving mother waiting for me. So with the confidence, faith, and certitude of a child, I surrendered myself to him, placing myself entirely under his care. I was certain that at last I had found him for whom I had been searching all these days. From then on I looked upon the Master as my mother. After this momentous visit, my life at home and work at the office became a burden. I often ran to see him, either in Dakshineswar or Calcutta.

During my second or third visit I was serving him when he suddenly touched my chest in an ecstatic mood. That touch made me lose outer consciousness and sent me into a deep meditative state. I do not know how long I remained in that state. As a result, everything became revealed to me. I realized that I was the Atman, eternal and free. I realized that the Master was the Lord born as man for the good of humanity, and that I was on earth to serve him. He gave me a similar blessing another day under the banyan tree in the Panchavati.

Nevertheless, the Master would not allow us to rest on our laurels, but would constantly urge us, with infinite patience, to taste the fruits of realization through our own efforts. He watched our efforts and directed us to go forward according to our temperaments and at our own pace. Bigotry and fanaticism had no place in his life or teaching. He would accept people of all denominations with the same love and sympathy. To come in contact with him was to become spiritual forever. To live with him was to live in the presence of God.

When we visited him, the thought of whether or not he was a Divine Incarnation never crossed our minds. We could not foresee that he would create such a superhuman movement throughout the world. Who could know then that the whole world would become intoxicated with this man, only three and a half cubits tall? He loved us very much. It was the depth of his love that drew us to him. How shall I describe his love? It was ineffable! In our childhood we had had the experience of parental affection and did not think there could be anything greater. But when we came to the Master and felt his love, we found the affection of our parents to be of a lesser kind. After coming to him, we felt that we had arrived home, that all those previous years we had been roaming about in a strange country. Whenever I came to Sri Ramakrishna, that was how I felt. I do not know how others felt. The Master won me over at my very first meeting.

One day Sri Ramakrishna said: "Well, so many people come here. I seldom ask anyone about his home and family, or desire to know anything about these things. But when I first met you I felt that you belonged here, that I would like to know the particulars of your home, parents, and the like. Can you tell me why? Where is your home and what is your father's name?" In reply I told him I came from Barasat and my father's name was Ramkanai Ghoshal.

Hearing this, the Master said: "Indeed! You are Ramkanai Ghoshal's son! Now I understand why the Mother aroused this desire in me for information about your home. I know your father very well. He is the attorney for Rani Rasmani's estate. The Rani and her family think highly of your father, and whenever he visits the garden at Dakshineswar, they do everything to make him comfortable, carefully arranging his accommodation, meals, servants, and the like. He is certainly a highly developed sadhaka [spiritual man].

"[In the early days — 1850s] whenever he came here, he would take his bath in the Ganga, put on a red silk garment, and enter the Mother's temple. He looked like a veritable Bhairava [celestial attendant of Shiva]. He was tall, stout, and fair-complexioned, and his chest was always red. He meditated for long periods in the Mother's temple. And he used to bring with him a musician who would sit behind him singing songs symbolically describing the nerve centres in the human body, as well as songs about Mother Kali. Your father would be absorbed in meditation, with tears streaming down his cheeks. When he left the temple after meditation his face would be flushed with spiritual emotion and nobody would dare approach him.

"At that time I was suffering from an unbearable burning sensation all over my body. When I met your father, I said: 'Well, you are a devotee of the Mother and so am I. I also have a little meditation, but can you tell me why I feel a burning sensation all over my body? Look! The burning sensation is so intense that the hairs of my body have been singed. It is sometimes excruciating!' Your father recommended that I wear an amulet bearing the name of my Chosen Deity. Strange as it may seem, with the wearing of this amulet, the burning sensation at once diminished. Would you ask your father to visit me sometime?"

In those days I was living in Calcutta, going home only occasionally. My father was very pleased when I told him about Sri Ramakrishna, and he came one day to see the Master. On another occasion the Master said: "Your father's spiritual practices were attended with some desire for worldly objects. As a result of his spiritual practices, he amassed much wealth and also spent it nobly."

When I first started visiting the Master, I often felt inclined to cry. One night I was crying uncontrollably by the riverside near the bakul tree. The Master was in his room, and he inquired where I had gone. When I returned he asked me to sit down and said, "The Lord is greatly pleased if one cries to him. Tears of love wash away the mental impurities accumulated through the ages. It is very good to cry to God."

Another day when I was meditating in the Panchavati grove, my concentration became very deep. The Master came towards me from the pine grove, and as soon as he looked at me, I burst into tears. The Master stood still. I felt something creeping up inside my chest, and I was overcome by a fit of shaking. The Master said that my crying was not insignificant. It was a type of ecstasy. I then followed him to his room where he gave me something to eat. The awakening of the kundalini[1] was an easy matter for him. He could do this even without a touch, but by a mere look.

Days in Dakshineswar

Dakshineswar is our heaven on earth. It is our Kailasa, our Vaikuntha. Is it an ordinary place? Sri Ramakrishna lived there about thirty years. The Panchavati is a great site of spiritual perfection, where the Master had innumerable spiritual experiences of a very high order. For twelve years he practised different modes of divine communion at Dakshineswar, and the divine visions and spiritual realizations he had there are without parallel. In the history of religion there has never before been

---

[1] Kundalini — lit., "coiled-up," the spiritual energy that lies in a dormant state at the base of the spine. When awakened through the practice of yoga, the kundalini rises through the sushumna, and various spiritual experiences occur as it passes through and arouses each of the chakras, or centres of consciousness.

recorded such intense and diversified spiritual practices and such high spiritual experiences in the life of any other Incarnation. The Master used to say, "The experiences that have occurred here [*meaning, in himself*] transcend all those recorded." That is why Swamiji used to refer to the Master as "the greatest avatara."

The Master brought some dust from Vrindaban and spread it on the ground in the Panchavati. Every particle of dust in Dakshineswar is holy. Blessed by the touch of the holy feet of God himself, Dakshineswar has become a great place of pilgrimage. It is a source of spiritual inspiration to people of all denominations — be they nondualists or dualists, Shaktas or Vaishnavas, Shaivas or Tantrikas, for the Master practised all those modes of divine communion and attained perfection in them. This time God manifested his greatest sattvic [pure] qualities. It was that Primordial Power, the great Mother of the Universe, the source of all creation, who freely and joyfully expressed herself, as it were, through the body of our Master. The Master's intense spiritual sadhanas [disciplines] will exert their influence not only on this earth, but also in the higher regions, even to heaven. Ah, what a play of divine power it was!

[*Before meeting the Master*] I had frequented the Brahmo Samaj. When I met the Master at Dakshineswar, he asked me, "Do you believe in Shakti [Cosmic Power]?" I replied: "No, sir, I prefer the formless aspect of God. And yet I feel that some Power pervades everything." Then he went to the Kali temple and I followed him. As he proceeded towards the temple, he was caught up in a divine mood, and when he reached the temple, he prostrated with great devotion before the Mother. I was in a difficult situation. I hesitated to bow down before the image of Kali. And yet I thought that, after all, Brahman is all-pervading. Therefore it must be in this image as well, so I should not hesitate to bow down before it. As soon as this thought arose, I too prostrated before the Mother.

Later on, as I began to visit the Master more frequently, my faith in God with form became stronger. It was my good fortune to have such association with the Master and to receive his grace.

[*In response to a devotee's question regarding Sri Ramakrishna's relationship with Sri Sarada Devi:*] When Holy Mother came to Sri Ramakrishna at Dakshineswar, he did not send her away. On the contrary, he kept her by his side, gave her advice on spiritual matters, and with great care encouraged and helped her in every way. But the Master did so after attaining nirvikalpa samadhi. "The Mother who is there in the temple," the Master said, "is the same Mother who is within this [*referring to his own body*]. Again, the Mother who is within me is the same Mother who is in the form of the Holy Mother." We never wished nor tried to understand why the Master acted the way he did. If you think you can understand his ways, you are welcome to do so. The Master acted that way. This is as much as we know.

His hands were very tender. But why speak just of his hands! His entire body was so. For instance, a type of luchi [fried bread] with a hard crust once cut his finger.

At night the Master would eat perhaps one or at the most two small luchis with a little porridge. Because he could not digest whole milk, they would add water and cook it with cream of wheat, making a pudding. He would take a little of that. In the cupboard there would be sweets made of fresh cheese. Whenever he was hungry he would eat one or two pieces or perhaps half of one piece, giving the rest to others who were there. His ways were like those of a child. It was as if he himself were a child.

Although there was nothing special in his eating habits, he did not eat like other people. He was like a boy and would eat according to his whim. Sometimes he would ask for eggplant soup seasoned with cumin. When it was prepared, he would taste a little of it and leave the rest. He was very fond of jilipi [a type of sweet, fried in butter and soaked in syrup] and also sandesh [a sweet made with cheese and sugar]. He used to call the jilipi the wheel of the Viceroy's car. [*All traffic on the street had to make room for the Viceroy's car to pass. Similarly the jilipi always finds room in the stomach, even if it is full.*] The Master was never a big eater. One day he said, "I have a desire to eat cheese pudding." At that time it was not possible to get cheese in Dakshineswar. One could only get it from a Calcutta market. Meanwhile, Swami Premananda's mother brought homemade cheese pudding for the Master, and he ate it with joy. What a divine play of the Mother we saw at Dakshineswar!

Once the Master said, "In the future many white-complexioned devotees will come here." God is all-merciful. He is not limited by time, place, or person. Blessed we are! We had the opportunity to serve the Master, making betel rolls and preparing tobacco for him. How fortunate we are! We served the Master and we received so much love and affection from him! His compassion and love for us were infinite.

In those days we used to sleep on the floor of his room. At bedtime the Master would tell us how to lie down. He would say that if we were to lie flat on our backs and visualize the Mother in our hearts while falling asleep, then we would have spiritual dreams. He asked us to think of spiritual things while going to sleep. During the summer we used to sleep on the verandah and were bothered by mosquitos.

The Master looked upon Swami Brahmananda as Gopala [the boy Krishna]. Occasionally he would send him to visit his relatives at home, but when Swami Brahmananda was not with him the Master had great difficulty managing himself. One night at 1:00 A.M. the Master came out to the verandah where I was sleeping and asked, "Could you chant the name of Gopala for me?" I chanted for an hour. Some nights when he did not have anybody around him, he would call the night guard to chant the name of Rama for him. What love the Master had for the name of God!

We saw how little the Master slept. Now and then he might get an hour or half an hour of sleep at the most. Most of the time he was absorbed in samadhi, and the remaining time he spent in spiritual moods. These moods became very pronounced at night. He would spend the whole night repeating the name of Mother or Hari. When we stayed with the Master at Dakshineswar we were filled with awe. He had no sleep at all. Whenever we awoke we would hear him talking with the Divine Mother in a state of spiritual inebriation. He would pace back and forth in the room, all the while muttering something inaudibly. Sometimes he would wake us in the middle of the night and say: "Hello, my dear boys! Have you come here to sleep? If you spend the whole night in sleep, when will you call on God?" As soon as we heard his voice, we would quickly sit up and start to meditate.

Some days he would start kirtan [devotional singing] accompanied by drums and cymbals, and we would join him. Usually he would sing only the names of God, occasionally improvising words and phrases. Sometimes he danced in ecstasy. Ah! How graceful was his dancing! He would then be transformed beyond recognition. It is impossible to describe his unique spiritual raptures! He had an unusually sweet voice, the like of which we never heard anywhere else. The kirtan would continue till the late hours of the morning. The Master's ecstasies were contagious, making all those around him ecstatic, and the constant repetition of the Lord's name made the place a heaven on earth. In what joy we passed our days with the Master!

We saw how the Master went into samadhi more frequently on a day like this [Janmashtami day, the birthday of Sri Krishna]. In spite of his efforts he would not be able to control his spiritual fervour. The natural tendency of his mind was to go high. By sheer force he would bring it down to this earthly plane. The Divine Mother kept his mind on a lower level for the good of the world. Ah! What a sight! He would be so beside himself with spiritual emotion that he could hardly speak. How great was his love for God! Tears would roll down his cheeks in streams. We have never seen anyone else shedding such tears of love and devotion. Here and there in *The Gospel of Sri Ramakrishna* we find brief descriptions of that love. Can it be described in any way? Only he who saw it can understand. Spiritual emotion, samadhi, and experiences of that kind were daily events with him. Master Mahashaya [M.] could not be present every day. He would visit the Master at Dakshineswar or elsewhere on Saturday, Sunday, or some such holiday, and he tried to keep a record of whatever happened in his presence.

While coming down from nirvikalpa samadhi [transcendental experience] and still under its influence, Sri Ramakrishna would try to describe that state, but he was never successful. Eventually he would say: "I wish very much to tell you about it, but I cannot. Somebody shuts my mouth." Really, that state cannot be described. "Only he who has had the experience can understand it."

One day a great musician came to Dakshineswar with the idea of entertaining Sri Ramakrishna. He was an accomplished musician and he sang beautifully. He began by singing songs about Shiva, but after hearing only one or two songs, the Master became absorbed in nirvikalpa samadhi. His face became flushed, and he throbbed with a divine presence. Moreover, his figure appeared larger than usual, and his hair stood on end. How can I describe that sight? A long time passed, and the Master still did not come down to the normal plane. As the singing continued, all were speechless with wonder. Never had we seen the Master in such deep samadhi nor had we seen his figure appear so large.

After some time the Master suddenly exclaimed, "Oh! Oh!" as if he were suffering unbearable pain within. With great difficulty he said, "Sing about the Mother." We understood what he wanted, and the singer was requested to sing about the Mother. As the songs continued, the Master's mind slowly came down to the normal plane. Later on he said that on that day his mind was plunged into such deep samadhi that he had had a hard time bringing it down.

The Master did not like to stay long in nirvikalpa samadhi. He had come for the good of the world, and if he remained in the nirvikalpa state, he could not continue his work. That is why he wanted to maintain the attitude of a devotee and be in the company of devotees. Meditation on Shiva represents the nirvikalpa state. In that state there is neither creation nor this world of living beings. The natural tendency of Sri Ramakrishna's mind was to go to the nirvikalpa state, so he would cherish some trivial desire in order to bring his mind down. Everything about him was unique!

We observed that the Master could not listen to the entire Shiva Mahimnah Stotram [Hymn on the Greatness of Shiva]. After hearing one or two verses he would be absorbed in samadhi. He himself would sometimes recite the two verses [32 and 41] which begin: "O Lord, if the blue mountain be the ink" and "O Lord, I do not know the true nature of thy being." As he repeated the last verse he would burst into tears and say: "O Lord, who wants to know thy nature? Who knows who thou art? I do not want to know thee or understand thee, O Lord! Give me pure devotion for thy lotus feet! Who can know thee?"

A monk from northern India came to Ram Babu's Kankurgachi garden and stayed there for a few days. He had a very gentle disposition and was extremely reserved. He meditated under a tree beside the path leading to the garden. Probably Ram Babu supplied his food and other necessities. One day Ram Babu mentioned this monk to Sri Rama-krishna, and the Master said, "Why not bring the holy man here some-day?" Consequently, Ram Babu hired a carriage and brought the monk to Dakshineswar. The Master received the man very kindly in his room, asked him to sit on the small cot, and sat by his side.

The conversation then turned to spiritual matters, and they began to discuss samadhi, both savikalpa and nirvikalpa. All of a sudden, as the Master was describing nirvikalpa samadhi, he became perfectly still, lost in that very state. One of his feet rested on the cot and the other hung down beside it. The monk mistakenly thought that Sri Ramakrishna was just getting ready for meditation. Seeing him in that unusual position, the monk said, "Why not sit in the proper meditation posture?" But how could the Master hear him? Sri Ramakrishna had reached a state of consciousness far above the body and the senses. How could one under-stand the Master's samadhi? Nobody knew when, how, or under what conditions he would have it. One could not tell by looking at him. In bed, apparently dreaming or sleeping — why, at any time, under any condi-tions, samadhi was natural to him.

The Master would not readily allow me to render personal service to him. This often pained me very much. Then, from an incident that happened one day, I learned why he was so unwilling. Who, indeed, can understand his motives? On that day I stayed at Dakshineswar. Other devotees were there also. After spending a long time in his room talking about religious matters, he got up and proceeded towards the pine grove to answer the call of nature. Usually one of the devotees would follow him on such occasions with his water vessel to pour water on his hands, as he could not touch anything metal. When he went to the pine grove that day, I carried the water pot and waited at the proper place for his return. On his way back, when he found me standing there with the water pot, he said: "Now, look here. Why did you do such a thing? Why did you come with the water pot? How can I accept water from your hand? Can I accept service from you? I honour your father as a guru." I was struck with wonder. Only then did I realize why he would not allow me to render service to him. The Master had infinite moods. How could we fathom them? We can understand only that which he allows us to understand.

I had to marry against my wish, and that was a great trial. My determination to renounce the world deepened as I prayed night after night with tears in my eyes, asking God not to bind me with worldly chains. I spoke about it to the Master and prayed that my worldly bonds be destroyed. After hearing my story the Master asked me to perform a certain ritual. Then he said in a tone of assurance: "Have no fear. I am here to protect you. Think of me and perform this ritual. Nothing adverse will happen to you. I am telling you that even if you sleep in the same room with your wife, you will be free from danger. You will see, your spirit of renunciation will instead be intensified."

On the death of my wife I was free from all bondages, and I ran straight to Dakshineswar. I begged the Master to allow me to stay with him, and he kindly accepted me. For those last three years of his life I lived almost constantly with him. At Dakshineswar I met Swamiji [Swami Vivekananda] as well as Swamis Brahmananda and Premananda. Among us Swamiji was most loved and trusted by the Master.

The Master had prescribed the same ritual for Swami Brahmananda as he had for me. I went through it as instructed and didn't have any trouble. Once, in the course of conversation, I mentioned this fact to Swamiji. He was very surprised and remarked: "What do you say? That is the characteristic of a Mahapurusha [great soul]. You are certainly one." After that he started calling me by this name, and others did the same. Previously Swamiji had called me "Tarak-da." One day at Balaram Babu's house, when Swamiji called me Mahapurusha, Swami Premananda's mother said: "What? Isn't a Mahapurusha one who lives in a tree? [*She meant a ghost.*] What kind of Mahapurusha is he?" Swamiji explained that I was a genuine Mahapurusha. It pleased her very much.

In the course of time, as a result of my frequent visits to the Master, I made up my mind to give up all connection with the world, and I went to say goodbye to my father. Tears began to trickle down his cheeks. He asked me to salute the deity in our shrine, and then he blessed me. Placing his hand on my head, he said: "May you realize God! I myself tried to renounce the world and realize him, but I failed. Therefore I bless you that you may attain God!" I repeated this to the Master. He was quite pleased to hear it and said, "It is good that this has happened!"

We heard from the Master that a few days before Maharaj [Swami Brahmananda] came to Dakshineswar for the first time, the Master had a vision: The Mother brought a child and placed him on his lap, saying, "Here is your child." The Master was startled and said to the Mother:

"How can I have a child? I am a monk." The Mother smiled and said: "He is not a child in the worldly sense. He is your spiritual son." Upon hearing this, the Master felt relieved. Later, when Maharaj came to Dakshineswar, the Master at once recognized him [*as the child in his vision*]. From the very beginning of his relationship with the Master, Maharaj behaved like a five-year-old child. And like a petulant boy he often made demands upon the Master. Sometimes he even climbed up on his shoulders or sat on his lap, and how many other childlike things he did! Those were unique sights to behold — divine phenomena. From the ordinary human standpoint one cannot understand these things.

At one time M. stayed for a while at Dakshineswar. His food was very simple, consisting primarily of milk and rice. The Master himself arranged to have a pint of good milk brought to him every day. M. had a very strong body, which enabled him to do so much of the Master's work. Whatever he heard from the Master he would note down in his diary after returning home. He had a prodigious memory. By exercising his memory through meditation, he was able to compile *The Gospel of Sri Ramakrishna* from the meagre notes he had jotted down. He belonged to the group of Sri Ramakrishna's intimate disciples. The Master brought M. with him for that particular work. M. visited the Master every Saturday or Sunday or on holidays. He also saw the Master in Calcutta and elsewhere. On such occasions interesting subjects were sure to be discussed, with a big crowd present. During these discussions, Sri Ramakrishna would suddenly turn to M. and ask: "M., did you understand? Note that point well." Sometimes the Master would repeat certain points. We did not realize then why he spoke to M. that way.

The Master's words were so impressive and instructive that I too felt tempted to take notes. One day at Dakshineswar I was listening to him and looking intently at his face. He was explaining many beautiful things. Noticing my keen interest, the Master suddenly said: "Look here! Why are you listening so attentively?" I was taken by surprise. He then added: "You don't have to do that. Your life is different." I felt as if the Master had divined my intention to keep notes and did not approve of it, and that was why he had spoken in that way. From that time on I gave up the idea of taking notes of his conversations, and whatever notes I already had I threw into the Ganga.

The Master was very fond of the Adhyatma Ramayana, a devotional scripture on the life of Ramachandra. There were two books on his small cot — the Adhyatma Ramayana and *Mukti O Tahar Sadhan* [Liberation and Its Practice]. It was not possible for him to read those books, because most of the time he was in an ecstatic mood, but he would often ask someone to read them to him.

Anyone who takes shelter in the Master with all sincerity and with his whole being, anyone who loves the Master, will surely attain liberation. There is a story about a sweeper named Rasik who lived at Dakshineswar. He used to call the Master "Father." One day the Master was returning from the direction of the Panchavati, absorbed in a spiritual mood. At that time Rasik knelt down before him and prayed with folded hands: "Father, why don't you bless me? What will happen to me?" The Master assured him: "You have no need to fear. You will have your wish fulfilled. You will see me at the time of death." And that is exactly what happened. Shortly before his death, Rasik was carried to a holy spot near the tulsi plant. [*Its leaves are used for worshipping Vishnu.*] As the moment of death approached, Rasik cried out: "You are here! You have come to me, Father! You have really come, Father!" And thus he breathed his last.

Sri Ramakrishna Taught Us

We met Sri Ramakrishna, associated with him, and received his grace. And yet he made us practise such severe spiritual disciplines. We too at first did not realize that he was God himself, born to bring deliverance to the world. Gradually, through spiritual discipline, we understood. Of course, nothing can be attained without divine grace. That the Master is God himself, the Supreme Being, the Lord of the Universe, we have come to know in the course of time. He himself has graciously revealed to us his true nature.

He did not give initiation in the ordinary way, by simply whispering a mantram in the disciple's ear. Instead, he would awaken the spiritual consciousness of a disciple by a touch or by writing the sacred mantram on his tongue, or perhaps he would transform the disciple's mind by his mere will. Being a world teacher, his ways of initiation were unusual. "A world teacher gives the mantram in one's heart, and an ordinary teacher gives the mantram in one's ear." Moreover, by prescribing different kinds of spiritual disciplines for different types of aspirants, Sri Ramakrishna could quicken the spiritual impulse and awaken the divinity within. He was not one-sided. Whatever path one chose, one could receive help from the Master.

As time passes, we understand why the Master practised various forms of spiritual discipline. All religions are true, and through each path people can realize God, the embodiment of Truth. He did not practise different religions only to discover and realize the harmony of religions. His spiritual practice had a deeper meaning. That is why men belonging to different sects of Hinduism have made him their ideal. He is also the ideal of many Christians. They worship him as Jesus, and it must be remembered that this is not the result of someone's preaching. Tell me who can preach Sri Ramakrishna? Who can reveal the one who is Truth itself? The Lord says in the Gita (15.6), "Him the sun cannot reveal, nor the moon, nor the fire."

Ah, how charming was the Master's singing! He would become lost in spiritual moods as soon as he started to sing. I have never heard such soul-enchanting singing from anyone else. My heart and soul were filled with his singing.

And how beautifully he danced! This was because he danced in the ecstasy of divine communion. His body was very well-proportioned and supple. When he danced he was absorbed in a divine mood, and those scenes are still very vivid to me. That charming dance of his would rouse us to dance also. And he, too, would force us to join in. "Why should you feel shy?" he would say at such times. "You should dance in the name of Hari. Certainly that's not something to be ashamed of. Nothing can be achieved until one is rid of three things — shame, hatred, and fear. One who cannot become mad in the name of Hari and dance, lives a vain life indeed."

The Master used to say: "As long as the child is busy with his lollipop, he is forgetful of his mother and she attends to her duties. But the moment the child tires of the lollipop, throws it away, and begins crying for the mother, she drops everything, runs to the child, and takes him up in her arms." As long as one remains attached to the lollipop of this world, one will not see God. It is most unfortunate if one does not avail oneself of the blessed privilege of being born a human being. In order to bring home this idea, the Master would often sing this song:

> O mind, you do not know how to farm!
> Fallow lies the field of your life.
> If you had only worked it well,
> How rich a harvest you might reap!

In the song is this line:

> Sooner or later will dawn the day
> When you must forfeit your precious field;
> Gather, O mind, what fruit you may.

The Master was right when he said that spiritual aspirants become sidetracked — nay, lost for a while — if they direct their minds to supernatural powers. The Mother told the Master that psychic powers should be shunned as filth. But in the case of Jesus, the miracles he performed were done not with the idea of showing off, but out of compassion to mitigate the sufferings of people. It is mentioned in the Bible that Jesus, while giving sight to the blind and healing a leper by a touch, cautioned them not to make it public. He did not do those things for name and fame or popular applause. The scriptures say that knowers of Brahman who survive after illumination are supremely compassionate and live in the world to do good to humanity. They do not have any other desire or wish.

Furthermore, Jesus was not an ordinary illumined soul. He was an Incarnation of God. His identity was merged with God, the Heavenly Father. In his case, performing miracles was neither unnatural nor wrong. While common people think those acts are extraordinary or impossible, for Divine Incarnations they are as easy as breathing. By their mere wish the impossible becomes possible. In certain cases Jesus used supernatural powers in order to create in the minds of unbelievers faith in God's existence. It is often difficult to comprehend the significance of the actions of Divine Incarnations.

To heal physical ailments by a touch is not so miraculous. It is rather an easy thing. Sri Ramakrishna demonstrated greater supernatural powers when by a touch he gave God-vision or samadhi. The greatest miracle consists of instantaneously directing a person's mind to God by reducing the layers of his strong impressions stored from birth to birth. No other Divine Incarnation did this. Oh, what marvellous things we saw the Master do! It makes our hair stand on end to think of them! He could play with a human mind and fashion it as he liked. By his touch the sickness of a mind could be cured. What stupendous spiritual powers he possessed! Outwardly he behaved like an ordinary man, but within him acted the Omnipotent God.

The Master used to say that pure devotion is a rare thing and seldom comes to ordinary souls. He would sing with intense feeling [this song of Krishna]:

> Though I am never loath to grant salvation,
> I hesitate indeed to grant pure love.
> Whoever wins pure love surpasses all;
> He is adored by men;
> He triumphs over the three worlds.
>
> Listen, Chandravali! I shall tell you of love:
> Mukti a man may gain, but rare is bhakti.
> Solely for pure love's sake did I become
> King Vali's door-keeper
> Down in his realm in the nether world.
> Alone in Vrindaban can pure love be found;
> Its secret none but the gopas and gopis know.

> For pure love's sake I dwelt in Nanda's house;
> Taking him as My father,
> I carried his burdens on My head.

Ah, with what feeling would the Master sing this song.

It was to save the sinners and the afflicted that the Master incarnated. If anyone takes shelter in him with all sincerity, he passes his merciful hand over the supplicant and wipes away all his sins. By his divine touch one immediately becomes sinless. What is needed is sincere love for him and absolute surrender to him. Girish Babu had committed many sins, but the Master was impressed by his devotion and so accepted him as his own. That is why Girish Babu used to say at the end of his life, "Had I known there was such a huge pit in which to throw one's sins, I would have committed many more." The Master is full of compassion. He is a veritable sea of mercy.

Whether the Master is only a wave of the ocean of Satchidananda or the ocean itself, I do not know. But this much I do know — that he alone is true and all else is illusory. By realizing him one can know everything — ocean, creek, canal, and pool. And the means of realizing him are faith and devotion. Anyone can pray to him according to his own liking. By merely knowing the world, one cannot realize him. But through discrimination and reasoning, one can gain true understanding. Philosophical speculations ultimately lead to the conclusion that the world is illusory and the Lord, who is Infinite, alone is true. That perfect Godhead is Sri Ramakrishna. He himself graciously assumed the form of a man so that human beings might be able to understand him.

There is nothing very striking in the incidents of my life to write about except one incident which is most special: my meeting with Sri Ramakrishna and the mercy granted to me out of his goodness. I had no special virtue to merit his mercy. He is self-willed, free, and independent. He, through his own will, has blessed me. This is the only incident worth mentioning in my life.

At Cossipore Garden House

Sri Ramakrishna was seriously ill and was staying at the Cossipore garden house while under treatment. Most of us were living there with him to nurse him. Taking turns, we waited on him day and night. Surendra, a well-to-do householder devotee, arranged for all the necessities.

A cook had been engaged, but when he fell ill, we had to take turns cooking. Our meals were very plain, usually consisting of rice or unleavened bread, lentils, vegetables, soup, or similar dishes. We were in such a mental state that we didn't pay any attention to food at all. We ate whatever we could get. In the first place, the Master was so sick, and then we were all deeply absorbed in severe spiritual disciplines.

One night it was my turn to cook for the household. As I was adding the final spices to the vegetables, the smell spread through the house and reached the Master upstairs. He asked the nearby attendant: "What is cooking? Excellent! The aroma of the spices is everywhere! Who is the cook?" When he learned that I was the cook, he said, "Go and bring me a little of it," and he tasted a tiny bit of the preparation. Because of the cancer in his throat he could hardly swallow anything. He would eat with great difficulty a little cream of wheat cooked in milk, but most of the time he was not able to swallow even that.

Because of his repeated spiritual experiences the Master hardly had any consciousness of the external world. How happily we passed our days serving him and practising austerities at the Cossipore garden! It seemed the Master took this sickness upon himself in order to gather us together and lay the foundation of his future Order. Inscrutable are the ways of a Divine Incarnation.

At one time we discussed Buddhist philosophy at length. Swamiji was well versed in Buddhism. The rest of us had read a little. We used to have heated arguments. In those days we didn't believe in the existence of God. Some of the devotees were very hurt by this. Swamiji himself would not say much, but he would egg me on. I would argue my point vigorously, and Swamiji would listen quietly and enjoy the fun. Sometimes I would even say that it was harmful to have body-consciousness, for it interfered with meditation. Even the thought of God would not allow the mind to be free from modifications. It was not just that we expressed ourselves that way — our meditations and experiences also were of that nature. We couldn't think otherwise in those days. We were so absorbed in those ideas.

Some devotees brought this matter to the notice of the Master, and he told them: "What they say is also true. There is a stage in spiritual life when the seeker does not admit the existence of God." This phase of ours lasted quite awhile. Even after the Master had passed away and we were living at the monastery in Baranagore, these ideas persisted. We were still atheistic.

One day the Master appeared to me and said: "The guru is all in all. There is no one higher than the guru." The moment I had that vision these ideas left me and did not return. Sri Ramakrishna was a Divine Incarnation, born to establish religion.

[*When Sri Ramakrishna was ill in Cossipore, Swamis Vivekananda, Shivananda, and Abhedananda went to Bodh Gaya without informing the Master.
Swami Shivananda was later asked if the Master had said anything about it on
their return to Cossipore.*] Yes, of course the Master said something.
Moving a finger in a circle and shaking the thumb, he said, "No spirituality anywhere!" Then pointing to himself he said: "This time all is here.
You may roam about wherever you please, but you will not find anything [spirituality] anywhere. Here all the doors are open!"

Why should the Master have been a kalpataru only on one day?[2] To
tell the truth, he is a kalpataru every day. His only work is to shower his
grace on all creatures. We saw with our own eyes how he blessed
innumerable people in so many ways. It is true that on that particular
day, in the Cossipore garden, he blessed quite a number of devotees all
at one time. In that sense, this day has a special significance, for it was
on this day that the devotees palpably felt his infinite grace.

None of the monastic disciples of the Master was present at that time.
The Master was seriously ill, and our hearts were then full of the spirit
of renunciation. He was passing through such a critical period of his
illness that we kept vigil twenty-four hours a day. The lay devotees
would come during the daytime according to their convenience and
arrange for the medicines, diet, and all other necessary expenditures. But
we shouldered the entire responsibility of nursing him. And along with
that we continued our intense spiritual practices. The Master also encouraged us in this. He would call us individually and guide our
spiritual disciplines. He kept himself informed on the progress we made
in meditation and the kinds of visions we were having. At night Swamiji
would sit in meditation with us around a blazing fire under the sky, and
sometimes we would sing devotional songs. The whole night would
pass thus in divine ecstasy while we served the Master by turns.

Since we had to keep awake at night, most of us would take a nap
after lunch. On that January 1, we were resting after lunch in the small
room adjacent to the downstairs hall, when for the first time at Cossipore
the Master came downstairs for a stroll in the garden. It was a holiday
and many devotees were present in the garden. Seeing the Master, they
followed him joyously. He was walking slowly towards the gate of the
garden when Girish Babu, after prostrating himself at the Master's feet,
began to sing his praises with folded hands. These words, full of sincere
devotion and faith, sent the Master into deep samadhi while he was

---

[2] The day (January 1, 1886) on which Sri Ramakrishna blessed the devotees at the Cossipore
garden house, fulfilling their spiritual desires like the mythological kalpataru, the wish-
fulfilling tree.

standing. Finding him in a divine mood, the devotees started exclaiming in great joy: "Victory to Sri Ramakrishna! Victory to Sri Ramakrishna!" and saluted him again and again.

Gradually the Master regained partial consciousness, and he turned his benign eyes on them, saying: "What else shall I say? May you all have your spiritual consciousness awakened!" No sooner had he uttered these words than the devotees felt an upsurge of ineffable bliss within themselves. They exclaimed repeatedly: "Glory to Ramakrishna! Glory to Ramakrishna!" and saluted him.

Then, still in a state of divine absorption, he touched most of them one by one, saying, "Be illumined!" As a result of that divine touch, the devotees felt wonderful spiritual stirrings within themselves. Some of them were lost in meditation, some danced with joy, some wept, and some shouted his praises like madmen. It was an unimaginable sight. The Master stood looking at them with great joy.

Their joyous uproar roused us from our sleep. We rushed out and saw the devotees all around the Master, behaving like lunatics, and he himself looking at them graciously with a smiling face, full of affection. By the time we joined them the Master's mind had returned to the human plane, but the devotees were still in an ecstatic mood, intoxicated with divine bliss.

Later on we learned about the incident from the devotees. All of them acknowledged that the Master's touch had given them wonderful spiritual realizations, and that that experience had lasted quite a long time. And why shouldn't his touch be that effective? Wasn't he God himself? Yet even on that day the Master did not touch one or two devotees, saying that they would have illumination later. From this it is clear that nothing happens unless the time is ripe. One has to wait for the right moment.

[*It was at Cossipore that*] the Master gave up his body [*on August 16, 1886*]. At first none of us realized that he was actually dead. We thought he was in samadhi, since occasionally the Master's samadhi was so deep that he would remain in it for two or three days at a time. Thinking he was in deep samadhi, we started loudly chanting the name of the Lord. The night passed in this manner without any change in his condition. The next morning we sent word to Dr. Sarkar. He came and examined the Master in detail and said he had given up the body. The doctor found no signs of life. He then suggested that we have a photograph of the Master taken, which we did. At about two or two-thirty in the afternoon the Master's body was cremated at the Cossipore cremation ground.

We never felt any strain or hardship [at Cossipore]. In those days we spent our time immersed in a particular mood. We were so absorbed in doing personal service for the Master, in practising meditation and austerity, that we often were not aware of the passing of day or night. Those were indeed unique days. After Sri Ramakrishna's passing away, most of the young disciples, except Swami Adbhutananda and me, went back home. Though Swamiji also returned home, he used to visit the garden frequently and was in close touch with us.

The Master's relics were preserved at the Cossipore garden, and we worshipped them daily. We could stay at the garden for a few days because the rent had been paid for the whole month. Swamiji and a few of us decided that the relics must be preserved and buried somewhere on the bank of the Ganga, as this had been the Master's wish. But we could not find a suitable place.

Meanwhile Ram Babu had arranged to take the relics to his garden house in Kankurgachi, Calcutta. We felt very sad, especially at the thought that the Master's wish would not be fulfilled, so a message was sent to Balaram Babu asking him to bring an earthen jar. He came at once. That very night we removed all the bones from the ashes, put them in the earthen jar, sealed it with clay, and sent the jar to Balaram Babu's house in Calcutta where the family deity was regularly worshipped. The relics began to be worshipped there daily.

In the meantime Ram Babu took the remaining ashes to Kankurgachi. As we did not tell him about our having removed the bones from the ashes, he did not know what had happened. The relics we kept then [at Balaram Babu's house] are now worshipped daily at the monastery here [at Belur Math]. Swamiji used to refer to that jar of relics as the urn of Atmarama [one who rejoices in himself]. We also call it by the same name.

The Master once told Swamiji, "Wherever you place me, carrying me on your head, I shall live." On the day this Belur monastery was consecrated, Swamiji carried Atmarama's urn on his head and installed it here. There was an elaborate worship, fire sacrifice [homa], and an offering of food. I cooked the rice pudding to offer to the Master. After installing the Master in this monastery, Swamiji said: "Today the heaviest responsibility in this world is off my head. Now it matters little even if I leave this body." Thereafter all our spiritual practices centred on this Atmarama.

It was the Master himself who instituted the monastic Order that bore his name. And Swamiji organized this Order to maintain the spiritual power with which the Master came to this world. Swamiji started the work with this Math as its main centre. This is the powerhouse of that spiritual energy. It is from here that the spiritual current will rush forth to deluge the entire world.

Sri Ramakrishna[3]

Even as a child I had an inherent tendency towards spiritual life and an innate awareness that enjoyment was not the object of life. As I grew in age and knowledge, these two ideas took a firmer hold on my mind. Seeking the knowledge of God, I went to various religious societies and temples in Calcutta. But I couldn't find satisfaction anywhere. None of them emphasized the beauty of renunciation, and none had among them someone who possessed true spiritual wisdom.

Then in 1880 or 1881 I heard about Sri Ramakrishna and went to see him in Calcutta at the house of one of his devotees. [*It was at this time that*] Swami Vivekananda and the other disciples of Sri Ramakrishna, who later renounced the world to carry on his divine mission, had begun to gather around him. On the first day of my visit I saw Sri Ramakrishna merge into samadhi, and when he returned to normal consciousness, he spoke in detail of the nature of samadhi. I felt in my innermost heart that here was a man who had indeed realized God, and I surrendered myself forever at his blessed feet.

I have not yet come to a final understanding of whether Sri Ramakrishna was a man or a superman, a god or God himself. But I have known him to be a man of complete self-effacement, a master of the highest renunciation, a man possessed of supreme wisdom, and an Incarnation of love. As time passes and I become more and more acquainted with the domain of spirituality, I feel the infinite extent and depth of Sri Ramakrishna's spiritual moods. Because of this I am more and more convinced that to compare him with God, as God is popularly understood, is to minimize and lower his greatness. I saw him shower his love equally on men and women, on the learned and the ignorant, on saints and sinners. He evinced earnest and unceasing solicitude for them in their sufferings and gave them infinite peace through the realization of the Divine. And I dare say that the modern world has not seen another person like him, so devoted to the welfare of human beings.

Sri Ramakrishna was born at Kamarpukur in the Hooghly district [of West Bengal] in 1836. Name and fame were extremely distasteful to him. His example and teachings deeply impressed on us the pettiness and insignificance of worldly pleasures compared to the inexpressible bliss of God. Day and night he lived in divine ecstasy. That rare and almost inaccessible state of samadhi was perfectly natural to him. It is no

---

[3] This article on Sri Ramakrishna was originally written by Swami Shivananda in reply to inquiries made by Romain Rolland. The swami briefly but clearly narrated his own experience and understanding of his Master.

wonder then that the idea of a God-intoxicated man being familiar with the details of everyday life and instructing people on them, as well as yearning to remove the sorrows of people who came to him with their worldly problems, should appear contradictory to those who did not witness his life. We saw innumerable such instances in his life. And there may be a few householders still living who feel themselves blessed remembering his infinite mercy and his eager attempts to relieve the sufferings of people.

When Mani Mallik lost his son he came to Sri Ramakrishna with a broken heart. Sri Ramakrishna not only sympathized with him but entered so deeply into Mani Mallik's grief that it almost seemed as if he were the bereaved father and that his sorrow surpassed Mani Mallik's. After some time Sri Ramakrishna suddenly went into a different mood and sang a song encouraging Mani to prepare for the battle of life. I remember how the father's grief was assuaged. The song gave him courage, calmed him, and instilled peace in him.

To Sri Ramakrishna there was neither good nor evil. He saw the Divine Mother abiding in all beings and differing only in degrees of manifestation. All women he revered and addressed as his own mother, seeing the Divine Mother in them.

By practising the doctrines of Hinduism, Christianity, Islam, and other faiths, he demonstrated the truth of all religions. He found that his own realizations tallied with descriptions of them in other scriptures — the Upanishads, the Bible, the Koran, etc. — and he declared that Truth is one, though defined and worshipped variously by the different religions of the world. I saw many true seekers of God, professing different creeds, come to him for spiritual guidance. And it was by seeing him that I came to believe in the truth of such Incarnations and prophets as Buddha, Jesus, and Muhammad, and to feel their infinite mercy. He never criticized anyone's spiritual mood or ideal. He helped all who came to him — rich or poor, learned or ignorant, high or low — to advance along the spiritual path according to their individual inclinations.

He was very much aware of the tremendous sufferings of the world. He not only relieved the suffering of those who came to him, but also removed collective suffering on several occasions. And he advised Swami Vivekananda and his other disciples to do the same. I should mention here that Swami Vivekananda also was a person of high spiritual attainments. We heard from the Master that the swami's spiritual capacity was of a very high order.

Once the Master accompanied Mathur Babu, a son-in-law of Rani Rasmani [owner of the Dakshineswar temple], to his estate in the district of Nadia. It was time for tax collection, though the tenants were in dire straits because their crops had failed the previous two years. The sight of the starving and ragged villagers deeply pained Sri Ramakrishna. He sent for Mathur Babu and asked him to remit their taxes and give them a sumptuous feast and some clothes. Mathur Babu replied: "Father, you do not know how much suffering there is in the world. But it will not help much to remit people's taxes." "You are merely Mother's steward, and these are Mother's tenants," said Sri Ramakrishna. "Let Mother's money be spent. They are suffering so much and won't you help them? You must." Since Mathur Babu regarded Sri Ramakrishna as an Incarnation of God, he had to accede to the Master's request.

I shall mention a second incident. It happened at Deoghar in Bihar. The Master was going on a pilgrimage with Mathur Babu and others. In those days the Master lived almost constantly in a high spiritual state. When they arrived at Deoghar, Sri Ramakrishna found the local people [Santhals, an aboriginal tribe] practically naked and extremely emaciated from starvation. Seeing their pitiful condition, he left the palanquin and asked Mathur Babu who they were. The people had been suffering from a terrible famine for the past two years, and the Master had never seen such misery before. When Mathur Babu explained everything to him, Sri Ramakrishna said that they must be given oil, bathed, clothed, and fed well. Mathur Babu resisted, but Sri Ramakrishna said he would not leave — he would live with them until their misery was relieved. Mathur Babu had no choice but to do what he was told. Those two incidents happened before I met the Master, but I heard about them from his own lips.

I will mention here two incidents that occurred in our presence which illustrate how Sri Ramakrishna was not satisfied with the mere verbal expression of sympathy and love for the afflicted. He actually instructed Swami Vivekananda and us to remove their misery. One day at Dakshineswar Sri Ramakrishna said in an ecstatic mood: "Jiva is Shiva [human beings are Divine]. Who can show mercy? Not mercy, but service — by looking upon human beings as God." Swami Vivekananda was present, and after hearing the Master's words, full of deep meaning, he said to us: "Today I have listened to noble words. If the opportunity ever comes, I shall proclaim this great truth to the world." If anyone seeks the origin of the innumerable works of service that are being done by the Ramakrishna Mission in various places, he will find it in this incident.

The other incident took place in the beginning of 1886. The Master was ill and under medical treatment at the Cossipore garden house near Calcutta. It was there in that same year that he entered into mahasamadhi [departure from the body in a superconscious state]. Swami Vivekananda and about fifteen others of us then lived in the garden house, attending on him. Swami Vivekananda often begged the Master during those days to give him nirvikalpa samadhi [the highest super-conscious realization]. One day while meditating, Swami Vivekananda actually reached that state. Seeing him unconscious with his body cold like a corpse, we hurried to the Master in great fear and told him what had happened. The Master showed no anxiety. He merely smiled and said, "Very well," and then remained silent. Some time later the swami regained outer consciousness and went to the Master, who said: "Well, now do you understand? This [the highest realization] will henceforth remain under lock and key. You have to do the Mother's work. When it is finished she will undo the lock." Swami Vivekananda replied: "Sir, I was happy in samadhi. In my infinite joy I forgot the world. I beg you to let me remain in that state." "Shame on you!" cried the Master. "How can you ask such a thing? I thought you were a large receptacle, and now I find you want to stay absorbed in personal joy like an ordinary person! By the grace of the Mother, this realization will become so natural to you that even in your normal state you will realize the One Divinity in all beings. You will do great things in the world. You will bring spiritual knowledge to people and assuage the misery of the humble and the poor."

Sri Ramakrishna had the power to transmit spirituality to others and lift them to higher states of consciousness. This he could do either by thought, look, or touch. Like Swami Vivekananda, many of us used to visit the Master and we had the good fortune to be lifted to higher planes of consciousness according to our capacities. I myself was privileged to attain that high spiritual consciousness [samadhi] thrice by his touch and wish during his lifetime. I am still living to bear testimony to his great spiritual power. It was neither hypnotism nor a mere state of deep sleep, for such realizations brought about changes of character and outlook which were more or less permanent.

Naturally it was not always possible for one like Sri Ramakrishna, who was constantly in a high spiritual state, to relieve the earthly sufferings of the poor. But it would be wrong to think that he was unconcerned about them. What he himself practised and taught in a few words were and are being subsequently realized and practised by Swami Vivekananda and others. It was impossible for him to look after even his own requirements while dwelling in high spiritual planes. He therefore transmitted his spiritual ideas, apparently under Divine guidance, to those who were fit to assimilate them quickly and devote themselves to the welfare of mankind. The greatest of them was Swami

Vivekananda — this we heard from the Master and we ourselves felt it to be true.

Therefore, as we study the life of the swami, we find that on the one hand he preached the wonderful message of religious harmony, and on the other he preached the universal creed of service — that is, giving secular and spiritual knowledge, food, medicine, and so forth to the needy, so that with all their wants met, they may eventually be led to the spiritual realm. In fact, Swamiji was the greatest interpreter of the Master's life and commentator on the Master's deep and noble spiritual teachings. I doubt that anyone will ever be able to fully determine the infinitude of Sri Ramakrishna's spiritual realizations.

Some see a contradiction between the realization of the Divinity in human beings and the acceptance of universal suffering, a primary motive for service. It seems to me that these are merely two aspects of the same thing and not two different things. It is only by realizing the inherent Divinity of human beings that we can truly feel the depth of their misery — for only then does the state of people's spiritual bondage and the deprivation of Divine perfection and bliss become evident. It is the painful awareness of the contrast between the Divinity within human beings and their present ignorance of it and consequent suffering, that inspires the heart to serve them. Without the realization of the spirit within oneself and others, true sympathy, love, and service are impossible. This is why Sri Ramakrishna wanted his disciples to attain Self-realization first. Then they could devote themselves properly to the service of humanity.

[From: *A Man of God*, by Swami Vividishananda (Madras: Sri Ramakrishna Math), 1957; *Spiritual Talks*, by The First Disciples of Sri Ramakrishna (Calcutta: Advaita Ashrama), 1968; *For Seekers of God*, By Swami Vividishananda & Swami Gambhirananda (Calcutta: Advaita Ashrama), 1975; *Sri Sri Mahapurushjir Katha*, (Calcutta: Udbodhan Office), 1934; *Mahapurushjir Patravali* (Calcutta: Udbodhan Office), 1953; *Prabuddha Bharata* (Advaita Ashrama), March 1930]

Swami Ramakrishnananda in Madras

9
Swami Ramakrishnananda

Swami Ramakrishnananda (1863-1911) came to Sri Ramakrishna with his cousin, Swami Saradananda, when they were both college students. Because of his devoted service to Sri Ramakrishna, he was given his monastic name after the Master. When Swami Vivekananda returned to India after his first trip to the West, he sent Swami Ramakrishnananda to Madras to start a centre there.

I
Sri Ramakrishna's Personality

Everything about Sri Ramakrishna is superhuman. I heard from his own lips, "The key to this room has to be turned the reverse way." This means that if anybody wants to attain knowledge, worldly means will be of no avail. Sri Krishna also taught the same thing: "In that which is night to all beings, the man of self-control is awake; and where all beings are awake, there is night for the sage who sees." Sri Ramakrishna's pure life is a glowing example of this teaching of the Gita [2.69]. His life is beyond ordinary human understanding. For what people regard as good was bad in his eyes, and what people regard as giving them happiness and peace he knew to be the cause of all misery and restlessness. His divine power was unparalleled and irresistible. In order to explain this phenomenon it is necessary to cite a few instances from his life.

Wherever there is the play of great power, there God manifests. Now one may ask: What greatness can be found in a temple priest, who draws a monthly salary of only seven rupees, that would make people revere him as a manifestation of God? From a human viewpoint it seems to be impossible. A few years ago Sri Ramakrishna's greatness was not known to the world at large, but today there is no nation that has not heard of him and does not regard him with great reverence. What is the reason? His poverty and lack of education are two factors that highlight his greatness. A desired object is attained by a certain means, and practice of that means brings perfection. It does not require proof, therefore, to understand that he who can attain a desired object without any visible means or effort on his part, possesses great powers.

One will have to admit unequivocally that divine power is manifested in a person who, singlehandedly and without any arms and ammunition, defeats a well-equipped army. Nowadays, if people want to be scholars, they study many books. The greater the number of books one has read the more learned he is supposed to be. But Sri Ramakrishna did not study books. Sometimes he would say, "Grantha granthi" — that is, books are knots. Mere book learning usually increases a person's ego, binding him to this world.

When Sri Ramakrishna was young he met a pandit of the Vedanta philosophy, who taught him about the impermanence of the world and the reality of God. From their talk the Master thought that the pandit was free from all worldly attachments. One day, however, he saw the pandit performing rituals as a priest for a little rice. This convinced him that mere book learning does not help a person attain true knowledge, and that there must be some other means to attain it. Thus he became disgusted with book learning. Later, seeing the pandits talk about the transcendental truths of Vedanta, he often compared them to vultures. As vultures soar very high though their eyes are always on the charnel pits, so the pandits constantly talk about high spiritual matters but their minds are on money. Once one of his disciples was studying the literature of the Parsis, neglecting his service to the Master. Sri Ramakrishna told him: "My boy, this book learning will make your mind more restless. It may even destroy your love for God." This scolding brought the disciple to his senses.

By reading too many books the mind becomes filled with other people's thoughts and loses the capacity of thinking for itself. If book learning stimulates one's thinking it is good, but if it destroys one's capability to think, then it is to be avoided.

Sri Ramakrishna shunned such learning and sought spiritual knowledge in his own pure mind. Within a short time he acquired so much knowledge that from his inexhaustible supply he freely distributed it to people. The rich, the poor, the learned, and the ignorant — all felt themselves blessed by listening to his holy words.

We had read in the Upanishads that there are two types of knowledge — the higher and the lower. The lower knowledge is considered to be the study of the scriptures, while the higher knowledge is that through which one realizes God. We could not understand this truth until we came in contact with Sri Ramakrishna. With the help of this higher knowledge [the knowledge of Brahman] the Master could dispel the ignorance of both the pandits and the illiterate. Nowhere else has such a phenomenon been seen. This proves that he was God incarnate.

Nowadays it is almost impossible for a person to be respected without wealth. Wealth makes even a fool appear learned and the impossible possible. So nowadays wealth is worshipped everywhere. But Sri Ramakrishna realized that attachment for wealth binds the soul and it is the root cause of all evil. He had such great repulsion for coins that he could not even touch a metallic object. If his hand touched any such object, it would become numb. It is because of his complete renunciation of money that wealthy people regarded themselves as blessed when they could serve him and spend money for him. Wealth flows to that person who has renounced it. This fact is proved in Sri Ramakrishna's divine life.

Saving for the future is essential for a person who lives in the world as no one knows what need may unexpectedly arise. But Sri Ramakrishna could not save anything even for the next moment. Because he was so nonattached, other people used to procure things for him. We had read in the Gita: "Persons who meditate on me, without any other thought, to them, thus ever zealously engaged, I carry what they lack and preserve what they already have." [9.22] But at that time we could not understand the true significance of this statement. Later Sri Ramakrishna's divine life made it quite clear to us.

In this world the tie of love alone is the cause of happiness. People enjoy family life because of this sweet bondage. It is for this bondage that a person builds a home, weaves a cloth, saves things in a safe, locks the door, and dresses himself with knots. A man who has no such bondage is a mendicant. Even a beggar ties into a bundle his old torn and tattered rags lest he should lose them. So bondages of some kind or other are indispensable for a person living in the world. But Sri Ramakrishna feared any kind of bondage. Bondages bind the soul to the world and do not allow him to reach God. They rob a person of his precious freedom. Bondages do not let a person's heart expand. He who wants to drink the divine nectar of God, or wants to move freely and fearlessly in the realm of maya, should not have any ties of attachment in his heart. In fact, Sri Ramakrishna had such a terrible aversion to being bound that he could not lock anything in his room. Also, he could not even tie his own cloth around his waist — someone had to do it for him. His nature was like that of a five-year-old boy. For this reason the Divine Mother engaged several attendants to look after him, and they felt blessed to be able to serve this great soul.

Sri Ramakrishna knew the Divine Mother Kali was his real mother. As a child is unwilling to leave its mother's lap, so also was he reluctant to be separated from his beloved Mother. He lived with the Divine Mother all the time and fearlessly floated in an ocean of bliss. He knew very well that one cannot have pure bliss anywhere in this world except from the Divine Mother. For this reason he used to guide the seekers of bliss to the Mother. In reality, as long as you regard all women as your mother, they also look upon you as their child. But the moment you look at them with lust, you are possessed by a strong desire to marry. And once you are married, the responsibility of maintaining your wife is on your shoulders. A wife has to be taken care of. Before your marriage you were living without responsibilities and in great bliss. You were taken care of by others. But once you accept the bondage of married life you become scorched by the fever of anxieties. You carry on your head the burden of misery and lead a troubled life. Your forehead is wrinkled with anxieties, and peace of mind has left you forever. That is why Sri Ramakrishna used to say: "Look at the newborn calf, how it skips about in great glee as though it is born to live in joy. But from the day the rope is put around its neck it looks depressed and its happiness gradually diminishes. Before marriage a person is as happy as that calf, but when the rope of worldly ties is put around his neck, happiness deserts him."

Freedom is the source of happiness. Freedom makes a person all-powerful. Sri Ramakrishna never lost his freedom. No ties could bind him. Moreover, his heart was as broad as the infinite space, and that is why he could appreciate all the religions of the world. He used to say: "Never say that God is this or that. No one has yet been able to know God as he really is, and no one ever will. He is the ocean of consciousness. Sages like Shuka, Sanaka, and Narada drank a drop of that ocean and became God-intoxicated. I have experienced God as with form, without form, and again beyond both. But what he really is I do not know. All religions of the world are but different paths to reach him. Follow sincerely that path laid down by the religion you were born in and you will in time reach the abode of Eternal Bliss."

There was not the least trace of egotism in Sri Ramakrishna. He could not say the words *I* and *mine*. Instead of using the word *mine*, he used to say "of this place" and point to himself with his finger. For example, when he wanted to say that something was not his opinion, he would say, "It is not the opinion of this place." Because there was no ego-consciousness in him, the Cosmic Ego of the Divine Mother worked through him. The playful Kali, the Mother of the Universe, incarnated herself in the form of Sri Ramakrishna to give her innumerable children knowledge and devotion.

I have tried to give the readers some glimpses of Sri Ramakrishna's personality, but it is beyond my power to describe in full even a particle of his infinite glory. If you are eager to know the Truth, then meditate on the all-purifying, all-compassionate life of Sri Ramakrishna. Gradually the self-luminous Truth will reveal itself in your heart, and you will attain infinite strength, peace, and joy. You will consider yourself as blessed.

II

Sri Ramakrishna and Keshab Chandra Sen

It was really Keshab Chandra Sen who may be said to have discovered Sri Ramakrishna and made him known to the world. At that time Keshab was the most prominent figure in Calcutta. His church was always crowded, and many young men were his ardent admirers. It was indeed impossible not to be moved by him. When he stood in his church, dressed in his white robe, and talked with God, the tears streaming down his face, there was not a dry eye in the whole congregation. He was a really great soul and a true devotee. Sri Ramakrishna had heard of him, and, learning that he was staying in a garden not far from Dakshineswar, he expressed a desire to go to see him.

When he entered, Keshab was sitting in meditation surrounded by a number of his disciples. These half-Europeanized youths looked scornfully at the plainly clad sadhu [monk] and when, as soon as Keshab opened his eyes, the visitor said, "I see that your tail has dropped off," they all began to laugh aloud, believing the stranger to be mad. Keshab checked them. Then the Master, apparently unmindful of the rudeness of the boys, explained: "You see, when a tadpole is young and has a tail, it can live only in the water, but when its tail drops off, it can live both in water and on land. So I see you can live both in the world and in God." Then Keshab turned to his disciples and said, "You see what words of wisdom this holy man speaks," and they were all abashed.

I had a desire to see the paramahamsa at Dakshineswar because Keshab had spoken of him in such high terms, so one day I went with fifteen or twenty other boys. I was then reading for F.A. [First Arts] and the others were all preparing for their matriculation. Being the eldest of the band, the conversation was addressed to me.

The first time anyone went to the Master, he would ask the visitor a question which was always on the subject about which that person knew most. The visitor would begin at once to talk eloquently, as if he were teaching the Master, who would listen most intently. The man would talk on confidently, but he was sure to commit some blunder.

Then the Master would check him gently and point out his error with so much wisdom that the man would hear in wonder, suddenly realizing that this man to whom he was talking so freely was in reality a great sage. And never again would the visitor venture to speak in his presence. This happened to me. Sri Ramakrishna asked me whether I believed in a formless God or God with form. I began talking very glibly about whether there was a God at all. But it was the last time I ever talked before him.

It cannot be said that any of Sri Ramakrishna's disciples came to him directly through Keshab Sen, but Keshab's devotion to him undoubtedly had much influence in leading them to the Master. Keshab used to urge Sri Ramakrishna to come to his Brahmo Samaj, and once the Master went there. When Keshab saw him enter he came down from his high seat and indicated to Sri Ramakrishna to take his place there. But the Master said: "No, no. Go on with your exercises as you always have them." He had no desire to enter into rivalry with Keshab or to usurp his high place. The Master used to pray: "Let all name and fame belong to Keshab, O Mother! Grant only that I may have true devotion for thy Holy Feet."

Once he was invited to attend a theatrical performance given by Keshab's Samaj. One of the members of the Samaj, in talking with the Master, said: "Keshab is such a great lover of God. He must be an incarnation of Lord Gauranga, and Pratap Majumdar is always his companion, so he must be an incarnation of Nityananda. Now who are you?" The Master clasped his hands, bowed his head, and replied, "I am their servant." When Keshab heard of this conversation he turned to the man and said: "You fool! How could you talk in such a senseless way?"

One day the Master was explaining to Keshab the different stages of bhakti [devotion]. Keshab asked eagerly, "And then what comes?" "Keshab, if I tell you," the Master replied, "you will have to give up your teaching. All idea of teacher and student will disappear. Are you ready for that?" "No," Keshab replied, "I do not wish to go so far." At that time he was the guru of thousands who looked to him for guidance, and he felt it his duty to help humanity. Sri Ramakrishna used to declare that Keshab was an eternal worker of God and would have to come again and again to help mankind.

Sri Ramakrishna as a Teacher

The Master actually was teaching from his very birth. His entire life was one long lesson. . . . It was characteristic of him that though he used the simplest language such as a child could understand, yet still that language carried thoughts that only a great sage could think.

People would come to him and ask for initiation into spiritual life and he would say: "My dear sir, you are not meant to be a sadhu. You had better get a position and take care of your family." He was able to tell at a glance what a man was fit for. A disciple once told me that when asked how he knew so clearly what was in others' minds, the Master replied: "When you look through a window, you see everything in the room, do you not? So when I look into a person's eyes, I see all that is behind."

Sri Ramakrishna never preached. If he went anywhere it was to be among good men and be blessed by their holy association. That was his idea. But when he was with them the Divine Mother would rise up in him and he would begin to talk. It mattered not whether there were a few listeners or many.

Sri Ramakrishna was most careful in his speech and manner. Compared to him we are all boors. When do we call a man mad? When there is incoherence in his thought and words, or when he behaves differently from others. But neither of these was true of Sri Ramakrishna. He was always most courteous, and every word he uttered was full of wisdom. Even when he would sit and talk to his Divine Mother people could not possibly have taken him to be mad. For what was he doing? He was shaping the lives of those who sat there before him awe-struck by his words. He was satisfying the needs of each of those hearts and lifting their burdens.

He had such wonderful power. Every time one went to see him one felt as if a great load had been taken off one's back and mind. Whatever doubt was in one's mind was sure to be cleared, without putting any question. Yet the Master was always simple and humble in his manner towards everyone, always ready to learn even from a baby.

[*Sri Ramakrishna once asked a pandit:*] "Have you a commission from the Lord? Has he commanded you to teach?" When the pandit admitted he had not, Sri Ramakrishna said: "Then all your lectures are worthless. People will hear you for a time but it will not last." What he said proved true. Soon the pandit lost all his popularity, everyone began to criticize him, and he had to give up. Then one day he came to Dakshineswar and prostrated before Sri Ramakrishna, saying: "All this while we have been chewing the chaff and you have been eating the kernel. We have been content with dry books while you have been enjoying life."

When the Master spoke of Sita, he would become Sita altogether, so that there would be absolutely no difference between him and Sita. If Vaishnava devotees came to him, at once he would become like Lord Gauranga. He would act, speak, and look like him — so much so that the devotees would prostrate before him, saying, "We see Lord Gauranga in you."

Once a Christian Quaker came to him, and as Sri Ramakrishna talked of Christ, tears began to trickle down the man's face and he fell down clasping his feet and crying, "I have found Christ in you." In the same way, when Muslims came he would so completely identify himself with

Muhammad that they would see their Prophet in him. Yet behind all these different manifestations there was always the one Sri Ramakrishna.

The Vaishnavas were in the habit of holding bhajans [devotional singing], and since they regarded Sri Ramakrishna as a paramahamsa [illumined soul], they once asked him to attend one of their meetings. In the hall where they met there was a high seat which was regarded as Lord Gauranga's seat. It was the custom to begin their singing by invoking Lord Gauranga to come down and occupy his place. Otherwise it would not be possible for them to praise the Lord properly. It was actually believed that he did come down and sit on the seat.

On that day when the Master was present, as soon as they began their invocation, he immediately got up and went and sat down on the sacred seat. Some people thought it was all right, for he was known to be a very holy man, but others were indignant. Seeing, however, that he was in samadhi and also perhaps being afraid of Hriday, who was with him and who, being a very stalwart man, always acted as the Master's bodyguard, they did not dare disturb him. The meeting therefore continued, and Sri Ramakrishna remained in his place.

Among those who objected to the Master's sitting in Lord Gauranga's seat was a famous monk, Bhagavan Das. He expressed his disapproval very boldly. Some time after, hearing of the many things Bhagavan Das had said against him, Sri Ramakrishna expressed a wish to go to him. Mathur Babu procured a boat and they set out, but all the time Mathur Babu kept on saying: "Why, Baba [Father], do you want to go to that man? He must be a very wicked person to talk as he has. Why should we go there?" But Sri Ramakrishna answered, "Let us go." When they reached the place, instead of getting down himself from the boat, he sent Hriday to see whether the sadhu cared to receive him. When Bhagavan Das heard that he had come, he ran to the boat and prostrated before him, crying: "Oh, forgive me, forgive me. I did not know who you were." Sri Ramakrishna at once comforted him and restored peace to his mind.

Bhagavan Das was a really great monk, and he had the power now and then of entering into samadhi. It seems that while he was in that state, it was revealed to him who Sri Ramakrishna was, and when he realized what a great mistake he had made, he was inconsolable. After that he went around telling everyone that Sri Ramakrishna had a right to take Lord Gauranga's seat, for he was a Divine Manifestation.

The Master never condemned any man. He was ready to excuse everything. He used to tell us that the difference between man and God was this: If a man failed to serve God ninety-nine times, but the hundredth time served him with even a little love, God forgot the ninety-nine times he had failed and would say, "Oh! my devotee served me so well today." But if a man served another man well ninety-nine times and the hundredth time failed in his service, the man would forget the ninety-nine good services and say, "That rascal failed to serve me one day." If there was the least spark of good in anyone, Sri Ramakrishna saw only that and overlooked all the rest.

Sri Ramakrishna and His Disciples

In telling the story of Naren's [Swami Vivekananda's] first coming to him, the Master said: "When I saw this boy enter the room I thought, can such a boy come out of Calcutta where everyone is mad after money and pleasure — where everything is rajasic [extremely active]? I could see that his mind was three-fourths turned inward, and that only with the other fourth was he doing all these outer things. One corner of his shawl was dragging on the ground, and his hair was a little dishevelled, as if he were careless about such things."

[*During Naren's second visit to Dakshineswar,*] when Naren had sat down, Sri Ramakrishna leaned over and touched his heart through the front of his shirt, which was unbuttoned. Naren told me afterwards: "The walls of the room began to recede and disappear. Then the river and all of Calcutta vanished. The floor of the room seemed to sink down into the earth, until at last I seemed to be in a vast vacuum in which there was nothing but this brahmin [Sri Ramakrishna] standing before me." This is how he told it, but the Master, in speaking of it afterwards, said that as he felt all this happening, Naren exclaimed: "What are you doing? I have my mother, my brothers to look after." But Naren did not remember this.

Later, when I asked Sri Ramakrishna whether there was a God, he told me to go to the boy Narendra and ask him. I went and asked him. Then Naren told me this story, and he added that for fifteen or twenty days after this he seemed to see God everywhere. Everything seemed to be living — the ground, the wall, everywhere there was life. So he came to know that this brahmin was no ordinary paramahamsa.

Once a drama by Keshab was to be performed, and Naren was assigned the part of a sannyasin [monk]. The Master expressed great satisfaction when he heard of it and insisted on being taken to see the performance. Naren acquitted himself most creditably of his task, and after the play was over the Master had him brought out in the hall that he might again see him in the orange cloth. It seemed to give him the greatest pleasure to have him dressed as a sannyasin.

From the outset Sri Ramakrishna's love for Naren was unbounded. When Naren did not come to the temple for a time the Master would grow so restless that he would even weep. Once when I was with him, he kept running first to the Ganga side of his room, then to the road side, to see whether Naren was coming. At last he told me to bring a carriage. I ran two miles to get one, and together we drove to Naren's house. We found him in his dingy room on the ground floor. "Why have you come?" he asked, with evident annoyance on seeing the Master. "What will my family think when they see a sadhu coming to see me like this?" In reality, however, he was annoyed that the Master was paying him so much honour.

Sri Ramakrishna used to explain that among his disciples there were certain ones who were his antar-anga — that is, his inner circle — that they would always come with him whenever he incarnated. These were Narendra, Rakhal, Baburam, and Niranjan. He always predicted that Niranjan would not survive him long, and he did not. Of these antar-anga, he said that Naren would be the one who would understand him most fully.

This understanding did not come at once, however. Again and again doubt of the Master rose, and Naren would shed bitter tears over his lack of faith. Instead of reproaching him, Sri Ramakrishna would weep with him and strive to comfort him. Still doubt came. Even at the end, only a short time before the Master left the body, it rose, but found no expression. The Master caught his thought, however, and he repeated three times with great emphasis, "He who was Rama, he who was Krishna, has now become Ramakrishna." The threefold repetition indicated the unquestionable truth of the statement.

While Naren was still attending college he used to study all day and spend the night in meditation. This constant use of the brain brought on a severe pain in his head, which kept him rolling on his bed for several days. Hearing of it, the Master came to the house of a devotee nearby and sent for him. "But he cannot get up from his bed," someone explained. "Just tell him. He will come," the Master replied. Naren came and as he sat down by the Master, the latter ran his hand lovingly through his hair, saying: "Why, my boy, what is the matter? You have a headache, have you?" Naren said that at once all the pain left him.

It was only on Sundays that there was a crowd at the temple. On other days the Master was left alone with his few chosen ones. Not everyone could stay with him — only those whom he chose to have. And why did he keep them? In order that in one night he might make them perfect. Just as a goldsmith gives shape to a lump of gold, so he would mould them so that their whole life would be changed and they could never forget the impression he had stamped on them.

He possessed the peculiar power to discern at once whether a man was fit or not. Sometimes people would come and want to stay with him, but he would see that they were not fit and he would tell them with childlike frankness, "You had better go home." When now and then there would be a feast and the Master would be sitting with his disciples, a man would sometimes come who was not really good but who by sitting with him wanted to appear good. At once Sri Ramakrishna would make him out and would say: "Here is a man who is not pure. He will spoil my children." Without hesitation he would send him away. When he was alone with his special disciples, they would sing and talk and play together. If a visitor came, he would tell him, "Go and have a bath, eat something, and rest awhile." Then about two o'clock he would begin to talk, and he would go on teaching for five or six hours continuously. He would not know when to stop.

Sometimes the Master would wake at four in the morning, and he would call the disciples who were sleeping in his room, saying: "What are you all doing? Snoring? Get up, sit on your mat, and meditate." Sometimes he would wake up at midnight, call them, and make them spend the whole night singing and praising the name of the Lord.

All the disciples were still at a malleable age, in their teens or early twenties — two were scarcely sixteen — and the Master played with them as if they were little children. He was very fun loving and was discovered near the Panchavati one day by a visitor having a game of leap-frog with his boys. Sometimes he would send them into peals of laughter by his mimicry. Then again he would be grave and wake them long before the dawn and make them sit in meditation on the mats on which they had been sleeping. Again at the evening hour he would tell them to go to the banyan tree and meditate.

The Master said, "If you will practise even one-sixteenth part of what I have practised, you will surely reach the goal." That sixteenth part of individual striving, however, was essential. He could not impose realization as one pastes a picture on a page. Someone said to him once, "You have the power by a touch to make a man perfect, so why do you not do it?" "Because if I did," he answered; "the person would not be able to keep perfection. He must grow to it and be ready to take it."

His method was peculiar. He did not tell a man to give up everything. On the contrary, he would say: "Go on, my children, and enjoy all you wish. The Divine Mother has given this universe for your enjoyment. But as you enjoy remember always that it does not come from yourself but out of the Mother's bounty. Never forget her in your pleasure, but always recognize that it is from her." In this way, by having become mindful of the Mother, the person would gradually lose all taste for the pleasures of the senses.

The Master never told us that anything was "wrong." On the contrary, he used to say: "Go and have a good time. The responsibility will be mine." He knew there was nothing wrong in the pleasures of the world — that by tasting them his children would come to realize their worthlessness and be satisfied only with higher pleasures. He was not merely the helper of the good, he was also the helper of the wicked. He tolerated and loved both. He wanted his children to be always happy. And if one of us came with the least shadow on his face, the Master could not bear that, and he would at once scold us.

Just by looking at a man he could tell what that person was fit for. If he saw that he was falsely leading a religious life, he would say to him, "Go and get married." If he saw that a man was ready to renounce, he would not ask him directly to give up, but he would direct his mind in such a way that the man would, of his own accord, renounce. He used to say that by seeing even one corner of a man's toe, he could make out just what sort of man he was.

At one time there was a very poor boy who used to come almost daily to Sri Ramakrishna, but the Master would never take any of the food he brought. We did not know why. Finally one day Sri Ramakrishna said: "This poor fellow comes here because he has a great desire to be rich. Very well. Let me taste a little of what he has brought." And he took a small quantity of the food. The boy's situation began to improve immediately, and today he is one of the most prosperous men of Calcutta.

Our Master never asked anyone to renounce, but he would give such a direction to the mind that the man would do so of his own accord. I had heard a great deal about the beauties of the Sufi poets, so I determined to learn Persian in order to be able to read them in the original. I bought several Persian textbooks and began to study most diligently. Often when I was at Dakshineswar I would go off to some corner with my books instead of staying to serve the Master. One day he called to me and I did not hear him. He had to call a second time. When I came to him, he asked, "What were you doing?" I told him. He said, "If you neglect your duty in order to learn Persian, you will lose what little devotion you have." Not many words, but they sufficed. By that time I had purchased fifteen or twenty rupees' worth of books, but I threw all of them into the Ganga, and for fourteen years I did not read a book. Only when I came to Madras, where people care so much for learning, did I begin to study again.

There was one boy who often came to Dakshineswar to see the Master. One day the Master took him into the temple and, touching his heart, gave him a vision of the Divine. Afterwards he explained that the boy would not be able to realize God in this life, but he wished to show him what he would attain in his next birth so that he might be encouraged to struggle for it. I remember that once he took the karma [the effect of past actions] of a certain devotee on himself and suffered from a serious bodily disorder for six months.

Religion as Sri Ramakrishna taught it was never vague or dismal. It went to the man where he was and lifted him up. It was not like an eagle, which soars high in the air and calls to the tortoise, "Come up here." Can the tortoise ever hope to rise so high? No, it can only say, "If you will come and lift me up, then I can go up there." So Sri Ramakrishna in his teaching came down and carried the man up by degrees. It gave him new hope and courage.

"God may come at any time," he would say, "but this need not frighten us. When the king wishes to visit one of his servants, he knows the servant will not have soft cushions and the proper things with which to receive him, so the day before he comes, he sends other servants to cleanse everything and prepare for his reception. Similarly, God, before he comes to the heart, sends his servants to make it ready for his coming. And who are those servants? Purity, chastity, humility, loving-kindness. Or again, as in the east the red glow in the sky tells us that the sun is about to rise, so just by looking at a man one can tell whether God will come soon to him."

Bhavanath was one of those whom the Master spoke of as having been "born perfect." He also said that Bhavanath and Narendra had a special affinity. But Bhavanath married. One day the Master told me to go to him, saying I could learn much from him. I wondered why he should send me to a householder to learn, but when I saw Bhavanath I understood. As we sat talking of God, he went into meditation, and tears of bliss and devotion poured down his cheeks. One could see that he was completely immersed in God.

Purna was another beloved disciple of Sri Ramakrishna. He was brought to see the Master when he was only nine years old. "Who am I?" the Master asked the boy. Purna replied without a moment's hesitation, "You are an Incarnation of the Deity." Then the Master asked him if he spent some time each day thinking of God. The boy replied that he often meditated and that when he did, tears of joy streamed out of the outer corners of his eyes. The Master always said of him that he had attained the highest stage of bhakti. He loved him so much that he would now and then stand and wait at the gate of his school to give the boy some sweetmeat. And whenever he went to the house of any devotee in Calcutta, he always asked that Purna be brought to see him.

Purna, however, was a rich man's son, and his parents were afraid that he might be led away from them and become a sannyasin, so they did not let him go about freely.

One day the Master, who was in Calcutta for the day, sent one of his disciples to bring Purna. The gatekeeper said the boy was sleeping and should not be disturbed, so the disciple came back to the Master without Purna. Then the Master sent me, and I somehow always managed to do whatever he asked of me. I went, pushed my way past the gatekeeper at Purna's house, and went upstairs to the hall where he lay asleep beside his brothers. I stooped down and pinched him gently. The boy woke up. I whispered to him why I had come, and together we slipped out softly, told some story to the gatekeeper, and ran to the Master.

Suresh [Surendra Nath Mittra] was an arch-sceptic and he laughed at the devotion which Balaram and some of his friends showed for the paramahamsa at Dakshineswar. One day he accompanied Balaram to the temple, determined to confound him by his arguments against belief in God. But when he sat down in the presence of the simple sadhu, his mind, so he told me afterwards, became a perfect blank. He could remember nothing of all the fine arguments he had intended to present. The Master spoke kindly to him as he did to everyone. Then with apparent unconcern he began to tell him certain facts about his life. Suresh at once recognized his divine power and, falling at his feet, became his devoted follower. It was he who contributed much towards the maintenance of the disciples when they came to live with their Master, and who provided meals for those who visited him at Dakshineswar.

On one occasion when the Master was talking with his disciples [at Shyampukur], he suddenly became entirely abstracted and for ten or fifteen minutes remained in that state. When he returned to outer consciousness, he explained, "I have been with Suresh." Suresh himself told later that he was sitting before the newly set up image of the Divine Mother [in his home], weeping because the Master had not come to see it, for it was the first time he had remained away from the Durga Puja [worship of the Divine Mother]. Suddenly he saw the Master before him, consoling him. [*The Master stayed with him for a little while, and then went away, leaving Suresh's mind perfectly pacified.*]

Sri Ramakrishna had practised pranayama [breath control] so much that he had formed a habit of remaining for long periods without breathing. Now and then he would stop breathing entirely. Even after we came to him, he used to tell us, "Whenever you see that I am not breathing, please remind me." Sometimes when he was sleeping, we would see that the breath had stopped. Then we would wake him up and tell him, "Master, you are not breathing." "Oh, thank you!" he would say and again begin to breathe.

[*During his twelve years of sadhana*] the Master did not know when the sun rose or when it set. He did not know whether he had taken food or not. Occasionally when a moment's consciousness would come, he would feel as if someone were dwelling inside him and he would ask: "Who are you? Why are you here?" So completely had the Mother possessed him!

His body was especially manufactured to stand the shock of these manifestations. It was not an ordinary body. He used to say, "If one-millionth part of the emotion I feel should come to an ordinary man, his body would break to pieces, just as when a mad bull gets into a garden, it tears and uproots everything there." He would compare his religious devotion to a mad elephant.

His mind was so constantly turned towards God that even when he was eating he would often not be conscious of it and someone would have to tell him when he had eaten enough. "Have I taken enough?" he would ask, and if the person said that he had, then at once he would stop.

Once none of his own people were with him and when he asked some other man who happened to be there, "Have I had enough?" and the man replied, "Yes," the Master said, "Very well, I will not take anymore." Just then Hriday came in and seeing that the Master had taken only one-half his usual quantity of food, he insisted on his eating more. The Master then perceived that he was still feeling hungry, but he said, "No, I have said I would eat no more and I cannot break my word."

The Master was extremely fond of ice. One day when it was very hot I walked from Calcutta to Dakshineswar [six miles] to carry him a piece of ice wrapped in paper. It was just noontime and the sun's rays were so strong that they blistered my body. When the Master saw me, he began to say, "Oh! Oh!" as if he were in pain. I asked him what was the matter, and he said that as he looked at my body, his own began to burn. Strange to say, the ice did not melt at all on the way.

Days in the Cossipore Garden House

Sri Ramakrishna did not give formal sannyas [monastic vows] to any of his disciples. Formalism and calculation were not in his nature. He moved wholly by the impulsion of the Divine Mother's will. His actions were always spontaneous and unplanned. He gave the first initiation to his boys, thus laying the foundation of their spiritual life; but he left the second [initiation] to be given by Naren, who became the leader of the group after the Master had gone.

Among the devotees, however, was a cloth merchant. One day Sri
Ramakrishna requested him to dye a bolt of cloth ochre and bring it to
him. When it was brought, he told the boys to put the cloths on, take
begging bowls, and go out to beg [food] for him. This was his simple
way of making them sannyasins. He needed no rites or ceremonials. The
spirit of renunciation wound itself about them with the ochre cloth and
bound them to holy self-denial for all time. The fire of the Master's word,
the purifying power of his touch, were sufficient consecration.

[*During the Master's last months, when he lay ill in an upstairs room at the
Cossipore garden house, his privacy was strictly guarded by one disciple who
acted as gatekeeper. One day Manmatha, a ruffian youth, came to Cossipore to
see the Master, but he was not allowed to go upstairs to his room.*] When the
Master heard that Manmatha was downstairs, he had him brought up
at once. I was in the Master's room at the time, but he sent me out and
the two were alone for a long while. Then the Master called me back and
told me to bring one of his photographs. This he took and with his own
hand gave it to Manmatha. That young man took it and without speaking a word to anyone ran out of the house as if he were mad. From that
moment he lost all consciousness of the world, of everything, and day
and night he sat repeating "Priya Nath, Priya Nath [Beloved Lord,
Beloved Lord]." When all the rest of the community was sleeping, one
could hear those words sounding out in the silence of the night.

Manmatha never returned to the Master. Like the pearl oyster, he had
got the drop of Svati rain[1] and needed nothing more. But after the Master
passed away, he used to come often to our Math [monastery] at Baranagore. For several months he came every evening. He would go straight
to the shrine, sit and meditate there for some time, then go away without
even coming to the part of the house where we lived. Sometimes he
would sing and he had a very beautiful voice. There was one song of
which Sri Ramakrishna had been particularly fond, and Manmatha
would sing it again and again. In this way would our Master transform
a life.

In Sri Ramakrishna there was absolutely no ego left. He could not use
the first personal pronoun "I." He would say instead, "Why do you not
come here [*meaning, to him*]?" "Mother will illumine you," he would say.
In him the Divine was fully manifested. He preached God, nothing but
God, and his whole nature was God-like. We never knew what purity
was, we never knew what perfection was, what God was, until we saw
him.

---

[1] The rain that falls when the star Svati ascends. It is believed that the oyster waits for a
drop of that rain and makes a pearl out of it.

He knew everything. Did anyone go to him with a morose or sorrowful heart? At once he would feel it in his own heart and would give peace. Everything he did was for others. He was not forced to come to this world, but he came to help mankind. And every movement of his body, every movement of his mind, was directed towards the amelioration of his fellow men.

The Master was able to supply to every man just what he needed. Sometimes a man would come from a distant place with his heart panting for God, but seeing the room full of people, he would shrink back and hide himself in a dim corner. Without a word, Sri Ramakrishna would walk to him and touch him, and in a moment he was illumined.

By that touch, Sri Ramakrishna really swallowed ninety-nine percent of the man's karma. Taking others' karma was the reason he had his last long illness. He used to tell us: "The people whose karma I have taken think that they are attaining salvation through their own strength. They do not understand that it is because I have taken their karma on me." We do not know how much we owe him, but someday we shall realize what he has done for us, and then we shall know how to be grateful to him.

It was winter when Sri Ramakrishna arrived at Cossipore garden house, and many days were quite cold. Once while attending to the Master's needs, I hurried outdoors in the middle of the night with just a thin cloth on. When I came back to his room, I saw that, sick as he was, he had gotten out of the bed and had somehow crawled across the room and was now reaching up for something hanging on a hook.

"What are you doing?" I asked him in a scolding tone. "The air is very chilly, and you should not be up." The Master held out his own dressing gown [a shawl] and in a weak voice filled with concern and love he said: "I didn't want you to be cold. Please take this."

I never felt worthy of keeping the Master's own cloth and later gave it to Swami Brahmananda.

The Master's Passing Away

[*During the Master's last day at Cossipore*] we all thought he was better because he ate so much more supper than usual, and he said nothing of going. In the afternoon he had asked Yogin [Swami Yogananda] to look in the almanac and see whether it was an auspicious day. Also he had been telling us for some time that the vessel which was floating in the ocean was already two-thirds full of water, and soon the rest would fill up and plunge into the ocean. But we did not believe that he was really going. He never seemed to mind the pain. He never lost his cheerfulness. He used to say that he was all well and happy, only there was a little something here [*pointing to the throat*]. "Within me are two persons," he would declare. "One is the Divine Mother, and the other is her devotee. It is the devotee that has been taken ill."

When Sri Ramakrishna gave up his body I think it was the most blissful moment of his life. A thrill of joy ran through him. I myself saw it. I remember every incident of that last day. Our Master seemed very well and cheerful. In the afternoon he talked for fully two hours to a gentleman who had come to put some questions to him about yoga. A little later I ran some seven miles to bring the doctor. When I reached the doctor's house he was not there, but I was told that he was at a certain place, so I ran another mile and met him on the way. He had an engagement and said he could not come, but I dragged him away just the same.

On that last night Ramakrishna was talking with us to the very last. For supper he had drunk a half glass of payasam [pudding] and seemed to relish it. There was, no doubt, a little heat in the body, so he asked us to fan him, and some ten of us were all fanning at once. He was sitting up against five or six pillows which were supported by my body and at the same time I too was fanning. This made a slight motion and twice he asked me, "Why are you shaking?" It was as if his mind was so fixed and steady that he could perceive the least motion. Narendra took his feet and began to rub them and Sri Ramakrishna was talking to him, telling him what he must do. "Take care of these boys," he repeated again and again as if he were putting them in Naren's charge. Then he asked to lie down.

Suddenly at one o'clock [*in the morning*] he fell towards one side. There was a low sound in his throat, and I saw all the hairs of his body stand on end. Narendra quickly laid his feet on a quilt and ran downstairs as if he could not bear it. A doctor, who was a great devotee and who was feeling his pulse, saw that it had stopped and began to weep aloud. "What are you doing?" I asked, impatient with him for acting as if the Master had really left us.

We all believed that it was only samadhi, so Naren came back and we sat down, some twenty of us, and began repeating all together: "Hari Om! Hari Om!" In this way we waited until between one and two the next day. Still the body had some heat in it, especially around the back, but the doctor insisted that the soul had left it. About five o'clock the body had grown cold, so we placed it on a cot, covered it with garlands, and carried it to the burning ghat.

[*At the Baranagore monastery, where the young disciples gathered and lived after the Master's passing,*] we had no thought yet of a mission. We believed that all we had to do was to realize the ideal the Master had set before us, which meant living and serving humbly. He never talked to us of a special mission or special work. If we had believed we had some special work to do, probably we would have lived very differently. We would not have spent our strength in so many severe austerities.

III
Sri Ramakrishna in Vrindaban
(Two Letters of Swami Ramakrishnananda to Swami Premananda)

Alambazar Math
26 December 1895

Dear Brother Baburam:

Yesterday Hriday Mukherjee [a nephew of Sri Ramakrishna] came to the Alambazar monastery. I am reporting exactly what I heard from him about the Master's visit to Vrindaban. The Master first landed at Mathura and visited Dhruva ghat and other important spots associated with Krishna. Next he went to Vrindaban and lived in a house near the Govinda temple. Mathur, Hriday, and several others were with him. In Vrindaban he was always in ecstasy and as a result he could not walk even a step. Consequently, a palanquin was engaged for his visits to the holy temples. The doors of the palanquin were kept open so that he could see the deities. Sometimes, out of excessive ecstasy, he would try to jump from the palanquin, but Hriday, who was walking alongside holding the rod of the palanquin, would stop him. Thus the Master visited Shyamkunda, Radhakunda, and the adjacent temples with Hriday. Mathur did not go on that occasion.

Along the way the Master saw a flock of white peacocks ahead and called Hriday's attention to it. He was so excited that he was about to jump from the palanquin. Later he saw a herd of deer and that also overwhelmed him. Mathur had provided Hriday with one hundred fifty rupees in coins for distribution. Whenever the Master came across a holy man or a Vaishnava, he would ask Hriday to give him a few coins.

He then went to see the Govardhan hill, where he ascended to the top. The priests helped him come down.

Gangamata [a woman saint of Vrindaban who lived near the Nidhuban] recognized the Master's divine nature at first sight, and at her invitation he lived with her for six or seven days. The Master was so drawn to the saintly woman that he did not want to leave. Mathur Babu, when he heard of this, asked Hriday to get the Master away from Gangamata at any cost. "How can we leave the Master here and return home with empty hearts?" Mathur said. So Hriday took the Master away from the Nidhuban against the will of Gangamata, who cried out in protest.

Thus he finished the visit to Vrindaban, went back to Mathura with Mathur, and then left for Calcutta. While in Vrindaban he wore the garb of a Vaishnava. In my next letter I shall write further details.

> Yours, etc.,
> Shashi (Ramakrishnananda)

*   *   *

> 14 Paush
> (December, year unknown)

Brother Baburam:

The Master received the Vaishnava garb from a priest at Radhakunda whose name was Chatura. While at Vrindaban he always carried a bamboo stick. Sometimes Hriday took it away from him and this upset the Master. He was unhappy until he got it back. In Vrindaban he could not walk even a step. He took his bath in the Jamuna sitting inside the palanquin.

> Yours, etc.,
> Shashi (Ramakrishnananda)

[Part I from: *Udbodhan* (Calcutta: Udbodhan Office), vol. 8, no. 2, 1905; Part II from: *Sri Ramakrishna and His Disciples* and *Days In An Indian Monastery*, by Sister Devamata (La Crescenta: Ananda Ashrama), 1928 & 1927; Part III from: *Udbodhan*, vol. 44, no. 12, 1942]

10

Swami Saradananda

Swami Saradananda (1865-1927) met Sri Ramakrishna in 1883 and became an ardent disciple of the Master. His premonastic name was Sharat Chandra Chakrabarty. After the Master's passing away he travelled all over India as an itinerant monk, and he then went to England and America in 1896 at Swami Vivekananda's request to preach the message of Vedanta there. In 1898 Swami Saradananda was recalled to India by Swamiji to become the General Secretary of the Ramakrishna Math and Mission. He held that office until his death in 1927. He is the author of Sri Ramakrishna, the Great Master, *the authoritative biography of Sri Ramakrishna.*

An Evening with Sri Ramakrishna

It was Monday, November 26, 1883. I was then studying at St. Xavier's College in Calcutta and had had the privilege of meeting Sri Ramakrishna only two or three times. As the college was closed that day, we [Barada Pal, Hari Prasanna — later Swami Vijnanananda, and Swami Saradananda] decided to visit the Master in the afternoon. We went by boat and reached Dakshineswar at 2:00 P.M.

As soon as we entered the Master's room and bowed down to him, he said: "Ah, you have come today! I would not have met you had you come a little later. I am going to Calcutta to attend the Brahmo festival, and a carriage has been called. But it is nice that you could see me. Please sit down. What a disappointment it would have been if you had been forced to return home without seeing me."

We sat on a mat spread on the floor of his room and asked him, "Sir, would we be allowed at the Brahmo festival which you are attending?" The Master replied: "Why not? You are free to go there if you like. It is at the house of Mani Mallik of Sinduriapati." Seeing a slender, fair young man enter the room, the Master asked him, "Could you tell these boys the number of Mani Mallik's house?" The young man humbly said, "81

Swami Saradananda in America

Chitpore Road, Sinduriapati." Later we learned that he was Baburam [later, Swami Premananda].

The carriage arrived shortly after. The Master asked Baburam to carry his towel, warm clothes, and a small spice bag. Then bowing down to the Mother he entered the carriage. Baburam took the Master's things and sat on the other side of the carriage. Another person also went with the Master to Calcutta. On inquiry we learned that he was Pratap Chandra Hazra.

Fortunately a passenger boat was available, and we took it to Barabazar, Calcutta. Then in the evening we went to the festival. Scarcely had we reached the road in front of the house when sweet music and sounds of a mridanga [a drum] greeted our ears. Knowing that the kirtan [devotional singing] had begun, we hurried to the parlour. What we saw defies description! There were crowds of people both inside and outside the hall. So many people were standing in every doorway and on the western roof that it was almost impossible to push through the crowd into the room. All were craning their necks and intently watching what was going on inside the hall. Full of devotion, they were totally unaware of their surroundings. Seeing that there was no possibility of entering the room through the front door, we went around the house, crossed the western roof, and reached the northern door of the hall. As the crowd there was somewhat thinner, we were able to thrust our heads into the room and we saw a wonderful scene.

We felt that high waves of heavenly bliss were flowing in the room. All were completely lost in the kirtan. They were laughing, crying, and dancing. Some, unable to control themselves, fell on the ground. Overwhelmed with emotion, others acted crazy. The Master was dancing in the centre of that God-intoxicated group, now rhythmically going forward with rapid steps and again going backward in a similar way. In whichever direction he would move, the people, as if enchanted, would make room for him.

An extraordinary tenderness, sweetness, and leonine strength were visible in every limb of the Master's body, and his face shone with a divine smile. It was a superb dance! In it there was no artificiality or affectation, no jumping, no unnatural gestures or acrobatics. Nor was there seen any absence of control. Rather, one noticed in the Master's dancing rhythmical and natural gestures and movements of limbs. It seemed as if an overflow of grace, bliss, and sweetness surged from within, like a big fish happily swimming all over a vast, clear lake, sometimes slowly and sometimes fast. It was as if the dance was a dynamic physical expression of the surge of the blissful ocean of Brahman, which the Master was experiencing within. As he danced this way, sometimes he lost outward consciousness and sometimes his cloth fell. When that happened, someone would fasten it tightly around his waist. Again, if he saw someone lose normal consciousness, imbued with spiritual emotions, he would touch that person's chest and bring him back to consciousness.

We felt a current of divine bliss emanating from the Master and spreading in all directions, making it possible for the devotees to see God face to face. It enabled those of lukewarm disposition to intensify their fervour, those with idle minds to go forward with enthusiasm in the realm of spirituality, and those who were attached, to become, for a while, free from their attachment. The waves of his divine emotion caught others and overwhelmed them. Charged by his purity, their minds ascended to an unknown high spiritual realm. On that day Vijay Krishna Goswami and some Brahmo devotees experienced ecstasy and from time to time lost outer consciousness. Chiranjiv Sharma, accompanied by a one-stringed instrument, sang with his sweet voice, "Dance, O Children of the Blissful Mother, round and round." He also was beside himself. Thus the kirtan continued for more than two hours.

Afterwards the Master told all of us that one could attain supreme peace if one could raise the mind from sense objects to God. The women devotees, who were seated in the eastern part of the parlour behind a screen, also asked him various questions on spiritual matters and enjoyed his inspiring replies. While answering their questions, the Master now and then sang a few songs in praise of the Divine Mother composed by Ramprasad and Kamalakanta, in order to impress the subject deeply on their minds.

While the Master was singing the Mother's name, Vijay Krishna Goswami went to another room with a few devotees and began to expound the Ramayana by Tulasidasa. When it was time for the evening prayer, Vijay returned to the parlour to bow down to the Master before beginning the prayer. Seeing him, the Master joked: "Nowadays Vijay feels great delight in kirtan. But I am scared when he dances, for the whole roof may collapse!" (All laughed.) "Yes, such a thing actually happened in our part of the country. There people build two-storied houses out of wood and mud. A Vaishnava teacher went to a disciple's house and began kirtan on the upper floor. When the singing reached the right mood, people began to dance. Now that teacher was a little plump like you [*pointing to Vijay*]. After he danced for a while, the floor collapsed, and the teacher fell through to the ground floor! That is why I am afraid that your dancing might repeat the same scene!" (All laughed.)

Noticing Vijay's ochre cloth, the Master said: "Nowadays Vijay is very fond of the ochre colour. Generally people dye their cloths and chadars ochre, but Vijay even dyes his shirt and shoes. That is good. A state comes when one wishes to do so, and he does not wear clothes of any other colour. The ochre colour is indeed the mark of renunciation. It reminds the aspirant that he has renounced everything for God." Vijay then bowed down to the Master, who blessed him heartily, saying: "Peace! Peace! Peace be unto you."

When the Master was singing the Mother's name, another thing happened. It shows how keen was his power of observation, though he always remained in an indrawn state. While singing, the Master looked at Baburam and immediately realized that he was hungry and thirsty. The Master knew that Baburam would not eat before him, so he asked for some sweets and water for himself. He then took a little and gave the rest to Baburam and other devotees.

Vijay began his evening prayer downstairs, and the Master was taken to the inner apartment for supper. It was nine o'clock. Meanwhile we came downstairs to attend Vijay's prayer. After some time the Master also joined the prayer and sat there for fifteen minutes. About ten o'clock the Master asked for a carriage so he could return to Dakshineswar. He then put on his socks, coat, and the cap that covered his ears in order to protect himself from the cold. He slowly got into the carriage with Baburam and others, and we left for home.

Sri Ramakrishna's Method of Teaching

Although we had had the good fortune of meeting the Master only very recently, we felt a tremendous attraction for his fascinating teachings from the very first day. Of course we did not then understand the reason for it. Now we realize how unique his method of teaching was. There was no parade of scholarship, no logic-chopping, no festooning of fine phrases. Neither was there any studied artificiality in the use of words — any attempt to bolster commonplace ideas by clothing them in pompous words, or to obscure profound thoughts by using very few words, as was done by the Indian writers of philosophic aphorisms [i.e., the sutra literature]. We cannot say whether the Master, who was the living embodiment of the ideas he expressed, paid any attention at all to the language he used. But whoever even once heard him speak must have noticed how he held before them picture after picture drawn from incidents of daily life, from the things and experiences the audience was likely to be familiar with, in order to imprint these ideas on their minds. The listeners also became freed from doubts, and were fully convinced of the truth of his words, as if they saw them enacted before their very eyes.

On wondering how these pictures could immediately come to his mind, we point out that the cause lies in his extraordinary memory, his wonderful comprehension, his keen power of observation, and his unique presence of mind. But the Master always said that the Divine Mother's grace was the only cause of it. He used to say: "Mother sits in the heart of him who entirely depends on her, and she makes him say whatever he has to say by showing it to him through unmistakable signs. Mother keeps his mind filled with a stock of knowledge which she continually supplies from her never-failing store of wisdom, whenever it appears to run short. Thus it never gets exhausted, however much he may spend from it." Explaining this fact one day, he mentioned the following event:

There was a government magazine to the north of the Kali temple at Dakshineswar where some Sikh soldiers lived in order to guard it. All of them were very devoted to the Master, and sometimes they would take him to their quarters and have him clear their doubts on various religious matters. The Master said: "One day they asked, 'How should a person live in the world so that he may realize God?' I immediately saw before my eyes a picture of a husking machine. Paddy was being husked and one person was carefully pushing the paddy into the mortar where the pestle was falling. As soon as I saw it, I realized that Mother was explaining to me that one should live in the world as cautiously as that. Just as the person who sits near the mortar and pushes the paddy is always careful that the pestle does not fall on his hand, so a person engaged in worldly activities should always take care that he does not get entangled in them, by being conscious that the worldly affairs are not his. It is only then that he can escape bondage without being hurt and lost. As soon as I saw the picture of the husking machine, Mother raised this idea in my mind, and I then told it to the soldiers. They were highly pleased to hear it. Such pictures come before me when I talk to people."

Another characteristic was observed in the Master's method of teaching: He never confused an inquirer by speaking unnecessary words. He used to carefully discern the subject and the aim of the person's question and then answer it in a few conclusive sentences. Furthermore, in order to convince that person, the Master would present illustrations in the aforesaid manner. His "statement of conclusion" was the special characteristic of his method of teaching. He would state as an answer only that which he knew to be true in his heart of hearts. He would not say that no other solution of the problem was possible. Nevertheless, that impression would be firmly imprinted in the mind of the hearer because of the Master's deep-seated conviction and the stress he laid on his expressions. If, on account of education and past impressions, a person brought forward contrary reasons and arguments and would not accept his conclusions, which the Master knew by experience to be true, the Master would wind up the topic, saying: "I have said whatever came to my mind. Now you take whatever you like, discarding the head and tail." Thus, he never tried to disturb a person's understanding by interfering with his freedom. Was it that he thought the hearer would not accept the true solution of the subject under discussion until he had reached a higher mental state by the will of God? It seems so. Again, the Master did not stop there but reinforced his statements by interspersing them with songs composed by well-known saints and sometimes by quoting examples from the scriptures. Needless to say, it would remove the inquirer's doubts about the conclusion of the truth, and being convinced, he would start to mould his life accordingly.

It is necessary to say one thing more. The Master told us again and again that ultimately the aspirant attains nondual knowledge by realizing his identity with the object of his worship, whether he treads the path of devotion or knowledge. As proof of this, the Master's sayings are cited: "Pure devotion and pure knowledge are the same thing." "There [*in the ultimate state*] all jackals howl alike [*all knowers of God speak of the same realization*]." Thus, although he was of the opinion that nondual knowledge was the Ultimate Truth, he always instructed people living in the world on the teachings of qualified nondualism [*which teaches that all living creatures and matter are parts of Brahman*], and also how to love God in a dualistic way. He felt disgusted with those people who had no high spiritual experience nor intense love for God, and yet held forth, with high-sounding words, on the philosophies of nondualism and qualified nondualism. He did not hesitate to condemn such behaviour in harsh words. One day the Master asked our friend Vaikuntha Nath Sanyal whether he had read the *Panchadashi* and other such books. Receiving a negative reply, the Master said with relief: "It is good that you have not. Some boys read those books and, giving themselves airs, come here. They do not practise anything. They simply come to argue. It is a torment to me."

Sri Ramakrishna Taught Us

We did not go to Sri Ramakrishna as devotees. I had joined the Brahmo Samaj, and I had an atheistic attitude and little faith. We did not gather around the Master to make him an avatar. Gradually we had to admit his divinity. When we found that the Master knew more about us than we knew about ourselves, and that his words always came true, then we had no choice but to accept him.

*   *   *

One day the Master was seated in the Panchavati grove when the Divine Mother Durga came over the Ganga. Slowly, she walked towards him and merged into his body. The Master later told Hriday: "Mother Durga came. Look, her footprints are still in the dust."

*   *   *

Sri Ramakrishna experienced the sound of Om resonating all over the world. He heard the mystical sound of Om in the singing of the birds, the gentle flow of the river, and the waves of the ocean. That sound of Brahman is continually moving like a wave through every place and every sound.

*   *   *

Sri Ramakrishna had a strong, healthy body. Otherwise he could not have practised so much sadhana [spiritual disciplines]. He had no regularity in his food and sleep. Normally the Master could eat half a pound of rice, but when he was in ecstasy he would sometimes eat a large quantity of food and had no problem digesting it. His body was very delicate and soft. He wore slippers, as he was unable to walk barefooted.

Once during the Master's samadhi a doctor put a stethoscope on his chest but could not find a heartbeat. On another occasion a doctor touched the Master's eyeball with his finger to check whether or not his eyelid would blink, and he was convinced that there was no sign of life in his body.

*   *   *

Sri Ramakrishna had tremendous power to transmit and awaken the spirituality in others' minds. If anyone with an occult or supernatural power came close to the Master, the Master absorbed that power and the visitor lost it. In fact, occult powers are terrible obstacles to God-realization. Thus, holy association with the Master would remove the obstacle to spiritual growth for the person endowed with such power.

*   *   *

Those who have lived with holy people know how they constantly talk about God even when besieged with dangers and misfortunes. We witnessed this in Sri Ramakrishna's life. He was then suffering from terminal cancer, and he lived for six months with almost no food. But the people around him were experiencing a current of bliss. During that critical time of his life, he gave secret instructions in sadhana to his disciples, answered their vital questions, and distributed uninterrupted bliss of God. We did not see any sign of pain or suffering in him.

*   *   *

Sri Ramakrishna used to say, "God dwells even in stones and trees, but he manifests especially in human hearts and he plays with human beings." He further said: "If there were no human beings or devotees, who would recognize or respect God? Who would comprehend the infinite power of God and spread his glory by writing the Vedas and Vedanta? The lives of the devotees testify to the existence of God. These three — the Bhagavata [the scriptures], the bhakta [the devotee], and the Bhagavan [the Lord] — are one and the One is the three."

Sometimes avatars, or Divine Incarnations, come to this world incognito. About this the Master said: "Sometimes a king visits his capital publicly with his convoy and trumpeters, but at other times, in order to observe the true conditions and activities of his subjects, he moves around in disguise. As soon as the people recognize him they whisper among themselves: 'He is the king. He is visiting us disguised as an ordinary person.' Then the king immediately leaves that place. Similarly the avatar appears sometimes publicly and sometimes secretly."

The Master further said about avatars: "An avatar will never get liberation. As an executive officer of an estate rushes to a place where there is chaos or disturbance, so the avatar comes to relieve the sufferings of people whenever there is any unusual condition in the Divine Mother's vast empire — that is, in the world." From this statement do not think that the avatar is ever under the control of maya. He is, by nature, the master of maya and is established in his own Self. He is never bound. So the question of his liberation does not arise at all. He is the beacon light of the spiritual world, and his pure life will be the object of worship all through the ages.

*   *   *

The Master came to make religion easy. People were being crushed under the weight of rules and regulations. According to the Master, no special time and place are necessary to repeat the Lord's name and to worship him. In whatever condition one may be, one can repeat his name. The Master never gave too much importance to external observances. As to means, he taught that one should adopt whichever suits one best. If you like God with form, that will lead you to the goal. If you like God without form, well and good. Stick to it and you will progress. Even if you doubt his existence, then ask him thus: "I do not know whether you exist or not, whether you are formless or with form. Please let me know your real nature." As to changing clothes, taking a bath, and other external observances, if you can observe them, well and good; if not, go on calling on him without paying much attention to all of these.

The Master once sang a song to me and said, "Assimilate any one of these ideas and you will reach the goal." The song runs as follows:

Thou art my All in All, O Lord! — the Life of my life,
  the Essence of essence;
In the three worlds I have none else but thee to call my own.
Thou art my peace, my joy, my hope; thou my support,
  my wealth, my glory;
Thou my wisdom and my strength.
Thou art my home, my place of rest; my dearest friend,
  my next of kin;
My present and my future, thou; my heaven and my salvation.
Thou art my scriptures, my commandments; thou art my
  ever-gracious Guru;
Thou the Spring of my boundless bliss.
Thou art the Way, and thou the Goal; thou the Adorable One, O Lord!
Thou art the Mother tender-hearted; thou the chastising Father;
Thou the Creator and Protector;
Thou the Helmsman who dost steer my craft across the sea of life.

*   *   *

The Guru Gita says: If God is displeased with a person, he can again please God through devotion to the guru, but if the guru is displeased, none can help that person transcend the terrible darkness of maya. For that reason Sri Ramakrishna used to say to his westernized young disciples (*pointing to his own body*): "Look! This body is only a case, and holding it, the ever-conscious, blissful Mother is teaching people. For that reason those who come to me, touch me, and serve me, will be inspired and soon realize God. But serve me with special love and care. If you do not pay me respect, I shall not be mad at you. But the Mother who is within me, if she, being neglected, hisses at you, you will suffer." Once a bohemian devotee of Sri Ramakrishna was disgusted with his shameful life. He could not cope with his pain and mental despair, so he released his tension by saying abusive words about the Master. When Sri Ramakrishna heard about it he became worried about the devotee and said affectionately: "Let him say to me whatever he wants. Has he said anything to the person who is within me? I hope he has not said those abusive words to my blissful Mother."

*   *   *

We think we are very weak, and this is a great defect with us. The more we think this way, the weaker we become. Such an attitude is as harmful as pride. Both are impediments to real progress and should be shunned. This is what Sri Ramakrishna used to say. Once the Holy Bible was read out to him. From the very beginning there were references to the doctrine of sin in it. After hearing a little and finding that it talked of nothing but sin, he refused to listen anymore. He used to say: "Just as in the case of snakebite, if the patient can be made to believe that there is no poison at all, he will be all right. Similarly, if one constantly thinks, 'I have taken the name of the Lord, so I am sinless,' one becomes pure." The more we give up such ideas as "I am sinful," "I am weak," the better for us. The Almighty God dwells in human beings. We are part of God. We are his children. How can we be weak? Our strength comes from him. We can never be weak. So the greatest sin is to think oneself weak and sinful.

*   *   *

Is it possible to realize the Truth while living the life of a householder? Many people think that if one gets married and has a family, it is almost impossible to practise self-control. This is utterly wrong. What stands in the way of a householder's controlling his senses? Sri Ramakrishna used to say: "Make your mind and speech one and you will attain everything. Do not limit it [spiritual practice] to restraining the senses. Many other excellent qualities will be reflected in your life."

Sri Ramakrishna used to say that all his spiritual attainments were for the sake of others. If people would do one-sixteenth of what he did, they would be blessed. That is why he assumed the responsibilities of married life and exemplified the noble ideal of the householder. Had Sri Ramakrishna not married, some of his critics would probably have remarked that he talked so vehemently against lust and gold and preached the ideal of renunciation so eloquently because he himself was not married.

Sri Ramakrishna's marriage has a deep meaning. He entered into it with the idea that people might learn from his example that marriage is a sacrament and has an ideal much higher than the gratification of the senses. This ideal was not exemplified in the lives of Rama, Krishna, Buddha, Jesus, Shankara, and the other avatars. It was demonstrated in Sri Ramakrishna's life to fulfill a great need. For the first time in the history of the world an absolutely pure married life was expressed through lifelong spiritual practices and austere disciplines. Sri Ramakrishna would say, "Let men cast their own lives in this mould and fashion an image of purity and perfect beauty."

*   *   *

Our Master, Sri Ramakrishna, warned against depending upon such external means as pranayama and other hatha yoga exercises. He told us repeatedly not to pay much attention to them. When over-zealously done, they may upset the brain or lead to some dangerous results. He advised us especially to meditate. He was insistent on it. All his emphasis was laid on prayer and meditation.

*   *   *

There are no contradictions in Sri Ramakrishna's teachings. He did not make one rule for all. He used to see the inner tendency of a person and then advise him accordingly. His instructions were given differently to different people because of their varied temperaments and abilities to apply his principles in life. To those who were young, energetic, intense with fiery enthusiasm, and in whom he saw the potential for becoming monks, his inspiring words were: "Now overlook all desires for name and fame and plunge headlong into spiritual disciplines. Never rest content until the realization of God has become an accomplished fact." He would enkindle the smouldering fire in their hearts, saying: "Is it possible to realize God without renunciation? Renunciation of lust and greed is the most essential prerequisite for entering into spiritual life. What is there in the world except anguish, misery, and trouble? Tell me, who is happy in the world? If you seek the world and long for sense objects, the world will drag you down. But if you seek God and renounce everything for him, God will lift you up and your consciousness will be filled with unending bliss."

To those who were encumbered with life's heavy responsibilities, who were caught in the net of *samsara* [the world] and had become old, his advice was: "I have cooked the food and placed it on the plate. Your task is simply to sit and eat. You will not have to do anything. You are merely to lift it up to your mouth and enjoy. I have taken the responsibility. You will not have to do any spiritual disciplines. I have already done them for you. It will be enough if you give me the power of attorney and be at ease." He knew that conditions were not favourable for them to do spiritual practice, and if asked, it would not be in their power to follow his instructions. Therefore he would advise them to rely on him and take refuge in the Lord.

*   *   *

Wherever there is want, there is also fulfillment. Where there is demand, there is also supply. Whenever an aspirant longs intensely for God, he finds the way towards the fulfillment of his desire. Sri Ramakrishna often said: "The Mother will not allow any of her children to go hungry. He who is hungry in the morning will be fed in the morning. He whose appetite is aroused late in the evening will be fed in the evening." Every sincere wish of a person will be fulfilled.

How Sri Ramakrishna Tested His Disciples

Sri Ramakrishna said to Keshab Chandra Sen, when the Brahmo Samaj was split over the Cooch Bihar marriage:[1] "It is no wonder that your Samaj broke up. You accept all as your followers without testing them. But I do not accept anyone without doing so." It was indeed wonderful in how many different ways the Master used to examine the devotees that came to him. He had had no formal education, yet he had mastered many wonderful methods of gauging human character. Was it due to the revival of knowledge acquired in past lives? Or to his supersensuous vision and omniscience attained through sadhana? Or to his being a Divine Incarnation, as he sometimes described himself to his intimate disciples?

We always found that when a person first came to him, he would look at him with special attention. If he felt attracted towards the visitor, he would talk about spiritual things with him and ask that person to visit him occasionally. As days passed and the visits continued, Sri Ramakrishna would observe, unknown to the visitor himself, the shape of his body and limbs, the nature of his thoughts, the intensity of his carnal desires, and the extent of his love for the Master. From these minute observations, he would arrive at a sure conclusion about his latent spirituality, and before long he would have a firm grasp of the person's character. And if he felt the necessity of knowing any hidden facts about the person's inner nature, he would learn about them through his keen yogic vision. About this he once said to us: "During the early hours of the morning, while awake and alone, I think of your spiritual welfare. The Divine Mother shows me how far one has advanced on the spiritual path, why another cannot progress, and so on." From this, however, let us not conclude that his yogic power was active only at that time. From his conversations at other times we understood that he could ascend at will to high states of spiritual consciousness and obtain similar visions. For he said, "Just as by merely looking at a glass case one can see all of its contents, so I can know the inmost thoughts, tendencies, and everything of a person by merely looking at him."

The above, however, was only his general method of judging character. In the case of his special devotees, he used to apply other methods also. In fact, their case was special in various senses. His first meetings with them always came about in a peculiar manner. He was generally

---

[1] According to the Brahmo Marriage Act of 1872 no girl in a Brahmo family could be married under the age of fourteen. But Keshab broke the rule when he arranged for his thirteen-year-old daughter to be married to the Hindu Prince of Cooch Bihar.

in an exalted mood at those times. And he would intuitively know their natures — the facts of their inner life would be spontaneously revealed to him. The explanation is simple: By wonderful spiritual practices, he had made his body and mind excellent instruments for retaining and communicating subtle spiritual forces. Thus, whenever any devotee approached him, the Master's mind would be at once coloured by the same spiritual outlook as that person's, and he could automatically respond to that spiritual level. The facts of the person's inner life would become instantly clear to the Master. This, it must be admitted, was a special method. It was an intuitive process. But, as we have said, he also applied the general methods, the methods of observation, to his special devotees, and these can be described under the following four categories:

1. Sri Ramakrishna would ascertain the predominant tendencies of his devotees by observing their physiognomy and other bodily signs. Physiology and psychology now prove that every definite thought, when it becomes active, leaves an impression on the brain and the body. The Vedas and other scriptures have always affirmed this fact. All Hindu philosophical and religious books declare that the mind builds the body, and that a person's physical form changes accordingly as his thoughts and propensities are good or evil. Therefore many proverbs are current about ascertaining a person's nature from the shape of his body and limbs. And that is also why on the occasions of marriage, initiation, and other ceremonies, an examination of the hands, feet, and other parts of the persons concerned is considered necessary.

It is no wonder that Sri Ramakrishna, believing as he did in the scriptures, should examine the shape of the body and the limbs of his disciples. He would relate many facts about this in the course of conversation. And we would listen wonder-struck to his descriptions of the various limbs and features of a person as he compared their shape with the objects of everyday life and explained their special significance. About the eyes he would say: "Some have eyes like lotus petals, some like a bull's eyes, and some possess the eyes of a yogi or a deva [god]. Those who have eyes like lotus petals are endowed with good and spiritual tendencies. Those whose eyes are like a bull's have a strong sex drive. The yogi's eyes have an upward look and a reddish tinge. The divine eye is not very large but is long and stretches to the ear. If a man glances to the side or looks from the corner of the eye while talking, know him to be more intelligent than the average person."

Or he would speak of the peculiarities of the body: "Those who have a devotional temperament have a naturally soft body, and the joints of their hands and feet are supple. And even if their body is lean, the muscles and tendons are so shaped that it does not appear as angular." In order to ascertain the tendency of a person's mind, whether it was towards good or evil, he would weigh the person's hand from the fingers to the elbow in his own hand. If he found the weight less than usual, he would conclude that the mind was towards good. We will cite an example. While Sri Ramakrishna was staying at the Cossipore garden, suffering from cancer, the younger brother of the present writer came one day to visit the Master. The Master was very pleased to see him. He made him sit near him, questioned him about various things, and gave him many spiritual instructions. When I came in to see Sri Ramakrishna, he asked me: "Is this your younger brother? He is a fine boy and more intelligent than you. Let me see if he has good or bad tendencies." So saying, he took my brother's hand into his own and weighing it said, "Yes, he has good tendencies." He then asked: "Shall I draw him [that is, draw his mind away from the world and turn it towards God]? What do you say?" I replied, "Yes, sir, please do so." But Sri Ramakrishna thought for a while and said: "No, no more. I have taken one, and if I take this one also, your parents, especially your mother, would be very grieved. I have displeased many a Shakti [woman] in my life. No more now."

The Master used to say: "People having different mental tendencies also have different ways of functioning physiologically, such as sleeping. Experts can find indications of character in these things. For example, all people do not breathe the same way in sleep. A worldly man breathes one way, a man of renunciation another way."

Of women, Sri Ramakrishna used to say that there are two kinds: vidya Shakti, of god-like nature, and avidya Shakti, of asuric nature, or low nature. "Those of godly nature," he said, "eat and sleep little. They do not care for sense enjoyment, they like to talk with their husbands about religious subjects, and they save their husbands from evil thoughts and impure acts by inspiring them with spiritual thoughts. They help their husbands to live a spiritual life so that they [the husbands] may ultimately realize God." But the avidya Shaktis are just the opposite. "They eat and sleep a lot, and they want their husbands to think of nothing but their happiness. If their husbands talk about religion they become annoyed."

In this way Sri Ramakrishna told us many things. Once he examined Naren's [Swami Vivekananda's] body that way. He was very much pleased with the result. He said: "You have all the good marks on your body, only during sleep you breathe heavily. Yogis say that this indicates a short life."

2. & 3. The Master's second and third means of knowing a person's nature were the observation of his mental tendencies and his attachment to lust and gold as expressed in small, ordinary actions. He would silently watch all those who came to visit him at Dakshineswar. When he had decided to accept someone as his disciple, he would teach him in many ways and would sometimes scold him to correct his defects. After studying a newcomer, he would decide whether he would train him to become a good householder or a monk. First he would ask whether he was married or single and whether he had sufficient means to maintain himself. Or, if that person was going to renounce the world, the Master would ask whether he had anyone to take his place in maintaining his family.

His love went out especially towards young students. He used to say: "Their minds are not yet divided between many interests, such as wife, children, desire for wealth, fame, etc. If they are properly trained, they can give their whole mind to God." Therefore he loved to instruct them in the spiritual path. He used to say: "The mind is like a packet of mustard seeds. If you once let it be scattered, it is very difficult to gather the seeds again." Or he would say, "Once a bird is full grown, it is difficult to teach it to say Radha-Krishna." Or again he would say: "If a cow steps on an unburnt tile the footprint can easily be smoothed over. But when the tile is burnt, the impression cannot be removed." He would, therefore, question the young boys carefully to learn the natural tendency of their minds — whether towards pravritti, or worldly enjoyment, or towards nivritti, or renunciation. He would train them towards renunciation if he found them fit for it. Through questioning he would also learn whether the boy was unsophisticated and truthful, whether he really practised what he professed, whether he used discrimination or not in all his actions, and how far he could understand the Master's instructions. All these he would ascertain very carefully.

Once he asked a young student who came to him, "Why don't you marry?" The boy replied: "Sir, my mind is not yet under my control. If I marry now, I shall have no discrimination of right and wrong in my attachment to my wife. If I can conquer lust, then I shall marry." Sri Ramakrishna understood that though the boy had strong attractions for sense enjoyment, yet his mind was tending towards the path of renunciation. He laughed and said, "When you have conquered lust, you will not need to marry at all."

Talking to another boy at Dakshineswar, he said: "You see, I cannot always keep my cloth on. Sometimes it comes loose and drops off without my noticing it. I am an old man and I move about naked, yet I do not feel ashamed. What is the reason? Formerly I did not notice at all whether people saw me naked or not. But now I notice that some people feel embarrassed, so I keep my cloth in my lap. Can you go naked, like me, before others?" The boy said: "Sir, I do not know. But if you tell me to do so I think I can." Sri Ramakrishna said: "Try it. Take off your cloth, wrap it around your head, and walk around the temple courtyard." The boy said: "No, sir. That I cannot do. I can do that only before you." Sri Ramakrishna said: "Yes, others also say that they feel the same way. They feel no shame before me, but they do so before others."

Once it was the second day of the bright fortnight. We had all retired. The moonlight was beautiful. The flood tide coming in on the Ganga was always a grand sight on such evenings. In the middle of the night Sri Ramakrishna called us and said, "Come, come and see the incoming flood tide." He himself then went to the embankment. Seeing the calm waters of the Ganga rising in huge waves with the tide and splashing against the embankment, he felt as happy as a boy and began to dance.

Now, on getting up, we had to fasten our clothes properly before we could follow him, and that made us a little late. By the time we got to the embankment, the moments of greatest beauty had passed. Only a few were in time to see a part of it. Sri Ramakrishna was absorbed in his own joy. When it was over he turned to us and said, "How did you enjoy it?" Hearing that we had come too late because we had to dress, he said: "You fools. Do you think the tide will wait for you to dress? Why didn't you leave your cloth behind as I did?"

Sometimes he would ask a disciple if he wanted to marry and earn money. If he replied that he would not marry but would have to enter service for earning money, it would not satisfy the Master, who was a great lover of freedom. He would say: "If you do not marry, why then be the slave of someone all your life? Give your whole heart to God and worship him. Having been born in the world, this should be your highest ambition. If that is not possible, then marry, but make the realization of God your highest goal and always maintain yourself honestly." Such were Sri Ramakrishna's views. If, therefore, any disciple whom he considered especially, or even fairly, gifted spiritually, married or entered service to earn money, or worked for fame and wasted his energy, he would take it very much to heart.

One of his young disciples [Swami Niranjanananda] accepted employment to support his mother. When Sri Ramakrishna heard about it, he said, "If it had not been for the fact that you did so for your old mother, I would have never looked at you again." When another disciple came to Cossipore garden to see Ramakrishna after his marriage, Sri Ramakrishna wept as if he had lost a son. He put his arms around the young man's neck, and crying, said repeatedly, "Try not to sink in the world forever by forgetting God."

All scriptures teach that progress in the spiritual path is impossible without sincere faith. Knowing this, some of us would make it a point to believe in everything and every person. But Sri Ramakrishna warned us against that. Though he asked us to travel along the spiritual path with faith, he never asked us to cease discriminating. One should use one's sense of right and wrong both in the spiritual path and in worldly matters — such, we think, was his view.

Once one of the young disciples [Swami Yogananda] went to a shop and bought an iron pot. He appealed to the religious feeling of the shopkeeper and did not examine the pot closely. Afterwards he found that the pot leaked. Sri Ramakrishna scolded him and said: "Because you are a devotee of God, does that mean that you should be a fool? Do you think a shopkeeper opens a shop to practise religion? Why did you not examine the pot before you purchased it? Never act so foolishly again. When you go out shopping, first determine the usual price of the item by going around to several shops and then thoroughly examine the thing you want to buy. And do not fail to demand the little extras where allowed."

Sometimes some persons, having begun the practice of religion, become so kindhearted that their kindness itself becomes a bondage to them and even drags them down from the path of spirituality. Such is often the case with softhearted persons. Sri Ramakrishna would instruct such people to be firm and resolved. But those who were by nature domineering and harsh, he would ask to be gentle. Swami Yogananda was of a very mild nature. We never saw him get angry or abuse anyone, even when there was reason enough for it. Though it was quite against his nature and inclinations, because of his tender heart he suddenly got married. His mother entreated him, and seeing her weep he did not have the strength to refuse. It was only through the grace of Sri Ramakrishna that he was saved from a life of bitter disappointment and repentance. Sri Ramakrishna watched over him with great care and tried in every way to cure his excessive mildness. The following is just one instance that shows how even through the smallest things Sri Ramakrishna instructed us:

A cockroach was once found among Sri Ramakrishna's clothes, so he asked Swami Yogananda to take it out and kill it. But Swami Yogananda took it outside the room and let it go without killing it. Sri Ramakrishna asked, "Have you killed it?" Swami Yogananda said, "No, sir, I let it go." Then Sri Ramakrishna scolded him and said: "I told you to kill the cockroach, but you let it go. You should always do as I ask you to do.

Otherwise, later in more serious matters also you will follow your own judgment and come to grief."

One day Swami Yogananda came in a rowboat from Calcutta to Dakshineswar. One of the passengers asked him where he was going, and he told him that he was going to Dakshineswar to see Sri Ramakrishna. Hearing this, the other passenger began to vilify Sri Ramakrishna's character, saying: "Sri Ramakrishna only pretends. He eats well, sleeps on a bed, and still he claims to be a saint, and he spoils young boys." Swami Yogananada was very much pained to hear the man talk like that about Sri Ramakrishna. He thought of rebuking him, but his gentle nature prevailed and he thought: "Well, people do not know Sri Ramakrishna, so they have odd ideas about him and criticize him. What can I do?" He kept silent.

Coming to Dakshineswar, he told Sri Ramakrishna about the incident. He thought Sri Ramakrishna did not care what people thought or said about him, and so the matter would end there. But he was mistaken. Sri Ramakrishna took it quite seriously. He said: "That man abused me for nothing and you kept silent! Do you know what the scriptures say? You must cut off the head of him who speaks ill of your guru, or leave his presence at once. And you did not even protest against these false accusations?"

Sri Ramakrishna trained each disciple in his own way, according to his needs, so the treatment of one would sometimes be quite the reverse of the treatment of another. In similar situations, under similar circumstances, Sri Ramakrishna taught his different disciples different ways of conduct. Let us illustrate this. We have just had Swami Yogananda's case. Now let us see what happened to Swami Niranjanananda under similar conditions.

Swami Niranjanananda was of a rough and ready temper. Once while he was going to Dakshineswar in a rowboat some fellow passengers spoke ill of Sri Ramakrishna. At first Swami Niranjanananda protested vehemently. But when they continued their slandering talk, he became very angry. He was so angry that he threatened to upset the boat and drown them all. He was a strong man and a good swimmer. They all got frightened and to save themselves began to pacify him in many ways. Then he calmed down.

When Sri Ramakrishna heard about it he scolded Swami Niranjanananda, saying: "Anger is like a pariah — an untouchable. You should never yield to it. The anger of a good man disappears like a line drawn in the water. Mean people will say many things, and if you want to quarrel about that, you will pass your whole life quarreling. You should think in such cases: 'What are people? They are like worms.' Pity them and overlook their weakness. Think of what an awful deed you were about to do through your anger. What was the fault of the boatmen that you should have put them also in danger?"

He would train his women disciples similarly. Once he said to one of them who was particularly softhearted: "Suppose someone you know takes great pains to help you on all occasions, but you feel that it is because he is under the spell of your beauty, which he is too weak to break. Would you be kind to the man? Wouldn't you, on the other hand, deal a hard kick to his chest and stay away from him? So you see, you cannot always be kind to all persons under all conditions. There must be a limit, and you must discriminate."

We remember the case of a young man named Harish. He was a strong man. He had a beautiful wife and a son and had enough means to support them. Coming to Dakshineswar a few times he felt a strong disgust for worldly life. His simple nature, his devotion and gentleness made him very dear to Sri Ramakrishna, so Sri Ramakrishna accepted him as a disciple. From then on he passed most of his time at Dakshineswar serving Sri Ramakrishna and meditating on the Lord. His guardians began to oppress him, his father-in-law asked him to go back to his home, his wife wept, but nothing could dissuade him from his purpose. He paid no attention to all these entreaties and threats. He remained silent and went on in his own way. The Master, to teach us through his example, pointed out to us how calm and steadfast Harish was, and he would say, "Those who are real men should be dead though living, like Harish."

One day Sri Ramakrishna was told that because Harish had left them, the whole family felt very sad and his wife was refusing to eat or drink. Hearing this, Harish remained silent as before. But Sri Ramakrishna, in order to test his mind, said to him: "Your wife is so very anxious to see you. Why don't you go to see her once? She has no one to look after her. What is the harm in consoling her once this time?" Harish became sad and answered: "Sir, this is not the proper occasion to show compassion. If I go there, I may fall into bondage again and forget the highest object of life. Pray, do not ask me to do that." Sri Ramakrishna was highly satisfied with his reply, and he often repeated Harish's words to us, praising his spirit of renunciation.

We may cite many instances of Sri Ramakrishna's noticing the trifling details of our daily lives and thereby understanding our mental qualities and defects. Once he saw Swami Niranjanananda taking too much ghee [clarified butter], and he said: "Why do you take so much ghee? Will you afterwards run away with somebody's daughter or daughter-in-law?" [*He meant that such rich food would make it difficult for the disciple to control his passions.*] When one of the boys, despite his disapproval, began the study of medicine, he said: "You are supposed to renounce your desires, but you are increasing them instead! How then will you make any spiritual progress?"

4. He was never satisfied with merely knowing the character of his disciples; he would also try to remedy their defects. And he would often inquire about their spiritual progress. In order to ascertain it, he always adopted a special means, which was his fourth method in examining his disciples.

Sri Ramakrishna would often inquire if the regard and devotion for him, which had first brought his disciples to him, were increasing or not. This inquiry would take the following forms: He would sometimes question his disciples about how far they could understand his spiritual conditions and conduct. Or he would observe if they put complete faith in his words. Or he would introduce them to other disciples, an intimacy with whom, he thought, would deepen their own spiritual moods. And he would not be finally certain of the spiritual future of a disciple until he had learned to accept Sri Ramakrishna, intuitively and of his own accord, as the expression of the highest spiritual ideal of the world.

This may astonish some, but a little thought will indicate that it was only reasonable and natural. For what else could he do, knowing as he did that there was an unprecedented influx of spirituality through him? He had gone through long and superhuman austerity and meditation and had attained samadhi. As a result, all his egoism had been totally destroyed, and all chance of any delusion or error had been eliminated forever. Necessarily, therefore, the complete memory of his past and omniscience was revived in him. He felt in his inmost soul that the spiritual ideal that was manifested through his mind and body had never before been witnessed in the world, and he naturally concluded that whoever would, in this age and with full understanding, seek to mould his life in the light of the ideal that was embodied in him, would find his spiritual progress easy and smooth. Need we wonder that he inquired of his disciples if they understood him to be the highest spiritual ideal, and if they were trying to build their lives in accordance with it?

The Master expressed this conviction of his in various ways. He would say: "The coins current in the reigns of the Nawabs [Muslim kings] became invalid during the Emperor's rule." "If you follow my instructions, you will directly reach the goal." "Those whose present birth is the last [that is, those who have been freed from their past karma so that they will not have to be born again], will come here and accept the spiritual ideas and ideals of this place." "Your Ishta [Chosen Deity] is [*pointing to himself*] within this. If you meditate on this, you meditate on your Ishta." We shall give a few illustrations.

All the disciples of the Master experienced that at one time or other he asked them what they thought of him. This question was usually put after a disciple had been intimately known to the Master, but not always. Sometimes he would put this question to a disciple at the first meeting. But such disciples belonged to the group whom he had seen previously in a superconscious vision. The replies that he received varied. Some said, "You are a true saint." Some said, "You are a true devotee of God." Some said, "You are a *Mahapurusha* — a great soul." Some said, "You are an emancipated person." Some said, "You are an Incarnation of God." Some said, "You are Sri Chaitanya himself." Some said, "You are Shiva himself." Some said, "You are God." And so on. Some who belonged to the Brahmo Samaj and did not, therefore, believe in Divine Incarnations, said, "You are a lover of God, of the same rank as Sri Krishna, Buddha, Christ, and Sri Chaitanya." A Christian named Williams[2] said, "You are the Christ himself, the Son of God."

We cannot say how far the young disciples really understood the Master. But their answers at least indicated what they thought of him and what their conception of God was. The Master evidently took the answers in that light and behaved with and instructed them according to their spiritual outlook and temperament. For the Master never interfered with anyone's moods and outlook. On the other hand, he helped each to grow in his own way so that he might eventually realize the Highest Truth. But he always carefully observed whether the disciple was replying from sincere conviction or merely copying others.

We shall mention the instance of Purna. The Master himself testified to his deep spirituality and regarded him as one of his chief disciples. In fact, he gave him a place next to Swami Vivekananda. Purna was only thirteen years old when he first met the Master, but he felt deeply moved even at the first meeting. When he next came to the Master, the Master asked him in what light he regarded him. Purna replied with a good deal of emotion: "You are God himself, incarnated in flesh and blood!" Sri Ramakrishna was surprised and delighted with the answer. He blessed him from the bottom of his heart and initiated him into the mystery of Shakti worship.

---

[2] We are reliably informed that Williams, after he had seen the Master a few times, became convinced of his divinity. He gave up the world at the Master's advice, went to the Himalayas to the north of the Punjab, and passed away there after practising hard austerities.

Here is another instance: There was a picture in Sri Ramakrishna's room in which Sri Chaitanya and his devotees were shown absorbed in singing the praises of God. One day Sri Ramakrishna pointed it out to a friend of ours and said, "Do you see how absorbed they are in singing the praises of the Lord?"

Friend: "They are all low class people."

Master: "What do you say? You must not say so."

Friend: "Yes, sir. I come from Nadia.[3] I know only low class people become Vaishnavas."

Master: "Oh, you come from Nadia? Then I salute you a second time.[4] Well, Ram and others say that this [*pointing to himself*] is a Divine Incarnation. What do you think?"

Friend: "They estimate you very poorly, sir."

Master: "What! They call me a Divine Incarnation and you think that a poor estimate?"

Friend: "Yes, sir. An avatar is a part of God, but I look upon you as Shiva himself."

Master: "Indeed!"

Friend: "So indeed I think of you. What can I do? You asked me to meditate on Shiva. But though I try daily, I cannot do so. Whenever I sit in meditation, your loving and blissful face appears before me in a luminous form. I cannot replace it by the form of Shiva, nor do I want to do so. So I regard you as Shiva himself."

Master (*smiling*): "Is that so? But I know I am like an insignificant hair on your head." (*Both laughed.*) "However, I am satisfied. I had been anxious about you."

The significance of the Master's last words was not perhaps quite evident to our friend at that time. We remember that whenever in such cases the Master expressed satisfaction with us, we would be filled with great joy and care little to go into his inner meaning. Now we understand the reason for the Master's satisfaction with our friend. He had accepted him as the highest spiritual ideal.

The Master was very careful that the disciples properly study all his ways before accepting him as the highest ideal. He would often say to us, "Watch a sadhu [holy man] by day and by night, and then trust him." He encouraged us to see if a sadhu practised what he taught and told us never to trust a person whose actions did not tally with his words and whose mind was not one with his lips.

---

[3] Nadia was the birthplace of Sri Chaitanya and the place of origin of Bengal Vaishnavism.

[4] It was the custom of Sri Ramakrishna to salute a person as soon as he met him. That is why he said "a second time."

Thus encouraged, we would carefully observe the Master's habits. Some of us even went so far as to test him. But he gladly put up with all the troubles we caused him in our sincere desire to confirm our faith in him.

Yogin, who afterwards became Swami Yogananda, was one of the principal disciples of the Master. His home was very near the Dakshineswar temple, and he could, therefore, pass long hours in the company of the Master. One evening Yogin, with the Master's permission, decided to spend the night with him in order to serve him in case of need. They went to bed. About midnight Yogin suddenly woke up to find the door of the room open and Sri Ramakrishna missing. At first he thought he might be taking a walk outside, but he did not find him there. Suddenly a suspicion flitted across his mind: Could he have gone to meet his wife, thus acting contrary to what he professed? Unpleasant though it was, he resolved to ascertain the truth and watched the door of the concert room where Holy Mother lived. Suddenly he heard the sound of slippers coming from the direction of the Panchavati. A moment later Sri Ramakrishna stood by his side. "Well, what do you want here?" he asked. Yogin hung his head in shame for having doubted the Master's sincerity and could not utter a word. The Master understood the whole thing in a moment and reassured the penitent boy, saying: "Well done! You must examine a sadhu by day and by night and then believe in him." Though forgiven, Yogin could not sleep anymore that night.

In conclusion, we may briefly delineate how Sri Ramakrishna examined Narendra and what conclusions he formed about him. Sri Ramakrishna carefully observed all of Narendra's actions and movements from the time of his first visit to Dakshineswar. From this he came to feel that spiritual earnestness, courage, self-restraint, heroism, self-sacrifice for noble causes, and similar other noble qualities existed in a developed form in him. He understood that noble qualities were naturally so predominant in Narendra that even under adverse circumstances and temptations he would never succumb to them and do anything mean. As regards his devotion to truth, the Master had noted his utter truthfulness. He thus implicitly trusted in whatever Narendra said, and he deeply felt that very soon Narendra would reach a state where nothing but truth would issue from his lips even under confusion, and that whatever casual desires arose in his mind would be fulfilled. He would, therefore, encourage him still further in truthfulness, and say: "Whoever holds to truth in word, thought, and action is blessed by the vision of God who is Truth itself"; and "One who observes truth for twelve years in thought, word, and deed reaches a state in which whatever he resolves comes true."

We remember a funny incident about Sri Ramakrishna's faith in Naren's truthfulness. In the course of conversation Sri Ramakrishna once mentioned that there comes a stage in the life of a devotee when he is like a chataka bird. This bird will drink only rainwater, and that, as it falls from the clouds. So it is always watching the sky in the hope that rain will fall. Devotees in that state depend on God alone to appease the thirst of their heart. As the bird watches the sky, so the devotees always look to God for all their needs. Naren was listening to this. Suddenly he exclaimed: "Sir, though it is the common belief that the chataka bird drinks only rainwater, it is not a fact that it does not take other water. I have seen these birds drink from rivers and ponds." Sri Ramakrishna said: "Is that so? Do they drink like other birds? Then I am mistaken. If you have seen it, then there is no doubt about it." But Sri Ramakrishna, simple as a boy, was a little disturbed in mind. He thought, "If I am mistaken in this, then I may also be mistaken in other ways." It made him very sad.

After a few days Naren called Sri Ramakrishna and said: "Sir, see, a chataka bird is drinking Ganga water." Sri Ramakrishna rushed out of the room and said: "Where? Where?" When they came near the spot, what did they see but a small-sized bat. Sri Ramakrishna laughed and said: "You rogue, it is a bat. You have given me so much trouble for nothing. Now I shall be wiser and not believe everything you say."

It is often seen that men, as soon as they come into the presence of women, become softer than is accounted for by a mere sense of politeness, respect, and appreciation of beauty. This, according to the scriptures, is the result of certain *samskaras* [impressions] hidden deep in the heart. But in Naren we did not find that. Sri Ramakrishna noticed this, and he was therefore convinced that Naren would never forget himself under the spell of feminine beauty. Once Sri Ramakrishna compared Naren with a well-known devotee who often went into spiritual ecstasy and was thus highly respected by us. He said: "That man gets beside himself on meeting women, but Naren never does. I have watched him carefully. Though he does not say so, I find that he seems rather annoyed when they come. It seems as if he thinks with some disgust, 'Why are they here?'"

It was characteristic of Naren that though jnana [knowledge] was so strong in him and he was so manly in every respect, still he was very gentle and full of devotion. Sri Ramakrishna often remarked on this, and once he said, looking at Naren's face: "Could one who is only a dry jnani have such eyes? You have, along with jnana, all the tender feelings of the devotee. You have the strength of a man and the devotion of a woman. Those who have only manly qualities do not have black circles around their nipples. In the great hero Arjuna these marks [black circles around the nipples] were not present."

Besides the four methods described above, the Master also tested Narendra in other ways. We shall cite two instances: One day he told Narendra that he possessed many supernatural powers and that he would like to transfer them to him. Narendra asked him if they would help him to realize God. When the Master answered in the negative, he sternly refused to have anything to do with them. This reply greatly pleased the Master.

But the other test was more severe. Narendra's visits to Dakshineswar were always hailed by Sri Ramakrishna with intense joy — so much so that sometimes even a distant sight of Narendra would plunge him into samadhi. But a day came when all this changed. Narendra came, saluted, and sat before him, but there was no response from the Master. The Master talked with others, but not with him. He even turned his face away from him. The whole day passed in this way. In the evening Narendra saluted him and returned home. Several days after this he again went to Dakshineswar. On that day also he met with the same reception. The third and the fourth time also it was the same. Thus passed one month.

Then one day Sri Ramakrishna called him to his side and said, "Tell me, how is it that though I do not speak a word to you, you still continue to come here?" Narendra replied: "Sir, it is not your words alone that draw me. I love you and want to see you. Therefore I come." Sri Ramakrishna was highly pleased with this answer. He said: "I was only testing you. I wanted to see if you would stay away when I did not show you love and attention. Only one of your calibre could put up with so much neglect and indifference. Anyone else would have left me long ago and would never have come again."

[From: *Sri Ramakrishna, The Great Master*, by Swami Saradananda (Madras: Sri Ramakrishna Math), vol. 2, 1979; *Swami Saradanander Jivani*, by Brahmachari Akshay Chaitanya (Calcutta: Model Publ. House), 1955; *Gitatattva* and *Bharate Shaktipuja*, by Swami Saradananda (Calcutta: Udbodhan Office), 1966, 1967; *Spiritual Talks* and *The Message of Our Master*, by The First Disciples of Sri Ramakrishna (Calcutta: Advaita Ashrama) 1968 & 1944; *Glimpses of a Great Soul*, by Swami Aseshananda (Hollywood: Vedanta Press), 1982; *Prabuddha Bharata*, March 1930; *Udbodhan*, vol. 35, no. 8, 1933]

11

Swami Turiyananda

Swami Turiyananda (1863-1922) was born in Calcutta, and his premonastic name was Harinath Chattopadhyay. From his boyhood he led an austere life. He met Sri Ramakrishna in his early teens and was regarded by the Master as the embodiment of renunciation as taught in the Gita. In 1887 he joined the Ramakrishna monastery, and afterwards he travelled all over India, practising austerities. He went to America in 1899 to preach Vedanta and established the Shanti Ashrama in Northern California. In 1902 he returned to India and led a contemplative life. His life was an inspiration to all who came in contact with him.

First Meetings with Sri Ramakrishna

I first saw Sri Ramakrishna at Dinanath Basu's house in Baghbazar. That was long, long ago. In those days the Master would frequently go into samadhi. About that time Keshab Chandra Sen had become acquainted with him. Kalinath Basu, Dinanath's brother, was a follower of Keshab Sen. He happened to see Sri Ramakrishna and was deeply impressed, so he asked his brother Dinanath to bring Sri Ramakrishna to their house. That is how the Master came to visit Baghbazar. We were all young, about thirteen or fourteen years old. People referred to Sri Ramakrishna as the Paramahamsa, so they were all talking about the Paramahamsa's visit. Some other boys and I were curious, and we went to see him. We saw a carriage with two men in it stop in front of Dinanath's house. Immediately people around began to say, "The Paramahamsa has come, the Paramahamsa has come," and began moving towards the carriage. First, one of the men in the carriage got down. [*This was Hridayram Mukhopadhyay, Sri Ramakrishna's nephew.*] He was well built, and there was a large vermilion mark on his forehead and a golden amulet tied around his right arm. Looking at him, one felt that he was a strong and very active person. He stood close to the carriage and helped the other person alight. The other man appeared very thin. He had a shirt

Swami Turiyananda at Shanti Ashrama in California (c. 1901)

on, and his cloth was securely tied around his waist. One of his feet was on the step of the carriage, and the other was inside. He was in a semi-conscious state, and it seemed as if someone quite drunk were being taken out of the carriage. But when he got down, what a wonderful sight! There was an indescribable radiance over his face. I thought: "I have heard from the scriptures about the great sage Shukadeva. Is he the same Shukadeva?" By that time many others had joined them, and they were taken to the second floor of the house. I followed them. When the Paramahamsa became a little conscious of the outer world, he opened his eyes and saw a large picture of Mother Kali on the wall. Immediately he saluted her and started to sing in a soul-bewitching manner. It stirred a wave of devotion in all who had gathered there. The song expressed the idea that Kali and Krishna are identical: "O Mother, for Yashoda thou wouldst dance, when she called thee her precious Blue Jewel. . . . " It is impossible to describe the extraordinary feeling this song aroused in everybody. Two or three years later I went to Dakshineswar and saw Sri Ramakrishna in his room.

I have done what a man ought to do. My aim was to live a pure life. I used to read a great deal, eight or nine hours daily. I read many Puranas and then Vedanta, and my mind finally settled on Vedanta. Once the Master jokingly said to me: "Tell me something of Vedanta. Does not Vedanta say that Brahman is true and the world false? Or does it say something else? Then give up the false and take up the truth." This was a turning point in my life. When I first met Sri Ramakrishna and saw his spiritual moods — his devotion and his samadhi — I knew I had found someone who lived the ideal. I felt as if I had come home at last, and I thought, "If there is anything to be attained in life, it is God."

Who can know God? If he, out of mercy, lets one know him, only then is it possible. One day the Master made me shed tears by singing this song:

> O Kusa and Lava, why are you so proud?
> If I had not let myself be captured,
> Could you have captured me?[1]

I was deeply moved. That very day the Master deeply imprinted on my mind the fact that one cannot attain God through self-effort, by performing sadhana [spiritual practice]. Only if God reveals himself is it possible to attain him.

Once when I told Sri Ramakrishna that the goal of my life was to attain nirvana [liberation], he reproached me for entertaining such a low ideal.

---

[1] This is what Hanuman, a devotee of Rama, said to the latter's two sons.

He said: "Those who seek nirvana are selfish and small-minded. They are full of fear. They are like those parcheesi players who are always eager to reach home. An amateur player, once he sends his piece home, doesn't like to bring it out again. Such players are unskilled. But an adept player is never afraid of coming out again, if by doing so he gets the opportunity to capture an opponent. Then he rolls the right number and returns home once more. It seems that whenever he rolls the dice, the right number comes up for him. So do not fear. Play without any fear."

I asked, "Does it actually happen?" The Master replied: "Of course it happens. By Mother's grace everything takes place. Mother likes people to play. Take the game of hide-and-seek. [*There is a granny, there is a thief who is blindfolded, and there are children trying to escape being caught by the thief.*] The granny likes to have the children run about and make the game go on. She may extend her hand to help a child so he will not be caught by the thief, if she thinks it necessary. Similarly, the Divine Mother is not really pleased with those who seek nirvana, for they want to retire from the game. She wants the game to continue. That is why devotees do not seek nirvana. They say, 'O mind, it is not good to become sugar. I want to eat sugar.'"

The Master told me many times: "What is there in the scriptures? They are like sheets of paper with a shopping list on them. The list is useful only to check off the items once purchased. When you have done that, the list is thrown away. So you should check your knowledge, your devotion, and consult the scriptures to see whether they agree. It is said, 'When you have the knowledge of the Absolute, the scriptures are worth only a straw.'" The Divine Mother had shown Sri Ramakrishna what was in the scriptures, the Puranas, and the Tantric literature. So, though he was an unlettered person, he was able to lower the pride of the pandits. He used to say, "If you get a tiny ray of light from the Divine Mother, it makes all learning pale into insignificance."

Sri Ramakrishna sounded like a drunkard when he talked to the Divine Mother, saying: "Do not give me the knowledge of Brahman, Mother! I don't want it! I spit on it!" I was an extreme Vedantist at that time, and his words shocked me very much. I thought to myself: "My goodness! What can be greater than the knowledge of Brahman?"

Days in Dakshineswar

Ah, those days at Dakshineswar were like heaven itself! From morning till one o'clock in the afternoon everyone would be busy picking flowers and making other preparations for worship until the poor were fed. In the meantime Sri Ramakrishna would discuss spiritual subjects, and the devotees would listen to him with rapt attention. Even his fun and jokes were related to God. There was no other topic. Everything culminated in his samadhi [transcendental state of consciousness]. After lunch, Sri Ramakrishna would rest for a short period and again would speak on spiritual matters. At vesper time he would go to the temple of Mother Kali and fan her a little. He would become God-intoxicated there and would return to his room reeling in a state of ecstasy. He used to ask those of us who were practising spiritual disciplines under his guidance, "Tell me, do you feel divine inebriation when you meditate in the mornings and evenings?" At night Sri Ramakrishna slept very little. He used to get up and wake those who were sleeping in his room, saying: "Don't sleep too much! Wake up and meditate!" Again he would lie down a short while, and then rise before dawn and chant the name of the Lord in his inimitable sweet voice. The disciples would sit and meditate in their own way. Now and then the Master would go to them and correct their posture.

Sri Ramakrishna used to say: "I cannot stand anyone calling me guru. It irritates me. Who is the guru? Satchidananda [God] alone is the guru." The external guru shows the path; the inner guru awakens the spirit. Ordinary men who pose as gurus do not know this and ruin themselves by feeding their egos.

An hour of congregational singing in the company of the Master would fill us with such exuberant joy that we would feel transported, as it were, into an ethereal region. But now, even meditation fails to evoke that celestial bliss, or even a semblance of it. That bliss would stay with us continuously for a week. We used to feel intoxicated, though we did not know why or how. Who would believe it? It is difficult to convince anyone. Yet I must speak out. The ordinary man seeks nirvana because he has suffered. But he does not know the tremendous joy in divine communion.

One day I arrived at Dakshineswar when the Master was having his dinner. A number of bowls containing various cooked items were placed before him. Someone might have thought this an unbecoming luxury, fit only for a rajasic [worldly] life. The Master at once said: "Well, the tendency of my mind is always towards the Infinite. It is by such rajasic devices that I hold it down to the lower planes. Otherwise I could not talk with you." "How strange!" I said to myself on hearing him. "Others seek to attain sattva by overcoming rajas through a rigorous discipline of diet, whereas he has to forcibly check his mind from rising to the sattvic [spiritual] plane!"

On another day when I went to see Sri Ramakrishna, there were many other visitors. Among them was a great Vedantic scholar. The Master said to him, "Let us hear some Vedanta from you." The scholar with great deference expounded on Vedanta for more than an hour. Sri Ramakrishna was very pleased. The people around were surprised at this, but after eulogizing the scholar, the Master said: "As far as I am concerned, I do not like all those details. There is nothing but my Mother and I. To you, knowledge, knower, and known — the one who meditates, meditation, and the object of meditation — this sort of triple division is very good. But for me, 'Mother and I' — that is all and nothing else." These words, "Mother and I," were said in such a way that it made a very deep impression on all present. At that moment all ideas of Vedanta paled into insignificance. The Master's "Mother and I" seemed easier, simpler, and more pleasing to the mind than the three divisions of Vedanta. I realized then that "Mother and I" was the ideal attitude to be adopted.

Whatever evil tendencies one may have, one is sure to improve in holy company. When you go to a perfume shop, the scent enters your nostrils, whether you will it or not. Nevertheless, people are not often inclined to associate with holy persons, and few have the capacity to do so. Sri Ramakrishna would talk and the devotees would listen, but their companions would whisper: "Well, let us go. How long are you going to listen?" The devotees, of course, would have no inclination to leave, so their friends would say in exasperation: "You remain here. We shall wait in the boat." Sri Ramakrishna would describe this so beautifully!

Once a singer came to visit Sri Ramakrishna. He sang song after song about Shiva. The Master went into samadhi on hearing the very first song and remained in that state for a long time. Seeing him so absorbed, we thought we should ask the singer to stop. Suddenly the Master came down from his samadhi and said to the singer: "Oh, I can't stand it any more! Sing songs of the Divine Mother!" As the Master listened to songs about the Mother, his mind returned to the relative plane. Later he remarked that he had been in a very high state of consciousness.

One day I saw Sri Ramakrishna waving a fan before Mother Kali in her temple. He was singing:

> Awake, O Mother!
> Long hast thou been sleeping
> In thy primal abode
> In the lotus of the muladhara.
> Awake, O Mother!
> Perform thy own true function:
> Pierce the six centres of spirit
> And unite thyself with the great Lord Shiva
> In the thousand-petalled lotus

In the centre of the brain.
Thus, Mother, wipe out my sorrow,
Thou who art purest consciousness.

The Master once told Swamiji, "Whenever you start singing, the Mother wakes up and listens to your song."

Ah, what a fund of humour we found in Sri Ramakrishna! It was unique. One day Keshab Babu was to come to Dakshineswar. Even before the appointed time Sri Ramakrishna put on a red-bordered cloth, covered his body with a good chadar, and with his lips crimson from chewing betel, began to pace the verandah of his room in expectation of Keshab. When Keshab saw him in that state he remarked: "Ah, today you have dressed yourself with extraordinary care. What is the matter?" "Why, today I have to charm Keshab!" replied the Master, smiling. "That's why all this trimming!" At this Keshab began to laugh.

Swamiji also was very humorous. But his humour was nothing compared to Sri Ramakrishna's, which used to create sidesplitting laughter. He would say, "I keep people in the right mood by introducing secular topics now and then." Once a Brahmo devotee referred to Keshab Chandra Sen and Pratap Majumdar, in their very presence, saying that they were like Gauranga and Nityananda. Sri Ramakrishna was nearby. Keshab asked him, "What then are you?" Sri Ramakrishna at once replied, "I am the dust of your feet." At this Keshab said, "He is never to be caught napping."

It was Sri Ramakrishna who taught the Brahmos to salute in the proper fashion. The idea of the Motherhood of God was also his contribution to the Brahmo Samaj.

The Lord is the protector of the humble — their friend and helper. But it is very difficult to be humble. Humility does not come as long as there is any egotism left. Sri Ramakrishna would often tell of a sweeper woman. Her work is the lowest that can be imagined, but no sooner does she put on an ornament than her vanity knows no bounds.

Every word of the Master's was instinctive and carried great power. He used to snatch the hearts of people, as it were.

The Vedanta practised in some parts of India is rather diluted. "I am Brahman," they say, and go on doing all sorts of things as if these did not affect them. Discrimination, according to them, is not a sign of knowledge. Once a monk came to live in the Panchavati at Dakshineswar. Gossip went around about his character, and at last it reached the Master's ears. When he reprimanded the monk, the monk said, "If the world is unreal, are my slips of character alone real?" Sri Ramakrishna replied, "I spit upon such knowledge as yours!" Falsehood should never be allowed to flourish. Knowledge dawns when discrimination is perfect.

How difficult it is to keep the mind above the world! It wants to come down. It is indeed very hard to escape from the grip of desires. As the Master would say, "Even he who has no one to call his own will raise a cat and create attachment."

Love and lust are very much allied. Sri Ramakrishna used to say, "Lust is blind, but love is pure and resplendent." It is lust if you have the idea of man or woman, and love if you have the idea of God in your beloved. One must analyze one's mind very carefully. The Master asked me to increase my lust infinitely. I was amazed that he would say this. Then he explained: "What is lust? It is the desire to get. So desire to get God and strengthen this desire greatly." Through discrimination and devotion to God one can be free from lust. With the gradual increase of love for God, lust, anger, etc., wane.

While going to visit the Master, as soon as I would enter the gate of the Dakshineswar temple garden, I would feel a throbbing sensation in the heart. Many others would also feel the same way, because the thought of going near a very holy presence would create a sense of awe. When one goes near a holy presence, one's bad samskaras within begin to tremble. For who was as pure as Sri Ramakrishna? Even the purest among us was insignificant compared with the Master. When any contrary thought would cross my mind, he would at once detect it and say: "Why do you look this way? Perhaps this is the reason." And to my amazement he would say the correct thing. How fearless is he who can say with a clear conscience that he has done no wrong!

One day at Dakshineswar the Master said to me: "Go to the Panchavati. Some devotees had a picnic there. See if they have left anything behind. If you find anything, bring it here." I went and found an umbrella in one place, a knife in another place, and some other articles. I gathered them up and took them to the Master. The knife had been borrowed from him. I was just placing it on the shelf when he said: "Where are you putting it? No, not there. Put it underneath this small bedstead. That is where it belongs. You must put everything in its proper place. Suppose I need the knife during the night. If you put it anywhere you please, I will have to go around the room in the dark, stretching out my arms in search of it, wondering where you put it. Is such service a service? No! You do things as you like and thereby only cause trouble. If you want to serve properly, you should completely forget yourself."

Swamiji used to say, "Be ready to attach yourself and detach yourself at any moment!" We take up a job and become attached to it — we cannot detach ourselves from it. But this should not be. Look at Sri Rama-krishna. Hriday was ordered to leave Dakshineswar. The temple guard came and said to the Master, "You will have to leave this place." "What do you mean? It is Hriday, not I," replied Sri Ramakrishna. The man said, "No, my master has ordered that both of you go." Sri Ramakrishna put on his slippers and moved towards the gate. Trailokya Babu [grandson of Rani Rasmani, the founder of the Dakshineswar temple] saw this from the kuthi [mansion], and ran and fell at the Master's feet, saying: "Sir, why are you going? I have not asked you to leave." Without speaking a word the Master went back to his room. Imagine! There was not a bit of haughtiness in his renunciation. And how we raise dust over our deeds! Had we been in his place we would surely have given Trailokya Babu a piece of our mind. But the Master said nothing. He was as ready to go away as to return.

The Master used to be shabbily dressed, so much so that one day a man mistook him for a gardener and ordered him to pick a rose for him. The Master did so immediately. Some time later the man learned about his mistake and stammered out an apology. At this Sri Ramakrishna said that there was nothing wrong in what was done, as one asking for help should be assisted by all means! Isn't it grand?

Can God be attained by a little cursory study or meditation? One must have intense yearning for the Lord! Life must seem unbearable without seeing him! Sri Ramakrishna said to us: "Because I had that yearning, the Divine Mother took care of all my needs and provided this Kali temple and Mathur Babu [son-in-law of Rani Rasmani and a great devotee who provided for and served the Master]." The heart must burst with longing for God. Then one attains everything.

The practice of excessive physical mortification and of harming the body in any way stems from tamas [delusion]. People may point out that Sri Ramakrishna used to rub his face against the ground, thus mortifying the body, but he was in an ecstatic state at the time. His yearning for God was so intense that he completely forgot the world and his ego.

When I used to meditate in the Master's presence, I would experience a sensation in my spine and feel energy rising. The body was like a desert. Then the guru gave the holy name of God, and through its power the desert was transformed into a beautiful flower garden. My life had previously been aimless, but after receiving the touch of the guru, I gained my life's ideal.

Sri Ramakrishna used to pray, "Mother, may these children of mine surpass me in spirituality." There is a saying, "Welcome defeat at the hands of the son or disciple."

I have meditated much on the teachings of the Gita, which contains the essence of all scriptures. Sri Ramakrishna said that I was a monk according to the precepts of the Gita.

Living with Sri Ramakrishna

Sri Ramakrishna said that the physiognomy of a person was the index to his character. He used to examine us thoroughly, measure the proportion of our limbs, and weigh our hands. He could easily detect a person's nature from his physical characteristics. He had a way of classifying aspirants into grades, but there was room for all.

Sri Ramakrishna used to say: "A fingerprint is clear when the ink is all right, but if the ink is bad, the impression also is bad. Spiritual instructions make a lasting impression on the mind possessed of discrimination and renunciation, but when there is deficiency in these the impression produced is proportionately small."

The Master disliked a happy-go-lucky attitude. He used to say of Swamiji: "See what a heroic temperament he has! As soon as he sets his mind on something, he applies himself heart and soul to it." Circumstances may or may not be favourable, but who cares? We must strain every nerve to accomplish what we set out to do. If one is determined to do it at any cost, one finds that great obstacles, which had appeared overpowering, ultimately turn out to be a great help. But one must struggle sincerely.

We ourselves will have to apply our minds. Others cannot do it for us. The Master said again and again: "You must try a little. Only then will the guru reveal the Truth." Let me tell you from our experience that if anyone advances towards God a single step, God advances towards him ten steps. This is our personal experience. If we do not exert ourselves, no one can do anything for us.

Once I heard a person arguing in front of our Master. He was saying that this world is real. After listening to him, the Master said: "Ram, why don't you say in simple words that even now you have the desire to enjoy the sour dish of hog-plum [the worthless pleasures of the world]! What is the need for all this vain argument?" What response could have been more forceful and irrefutable? The truth is that if one has attachments one is afraid to renounce the world. But to hide this attitude and imagine that one can realize God without giving up the attachments only indicates one's natural inner weakness.

Truth is God. Falsehood is maya. Everything is achieved by holding onto truth. Sri Ramakrishna taunted Pandit Shivanath Shastri, saying: "If you are all such sane people, how can you speak an untruth? You call me insane, but never does an untruth escape my lips!" Once a Kalighat priest kicked Sri Ramakrishna. He knew the priest would be punished, so he wanted to keep it a secret. The Master asked Hriday to elicit from him a promise not to mention it to anybody. Hriday at first objected, but the Master made him elicit the promise from him three times, and then he said, "Now it will never escape my lips." For the protection of the priest he thus put himself under a vow to observe silence on the matter.

Once the Master made an engagement with Jadu Mallik but later forgot about it, being engrossed in conversation with a number of visitors. At eleven o'clock, when he was about to retire for the night, he suddenly remembered it. Immediately he had a lantern lighted and, accompanied by Swami Brahmananda, went to Jadu's garden. Finding the gate closed, he put one foot inside and shouted, "Here, I have come!" Sri Ramakrishna had given up everything, but he could not give up truth. It is a tremendous ordeal to abide by truth.

To transcend the mind is to manifest the intellect fully. It is not that the mind is altogether annihilated, but the mind which formerly had relations with the phenomenal world no longer exists. Sri Ramakrishna used to say that the pure mind and the pure Self are one. The mind becomes purified as soon as its worldly character is destroyed. A pure mind is that which, fully believing in the unity of Self, sees the same Atman [Self] in all, and deals with others accordingly. Sri Ramakrishna used to say: "First be converted into gold. Then you may even stay in an unclean place and still remain gold."

We must make everyone our own. The more we approach God, the more we become frank, sincere, and generous. Our Master was the very personification of guilessness and sincerity.

The Lord of the devotee can be both angry and pleased. The Master used to say that he could not bear the sight of egotistic people. Those who go to God without seeking nirvana are Ishvarakotis [great souls].

The Master had two moods: Sometimes he would say that he did not like divine forms — not even Kali — and his mind would remain immersed in the Absolute. At other times he would say that he could not do without divine forms, and he would tell the Divine Mother that he did not want to see her formless aspect or have the knowledge of Brahman. He who rejects everything and gets lost in the formless Brahman is one-sided. The jnani [the follower of the path of knowledge] is afraid of rebirth lest he be caught in the meshes of ignorance. But the expert player is not afraid of anything. Similarly, he who has realized only the forms of God, but not his formless absolute aspect, is also one-sided.

When God is realized, all religious practices are left behind. The Master used to say: "When a prospective husband is expected, a woman dresses herself nicely, combs her hair, and tries to look her most attractive in anticipation of getting a husband. But after she gets one, everything is neglected, for where is the necessity for such cosmetics?"

Sri Ramakrishna Taught Us

When I was in my early twenties I was an extreme Vedantist. My one ideal at that time was to attain nirvana. I considered that to be the supreme goal. But Sri Ramakrishna scolded me again and again and gave me another ideal. He pointed out that the path of knowledge was not my way. He made me a devotee instead. I still clearly remember how the Master disciplined me.

Considering myself a follower of the path of knowledge, I used to study the scriptures, thinking, "I will attain samadhi [union with God] immediately." After I came to Sri Ramakrishna, I learned what spiritual realization and samadhi meant.

Sri Ramakrishna's example solved all the problems of my life. I have no problem left to solve. While I was in the West, whenever anyone asked me a question I would look at the person and see his problem, and the answer would immediately come to my mind.

"Be a devotee, but don't be a fool!" One must be alert at all times. Sri Ramakrishna used to say: "Look at me! The Divine Mother has placed me in such a state that I can hardly keep clothes on my body, yet I am not forgetful." The Master told us, "He who is careless is foolish."

Sri Ramakrishna used to scold anyone who was careless. Carelessness is a defect of character. The Master was never slow in his actions, but at the same time he did not like to hurry or bustle.

To be a human being is to be alert, conscious. If one must lose consciousness, he should do so with full consciousness [in samadhi] — like Sri Ramakrishna. The Master used to lose external consciousness in ecstasy when someone would sing a devotional song. But even a slight mistake in the music would cause him pain, bringing him back to ordinary consciousness.

The Master instructed some in different kinds of sadhana [spiritual disciplines]. To me, however, he said only to practise meditation and japam. But he told me to meditate at midnight, completely naked. The Master was never satisfied with merely instructing. He would keenly observe each disciple to see how well his instructions were being executed.

A few days after giving me that particular instruction, he asked me, "Well, do you meditate at midnight naked?" "Yes, sir, I do," I replied. "How do you feel?" "Sir, I feel as if I am free of all bondage." "Yes, go on with the practice. You will be greatly benefitted."

On another occasion he told me that sadhana was nothing but "making the mind and speech one." In those days I was studying the Vedanta of Shankara intensely. The Master said to me: "Well, what is the use of merely saying that the world is false? Naren can say that. For if he says that the world is unreal, at once it becomes unreal. If he says there is no thorny plant for him, the thorny plant cannot affect his body. But if you put your hand on the thorns, you will at once feel their pricks."

In the early days I used to practise a spiritual mood earnestly for a time. Once I practised with great intensity the mood of being the Lord's instrument: "I am the machine, and He is the operator." I would carefully watch every thought and action of mine to see if they were inspired and filled with that mood. I practised this for some days. Then I practised "I am Brahman" for a while.

What we know we must put into practice at least once. But Sri Ramakrishna practised everything three times. Through practice new knowledge comes. Do something. Practise! Bondage and freedom are both in the mind. Atman is beyond the mind.

Embracing the monastic life is not a joke. Sri Ramakrishna used to say, "That person alone is fit for the monastic life who can allow himself to fall from a palmyra tree without moving his limbs." Is that an easy feat?

What will mere words do if there is no character behind them? That is the great stumbling block for all. Sri Ramakrishna would say: "Almost all have been caught in the snare of sex attraction. Only a few have been saved by the Divine Mother." It is a most dreadful attachment. People are all right as long as they do not come under its influence. But a man under its spell can stoop to anything. "Lust and gold" and "the palate and sex-impulse" are short expressions denoting the same thing. If one gives up these enjoyments, one verily renounces the world. One who can do this indeed negates the whole world.

If someone hurts you and you retaliate, you hurt yourself more. You become as evil as he. The Master used to say, "He who curses another and holds resentments cannot attain liberation."

[*Addressing the monks:*] Days, months, and years pass by, while you are idling away your time. Where is your yearning for God? Don't you remember how Sri Ramakrishna used to weep, "O Mother, another day is gone and still I have not seen you"? You have become dry! You have lost your spirit! "Who is dead-while-living? He who does not long for the truth of God." Swamiji once said, "At the age of twenty-nine I finished everything."

Has it been revealed to you what the purpose of this human birth is? Sri Ramakrishna's life is an example for us. The Master had the vision of the living Mother of the Universe and entered into an intimate relation-ship with her. He surrendered himself to her.

There must be self-effort. Sri Ramakrishna used to say: "Struggle a little! Then the guru will help you further." The Master used to sing, "Mind, struggle unto death. Can a pearl be found in knee-deep water? If you want to realize him, dive into the very depths of the ocean."

Don't expect anything from anyone! Learn to be the giver! Otherwise you will become self-centred. This is the teaching in the family of Sri Ramakrishna. I have seen so-called holy men who thought that they had become detached from the world and would have nothing to do with others. They were dry. . . . Sri Ramakrishna taught us, "Work with your hands, but let your mind remain at the feet of the Lord."

We have seen with these eyes. We have heard with these ears. When we came to Sri Ramakrishna he made us feel that God-realization was within our grasp. Yet occasionally we would become discouraged and worry whether our lives would pass without reaching the goal. In the course of time, however, the Master did everything for us.

Our Master could not bear the word *sin*. He told people not to consider themselves sinners, and taught them to think: "I am chanting the name of God. Why should I worry? Whom shall a child of the Mother of the Universe fear?"

Sri Ramakrishna also said, "Forbear, forbear, and forbear" — as if he were pleading that there was no other way. Again he said: "He who endures, lives. He who does not endure is destroyed." Therefore we must endure. Always remember the words of the Master, "Let the body endure its ailments, but you, O my mind, engage yourself in the thought of God and thus enjoy bliss." This attitude will save you from being overwhelmed by suffering.

Sri Ramakrishna said, "If you see an artificial fruit, you are reminded of the real fruit." In the same way, seeing a photograph of the Lord, one is reminded of him. Imagining him to be actually present in the photo-graph, we must know him to be real and serve him. He will fill us with inspiration.

My Master was a perfect yogi. Nothing remained hidden from him. He knew our minds through and through. We didn't have to ask him anything. He anticipated all our thoughts. We never had the impression that he was teaching us, yet he watched us all the time. Nothing escaped him. He knew what pitfalls stood in our way, and he made us avoid them.

Once our Master told us that he had other disciples who spoke a different language, who had different customs, somewhere far away in the West. "They also will worship me," the Master said. "They also are Mother's children."

Sri Ramakrishna and His Disciples

It is very difficult to realize God. The slightest desire blocks the way. The Master often said, "The thread does not pass through the eye of a needle if even the most minute fibre is sticking out." Swami Vivekananda once said to him, "Please pray to the Mother that they [Swamiji's relations] may have a bare subsistence." The Master sent him to the temple to ask the Mother himself. But when Swamiji entered the temple, he could not plead for anything but *viveka* [discrimination] and *vairagya* [dispassion]. How could he? He had no attachment within. When he said this to the Master, the Master remarked to us: "Do you see what a great soul he is? He could not ask the Mother for anything but viveka and vairagya."

Swamiji used to bring all sorts of people to Sri Ramakrishna. At this the Master would say: "What worthless people you bring — one-eyed, lame, and so forth. You don't know good people from bad people. Don't bring anyone and everyone."

Swamiji would always help the weak. He would say: "The weaker the man, the more help he needs. If a brahmin boy needs one teacher, engage four for a pariah." What a grand sentiment! Once Sri Ramakrishna was very angry with a lady devotee. He asked all of us not to go to her house or eat her food. He also asked her not to come to Dakshineswar. Against this serious injunction of his, who would dare visit her house? Nevertheless, one day Swamiji said to Swami Shivananda, "Come, let us go for a walk." In the course of the walk they came upon the lady's house and Swamiji asked her for something to eat. The lady was beside herself with joy and fed him heartily. Afterwards Swamiji went to Sri Ramakrishna and told him what he had done. The Master said: "Well, I forbade you and yet you went there and ate!" Swamiji replied: "Well, what harm was there? I have also invited her to come here."

Once at Cossipore Swamiji pleaded with the Master on Hazra's behalf. Swamiji would not leave him alone! His persistent demand was: "You must do something for Hazra. You must bless him." Sri Ramakrishna said, "He will get nothing now, but he will get it at the time of death." It actually came to pass. At heart Swamiji was a believer in grace.

Latu used to fall asleep early, and once the Master was very irritated with him. He wanted to send him away from Dakshineswar, but Swamiji interceded and the matter ended peacefully. It was for this reason that

Latu used to say, "If anyone is really a brother disciple, it is Vive-kananda."

Sri Ramakrishna gave no other blessing than: "Mother, let them have illumination. Let them be conscious of their real nature." Rakhal Maharaj [Swami Brahmananda] was living with him at the time. Rakhal Maha-raj's relatives first brought him to the Master, but when they discovered he was about to renounce, they did not like it. They spoke to Sri Ramakrishna, but he did not pay much attention to what they said.

Suresh Babu [Surendra Nath Mittra] was spending money for the comforts of the devotees. One day Manomohan, a devotee of Sri Rama-krishna and a relative of Rakhal Maharaj, said, "Suresh Babu does not like Rakhal living here." Immediately Sri Ramakrishna called out: "What! Who is Suresh? What does he do here? Throw away all that bedding Suresh brought. Remove those things at once. [*When the Master became excited everyone would be terribly afraid, and no one would dare come near.*] Because these boys have good characteristics that tend to spirituality, I keep them with me, and I pray to Mother to bless them so they may realize the Self. My idea is that they should first attain realization and then they may live anywhere they like." Hearing this, Suresh Babu fell at his feet and with tears in his eyes said that he had never said such a thing — that it was all false.

Sri Ramakrishna's life had two aspects. One must try to understand both. If one accepts only one aspect, there will be misunderstanding and confusion. For instance: The Master used to give presents to the musi-cians who played for him. When he had nothing else to offer, he gave them the very cloth he was wearing. Wasn't that an example of supreme renunciation? On the other hand, when that same Ramakrishna did not receive the customary food offering from the temple, he anxiously inquired about it and asked Swami Yogananda to go and get it. Swami Yogananda asked, "Why bother?" But the Master rebuked him, saying: "Oh, yes. I know you are a man of great renunciation. You don't care!"

How are these two attitudes reconciled? Of course Sri Ramakrishna did not take a morsel of that food offering himself. He had it brought for distribution among the devotees.

One day Sri Ramakrishna told Yogananda: "Be a devotee, but don't be a fool! When you want to buy something, go to different shops, compare prices, and take the best and cheapest. If you save money in this way, give it to the poor."

There is another instance. When Maharaj [Swami Brahmananda] found a pice that someone had lost and he showed it to the Master, the latter said: "Why did you take it? You don't need it. Why would a person who doesn't want fish go to the fish market and haggle over prices?"

How can one reconcile these contradictory attitudes? One time Sri Ramakrishna apparently behaved like any other worldly man, carefully calculating everything. Then again he exemplified the ideal of renunciation. You see, he was a man of principle. He represented the ideal [householder or monastic] in whatever he did. This is what I would call a perfect soul.

A worldly man is very grasping. And if an ordinary man feels a little renunciation, he completely loses his head. As we associated with Sri Ramakrishna, our eyes were opened. He showed us the ideal life by his own example.

When a Marwari devotee, Lakshminarayan, offered Sri Ramakrishna ten thousand rupees, the Master fell unconscious. Regaining consciousness, he told the devotee to get away from him. When Lakshminarayan suggested giving the money to Hriday for the Master's use, the Master exclaimed: "Oh no! He will accept it in my name, and I can't bear the thought of possessing money!" The devotee then said: "Ah, I see. You have not yet overcome the idea of acceptance and rejection." The Master simply replied, "No, I haven't."

How wonderfully Sri Ramakrishna taught each person so as to remove his particular wants! He used to illustrate this method of teaching by saying: "A mother has made various curries out of a fish. She doesn't give all her sons the same thing. She gives to each what will exactly suit his stomach." The Master followed this in practice also.

Swami Yogananda once overheard several men criticizing Sri Ramakrishna. He pocketed the affront and later reported the incident to the Master. Hearing of it, the Master said, "They abused me and you kept quiet!" Then he rebuked Swami Yogananda. On another occasion, some time after this event, Swami Niranjanananda was on his way to Dakshineswar by boat. Several of the passengers were criticizing Sri Ramakrishna. The swami was exceptionally strong, and he at once came out of the cabin, placed his legs across the deck, and began to rock the boat. "You are abusing Sri Ramakrishna," he said. "I shall now sink this boat. I would like to see who dares stop me." They were all frightened and begged him to stop. When Sri Ramakrishna heard about this incident, he said: "You fool. If they abused me, what was that to you? Let people say what they like. What does it matter to you?"

See the fun! The teaching was different, according to each recipient's need. Where can one find another teacher like him?

At one time Kali Maharaj [Swami Abhedananda] would catch fish, reasoning that the Atman is immortal — it neither slays nor is slain. Hearing of this, Sri Ramakrishna sent for him. He told Kali Maharaj: "What you are saying is true. But at your state of development, before you have realized the Atman, it is not good to discriminate in that way and kill any creature. You should know that realization of the Atman is a state of attainment beyond all logic and reason. He who attains that state feels compassion for all beings. A holy man is freed from all samskaras [past impressions], but the thought-wave of compassion stays with him to the last moment of his life. Never give up the ideal of a holy man!"

Once the Master asked B., "Whom do you love most of all?" The answer was, "Well, sir, I don't think I love anyone." At this the Master exclaimed: "Oh, what a dry rascal! Fall either into one pit or the other — into the pit of filth or into the pit of gold!" But who is foolish enough to want to fall into the pit of filth?

Advice to the Householders

Can one give up the householder's life, even though it is no longer appealing, when one has a wife and children? What then will be their fate? It is selfishness, pure and simple. To be in the world and maintain a family, to fulfill one's duties — certainly this too is religion. Nothing is gained by suddenly giving up everything. One cannot climb to the roof at one bound. One must ascend step by step. Sri Ramakrishna used to say: "A fruit picked before maturity rots and becomes spoiled. A sore bleeds if you take away the scab too soon, but it drops off by itself when the sore is healed." What fine illustrations these are! Everything depends on the mind alone. If one happened to be married but later regretted it and informed Sri Ramakrishna of his intention to embrace the monastic life, the Master would say: "Wait. Don't give up the world. If you are sincere, everything will fall into place. You only have to pursue faithfully the course laid down in the scriptures."

Sri Ramakrishna used to tell us about a man named Mukherji, who had left his home and had come to Dakshineswar. He used to pass his days at the Kali temple, living on the food regularly given there. One day the Master said to him: "You are a married man. Do you have children?" On being answered in the affirmative, he next inquired as to who was looking after them. As soon as he heard from Mukherji's lips that his wife was pining away at her father's place, he shouted: "You rogue. You were the man who married and who had children, and now they must be fed and clothed by your father-in-law! And here you are living on food that is meant for the poor!" Hearing these words Mukherji went home and began to look after his household duties with zeal.

Sri Ramakrishna would also tell us the parable of a woman in love. She attends to all her household duties, but her thoughts are on her lover. When in this way her whole mind is on her lover, she breaks the family ties and follows the man of her heart. Isn't it a beautiful parable? Work with one hand and serve the Lord with the other. When the time comes, one will be able to serve him with both hands. And the time does come if one is sincere.

Once a gentleman came to Sri Ramakrishna from Jabbalpur. He was a scholar, an M.A., and was very frank, but he had an agnostic turn of mind, so he had much discussion with the Master. He confessed that he had great mental unrest, but he would not pray to God, because, as he said, there was no proof of his existence! Sri Ramakrishna said to him, "Well, I suppose you have no objection to praying like this: 'If thou really art, then listen to my prayer.' If you pray like this, it will do you good." The gentleman thought it over and then said he had no objection to that sort of prayer. Sri Ramakrishna asked him to follow this advice and come to him again. Some time later the gentleman returned, and he was a changed man. Touching the Master's feet, he wept as he said, "You have saved me!"

After M.'s eldest son died, his wife came to Sri Ramakrishna weeping bitterly. I was there. Seeing her weep so much, Sri Ramakrishna said to her sternly: "At other times you talk of knowledge, devotion, etc. Where are those things now? Have they vanished?" His words greatly appealed to me. Often if one speaks sternly to a person in grief or sorrow, it is very effective. The influence of tamas goes away at once.

If anyone lost or misplaced anything, Sri Ramakrishna would be very annoyed. Once Hazra lost a towel in the Ganga. At this Sri Ramakrishna was very displeased and said to him: "I am often beyond the normal plane of consciousness, yet I have never lost anything. And you are so forgetful!" The Master kept everything in his room in perfect order. Every object had its proper place so that even in the dark he could find what he wanted. An orderly mind is as necessary as external order.

Man is entirely absorbed in sense enjoyments. Eating, sleeping, and sexual pleasure — in these he spends his whole life. Sri Ramakrishna used to say: "Many rice merchants place parched rice at the front entrance to keep rats from entering the storerooms. As soon as the rats come, they eat the parched rice instead of the bags of rice inside. The rats do not even smell the rice in the storerooms. In the same way, the Divine Mother has kept man deluded with many tempting things — lust and gold. Man cannot go beyond them and get to the rice bags — i.e., God. This world is like a labyrinth. Once one enters it, one finds it difficult to get out. With human birth there comes an opportunity to escape. But of what avail is it? Man forgets all, busying himself with things pertaining to the senses." Sri Ramakrishna did not have much regard for people who were immersed in sex. He said that they had lost all substance.

The Master used to say: "The hog-plum is all peel and stone. It has no pulp and causes colic when eaten. But it does have an attractive taste. So is this world." Where is happiness in the world? It is full of suffering, an abode of misery. Sri Krishna said to Arjuna, "Those who take refuge in me alone, cross over this maya."

Rather than smearing the body with mud only to undergo the trouble of washing it off, isn't it better to stay away from mud? But how many can do that? So Sri Ramakrishna would often say that it is better to have a little worldly enjoyment. But then it must be accompanied with due discrimination. Through this cycle of birth and death one gradually moves towards God.

Divine love must be awakened within the heart and be intensified and crystallized. Only then does the vision of God open up. Take for instance the life of Gopaler-ma [a woman disciple of Sri Ramakrishna, who had a continuous vision of Gopala, Lord Krishna as a child]. She would see Gopala accompanying her and gathering fuel for her. And Sri Ramakrishna used to have visions of Ramlala [the child Rama] walking and playing with him. Oh, how wonderful was the Master's play with the brass image of Ramlala! When he spoke to us of these strange happenings, we understood little. Once Ramlala went frolicking in the Ganga to bathe and he got into deep water. Sri Ramakrishna asked him to come out, and when he refused the Master gave him a slap on the cheek. Another time, the Master wept bitterly, saying: "He who was fed with butter and cream by Mother Kaushalya was offered unclean puffed rice by me!" We were dumbstruck with wonder. Intense devotion for God is the important thing in spiritual life. What does it matter whether one worships him as formless or with form?

Girish Chandra Ghosh and Other Devotees

Even a man like Girish Babu was accepted by Sri Ramakrishna. The Master could mix with all types of people. We try to mould everyone according to our own ideas, but he took each person from where he was and pushed him forward. He never disappointed anyone by failing to mould them according to their own light. He had a unique relationship with each devotee and maintained it through the years. Often he would teach them through humour. Ah, what a teacher! Where can one find another like him?

Girish Babu used to say: "My younger brother would walk, taking hold of my father's hand, but I used to sit on his lap. I would say all sorts of things to Sri Ramakrishna, but he was never displeased with me. Often when I was dreadfully intoxicated, I would go to him. Even then he would receive me cordially and say to Latu: 'See if there is anything in the carriage. If he wants to drink here, how can I provide it?' He knew there must be a bottle in the carriage. Then he would gaze into my eyes and completely destroy the effect of the intoxication. I would say, 'Why, you have spoiled the effect of a whole bottle!' He used to inquire about the past of each person who came to him, but he never asked me anything about my past life. Nevertheless, I told him the whole story. He never forbade me to do anything. Is it for nothing that I adore him so much?"

Sri Ramakrishna used to say, "If a water snake bites a frog, it produces no effect, but if the frog is bitten by a cobra the poor thing expires before it can croak thrice."

There were few sins in which Girish Babu had not indulged. He once said to us, "I have drunk so much wine in my life that if the wine bottles were placed one upon another, they would stand as high as Mount Everest." He was a poet, so he spoke poetically like that. Truly speaking, he did drink a lot. When he was asked by the Master to repeat the name of God morning and evening, he refused to do so. He said: "I am not sure I can do it. I do not know in what condition or where I may be at those hours." Then Sri Ramakrishna asked him to remember God before meals. "That also I cannot promise you," replied Girish Babu. "I am often engrossed in lawsuits and have to attend to all sorts of things. I can't even do that." At this Sri Ramakrishna said, "Then give me the power of attorney."

Referring to this conversation later, Girish Babu said to us: "I readily agreed to give him the power of attorney, but later on I realized how difficult it was. I had told him I wouldn't be able to repeat the name of God even once in the evening, but afterwards I found I could not do the least bit of work without remembering him at every step."

In one day Girish Babu gave up his fifteen-year habit of taking opium. He said the first three days he suffered tremendously; his entire body became inert. By the fourth day though he was all right. Later in life he did not even smoke.

Sri Ramakrishna was knowledgeable on a variety of subjects. Girish Babu once said to him, "You are my superior in every respect — even in wicked things." At this the Master said: "No, no, it is not so. Here [*meaning himself*] there are no samskaras [past impressions]. There is a world of difference between knowing something by actual experience and learning about it through study or observation. Experience leaves impressions on the mind which are very difficult to get rid of. This is not the case with knowledge through study or observation."

Once Girish Babu asked the Master, "Why do you have to practise so hard?" The Master replied: "You know, there is eternal union of Hara

[Shiva] with Gauri. Still, why did she practise so much austerity? It was
to set an example for others. If I do so much, others will do at least
one-sixteenth part of it. Isn't that so?"

The Master once said to Girish: "What are you saying about knowledge of Brahman! Shukadeva saw and touched the Ocean of Brahman.
And Shiva drank only three handfuls of Its water and became a shava
[corpse]." Girish Ghosh clasped his head and exclaimed: "Stop, sir, say
no more. My head is reeling."

A householder devotee once had a wonderful experience. He had
freely drunk and was very excited. Stopping his carriage before a house
of ill repute, he went upstairs. But at the top of the staircase he found Sri
Ramakrishna standing in front of the door! He fled in shame. Unless God
saves us, there is no way out. Blessed are those who have no evil
tendencies in their minds. They alone are saved. None can escape this
attraction by personal exertion. But as Sri Ramakrishna used to say, "If
you are sincere, Mother will set everything right."

Generally, people try to show their good side. They want to make a
good impression, rather than trying to be good themselves. The first
thing we learned from Sri Ramakrishna was to pay no attention to the
opinion of others. He used to say: "Spit on public opinion! Look towards
God and try to please him!" Swamiji was also like that.

Vishnu [a devotee of Sri Ramakrishna] would meditate with great
absorption. As soon as the Master touched him, however, he would
wake up and gaze at him. Nityagopal [a devotee of Sri Ramakrishna]
used to live in ecstasy all the time. The Master used to tell him: "Don't
be so intense! You have to keep your mind down enough to live with
other people." Nityagopal attained a very high state. His body would
become luminous. It seemed as though he had no tamas [lethargy] in
him. In his company I learned forbearance. We used to pass the whole
night meditating and chanting the Lord's name in places like Kalighat,
Beadon Square Gardens, the College Square, and other parks of Calcutta.
The Master used to say that Nityagopal had attained the state of a
paramahamsa [the highest state of consciousness]. I can frankly say that
at any time I can raise myself to that state and forget the world.

At Calcutta and Cossipore

One day Mathur Babu was returning to Jan Bazar in his deluxe
phaeton [a light four-wheeled carriage], bringing Sri Ramakrishna with
him. When the carriage reached Chitpore Road the Master had a wonderful vision. He felt that he had become Sita, and that Ravana was
kidnapping him. Seized by this idea, he merged into samadhi. Just then
the horses tore loose from their reins and stumbled and fell. Mathur Babu

could not understand the reason for such a mishap. When Sri Rama-krishna returned to normal consciousness, Mathur told him about the accident with the horses. Sri Ramakrishna then said that while in ecstasy he perceived that Ravana was kidnapping him, and that Jatayu [the great bird who had attempted to rescue Sita] was attacking Ravana's chariot and trying to destroy it. After hearing this story, Mathur Babu said, "Father, how difficult it is even to go with you through the street!"

One day Sri Ramakrishna came to Balaram mandir [Balaram's Cal-cutta residence] from Dakshineswar. He took his seat in the hall where the devotees had also assembled. Desiring to test the omniscience of the Master, Balaram Babu brought one full plate of sandesh [sweets] and placed it in front of him. Beforehand he had earmarked the sweets mentally: this one for the Master; this one for Naren; this one for Baburam; this one for Rakhal, etc. The Master took the very one which Balaram Babu, in his mind, had reserved for him. And thus Balaram Babu's doubt was dispelled.

Our Master visited Balaram's house many times. One day he was illustrating his teachings with some very apt tales. I was surprised at the spontaneity with which these stories cropped up in his talk, and I asked, "Sir, do you prepare your similes before you go out?" He said: "No. Mother is always present. Wherever I am, Mother supplies me with ideas."

I was reading about Hirananda's life today, and I liked it very much. He, too, was a disciple of Sri Ramakrishna and was loved by the Master. During the Master's last illness, Hirananda came from Sindh to see him. He brought some sweets and loose trousers for Sri Ramakrishna, who wore the trousers for a day. One day the Master set up a debate between Hirananda and Swamiji. Swamiji spoke from the standpoint of knowl-edge, while Hirananda spoke from the standpoint of devotion. He did not do well. He was also a disciple of Keshab Babu.

One day Sri Ramakrishna talked about his disease. He was asked if he felt pain in his throat, and he answered: "What foolishness! The body does not become spiritual! It is the mind that becomes holy!"

A man may have Spartan fortitude. He may be able to bear physical suffering patiently, and he may hide his suffering. That is nothing. But when a man knows his pain is of the body, not of the Atman, then he is able to keep his mind detached from disease and suffering, and he lives immersed in the consciousness of God.

I heard a beautiful story about Holy Mother, which she herself told. After the passing away of Sri Ramakrishna she was crying, when he appeared before her and said: "Why do you cry? Do you think I am gone? Here I am! I have, as it were, passed from one room to another — that's all. You may not see me physically, but you *know* in many ways that I exist."

Sri Ramakrishna's Philosophy

In one of the Puranas [narratives amplifying the scriptural truths declared in the Vedas] it is written that the divine forms remain even after the universe is dissolved. Sri Ramakrishna used to say that there are places in the ocean where the ice never melts. It seems to me that in this state one worships God in his eternal form after the realization of both his personal and impersonal aspects. Here the ice does not melt because the rays of the sun do not enter. We never knew of these things until we came to Sri Ramakrishna. His words were scripture. He taught more than even the scriptures do. But he himself used to say that everything he taught could be found in our scriptures.

Shankara taught only one aspect: the way to freedom, or nirvana. Our Master first made a person free, and then taught him how to live in the world. His touch could make one free. But those who follow his instructions, also attain freedom. His words had such shakti [power]. Be free first. Do away with name and form and the entire universe. Then see Mother in all. Be her playfellow. We don't care for nirvana. We want to serve the Lord. We have touched the granny and cannot be made thieves again. When life is painful we go to Mother, and thinking of her brings peace.

Sri Ramakrishna taught using simple examples from everyday life. Because of this, we are constantly reminded of him. He taught us to see Mother in everything — in trees, in flowers, in insects, in human beings. Whether living or dead, we are always in Mother. Realize this and remember it constantly. Then the world cannot taint us. How difficult life is without her. With her, however, it becomes easy. With her, we are fearless.

How inspiring is *The Gospel of Sri Ramakrishna!* It always seems new. As one reads it, one feels like calling on the Lord.

The Master used to tell us: "First tie the knot of nondual knowledge in the corner of your cloth; then do as you please. And adore him." That is to say, first know him to be your innermost Self — the life of your life, the eye of your eye — and then devote yourself to him.

Sri Ramakrishna used to repeat: "Not I, not I, O Lord! Thou, thou alone! I am thy servant." A devotee must completely renounce his ego.

It is not possible to have a clear conception of God all at once. Listen to our words. Reflect on them. Then one day in a flash of illumination you will realize for yourself the truth of our words. We also had to pass through some doubts about God. Studying the scriptures made us even more confused. Then Sri Ramakrishna taught us the truth which we later experienced for ourselves in a burst of realization. Now we are established in it.

Sri Ramakrishna used to say that for him there was no mukti [liberation]. I heard this from his own lips. Mukti here means nirvana-mukti — that is, upon attaining this liberation, one does not have to be reborn in the world. The jivakotis [ordinary beings], sorely afflicted by the miseries of this world, do not want to be reborn. They seek to escape from these miseries once and for all. That is why they strive for liberation.

How is nirvana possible for him who, afflicted by the sufferings of jivas, must repeatedly come to this world? This is why Sri Ramakrishna said that for him there would be no liberation. Again, Sri Ramakrishna said to Swami Vivekananda, "He who was Rama and Krishna is now Ramakrishna in this body, but not from the standpoint of your Vedanta." The point stressed here is that the Advaita school of Vedanta holds jiva and Brahman to be one. Some take this to mean that everyone is equal to Rama and Krishna, and that they (Rama and Krishna) have no distinctive qualities. Lest Swamiji misinterpret the saying, "He who was Rama and Krishna is now Ramakrishna in this body," Sri Ramakrishna qualified this statement with the words, "not from the standpoint of your Vedanta." That is to say, the consciousness of Sri Ramakrishna was the consciousness of Ishvara and not that of the jiva. According to Advaita, the jiva can attain the knowledge of his identity with Brahman by removing his ignorance through spiritual practices culminating in samadhi. Yet, despite all imaginable efforts, the jiva can never become Ishvara. He who is Ishvara is eternally the Ishvara. Even when he assumes a human body and appears like a jiva, he remains the same Ishvara and does not become the jiva.

Those who profess to be the children of the Master must have yoga, bhakti, karma, jnana — nay, everything. For Sri Ramakrishna stands for the synthesis and harmony of all religious paths. In the past, the rule was to follow one particular path for spiritual growth. But now one needs an all-round development combined with a magnanimity of heart to love others.

A Letter by Swami Turiyananda

Dear Sharvananda,

I received your letter some time ago, but I could not write to you until now because I was ill. Though the subject [*What is Sri Ramakrishna's Philosophy*] is extremely difficult, with the Lord's grace, I will try my best to answer your questions.

It is not so easy to speak about Sri Ramakrishna's philosophy. It seems to me that to encourage the followers of all religions, he declared, "As many faiths so many paths." He made this statement after he himself practised disciplines of various religious paths and experienced that their paths lead to the same Truth.

The ultimate Truth is one and nondual. It is called by various names: Brahman, Paramatman, Bhagavan [Lord], God, and so on. Whoever has realized that Truth has tried to express it according to his own temperament and understanding by giving it a particular name. But nobody has been able to express the *whole* truth. "What he is, he is" — that is the final conclusion of those who have realized him.

From different standpoints, Gaudapada's doctrine of no creation, Shankara's doctrine of superimposition, Ramanuja's doctrine of transformation, and [Sri Kantha's] doctrine of Shivadvaita — each one of these is true. Again, apart from all these doctrines, he is beyond all human expression and beyond the cognition of mind. The founders of all these philosophical systems practised austerities, and having received God's grace, they preached the various doctrines at his command. God is the subject from which these doctrines evolved, but he himself is beyond them. To express this truth is the philosophy of Sri Ramakrishna. That is what I think.

Hanuman said to Rama: "O Lord, while I identify myself with the body I am your servant. When I consider myself as an individual soul, I am a part of you. And when I look upon myself as the Atman, I am one with you — this is my firm conviction." Sri Ramakrishna referred to this statement as the best conclusion of different phases of spiritual experience.

Why should it not be possible to see the worship vessels as Brahman, saturated with consciousness? [*This is a reference to Sri Ramakrishna's vision in the Kali temple, where it was revealed to him that everything is Pure Spirit.*] "Throughout the universe he exists, pervading every being and thing, animate and inanimate." There is nothing but he. He verily is all. Because we cannot see him we see objects instead, but the fact is that he is everything. Names and forms originate from him and remain in him. The waves, the foam, the bubbles — they are all nothing but water. Who cares if your doctrine of superimposition stands or falls! He who has known this truth [that Brahman is all] cannot be content with a lesser standpoint.

The Master used to experience a state beyond all thought and idea. That state transcends name and form, words and mind. There exists only One without a second, beyond the realm of prakriti [that is, beyond relativity]. Where is the doctrine of superimposition or the doctrine of no creation in that realm of Oneness? And yet again, all doctrines — whether of superimposition, or of no creation, or of transformation, etc. — originate from him.

He alone is the Reality, the Truth. And again he is the source of all individual beings and of the universe. This manifestation is also true if he is not forgotten. Name and form become unreal if we forget God, because they cannot exist without him. [*Sri Ramakrishna said: "Zeros added together amount to zero. Place the digit one before them, and they add in value." The digit one is God.*] But if he dwells in our thoughts, only then can we understand the truth that "the pith belongs to the sheaths and the sheaths belong to the pith." [*A reference to Sri Ramakrishna's saying that as long as the plantain tree contains sheaths, it also contains pith. He was illustrating the point that while God keeps the "ego of a devotee" in a person, the Relative (the sheaths) is real as well as the Absolute (the pith).*] At that time one can understand these sayings of the Gita: "All things in this universe are pervaded by Me" (9.4); "All is strung on Me as a row of gems on a thread" (7.7).

The *main thing* is we must see him. When we see him, everything else disappears. One experiences him as everything. Before we see him we have doubts and confusion, and all sorts of theories and controversies. But these cease to exist as soon as we see him. Then one experiences uninterrupted peace and bliss.

Sri Ramakrishna's philosophy therefore is: In whatever way and at any cost we must attain God. The Master said, "Tie the nondual knowledge in the corner of your cloth and then do as you please." This means: Once you attain him, it does not matter which doctrine your temperament bids you to uphold. Liberation is assured when you know him. Then there is no more bondage. After death, whether you take another body or not depends upon your wish.

The seekers of nirvana [final liberation] consider this world a dream. They merge their minds in the impersonal aspect of Brahman and become one with It. And the devotees who are attached to the Personal God, consider this world a manifestation of God's power. They attach themselves to the Lord, who is Existence-Knowledge-Bliss Absolute. They are not afraid to be born again and again. They consider themselves to be playmates of God, and they come to the world to join his divine play. They delight in the Atman and at the same time remain devoted to God. They covet nothing in this world. They even refuse to accept nirvana if it is offered to them. That is enough for today.

Varanasi   Turiyananda
April 18, 1919

[From: *Swami Turiyanander Patra* (Calcutta: Udbodhan Office), 1963; *Prabuddha Bharata*, 1924, 1925, 1930, 1974; *Spiritual Talks*, by The First Disciples of Sri Ramakrishna (Calcutta: Advaita Ashrama), 1968; *Swami Turiyananda*, by Swami Ritajananda (Madras: Sri Ramakrishna Math), 1963; *Udbodhan*, vol. 49, no. 10, 1942; *Vedanta and the West* (Hollywood: Vedanta Press), nos. 123, 130, 131, 132, 145, 151; *Vedanta Kesari* (Madras: Sri Ramakrishna Math), September 1951; *With the Swamis In America*, by A Western Disciple (Mayavati: Advaita Ashrama), 1946]

12

Swami Abhedananda

Swami Abhedananda (1866-1939) met Sri Ramakrishna in 1884. His premonastic name was Kali Prasad Chandra. He was very devoted to the Master and served as one of his attendants during his last illness. After the Master's passing away he became an itinerant monk and travelled to various parts of India. In 1896 Swami Vivekananda asked him to carry on the Vedanta work in England and America, which he did for the next twenty-five years. He returned to India in 1921 and soon afterwards founded the Ramakrishna Vedanta Math to propagate the message of Vedanta in Calcutta. He was a great scholar and wrote many books.

First Meeting with Sri Ramakrishna

My father once told me about a hatha yogi who was immersed in samadhi in the deep forest of Sunderban, near the coast of the Bay of Bengal. Hearing about him brought a desire to my mind to remain in samadhi by practising yoga, and I became restless to find a guru who could teach me yoga. I confided my desire to my classmate Yajneshwar Bhattacharya, who was very fond of me. Yajneshwar told me: "I know a wonderful yogi. His name is Sri Ramakrishna Paramahamsa, and he lives in Rani Rasmani's temple garden in Dakshineswar. He has no pretensions. Many respectable people visit him, and he sometimes comes to Calcutta. Perhaps he can fulfill your desire to learn yoga." My joy knew no bounds when I heard this from Yajneshwar, and I at once resolved to meet Sri Ramakrishna, though I had no idea where Dakshineswar was.

One Sunday morning I started for Dakshineswar by asking directions from people on the street. I crossed the Baghbazar bridge and walked north on the Barrackpore trunk road. It was quite a distance. I then asked a person on the road about the temple garden of Dakshineswar. He told me: "You have gone the wrong way. The Kali temple is on the bank of the Ganga." At last I reached the temple garden at eleven o'clock. When

Swami Abhedananda in America

I asked about Sri Ramakrishna, a temple worker informed me that he had gone to Calcutta that morning. I was exhausted, having walked all that way barefoot in the sun. Disappointed, I sat on the steps of Sri Ramakrishna's northern verandah and wondered how I could ever go back to Calcutta. I was hungry and thirsty, I was dead tired, I had no money, I had not informed my family as to where I was going, I had no acquaintance in Dakshineswar, and moreover I had no strength to walk back to Calcutta. I began to cry.

Just then another young man arrived and asked me about Sri Ramakrishna, and I told him that he had gone to Calcutta. The young man was also disappointed. We then talked and got acquainted with each other. On inquiry I learned that his name was Shashi [later, Swami Ramakrishnananda]. He advised me about my circumstances, saying, "Have a bath in the Ganga, take prasad, and then return to Calcutta after a rest." Later in the afternoon, when I expressed my intention to return to Calcutta, Shashi told me: "You should not return home without seeing the Master. Is there any certainty that such an opportunity will come again in your lifetime? Since you have come to see him with so much difficulty, it is better for you to wait." I knew my parents would be worried about me because I had not told them where I was going. Understanding how I felt, Shashi said to me: "Look, brother, I have also come here without informing my parents. Don't worry. We shall stay here tonight. The Master will positively return from Calcutta by late evening, as he never stays overnight at any devotee's house in Calcutta."

Shashi showed me around and in the evening took me to the Kali temple to attend the vesper service. I felt tremendous peace and joy. Ramlal, the Master's nephew, gave us some luchis [fried bread] and sweets for refreshments. We waited on the northern verandah for the Master's arrival. Finally a horse carriage arrived at the northeastern corner of the Master's room, and Shashi and Ramlal went to receive the Master. My heart was beating hard. I stood where I was, motionless. After getting down from the carriage, Sri Ramakrishna said, "Kali, Kali, Kali," entered his room, and sat on his small cot.

Ramlal and Shashi informed the Master about me while I waited on the verandah. Then Ramlal came out and said that the Master was waiting for me. I entered the room and bowed down to him. The Master asked about me and I told him: "I have a desire to learn yoga. Will you kindly teach me?" The Master kept quiet for a while and then said: "It is a good sign that you have a desire to learn yoga at this young age. You were a yogi in your previous life. A little was left for perfection. This will be your last birth. Yes, I shall teach you yoga. Rest tonight and come to me again tomorrow morning."

The next morning Ramlal told me the Master was waiting to see me. Entering his room I bowed down to him. He then asked me what I was studying, and I replied, "I am now in the entrance class [i.e., tenth grade]." "Very good," said the Master. Then he took me to the northern verandah. He asked me to sit on a cot. When I was seated in the lotus posture, the Master asked me to stick out my tongue. As soon as I did that, he wrote a mantram on it with the middle finger of his right hand and advised me to meditate on Kali, the Divine Mother. I did what he said. Gradually I lost outer consciousness and sat in deep meditation. I felt an unspeakable joy within. I don't know how long I stayed in that condition. After some time the Master touched my chest and brought me back to outer consciousness. He then asked me what had happened, and I told him about my blissful experience during meditation. He was very pleased. Afterwards the Master instructed me on meditation and sang these lines of a mystical song:

> When will you sleep in the divine chamber
> With the clean [good] and the unclean [evil]?
> When these two wives are friendly to each other,
> Mother Shyama will be within your reach.

The Master further told me to meditate every morning and again at night and to report to him my visions and spiritual experiences. Then the Master asked me to go to the Kali temple and meditate there. When I returned from the temple the Master gave me prasad and asked me to visit him again. He even offered to provide my fare if I could not get it from home. In the meantime a devotee had arrived by carriage from Calcutta to visit the Master, and the Master asked me to return home with that devotee. On my way back home I thought of the Master's overwhelming love and compassion. I arrived home before noon, and my parents were exceedingly happy to see me.

Days with Sri Ramakrishna

After my first visit I felt an irresistible attraction for the Master. Sometimes I would feel that the Master was drawing me. During my meditations at night I was having various kinds of visions. One day I told my father of my desire to visit the Master, but he locked the main door of our house so that I could not get out. Later in the afternoon, however, I found the door open, and I ran to the Ahiritola ghat [in West Calcutta] and went to Dakshineswar by boat. Seeing me, the Master was pleased. He listened to the report of my spiritual experiences and said: "You are doing well. Continue it." That night I stayed at Dakshineswar.

After that, whenever I went to Dakshineswar I would give personal service to the Master. I would carry his towel and water pot when he went to the pine grove to answer the calls of nature. Sometimes the Master would walk around the Panchavati with his hand on my shoulder. I also went with the Master to Girish Ghosh's Star Theatre to see the *Chaitanya Lila* and *Prahlad Charitra* plays. Every Saturday and Sunday devotees would gather at Dakshineswar to see the Master. I also began visiting him on Saturday afternoons, returning to Calcutta the following day with some devotees. Thus I became acquainted with other disciples of the Master.

I felt immense bliss in my heart when I heard Sri Ramakrishna's teachings. When in ecstasy, he would sometimes laugh, sometimes cry, sometimes dance, and sometimes go into samadhi. Again at other times he would joyously sing in his melodious voice the songs of Ramprasad, Kamalakanta, and other mystic composers. Occasionally he would sing kirtan depicting Radha and Krishna's divine play in Vrindaban. Sometimes while describing the divine play of Rama and Sita, he would, like the great saint Tulasidasa, float in an ocean of bliss. The spirit of the harmony of religions was reflected in Sri Ramakrishna's everyday life, and he constantly taught his followers the liberal, universal message, "As many faiths, so many paths."

Sri Ramakrishna also taught us to chant the name of God, "Hari-bol, Hari-bol," loudly while clapping our hands. When somebody asked him the reason for clapping the hands, he said: "As the birds of the tree fly away when one claps one's hands loudly, so the sinful thoughts of the mind go away when one chants God's name while clapping one's hands." In Dakshineswar we observed that every evening the Master would sit on his bed facing the north and repeat aloud "Hari-bol, Hari-bol" while clapping his hands. Sometimes he would repeat thus: "Hari is my guru, my guru is Hari." "O Krishna, O Krishna." "O Govinda, you are my life and soul." "Not I, not I — but Thou, Thou." "I am an instrument, you are the operator." Then he would go into ecstasy. In that state he would importune Mother Kali, but his words would not be audible to us. Watching his God-intoxicated state we were amazed. We felt that the Master was in communion with the Divine Mother, that he was talking to her, and that the Mother was answering his questions. We realized that Sri Ramakrishna was not a human being. He was God.

Sri Ramakrishna taught us to practise japam and meditation every morning and evening. About meditation, he sometimes referred to his naked guru Tota Puri's illustration, telling us, "Tota used to say that if a brass water pot is not cleaned every day, stain accumulates on it, and that likewise, if the mind is not cleansed by meditation every day, impurities accumulate in it."

Sometimes while teaching us, the Master would tell us about his own sadhana. He said: "When I meditated I became like a motionless stone image. Sometimes birds sat on my head, but I could not feel them." In fact, during deep meditation, when the mind becomes still and motionless, one does not notice if flies or mosquitoes sit on the body. The Master used to say that this is a sign of a concentrated mind.

Towards the End of the Journey

At the time of the car festival of Jagannath [July 14, 1885] I visited the Master at Balaram Basu's house in Calcutta. Many devotees were present and Vaishnav Charan sang kirtan:

O tongue, always repeat the name of Mother Durga!
Who but your Mother Durga will save you in distress? . . .

As soon as Sri Ramakrishna heard a line or two of the song he went into samadhi. Then the Master sang, "O Mother, for Yashoda thou wouldst dance when she called thee her precious 'Blue Jewel' . . . "

In the meantime a small decorated chariot of Lord Jagannath [Krishna] had been brought to the upper verandah, and the Master pulled it along with the devotees. While pulling the chariot the Master sang:

Behold, the two brothers [Gauranga and Nityananda] have come,
Who weep while chanting Hari's name. . . .

He sang again:

See how all Nadia [birthplace of Gauranga] is shaking
Under the waves of Gauranga's love! . . .

It was a divine sight! The Master sang and danced in ecstasy, and the devotees joined him. Afterwards the Master sat in the big hall and told Pandit Shashadhar: "This is called *bhajanananda*, or the bliss derived from the worship of God. Worldly people enjoy pleasure derived from lust and gold, and devotees attain the bliss of Brahman through the worship of God."

Thus the devotees passed joyful days with the Master. One day when I went to Dakshineswar I learned that the Master had a sore throat. Like a child he was showing his throat to everybody, and he was trying to follow whatever advice was given to him. He was fond of ice cream, and it was a hot summer. A devotee had recently given the Master a large can of ice cream, and the Master had thoroughly enjoyed it, but as a result, a sore in his throat had developed. Moreover, the pain gradually increased, and he could not get any relief from it. He had great difficulty in swallowing, eating, and talking.

One day Golap-ma said to the Master: "Dr. Durga Charan of Calcutta is a reputable physician. Perhaps he can find some remedy for you." Immediately the Master agreed to visit him. That night I stayed at Dakshineswar. Latu and Golap-ma were also there. The next morning the Master, Golap-ma, Latu, and I went to Calcutta by boat. Landing there, we rented a horse carriage and reached the doctor's office at Beadon Square. Out of his mercy the Master asked me to sit next to him, and Golap-ma and Latu sat on the opposite seat.

The doctor examined the Master's throat and prescribed some medications. Then we went to the Ahiritola ghat and rented a boat for Dakshineswar. It was about 1:30 P.M. and none of us had had any food. The Master was hungry. He asked the boatman to anchor the boat at Baranagore ghat and then asked me to buy some sweets from a nearby market. Golap-ma had four pice with her which she gave me. I immediately went to the market and bought some chanar murki [small sweet cheese balls]. The Master took the packet of sweets from my hand and joyfully ate them all. He then threw the empty packet into the Ganga and drank some water from the river with his hands. He showed his satisfaction. The Master knew that the three of us were hungry, but without sharing any sweets he had eaten everything. It was amazing though that as soon as he showed his satisfaction, our own stomachs felt full. We looked at each other silently. Then the Master smiled and like a boy began to make jokes — continuing all the way to Dakshineswar. We all got out of the boat, and later the three of us discussed among ourselves what had happened and realized that it was a miracle.

Such an event occurred when Krishna was alive and enacted his divine play. When the five Pandavas and their wife Draupadi were living in the forest during their exile, the sage Durvasa went to their cottage with his twelve hundred disciples and asked for food. According to the custom guests had to be fed, for otherwise it would be very inauspicious. Durvasa and his disciples went to the river for a bath, and while they were gone, the helpless Draupadi called on Krishna to come to the rescue. Krishna came and asked Draupadi for some food. There was nothing but a few particles of rice and a little spinach at the bottom of a cooking vessel. Krishna ate this and drank a glass of water and by doing so, filled the stomachs of Durvasa and his disciples. So it is said, "If God is pleased the whole world becomes pleased." That day I realized this truth by observing Sri Ramakrishna's life.

Almost every year Sri Ramakrishna would go to the Flattened Rice Festival at Panihati. In 1885, in spite of his sore throat, he decided to attend the festival. A boat was rented, and Latu and I, as well as some other devotees, accompanied the Master. Arriving at Panihati, the Master joined the kirtan party and became absorbed in bhava samadhi. He sang and danced in ecstasy. It was a wonderful sight! In the evening we all returned to Dakshineswar by boat. The Master's sore throat was aggravated from exposure during the journey.

In September 1885 Sri Ramakrishna had to be moved from Dakshineswar to 55 Shyampukur Street, Calcutta, for treatment of throat cancer. The Master lived there for three months. Golap-ma took the responsibility of cooking for the Master and his attendants. Then later, with the Master's consent, Holy Mother came to Shyampukur so that she could serve him. At that time I left home in order to serve the Master on a full-time basis.

One day the Master was in deep samadhi, seated on his bed like a wooden statue. He had no outer consciousness. Dr. Mahendralal Sarkar checked his pulse and felt no throbbing. He then put his stethoscope on the Master's heart and did not get a heartbeat. Next, Dr. Sarkar touched the Master's eyeballs with his finger, but still the Master's outer consciousness did not return. The doctor was dumbfounded. After some time the Master returned to the normal plane of consciousness and began talking about God with the doctor.

It may be asked why the Master had cancer. It is really difficult to answer this question. Once while staying at the Shyampukur house the Master said: "The Divine Mother has shown me that people are getting rid of their sins by touching my feet. I am absorbing the results of their sinful actions, so I am suffering from this terrible cancer." This is called "vicarious atonement." Jesus Christ also suffered this way in his life. One day Narendra [Swami Vivekananda] remarked: "All this will appear like a dream in our lives. Only its memory will remain with us." Narendra's words are still ringing in my ears.

Sri Ramakrishna at the Cossipore Garden House

At Shyampukur, the Master's cancer, instead of abating under the treatment of Dr. Mahendralal Sarkar, began to increase more and more. The doctors then advised that he be moved to the country. After searching for a place, the devotees found a spacious garden house at Cossipore. They rented it for eighty rupees per month, and on December 11, 1885, the Master was taken there. He was accompanied by Holy Mother, Golap-ma, Lakshmi, and his young attendants. One day the Master told us: "This cancer in my throat is a ruse. It is because of this that you have gathered together."

In the beginning two or three of us would look after and nurse the Master. Holy Mother would prepare his special diet, and Golap-ma and Lakshmi would help her. Golap-ma would also cook for the attendants. But gradually the number of attendants increased, so a brahmin cook and a maidservant were hired.

After a few days at Cossipore the Master felt a little relief. The large room on the upper floor of the house was used as the Master's bedroom. To the south of that was an open terrace over the portico. Standing on the open terrace, the Master used to gaze at the trees and creepers of the garden. The fresh air of the place proved to be beneficial for his health, and this raised hopes in the minds of the devotees that he might completely recover.

There were two ponds at the Cossipore garden house, and there were plenty of fish in both of them. One day Narendra said, "Come, let's catch fish from this pond." I got ready. While living at home, I had learned angling. Niranjan also came and the three of us went fishing. Narendra and Niranjan did not have much experience in angling, so by the time they had caught one fish I had caught four or five. News of my angling skill reached the Master. One evening while I was serving him, the Master asked me, "Is it true that you have been catching many fish with a fishing rod?" "Yes, sir," I replied. The Master said, "It is a sin to catch fish with a fishing rod, for thereby living beings are killed."

In defense I quoted from the Gita: "He who thinks that the Atman [Self] is the slayer as well as he who thinks that the Atman is slain is ignorant, for the Atman neither slays nor is slain." Then I added, "So why should it be a sin to catch fish?"

The Master smiled and tried to make me understand through various arguments. He said, "When a person attains true knowledge, he does not take a false step." All of a sudden the Master began coughing, and there was a trace of blood in his sputum. I was frightened. I told him: "Sir, if you talk it will aggravate your disease. Please do not talk anymore." Then the all-merciful Master said to me: "I consider you to be one of the most intelligent of the boys. You will understand if you meditate on what I have said."

I then took leave of him, and according to his instructions I began to meditate. After three days I realized the meaning behind the Master's advice. I went to him and said: "Sir, I have now realized why it is wrong to catch fish. I shall not do it again. Please forgive me." The Master was very pleased to hear this. He said: "It is deceitful to catch fish in this way.

To hide the hook inside the bait and to hide the poison in the food offered to an invited guest are sins of the same kind." I humbly accepted what the Master said and felt his infinite compassion for me. He further said: "It is true that the Atman does not die nor is it killed. But he who has realized this truth is the Atman himself, so why should he have the tendency to kill others? As long as the tendency to kill remains, he is not identified with the Atman nor does he have any Self-knowledge. That is why I say that when one attains true knowledge one does not take any step out of rhythm. You should realize that the Atman is beyond the body, the sense organs, the mind, and the intellect, and that it is the witness of phenomena." The Master's words penetrated inside me and I realized the truth.

One day while I was serving the Master, he said: "Your father came today and said that your mother had been crying bitterly. He requested me to ask you to visit your mother at home. I am therefore telling you that you should go home to see your mother." I agreed. In the evening I left for home on foot. My parents were very happy to see me. With tears in her eyes my mother asked me to have supper and to stay for the night. But within half an hour I felt uncomfortable at home. I felt as if I were in hellfire. My heart was restless and thoughts of the Master haunted me. I tried to control my desire to run away from home, but failed. After hurriedly eating some refreshments I said goodbye to my parents and returned to Cossipore. The Master was surprised to see me and asked, "Did you not go home?"

"Yes, sir. I did."

"Your parents must have asked you to stay at home. Why did you not stay?"

"I did stay."

"How long?"

"For half an hour."

"But why did you return?"

"I went with the idea of staying at home tonight. My parents also begged me to stay. But I felt great agony while I was there. My mind longed to return to you. While there I felt as if I were in hell, so I ate a few sweets and hurried back here after saying goodbye to them. My mind was pacified only after arriving back here."

With a faint smile the Master said to me affectionately: "Very well! There is no doubt that you will have peace here." In fact I always felt peace and joy when I was around the Master. Parental affection seemed insipid compared to the Master's pure love.

One afternoon, while the Master was lying on his bed, a man was pacing back and forth outside on the green lawn of the garden house.

The Master said to me: "Please ask that man not to walk on the grass. I am in great pain, as if he were walking on my chest." I was amazed when I heard his words and actually saw this. I hurriedly went and asked the man not to walk on the grass. Then the Master was relieved.

A crazy woman used to come to visit the Master at Cossipore. She had a sweet voice, and when she would sing the Master would be in ecstasy. One of her songs was:

Come! Come, Mother! Doll of my soul! My heart's Delight!
In my heart's lotus come and sit, that I may see thy face.
Alas! sweet Mother, even from birth I have suffered much;
But I have borne it all, thou knowest, gazing at thee.
Open the lotus of my heart, dear Mother! Reveal thyself there.

The devotees were overwhelmed listening to her song. The woman was very obstinate and unpredictable, however. Whenever she had a chance, she would run upstairs to the Master's room. The Master forbade her to come there as she had adopted the same attitude towards him as the gopis had had towards Krishna. Finding that the disciples would not permit her to visit the Master, she eventually stopped coming. Girish Chandra Ghosh was inspired by seeing and hearing this crazy woman and he depicted her in the character of the mad woman in his drama *Vilwamangal*.

Pandit Shashadhar had great love and respect for Sri Ramakrishna. One day he came to see the Master at Cossipore when the cancer was in an advanced stage. Shashadhar said to the Master, "Sir, if you put your mind on your throat a little, your cancer will surely be cured." The Master answered: "How can the mind which I have already offered to the Lord be diverted again to the body of flesh and blood?" But still Shashadhar pleaded, "Sir, when you talk to the Divine Mother, please ask her to cure your cancer." Then the Master replied: "When I see the Mother of the Universe, I forget my body and the universe. So, how can I tell the Mother about this insignificant body of flesh and blood?" The pandit was dumbfounded. We too remained still. No one spoke a word.

The Passing Away of Sri Ramakrishna

The day Sri Ramakrishna began to hemorrhage, Narendra, Rakhal, Niranjan, and I, as well as others were present with him. The loss of blood made him terribly weak. A few days later, on August 16, 1886, at 1:06 A.M. [actually 1:02], the Master passed away. We saw the Master suddenly merge into samadhi as usual. His eyes remained fixed on the tip of his nose. Narendra began to chant "Om" aloud, and we all joined him. We expected the Master to come back from samadhi soon and regain normal consciousness. We waited for hours and consoled our-selves, remembering that once the Master had been in samadhi for three days and three nights and that he had then returned to the normal plane. We told ourselves that perhaps that might happen this time also. But as the whole night passed and his outer consciousness did not return, we lost hope and were at a loss about what to do.

The Holy Mother was informed. She came upstairs and, sitting by the side of the Master's bed, cried out, "Mother, where have you gone?" It was a heartrending scene. Standing on one side of the room, we wit-nessed with wonder that sweet relationship between the wife and the husband and thought that we had never before seen such a scene and such expression of love. In fact the Master used to regard Holy Mother as the living image of Mother Kali, and Holy Mother in return addressed the Master as Mother Kali. What a sweet relationship existed between the Master and Holy Mother!

Captain Vishwanath Upadhyay of Nepal arrived immediately after receiving news of the Master's mahasamadhi [passing away]. He sug-gested rubbing ghee [clarified butter] on the Master's backbone so that his consciousness might come back. Immediately Shashi [Swami Rama-krishnananda] began to rub some ghee on the Master's backbone, but there was no sign of outer consciousness.

Gradually the news of the Master's passing away spread and people began to flock to the Cossipore garden house. At 10:00 A.M. Dr. Mahen-dralal Sarkar came. He checked the Master's pulse and examined him carefully. Then he declared that the Master had breathed his last a half hour earlier and that rubbing would not be of any use. Listening to the doctor's report, we lost all hope. Arrangements were then made for cremation of the Master's divine body. Dr. Sarkar gave ten rupees so a photograph could be taken and then left with a heavy heart. At that time we all felt completely helpless. We felt that our entire source of strength and hope had gone. We thought: Now what shall we do? On whom shall we depend? And how shall we pass our days?

It was an unforgettable day in our lives. It was not apparent that the life force had left the Master's body. There was a sweet smile on his face, and it seemed as if a divine glow were emanating from his whole body. The Bengal Photographers Studio was called to take photographs of the Master's mahasamadhi. Sri Ramakrishna's body was placed on a cot, which was decorated all over with flowers. Then the Master's body was adorned with sandal paste on his face and garlands around his neck. Ram Datta stood in front of the cot and asked Narendra to stand by his side. The rest of us stood silently behind on the staircase. The Bengal Photographers took two group photographs.

Gradually the crowd began to grow. In the meantime all materials required for the cremation had been collected. At 5:00 P.M. the Master's body was carried by his disciples from the Cossipore garden house, and a large crowd followed the funeral procession singing kirtan [devotional songs]. The sounds of drums, cymbals, and singing reverberated everywhere. In that procession people carried emblems of different religions, such as the Om symbol, the Trident, the Cross, the Crescent, and so on. At last we reached the Cossipore cremation ground.

According to the custom, the Master's body was washed with Ganga water and then covered with a new cloth and garlands. Finally it was placed on the funeral pyre. The devotees of the Master had brought ghee, sandalwood, firewood, and perfume. Gradually the fire of the funeral pyre grew into flames with hundreds of tongues. The disciples and devotees showered flowers into the fire. The cremation ground also reverberated then with drums, cymbals, and kirtan. It was an indescribable sight! The disciples and devotees gazed at their Master's divine body for the last time and then bowed down to him with reverence. Hymns were also chanted.

At last the Master's body was reduced to ashes. Three of us collected the relics of the Master and put them in a copper urn, which we carried to the Cossipore garden house with heavy hearts. We then placed the Master's relics in his bedroom and passed the whole night in japam and meditation. Trying to assuage our grief over the Master's absence, we talked about his divine life. Narendra sat in front and occasionally consoled us by telling stories of the Master's unselfish love and wonderful grace.

The day Sri Ramakrishna passed away a miraculous incident took place. Holy Mother was in her room overwhelmed with grief. She decided to remove the bracelets from her arms, which signified that her husband was alive. [*According to the Hindu custom a widow is supposed to take off her jewellery, wear a plain white sari, and lead an unostentatious life.*] Just as she was taking them off, Sri Ramakrishna appeared before her in his physical form and forbade her to do so. Pressing her hand, he said: "Do you think I have gone elsewhere? I have just gone from one room to another." Holy Mother realized that though the Master's earthly body was destroyed, he was ever present in his divine form. After that, she continued to wear her bracelets as well as a sari with a small red border.

We wanted to stay at the Cossipore garden house after the Master passed away, but who would pay the rent? The householder disciples had paid the rent when the Master was alive. Ram Babu [Ram Chandra Datta] suggested that the young disciples return to their homes and that the Master's relics be installed in his Kankurgachi Yogodyana.

Narendra and the rest of us were very sad to hear Ram Babu's proposal. We expressed our wish to Ram Babu that the Master's relics be installed on the bank of the Ganga and a temple built there. But Ram Babu did not listen to us. He made the final decision that the Master's relics would be installed at Kankurgachi and left for his Calcutta residence that night.

The night deepened. Narendra and the rest of us sat in silence around the urn containing the Master's relics. We did not know what to do. Then Niranjan suddenly said, "We will not hand over the Master's sacred relics to Ram Babu." We all agreed with Niranjan. Then we decided that the major portion of the relics be transferred from the urn to a casket, which would then be concealed in Balaram Babu's house at Baghbazar so that Ram Babu would not know at all. Afterwards, when Ram Babu would come, the urn would be given to him. Action was taken accordingly. That night almost all the relics were transferred from the urn to a casket, leaving only a small quantity of bone dust and ash mixed with Ganga clay in the urn. Narendra then said: "Look, our bodies are living shrines of the Master. Let us all sanctify ourselves by taking a little of the relics of his holy body." Narendra first took a small quantity of bone dust from the urn and swallowed it, saying, "Glory be to Ramakrishna." All of us then did likewise and we felt blessed.

On August 24, 1886, Ram Babu came to the Cossipore garden house to take the urn to Kankurgachi Yogodyana. It was Janmashtami day [the birthday of Sri Krishna]. Narendra led the procession, singing devotional songs. Ram Babu and other devotees accompanied us. Shashi carried the urn on his head with great care. At last the holy relics of Sri Ramakrishna were installed ceremoniously at the Kankurgachi Yogodyana. That night we stayed at the Yogodyana.

[From: *Amar Jivankatha*, by Swami Abhedananda (Calcutta: Sri Ramakrishna Vedanta Math), 1964]

13

Swami Akhandananda

Swami Akhandananda (1864-1937) was born in Calcutta, and his pre-monastic name was Gangadhar Ghatak. When he met Sri Ramakrishna he was a young boy. The Master praised his ascetic habits and attributed them to the spiritual disciplines performed in his past life. Swami Akhandananda travelled with Swami Vivekananda to many places of India and also crossed the Himalayas and went to Tibet. He later became the third president of the Ramakrishna Order.

First Meetings

It was in the summer of 1883 that I first met Sri Ramakrishna at Dakshineswar. I was then in my teens. The Master received me cordially and made me sit beside him. Then he asked, "Have you ever seen me before?" "Yes," I replied. "I saw you once when I was very young at the house of Dinanath Basu in Calcutta." Swami Advaitananda was also present. Addressing him, the Master said with a smile: "O Gopal, listen to this! This boy says that he met me when he was very young. This little one had an early boyhood!"

In the afternoon the Master asked me to go to the Panchavati after saluting the deities at the Kali and Vishnu temples. Later in the evening, as I returned to the Master's room, I heard music being played from the two nahabats [concert towers], and the temple garden was filled with the melodious sound of the vesper bells. The Master's room was dark, and there was a sweet smell of incense. The Master was seated on his cot, barely visible. He did not have any outer consciousness. As he had asked me to stay overnight at the temple garden, I did. The next morning, when I was about to leave for Calcutta, he said to me with a smile, "Come again on Saturday."

After a few days I went to Sri Ramakrishna for the second time on a Saturday, and I was again made to stay overnight. In the evening, after the vesper service was over, the Master handed me a mat and asked me

Swami Akhandananda

to spread it on the western verandah. He took his pillow and sat down on the mat. He then asked me to sit in a comfortable posture and meditate. "It is not good to sit leaning forward or to hold the body too straight," he said.

That evening the Master initiated me by writing a mantram on my tongue. He then lay down putting his feet on my lap and asked me to give them a little massage. I was quite strong, as I practised wrestling. No sooner had I begun to press his feet than he cried out: "What are you doing? The legs will be crushed! Press them gently." Immediately I realized how soft and tender the Master's body was, as if his bones were covered with butter. I was embarrassed, and I asked with some fear, "How then should I massage?" "Pass your hands over them gently," he replied. "Niranjan [Swami Niranjanananda] also did like you at first."

After that meeting I visited the Master often, usually arriving in the afternoon, staying overnight, and returning the next morning. Many other disciples would visit the Master, but Harish and Latu [Swami Adbhutananda] lived with him.

I was extremely orthodox in those days and scrupulously observed all the brahminical customs in accordance with the scriptural injunctions. For example, I used to bathe four times a day in the Ganga without applying any oil to my body, and as a result my skin and hair became very dry. I was a vegetarian and cooked my own food. Fearing that I might have to eat the nonvegetarian prasad [sanctified food] of Mother Kali, I always left Dakshineswar before noon. Also, I was in the habit of chewing a myrobalan[1] [a bitter nut] after meals, so my lips became white. One day the Master noticed this and said to me: "What is this? You are a youngster. Why have you imbibed these old people's ideas? This is not good."

Before I went to the Master I used to practise pranayama [breathing exercises] along with my other morning and evening spiritual disciplines. I increased the volume of pranayama so much that my body began to perspire and shiver. I practised kumbhaka [breath holding] by diving into the Ganga and grabbing a stone. I was fascinated by this play with the prana. As soon as I told the Master what I was doing, he forbade me to practise pranayama, saying that it might cause a fatal disease. He told me: "Repeat the Gayatri mantram every day as much as you can."

One ekadasi day [the eleventh day of the moon, which orthodox people observe by fasting] I fasted and went to see the Master in the

---

[1] A Sanskrit verse: O King, chew daily a myrobalan, which is as beneficent as a mother. A mother sometimes gets angry, but not the myrobalan. To remove the inner impurities, remember God, eat a myrobalan, repeat the Gayatri mantram, and drink Ganga water.

afternoon. It was a hot summer day, and my face had become red from sunburn. He was very pleased that I had brought a watermelon for him. When I bowed down to him he asked, "Are you planning to return today?" "No, sir," I replied.

The next morning Sri Ramakrishna asked me to accompany him to the Panchavati, and there he told me to meditate facing the east. He left for a while, and when he came back he set my body straight. He remarked, "You become a bit bent during meditation." We then returned to his room. After that he asked me to carry a waterpot and go with him to the chandni, the bathing ghat on the Ganga. He had his bath and returned to his room in his wet cloth. Before he put on his fresh cloth he asked me to sprinkle a little Ganga water on it. There was a picture of Mother Kali of Kalighat [Calcutta] in his room, which he saluted. Then he ate a little dry prasad of Lord Jagannath and gave some to me. Standing in front of the picture of Kali, he said several times, "Om Kali." He then put the palm of his right hand on his chest with the three middle fingertips touching the palm, and he stood there with half-closed eyes for some time. After that he took the offered fruits and sweets that had been sent to him from the Kali and Vishnu temples. He then drank a little bel sherbet and gave me the prasad, after which he sat on his small cot and smoked from a hubble-bubble.

When the food offering was over in the temples the Master took me to the eastern verandah of his room and said: "Go and take the prasad of Mother Kali. It is cooked in Ganga water and is very holy." I agreed. While walking through the courtyard I looked back and noticed that the Master was watching whether I was going to the kitchen of the Vishnu or Kali temple. I wondered why he had asked me to go to the nonvegetarian kitchen of Kali instead of the vegetarian kitchen of Vishnu. I did what the Master said, but I ate only the vegetarian dishes. I still remember the thick preparation of chana dal [lentils].

When I returned to the Master's room I found him waiting near the east door with a betel roll in his hand. Giving it to me he said: "Chew it. It is good to chew a couple of betel rolls after meals. It removes bad breath." Then he said: "Naren [Swami Vivekananda] eats whatever is given and chews a hundred betel rolls a day. His eyes are large and indrawn. When he walks through the streets of Calcutta he sees the buildings, horses, carriages, and everything as God. His home is at Simla [in central Calcutta]. Go and see him one day."

The next day I went to Swami Vivekananda's house at Simla. He was lying on a bed in his room and studying *Buddha-Gaya*, written by Dr. Rajendralal Mittra. The book was very thick, like a Webster's Dictionary. His room was not very tidy, nor was his bed, but I was quite impressed seeing Swamiji's serene, loving face. I told him, "The Master has asked me to visit you." "Please sit down," he said. He was pleased to hear that I was acquainted with the Master. He talked to me for some time and then said, "Come again."

The next time I visited the Master, he immediately asked me, "Did you visit Naren?" "Yes, sir," I replied. I told him all about my short meeting with Swamiji. "I saw his large, captivating eyes," I said. "He was completely oblivious of his surroundings, as if his mind was not in this world. What you said about him, sir, was true." The Master was very pleased to hear this. He then said, "Visit him frequently and enjoy his company."

Swamiji did not go to see the Master for a long time after his father's death. The Master was very anxious about him and sent for him many times, but Swamiji was not in a mood to go. Probably he stopped coming lest the Master become worried about his financial difficulties. Later, whenever I visited the Master, I usually saw Swamiji, Swami Brahmananda, Swami Abhedananda, or Swami Saradananda.

One day a number of devotees came to see the Master, both men and women, including Yogin-ma, Gauri-ma, and Krishnabhavini. Towards evening, as I was about to return to Calcutta, someone suggested that I walk back with one of the gentlemen. But the Master intervened: "No, no. He is a young boy. How can he keep pace with a tall man who walks with big steps? Let him accompany these ladies." After the vesper service Swami Saradananda and I returned to Calcutta with the ladies in their carriage.

Sometimes I would think: "The Master says that most of my habits, such as taking only self-cooked food, being a vegetarian, practising austerity, chewing myrobalan, and so on, are for old people. If they are not good, why shouldn't I give them up?"

One day I visited the Master and had prasad at the temple. A group of lay devotees came after his noon rest and I spread a mat for them on the floor. One of them asked the Master, "Sir, is it good that these young boys come to you to embrace the monastic life, disregarding the householder's life?" The Master replied: "Look, you only see their present life, and not their previous lives in which they passed through these other stages. For instance, a man has four sons. One of them, having grown up, says: 'I shall not put oil on my body or eat fish. I shall eat only self-cooked vegetarian food.' The parents try to dissuade him from these habits and even threaten him, but the boy will not give up the path of renunciation. Yet the other three sons are mad after enjoyment and swallow whatever they get. Look, it is because of the preponderance of the sattva quality that this boy wants to renounce everything before he reaches manhood." Listening to this from the Master, my faith in keeping up my orthodox customs became doubled.

The Master used to say, "In this kali yuga [iron age] the path of devotion as taught by Narada is beneficial and easy to practise." All those whom the Master loved he asked to come and see him on Tuesdays and Saturdays. He also encouraged us to practise more japam and meditation on those days. According to him, Saturday is sweet and sacred.

Another day I went to Dakshineswar early in the morning. The Master bathed in the Ganga, ate some prasad, and then lay down for a rest. Part of the eastern verandah of his room was enclosed by a bamboo partition so we could rest and chat. After a while I entered his room and found him sitting on his bed and sweetly singing, "Radha, who wanders joyously in Vrindaban, is ours and we are hers." While singing, his chest became wet with tears, and gradually he went into samadhi. I was dumbfounded, because I had never seen such a wonderful thing as this in my life. The rest of the afternoon we spent in kirtan [devotional singing]. Manomohan Mittra, a devotee of the Master, was present on this occasion.

Whenever I went to the Master I noticed that he talked about nothing but God and religion. He was never dry or boring. During talks on the most exalted topics he created much laughter by making jokes. One day he said: "You know there are various kinds of siddhas [perfected souls]. Do you know what siddha means? Literally, it means 'boiled.' As potatoes and squash become soft when boiled, so men are when perfected or illumined."

Once I spent a night at Dakshineswar with several other disciples, and the Master had us all sit for meditation. While communing with our Chosen Deities, we often laughed and wept in ecstasy. The pure joy we experienced in those boyhood days cannot be expressed in words. Whenever I approached the Master he would invariably ask me, "Did you shed tears at the time of prayer or meditation?" And one day when I answered yes to this, how happy he was! "Tears of repentance or sorrow flow from the corners of the eyes nearest the nose," he said, "and those of joy from the outer corners of the eyes." Suddenly the Master asked me, "Do you know how to pray?" Saying this he flung his hands and feet about restlessly — like a little child impatient for its mother. Then he cried out: "Mother dear, grant me knowledge and devotion. I don't want anything else. I can't live without you." While thus teaching us how to pray, he looked just like a small boy. Profuse tears rolled down his chest, and he passed into deep samadhi. I was convinced that the Master did that for my sake.

One day the Master talked about dreams: "One may dream that someone has come and lit a lamp, or that something has caught fire, or that one is calling oneself by one's own name. All these dreams are auspicious — but the last one is the best."

Whoever visited the Master at that time was blessed with various spiritual visions during meditation. People visualized and talked with their Chosen Deity as they sat with half-closed eyes. Seeing all this, the hairs of my body would stand on end. The eight sattvic signs of spiritual ecstasy [tears, shivering, horripilation, perspiration, etc.] in one form or other were visible in almost all the Master's intimate disciples. But Swamiji was exceptionally reserved and never yielded easily to any spiritual mood.

There was another day at Dakshineswar when several unforgettable incidents took place. I had stayed at night with the Master, and in the morning after visiting the temples I returned to him. He asked me to accompany him to the chandni ghat, where he took his bath. I carried his *kamandalu* [water pot]. As we went down the steps of the ghat, I saw the temple manager. He was sitting at the edge of the water with one foot in the Ganga and rubbing the heel of the other foot on the step. The Master went to the other side of the steps and did not even glance at the manager. As he started to bathe, the Master put his foot in the water very carefully and then got in waist-deep, throwing a little water on his head. The respect and reverence he showed while taking his bath was consistent with his saying a few days earlier that the water of the Ganga was divine.

Meanwhile an old brahmin appeared on the steps of the ghat. He looked like he was from a village. Approaching the temple manager, he started asking him questions in a loud voice, such as how much fish do they get from the temple pond, how much money do they receive by selling the fruits and vegetables grown in the temple garden, and so on. The Master overheard all this and looked at the old brahmin out of the corner of his eye with displeasure. After the Master had bathed I followed him back to his room and sprinkled a little Ganga water on his cloth. He then went to the temples and bowed down to the deities, after which he returned to his room and ate a little prasad.

The Master was sitting on his cot enjoying a smoke when the old brahmin appeared at his door and asked, "Is Harish here?" Instead of answering him, the Master said: "Well, you are a brahmin and three-fourths of your life is already over. You have now entered the last part, and yet you do not remember your Chosen Deity even on the banks of the Ganga. Fie on you, that you should inquire at such a sacred place how many fish there are in the pond and what quantities of vegetables and fruits grow in the garden!" The brahmin was evidently not in the least repentant, however, and went away in annoyance. The Master asked me to sprinkle some Ganga water on the place where the old man had stood.

A little later a beggar appeared and asked for some money. The Master called me and, pointing to four pice, asked me to give them to the beggar. When I had done this Sri Ramakrishna said, "Wash your hands with Ganga water." So I washed my hands with the water in the large earthen jar in a corner of his room. Then he made me stand with him in front of one of the pictures on the wall — that of Kali of the Kalighat temple. He clapped his hands and repeated "Hari, Hari," making me do the same. This incident indelibly impressed on my mind the idea that *money is rubbish, dirt*. Later in life I wandered fourteen years all over the country as a penniless monk and never touched money. The indifference for it which I cherish even now is the result of that blessed incident.

Experiences at Dakshineswar

Generally the Master travelled to Calcutta in a hired second-class coach belonging to Beni Pal [*according to* Sri Ramakrishna, The Great Master, *Beni Saha*]. If the coachman whipped the horses, the Master would become restless and cry out, "He is beating me!" Hearing about this, Beni Pal thenceforth arranged to provide the Master always with his strongest and fastest horses, which did not require beating.

Once Latu and I accompanied the Master on a drive to Calcutta. When we reached Baghbazar Street the Master asked the driver to stop and, turning to me, asked, "Well, can you go and call Narayan?" Narayan was a boy who visited the Master now and then. So I found him and brought him to the carriage. The Master asked him why he hadn't been to Dakshineswar for a long time and advised him to go there soon. Then we drove to the house of Vishwanath Upadhyay, the ambassador of Nepal, whom the Master called "Captain." We all went upstairs, where members of the family saluted Sri Ramakrishna. Then the Master drank a little iced water, of which he was very fond. From there we went to Balaram Basu's house and after that returned to Dakshineswar. The Master hardly ever spent a night away from Dakshineswar, except on perhaps one or two occasions when he stayed at Balaram Basu's place. Once Swamiji said to me, "The Master never took a cooked meal [*outside of the temple garden*] except at Balaram Basu's, because he knew the food there was pure."

In those days two hundred and fifty to three hundred monks, visitors of all kinds, and poor people were given a sumptuous meal every noon at the Kali temple. Many great souls of all the religious orders visited

Dakshineswar then and lived secluded lives in that sacred place. During Sri Ramakrishna's stay there the place vibrated with a holy atmosphere like that of heaven. Many great saints came there and enjoyed the holy company of the Master and benefited from his inspired teachings. Whenever such a person came to Dakshineswar the Master always sent us to him to receive his blessings.

Once I went to the Master with a group of people who were nondualists. The leader of the group said to Sri Ramakrishna, "Sir, we have brought the devotees of Varanasi."

"Is that so?" the Master replied. "Then you have brought a group who say, 'I am He.'" He welcomed them warmly and asked them to sit down.

One person asked, "Sir, how can he who is the absolute Brahman, omnipresent and pervading the whole universe, incarnate himself as man?"

"You see," was the reply, "he who is the absolute Brahman is the witness and is immanent everywhere. The Divine Incarnation is an embodiment of his Power. The power is incarnate somewhere a quarter, somewhere else a half, and very rarely in full. He in whom the full power is manifest is adored as *Purna Brahman*, like Krishna. And three quarters of the Divine were manifested in Rama."

To this, one of the gentlemen said: "Sir, this body is the root of all evils. If it can be destroyed, all troubles will cease."

"The raw earthen pots when broken are made into pots again," the Master said, "but the burnt ones, once broken, can never be remade. So if you destroy the body before the attainment of Self-realization, you will have to be reborn and suffer similar consequences."

"But, sir," the gentleman objected, "why does one take so much care of his body?"

The Master answered: "Those who do the work of moulding, preserve the mould with care till the image is made. When the image is ready, it does not matter whether the mould is kept or rejected. So with this body. One has to realize the Supreme Self. One has to attain Self-knowledge. After that the body may remain or go. Till then the body has to be taken care of." The gentleman was silenced.

Then the Master sang a few devotional songs — favourites of his, addressed to the Divine Mother. One of the gentlemen present burst into tears. The Master was very pleased to see this and said: "They talk in this manner like a pan of ghee in a blazing oven. After this they will be quiet." At the end of the long discussion the Master got up and we all visited the temples and wandered about in the garden. One of these visitors, Gadashankar, was a follower of Keshab Chandra Sen. The Master talked with him on the eastern verandah while I was there.

"Do you practise the brahminical devotions?" the Master asked him.
"I do not like all these rituals," he said.

"You see," the Master went on, "do not give up anything by force. If the blossoms of gourds and pumpkins are plucked off, their fruits rot, but when the fruits are ripe the flowers fall off naturally. Do you believe in a God with form or in a formless God?"

"In the formless aspect," was the reply.

"But how can you grasp the formless aspect all at once?" the Master asked. "When the archers are learning to shoot, they first aim at the plantain tree, then at a thin tree, then at a fruit, then at the leaves, and finally at a flying bird. First meditate on the aspect with form. This will enable you to see the formless later."

One morning the Master took me to the Kali temple. Whenever I went there alone I stood outside the threshold, but on this occasion Sri Ramakrishna took me into the sanctum sanctorum and showed me the face of Lord Shiva, who was of course lying on his back while Kali stood on him. His face was not visible from outside the shrine, where one could only see the top of his head. The Master said, "Look, here is the living Shiva." I felt that Lord Shiva was conscious and breathing. I was astonished. How potent were the Master's words! Up to that time I had thought that this image was just like all the other Shiva images I had seen.

Sri Ramakrishna then gently pulled Mother Kali's cloth and placed her ornaments properly. When we left the temple he was reeling like a drunkard. He was escorted to his room with difficulty and remained for some time in samadhi. I cannot describe the details of that day — the joy the Master poured into my heart cannot be communicated. After coming down from samadhi the Master sang many songs in an ecstatic mood.

*   *   *

Once I heard a great saint, who was staying at Dakshineswar, singing a Hindi couplet which went as follows: "Hear, O mortals of the earth! There is none high or low among mankind. The God who is in the elephant is also in the ant." I translated this for the Master, who said: "How can that be? The power of an elephant and that of an ant are not the same. As Spirit they are one, but as power they are different."

On another day I arrived at Dakshineswar in the morning and found the Master taking a shave on the eastern verandah of his room. "Stay here today," he said to me. So I did and had a long talk with Kali [Swami Abhedananda]. He was truant from school, very active, smart, and strong. The Master loved him intensely.

A few days later the Master had his arm in a splint, hanging from his neck in a sling. I heard that while in ecstasy he had fallen down and broken his arm. But all these are random recollections of long ago. I was a mere boy then and how can I remember everything?

At the House of Balaram Basu

I shall now try to record what I can remember of Sri Ramakrishna's visits to Balaram Basu's house on the occasions when I accompanied him. One day there were many devotees present, among them the famous pandit Shashadhar Tarkachudamani. The pandit was thin, and he wore a white dhoti [cloth], a white wrapper on his shoulders, and a garland around his neck. His face was cast down, his eyes fixed on the ground.

"Well, here is a good gathering!" the Master said to him. "Why don't you tell them something?"

"I speak to the atheists," the pandit answered, "but here all are theists. What should I say to these devotees? You alone are worthy to speak to them."

The Master then said, "You see, I thought you were a pseudo-pandit. But today I see that you are a spiritual aspirant." The pandit then shed tears of devotion on hearing this. Later the Master held a kirtan for a long time in an ecstatic mood.

Another day at Balaram Basu's place the Master was surrounded by devotees. Swami Vivekananda sat near, and from time to time the Master asked him a casual question, such as, "My boy, why didn't you go there [*meaning, Dakshineswar*]?" Then Swamiji sang a song beginning with: "My mind, take the name of Rama. Repeat it daily wholeheartedly." The Master was charmed by this. Crowds gathered, and he fell into an ecstatic mood. Seeing him, many of the devotees were greatly moved. Some wept, some laughed, some meditated and were greatly inspired, and some started shivering. A wonderful sight! Those who had come only out of curiosity or to scoff remarked while leaving: "Wonderful indeed! How sweetly the Paramahamsa sings the name of the Mother. It goes straight to the heart and inspires one."

The Master came one day to Balaram Basu's home during the time of the car festival. Sankirtan [singing] and dance created a flood of joy there. The Master told his young disciples jokingly: "Well, my boys, sing and dance well. Then Balaram will give you malpo [a Bengali sweet]." So we all sang loudly.

Another day the Master went to Balaram's in the morning. He was seated in the small room to the right of the stairs with several devotees. I bowed to him and sat by his side. The Master's mind that day was turned completely inward. He would mutter a few words and then pass into ecstasy. In that state he started talking about Ramlala [an image of the child Rama]. He described how Ramlala had played with him, how he [the Master] had bathed and fed him, and so on. While feeding Ramlala one day, the Master said, a husk scratched Ramlala's tongue. The Master told us with tears, "How unfortunate am I that I put husk into the mouth in which Mother Kaushalya hesitated to put butter, cream, and thickened milk!" Then he went into samadhi, and as he came back to normal consciousness he went on talking about Ramlala, singing his glories in a sweet voice. Later he was silent for a while, and then he began speaking with the Divine Mother thus: "Beloved Mother, how can I offer my life and mind to you? It is you who have become my life and mind."

When this mood had passed, the Master closed his fist, and holding it before him, said with half-closed eyes in a God-intoxicated state: "I spit upon lust and lucre. Those who are attached to them will never have God-vision." He repeated this several times. The godly scene I witnessed that day has become the source of lifelong inspiration — not only for myself but also for my brother disciples who were present.

The Story of Manmatha

It will not be out of place here to relate a story about Manmatha, an expert wrestler and noted ruffian, who was, as we shall see, completely transformed by contact with Sri Ramakrishna. It happened like this: Yogin-ma, a great woman devotee, had a brother, Hiralal, who objected to his sister's visiting Sri Ramakrishna at Dakshineswar. The first time that she invited the Master to the house I accompanied him there. Her brother had asked Manmatha to be present in order to frighten Sri Ramakrishna away. But Manmatha, after seeing the Master and hearing a few of his words, fell at the Master's feet and wept, saying: "My Lord, I am guilty. Please forgive me." The Master told him to come to Dakshineswar. I knew Manmatha very well, and he asked me: "Please take me to him. He has graciously invited me to go there." So a day was fixed and we both set off together in a coach with a pot of rasagollas [sweet cheese balls]. The Master treated him very kindly.

I said to Sri Ramakrishna in front of Manmatha, "This man is a noted ruffian of whom all the boys are afraid, and in riotous clashes he is always the ringleader."

The Master touched Manmatha's body and said, "How hard!" Hearing that Manmatha had cast off his sacred thread, the Master asked him, "Why don't you put it on?"

"Sir," he replied, "when I perspire it sticks to my body causing me to scratch. So I quit wearing it."

The Master gravely said, "You should put on this brahminical symbol." Then he took Manmatha to the Kali temple and while circumambulating, blessed him in a solitary corner and asked him to visit him on another Sunday. Another time I took Manmatha to see the Master. They met only three times in all.

This is what I heard some years later from my brother disciple Swami Shivananda: "When I passed by Manmatha's house in Baghbazar, I heard him repeating 'Mother, Mother!' And his appearance is quite different these days. His body is no longer bulky and his hair is long. If you could see him now, you would be astonished." Then in 1890 [*four years after the Master's passing*] Manmatha came to our first monastery at Baranagore, barefooted and with only one piece of cheap cloth around him. He kept repeating with folded hands, "My beloved Lord! My beloved Lord! [Priyanath! Priyanath!]" Many of us brother monks were present, including Swamiji, Ramakrishnananda, Niranjanananda, Shivananda, Advaitananda, Abhedananda, and others. Manmatha smiled sweetly at me from time to time. Swamiji said to me, "You were instrumental in his having the Master's grace and this transformation."

Then a few years after that I went with a friend to see Manmatha at his home. He was gazing at the sun without blinking and without any outward consciousness. His body was emaciated and he wore an ochre cloth. The sight of his divine madness moved me exceedingly. That day I realized that what is not gained by austere penances in the mountains and forests is easily attainable at home through the Master's grace. Shortly after this I heard that Manmatha had died of cholera.

Other Experiences with the Master

One day Swamiji, Swami Yogananda, Swami Niranjanananda, and others arranged a picnic in the Panchavati. The Master came and joined in our games for a while. Another day I saw the Master passing frequently into samadhi. When he came down to normal consciousness he spoke of God-vision and Self-realization, saying: "One's own Chosen Deity is one's own Self. The Chosen Deity and the Atman are identical. The vision of the Chosen Deity is equivalent to Self-knowledge." The Master continued: "Ah! How wonderful was the attitude of Prahlada. Sometimes he said, 'Not I,' and in another mood, 'I am thy servant, Oh Lord!' But there were moments when his mind soared to the absolute state when he said, 'I am He,' and remained still and speechless."

Another day I went to Dakshineswar. The northern verandah at that time was enclosed and contained two bedsteads on the east and the west sides respectively. That night I slept on one and Harish on the other. In the small hours just before dawn the Master got up and chanted "Om" and passed into samadhi. At the same time Harish began to sing the names of the deities — Durga, Shiva, and others. In that blessed moment in the Master's room, the sky above and the air around were all over-powered by the silence of samadhi. Like a fruit in my palm, God became perceptible to me inside and outside.

Then a few days later I came to Dakshineswar, took my bath in the Ganga, and sat in the Master's room. Many devotees arrived, and talks about God poured out in a torrent through the Master's lips. Shortly after the meal he rested awhile and stretched himself on his smaller cot, placing his head southward. He called me and asked me to massage his feet. I drew his legs onto my lap and was passing my hands over them when he began to tell me with a smile many beautiful things on spiritual life. I later communicated these to Swami Brahmananda, who said he had been told the same things by the Master previously. While massaging his feet I rubbed his two big toes on my forehead, as if I were drawing the Vaishnava marks.

The Master smiled, "What are you doing, my boy?"

"Why," I replied, "you told me that those who are of a sattvic nature, while bathing in the Ganga, draw marks on their foreheads with its sacred water, whereas those who are rajasic [active or passionate] cover their bodies with marks of vermilion and white and red sandal paste. Today I am putting the sattvic marks on my forehead. What is there on earth more sacred than your holy feet?" The Master seemed happy to hear this and smiled joyfully.

Other gurus teach their disciples to follow a set of fixed rules and regulations and thereby help their spiritual unfoldment. But the case of our Master was very different — even extraordinary. He was a unique type of spiritual teacher. He blessed those who came to him by a mere touch, by a mere look, or by a mere wish. In this way he transmitted spiritual powers through which the recipients got spiritual experiences. He wanted all of us to enjoy the bliss of God-union. How eager was he to rouse the dormant spirituality in us and awaken our souls to God-consciousness! To his intimate disciples he spoke of his spiritual illuminations and inspired them to attain those realizations. Hari Om!

[From: *Smriti Katha*, by Swami Akhandananda (Calcutta: Udbodhan Office), 1937; *Vedanta and the West* (Hollywood: Vedanta Press), no. 113, May-June 1955]

14

Swami Vijnanananda

Swami Vijnanananda (1868-1938) met Sri Ramakrishna when he was a boy and later was initiated by the Master. His premonastic name was Hari Prasanna Chattopadhyay. After graduating from college, he became a District Engineer for the Government, but in 1896 he resigned from his job to join the Ramakrishna monastery at Alambazar. Later, Swami Vijnanananda established a monastery at Allahabad and practised spiritual disciplines there. He was a Sanskrit scholar, and translated Devi Bhagavatam and Valmiki Ramayana into English. He was the fourth president of the Ramakrishna Order.

I first saw Sri Ramakrishna in 1875 at Belgharia [near Dakshineswar] in the garden house of Jaygopal Sen. The Master came to visit Keshab Sen in that retreat house. I was then a little boy. I was playing with my friends and then just by chance saw the Master there. At that time the paths of the garden house were covered with red brick dust. Many people came. The Master was seated in a room. After seeing him, I returned to my home nearby.

I met the Master again in Belgharia when I was studying in class IX or X. One day at about four o'clock in the afternoon, I was playing at Sarada's [Swami Trigunatitananda's] house, when a friend of ours came and asked, "Would you like to visit a paramahamsa [literally 'great swan' — an illumined soul]?" "Where is he?" we inquired. "At the Dewan's house nearby," he replied. I had no idea what a paramahamsa was. Moreover, I was a little afraid of monks who wore ochre cloth, but we all went to meet him.

As we entered the house of Dewan Govinda Mukhopadhyay, we encountered a wonderful scene. A young man [Swami Vivekananda] was singing a devotional song, "Jai, Jai Dayamaya, Jai Dayamaya [Victory to the compassionate Lord, Victory to the compassionate Lord]." Sri Ramakrishna was standing in the centre of the group, and another young

Swami Vijnanananda in Allahabad

man [Swami Premananda] was holding him so that he would not fall. The Master was completely oblivious of his surroundings. He wore a white cloth. His face shone with a heavenly lustre and a smile played over his lips. His teeth were visible, and there was such a joyful expression on his face that it seemed as if it would crack — like a cracked melon! His eyes seemed to be gazing at something, and he appeared to be immersed in an ocean of bliss. I pointed out the Master's blissful expression to my friend Rajen Sarkar, and he agreed, saying, "Yes, you are right."

After a while the Master sang a song in praise of the Divine Mother, composed by Ramprasad: "Is Mother merely a simple woman, born as others are born? . . . " He was still in an ecstatic mood. It seemed to me that he was having a direct vision of the Mother and was singing to her. On this occasion I saw another person in ecstasy. Later I learned that he was Nityagopal. He was seated next to the Master, and his face, eyes, and chest were red from spiritual emotion. The Master sat down and began to speak to Nityagopal in a mysterious language. When the Master was standing, his mood had been like that of the Divine Mother. Now, when he was seated, his mood was like that of Krishna. At that time I observed another amazing thing that would remain in my memory all through my life. I saw that the Master's spinal cord was swollen like a thick rope and that his kundalini power had reached his head. It looked like the hood of a snake moving with joy.

In the evening, after the kirtan, Govinda Babu accompanied the Master, Swamiji, Swami Premananda, and others upstairs for refreshments. We then returned home.

A couple of years passed. I was then a second-year student at St. Xavier's College, Calcutta. Sharat Maharaj [Swami Saradananda] and Barada Pal were my classmates. One day [November 26, 1883] the three of us decided to visit the Master. We rented a boat and reached Dakshineswar in the afternoon, but the Master was busy. A carriage was waiting to take him to Mani Mallik's house in Calcutta. He called his nephew: "Ramlal, the carriage is ready. Let us go. People are waiting there for us. Hello, driver! Please start." The Master also invited us, saying: "You boys come to Mani Mallik's house. There will be a great festival. Tell the gatekeeper there that you have come to meet the paramahamsa."

We bowed down to the Master and returned to Calcutta by boat. I remember that after attending the festival at Mani Mallik's house, I returned home and my mother scolded me. When she heard that I had gone to see Sri Ramakrishna, she said: "My goodness! You went to that crazy brahmin! He has deranged the brains of three hundred and fifty young men." It was indeed the derangement of brains! Even now my brain is hot. I did not pay any attention to my mother's scolding.

Thus four or five times I visited the Master at Dakshineswar. A few times I also spent the night with him. Once [June 8, 1883] the Master blessed Swami Shivananda when I was there. Swami Shivananda still remembers that episode. On his first meeting, the Master had told him, "You will attain God-realization in this life." Swami Shivananda later told me that after meeting the Master, sense pleasures and the world became repulsive to him.

Another day I went in the afternoon to visit the Master at Dakshineswar. Many devotees were seated in his room. After saluting the Master I sat quietly in a corner. The Master was conversing with the devotees seated on his small cot. In physical appearance he was like any other man, but his smile was something divine. I have never seen such a smile in my life. When he smiled, a wave of bliss rolled not only over his face but over his whole body. And that blissful smile would wipe out the worries and troubles of those who looked at him. His voice was so sweet and melodious that one never tired of hearing it. His eyes were keen and bright, and when he would look at a person, it seemed that he was seeing everything inside him.

I felt Sri Ramakrishna's room vibrating with a tangible atmosphere of peace, and the devotees present seemed to be listening in blissful absorption to the words that poured from the Master's lips. I don't recall what he said, but I experienced tremendous joy within. For a long time I sat there, my whole attention concentrated on Sri Ramakrishna. He did not say anything to me, nor did I ask him anything. Then one by one the devotees took their leave, and suddenly I found myself alone with him. The Master was looking at me intently. I thought it was time for me to depart, so I prostrated before him. As I stood up to go, he asked: "Can you wrestle? Come, let me see how well you wrestle!" With these words he stood up, ready to grapple with me. I was surprised at this challenge. I thought to myself, "What kind of holy man is this?" But I replied, "Yes, of course I can wrestle."

Sri Ramakrishna came closer, smiling. He caught hold of my arms and began to shove me, but I was a strong, muscular young man and I pushed him back to the wall. He was still smiling and holding me with a strong grip. Gradually I felt a sort of electric current coming out of his hands and entering into me. That touch made me completely helpless. I lost all my physical strength. I went into ecstasy, and the hair of my body stood on end. Releasing me, the Master said with a smile, "Well, you are the winner." With those words, he sat down on his cot again. I was speechless. Wave after wave of bliss engulfed my whole being. I was pondering the fact that the Master had not won physically but his spiritual power had completely subdued me. Some time passed. Then the Master got up from his seat. Patting me gently on the back, he said: "Come here often. It is not enough to come once." Then he offered me some sweets as prasad, and I returned to Calcutta. For days the spell of that intoxicating joy lingered, and I realized that he had transmitted spiritual power to me.

One day [Janmashtami (Krishna's birthday), August 18, 1884] Girish Ghosh came to visit the Master at Dakshineswar. I was also there. That evening Girish sang a song to the Master from his play *Chaitanya Lila*: "O Keshava, bestow thy grace upon thy luckless servants here. O Keshava, who dost delight to roam Vrindaban's glades and groves!" The Master, out of ecstasy, embraced Girish and sat on his lap. Tears of joy flowed from the Master's eyes. After a while Girish left for Calcutta. Since it was too late for me to return home the Master said to me: "It is late. You will not have to return home. Stay here tonight." So I decided to pass the night at the temple garden of Dakshineswar. Some time later the Master gave me some luchis [fried bread] and sweets, which were prasad of the Divine Mother. Sri Ramakrishna made a bed for me and set up the mosquito curtain. I fell asleep as soon as I lay down. At midnight I woke up and found the Master walking around my bed, saying, "Mother, Mother." I was dumbfounded and could not understand what was going on. That night Sri Ramakrishna blessed me.

It is hard to describe Sri Ramakrishna's fascinating power. He who saw him once was attracted to him forever. One evening I went to Dakshineswar and expressed to the Master my desire to stay overnight. He gladly gave his consent. There was no good eating arrangement at night in Dakshineswar. Every night some prasad of the Divine Mother would be sent to the Master for his supper, and from that he would eat a little and distribute the remainder among those who stayed with him. The Master's night meal was very small — like a bird's food. He would eat a couple of luchis, a little farina pudding, and some sweets. However, seeing the small quantity of prasad, I was upset. I realized that I would have to fast that night. I was then young with a well-built body and a good appetite. That little bit of prasad was not enough for me. Knowing what was in my mind, the Master asked somebody to bring some chapatis [bread] and vegetable curry for me from the nahabat. Even that amount of food was not sufficient for me, but I ate it and lay down on the floor of the Master's room.

Suddenly at midnight I woke up and saw the Master pacing back and forth in his room. Sometimes he would go to the front verandah, muttering something, or he would chant the names of gods and goddesses while clapping his hands. During the day the Master talked and joked with the devotees, but now, at night, he was so different. I was scared to death. I lay in bed, quietly observing the Master's madness. I could not get back to sleep. Sometimes the Master sang and danced, and sometimes he talked with someone. At last the night passed and I was relieved. In the morning the Master was normal again. I talked to him as usual. As I looked at him, I could not believe that this was the same person who had acted so abnormally the night before. Everything about the Master was mysterious! Outwardly he looked like an ordinary human being, but truly he was a living god. We are fortunate that we came in contact with him, and he, out of mercy, gave us shelter.

When I returned home, my sister asked, "Where did you stay last night?" "At the temple garden of Dakshineswar," I replied. Immediately she exclaimed: "Did you stay with that mad brahmin of Dakshineswar? Don't go to that man again. He is really mad. Very often I go there for a bath in the Ganga. I have seen him and I know about his madness." I listened to her words and smiled.

Sri Ramakrishna was very concerned about our welfare. If any of his disciples did not visit him for a while he would ask someone to inquire about that person. Sharat Maharaj sometimes gave me news about the Master. Once when I had not come for a long time the Master sent for me. I went to Dakshineswar, and that day not too many people were around him. As I entered his room he asked in a complaining but affectionate tone: "Hello, how are you? What is the matter? Why haven't I seen you for so long?" I replied truthfully, "I did not feel like coming." "That's all right," the Master said, smiling. "But I hope you have continued your practice of meditation." I said, "I try to meditate, sir, but I find I can't."

The Master seemed surprised at my reply and exclaimed: "What do you mean you cannot meditate? Surely you can." He remained silent for a few moments. I was looking at him, waiting for him to say something more. Soon I noticed a change coming over his face and eyes. He looked at me intently. After a little while he said, "Come near me." As I approached the Master, he asked me to stick out my tongue. When I did, he drew a figure on it with his finger. My whole body began to tremble, and I felt an unspeakable bliss within. Then the Master said, "Go to the Panchavati and meditate there." Following his instruction, I slowly moved towards the Panchavati. I walked with difficulty, intoxicated with joy from the Master's touch. Somehow I reached there and sat for meditation. Then I lost all outward consciousness. When I regained my ordinary state of mind, I saw the Master seated by me. He was rubbing my body with his hands. His face shone with a heavenly smile. I was

still in an intoxicated mood. He asked me, "Well, how was your meditation?" "It was very good, sir," I replied. Then the Master said, "From
now on you will always have deep meditation." He further asked, "Did
you have any vision?"

I reported my experience to the Master as faithfully as I could. Then
I followed him to his room. I was alone with him. That day he talked to
me for a long time and gave me many spiritual instructions. I was
overwhelmed by the Master's love and compassion for me. I had not
realized before that he had so much feeling for me. Sri Ramakrishna's
grace was unbounded.

On that day the Master said to me: "Never get involved with women.
Always be careful. Let there be no stain in your character. Never look at
a woman, even if she is made out of gold. Do you know why I am saying
all this to you? You belong to the Divine Mother, and you will have to
do a lot of work for her. A pecked fruit cannot be offered to the Mother.
So I tell you, be careful."

On one occasion I was massaging the Master's feet when a gentleman
came to visit him from Konnagar. After he had left, the Master said, "You
know, I can see the inside of a man's mind just as I can see the objects
inside a glass case." I thought to myself: "Well, then he can also see
everything in me. What a dangerous man he is!" But the Master would
only speak of the goodness in others, not of their evil deeds or tendencies.

In Sri Ramakrishna we found manifest aspects of other Divine Incarnations of the past. Once, standing in his room, the Master said in a
serious mood, "In my incarnation as Krishna I played with the shepherd
boys and girls of Vrindaban." I was then a college student, and it was
hard for me to believe these words. He knew my doubts and so he began
to talk of the deep love the gopis [shepherd girls] had for Krishna.

The Master said: "The gopis' love was pure, divine love. They were
so intoxicated with love that whenever they heard the sound of
Krishna's flute, they would rush to him, leaving home, husband, and
children. Krishna was a shepherd boy. He did not have any wealth. Still
the gopis loved him dearly. They surrendered their bodies, minds, souls,
and everything to their beloved Krishna. It is said in the Bhagavatam
that Krishna played the *raslila* [the divine sport with the gopis on a full
moon night in autumn]. At that time his entire energy went to the
sahasrara [seventh chakra in the crown of the head], and he was immersed in deep samadhi in the realm of light and bliss. And the gopis
also had the same experience."

While talking about this divine attraction, the Master suddenly became speechless and lost all outward consciousness. He was deeply
absorbed in samadhi. I was also beside myself, thinking about the divine

sport of Krishna with the gopis of Vrindaban. The Master created a palpable atmosphere of divine love in the orbit of his power, as Krishna had done in Vrindaban. Since I happened to be inside that orbit, my veil of ignorance about the raslila disappeared. For the first time I realized the true significance of Krishna's play with the gopis. When the Master returned to the normal plane of consciousness he smiled sweetly. I kept silent.

Once during my college days when I went to visit the Master at Dakshineswar, I asked him, "Is God with form or without form?" The Master replied: "God is with form as well as without form, and again he is beyond both form and formlessness." Then I asked, "If God is all, is this cot also God?" He answered emphatically, "Yes, this cot is God, this glass, this utensil, this wall — everything is God." As he spoke, I experienced an inner transformation and was lifted beyond ordinary consciousness. My heart was illumined, and I saw the light of Brahman everywhere.

After a while I again asked the Master, "If God has become everything, then why do people discriminate during meals, thinking that if their food is touched by a certain person they won't eat?" The Master replied: "Look. When some monks were eating here at Dakshineswar, a prostitute came and ate the leftovers from their leaf plates. She had no discrimination about food. Do you then mean to say that she was a knower of Brahman?" I said, "No, sir, her character was not good." Then the Master said: "So the knowledge of Brahman does not only depend upon nondiscrimination in eating. It depends upon something else." Listening to the Master's logical answer, I was dumbfounded. The Master had such a gigantic personality that sometimes I was afraid to be near him. He had all powers. He could fulfill the wishes of others.

During my youth I had read the philosophies of Kant, Hegel, and other thinkers. One day I said to the Master: "Sir, what do you know about philosophy? Have you read the works of Kant and Hegel?" He replied: "What are you saying? Throw away all those books. Knowledge of God is not in any book. Those books are all products of ignorance." What a great statement the Master made! Later, finding no way out, I gave up arguing. In the beginning we need faith for God-realization.

Once at Dakshineswar the Master gave me an English book and asked me to read and explain it to him. It was stated in the book: "Speak the truth. Do not covet what belongs to another. Control your senses." On hearing this, the Master felt elated like a boy and expressed his great delight. The Master's joy is even now deeply impressed on my mind. I think that his expression of great delight was due to the fact that if a person attains perfection in those three disciplines he is sure to reach

God. Whenever he heard any discussion about God, he would go into ecstasy.

Our Master did not have any school education, but he could read and write. In his presence we would feel that our book learning was a very inferior type of education. Of course book learning does refine the intellect to some extent, but of what use is it unless this refined intellect is profitably employed? The Master wanted us to acquire the wisdom that comes from the direct vision of God.

Blessed is this country that held in her bosom such a God-man. I am very fortunate that I met him.

The Master was the living embodiment of holiness and purity. People may think I say this because I am his disciple. It is not so. I tell you frankly that I have never seen anyone to compare with the Master. He was always in an ecstatic mood and his nerve current always flowed towards the highest plane.

What childlike simplicity the Master had! During his fatal illness if somebody would say, "Sir, please use this medicine and you will be cured," he would believe that person like a child. Once he called Ramlal and said: "This person says that if I take this medicine I will be cured. Please get it for me." With his natural innocence and frankness, he was, like a child, as quick to believe as to disbelieve a person's words. He would take the medicine, but his disease did not abate. Later when he met the person who had suggested it, he said: "Your words are not true. I am not going to believe you anymore." It was extremely difficult to talk to the Master. When I talked with him, I always chose my words carefully. I understood the Master very little.

Even looking at him one could see that he observed people in silent amazement. He would say: "People in this world are entrapped by maya and engrossed with impermanent, mundane things. They are so deluded and attached to momentary pleasures that they turn away from eternal bliss." His spiritual mood was absolutely incomparable.

He was a man of renunciation. He could not touch any money or metallic object. As our nerves contract when we touch a thorny plant, similarly, when touching a coin or piece of metal, his whole body would contract. He considered money as negligible as clay. He said, "The goal of human life is to realize God." And he constantly emphasized one thing: "Let there be knowledge and devotion." No one ever heard him say, "Let there be riches and supernatural powers." He looked down on those things with disgust.

Before accepting a person as his disciple, the Master would check the signs of that person's whole body. He did this to me. I didn't care. I was then a teenaged boy. After examining me he asked me to massage his feet. I began to press his feet vigorously, but he asked me to rub them gently. I vividly remember the Master saying to me, "I see a light like the flame of a matchstick inside you." I did not understand what he meant. He could clearly see what was inside every human being.

Once a gentleman came to visit the Master at Dakshineswar. As he was taking his leave, the Master asked him, "When are you coming again?" He replied, "I shall come at about 3:00 P.M. the day after tomorrow." On that day, at the appointed time, the Master became very restless and began to pace back and forth, in and out of his room. At last when the Master realized definitely that the man was not coming, he remarked indignantly: "So he has not turned up at all! His words cannot be relied upon."

A few days later, when that gentleman came to visit him, the Master asked: "How is it that you did not come the other day though you had said you would? Did your wife pull you by the cloth and thus persuade you not to come here?" The man was dumbfounded, for that was actually what had happened. The Master could read the thoughts of others as one does the open pages of a book.

About caste distinctions, the Master once said to me: "When a matchstick burns, if you put some dry wood on it, will that stick continue to burn?" I answered, "No, because that little flame of the matchstick will be extinguished by the pressure of the heavy firewood." Again he asked, "When a forest of dry wood catches fire, if you throw a raw plantain tree into it, will it not burn?" "Yes, it will burn," I replied. Then the Master said: "When a little spirituality dawns in a human mind, one should observe caste rules, the distinction between the guru and Chosen Deity, and other current traditions and customs. Otherwise, nonobservance of these religious rituals and conventions will diminish this little spirituality. But when the blazing light of Brahman illumines the heart, all distinctions between guru and Chosen Deity, caste, customs, and practices disappear."

The light of Brahman was constantly ablaze in the Master. He experienced Brahman in everything and every being. The Master said: "I passed through such a state when I ate the discarded leavings of food alongside a dog in a dirty place. I was then carried by a spiritual tempest, and everything appeared to me as nondual Brahman."

Sri Ramakrishna set the example of a sincere seeker of God. He could not bear coming into contact with lust and gold. The touch of money would contort his hands. At one time he could not accept salutations from just anyone.

Our Master was the embodiment of purity. As soon as there was any talk on a spiritual subject, he would immediately go into ecstasy. People of all communities derived great pleasure from his holy company, and they would look upon him as their own. He practised universality. He was not bound by any limitations.

The Master's mind soared constantly in the highest realms of the spirit. The world was almost nonexistent to him. When he talked with people of this world, he had to forcibly bring his mind down to a lower plane of consciousness.

The Master was a spiritual dynamo. While chanting the Lord's name he would become intoxicated and lose body consciousness. A piece of live charcoal once touched his body while he was in samadhi but he did not feel it.

One day a wealthy man came and offered some money to Sri Rama-krishna, but he refused to accept it. He said, "This devil has come to drag me away from the Divine Mother." A pandit prayed to the Master for wisdom. The Master told him: "I don't know anything. The Mother knows everything." When the mind is detached from sense objects, the light of Brahman is seen in all beings. People are scorched by the fire of the world because of attachment to sense objects. As the Master was absorbed day and night in the thought of the Divine Mother, the fire of the world could not touch him. As a result of constant absorption in the Divine, the Master enjoyed perennial bliss. He was overwhelmed with bliss — sometimes laughing, sometimes weeping in the joy of ecstasy. I never saw him devoid of bliss. It pained him to see us cheerless. He was eager to share with us the eternal joy in which he remained immersed twenty-four hours of the day. In the presence of the divine light, all work and study in this world seem mere trash. As our eyes always see the world of matter, so the Master's eyes constantly saw the light of Brah-man.

Sri Ramakrishna was an embodiment of truth and purity, but he practised hard austerities to achieve that exalted state. Once he decided that he would see the Divine Mother in the sun. For three days he gazed at the sun from sunrise to sunset. The following day he saw the Divine Mother in the sun. The secret of obtaining God-vision and spiritual illumination is to possess infinite longing for them both. [*One should not practise this type of sadhana without the instruction of the guru.*]

Sri Ramakrishna would be annoyed if he was addressed by any of these three words: guru, karta [master], and baba [father]. He did not give mantras in the way it is usually understood and done. But his advent was for the good of humanity — to give liberation to people. He bestowed his grace on numerous persons. Even during the course of a conversation he could vouchsafe to a person the vision of his Chosen Deity by a mere touch or wish. He would make him realize God in his heart. There was not the least ostentatious display when giving a mantram.

When the Master was blessed for the first time with the vision of the Divine Mother, he thought, "If this vision of mine is true, then let this big stone [*which was in front of the nahabat*] jump up thrice." What he thought immediately happened, and seeing that, the Master was fully convinced of the genuineness of his vision.

The Master had passionate love for truth. He always kept his word. Whenever the carriage reached Dakshineswar to take him to Calcutta, he would immediately get ready and enter it. Then he would call the driver, who was perhaps smoking. The Master would hurry because devotees in Calcutta were waiting for him, and if he were late they would be worried. When the carriage started, he would be relieved. Once he said, "If one word of mine is untrue, then whatever I have said is untrue." What a great statement! It is something new. Can anybody speak such words if his life is not firmly established in truth?

The Master was a wonderful person. I noticed that a wave of spiritual power played on the Master's body all the time. A little power in the brain makes an ordinary person a famous chemist or physicist or politician. On the other hand, a tremendous spiritual current flowed in every centre of the Master's body. What terrific power he had!

Once the Master told me, pointing to his own picture: "Look. I dwell in this picture. Meditate on me." "Yes, I will," I told him. All the forms of gods and goddesses are within Sri Ramakrishna's form. His photograph symbolizes the piercing of the six centres of kundalini. When I look at his luminous form, it seems to me that the Master is immersed in the blissful ocean of Satchidananda transcending the six centres of the kundalini. I see many wonderful things in the Master's picture. Sri Ramakrishna manifests himself to those people who are pure in heart.

The last night I stayed at Dakshineswar with the Master was the very night he got his sore throat [cancer]. In the morning he said to his nephew, "Ramlal, I have a pain in my throat." A young boy who was nearby suggested, "Sir, if you apply the juice of the *tejbal* leaf, your pain will subside." The Master immediately believed his words and said to Ramlal: "Look. This boy is suggesting that I apply the juice of tejbal leaf to relieve this pain. Why don't you make some for me?" Ramlal knew the Master's nature. He said, "All right, I will make it right now."

That was my last visit to the Master. Afterwards I went to Bankipur [in Bihar] for my last two years of college. The house where I lived is now an ashrama. The day the Master passed away I saw him standing in front of me. I wondered: "How did the Master come here? What is the cause of this vision?" The next day I read of the Master's passing away in the *Basumati* newspaper.

Once at Dakshineswar the Master said to me: "Do you know why I love you? You boys are my very own. The Divine Mother has asked me to love you." I cannot express how much love the Master had for us. We don't have that capacity to love others. We became intoxicated seeing the Master, and now people are intoxicated just by hearing his name. How blessed they are!

[From: *Satprasange Swami Vijnanananda*, by Swami Apurvananda (Allahabad: Sri Ramakrishna Math), 1953; *Swami Vijnanananda*, by Swami Jagadiswarananda (Allahabad: Sri Ramakrishna Math), 1947; *Pratyakshadarshir Smritipate Swami Vijnanananda*, by Suresh Chandra Das & Jyotirmay Basu-Roy (Calcutta: General Printers & Publ. Pvt. Ltd.), 1976; *Udbodhan*, vol. 43, no.7, 1941; *Prabuddha Bharata*, 1950-51; *Vedanta and the West*, no. 112, March-April 1955]

Swami Trigunatitananda in San Francisco

15

Swami Trigunatitananda

Swami Trigunatitananda (1865-1915) met Sri Ramakrishna in 1884 through M., the recorder of The Gospel of Sri Ramakrishna. *He served the Master at Cossipore and took his final vows at Baranagore monastery. He was the first editor of* Udbodhan *magazine, which was started by Swami Vivekananda. In 1902 he became the head of the Vedanta Society of San Francisco, and through his efforts the first Hindu temple in the West was built in 1906.*

This article is an edited version of a lecture given by Swami Trigunatitananda in San Francisco under the title "The Great Prophet of the 19th Century — Life of Sri Ramakrishna."

Sri Ramakrishna was born in 1836 in a little village, the inhabitants of which gained their livelihood by tilling the soil. His parents were very poor in material things, but in the most important things — the culture of the Self and deep religious feeling — they were very rich. That little family did not care for worldly prosperity. Belonging to the brahmin caste — the highest in India — they were supposed to cultivate the Self, to devote themselves to religious practices, to teach, but nothing else.

The boy was sent to school to learn what the teachers had to tell, but in a very few days he understood that that kind of learning would not give him the truth for which his life was meant. He understood this at the early age of five, and said to his parents: "I am not meant to earn bread and butter in this world. I am meant for higher things. Others will look out for me. God has created me; God will give me food. Who has brought me to this world? Who has given me this life? God. God will sustain this life. When God thinks it is time, He will take me away from here."

We think we are taking care of ourselves; that is because we are ignorant. But that little boy was a born sage. He understood from the moment he came into this world what his mission was, so he gave up worldly education and commenced to study higher subjects. Where could he go for higher knowledge? Wherever he went in the world, he found a-b-c-d, he found 1-2-3-4. Wherever he went he found good or bad, money, men and women. Wherever he went he found nothing but worldliness. He could not find the place to get *his* kind of education.

A few years passed and he left his home and came to the city, Calcutta, where he thought he would find some higher help. He wanted to get some positive light by the practice of certain religious exercises. He felt the necessity of going in a methodical way. But he could not find anyone in the city able to teach him. Afterwards he was appointed as a priest in a big temple near Calcutta. Belonging to the brahmin priestly caste, he was eligible for the priesthood. There he worshipped the image of Mother Kali.

Some people in India worship Mother Kali as the embodiment of the great creative faculty — not only creative faculty (you know in everything there is a trinity) — but preservative and destructive as well. Destruction does not mean death, but liberation. Creation — that is birth. Preservation — that is bondage, our life. And liberation, the great salvation, unity with him from whom we have come. That is the image of Mother Kali.

Ramakrishna was appointed to worship that Mother Kali. He used to worship first as the religious rite dictates, with flowers, sandal paste, incense, food, water, etc. But the image did not eat the food, did not drink the water, nor accept the flowers. Everything was left there as it was. Nothing was diminished.

The young boy learned the mantram, the prayer which was used in offering those objects; he knew its meaning. He did not just repeat the words as the ordinary priests do in every country. He was of special make. He was made for some special purpose. He could not do anything without understanding the meaning of it. After meditation he found all the objects of offering there as they had been placed. He thought that was strange. He had meant that food for Mother Kali and she ought to have eaten it. He commenced praying, praying, praying, meditating and meditating, deeper and deeper. He went to this person and that person and asked why his offerings were not accepted. They said, those offerings cannot be accepted externally. If you are sincere, God will accept them internally and you will feel, you will understand that. But the poor boy's mind was not satisfied. He thought that if he worshipped that image as God, God should appear; that if he offered anything to God, God must accept it in every sense, internally and externally. If God did not do so with others, He should do it with him. He said he would not let God go without accepting his offerings. The brave soldier! Do or die, he had to succeed! His purpose must be fulfilled. He had to get the full effect of his work, to know that his offerings, his worship, were accepted.

He left the temple. He was still a young boy. He did not know where to go. He thought that he would enter into the deep forest and be merged in deep meditation and practise hard yogas. But some voice within told him: if there is such a thing as God, then he must be everywhere. So he commenced practising alone in the very garden of the temple. That garden is a very large, spacious compound, covering several acres of land, and with big buildings and many temples. And in a secluded place in the garden he commenced to practise yoga. He had all time at his command. He did not care what he ate nor what he put on. Hunger of the body is not as important as the hunger of the soul and he was hungry in spirit for the Spirit. He cared for *that* kind of food, for *that* kind of drink, for *that* kind of clothing. Along what line would he practise? Simply speaking, simply thinking, simply sitting would not do. Practice is quite different from study; practising means putting into practical life. You imbibe certain thoughts and ideas until your actions are nothing but the reflection of those ideas and thoughts. That is practice. We practise so many things, but we do not learn many, especially about religion. Practising religion is very difficult, very hard to understand, very hard to perform.

He thought of having a guru, a spiritual teacher, who would show him the proper way. As we have already heard, he never had before in his life any teacher to satisfy his soul, and he could not at that time get any teacher. There were many experienced teachers, but all their teaching fell short of his capacity. He used to say now and then to them: "I want to know more; what everybody knows, that I know. I want to know something beyond that, which will satisfy my soul." He saw many persons coming to the temple and shedding many tears and giving expression to their feelings of devotion, but he wanted something still beyond, which would satisfy his thirsty soul. God does not reveal himself when we look outside for him. His outside aspect is far, far distant. The nearest of the near is inside, and if we want to see God sooner we must look inside.

Some force, some power, some tendency, some inclination, dictated to Ramakrishna to sit quiet and to meditate. He did that. There was no other way open to him but that. When we sit quiet, we simply close our eyes, but we are not even physically quiet. We cough, we move, we swallow, and we do this and that, and many external things torment us. Internally the mind cannot be made to be quiet. That is against its nature. It is not built that way. It goes here and there and everywhere without any purpose. The mind is enslaved, but God has given us a little power of control so that we may get and keep that mind under our sway. That controlling power that we have from our birth is to be developed. That boy used to sit quietly; the external world used to vanish and he became merged in deep meditation. We often speak of meditation. What is meditation? Thinking of God. We have not seen God. We have heard of him. Can we believe what we have heard? Everything is doubtful, full of questions. If we meditate properly, doubts will become less. That is the kind of meditation that we should practise. It is not beyond our power.

Those very things that are in born sages, that are in all the prophets, Incarnations of God, are within every man, more or less. We can, if we try, if we wish, have them developed to the same extent. Ramakrishna used to meditate, to lose himself physically and mentally in God. "Oh God, if thou existest, show thyself, prove thyself, appear before me," was his prayer, and he used to analyze and listen. He would lose all his physical and mental faculties, and keep simply the spiritual faculty, the power of discrimination, the power of discovering the light inside. He used to search with that searchlight that he had kindled with his great love of truth that was within him from his birth. At last, after performance of hard asceticisms for twelve years, he attained the truth. He found that there was no difference between this and that, as we often say. Before, he had heard all those doctrines, all those tenets, but he could not believe in them, because whenever he prayed he found that his heart did not correspond with his words. He was sincere to the backbone. We fool ourselves at every step, at every moment of our lives.

He came out victorious after his great fight. We cannot describe properly what he went through in those twelve years of hard asceticism. We cannot realize, because we are not yogis, we are not practitioners of those hard yogas. If you search for God from outside, he is far, far away from you. Search inside. Inside means that you will forget the outside; your mind will not wander in your meditation, you will forget the external world. Ramakrishna understood all these things and he was very careful not to be led away by worldly temptations.

Those people who lived around him, and used to see him, told us the story. They used to see Ramakrishna sitting from morning to night in one seat, in one posture. He felt no hunger, no thirst, no heat, no cold, no fear, nothing except inside the burning desire for the truth. That was the way he lived. That love for the truth became his sustenance. Others used to come and call him by name: "Get up, get out, eat, drink, or you will die. We will drive you away from this garden, for we cannot see you dying here, committing suicide here." It was as though they were addressing a tree, or the river, for the boy could not hear. Then they used to thrash him, to bring him to consciousness so that he might eat. They understood that the boy was an extraordinary one, that they should take proper care of him; but they did not know how. They thought that if he did not eat a little fruit, or drink a little milk, every day or at least every other day, how could he continue his practice? So they used to beat him, to make him open his mouth for some milk. In that way twelve years passed.

You might have read in the *Light of Asia* of the great Buddha, and how many years he passed in hard asceticism without even a drop of milk and yet it was possible for him to live. That is possible for such people who are messengers, who are Messiahs, who are the great prophets and sages that come to teach the world.

You compare all the Bibles [scriptures] of the world. One and all will say the same thing. But who can explain until a Jesus, a Christ comes? Ramakrishna came to teach the Bible, to teach not one Bible, but all the Bibles of the world. Not to teach as we teach, from the platform, from the pulpit, either in church or in school, but in his own practical life. The great teachers impart that force, that spiritual life, that spiritual treasure that they earned for humanity out of their own struggle and experience. We know when we work how tired we get — our brows perspire. But their blood dries out of hard asceticism. And that young boy, when he practised those hard asceticisms, attained the object for which he was meant, for which he came to this world.

Such sages, or those who attain the truth, do not care to live afterwards in this world. Not that they have any independent will or judgment about their staying or going away, but it is the Law that makes them go. You can imagine that after twelve years of hard asceticism few people can live in flesh and blood — in the physical life. Spiritually, when in the deepest meditation they enter into *nirvakalpa samadhi* — that is, into the highest realization, where there is nothing but supreme bliss, the oneness of the spirit — they lose their individual existence; the ego and the body are left behind; the spirit is united with the One. How can they awake from meditation? But this young boy came back from his deep meditation and samadhi, owing to the force, to the necessity of the message he received. He came to give that message to the world.

That young priest Ramakrishna was born quietly. Nobody could understand his greatness in his boyhood. Nobody, in his childhood, could understand his grandeur. When as a young man, after his success in spiritual culture and he came out of his meditation, very few people understood him; and he went away quietly. Leaving what? Bequeathing what? Such a great energy, such a great force, such a great power, that *must* produce something very great. He used to tell us to follow what he said and did and we would see whether his words and actions corresponded. Those who have learned about his life have understood a little glimpse of the truth. After his spiritual success, externally he practised every religion. He became a Christian, worshipped Jesus the Christ, understood what Christ was, and what his words and the Bible were. He used to explain passages of the Bible which he never had read in his life. He never could read any sentence or utter a single word in English. He became a Muslim; he understood who Muhammad was and that he had taught the truth.

All the prophets, sages, and Incarnations of God are nothing else but messengers to bring the message from Heaven. Ramakrishna could explain beautifully that there is or can be not one messenger only, not one path only, not one Incarnation of God, but many, so that the different types of minds could be satisfied.

We cannot give up the world and go to God. We have been created in the materials of the world. Inside and outside there is nothing but the world. Outside it is worldly; inside it is worldly. How from such conditions can we raise our level, can we improve our state? He showed the way. In the Bible Jesus taught, "Be ye in the world but not of it." And this Ramakrishna came and showed what most Christians say but cannot understand — how to be in this world but not of it. He said: first keep before the mind the highest ideal, that you are one with the Absolute. "Thou art One. Philosophers represent thee variously." Keep that ideal before you and start from where you are. There is no need of renouncing the world. Ramakrishna did not go to the forest to practise his great asceticism after the truth. He stayed in the world; he even married.

If you want to see God in one life, sages, prophets, and messengers have shown the way in their practical life, and you will have to do as they have done. Or, if you have not that great energy, great power, great capacity, you may go slowly. But go surely. Know that you are going. Do not go back. Do not stop. Go, even if it be slowly, but advance all the time and there will come a time when you will see the light, when you will see the truth, be it in twelve years, be it in twelve lives, be it in twelve centuries. Time is eternal before us. God is infinite and eternal. But start your work right now, so that you may be on the right road and may not lose time and energy.

[From: *Voice of Freedom* (San Francisco: Vedanta Society), vol. VII, nos. 11-12, February-March 1916]

II

Householder Disciples and Devotees

Ram Chandra Datta in Calcutta

16

Ram Chandra Datta

Ram Chandra Datta (1851-1899) was a householder disciple of Sri Ramakrishna and a medical practitioner of Calcutta Medical College. He had great enthusiasm for preaching the message of the Master. Even as early as 1885 he published a book titled Tattwasara *containing the teachings of Sri Ramakrishna. He also founded the Kankurgachi Yogodyana (a retreat in East Calcutta), where he installed the Master's relics.*

In 1879 (November 13) we [Ram Chandra Datta, Manomohan Mittra, and Gopal Chandra Mittra] went to visit Sri Ramakrishna. We arrived at Dakshineswar at 1:00 P.M. The door of his room was closed, and we were wondering if we should call out to him. Just then someone opened the door.

As soon as we saw him our hearts became calm, but we did not know who he was. We entered the room, bowed down to him, and sat on the floor. We guessed that he must be Sri Ramakrishna, though he was not wearing an ochre cloth as monks normally do. For that reason many people did not recognize him to be a holy man.

We were rank atheists, but Sri Ramakrishna made us believe in God. His advice did not consist of mere words. Let me tell the story of how I accepted the Master as my guru.

When my first daughter died, the joy I felt in my family life was shattered. Many questions then arose in my mind: Does God exist? Can anyone see God? Is it possible to enjoy the bliss of God? A few days later our hereditary guru came to our house. Seeing him I thought he would be able to answer my questions. When I put my questions to him, however, he said that he did not know the answers, and he even doubted that there was anybody who could answer my questions except Lord Shiva. Listening to this, I was at first very disappointed, but later I thought that perhaps Lord Shiva might be gracious enough to give me a vision. It was after this that I went to the Master and all my questions were answered.

During our first visit we did not ask any questions. As soon as he saw us he began to speak: "Who wants God? Man weeps one jugful of tears for property, two jugfuls of tears for wealth and money, and ten jugfuls of tears for wife, children, and relatives. But who sheds a teardrop for God? He only finds God who wants him, who sees darkness all around without him, who feels terrible discomfort without him." These words from the Master solved all our problems. From that moment he captured our hearts.

One day we asked: "Does God exist? How can one see God?" The Master replied: "God really exists. You do not see any stars during the day, but that does not mean that the stars do not exist. There is butter in milk, but can anyone know it by seeing the milk? In order to get butter you must churn the milk in a cool place before sunrise. If you want to catch fish in a pond, you have to learn the art of fishing from those who know it, and then you must sit patiently with a fishing rod, throwing the line into the water. Gradually the fish will grab the bait. Then, as soon as the float sinks, you can pull the fish to shore. Similarly, you cannot realize God by a mere wish. Have faith in the instructions of a holy man. Make your mind like a fishing rod and your prana, or life force, like a hook. Your devotion and japam must be like the bait. Eventually you will be blessed by the vision of God."

Previously we did not believe in the existence of God. Furthermore, after associating with the Brahmo Samaj we had come to believe that God is formless. The Master read our minds and said: "Yes, God can be seen. Can God, whose creation is so beautiful and enchanting, be imperceptible?" We said: "Sir, whatever you say is true. Who can refute you? Is it possible to realize God in this life?" The Master replied: "You get what you desire. Faith alone is the key to success." Then he sang a song:

> As is a man's meditation, so is his feeling of love;
> As is a man's feeling of love, so is his gain;
> And faith is the root of all.
> If in the Nectar Lake of Mother Kali's feet
> My mind remains immersed,
> Of little use are worship, oblations, or sacrifice.

The Master continued: "The more you advance in one direction, the more you leave behind the opposite direction. If you move ten steps towards the east, you move ten steps away from the west." Then we said: "But one must have tangible proof. Unless we have direct experience of

God, how can our weak and doubting minds have faith in his existence?" The Master replied: "A typhoid patient in a delirious state clamours to take gallons of water and heaps of rice. But the physician pays no heed to those entreaties, nor does he prescribe medicine at the patients's dictation. He knows what he is doing." In spite of listening to the Master's convincing words, our minds were not satisfied.

A few days later I felt tremendous longing for God. One night I dreamed that I took my bath in a familiar pond and the Master came and initiated me with a sacred mantram. He then instructed me, saying, "Repeat this mantram one hundred times every day after your bath." As soon as I woke up I felt that my body was throbbing with bliss. The next morning I rushed to Dakshineswar and related my dream to the Master. Hearing about it, Sri Ramakrishna joyfully said, "He who receives divine blessings in a dream is sure to attain liberation." But due to my Western education, even this assurance from the Master did not convince me. I had learned from Western thinkers that dreams are fantasies of the mind. The Master's words had not removed my doubts, so I kept quiet.

As days passed I felt more and more discontented, and in my confused state of mind I cursed the day I met Sri Ramakrishna. I neither found pleasure in sense enjoyments nor could I definitely ascertain the existence of God. A few days passed this way. Then one morning at 11 o'clock, I was standing near the southwest corner of College Square in Calcutta with a friend. We were talking about our mental unrest. All of a sudden a dark-complexioned man appeared before us and said with a smile: "Why are you so anxious? Have patience." We were taken aback. Who was this man, we wondered, who had read our minds and lifted our spirits? We looked in all directions for the stranger, but he was gone. We were puzzled. It could not have been an illusion, for both of us had seen and heard him in broad daylight. I took this incident to be a message from God. When I related to the Master what had happened, he said, "Yes, you will see many such things."

For some time after this incident I felt great tranquility of mind. I began to taste the bliss of God. Sometimes out of ecstasy I would laugh for half an hour, or I would cry so much that tears would wet my cloth. One day I prayed to the Master to be initiated into sannyasa. But Sri Ramakrishna dissuaded me, saying: "Nothing should be done on the spur of the moment. God alone knows what he intends to do through a particular person. Have you not seen that if the mother fish is killed in a pond, her newborn children are eaten by other fish? Similarly, where will your wife and children be if you leave the world? You must not try to upset the arrangement God has made for you. Everything will come in time."

I considered myself to be an advanced soul, and I felt that renunciation was the summum bonum of spiritual life. Consequently, a few days
later I again approached the Master about becoming a monk. This time
he said sternly: "What will you gain by renouncing the world? Living a
family life is like living inside a fort. It is easier to fight an enemy from
inside a fort than from outside. You will be in a position to renounce the
world when you can put three-fourths of your mind on God, but not
before that." This time I respectfully accepted the Master's advice.

For a while I was happy and passed my days in joy. But after some
time my mind suddenly became restless again, and I felt an emptiness
inside me. Life seemed to be a barren desert. I could not find any way
out from that depression. I went to the Master and told him my sad story.
But this time the Master behaved differently. He gravely said to me:
"What can I do? Everything depends on the will of God." Surprised, I
said: "Sir, all these days I have been looking to you for help. If you treat
me like this what shall I do?" But he indignantly replied: "I don't owe
you anything. I should not be blamed. If you like, you may come here.
If not, don't."

This tone of cold reserve and indifference in the Master's voice
unnerved me. My first impulse was to drown myself in the Ganga during
the flood tide that night. Resolving to do just that, I left the Master. But
after a while I asked myself: "Why should I commit suicide? I have heard
that the name of the Lord is greater and more powerful than the Lord
himself. And the Master said that it was my good luck to have had
initiation in a dream. I shall test the efficacy of that mantram right now."
I lay down on the verandah outside Sri Ramakrishna's room and began
to repeat that mantram silently. At dead of night the Master suddenly
came out of his room, sat near me, and instructed me to serve the
devotees. The Master's compassion melted my heart, and my wounded
feelings disappeared.

I was reluctant to serve the devotees, however, because that required
money. [*Quite often devotees of Sri Ramakrishna would arrange to have
festivals in their homes and would invite the Master and other devotees. At such
gatherings the Master would talk about God and sing and dance in ecstasy,
filling the whole house with an intense atmosphere of spirituality. The host
would generally bear all expenses of such a feast, including the Master's carriage
fare, and sometimes the hiring of a musician. Ram was known for his miserliness.*] At that time I did not have any inclination to attain virtue by
spending money. But one day the Master asked me, "When are you
going to invite me to your home?" I casually replied, "Whenever you
wish, sir." The Master set a date: Saturday, June 2, 1883, the full moon
day of the Bengali month of Vaishakh [April-May]. Later I tried to cancel

the Master's visit, but then I felt ashamed to show my face to him. During that time I earned several hundred rupees which I entrusted to my wife. I then realized that it was only through the Master's grace that I earned that extra money, and I was so mean as to want to enjoy it by myself. Immediately I set about with heart and soul to arrange the festival. The Master came and many devotees participated in the function. After distributing bliss and peace in the hearts of the devotees he left for Dakshineswar.

The next evening [June 3, 1883] I went to Dakshineswar. The Master gave me various spiritual instructions, and we talked until 10 o'clock at night. It was a dark night. After taking leave of the Master I went to the outer verandah. Then I saw that he was following me, so I turned towards him. The Master came near me and said, "Well, what do you want?" *What do you want?* These words penetrated inside me like lightning. I thought: "What should I ask for? Should I ask for money?" Immediately I felt ashamed of craving for money. Then I thought: "Should I ask for supernatural powers?" My mind immediately reacted adversely, thinking of the dangerous results of those powers. "Then what should I ask for from the Master?"

Although I realized that Sri Ramakrishna was standing in front of me like a kalpataru [wish-fulfilling tree], ready to grant any boon I wanted, I was at a loss to know what to ask for. Finally, overwhelmed with emotion, I said: "Lord, I don't know what to ask for. You decide for me." "Give me back the mantram I gave you in that dream." Saying this, the Master went into samadhi. Immediately my heart overflowed with heavenly bliss. I wondered, "Is this really happening or is it a dream?" Without losing any time, I prostrated before the Master and offered the mantram mentally at his feet like a flower. The Master touched my head with his right foot, and I also lost outer consciousness. Gradually the Master came back to the normal plane of consciousness and took his foot away. Then he said to me, "If you wish to see anything, look at me." I looked up and saw my Chosen Deity, the object of my meditation, in him. Then he told me: "You do not need to practise any more spiritual disciplines. Just come here and see me now and then, and bring with you a pice worth of something as a present." From that moment I began to live in the realm of peace. I got the taste of divine bliss. I recognized my guru and realized that he and my Chosen Deity were one. I knew the Master to be my all in all.

Soon after I met Sri Ramakrishna I began reading *Sri Sri Chaitanya Charitamrita* [a biography of Chaitanya]. The more I read that book, the more I could visualize the Master. It seemed to me that Sri Chaitanya and Sri Ramakrishna were the same person. I was curious. Then one day the Master asked me to stay that night at Dakshineswar and I agreed. In the evening I was alone with him. Suddenly he asked me, "What are you looking at?" "I am looking at you." He again asked, "What do you think of me?" I replied, "I consider you to be Chaitanya." The Master was silent for a moment and then said, "Well, Bhairavi Brahmani used to say the same thing." The Master's words were significant.

As days went by I saw more and more of Sri Ramakrishna's extraordinary spiritual powers. Whenever I wished to hear the Master's words on a certain subject he would speak on that same topic. The Master knew everything one did. An example of his powers was shown when I took him some sweets. The Master was very fond of jilipis [a sweet], so one day on my way to Dakshineswar I bought some for him from a shop in Calcutta. As I was crossing the Baghbazar bridge, a little boy begged for one of those jilipis and began to run alongside my carriage. I tried to discourage him through scoldings, but he persisted. Then I thought that perhaps the boy was God in disguise, so I gave him a piece. Nobody else knew about this incident.

After arriving at Dakshineswar I put the sweets in the Master's room and spent the whole day there. In the afternoon Sri Ramakrishna asked for some refreshments, and I immediately placed the jilipis in front of him. Then a strange thing happened. He touched them and looked up. He then broke a few and, shaking his head, expressed his unwillingness to eat them. After this he washed his hands.

I was so perturbed and upset that I threw the jilipis away and went home. After a few days I returned to Dakshineswar and the Master said to me: "When you bring something for me, don't give any of it away beforehand. I can't take anything without offering it to God, and I can't offer anything to him that has been defiled by being offered to someone else first." Such events happened many times, convincing me that Sri Ramakrishna was an Incarnation of God.

Hriday [a nephew of Sri Ramakrishna] served the Master for many years, and as a result he received his uncle's blessings. Gradually, however, he became greedy and possessive. No one could talk to the Master or sit near him without first satisfying Hriday with some gifts. When the Master learned about this situation, he forbade Hriday to continue this behaviour. But Hriday paid no attention and did not change his ways. He spoke rudely to Sri Ramakrishna in public and bullied him into submission over trifles. Hriday even dared to put on airs of great sanctity, imitating the gestures Sri Ramakrishna made when in ecstatic moods, and singing and dancing as the Master did. Thus Hriday became a great nuisance. He began to rule the Master, and the latter could do nothing about it.

Once, when Sri Ramakrishna was in bed with a fever, a devotee [Ram himself] came to visit him while Hriday was temporarily away, bringing with him a cauliflower as a gift. The Master was very pleased and praised the thoughtful gift. But he added hastily, "Please hide it, though, and don't tell Hriday, or he'll be angry with me!" The cauliflower was immediately put away as he wished. Then the Master went on to defend Hriday, praising his past services and adding: "Mother has rewarded him well for his faithfulness. He has been able to buy land for himself. He can afford to lend money to people. And he's a very important person in this temple, highly honoured." No sooner had Sri Ramakrishna finished saying this than Hriday entered the room and spied the cauliflower. Sri Ramakrishna seemed dismayed. He said pleadingly to his nephew: "I never asked him to bring me this. He brought it of his own accord. Believe me — I never asked him to!" But Hriday flew into a rage and scolded the Master severely, saying that the doctor had forbidden him to eat cauliflower because it disagreed with him. I still shiver when I remember Hriday's terrible form. Meanwhile Sri Ramakrishna weepingly addressed the Divine Mother: "O Mother, you freed me from all worldly ties, and yet you let Hriday humiliate me like this!" Suddenly his mood changed. He smiled and said: "Mother, he only scolds me because he loves me dearly. He's still only a boy. He doesn't know what he's doing. You must not be angry with him, Mother." The Master then went into samadhi.

Towards the end of May 1881, Trailokya, one of Mathur's sons, arrived at Dakshineswar with his wife and children to take part in the annual festival commemorating the founding of the temple. Hriday went to the temple to perform the worship. Trailokya's ten-year-old daughter was then in the shrine of Kali. Suddenly Hriday felt inspired and began to worship the little girl as the goddess with flowers and sandal paste. He was imitating Sri Ramakrishna, but this act actually brought about his downfall. Later that day Trailokya's wife noticed sandal paste on her daughter's feet and found out what had happened. She began to cry, thinking that this was very inauspicious for her daughter. [*It was believed that if a brahmin worshipped a girl of a lower caste, she would be widowed soon after marriage.*] Trailokya became furious. He immediately ordered his guard to remove Hriday from the temple precincts.

Hriday did not go far, however. He settled down in the garden house of Jadu Mallik, just outside the temple grounds. Sri Ramakrishna used to visit him now and then, and he regularly sent him food from his own share. For a while Hriday kept trying to persuade the Master to leave Dakshineswar and go with him in search of another Kali temple where they could be together again. But the Master always refused. One day he said to Hriday, "Do you want to hawk me from door to door like a curio?"

Once three girls in my family died from cholera, and as a result I could not visit the Master the following Sunday. The Master told the Calcutta devotees: "Something terrible has happened in Ram's family. Please go and visit him." That night the devotees came to my house and informed me that the Master was very worried about me. I sent a messenger to the Master the next day with details of what had happened. The following Sunday, when I went to visit him, I saw that he was more grief-stricken than I.

The devotees of Sri Ramakrishna began observing the Master's birthday with an annual festival at Dakshineswar. Devotees would begin to assemble there in the morning. Trailokya and the temple staff would help in coordinating the function. At 10 o'clock in the morning the Master would take his bath and then put on a new cloth. The singers would then start kirtan [devotional singing], and the Master would join them, improvising words now and then. This brought life to the singing as well as to the gathering.

The devotees could not restrain themselves when the Master was in ecstasy. They also became overwhelmed with spiritual emotion. It was contagious. When the Master lost outer consciousness, the devotees would put white sandal paste on his forehead and feet and a garland around his neck. At such times he would look beautiful! We would gaze in awe at his wonderful form in samadhi. Some devotees would sing and dance around the Master. Then after regaining outer consciousness, the Master would throw away the garland and wipe off the sandal paste, because these were signs of rajas, which he could not bear. Later he would eat with the devotees.

Sri Ramakrishna was very compassionate to the poor, destitute, and dejected. One year, on his birthday celebration, a poor woman devotee of Calcutta brought four rasogollas [cheese balls soaked in syrup] for him and gave them to Holy Mother at the nahabat. Other women devotees were also present there, and they told her: "The Master is now busy with the devotees. How can Holy Mother carry these sweets to him? Moreover, the Master has already finished his meal. He won't eat anything more now. If he does, he will be sick." These words pierced the heart of that poor woman, and tears came to her eyes. She mentally cried to him: "Master, you are the Lord of the poor and the lowly. Your rich devotees have arranged this festival spending a lot of money, and you are in a festive mood with them. I am a poor, simple woman. Somehow I managed to save four pice, and with that I bought these sweets for you.

I don't know what to do! I am helpless. Now I feel that you are not the Lord of the poor." The Master was omniscient. He felt that someone was pulling him, and he immediately left the gathering, went to the nahabat, and ate the sweets that the poor woman had brought for him.

In 1884 Sri Ramakrishna went to the Star Theatre to see *Chaitanya Lila*, a play by Girish Chandra Ghosh on the life of Chaitanya. It was an auspicious day in Girish's life. He used to visit the Master quite often. In spite of his heavy drinking, Girish was undoubtedly an intelligent person. He knew that the guru was Brahma, Vishnu, and Shiva. And although he realized that Sri Ramakrishna was an extraordinary person, he still wanted to test his greatness. Sri Ramakrishna also went to another play of Girish's, and on that occasion Girish was drunk. When the play was over he publicly rebuked the Master, using the most coarse and brutal words. The devotees were very angry at Girish, but they controlled themselves, seeing the Master's serene face. Sri Ramakrishna did not react at all. He smiled as usual and left for Dakshineswar.

When the news of what Girish had done spread among the rest of the devotees, they became very upset. The next day I went to Dakshineswar and found the Master surrounded by devotees. As soon as he saw me the Master said, "Girish has scolded me."

"What can you do, sir? You will have to endure."

"Shall I have to digest his beating?" The Master seemed surprised at the suggestion.

"Yes, Girish should not be blamed. When the cowherd boys were killed by the venomous snake Kaliya, Krishna punished him by jumping on his head. Then Kaliya began to spew out poison in great quantities. Krishna asked him why he was emitting poison, and Kaliya replied: 'Lord, you yourself have given me this poison. It is all I have with which to worship you. Where shall I get nectar?' It is the same with Girish. Whatever rubbish or poisonous stuff was within him, he released on you. If he were to speak those same words to anyone else, that person would undoubtedly take revenge. If he were to say those things to me, I would sue him! Knowing all this, Girish flung his filthy stuff on you, and you accepted it as an offering."

Immediately the Master's face turned crimson and tears rolled from his eyes. He stood up and got ready to go to Girish's house. A couple of devotees asked the Master not to go out in the scorching sun, as it would be tiring for him, but he did not listen. He immediately got into [Ram's] carriage and went to Girish's house.

Meanwhile Girish had become very repentant for his bad behaviour. He was torturing himself, refusing food, and weeping profusely. He wondered how he could ever show his face again to the devotees. But when the compassionate Master arrived at his home, Girish realized that he had been forgiven. Sri Ramakrishna gave him much spiritual advice and sang devotional songs with the devotees, and this removed the shame and agony from Girish's mind. Thus the Master's spiritual power overwhelmed Girish and conquered his heart.

The Last Days of Sri Ramakrishna

Sri Ramakrishna passed blissful days with the devotees at Dakshineswar. His divine life, new thoughts and ideas, and fresh spiritual teachings filled our hearts with unspeakable joy. When I think of how each devotee experienced constant bliss while living with the Master, it seems like a dream. We had no idea then how quickly those happy days would pass.

The Master's room was always crowded on Sundays and holidays, and he inspired each and every one who came. In addition to this time with the Master, each devotee would seek an opportunity to be alone with him and talk to him privately. For this purpose they would come to him on weekdays. Once the Master said in ecstasy, "He who comes here for God-vision, knowledge, and devotion, will have his wish fulfilled."

One afternoon I went to Dakshineswar to see the Master. He was seated alone in his room. After bowing down to him, I sat on the floor, and he said to me: "Look. I told the Divine Mother that I couldn't talk to people anymore. I asked her to give a little power to Girish, Vijay, Kedar, Mahendra, and Ram. They will prepare the minds of newcomers through spiritual instructions, and I shall then give them spiritual experience by a touch." I was dumbfounded. At the time I could not understand why the Master had said that. Who knew then that he was preparing to depart from the world?

A few days later the Master started feeling a pain in his throat. At first he did not pay any attention to it, but when the pain increased, it became difficult for him to swallow food. Gradually he could not eat any solid food and had to live on a liquid diet. Moreover, the wound in his throat swelled and formed pus. At first Dr. Rakhaldas Ghosh treated the Master, but when his medicine was found to be ineffective, Dr. Pratap Chandra Majumdar was called in, and he administered homeopathic medicine. His treatment did not improve the Master's condition either. The devotees were now very worried, seeing that the disease was getting worse and the Master was getting weaker. In spite of all this, however, the Master did not stop singing about God or giving advice to people.

One day I discussed the Master's physical condition with Kalipada, Girish, and Devendra, and we all agreed that we should consult a

European physician for a diagnosis of the Master's disease. The next morning I went to Dakshineswar and found the Master sitting alone in his room. He seemed to be depressed. He told me that he had had terrible hemorrhaging the previous day. Moreover, it was now the rainy season, and the water of the Ganga had risen and was covering some parts of the temple garden. His room was damp. I suggested: "Sir, if you agree to move to Calcutta for a few days, then we can engage a European doctor for your treatment. We think we should not waste any more time."

The Master immediately agreed and advised me to rent a house at Baghbazar [in North Calcutta] near the Ganga. He then asked his nephew Ramlal to consult the almanac and find an auspicious time for moving to Calcutta. It was determined that the best time for moving would be on Saturday, after 3:00 P.M. As it was already Thursday, there was only one day left to make preparations. I immediately left for Calcutta and rented a new two-storied house in a lane near the Baghbazar ghat. On Saturday the Master went to the house, but after seeing it he did not want to stay there. He was then taken to Balaram's house.

In the meantime the news had already spread that Sri Ramakrishna was going to be living in Calcutta and gradually many people began to visit him. Balaram's house became a place of festivity. A couple of weeks later the Master moved to a rented house at Shyampukur, near Baghbazar.

After moving to Calcutta, the Master did not show much interest in the European doctors [*most probably because they would have administered allopathic medicine, which would have been very hard on his system*]. Dr. Pratap Majumdar carefully prescribed homeopathic medicine. When the Master's condition still did not improve, Dr. Majumdar suggested bringing in Dr. Mahendralal Sarkar. Dr. Sarkar treated the Master for the next three months.

At Shyampukur the Master was surrounded by devotees. Although the devotees asked him not to talk, he did not listen to them. Dr. Sarkar used to come every day, and after checking the Master's physical condition he would talk to him for a couple of hours about God and spiritual life. Thus, in spite of his deteriorating health, he continued to teach people. Days and nights were passed in singing, dancing, and talking about God. Every day we witnessed wonderful events in the Master's life at Shyampukur. I shall narrate what happened on Kali Puja night [1885].

Sri Ramakrishna told M. [Mahendra Nath Gupta] privately: "Today is Kali Puja, an auspicious day. One should worship the Divine Mother on this day." M. mentioned this to Kalipada Ghosh. Kalipada was a friend of Girish's, and his life had been transformed by the Master. He was a prominent devotee and took care of the Master at Shyampukur. Immediately Kalipada made arrangements for the worship of Mother Kali. He decorated the house with lights, and obtained the necessary articles for worship.

In the evening all articles — candles, incense, flowers, fruits, farina pudding, fried bread, sweets, etc. — were placed in front of the Master. The room was filled with people. Candles were on both sides of the Master. We all thought that the Master himself would perform the worship, although there was no image. The Master and the devotees sat there in silence. All of a sudden it came to my mind: "It is needless for the Master to perform worship. We shall worship him." I whispered this to Girish, who responded with excitement: "What do you say? Is the Master waiting to accept our worship?"

Girish then took some flowers and offered them to the Master, saying, "Victory to Sri Ramakrishna." Immediately the Master went into sama-dhi. The devotees were overwhelmed, and they began to dance and chant, "Victory to Sri Ramakrishna." When the Master came back to his normal plane of consciousness, a devotee offered a bowl of farina pudding to him and he ate it. The prasad was distributed among the devotees, and everyone was filled with joy. It is almost impossible to describe the festivity of that night.

Gradually the Master's disease took a serious turn, and it became difficult for him to swallow even blended food. His voice sounded hoarse and his body became emaciated. He did not have sufficient strength to walk. Since his body was not responding well to the current treatment, the doctors suggested that we move him to a healthy, spa-cious place outside Calcutta. A devotee [Ram] asked Sri Ramakrishna, "Master, tell us where we might find a suitable place for you." "What do I know?" replied the Master. The devotee asked, "Should we try at Cossipore or the Baranagore area?" The Master nodded his head. Imme-diately that devotee went to Cossipore and met Mahim Chakrabarty, who informed him of the Cossipore garden house. It was rented for the Master at eighty rupees per month.

The change improved the Master's health a little. The wound in his throat healed to some extent, and he gained a little strength. While he was at Dakshineswar the Master had made a forecast regarding his end, saying, "Before I go, I'll cast my whole secret to the winds." We heard it. On January 1, 1886, the Master felt much better. It was a holiday, so many people had come to visit the Master at Cossipore. During the previous week a devotee had asked Sri Ramakrishna to bless Harish Mustafi, but he had not said anything. On January 1, however, as soon as Harish went to the Master, the latter blessed him. Out of joy, tears came from Harish's eyes. He came downstairs and informed a devotee: "Brother, I cannot hold the surge of bliss within. What is this? I have never experienced such a thing in my life!" With tearful eyes the devotee said, "Brother, it is the grace of the Master."

We were all seated on the lawn of the garden house that day when the Master called for Devendra. After seeing the Master, Devendra told us: "The Master said to me: 'Ram has declared me to be an avatar. Can all of you verify Ram's statement? Keshab's disciples also call him an avatar.'" We could not figure out why the Master said that. In the afternoon the Master came to the lawn for a walk, and the devotees followed him. I vividly remember the scene and the Master's wonderful form. His body was covered with warm clothing, and there was a green cap on his head covering both ears. His face radiated light and joy. It was a sight to see.

Coming near us, he raised his right hand and said: "What more need I tell you? I bless you all. Be illumined!" Then he went into samadhi. The devotees picked flowers from the garden and offered them at the Master's feet, saying, "Victory to Sri Ramakrishna!" Some threw flowers in the air out of joy, and it looked like it was raining flowers.

When the Master regained outer consciousness, he touched Akshay Sen's chest. Immediately Akshay began to shed tears in ecstasy. The Master then touched Navagopal Ghosh, Upendra Nath Majumdar, Ramlal Chattopadhyay, Atul Ghosh, Ganguly, and some others. Touching Haramohan the Master said: "Not today. You will have to wait." Then the Master returned to his room. All the devotees were extremely happy that day. But alas! Who could realize that it was the Master's last play?

The cancer in his throat became worse after this. Dr. Rajendra Datta, Dr. Navin Pal, and Dr. Coats of the Calcutta Medical College treated the Master with great care but could not improve his condition. Then Pandit Shashadhar Tarkachudamani asked the Master to put his mind on the wound during samadhi, saying that that would heal the throat. But the Master refused, saying: "Shall I have to cure my disease through samadhi? The mind has been given to God once and for all. How can I withdraw it from him and turn it on this worthless body?"

Although the Master was in terrible pain he was always joyful. We never saw him sad or worried. He talked about God to whomever came to see him. If someone asked about his health, he would say: "Let the body and pain take care of each other. O my mind, you stay in bliss." Many times the devotees implored the Master, "Sir, if you do not cure yourself, none can cure you." The Master always answered calmly: "I see that the body is like a paper doll, and it has a hole in its throat. What shall I do with it?"

On Sunday morning, August 15, 1886, the last day of the Bengali month of Shravana, he asked a devotee to read the almanac to him. After listening to the descriptions of that day, he heard about the next day — that is, 1st Bhadra, which was an inauspicious day for journeying — and he asked the reader to stop. [*Actually this incident took place about eight or nine days before his passing away. Swami Yogananda read the almanac to the Master.*] In the afternoon he told the doctor that both of his sides were in pain, as if they were burning. He then extended his hand so the doctor could check his pulse. The doctor indicated that the Master's condition was serious. The Master then became indrawn. He did not talk anymore about his disease or pain.

After a while he said, "I wish I could eat a lot of rice and lentil." That night he ate farina pudding and milk more easily than on other days, and he slept peacefully till 1:00 A.M. Then at 1:06 A.M. [actually 1:02] the Master suddenly went into samadhi [August 16, 1886]. It was a full moon night. The disciples guessed that it was mahasamadhi [the great departure], and the news was sent to the Master's devotees. Immediately everyone rushed to Cossipore.

Vishwanath Upadhyay, the ambassador of Nepal and a devotee of the Master, came early that morning. He saw that the Master's body was stiff, his hair was standing erect, and his gaze was fixed. He checked the backbone and felt that it was still warm, so he doubted that it was mahasamadhi. Hearing Vishwanath Upadhyay's opinion, the devotees brought in Dr. Mahendra Sarkar, who declared that the Master had passed away. The devotees were now submerged in grief. They still kept vigil, however, until 5 o'clock that afternoon.

The devotees then carried the Master's body downstairs and placed it on a decorated cot. His body was bathed by his attendants with a wet towel and covered with an ochre cloth. After that they put white sandal paste, flowers, and garlands on it. A couple of photographs of the Master and the devotees were then taken. The Master looked beautiful. Meanwhile Surendra, a great devotee of the Master, arrived. He offered flowers and bel leaves at the Master's feet and said with tears: "Master, I am sad to see you in this condition. What more shall I say? All my hope and aspiration, perhaps, are going to be ended today! Please accept this flower offering from your wretched devotee."

At 6:00 P.M. the devotees formed a procession and carried the Master's body to the bank of the Ganga, singing kirtan with drums and cymbals. The funeral pyre was ready, and the Master's body was placed on it. The devotees ignited the pyre while Trailokya Nath Sanyal sang some suitable devotional songs. Gradually the Master's body was reduced to ashes, and the relics were collected in a copper urn.

When the devotees were returning to the Cossipore garden house, there was a terrible incident. Upendra Nath Mukhopadhyay, a devotee of the Master, was bitten by a snake. He fell on the street, and the other devotees immediately tied his leg with a string so that the poison might not spread all over his body. Then they cauterized the spot with a piece of red hot iron. By the grace of the Master, Upen's life was saved.

The disciples of Sri Ramakrishna placed the urn containing the Master's relics in his Cossipore room and began to worship it daily and offer food as they always had. Then on Janmashtami [Krishna's birthday], August 24, 1886, the relics of the Master [actually part of the relics] were installed at the Kankurgachi Yogodyana with ritualistic worship and a grand festival. Since then the daily worship of the Master has been going on at the Kankurgachi Yogodyana.

[From: *Sri Sri Ramakrishna Paramahamsadever Jivan Vrittanta*, by Ram Chandra Datta (Calcutta: Sri Ramakrishna Yogodyana), 1950; *Gurupran Ramchandrer Anudhyan*, by Mahendra Nath Datta (Calcutta: Mahendra Publishing Committee), 1958; *Mahatma Ramchandrer Vaktritavali*, by Ram Chandra Datta (Calcutta: Sri Ramakrishna Yogodyana), vol. I, 1948; *Tattwamanjari* (Calcutta: Sri Ramakrishna Yogodyana), vol. 20, Kartik 1323 (1916)]

Manomohan Mittra in Calcutta

17

Manomohan Mittra

Manomohan Mittra (1851-1903) was a householder disciple of Sri Ramakrishna whose whole family was devoted to the Master. Rakhal (later, Swami Brahmananda) was married to Manomohan's sister and was introduced to Sri Ramakrishna by Manomohan in 1880. Manomohan had an evangelistic nature. He wrote many articles about the Master in Tattwamanjari *and preached about him publicly.*

Long ago I heard about Sri Ramakrishna and read about him in the Indian Mirror and *Sulabh Samachar*. I talked about him with my friends and had a desire to see him, but my desire was not fulfilled until the fall of 1879. At that time it rained continuously for four days. One Saturday night I saw in a dream that the whole world was flooded with water. All of the tall buildings of Calcutta, including the Ochterloney Monument, were swept away by the terrible current. In whatever direction I looked I saw only water and not a single human being. I was drifting helplessly in the current. All of a sudden the thought came to my mind: "Where is my mother? Where are my wife, daughter, and sisters?" Immediately I heard a voice: "There is no one left in this world who is your own. All are dead."

"Then what is the use of my living?"

"Suicide is a great sin."

"Then where shall I go? I don't find any human habitation."

"No one is alive in this world. All are dead."

"When none is alive, then with whom shall I stay?"

"They only have survived from this deluge who have realized God. You will meet them very soon and live with them."

"I see only water all around. What shall I eat?"

"Search below your heart. You will get food."

I put my hand below my chest and found a plank of wood, which was helping me to float in the current. I was surprised to witness this play of

God. Without my knowing it he had sent a plank to save my life. I did not know how to swim well, so it would have been impossible for me to float for such a long time.

I woke up at four o'clock in the morning, but I lay there perplexed for some time. Then, seeing my wife, I cried out: "Where am I? Who are you?" Hearing this, she was dumbfounded. When I regained my normal consciousness, I realized that what I had seen was a dream.

Later that morning I told my cousin Ram Chandra Datta about my dream. Ram said: "What you have seen is true. To tell you the truth, all beings are submerged in maya. They are the living dead." Then I said to Ram, "For a long time I have been thinking about meeting Sri Ramakrishna Paramahamsa at Dakshineswar, but I'm sorry to say I have not made any time to do so." Ram immediately said: "Let us go today [Sunday, November 13, 1879]. It is an auspicious day, and moreover it's a holiday."

We immediately got ready. Gopal Chandra Mittra, Ram, and I first went to Prankrishna Datta, a close friend of ours and a member of the New Dispensation. Quite often I had heard from him about Sri Ramakrishna. But for some reason he could not join us. We three then went to Dakshineswar by boat. After landing at the chandni ghat we inquired about Sri Ramakrishna, and someone pointed out a room towards the north end of the compound. Accordingly we reached his room, but the door was closed. We did not dare knock at his door. Later someone encouraged us to knock, and so we did. An ordinary looking man opened the door, bowed down to us, and invited us to sit on his cot. We saw a tall man lying on the floor. Later we learned that he was Hriday, a nephew of Sri Ramakrishna. We were very much impressed seeing Sri Ramakrishna's serene face.

When I had left home that morning I expected Sri Ramakrishna Paramahamsa to be like other monks — with shaven head, wearing an ochre cloth, and sitting on a tiger skin. But when I met him I saw that there was no external show about him and he was very simple. He was wearing a dhoti [cloth] — using half of it to cover his upper body.

Sri Ramakrishna said to Hriday with a smile: "Hridu, these people are quiet by nature. They do not belong to the Brahmo Samaj." Hriday agreed. I then said to Sri Ramakrishna: "I have been connected with the Brahmo Samaj from my boyhood. I believe the Brahmo religion is the only true religion. I hate idolatry." Sri Ramakrishna said, "I meant that you do not belong to any group." I was a little embarrassed. Then he continued: "As an imitation custard apple reminds one of the real fruit, so the divine images enkindle the presence of God. He is all-powerful. It is possible for him to manifest in anything."

Then suddenly he said to Ram: "Aren't you a doctor? [*Pointing to Hriday*] He is suffering from fever. Could you check his pulse?" Ram had not introduced himself to Sri Ramakrishna as a doctor. We were all amazed. After examining Hriday, Ram reported that his body temperature was normal.

That day we stayed with Sri Ramakrishna till evening. In his presence we experienced wonderful peace and bliss, which we had never experienced before. We had not known previously how much peace one could have from the company of the holy in this sorrowful world. As we were leaving, Sri Ramakrishna said, "Come again." We promised him, "We shall come again next Sunday."

The next Sunday we left for Dakshineswar early in the morning. During that day's visit I said to Sri Ramakrishna: "Some people say that God is formless, others say he is with form, and again others call him Krishna, Shiva, or Kali. Could you tell us what the real nature of God is?"

Sri Ramakrishna smiled and said: "He is sometimes with form, he is sometimes formless, and again he is beyond both. He is all-pervading. It is difficult to ascertain his real nature. Just as there is nothing to compare gold with except gold, so there is nothing equal to God. He is the cause of the gross objects as well as of the subtle mind and intellect. For example: The same substance in its solid form is ice, in its liquid form is water, and in its gaseous form is vapour. According to the mental attitude of the spiritual aspirant, God manifests himself. A jnani experiences God as all-pervading, formless space, and a devotee perceives God with a particular form. So if you sincerely want to know the real nature of God, meditate on him in solitude. Have patience. Surrender yourself to him and pray. When the right time comes you will see him."

Again I told him, "We get peace when we feel the presence of God in our hearts; otherwise mere intellectual understanding of God and atheism are the same." Sri Ramakrishna then replied: "In the beginning one should move forward on the spiritual path holding to an initial faith [i.e., faith in the words of the scriptures and the guru]. One then attains direct perception. There are two kinds of faith — initial faith and real faith [i.e., faith that comes from direct experience]. Be steadfast in the first one and then you will see God."

We continued to visit Sri Ramakrishna every Sunday. One day the Master said, "This world is a 'framework of illusion.'" I laughed at this, but the Master's words penetrated into my heart and I realized the truth of them — that the world is indeed impermanent. The Master continued: "This world again is a 'mansion of mirth,' but one should know how to get joy here. Try to live in God, and then you will not suffer from misery.

Living in God means that one offers one's body and mind to him. Have constant recollectedness of God. Life in the world is fraught with fear, and moreover there are so many ways in which the mind can get polluted. But if you can somehow keep your mind in God, all obstacles will go away. There is tremendous power in the name of God. Sing his name and glories."

I then asked, "Does God listen to our prayers?" Immediately the Master got excited and said: "What are you saying? You call on God and he does not listen? He is omnipresent and omniscient. How do you know that he does not listen to your prayers? You have no faith, so you are doubting him." I humbly expressed my ignorance to the Master.

Then I asked, "Sir, would you tell us how to increase our longing for God?" The Master said with a smile: "As hunger and thirst arise spontaneously, so does longing for God. Everything depends on time. Mere thinking cannot make a person hungry. In the same way longing for God does not come simply by saying, 'Let there be longing.' Yearning is awakened in the mind automatically when a person feels the need for God. Yearning for God does not come until and unless a person has satisfied his cravings for mundane objects, renounced all attachment to lust and gold, and shunned worldly comforts and enjoyments like filth. How many people are restless for God-realization? People shed a jugful of tears for their wives, children, or money, but who weeps for God? He who longs for him will certainly find him. Cry to him. Call on him every evening with a longing heart. You will see him."

I fell at the Master's feet, and he went into samadhi. I then felt his grace as well as an inexpressible joy inside. When he came back to normal consciousness, he sang this song:

> Oh brother, persist joyfully,
> You will succeed gradually.
> What went wrong will be set right.
> Anka was saved, Banka was saved,
> And the butcher Sujan was saved.
> Teaching the parrot, the prostitute was saved.
> So was saved Mira Bai.
> Having the wealth and treasure of the world,
> The trader still drives the bullock,
> When misfortune overtakes him,
> No trace (of all these) will be left.
> Have deep devotion in your mind;
> Give up hypocrisy and craftiness.

Lord Ramachandra will be attained easily
By virtue of service, worship, and surrender.

It was evening, and we began to think about returning home. I humbly said to the Master: "Sir, I do not know God, but I have taken refuge in you. Please accept my responsibility." Sri Ramakrishna was quiet for some time. Again he went into an ecstatic mood and said: "Listen. He who comes here for God-realization or to attain knowledge will have his desire fulfilled. Let me say again: He will definitely have his desire fulfilled."

A few months after we began to visit Sri Ramakrishna at Dakshineswar, our friend and neighbour Surendra Nath Mittra and his brother Girindra Nath Mittra joined us. We were happy to have their company. In 1881 Surendra arranged the first birthday festival of Sri Ramakrishna at his own expense. On that auspicious day we gathered together for the celebration in the Panchavati at Dakshineswar.

Ram Chandra Datta began kirtan with this song:

Who is singing Hari's name upon the sacred Ganga's bank?
Is it Nitai that has come, the giver of heavenly love?
It must be that compassionate Nitai,
Otherwise who can bring peace to the heart?

Hearing this song Sri Ramakrishna joined the kirtan. He was in an ecstasy of love. He began to dance vigorously and rhythmically. Tears rolled down his cheeks, and he lost outer consciousness off and on. Encircling him we also began to dance and sing, forgetting our surroundings. The glorious sound of the Lord's name reverberated all around, and our inspiration increased a thousandfold. Some of us began to dance raising both hands, some began to clap, and some began to jump. Some, out of exuberant emotion, fell on the ground. Some, out of joy, began to laugh heartily and embrace each other. Some began to cry loudly, and then they also began to laugh. We had never seen such a scene in our lives. We were all overwhelmed with that current of divine bliss.

The kirtan ended with this song:

Thou art my All in All, O Lord! — the Life of my life,
    the Essence of essence;
In the three worlds I have none else but thee to call my own.
Thou art my peace, my joy, my hope; thou my support,
    my wealth, my glory;
Thou my wisdom and my strength.

Thou art my home, my place of rest; my dearest friend,
    my next of kin;
My present and my future, thou; my heaven and my salvation.
Thou art my scriptures, my commandments; thou art my
    ever gracious Guru;
Thou the Spring of my boundless bliss.
Thou art the Way, and thou the Goal; thou the Adorable One, O Lord!
Thou art the Mother tender-hearted; thou the chastising Father;
Thou the Creator and Protector;
Thou the Helmsman who dost steer my craft across the sea of life.

The Master was then in deep samadhi, seated like a lifeless wooden image with his eyes fixed. His face was luminous and blissful. We sat there looking at his wonderful face. Sri Ramakrishna's form on that day is still imprinted in my heart.

In January 1881, during the winter festival [Maghotsava] of the Brahmos, I went to Dakshineswar with Keshab Chandra Sen. On that occasion Keshab offered two bouquets at Sri Ramakrishna's feet and bowed down to him. The Master also saluted him. Sri Ramakrishna began to talk about Brahman, Atman, God, and spiritual life, and Keshab quietly listened. Observing Keshab's silence, some of his Brahmo followers felt uncomfortable. They repeatedly asked Keshab to say something. Finally Keshab said to them loudly: "As it is meaningless to sell a needle to a blacksmith [because he makes needles], so is it to give a lecture in front of Sri Ramakrishna. I don't have such audacity to lecture here. I have come to listen to him, and I request all of you to do the same. Please don't embarrass me."

On another occasion that same year I again went to Dakshineswar with Keshab. The devotees asked Sri Ramakrishna to give a spiritual talk, but the Master said: "Keshab is an orator. He really speaks well. I am not a lecturer. What can I tell you? However, I can tell you one thing that I say to everybody, but very few people appreciate it. I don't know whether you will like it or not." Being requested repeatedly, Sri Ramakrishna said, "Brahman alone is real, and whatever you see around you is maya [apparent]." Saying this, the Master went into samadhi. After some time, when he returned to the normal plane, he said: "I have finished my talk. Now Keshab will speak." Keshab then said: "Whatever Sri Ramakrishna has said, that is the greatest truth. Who will dare say more than that?"

We were astonished to observe Keshab's humility that day. Keshab was an extremely learned and famous person. At that time there were few well-known people like him in India, yet he had so much love and respect for Sri Ramakrishna!

One day I went to Dakshineswar and saw the Master talking to the devotees in the Panchavati. About the same time Keshab reached there with some of his followers. Seeing Keshab, Sri Ramakrishna was delighted. They talked for some time. Then Keshab said to the Master: "Sir, if you permit, I want to make your message known to the public. It will definitely do people good and bring peace to the world." Sri Ramakrishna replied in an ecstatic mood: "It is not the time to spread the message of this place [*i.e., his message*] through lectures and newspapers. The power and ideas that are within this body will automatically spread all around in course of time. Hundreds of Himalayas will not be able to suppress that power." As the Master said this his eyes were wide open and his face radiated a wonderful glow. All were quiet. Then the Master went into samadhi. On this occasion I realized that one day Sri Ramakrishna's message would spread far and wide.

[From: *Bhakta Manomohan* (Calcutta: Udbodhan Office), 1944]

M. (Mahendra Nath Gupta) seated near the Panchamundi at the Dakshineswar temple garden, where Sri Ramakrishna practised tantra sadhana

18

M. (Mahendra Nath Gupta)

*M. was the pen name of Mahendra Nath Gupta (1854-1932), the
headmaster of Vidyasagar's High School in Calcutta. M. met Sri Ramakrishna in 1882 and recorded in his diary many of the Master's conversations and teachings until the latter's passing away in 1886. Excerpts
from this diary were first published in Bengali in five volumes under the
title* Sri Sri Ramakrishna Kathamrita. *In 1942 Swami Nikhilananda
translated this into English and combined the five volumes into one,
entitled* The Gospel of Sri Ramakrishna. *In his later life M. was
surrounded by devotees, and his conversations with them about Sri
Ramakrishna and spiritual life were recorded by Swami Nityatmananda
from 1923 to 1932. These conversations were published in Bengali in
sixteen volumes under the title* Srima Darshan. *The following reminiscences have been translated from those volumes.*

My First Meeting with Sri Ramakrishna

What a great event it was when I first met Sri Ramakrishna. At that
time I could not get along with my father and brothers at home. Though
I tried my best to serve them, they mistreated me very much. Unable to
bear the mental agony any longer, I decided to leave home and commit
suicide. One night at ten o'clock I left with my wife in a hired carriage.
I asked the driver to take us to Baranagore, where my sister lived, but
on the way, near Shyambazar, a wheel of the carriage came off. We then
went to a friend's house and got a cold reception. He thought we wanted
to stay at his house overnight. Finally I was able to get another carriage,
and we reached Baranagore at midnight.

The next afternoon I went for a walk with my nephew Sidhu, and we
visited several gardens on the bank of the Ganga. Feeling tired and
depressed, I sat down in a garden. Sidhu then said: "Uncle, let us go to
Rasmani's garden. A holy man lives there." We entered through the

main gate of the temple garden at Dakshineswar. It was half an hour before sunset.

Having a poetic mind, I was deeply impressed with the beautiful flower garden. I picked some flowers and was overwhelmed by their fragrance. After some time we entered Sri Ramakrishna's room.

The Master was seated on his small cot and the devotees were on the floor. I didn't know any of them. The first thing I heard from the Master's lips was: "When, hearing the name of God once, you shed tears and your hair stands on end, then you may know for certain that you do not have to perform any more karma." (*Srima Darshan*, I. 339-40)

[Note: Further references to *Srima Darshan* will be referred to by part and page number only.]

My Ego Was Crushed

During my second visit to the Master he asked me, "Well, do you believe in God with form or without form?" I had a tendency to argue on religious matters. I answered, "Sir, I like to think of God as formless." And I further said: "It is meaningless to worship a clay image. One should explain to those who worship a clay image that it is not God, and that while worshipping it, they should have God in view and not the clay image." At that time there were so many lectures on this topic in Calcutta. But the Master immediately silenced me by saying: "That's the one hobby of you Calcutta people — giving lectures and bringing others to the light. Nobody ever stops to consider how to get the light himself. Who are you to teach others?" He continued: "You will not have to rack your brain on this matter. Look at the world — how it moves in an orderly way. It is God who sends the sun to shed light, the rain to give water, and the seasons to rotate. The earth produces the crops which help mankind to survive. God arranged everything for us. Look at the spiritual world. You can see temples and holy places all around the country. He created the scriptures and the holy people. These he arranged for people who want to lead a spiritual life. He thinks about everyone. We do not have to think of anything." Listening to this, I was speechless. My inclination for argument stopped forever. I realized that the Lord is the doer and we are his instruments. (II. 36)

My Family Trouble Was a Blessing

Seven or eight days after my first meeting with the Master, he was walking through the courtyard of the Kali temple and I said to him, "It is better to take one's life than to suffer such terrible pain." At once he replied: "Why do you say so? You have a guru. Why do you worry? Your guru is always behind you. He can remove your suffering by a mere wish. He makes everything favourable. A juggler threw a rope with many knots in it in front of a thousand people, and none could untie a single knot. But the juggler immediately removed all the knots just by a jerk of his hand. Don't worry. The guru will remove all your obstacles." What agony I was suffering, but I had found the Master. How he guided my life! Later my father came. We were reconciled with love and affection, and he took me back home. In retrospect we see that God is all-auspicious, but we judge things superficially. It was my family problems and my desire to commit suicide that led me to God. (I. 340-41)

Live at Home like a Maidservant

The Master used to say: "There are two types of devotees — the inner circle and the outer circle. Those of the inner circle easily get spiritual awakening, but those of the outer circle are a little egotistical. Those of the latter group think that they will not attain knowledge without practising austerity." The Master used to compare the two types of devotees with the inner and outer pillars of the natmandir [the hall in front of the Kali temple]. Those of the inner circle were like the inner pillars, and those of the outer circle, like the outer pillars. He had special love for devotees of the inner circle because they would carry on his mission.

The Master asked some of the devotees to live at home like a maidservant in a rich man's house. And some of them he trained to set an example for others. He said to me, "The Divine Mother has told me that she will make you do some teaching work for her." The Master even prayed to the Mother to give me a little power, because one cannot teach people without the power of the Divine. At that time I had a desire to renounce the world, which I expressed to the Master.

One night at nine o'clock the Master was alone in his room and I was standing on the western verandah. Leaving his room, he came and stood next to me. In front of us the Ganga flowed with a sweet murmuring sound. All was quiet. Suddenly he said to me: "Look. Let no one think that without him the Divine Mother's work will stop. She can make great teachers out of straws." He further said: "If a faucet in the bathroom leaks, the plumber replaces it with a new one. He has many spare parts. Similarly the Divine Engineer [God] can bring a new person to do his work. His work never stops." I wholeheartedly accepted what the Master said to be the will of the Mother.

The Master prayed for me: "Mother, as you are keeping him in the world, please give him your vision from time to time. Otherwise, how will he live in the world?" (II. 247, IX. 43, VIII. 295)

My Boyhood Memory

I remember an incident from my boyhood. I went to Rishra with my mother, and from there we visited the Car Festival of Jagannath at Mahesh. On our way back we stopped at the Dakshineswar Kali temple. I was then four years old. Standing in front of the Kali temple, I began to cry because I could not see my mother in the crowd. She was then visiting the other temples. I heard people saying, "This is the Kali temple of Rani Rasmani." In the meantime a man came and consoled me. Most probably it was Sri Ramakrishna. It was 1858 and he was then a priest of the Kali temple and practising austerity there. My next meeting with the Master was twenty-four years later. (VII. 198)

The Master's Training

Once the Master accompanied me to the Panchavati grove, and he bowed down at the spot where a branch of the old banyan tree had fallen. He then said: "I have had so many visions here. Please bow down." He was like my loving mother. Another time the Master asked me to buy a shirt for him, and I got three. He took one and returned the others. Lest I should feel hurt, he affectionately asked, "How many shirts did I ask for?" "One," I replied. Then he said: "Please keep these two extra shirts with you. When I need another one, I shall tell you. You are my own." What renunciation he had! He could not hoard anything. His mind dwelt only on divinity. He further told me, "Never do anything that would disturb my mind." The Master warned me that if he were disturbed it would be harmful for the devotees.

Another time he asked me to buy a carpet. He knew that I might ask someone else to get it, so he said, "You yourself should go and buy it." Why did he say this? Because the impression of serving the Master would stay in my mind, and I would be able to meditate on him throughout my life, thinking, "I presented a carpet to the Master." (II. 84)

Kali, the Mother

Once somebody asked the Master, "Is God with form or without form?" The Master answered: "I have seen the Mother both ways. She is the indivisible Satchidananda, and again she assumes various forms for the devotees. At Kalighat [in South Calcutta] I saw the Divine Mother playing with some children and chasing a butterfly. Another time I saw her walking on the Adi Ganga." On one occasion the Master told us: "Mother has come. She is wearing a red-bordered sari and has tied a bunch of keys in the corner of her cloth." He said this in the presence of

Keshab Sen and others in his room at Dakshineswar. People heard the Master's words, but the Master alone heard the Mother's words. Another day he said: "The Mother is going up and down the stairs in the temple. Her hair is dishevelled, and her anklets are making a *jhun-jhun* sound." Once in Cossipore he said, "Today I saw the Mother playing a vina [a musical instrument]." The Master was absorbed in the formless aspect of the Mother for six months at the time of his sadhana.

One day I went to Dakshineswar and found the Master sweeping the garden path to the north of his room. Seeing me, he said, "The Mother walks here, so I am cleaning the path."

The Master used to say, "Sculpture, painting, poetry, music — all these fine arts make one thoughtful." We also heard from him that Navin, a sculptor, used to eat only once a day, at three o'clock in the afternoon, a vegetarian meal of rice, boiled vegetables, and butter. When Navin made the image of Mother Kali at Dakshineswar he practised self-control and hard austerities for six months. That is why the image looks alive. Only when the sculptor is absorbed in the Divine can he project divinity in a stone image. (VIII. 166, IX. 119, III. 96, IV. 200)

The Master Talked with God

Before I met the Master I had been connected with the Brahmo Samaj for seven or eight years. During their formal service they would talk about God, and as I listened to their sermons, I would think that God was far away. But when I went to the Master, I saw that he would talk *with* God. What a great ideal the Master presented before us! He said, "The goal of human life is to realize God." Without that, life is meaningless. He not only saw God — he used to talk to the Divine Mother, as we talk among ourselves, in front of people. One day he said, "The Mother has come." Then he began to talk to her, saying: "Well, Mother, to whom should I listen? This person is saying this and the other person something else." Then the Divine Mother said something to him. Again the Master said: "I understand, Mother. I shall listen to you and no one else." At the beginning of his years of sadhana he would cry to the Divine Mother: "Mother, I cannot bear these worldly people. My body is burning." The Mother said to him: "Wait for some time. The pure-souled devotees will come." The Master had to wait nearly twenty-two years for his devotees. (VI. 193, II. 154-55)

From the Infinite to the Finite

When the Master was going to Vidyasagar's house he asked me: "My shirt is unbuttoned. Will that offend Vidyasagar?" I assured him: "Oh, no! Don't be anxious about it. Nothing about you will be offensive."

What a wonderful person the Master was! A few minutes earlier in the carriage he had been in samadhi, and when he alighted he was still absorbed in that mood, so his steps were faltering. But still he was quite aware of social formalities, such as the condition of his clothes. What a fantastic mind he had! At that time two opposite ideas were harmonized in his behaviour. On the one hand his mind had transcended the world and was merged in God, and on the other he was inquiring about human affairs. This should be the ideal: "True to the kindred points of heaven and earth." This we find in the lives of the avatars [incarnations]. The avatar brings the message of the Infinite to the finite world. (VI. 281)

"What Do You Think of Me?"

Once there was a big gathering at Jadu Mallik's house and Keshab Sen gave a lecture. The Master repeatedly asked Keshab: "Please evaluate my knowledge and devotion. How much am I worth?" Keshab was reluctant to answer, but at last he hesitantly said, "Sir, your knowledge is one hundred percent." Then and there the Master said: "I don't trust your words. You are attached to wealth, name and fame, and other worldly things. If the great sages like Narada and Shukadeva were to evaluate me, I would value their judgement." Sometimes for the sake of truth and justice the Master uttered unpleasant truths. He frankly spoke about Keshab in public. At that time Keshab was highly admired. The Master loved him, so he told him the truth without compromising. When Keshab died, the Master wept.

Another time the Master said, "It is the Divine Mother within who is making me do everything." He asked me: "Some say that I am the full manifestation of the Godhead. What do you say?" I replied: "Sir, I don't understand whether the manifestation is full, partial, or the like. But one thing you mentioned I have understood: 'There is a round hole in a wall and through it one can see a vast field on the other side.' You are that hole. Through you everything can be seen — that Infinite Meadow without end." The Master was extremely pleased and said, "Yes, one can see quite a bit." (I. 100-01, II. 62, VI. 177, I. 350)

Living with the Master

The Master could see the inherent tendencies of a person. When he first met each of his disciples, he immediately recognized him and tried to change his mental tendencies. He used to say: "There are some who have gold [i.e., knowledge of the Self] hidden beneath a half pound of earth, but for others it is beneath forty pounds. So let it be! Who is going to dig out forty pounds of earth?"

The Master knew the past history and samskaras [impressions] of his intimate disciples and would mould them accordingly. For example: Suppose he felt that a disciple should live with him for his spiritual growth. At that time he would not let the disciple visit his home in Calcutta. If the Master were told that a relative was sick at home, he would say: "Let it be. If there is any emergency, the neighbours will take care of it. You will not have to go." What he meant was, trials and tribulations, sorrows and sufferings, have always existed and will continue to exist in this world, but the Master would not live forever. For this reason he forced his disciples to live with him while they had the chance. As Christ said, "Me ye have not always."

Once he sent me to practise meditation under the bel tree of Dakshineswar. I closed my eyes and sat facing east. When I opened my eyes after meditation I found the Master, the object of my meditation, standing in front of me. Immediately I bowed down to him. He did not merely give instructions, he also kept an eye on each person to see whether he was practising the instructions or not. If somebody was unable to do it, he would help him like a loving mother.

I once lived at Dakshineswar for a few days at the Master's instruction. One day a messenger came from my Calcutta home with a letter for me. As soon as the Master saw the letter he cried out as if he were afraid of a snakebite: "What is this? What is this? Throw it away." I immediately threw it away as if it were poison. He did not allow me to read it, thinking that the spiritual mood that I was acquiring by living with him would be destroyed by worldly news. He led his disciples against the current of maya, so he was extremely cautious. The path of the world goes downward, but the Master went in the opposite direction and guided his disciples the same way.

Once the Master asked a devotee: "How is everybody in your family? Are they all right?" The devotee answered: "They are so so. You have told us that here there will be no talk other than about God." The Master was pleased to hear this reply. Later he would get information about the welfare of this devotee's family through someone else.

Girish Ghosh once said to the Master: "Sir, my servant was down with a fever for six days. Your prasad cured him." At once the Master scolded him: "Fie on you! What a small-minded person you are! You are asking for pumpkins and gourds from God! You should ask for immortality from him."

A visitor came one day to the Master and was introduced as an atheist. The Master patted him on the back and said, "Oh no, how can he be an atheist?" The Master knew what was inside that person. He used to say, "I can see what is inside each person, just as I see what is inside this glass case." The Master understood that since that person had come to see him, he could not be an atheist.

There was another person whose monthly salary was twenty-five rupees. He used to bring rabri [pieces of thickened milk, soaked in syrup] and other fancy sweets for the Master. The Master later told us: "Look. The things that man brought for me seem like filth." Afterwards we found out that though the man's regular salary was twenty-five rupees, he was making an extra thirty rupees by presenting false bills. The Master saw his food to be filth and could not eat it.

Once Ishan Mukherjee visited the Master wearing a gold ring on his finger. He was then fifty years old. Nothing escaped the Master's eyes. Seeing the ring, he remarked with a smile, "There was an old prostitute who lost all her physical beauty, but she always adorned herself with earrings." Hearing the Master's comment, everybody laughed loudly. (I. 40-42, 55, 64, 241)

An Evening with the Master at Dakshineswar

It was almost dusk. The Master said to me: "The mind of the yogi is always fixed on God, always absorbed in the Self. You can recognize such a person by merely looking at him. His eyes are wide open, with an aimless look, like the eyes of a mother bird hatching her eggs. Her entire mind is fixed on those eggs, so there is a vacant look in her eyes. Can you show me such a picture?" I said, "I shall try to get one." [M. was not able to find such a picture during the Master's lifetime, but fulfilled the Master's wish later.]

As evening came on, the temples were lighted up. Sri Ramakrishna was seated on his small couch, meditating on the Divine Mother. Then he chanted the names of God. Incense was burned in the room, where an oil lamp had been lighted. Sounds of conch shells and gongs came floating in the air as the evening worship began in the temple of Kali. The light of the moon flooded all the quarters. (IV. 100, VII. 225, and The Gospel of Sri Ramakrishna, p. 113)

We Watched the Master Twenty-Four Hours a Day

The Master was in such a state that he could accept things only after offering them to the Divine Mother. If someone presented a new cloth to the Master, he would first offer it to the Mother in the temple and then use it himself. In this way the Master demonstrated how one could be immersed in yoga while living in this world.

Once the Master was staying at Mathur's Calcutta residence. One morning at two o'clock he suddenly said to Mathur, "I want to go back to Dakshineswar." Mathur said: "Father, where shall I get a carriage now? You can go at daybreak." "If you don't get a carriage now I shall go on foot," said the Master. Mathur was compelled to go to his coachman and ask him to get the carriage ready and take the Master to Dakshineswar. After arriving at the Kali temple the Master said, "Mother, here I am." The Divine Mother was his all in all.

The Master said, "Gauranga and I are one." One day he was humming and chanting the name "Gaur, Gaur." A person asked, "Sir, why are you saying 'Gaur, Gaur' instead of chanting the Mother's name?" The Master replied: "What can I do? You people have many resources — wife, son, daughter, money, home, and so on — but I have only one resource, God. For that reason I say sometimes 'Gaur,' sometimes 'Mother,' sometimes 'Rama, Krishna, Kali, Shiva.' This is the way I spend my time."

The Master experienced the truth of Brahman as described in the scriptures not just once or twice but all the time. We lived with the Master and watched him closely twenty-four hours a day. He never deviated from God-consciousness. Even while lying in bed at night he would chant "Mother, Mother." He had very little sleep. He never slept more than fifteen to thirty minutes at a stretch. Such a thing is not possible for an ordinary God-realized person. Only when God incarnates in a human body is such a thing possible. He declared that in his body Satchidananda had manifested on earth. One day he told me, "Christ, Chaitanya, and I are one and the same entity." Is this the temple priest or God? We were bewildered when his real nature was revealed to us. "The Mother of the Universe," he said, "speaks through my mouth." He spoke out of inspiration. "I am an illiterate man," he said on several occasions, "but the Mother supplies knowledge from behind." (V. 34-35, XIII. 212, VII. 178, XI. 84, 130-31)

Days in Cossipore

Once when Sri Ramakrishna was ill at the Cossipore garden house, somebody said to him, "Sir, why don't you go to Dakshineswar?" "Why?" asked the Master. "Because Mother Kali is there," was the reply. "Is not the Mother here?" said the Master.

On the eve of the *holi* festival at Cossipore, the Master touched his heart with the palm of his hand and then made a circle around himself with a finger. He then said to Narendra, "Tell me what I have indicated." Narendra replied, "Sir, the whole universe has emanated from you." The Master was pleased and said to Rakhal: "Just see. Now he understands me." Previously Narendra had not accepted the concept of avatar, or Incarnation of God. But now he did, so the Master was happy.

Narendra sang this song at Cossipore:

O Lord, I am thy servant, I am thy servant!
   Thy servant am I!
O Lord, thou art my Master, thou art my Master!
   My Master art thou!
From thee I have received two pieces of bread and a kaupin;
When I sing thy name, devotion wells up in my heart and
   shields me from harm.
Thou art the Master, the All-compassionate; this I repeat, O Lord!
Thy servant Kabir has taken refuge at thy feet.

When the Master heard this song, tears fell from his eyes. Oh, what a sweet voice Narendra had! The Master also had a beautiful, sweet voice. After hearing them, I don't enjoy anybody else's singing. Their singing was not only sweet, but sublime and charming. It would raise the mind to a higher level of consciousness and unite it with God. I will never hear such singing again. During the last year of his life, the Master could not sing. Usually Narendra and some devotees would sing and the Master would listen. The frequent bleeding in the Master's throat reduced his body to a skeleton. By enduring this physical pain, he showed humanity that physical suffering is inevitable when one takes a body, and that there is no escape from it.

The Master was in terrible pain, but he never forgot God even for a minute. This is possible only when one attains supreme love. Whenever he listened to a song or talked about God, his mind would transcend the body and merge into God-consciousness. Saying "Mother, Mother," the Master would lose outer consciousness. This state is possible only for an incarnation of God and none else.

Even during his last illness at Cossipore, he played as he used to do when he was a child. There was a fair in the neighbourhood in celebration of the last day of the Bengali year. The Master had sent a devotee to the fair to buy a few articles, and when he returned the Master asked, "What have you bought?" The devotee replied, "Candy, a spoon, and a vegetable knife." "What about the penknife?" asked the Master. "I couldn't get one for two pice," said the devotee. "Go quickly and get one," said the Master.

At Cossipore the Master's body was so emaciated that it appeared bent like a bow. Once I was seated near his bed, dejected in mind. Seeing me the Master said: "Why are you seated like that? It is not right. Be strong and gird your loins. Give up this melancholy."

Once at Cossipore the Master asked me to buy a stone cup. Someone said, "Master, we have a cup." But he said, "Let him buy another one." It was noon. Without eating lunch, I went to Jorasanko [in West Calcutta] and returned to Cossipore after purchasing the cup. The Master took the cup in his hands and looked at it. Why did he do this? The Master knew I would remember this incident all through my life and that it would be helpful to me. The remembrance that I had bought a cup for an avatar would inspire my mind and become a living meditation. (XV. 161, III. 225, IV. 322-24, V. 209; *Gospel*, p. 950; IV. 19, VIII. 190)

My Crisis

While the Master was lying sick at the Cossipore garden house, I was working as headmaster of Vidyasagar's Shyambazar High School. I visited the Master quite often, and as a result I could not pay sufficient attention to the activities of the school. The students' test scores suffered a little. Vidyasagar was displeased with this and said to me, "You are visiting Sri Ramakrishna too much, so the results of the examinations were not good." I immediately resigned my job and informed the Master. He said three times, "You did the right thing." He knew that I did not have any savings and that I might have to starve, but still he said that I had done the right thing. Whatever one does for God is the right thing to do. First serve God and then the world.

When I quit that job I was worried about how I would feed my children. Within fifteen days I got another job. A teacher of the Hindu School was on leave, and the headmaster of that school called me and appointed me in his place, saying that the post was likely to be permanent. Even then I was worried. Another day I was abstractedly pacing back and forth on the verandah when I heard someone calling me from downstairs. I went down and found a messenger who gave me a letter from Surendra Nath Banerjee requesting me to visit him. When I met him, he said to me: "I hear you have given up your job. Why don't you work in our college?" So I joined the Ripon College [now Surendra Nath College] as a professor and worked there for five years. (IV. 308-9, VII. 37)

My Visit to Kamarpukur

I went to Kamarpukur in 1886 during Saraswati Puja when the Master was living at Cossipore. At that time the Master had raised my mind to such a high state that I perceived light everywhere in Kamarpukur. I saw trees, plants, birds, beasts, human beings — all as luminous forms and I bowed down to them.

While travelling on the road to Burdwan I reflected that the Master had walked on this road, so every bit of its dust was pure. Part of the way I went by bullock cart and the rest on foot. On the way I saw a man carrying weapons. I immediately rushed to the cart and asked the driver, "Is this man a robber?" The driver replied: "No, he is not a robber. He is a mailman. He has money with him so he carries a weapon. We are robbers." I was scared when I heard that.

When I returned the Master asked me, "How did things go in that place of robbers?" I told him everything in detail, including how I had seen everything there as luminous. When I told him that I had bowed down to a cat on the street in Kamarpukur, he laughed. I then expressed my desire to visit Kamarpukur again and he whispered, "Let me get well." But the Master was very sick by then, so my desire was not fulfilled. (VII. 189-90, XII. 54)

Pray in Solitude

The Master used to talk quite often about living in solitude. In a solitary place one develops a sense of infinity. There, nature imparts education. This cannot be understood unless one lives in solitude. The Master said: "The trees of the temple garden would remind me of the *tapovana* [forest hermitage] of the ancient *rishis* [sages], where they practised their austerities. They would watch the infinite sky, the morning sun, and the beauty of nature." The Upanishads originated in the forest, so they are also called *Aranyakas* [forest treatises].

Seeing the clouds in the sky, I am reminded of these ancient rishis. They passed through all the six seasons — summer, rain, autumn, fall, winter, spring — and realized God. The descriptions of these seasons are found in their hymns and conversations. The six seasons have also been mentioned in *The Gospel of Sri Ramakrishna*. Reading between the lines, one can find out what was spoken when. The Master said: "During my early days, a monk came to Dakshineswar. As soon as he would see the clouds in the sky, he would begin to dance."

The riverside, the ocean, the vast fields — all these awaken God-consciousness. After I returned from Darjeeling, the Master asked me, "Did you experience the presence of God when you looked at the Himalayas?" He said nothing else. I told the Master that when I saw the Himalayas from a distance I had burst into tears. At that time I did not realize the significance of it. Later on I read in the Gita where Krishna said, "Among the immovable things, I am the Himalayas." Without knowing it, I had had that awakening. The Master used to say, "Knowingly or unknowingly if you bite into a chili, your tongue will burn." (I. 38, 84, 30)

The Way of Meditation

The Master gave three illustrations regarding meditation: First, imagine a windless sky overcast with clouds. Second, think of a big lake with motionless water. Third, mentally visualize the unflickering flame of a lamp in a windless place.

Once the Master told me, "If you meditate on me that will do." Another time he taught me meditation on the formless Brahman. He took me to Mati Seal's lake at Belgharia. There were tame fish in the lake. Nobody harmed them. Visitors threw puffed rice and other bits of food into the water, and the big fish came in swarms to eat it. The fish swam fearlessly and sported joyfully in the water. The Master said to me: "Look at the fish. Meditating on the formless God is like swimming joyfully like these fish in the ocean of Bliss and Consciousness." He also gave an illustration of a bird flying freely in the infinite sky. Thus he pointed out how to imbibe the mood of meditation on the formless aspect of God. Meditation on the Master is the same as meditation on the nondual *Satchidananda* [Existence-Consciousness-Bliss Absolute], which is beyond mind and speech.

The Master would sometimes pace back and forth like a lion on the embankment of the Ganga at two or three in the morning. He could hear the *anahata* sound [Om] at that time. He said that yogis could hear it.

One day there was a terrible thunderstorm in Dakshineswar. The Master was pacing in his room and repeating his mantram. Perhaps he was watching the terrible form of the Divine Mother. He began to hum these two lines of a song: "O Mother, when assuming your terrible form you dance with your sword, the earth trembles. Mother, you are the embodiment of the three gunas, the destroyer of demons, the saviour, the consort of Shiva."

One day the Master, in an ecstatic mood, walked alone on the Barrackpore Trunk Road, which was straight and wide. Later he told us, "Seeing that beautiful road, I felt it was like a monk's heart, which is straight and vast." (I. 183, 231, 252, 370; *Gospel*, p. 256)

Plain Living and High Thinking

About food the Master used to say, "Eat a little rice and spinach and chant God's name the whole day." What is the necessity of many dishes, such as meat, fish, vegetables, and sweets? The focus of those who are earthbound is on external things and worldly enjoyments. On the other hand, those who have some knowledge about spiritual life or have a guru don't need many material things. They should be content with bare necessities and should practise sadhana as long as they live. Once the Master's parental home was being repaired by the Laha family. Seeing that ornamental designs were being put on the door, the Master said: "What is the need for all those decorations? Just put up a door so that the jackals cannot enter." But who has such insight?

The Master solved various human problems through the example of his own life. Eat simple food and the rest of the time chant the name of

Rama. He used to say: "My ideal is a brahmin widow who lives in a cottage, grows her own vegetables, eats simple food, and chants God's name all the time." When Swami Vivekananda's family was suffering from starvation, the Master blessed him, saying, "You will get rice and lentils — that is, plain food — and nothing more."

A beginner should practise japam and meditation daily at fixed times. Even when busy, he must sit for meditation in the morning and evening. Practice makes everything easy. The Master used to say: "One should get up at four in the morning, if not at three. Four or five hours of sleep is enough. One should think of God early in the morning. Holy people meditate at that time. This is called *Brahma-muhurta*, or the time of Brahman, when a spiritual current flows all around."

One should be careful about one's evening meal. If you eat too much then, you won't be able to get up early. So the Master used to say, "One may fill one's stomach at lunch, like a cannon which has been loaded with gunpowder, but supper must be light." He told me at Shyampukur: "Read the Bhagavad Gita. There you will find instructions concerning moderate eating for a yogi." The yogis eat neither too much nor too little. They eat food which is simple, substantial, and easily digestible. The Master advised some devotees to eat rice with ghee [clarified butter] and milk. He mentioned that it was the food of the ancient sages. (I. 23-24, 28, 36, II. 25-26)

Be a Devotee, But Don't Be Foolish!

The Master taught the devotees how to be practical in day-to-day life. It is extremely difficult for a person to make any progress in spiritual life if he is careless and unmindful in small matters. A person has to reach God with the help of this mind, so there should be no insincerity or inadvertence. The Master scolded Swami Yogananda when the latter bought a cracked cooking pot. He said: "Why did you buy the pot without examining it? The shopkeeper was there to conduct his business, not to practise religion. Why did you believe him and get deceived? Be a devotee, but don't be foolish!" The Master then sent him back to exchange the pot.

What a watchful eye the Master had! He did not miss any detail. Once a disciple paid a pice for six betel leaves instead of ten. Immediately the Master scolded him: "Why do you allow yourself to be cheated? You must get the right quantity. If there is any extra, distribute it among others. But by no means be cheated." This saying of the Master's has a deep significance. If a person is not careful, maya will cheat him through lust and gold. Out of carelessness, some people develop a mentality that permits being cheated by others.

Once I forgot to bring the Master's umbrella from the Panchavati. As soon as I reached his room he said to me indignantly, "While in ecstasy it is hard for me to keep the cloth on my body, yet I do not make such a mistake." Since the Master's whole life was based on dharma [religion], every action of his was perfect. It will not do to behave in a religious manner part of the time and in the opposite manner later. Whether eating, walking, sleeping, dreaming, telling beads, concentrating, worshipping, or reading the scriptures — in every condition, the mind should remain centred on one thought, one ideal — realization of God.

Nowadays some people consider dharma to mean an indifference to external matters. But the Master could not tolerate this. He said, "Such indifference is the result of *tamoguna* [inertia]." He was very particular about several things: First, cleanliness and tidiness. Generally people are unclean because of habitual laziness. How many people forget their bodies because they are thinking of God? God does not manifest himself to an unclean person. Both external and internal purity are necessary. Second, one should not be wasteful. The Master could not bear it if people wasted anything. Once at Cossipore he scolded a devotee who had cut six pieces of lemon instead of one. He said: "You are wasting the devotees' hard-earned money, which they are giving for my service. It is better to be miserly than extravagant." The Master also did not like it if anybody wasted food on his plate. Third, he could not bear people using torn or dirty clothes. He said, "The goddess of fortune leaves a person who wears patched clothes." Fourth, disorderliness. He wanted everything to be put in its proper place and handled artistically. Fifth, self-reliance, such as cooking one's own food. He mentioned: "A spiritual aspirant should cook his own food and then eat prasad after offering it to God. Thus he will not have to depend on others, nor will he lose his spiritual excellence."

He used to say: "A great worship is going on all the time. Nothing should be neglected. One should think of God during all activities of life, such as eating, walking, moving, talking, sleeping. This is called true religion." (I. 29-30, 145-47)

Be Perfect

[*M., noticing the orderliness of the kitchen storeroom at the Mihijam retreat, made the following comments:*] It looks beautiful, as if it were a shrine. When the Master came to Shyampukur from Dakshineswar for treatment, he first visited the kitchen storeroom to check on the household supplies. He noticed that the earthen pots didn't have coil stands and lids, so he immediately sent somebody to the market to buy those things. The Master couldn't tolerate disorderliness. He insisted on arranging things properly and putting them in their respective places. On the one hand he was in samadhi day and night, forgetting even his wearing cloth, and on the other, he was keenly alert to the details of everyday life. The Master used to say, "He who can keep an account of salt can also keep an account of sugar candy."

On the night of Phalaharini Kali Puja there was a theatrical performance of the *Vidyasundar* in the natmandir of Dakshineswar. The Master watched part of it. The next day the actors came to his room to pay him their respects. The Master was pleased with the young man who had skillfully played the part of Vidya. The Master said to him: "Your acting was very good. If a person excels in singing, music, dancing, or any other art, he can also quickly realize God, provided he strives sincerely." The power is the same. Instead of diverting it towards the world, direct it towards God. All knowledge comes from God, so no branch of learning should be neglected. Whatever you do, do it wholeheartedly. A sattvic worker does not do anything for himself. He does everything for God. One should care for one's personal things including clothing, house, etc., properly, because everything belongs to God. A great worship is going on everywhere all the time. (I. 330-31; *Gospel*, p. 427)

Three Practical Lessons

The Master taught us three practical lessons: First, have a charitable attitude towards all. One should remember that human beings are a mixture of good and evil. Second, show your manliness. Sometimes it is necessary to scold somebody if he does something wrong; otherwise he may exploit your goodness. Hiss but don't bite. Once I said to the Master, "My nature is so tender that I cannot hit a cat even if it steals the fish from my plate." He immediately protested and said firmly: "Don't be like that. If you push the cat away, it will not die." I had thought the Master would appreciate my pacifist attitude, but instead he was advising me to resist. Failure to act is not considered nonviolence; rather, it is tamas, or inertia. Third, if you find a person with predominantly evil tendencies, salute him from a distance as people do the tiger god. All are gods, but maintain a safe distance from the tiger god; otherwise, it may kill you. (I. 97)

Sri Ramakrishna, an Exemplar

I heard the following story from the Master. It happened during his early years at Dakshineswar when he was twenty-five years old. Before the arrival of Tota Puri, various monks visited the Master. One of these monks lived for a time in the Panchavati and served Gopala [the child Krishna]. The Master used to visit him and listen to his teachings.

According to tradition, one should serve the guru for three days. The Master served the monk by bringing him water, food, and so on for three days and then stopped going to him. The monk asked, "Why are you not visiting me anymore?" The Master replied, "I decided to serve you for three days and now that time is up."

Once a hatha yogi [one who practises postures and cleaning the body] was staying at the Panchavati of Dakshineswar. He was addicted to opium and also required one and a half seers of milk daily. He requested Rakhal to collect some money for his needs, so Rakhal said he would mention it to the Calcutta devotees. When the devotees arrived at the Master's room, the hatha yogi also arrived there, clattering his wooden sandals. As soon as the yogi reminded Rakhal about the money, the Master said to the devotees, "Will you give him something?" Perhaps the devotees felt he was not a worthy recipient, so they kept quiet. Then the Master continued: "Oh, you do not wish to give him anything. I see nobody is responding." The Master spoke tactfully, so that the devotees might not feel pressured.

A young disciple [Latu] used to live with the Master at Dakshineswar and serve him. Once a householder devotee presented a new pair of sandals to that disciple. As he was busy most of the time serving the Master, he had no time to wear them. One night a jackal took one of them away. When the Master learned about it, he searched around the garden and finally found the sandal after an hour. The Master returned it to his young disciple. At once the latter exclaimed: "Sir, what have you done? I am supposed to serve you and not the other way around." Saying this, he took the sandal from the Master's hand. What affection the Master had for the devotees!

Adhar Sen was an English-educated person. Once he went to Jadu Mallik's house with the Master. He bowed down to the goddess Simhavahini but did not make an offering. At once the Master said to Adhar, "You have not offered anything to the Mother!" Adhar said, "Sir, I didn't know that one should make an offering after saluting the deity." He then offered a rupee.

Occasionally the Master would say: "I don't usually say this lest you think I am egotistical, but when you come here bring a pice worth of cardamon or myrobalan or something." He did not ask for anything expensive, lest the devotees should stop coming. [*The Master said it for the welfare of the devotees. According to the Hindu custom, a person is supposed to offer a fruit or a flower or some money when visiting a deity or a holy man.*]

Shashi, a young disciple of the Master, used to live in Central Calcutta. As the Master was very fond of ice, he asked Shashi to bring one pice of ice from Calcutta. During summer Shashi would walk nearly six miles with the ice wrapped in a cloth to bring it to the Master. He ignored the scorching sun. He felt tremendous joy in serving the Master. The Master would mix the ice with water and greatly enjoy it. What service Shashi gave to the Master till the end! He offered his body, mind, everything at the Master's feet, and thus he became great. (III. 176, IV. 18-19, III. 249, 247-48, XII. 91)

There Are Two Paths

Once a person came to the Master and said that he was feeling great sorrow. The Master told him: "Look. Misery is better than joy. *Nivritti* [renunciation] is better than *pravritti* [attachment to sense objects]. Misery directs the mind towards God." Another time a woman came from Kamarpukur and said to the Master, "I have no one in this world." At this the Master began to dance with joy. He said to her, "He who has nobody has God." The woman returned home, at peace.

We heard from the Master that there are two paths: *vidya-maya* [the path of knowledge] and *avidya-maya* [the path of ignorance]. Through avidya-maya one can have money, home, name, fame, sense enjoyments, and so on. These things divert the mind from God. Compassion, holy company, austerity, study of the scriptures, and pilgrimage belong to the category of vidya-maya. They help one to realize God. (V. 225, X. 115)

The Value of Prasad (Sanctified Food)

The Master used to say, "In this kali yuga, the prasad of Jagannath, Ganga water, and the dust of Vrindaban are veritable manifestations of Brahman." It is not possible for us to understand his divine outlook. Every morning the Master would eat a particle of Jagannath prasad [dry rice] before eating anything else. He kept this prasad in a small cloth bag near the western wall of his room, and he used to share it with us. One day he gave a particle to Narendra, who refused to eat it, saying, "It is unclean dry rice." The Master then asked him: "Do you believe in the effect of food on the human body? For example, opium causes constipation, whereas *triphala* [myrobalan, amlaki, and baira — three kinds of tropical fruits] has a laxative effect." Narendra replied, "Yes, I believe that." Then the Master said, "In the same way, anybody who eats this prasad of Jagannath will attain knowledge, devotion, and faith." Narendra did not argue any further and ate it. He trusted every word of the Master's. He knew that the Master was truthful and an expert in metaphysical science.

Many times the Master told us, "I am Lord Jagannath of Puri." He sent me to Puri a few times and advised me about what to do in a holy place. Once he said, "Embrace Lord Jagannath." I was in a dilemma, because pilgrims are not supposed to embrace the Lord on the altar. But when I was inside the temple, the Master inspired me with an idea. I had some coins and other money in my pocket, which I intentionally dropped on the floor of the dark inner sanctuary of the temple. The priests rushed to pick up that money, and in the meantime I jumped onto the altar and embraced Lord Jagannath. Someone saw me and shouted, but I immediately got down and began to circumambulate the Lord. In the dark nobody could recognize me.

It was the Master who asked me to embrace Lord Jagannath and gave me the idea of how to do it, and then he made it easy for me by arousing greed in the minds of the priests. Now I wonder how I did that heroic deed! The Master never went to Puri. He said, "My body will not last if I visit Puri." When I returned from Puri the Master embraced me and said, "Now I have satisfied my desire to embrace Jagannath."

Once a Vaishnava monk came to Dakshineswar. The Master sent him some luchis [fried bread] and sweets that had been offered to Mother Kali. But the monk was such a fanatic Vaishnava that he threw away the prasad because it had been offered to Kali. The Master became angry. He said, "It would be good if somebody beats this rascal from head to foot and throws him out of this place." After three days that monk quarrelled with the gardeners, and they beat him and threw him out. Later the Master lamented: "That rascal threw away the Mother's prasad! If a person doesn't want to eat it, he should either give it to someone else or return it." (XIV. 243, VII. 19-20, XIV. 72, VII. 76)

Advice to Worldly People

Samadhi is the natural state of all human beings, but it seems to be unnatural. Why? Because of our craving for worldly enjoyment. When desires cease, samadhi begins. People are drowned in maya. When the Master would go to Calcutta by carriage, he would watch the people on the street through the carriage windows. Once he said: "I saw only one person with a high spiritual outlook, near the corner of the Criminal Court Building. All others had a worldly outlook." People with a worldly outlook are busy eating, sleeping, and begetting children.

Another time the Master went to Barabazar and found that a man had opened a shop in a small cell in a basement. Neither sunlight nor moonlight could penetrate there. One could not possibly enter it without bending one's head. The man was selling earthen cups and pipes for smoking tobacco. I did not pay any attention to the man, but later the Master told me: "See how people undergo so much hardship with intense concentration to earn money? They could divert this austerity and concentration towards God." But who has this perspective and who thinks this way? The Master came to do good to humanity. His mind was always on God, whereas man's mind is on the world.

The Master used to say that those who have an oily physical appearance want both God and enjoyment, yoga and bhoga. Those who have a dry physical appearance are devoted only to yoga. (II. 135-36, VII. 141, III. 320)

The Path of Degradation

Krishna mentioned in the Gita about the seven steps of a man's downfall from spiritual life.[1] The Master used to say, "The path of degradation is like a slope. A man has no inkling that he is going downward." The Master went to visit Fort William [a military barrack built several storeys below ground] in Calcutta. He said: "In the beginning I did not realize that I had descended so far. My goodness! When I looked up, I found myself below the level of a three- or four-storeyed building. Likewise, the mind, thinking of sense objects, unconsciously sinks to the depths."

Once the Master visited the Kali temple of Thanthania [in Central Calcutta] and saw that the priests were playing cards on the verandah. He plaintively said: "Look. In such a holy place they are playing cards!" A bound soul goes to his neighbour's house and wastes the whole afternoon playing cards, but he will never call on God. (I. 274, 337)

Worldly Talk

Aswini Datta's father, a subjudge, came to visit the Master after his retirement. Observing his good nature and physical traits, the Master asked him to stay at Dakshineswar for three days. One day the Master's room was full of visitors and Mr. Datta began to talk about some secular subject. At that time the Master was in samadhi. As soon as he regained outer consciousness, he heard that secular conversation. With folded hands he said humbly to Mr. Datta, "Sir, I don't like to hear talk about anything other than God."

Another time a man came to the Master and asked, "Sir, tell me how to realize God." The Master had previously heard that this person didn't

---

[1] Thinking about sense objects
Will attach you to sense objects;
Grow attached, and you become addicted;
Thwart your addiction, it turns to anger;
Be angry, and you confuse your mind;
Confuse your mind, you forget the lesson of experience;
Forget experience, you lose discrimination;
Lose discrimination, and you miss life's only purpose. (2. 62-63)

have a job, so he immediately said to him, "First try to get a job and then I shall tell you how to realize God." (IV. 267, VII. 38)

Sri Ramakrishna and Girish Chandra Ghosh

The Master went to see the drama *Chaitanya Lila* [The Life of Chaitanya] in September 1884. We went with him. Girish Ghosh arranged a box seat for the Master and engaged a man to fan him with a big palm leaf fan. The Master asked, "How much will they charge?" "Nothing," I replied. "They are happy that you have come to see the performance." Then the Master said joyfully, "I chant Mother's name, so they are doing all these things for me." It is amazing that he was reluctant to take any credit for himself. The Mother was doing everything.

Sri Ramakrishna went on another occasion to see Girish's performance at the Star Theatre. He gave him a rupee since he did not want to see it for free. Putting the money on his head, Girish began to dance. He regarded it as prasad from the Master and preserved it in his shrine.

One day while going to Balaram's house, the Master passed near the home of Girish Ghosh, who was then seated on his verandah. Pointing to him, Narayan, a young devotee, said to the Master, "There is Girish Ghosh, who wrote Chaitanya Lila." As the Master was by nature humble, he saluted Girish with folded hands. Girish followed the Master to Balaram's. There the Master said to him: "The play is well written. Many people will derive joy from it." Girish replied: "Sir, I am an unworthy person. I do not deserve such a compliment. Wherever I sit, the earth becomes impure seven cubits deep." Immediately the Master entered into an ecstatic state and sang this song:

> If only I can pass away repeating Durga's name,
> How canst thou then, O Blessed One,
> Withhold from me deliverance,
> Wretched though I may be?
> I may have stolen a drink of wine, or killed a child unborn,
> Or slain a woman or a cow,
> Or even caused a brahmin's death;
> But, though it all be true,
> Nothing of this can make me feel the least uneasiness;
> For through the power of thy sweet name
> My wretched soul may still aspire
> Even to Brahmanhood.

Listening to this song, Girish felt consoled. The Master blessed him. After that Girish would inquire about the Master's Calcutta visits and would wait for him at those places. Gradually his life was changed. One day he and a friend went to Dakshineswar by carriage. Both were dead drunk. Holding onto the Master, Girish began to sing, "O Lord, where is your sweetheart Radha?" Later the Master said: "What faith Girish has! It is so deep that it cannot be measured."

One day the Master asked Girish to take a dip in the Ganga and pray, "O all-purifying Mother Ganga, please bless me." Girish unwillingly did what the Master said. But after dipping into the Ganga, his mind became filled with bliss. Such was the greatness of Mother Ganga! The Master said, "In this kali yuga, Ganga water is the veritable manifestation of Brahman."

Another time Girish asked the Master, "Why do I feel depressed from time to time?" The Master replied: "As long as you are in the world, the cloud of maya will arise. Don't be afraid of it. It is the nature of the mind to go sometimes up and sometimes down." Girish said: "Sir, you have the power to make everybody pure and unattached, whether he is a householder or a monk. You are beyond all laws." What faith he had! The Master agreed and said to him: "Yes, it is possible. Exuberant devotion transcends all scriptural injunctions." Here the Master gave himself away. Who can admit such a thing except an avatar? Whatever Girish asked for from the Master he got. He said to the Master, "Sir, what I was and what I have become — just by thinking of you!"

What faith Girish had! The Master used to say, "Girish has one hundred and twenty-five percent faith." The Master didn't give importance to the external behaviour of a person. He saw a person's inside. Once he said, "I can see the inside of each person as one sees an object through a glass case." He could see not only the present life of a person but his past and future lives too. Though Girish's external life was to some extent unconventional, basically he was a spiritual person.

Once the Master visited Girish's house. Girish bought some refreshments at the market and served them on plates which were put directly on the carpet where the devotees were seated. Balaram Basu, a staunch devotee of the Master, was also present. Girish's style of service upset Balaram, because in his opinion it was not the proper way to serve the Master. Sri Ramakrishna looked at Balaram and told him with a smile: "This is the custom here. When I go to your house, you may serve me in your way." Balaram was a strict orthodox Vaishnava devotee. (VI. 130, VII. 156, I. 108-09, III. 86, II. 107, V. 210-11, III. 39-40)

The Story of Rasik

Rasik was a sweeper in the temple garden of Dakshineswar. The Master told us about him: One day Rasik asked him, "Master, what will happen to me?" [*The Master blessed him and said, "You will see me at the time of death."*] Rasik built a tulsi grove in his courtyard where he would practise spiritual disciplines. Later he became ill, and at last one day at noon he asked his wife to call his sons and have them carry him to the tulsi grove. There, fully conscious, he gave up his body while chanting the Master's name.

Rasik was a great soul. He not only saw the Master over a long period of time, but he also recognized him as an Incarnation of God. Through the Master's grace he was prompted to ask that vital question, "What will happen to me?" Though Rasik was a sweeper, the Master gave him immortality. The Master himself told us that once he cleaned the open drain of Rasik's house with his own hair while praying with tears in his eyes, "Mother, destroy my pride of being a brahmin." (VII. 170-71, 168)

Sri Ramakrishna's Humour

Sometimes the Master would tell funny stories that made the devotees laugh. One day he said: "Do you know how young boys talk among themselves? One says: 'Brother, once I was walking along a street flooded with water. Do you know what I saw? There were many shad fish jumping over the open drain near the street.'" [*Usually shad are confined to rivers.*]

The Master could accurately imitate the voice, gestures, and movements of a person. At such times it seemed to us that he had become identified with that person. He knew the devotees might not like to hear only talk about God, so he used to tell many humourous stories. When their mental tensions had subsided, he would lift their minds to a higher plane again. Wit and humour are necessary in the initial stages of spiritual life. They have the same effect as pickles. A person relishes his food more if he takes a little pickle with it now and then. The Master adopted various means for inspiring the devotees.

Once I went to Dakshineswar and found the Master lying on his small bed. It was a hot summer day and I was perspiring quite a bit. Mani Mallik was seated on the floor, and the Master said to him, "Since all these Englishmen [*meaning, people who have an English education*] are coming here, it proves there must be something within me." Thus, even through humour he disclosed his true nature.

The Master often went to Calcutta from Dakshineswar by horse carriage. If the horse were old and weak, it would pull the carriage only a short distance and then stop. Once when this happened he asked the coachman, "Hello, what happened?" The coachman replied: "There is nothing wrong, sir. My horse is just getting a little breath." Everybody laughed. What a humourous person the Master was! He meant that if a man were old and weak like that horse, he would not be able to see God. In an amusing way he would teach others.

The Master used to tell a story: When farmers go to the market to buy bullocks, they test each one by touching its tail. A gentle one closes its eyes and lies down on the ground, but a strong one jumps up as soon as its tail is touched. This indicates its mettle. A spirited bullock costs seventy-five rupees, whereas a gentle bullock is only five rupees. A seeker of God should be like the strong bullock, which does not care for comfort.

When the Master travelled by horse carriage, it would usually cost three rupees and two annas for a round trip. One day Balaram arranged for the Master's return trip to Dakshineswar at a cost of only one rupee and four annas. The Master asked Balaram, "Why is the fare so low?" "Sir, I got it at a cheaper rate," answered Balaram. On the way to Dakshineswar near Baranagore, the carriage lost one of its wheels, and the Master was stranded on the street. Just then Trailokya, Mathur's son, who was on his way to Dakshineswar, passed by in his luxurious phaeton. The Master was embarrassed and covered his face with his cloth. Later he would tell us about Balaram's miserliness and the accident, and we would all laugh. (VI. 163, VII. 282, I. 68, 71, VI. 55-56)

The Slide Show

Once a magician came with a magic lantern box, which contained many slides. There were two projectors to magnify the pictures. As soon as he pulled a string, the picture would change. He charged each child a pice to see them. The magician announced in a musical tone: "Look. This is Calcutta city, and this is Bombay. Here is the court of the king and queen." He thus showed various pictures. When he announced, "Now see Badri Narayan [a famous holy place in the Himalayas]," the Master immediately became curious like a child and peeped through the viewer. Seeing Badri Narayan, the Master went into ecstasy. What was the need of a picture then? Afterwards, when he came back to the normal plane, he asked a devotee to pay the magician. The devotee gave four pice. Then the Master said indignantly: "What! He showed Badri Narayan and you paid only four pice! Please give him a rupee."

What a mind the Master had! Day and night he was in a God-intoxicated state. The slightest stimulation would plunge him into samadhi. I have never seen another person like him in my life. (IX. 83)

Sri Ramakrishna at the Circus

One winter a circus company came to Calcutta. We bought tickets for the cheapest seats [half a rupee] and went to see it with the Master. Sitting on a bench in the upper gallery, the Master said: "Ha! This is a good place. I can see the show well from here." Like a child, he could not contain his joy. There were exhibitions of various feats. A horse raced around a circular track over which large iron rings were hung at intervals. The circus rider, an Englishwoman, stood on one foot on the horse's back, and as the horse passed under the rings, she jumped through them, always alighting on one foot on the horse's back. The horse raced around the entire circle, and the woman never missed the horse or lost her balance.

When the circus was over the Master and the devotees stood outside in the field near the carriage. Since it was a cold night he covered his body with his green shawl.

The Master said to me: "Did you see how that Englishwoman stood on one foot on her horse, while it ran like lightning? How difficult a feat that must be! She must have practised a long time. The slightest carelessness and she would break her arms or legs. She might even be killed. One faces the same difficulty leading the life of a householder. A few succeed in it through the grace of God and as a result of their spiritual practice. But most people fail. Entering the world, they become more and more involved in it. They drown in worldliness and suffer the agonies of death. A few only, like Janaka, have succeeded through the power of their austerity in leading the spiritual life as householders. Therefore spiritual practice is extremely necessary; otherwise one cannot rightly live in the world." (I. 72; *Gospel*, p. 154)

Sri Ramakrishna: An Ideal Teacher

The Master used to advise us to practise japam and meditation at fixed hours. He taught that one should follow one's routine rigidly. When he was ill in Cossipore, he said to one of his disciples, "In the evening practise japam and meditation." One should give up all activities in the evening and call on God. He further said: "The ancient rishis realized God after hard struggle. Early in the morning they would leave their ashramas and go into the deep forest so that nobody could disturb their spiritual disciplines. Then they would return in the evening. Thus they had visions of God." Their words have become Vedic mantras. Whatever the Master said also is a mantram.

Once someone asked the Master, "What is the way?" Without hesitating for a moment, he replied, "Faith in the words of the guru." He further said: "What are the words of the guru like? Suppose a man is being tossed up and down in a rough, choppy ocean and he is gasping for breath. Just at the critical moment a lifeboat arrives. The words of the guru are that lifeboat." One should have faith in the words of one's guru.

The Master also mentioned, "One should thoroughly scrutinize a person before choosing him as the guru." Once you have accepted a guru, you should not leave him. You cannot change gurus as you change the cleaners that clean your clothes.

Regarding initiation, the Master told someone: "Just visit this place [*meaning, himself*]. That will do." Sometimes he would write a mantram on a person's tongue, or to someone else he would give some specific instructions. Once the Master said, "He who has seen the avatar has seen God." Christ also said: "He that hath seen me hath seen the Father. I and my Father are one." The Master knew who he was, so he said: "Just visit this place. That will do." One could get spiritual awakening by just seeing the Master. Why do people practise japam and meditation? For this awakening.

One day Hazra was repeating the mantram with his rosary. The Master took the rosary from his hand and threw it away. He said to Hazra, "Even sitting here you are counting beads!" In other words, the aim of counting beads is to see God, and here the avatar is in front of you. What other purpose does japam have?

A devotee would come and look at the Master intently without blinking. Once after he had left, the Master told the others, "He has fixed his whole mind on me, so what else has he to do?" In other words, that man had achieved the goal of his sadhana [spiritual disciplines]. Another time the Master told me: "Please tell that person in Calcutta to meditate on me. Then he will not have to do anything else." At night the Master asked the Mother: "Well, Mother, did I do anything wrong in sending that message to the devotee? I see, Mother, that you have become everything — the five elements, mind, intellect, mind-stuff, ego — all the twenty-four principles." He was aware of his Divine nature. Who else could speak like this except God?

When his mother was dying at the bakul-tala ghat on the Ganga, he held her feet and cried, saying, "Mother, who are you who carried me in your womb?" He knew that he was the Supreme Brahman. He was telling his mother that she was not an ordinary mother because she had given birth to an avatar.

A devotee used to secretly practise spiritual disciplines in seclusion at Haritakibagan, in Calcutta. One day, without giving any intimation, the Master went to his house. The devotee was dumbfounded. He humbly said to the Master, "Sir, I am supposed to visit you, but instead you have found me after a long search and have come to my home." The Master said to him: "Call on God. Then someone will come forward to help you." That is why he was very anxious for the devotees. (II. 53-58, 34)

Only Longing Is Needful

No external objects are needed to attain God. The Master used to say, "Cry to the Divine Mother secretly in solitude and pray, 'Mother, please reveal yourself to me.'" A wealthy devotee built a large cottage for practising *purashcharana* [the repetition of the name of a deity a fixed number of times, according to a vow]. When the Master heard about it he scolded him, saying: "Fie on you! What low intelligence you have! You want to call on God by putting a signboard outside your house? God, the priceless treasure, dwells within the heart. One should call on him secretly."

Once I was carrying some grams [chickpeas] to keep count of my japam. I had decided to set aside one gram after each repetition of 108 japam. When the Master found out about it, he said: "This will lead to vanity. You will only dwell on how you have repeated the name fifty thousand times, or have performed so much purashcharana. God is a hidden treasure. Give me those grams. I would rather soak them and eat them."

The Master's mind remained in samadhi most of the time. Once a person closed an umbrella before him, and he at once went into samadhi. It reminded him of yoga, which teaches how to gather in the scattered mind. He had tremendous concentration. Another time, in an ecstatic mood, he fell into a fire and his hand was burned. When he regained external consciousness, he prayed like a boy, "Mother, heal my wound."

A person gave up eating fish and betel leaf. At this the Master said: "Do you consider this a big thing? Real renunciation is renunciation of lust and gold. What will one achieve by renouncing fish and betel leaf? Blessed is he who can fix his mind on God even while eating pork. On the other hand, wretched is he who, though eating sanctified vegetarian food, feels lustful and greedy." (III. 26-27)

Call on God Secretly

Once the Master visited Navin Sen's [a relative of Keshab Sen] house in Coolootola. Keshab Sen had passed away. I was living nearby at Shyampukur. When the people of my household fell asleep that night, I left for Navin Sen's house. I sat on the outside verandah and listened to the Master singing upstairs. Ah, what singing! I could not hear the conversation, but I heard the songs. Nobody knew I was sitting on the verandah. It was a full moon night, and I returned home alone. It seems to me as if it happened just the other day. The next day when I visited the Master, his room was full of people. I sat at a distance. Suddenly the Master came near me and said, "Secretly — very good." He knew that I had gone to Navin Sen's house. He then said, "It is good to call on God secretly." He thus encouraged me. (II. 247-48)

Sri Ramakrishna's Prayer

Every word of the Master's is a great mantram. Repetition of any one of them leads to perfection. His prayer too is a mantram. Is it necessary that all mantras be in Sanskrit? A mantram can be in Bengali too. The Master used to pray:

> Mother, here is thy virtue, here is thy vice;
>   take them both and grant me only pure love for thee.
> Here is thy knowledge, here is thy ignorance;
>   take them both and grant me only pure love for thee.
> Here is thy purity, here is thy impurity;
>   take them both and grant me only pure love for thee.
> Here is thy dharma, here is thy adharma;
>   take them both and grant me only pure love for thee.

The Master used to repeat the following prayer in a voice filled with pathos:

> Mother, I don't want any physical enjoyment;
> Mother, I don't want name and fame;
> Mother, I don't want the eight occult powers;
> Mother, I don't want the other hundred powers;
> Mother, give me pure, unchanging, selfless devotion to you.
> Mother, may I never be deluded by your bewitching maya.

This is our Lord's prayer or universal prayer. Jesus Christ also taught his disciples a prayer: "Our Father, who art in heaven, hallowed be thy name. Thy kingdom come, thy will be done on earth as it is in heaven. Give us this day our daily bread, and forgive us our debts as we forgive our debtors. And lead us not into temptation, but deliver us from evil. For thine is the kingdom, the power, and the glory forever."

The Master used to say another prayer:

> O Mother, thou art the operator and I am the machine.
> Thou art the indweller and I am the house.
> Thou art the driver and I am the chariot.
> I move as thou movest me.
> I do as thou makest me do.
> I speak as thou makest me speak.
> Mother, not I, not I, but thou, but thou.

Mother, thou art my refuge!
Thou art my refuge! Thou art my refuge!

(I. 199-200, III. 22, II. 145-46)

The Master's Samadhi

After renouncing karma one attains samadhi. Who knows what happens in samadhi? Only he who has experienced it knows. It cannot be described in words. Avatars and some great souls have reached this state. We are really fortunate that we lived with a person who was immersed in samadhi most of the time. Now by his grace I understand a little. It is not a matter of talk, but is felt in the depth of one's being. The Master could transmit this experience of samadhi by a touch or a mere wish.

It is extremely difficult to have samadhi even once, whereas the Master would experience samadhi many times a day — as if he were possessed by a spirit. While coming down from samadhi he would say, "The pandits are like straw to me [*which means they were dry intellectuals and could not taste the bliss of Brahman*]." We are indeed fortunate. By his grace we got a little glimpse of his message. A salt doll went to measure the depth of the ocean and got dissolved there. Who could bring back the information? This [samadhi] is the summum bonum of life. (II. 88)

Hold onto the Truth

The person who holds onto the truth has nothing to fear. He has already achieved seventy-five percent of his goal. I vividly recall one memorable night when I was riding in a carriage with the Master. As we came near the junction of Shobhabazar [in West Calcutta], the Master said to me, "If you hold onto truth, you will see God." What a great message!

Jadu Mallik had promised that he would arrange for the recital of the Chandi, but he forgot. The Master reminded him, saying: "Jadu, what is the matter with you? You have not yet arranged the Chandi recital."

Vidyasagar once gave his word to the Master that he would visit him at Dakshineswar, but he never came. One day the Master asked me: "What kind of man is this Vidyasagar? He has not kept his promise." The Master used to say, "The words of a person should be like the tusks of an elephant." He meant that just as the elephant never retracts his tusks, in the same way, whatever comes from one's lips should be followed. (X. 94-95)

The Master's Forbearance

The Master had to endure much criticism from the temple officials. Once a devotee offered a little money to Holy Mother as a gift. Trailokya, Mathur's son, remarked: "The young priest [Sri Ramakrishna] has brought his wife to the temple garden to earn money." The Master was shocked to hear Trailokya's comment. He said to the Divine Mother with tears, "Mother, the temple people say so many things that are not true." What can be done? Worldly people talk like that, but one has to adjust accordingly.

Another time Trailokya ordered his temple guards to remove Hriday, the Master's nephew, from the temple compound for misconduct. But by mistake the guard also went to the Master and asked him to leave. Without a word of protest, the Master left the room, putting his towel over his shoulder. Seeing the Master walking towards the gate, Trailokya asked, "Sir, where are you going?" The Master said with a smile, "You have ordered your guard to ask me to leave the temple garden." Trailokya was embarrassed and said: "No, sir, I didn't say that you must go. Please come back. The guard made a mistake." The Master again returned to his room with a smiling face. The Master was unconcerned about his dwelling place. The Divine Mother was always with him, so he was fearless. (VI. 74, 79-80)

The Master's Renunciation

What a state the Master had to pass through! He could neither touch nor accept money, and hoarding it was out of the question. Mahendra Kaviraj of Baranagore once gave five rupees to Ramlal for the Master's service. At first the Master thought the money could be used to pay the milk bill. But after a couple of hours he got up and called Ramlal, who was then sleeping. The Master asked: "To whom did Mahendra give that money? Is it for your aunt [meaning, Holy Mother]?" "No, it is for you," answered Ramlal. Immediately the Master said: "No, don't accept it. Go right now to Baranagore and return the money." It was midnight. Ramlal pacified the Master for the time being by promising to return the money the next morning, which he did.[2] Later the Master told the devotees: "Because of that money, I could not sleep at night. I felt as if a cat were scratching my chest."

Once when Doctor Bhagavan Rudra came to see him, the Master said to the doctor: "See what has happened to me! I cannot touch money." Saying this, he stretched out his hand and said, "Now put a rupee in my

---

[2] According to Swami Adbhutananda the money was returned that very night (see p. 89).

hand and see what happens." As soon as the doctor put a rupee in the Master's hand, his breathing stopped and his hand became stiff. The doctor was dumbfounded, as such a thing had not been mentioned in his medical books. While the Master was in samadhi, Dr. Mahendra Sarkar touched one of his eyeballs with his finger. There was no response. The Master was devoid of body-consciousness. (II. 79, III. 91)

The Master's Compassion

The Master used to pray to the Divine Mother for the devotees with tears falling from his eyes, "Mother, fulfill their desires." He had so much compassion for the devotees! They could not serve him to their heart's content while he was ill because of their family obligations, so he prayed to the Mother on their behalf: "Mother, they are very busy and have so many problems at home. Don't consider their shortcomings. Bless them, Mother."

Taking a few hours leave, some soldiers of the Dum Dum cantonment would sometimes come to visit the Master. The Master used to pray for them: "Mother, be kind to them. They come to you, undergoing so many difficulties."

Once some ornaments were stolen from the Radhakanta temple of Dakshineswar. Haladhari, a cousin of the Master, was then the priest of that temple, and the police arrested him as a suspect. The Master prayed: "Mother, your name is Durga [*meaning, one who saves the devotees from danger*]. Your name will be tarnished if misfortune befalls your child. Mother, remove all obstacles." [*As far as we know Haladhari was released.*]

A man came to the Master and said: "Sir, I am incapable of practising spiritual disciplines. If you wish, give me some experience." Immediately the Master went into samadhi. After some time he began to talk to the Divine Mother, saying: "Mother, this person does not want to do anything. Do I have to make curd from milk, butter from curd, and then put the butter into his mouth?" This attitude towards spiritual practice is prevalent in the modern age. (III. 68, 214, 26, V. 72-73)

The Master's Forgiveness

Christ prayed, "Father, forgive them, for they know not what they do." He said this prayer for those who were responsible for his death. The Master, too, prayed for evildoers. Mathur Babu's family priest lived at Kalighat, but he would conduct the worship service at Jan Bazar, Mathur's Calcutta home. This priest was very jealous of the Master because of Mathur's devotion to him. One day the Master was lying on the floor in ecstasy at the Jan Bazar house when the priest came to him and said, "Tell me, how did you cast a spell on Mathur Babu?" But the priest could not get any response from the Master, so he kicked him and left. The Master, knowing the priest would have been severely punished, never reported this incident to Mathur.

The Master went one day to attend the annual festival of the Brahmo Samaj at Nandan Bagan [in Calcutta]. The head of the family responsible for the festival had passed away, so his sons were conducting it. They did not treat the Master respectfully, but the Master remained unconcerned. Other people began eating, but the young hosts ignored the Master. Some of the devotees were very much upset and wanted to leave, but the Master said to them: "It is late. Where shall we get food at this late hour? Moreover, who will pay our carriage fare?" Later, he made a little room to eat in a dirty corner where people put their shoes. He ate a couple of luchis [fried bread] with some salt. Why did he do that? The Master understood that the boys were young and did not know him, so he compassionately accepted their food.

Once Trailokya [Mathur's son] arranged a garden party at the kuthi [mansion] in Dakshineswar, and he invited some young women. He sent a messenger to the Master asking him to come to the kuthi. The Master immediately went there and asked, "Why did you call me?" "Sir, we want to hear your singing," replied Trailokya. "Why?" said the Master. "Let these girls sing and we shall listen." Later the Master sang, and so did the women. They offered some refreshments to him, but he did not eat anything. Someone later brought refreshments to his room.

One night an officer of a rich man arrived at Dakshineswar in a phaeton. He approached the Master and said: "Sir, you will have to come with me right now. Our master at home is extremely ill." The Master told him: "You have made a mistake. There is a monk in the Panchavati who distributes medicines. I don't know those things. I simply eat and live in this temple garden."

One day a girl was waiting at the corner of the temple courtyard. When the Master passed by, she beckoned him with her hand. The Master went near her and she said: "My paramour has not visited me for some days. You are a holy man. Why don't you teach me some mantras or tricks so that I can attract him?" The Master replied, "Mother, I don't know such things." (I. 175-76, III. 151, VI. 15)

The Master's Simplicity

Once the Master ate at Keshab Sen's house, though Keshab was not a brahmin. He forbade us to tell anyone about it, lest the temple officials refuse to let him enter the Kali temple. The next day, however, when the temple manager was passing by, the Master told him: "Yesterday I went to Keshab's house and he gave me a sumptuous feast. I don't know whether the food was served by a washerman or a barber. Will it harm me?" Smiling, the manager replied: "No, sir, it is all right. Nothing can pollute you." The Master was simple like a child.

Most people call on God to fulfill their desires. As long as they get wealth and prosperity, they continue their worship. As devotees they are all right. But real devotees, those who love God for love's sake, are few in number. The Master's whole life was one of pure devotion. Wealth and power could not touch him. It was often difficult for him to keep his cloth around his body. Most of the time he would call "Mother, Mother," as if he were a child of the Mother.

Most of the Master's devotees were not well-to-do, and some were even penniless. He would often say things to amuse them. One day he asked, "How many carriages have come today?" "Nineteen," replied Latu. The Master laughed and said: "Only nineteen! That is nothing. Had there been many cabs, horses, and devotees, people would think this place must really be something." (II. 59, IV. 286-87, 283-84)

The History of the Gospel of Sri Ramakrishna

Once the Master said to me: "The Divine Mother has told me that you have to do a little work for her. You will have to teach the Bhagavata, the word of God, to humanity. God binds the Bhagavata pandit to the world with one tie; otherwise, who would remain to explain the sacred book? He keeps the pandit bound for the good of men. That is why the Divine Mother has kept you in the world."

To what extent can we foresee God's plan? The Master made me start keeping a diary in 1867 when I was a student of class eight at Hare School. Since then I recorded in my journal my daily activities, the places I had visited, and so on. I met the Master in the later part of February 1882. That is when my habit of maintaining a diary really became fruitful. When we look back on our past we realize that God is making us do everything. God determines beforehand what he will do through a particular person and then gets it done through him. There were many people around the Master, but he made me write the chronicle. As a result, *The Gospel of Sri Ramakrishna* came into existence. I was an apprentice for fifteen years. The hard discipline greatly helped me. It sharpened my memory and increased my skill in writing. I could recall the sequence of all of the incidents that had occurred during the day after I returned home at night. I would try to remember the first lines of the songs I had heard. This is the way the Master worked through me.

I was involved in worldly activities, bound to my work, and could not visit the Master whenever I wished. Therefore I used to note down his words so that I could think over what he had said between my visits to him. In this way the impressions made on my mind might not be counteracted by the stress of worldly work and responsibilities. It was thus for my own benefit that I first took notes, so that I might realize his teachings more perfectly.

I used to memorize the Master's words, and then after returning home I would write brief notes in my diary. Sometimes I would spend the whole night in completing my record. Later I would fill in all the details from memory. Sometimes I would spend seven days completing the record of one day's happenings. Thus *The Gospel of Sri Ramakrishna* appeared in book form from the notes of my diary. Sometimes I had to wait for a word of the Master's to come to my mind as a chataka bird waits for a drop of rainwater to fall. Sometimes I meditated on one scene over a thousand times. As a result I could vividly visualize the Master's divine play, though it had happened long before. By the grace of the Master I used to feel that his play had just happened. Therefore one can say that it was written in the Master's presence. At times I would not be satisfied with a particular description of an episode, so I would get absorbed in meditation on the Master. Then the correct picture would vividly appear in my mind. Therefore, from a human standpoint there was a great distance of time, but in my thought world I felt that it had happened just before I recorded it. My account is not culled from other sources. I recorded whatever I heard with my own ears from the Master's lips and whatever I saw of his life with my own eyes.

Swami Vivekananda wrote to me about the *Gospel*: "The move is quite original. Never was the life of a great teacher brought before the public untarnished by the writer's mind, as you are doing." *The Gospel of Sri Ramakrishna* is the world's only firsthand record of the life and teachings of an avatar. One can collect materials about Sri Ramakrishna in three ways: First, direct observation recorded on the same day; second, direct observation but unrecorded during the lifetime of the Master; and third, hearsay, also unrecorded during the lifetime of the Master. *The Gospel of Sri Ramakrishna* belongs to the first category. I was present during each scene of the *Gospel*.

I have published my diary very carefully. If there is any mistake in it, then its value will diminish. People do not realize that at one time I had to study the rules of evidence. If a witness makes a single mistake, the entire case becomes nullified. Addressing the judge, the lawyer says, "My Lord, this witness is not reliable." I used to visit the court and observe all these details. The evidence of an eyewitness is very valuable. For that reason the judge asks, "Did you see this yourself?" If a person has seen and heard something himself, his words carry weight. I checked all the facts and details before I published the *Gospel*.

[*When somebody asked M. to remove some of the repetitions from the* Gospel, *he replied:*] I cannot do that. The Master told the same parable to different people. If I remove a particular section, the train of the conversation will be broken. Moreover, you won't be able to see the effect of the *Gospel* on a particular person's life. The Master gave the same teaching to five different people in five different places. What he said to Bankim, he said to others also; and whatever conversation he had with Vivekananda, he had with others too.

You see, sometimes the brilliance of a diamond is enhanced by changing its setting. Putting it on the dusty ground produces one effect, and putting it on a green lawn produces another. But putting it in a casket lined with blue velvet produces the most brilliant effect of all. The same is true of the words in the *Gospel*. The rays of the sun look different when they fall on water, on the earth, and on glass, but the maximum brilliance is produced when the sun is reflected on glass. So I cannot avoid the repetitions in the *Gospel*, because removing them would disturb the Master's dialogue.

Once Hriday said to the Master: "Uncle, please reserve some of your best teachings. Otherwise, if you say everything all at once, and then repeat the same thing again and again, people will not come to you anymore." The Master replied: "You rascal! I shall repeat my words fifty times. What does it matter to you?"

[*The Gospel of Sri Ramakrishna was in the curriculum of M.'s school. When M. was accused by some people of trying to sell his books to the students, he calmly replied:*] The students will understand the effect of reading the *Gospel* when they enter family life. The Master used to say, "The world is a burning fire." And I fully realized it. After the boys enter the world and are tormented by sorrows and sufferings, the Master's immortal words will save them, like a loving mother. If they remember at least one of the Master's teachings, that will be like a boat to ferry them across the turbulent ocean of maya and it will bring peace to their lives.

[*In spite of his illness, M. read the proofs of the last part of the Bengali* Gospel *at one o'clock in the morning by the light of a kerosene lantern. Being lovingly chastised by his colleague, he said:*] People are finding peace by reading this book, the Master's immortal message. It is inevitable that the body will meet its end, so it is better that it be used for spreading peace to others. We are in the world and have fully experienced how much pain there is in it, yet I have forgotten that pain through *The Gospel of Sri Ramakrishna*. I am hurrying so that the book may come out soon. (*Srima Darshan*, I. 36; *The Gospel of Sri Ramakrishna*, pp. 718-19; *S. D.*, I. 13; *Disciples of Sri Ramakrishna*, Advaita Ashrama, p. 424; *S. D.*, XIV. 290, VI. 104-06, IX. 147-52, VI. 118-19, I. [Introduction], pp. 11-12)

"I Am an Avatar"

Standing in the pine grove of Dakshineswar, the Master said to me: "I am an avatar. I am God in human form." He also told me, "I will have to be born again." The Master proclaimed again and again, "The greatest duty of man is to realize God." And he himself fully demonstrated this ideal in his own life.

When an avatar descends, a current of bliss flows everywhere. So Christ said, "Can the children of the bride chamber mourn as long as the bridegroom is with them?" Christ was an avatar. One day the Master told me, "Christ, Gauranga, and I are one." A person experiences uninterrupted bliss while he lives with an avatar. But when the avatar departs, sorrow and gloominess come. I forgot the world for five years. When the Master was with us we floated in bliss. Now I experience happiness one day and misery another. What a wonderful time we had with the Master — festivals, feasts, singing, dancing! When the Master passed away I fasted for three days.

I am an insignificant person, but I live by the side of an ocean, and I keep with me a few pitchers of sea water. When a visitor comes, I entertain him with that. What else can I speak but the words of the Master?

If anybody asks me what the greatest event of my life was, I would say that I met Sri Ramakrishna Paramahamsa — my Master. (VI. 224, XVI. 29; *Disciples of Sri Ramakrishna*, Advaita Ashrama, 1955, pp. 265-66; S. D., VII. 25)

[From: *Srima Darshan*, by Swami Nityatmananda (Calcutta: General Printers & Publ. Pvt. Ltd.), vols. I-XVI, 1967-77; *The Gospel of Sri Ramakrishna*, tr. by Swami Nikhilananda (New York: Ramakrishna-Vivekananda Center), 1969; *Disciples of Sri Ramakrishna* (Calcutta: Advaita Ashrama), 1955]

19

Girish Chandra Ghosh

Girish Chandra Ghosh (1844-1912) was a well-known actor and play-wright even before meeting Sri Ramakrishna. Though he wanted to renounce the world after coming in contact with Sri Ramakrishna, at the Master's command he continued his writing career. He thus greatly inspired many people through his dramas as well as through his life.

When the responsibility of writing an article on Sri Ramakrishna fell on me, I thought it would be a very simple thing. But actually, I find the writing extremely difficult. I thought it would be easy, for I have enjoyed his unfathomable love. I have also heard from each disciple how Sri Ramakrishna showered his infinite love on him. Many a time with enraptured minds, we have discussed among ourselves that great love. Whenever a disciple would recount his personal experiences, immediately as a reaction, a hundred fountains would open up from within and a hundred streams would flow with a gushing torrent. Not so much from the actual words of the disciple, but from the manner of his expression a sympathetic chord in my heart would be touched, and his experience would become vivid and living before my mind's eye.

A single word of the disciple, a single incident described, would make me feel that I too had heard such words of affection — I too had seen many such acts of compassion. With a single word the disciple would relive the experience and the listener would feel himself to be a participant. But I wonder if my readers will be able to share with equal vividness my own experiences. Shall I be able to convey them in words? Let me ask a question: Can you describe the warmth of affection which you have received from your own mother? For myself, I could not. I could only exclaim, "Ah, mother's love, mother's love." In every act of my mother, in her every glance and movement, what I have felt is beyond my words to describe. Besides, could anyone really understand a mother's love without becoming a mother? Even were such under-

Girish Chandra Ghosh in Calcutta

standing possible, an understanding of Sri Ramakrishna's love lies far beyond it.

Our relationships in the world are conditioned by maya. Father's love or mother's love can also be said to fall within maya. Usually love prompted by maya, desires only the worldly happiness of the son. It seeks only his worldly prosperity and nothing more. Very often it is seen that if the son, for the sake of spiritual enlightenment, pays no attention to worldly duties, he becomes a source of annoyance to his parents. In spite of his possessing good qualities, if the son prefers monastic life to marriage, he becomes an object of displeasure to his parents. They advise him that there is time for everything, and that he should attend to spiritual life after finishing his life in the world and discharging his duties to the world in a proper manner. If the boy does not listen to their advice, they may not say in so many words that their son has gone astray, but will not refrain from saying to friends and relations with a sigh of regret that he is useless and lacking in purpose. There is selfishness in the love of parents. It is seen that the father is partial to an accomplished son. As long as the son is a mere boy and helpless, the parents are unselfish. But most parents expect that in their old age they will be looked after and provided for by their sons. Greater is the love of the mother for the son who has no talents. Father's love or mother's love is very high indeed. But it cannot be said that it is absolutely free from selfishness.

If I stretch my imagination I can have a glimpse of my parents' love. But the love of Sri Ramakrishna — that immaculately pure and absolutely unselfish love — how can I comprehend it? How shall I portray it in words? Without attaining the state of consciousness that is free from the touch of selfishness, free from the delusion of maya, how shall I understand the actions of a person who has broken the bonds of maya and is without faults? If I had attained that condition in which Sri Ramakrishna lived, the condition of being totally free from maya, and if I had had a disciple, I could then have gained the power of understanding Sri Ramakrishna's love in a small measure. But I don't know whether I would have been able to express it. I have grasped to some extent the love of Sri Ramakrishna by listening to the stories which other disciples have narrated to me and by comparing notes which I myself have gathered, but it is not possible to describe the story of the pilgrimage of the soul which a fellow traveller has made and paint a picture of the longings and aspirations of his heart. I may or may not know the story of my own life, but the story of another man's life is a completely sealed book to me. Therefore in this article I shall tell only my own tale, what I felt about the love of Sri Ramakrishna in relation to me. Beyond that I am helpless. I must speak about myself. My listeners, out of compassion for my pitiable condition, must kindly forgive me.

Another thing, those who went to Sri Ramakrishna were all gentle, good-natured, and virtuous. Boys like Narendra and others, who are considered as his own, visited the Master at an early age, when they were very young. Being drawn by his love, they left their hearth and home and later embraced the monastic life in order to carry out his mission. To describe his love for them will hardly give a correct picture of his love. His affection for these boys, who were pure and spotless and who had taken shelter in him after renouncing everything for his sake, was quite natural. But I too was the recipient of his love. This seems to me something extraordinary. Sri Ramakrishna loved me unstintedly. This was proof of the fact that he was an ocean of unconditional mercy and boundless compassion.

One of the names of God is "Saviour of the fallen." I, and no one else, can bear witness that he deserved that name. Some of those who have been with the Master may be fickle-minded, but in comparison with my fickle and restless nature they are all saints. They may have a few weaknesses, their feet may have slipped a few times, but in comparison with my Himalayan faults, those shortcomings are nothing. From my early boyhood I was moulded in a different way. I never learned to walk a straight path. I always preferred a crooked way. In spite of my faults, I was the object of his deepest affection. The manifestation of his love was revealed nowhere so clearly as in my case. The readers will get a glimpse of it from the story I shall tell below.

Sri Ramakrishna gave me refuge at a time when I was torn by conflicts and brutal agony of the heart. My early training, lack of a guardian from childhood, wayward youthful tendencies — all these conspired to lead me away from the path. Atheism was the fashion of the day. Belief in the existence of God was considered foolish and a sign of weakness. In my circle of friends if one could prove the nonexistence of God, one received the most extravagant praise and honour. I used to make fun of those who believed in God. After reading a few pages about science I jumped to the conclusion that religion was pure imagination and myth. Priests had concocted it to frighten people into morality and abstention from evil-doing. Wisdom lay in accomplishing one's ends by any means, fair or foul. An unworthy act became ignoble when it was discovered and not before that. It was daylight that made sin. To fulfill one's purpose secretly was a proof of talent. To satisfy one's desire through cleverness was a mark of intelligence. But in a world ruled by providence such intelligence does not last. Evil days are bound to come. When they come they teach hard truths. I learned from them one big lesson, that there is no way to hide a wicked deed. There is a saying, "Murder will out." Too true, as I learned. But the deeds had already begun to bear fruit. A terrible future was painted in vivid colours on the canvas of my mind. It was not the end but only the beginning of the episode that darkened my destiny. Punishment had begun, but the way to its escape had not yet been found. Friendless, and surrounded on all sides by enemies who took advantage of my misdeeds to ruin me, I felt that I was adrift on a sea of despair.

At such a crisis I thought: "Does God exist? Does he listen to the prayers of man? Does he show him the way from darkness to light?" My mind said, "Yes." Immediately I closed my eyes and prayed: "Oh God, if thou art, carry me across. Give me refuge. I have none." I remembered the words of the Gita: "Those who call on me only in the days of affliction, to them too I bring succour and refuge." These words sank deep in my consciousness and gave me solace in sorrow. I found the words of the Gita to be true. As the sun removes the darkness of the night, so the sun of hope arose and dispelled the gloom that had gathered thick in my mind. In the sea of trouble I found the harbour of repose. But I had nurtured doubt all these years. I had argued long, saying, "There is no God." Where would the impressions of these thoughts go? I began to reason in terms of cause and effect and argued that such and such a cause had produced such and such an effect, which was instrumental in bringing release from this danger. It is said that doubt dies hard. Again I fell victim to doubt. But I had not the courage to say boldly, "God does not exist."

Desire for inquiry came. Looking into the current of events, sometimes faith, sometimes doubt, emerged. Everybody with whom I discussed my problems said unanimously that without instruction from a guru doubt would not go and nothing could be achieved in spiritual life. But my intellect refused to accept a human being as a guru, for one has to salute the guru with the words, "Guru is Brahma, Guru is Vishnu, Guru is the Lord Maheshwara, the god of gods, etc." How could I say this to a man like me? This was hypocrisy. But the tyranny of doubt was intolerable. Terrible conflicts pierced my heart through and through. That condition can better be imagined than described. Suppose a man, all of a sudden, is forcibly dragged to a dark, solitary room with his eyes covered and kept confined there with no food and drink. What will be the state of his mind? If you can picture his mental condition, you will be able to understand something of my own. There were moments when I was breathless with emotion. Thoughts of despair bit through me like a saw. At other times the memory of the past was revived and the darkness of my heart knew no bounds. Just at this time I saw Sri Ramakrishna passing by our lane to the house of Balaram, the great devotee, and for the first time I felt irresistibly drawn to him. However, I shall describe this meeting later.

Some time previously I had read in the *Indian Mirror* that there was a paramahamsa [an illumined soul] who was living in Dakshineswar. Keshab Chandra Sen was visiting him frequently, accompanied by his disciples. With my little understanding I thought that the Brahmos, who had many strange ideas, had created a fake paramahamsa. He could not be the real thing.

A few days passed, and I heard that the paramahamsa would be coming to the house of Dinanath Basu, an attorney of the Calcutta High Court, in our neighbourhood. To satisfy my curiosity and to ascertain what kind of a paramahamsa he was, I went to see him. I returned with irreverence instead of reverence. When I arrived at Dinanath Basu's I saw that the paramahamsa had come and that he was giving instructions to Keshab Sen and others, who were listening with rapt attention. It was dusk. Lights were lit and they were placed in front of Sri Ramakrishna. But he began to make repeated inquiries, saying, "Is it evening? Is it evening?" At this I thought to myself: "What pretention! It is dusk. Lights are burning in front of him. Yet he cannot tell whether it is evening or not." Thinking I had seen enough of him, I left.

A few years later Sri Ramakrishna was to come to the residence of Balaram Basu at Ramkanta Bose's Street. High-souled Balaram had invited many in our neighbourhood to come and visit the Master. I too had an invitation, so I went. After arriving there I found Sri Ramakrishna had already come and Bidhu, a dancing girl, was seated by his side in order to sing a few devotional songs for him. Quite a large gathering had assembled in Balaram's drawing room. Suddenly my eyes were opened to a new vision by Sri Ramakrishna's conduct. I used to think that those who consider themselves paramahamsas or yogis do not speak with anybody. They do not salute anybody. If strongly urged, they allow others to serve them. But the behaviour of this paramahamsa was quite different. With the utmost humility he was showing respect to everybody by bowing his head on the ground. An old friend of mine, pointing at him, said sarcastically: "Bidhu has had a previous intimacy with him. That's why he is laughing and joking with her." But I did not like his insinuations. Just at this time Sishir Kumar Ghosh, the well-known editor of *Amrita Bazar Patrika*, arrived. He seemed to have very little respect for Sri Ramakrishna. He said, "Let us go. Enough of him!" I wanted to stay and see a little more, but he insisted and made me come with him. This was my second meeting.

Again some days went by. My play, *The Life of Chaitanya*, was being enacted in the Star Theatre. I was strolling in the outer compound of the theatre one day when Mahendra Nath Mukhopadhyay, one of the devotees of Sri Ramakrishna, came and said to me: "Paramahamsadeva has come to see the play. If you allow him a free pass, well and good. Otherwise we will buy a ticket for him."

I replied: "He will not have to purchase his ticket. But the others will have to." Saying this, I proceeded to greet him. I found him alighting from the carriage and entering the compound of the theatre. I wanted to salute him, but before I could do so he saluted me. I returned his salute. He saluted me again. I bowed my head and he did the same to me. I thought this might continue forever, so I greeted him mentally and led him upstairs and offered him a seat in the box. After arranging with an attendant to fan him, I returned home, feeling indisposed. This was my third meeting.

Before I narrate my fourth meeting I must tell you the condition of religion that prevailed in the country at that time. During my school days those who were called "Young Bengal" were the people who were recognized in society as respectable and learned. They were the first products of Western education in Bengal. The majority of them were materialists. A small minority had been converted to Christianity. Some of them accepted the creed of the Brahmo Samaj, but few of them had any respect for Hinduism. Orthodox Hindus were bitterly torn by sectarianism. Conflict between Shaktas and Vaishnavas was very strong. And Vaishnavism too was divided into many sects, each contending for supremacy over the other. Rivalry was growing fast between one sect and another. Moreover there were other faiths prevalent at the time. Each faith condemned the followers of the other faiths to the darkness of hell. Added to this, many brahmin priests were degenerate. They were completely ignorant of their own scriptures and were not even familiar with the formalities of religion, and yet they acted as priests and preachers. In a word, they lived a most hypocritical life.

On the other hand, the youths of the day, having studied a few pages of English, became iconoclasts at heart. The materialists were considered the most enlightened people on earth because of their erudition and scholarship, and so their words were accepted as the supreme authority. The sign of scholarship was not to believe in God. Under such circumstances, the young educated people lost all faith in their own religion. But there would be discussion now and then among ourselves about the existence of God. Occasionally I would attend the services of the Brahmo Samaj, and would sometimes visit the one in our neighbourhood, but I arrived at no conclusion. Whether God existed or not I was doubtful. If he existed, which religion should I follow? I argued much, deliberated much, but could not find any solution.

This made me uneasy. Then one day I prayed, "Oh Lord, if thou art, show me the way." But there was egotism in my heart, and I thought: "All the necessities of material life, such as air, water, and light, are abundantly supplied by nature and available for man to enjoy. Why should not religion, so essential for eternal life, be equally available. To me, it seems neither natural nor within my reach, and therefore it must be false. Materialism must be true." Thus I passed fourteen long years in a fog of gloom.

Then came evil days which allowed me no rest. There was darkness within, there was darkness without — darkness everywhere. I thought: "Is there any escape? I have seen people taking refuge in Taraknath Shiva when they suffer from some incurable disease." My condition too was very serious. To get release from my trouble was almost impossible. At this juncture, would it do me good if I prayed to Taraknath Shiva, the protector of his devotees? Let me test it! I made an honest attempt to resign myself to the will of the Lord, and my attempt was successful. A network of danger was pierced through in no time. A firm conviction arose that God was not unreal.

I was saved from the present danger, but was this the way to ultimate salvation? Terrible conflict was raging in my mind, and I was uncertain which way to take. I had seen the glory of Taraknath. Why not call on him again? Gradually faith in God began to grow in me. But they said that no liberation is possible without a guru. Furthermore, I was told that one must look upon the guru as God. My reason found this hard to accept. The very idea was revolting to me, for nothing seemed more blasphemous than to think of man as God. I must trudge on alone without a human guru. I would pray to Taraknath. Let him be my guru. I had heard of some people to whom the Lord had appeared as guru in a vision and who thus received their spiritual instruction without a human intermediary. If he would shower such grace on me, I would be saved. Otherwise I was helpless. But I had not seen Taraknath. What should I do then? Let me chant his name in the morning and then see what happens.

At this time I became acquainted with a painter who was a Vaishnava. I don't know if it was true or not, but he said to me one day: "I offer food to the Deity every day, and I am convinced by certain signs that he accepts it. Until one is initiated by a guru such a rare privilege will not happen in one's life." My mind became restless. I took leave of him, went to my room, closed all the doors, and began to weep.

Three days later I was sitting on the porch of a friend's house, which was at an intersection, and I saw Sri Ramakrishna slowly approaching, accompanied by Narayan and a couple of other devotees. No sooner had

I turned my eyes towards him than he saluted me. I returned his salute. Then he went on. For no accountable reason my heart felt drawn towards him by an invisible string. As soon as he had gone a short distance, I felt an urge to follow him. I could not keep calm, for the attraction I felt was not of this earth. It was something for which no former experience had ever prepared me. It was something unique, which no words could describe. Just at that moment a person, whose name I do not recall, brought me a message from him and said, "Sri Ramakrishna is calling you." I went.

Sri Ramakrishna went on to Balaram's, and there I followed him. Balaram was lying on a couch, seemingly ill. The moment he saw Sri Ramakrishna he got up quickly and with great reverence prostrated himself before him. After an exchange of a few words with Balaram, Sri Ramakrishna suddenly exclaimed, "I am all right, I am all right." So saying, he went into a state of consciousness which seemed very strange to me. Then he remarked, "No, no, this is not pretense, this is not pretense." He remained in this state for a while and then resumed his normal state. I asked him, "What is a guru?" He answered: "Do you know what the guru is? He is like a matchmaker. A matchmaker arranges for the union of the bride with the bridegroom. Likewise a guru prepares for the meeting of the individual soul with his Beloved, the Divine Spirit." Actually, he did not use the word matchmaker, but a slang expression, more forceful. Then he said: "You need not worry. Your guru has already been chosen." I asked, "What is the mantram?" He replied, "The name of God." And as an example he told the following story.

"Ramananda used to bathe in the Ganga early every morning. On one of the steps of the ghat a weaver by the name of Kavir was lying, and as Ramananda came down the steps his feet accidentally touched the body of Kavir. Being conscious of the divine presence in all, he uttered the word 'Rama.' Kavir, on hearing this name from the lips of a holy man, took it to be his mantram, and by chanting it he eventually realized God."

Then the talk drifted to the theatre, and he said: "I liked your play very much. The sun of knowledge has begun to shine upon you. All the blemishes of your heart will be washed away. Very soon devotion will arise to sweeten your life with profuse joy and peace." I told him that I had none of those qualities and that I had written the play only with the idea of making some money. He kept quiet. Then he said, "Could you take me to your theatre and show me another play of yours?" I replied, "Very well, any day you like." He said, "You must charge me something." I said, "All right, you may pay eight annas." Sri Ramakrishna said, "That will allow me a seat in the balcony, which is a very noisy place." I answered: "Oh no, you will not go there. You will sit in the same place that you sat last time." He said, "Then you must take one rupee." I said, "All right, as you please." Our talk ended.

Soon after this, Haripada and I saluted Sri Ramakrishna and came out of Balaram's house. On the way Haripada asked me, "What do you think of him?" I replied, "A great devotee." My heart was filled with unspeakable joy, for it seemed as though my search for a guru had ended. For did not Sri Ramakrishna say that my guru had already been chosen?

Looking back at my former objections to a guru, I understood the pride and vanity which had lain behind my rationalizations. I had thought: "After all, the guru is a man. The disciple is also a man. Why should one man stand before another with folded palms and follow him like a slave?" But time after time in the presence of Sri Ramakrishna my pride crumbled into dust. Meeting me at the theatre, he had first saluted me. How could my pride remain in the presence of such a humble man? The memory of his humility created an indelible impression on my mind.

A few days after my visit with him at Balaram's I was sitting in the dressing room of the theatre when a devotee came to me in a hurry and said with some concern, "Sri Ramakrishna is here in his carriage." I replied: "Very well. Take him to the box and offer him a seat." But the devotee answered, "Won't you come to greet him personally and take him there yourself?" With some annoyance I said: "Does he need me? Can't he get there himself?" Nevertheless I went. I found him alighting from the carriage. Seeing his serene and radiant face, my stony heart melted. I rebuked myself in shame, and that shame still haunts my memory. To think that I had refused to greet this sweet and gentle soul! Then I conducted him upstairs. There I saluted him, touching his feet. Even now I do not understand the reason, but at that moment a radical change came over me and I was a different man. I offered him a rose, which he accepted. But he returned it again, saying: "Only a god or a dandy is entitled to flowers. What shall I do with it?"

There was a special room on the second floor of the Star Theatre, which was intended for the visitors of the dress circle to sit in during the concert. Sri Ramakrishna came there, and a good number of devotees joined him. He started conversing with me. He spoke of several things while I listened longingly. I felt a spiritual current passing, as it were, through my body from foot to head and head to foot. All of a sudden Sri Ramakrishna lost outer consciousness and went into ecstasy, and in that mood he started talking with a young devotee. Many years earlier I had heard some slandering remarks against him, made by a very wicked man. Suddenly I remembered those words, and at that moment Sri

Ramakrishna's ecstasy broke and his mood changed. Pointing towards me, he said, "There is some crookedness in your heart." I thought: "Yes, indeed. Plenty of it — of various kinds." But I was at a loss to understand which kind he was particularly referring to. I asked, "How shall I get rid of it?" Sri Ramakrishna replied, "Have faith!"

Time rolled on. One afternoon I went to the theatre and saw on my desk a slip of paper with a note that Sri Ramakrishna would be going to Ram Chandra Datta's house at Madhu Roy's Lane, Calcutta. After reading that note I felt in my heart the same kind of strong urge to go to meet him as I had felt on that day when I saw the Master coming while I was sitting on the porch of a friend's house in our neighbourhood. I was very eager to go. But again I considered, "Should I go to a stranger's house without an invitation?" But the pull of the invisible string was strong. I had to go. I went as far as Anath Babu's market and stopped. Then I thought again, "No, I must not go." But I was helplessly drawn. I would go a few steps and then stop. I hesitated even after coming very near to the house of Ram Chandra.

At last I reached the gate. Ram Chandra was sitting there and ushered me in. It was evening. Sri Ramakrishna was dancing in ecstasy in the courtyard. There was singing accompanied by a drum, and the devotees were dancing in a circle around Sri Ramakrishna. The words of the song were: "Nadia is shaken by the surging waves of divine love emanating from the heart of Gauranga." The courtyard seemed a sea of bliss. Tears filled my eyes. Sri Ramakrishna suddenly became still, absorbed in samadhi. The devotees began to take the dust of his feet. I wanted to do the same, but I could not, as I was shy. I was thinking of what others might say if I went to Sri Ramakrishna and took the dust of his feet. No sooner had this thought crossed my mind than Sri Ramakrishna, coming down from samadhi, began dancing again. While dancing he came before me and stood still, once more absorbed in samadhi. Now there was no longer any hesitation on my part to touch his feet. I took the dust of his feet.

After the music Sri Ramakrishna came and sat in the drawing room and I followed him. Then he began to talk to me. I asked him, "Will the crookedness go out of my heart?" He said, "Yes, it will go." Again I asked him the same question, and he gave the same reply. I repeated it once more, and he said the same thing. But Manomohan Mittra, an ardent devotee of his, said to me rudely: "Enough. He has already answered you. Why do you bother him again?" I turned towards him to answer sharply, for no one who criticized me ever escaped the lash of my tongue. But I controlled myself, thinking: "Manomohan must be right. He who does not believe when told once will not believe even if he is told a hundred times." I bowed down before Sri Ramakrishna and returned to my theatre.

One night, in a happy and drunken mood, I was visiting a house of prostitution with two of my friends. But suddenly I felt an urge to visit Sri Ramakrishna. My friends and I hired a carriage and drove out to Dakshineswar. It was late at night, and everyone was asleep. The three of us entered Sri Ramakrishna's room, tipsy and reeling. Sri Ramakrishna grasped both my hands and began to sing and dance in ecstasy. The thought flashed through my mind: "Here is a man whose love embraces all — even a wicked man like me, whose own family would condemn me in this state. Surely this holy man, respected by the righteous, is also the saviour of the fallen."

After these meetings with Sri Ramakrishna I began to wonder: "Who is this man who speaks to me with such intimacy and makes me feel that he is my very own? No longer do I fear my own sins, for I feel sure he would not condemn me. Though he seems to know me through and through, a confession might do me great good. I must take shelter at his feet, for he alone can bring me peace."

I went to Dakshineswar and found Sri Ramakrishna seated on the southern porch of his room. He was talking with a young devotee named Bhavanath. I prostrated myself before Sri Ramakrishna and mentally recited the verse "Guru is Brahma, Guru is Vishnu, Guru is the Lord Maheshwara, the god of gods." He said: "I was just talking about you. And if you don't believe me, ask Bhavanath!"

After a while he started to give me some spiritual advice. I stopped him, saying: "I won't listen to any advice. I have written cartloads of it myself. It doesn't help. Do something that will transform my life." Hearing these words, Sri Ramakrishna was highly pleased. Ramlal, his nephew, was present. Sri Ramakrishna asked him to recite a particular hymn, which ran thus: "Go into solitude and shut yourself in a cave. Peace is not there. Peace is where faith is, for faith is the root of all." I saw a smile playing on the lips of Sri Ramakrishna, and I felt at that moment that I was freed from all impurities. And at that moment my arrogant head bowed low at his feet. In him I found my sanctuary and all my fear was gone. I prostrated myself before him and was about to return home. He followed me as far as the northern porch. There I asked him, "Now that I have received your grace, am I to continue the same kind of work that I have been doing?" Sri Ramakrishna replied, "Yes, why not?" From his words I understood that my connection with the theatre would not hurt my spiritual life.

My heart was filled with joy. I felt as if I were born anew. I was a totally changed man. There was no more doubt or conflict in my mind. "God is real. God is my sanctuary. I have found my refuge in this God-man. Now I can easily realize God." Thoughts like these cast their spell on me night and day. While awake or while dreaming, the same mood persisted: "Fearless am I! I have found my very own. The world can no longer bind me, for even the greatest fear, the fear of death, is gone."

Meanwhile, I would hear from various devotees that the Master had spoken affectionately of me. If anybody would criticize me, Sri Ramakrishna would say: "It is not true. You do not know. He has tremendous faith."

Sri Ramakrishna would come to the theatre now and then to visit me, bringing some sweets for me from Dakshineswar. He would first taste them and then give them to me. Immediately my mood would change, and I would feel like a little child, fed by a loving parent.

One day when I arrived at Dakshineswar, Sri Ramakrishna was just finishing his noonday meal. He offered me his dessert, but as I was about to eat it, he said: "Wait. Let me feed you myself." Then he put the pudding into my mouth with his own fingers, and I ate as hungrily and unself-consciously as a small baby. I forgot that I was an adult. I felt I was a child of the mother and the mother was feeding me. But now when I remember how these lips of mine had touched many impure lips, and how Sri Ramakrishna fed me, touching them with his holy hand, I am overwhelmed with emotion and say to myself: "Did this actually happen? Or was it only a dream?" I heard from a devotee that Sri Ramakrishna saw me as a little baby in a divine vision. And whenever I was with him, I would actually feel like a child.

Although I had come to regard Sri Ramakrishna as my very own, the scars of past impressions were not so easily healed. One day, under the influence of liquor, I began to abuse him in most unutterable language. The devotees of the Master grew furious and they were about to punish me, but he restrained them. Abuse continued to flow from my lips in a torrent. Sri Ramakrishna kept quiet and then silently returned to Dakshineswar. There was no remorse in my heart. As a spoiled child might carelessly berate his father, so did I abuse Sri Ramakrishna without any fear of punishment. Soon my behaviour became common gossip, and I began to realize my mistake. But at the same time I had so much faith in his love, and felt his love was so infinite, that I did not fear for a moment that Sri Ramakrishna could ever desert me.

Many of the devotees wondered why the Master put up with all my wickedness and suggested that he sever all connection with me. Ram Chandra Datta alone pleaded on my behalf and said to him: "Sir, he has worshipped you with abuse, according to his nature. The serpent Kaliya asked Lord Krishna, 'Since you have given me poison, how can I offer you nectar?'" Sri Ramakrishna said, "Just listen to what Ram says." But as the others continued to condemn me, the Master said abruptly: "Get me a carriage. I must go to see Girish!" My affectionate spiritual father then came to my house and blessed me by his presence.

As the days passed on I began to feel more and more remorse for my conduct towards this gentle holy man, who was the very soul of love. Thinking of the other devotees who worshipped him with adoration, I was full of self-reproach. It was in this state of depression that Sri Ramakrishna found me a few days later, and in an ecstatic mood he said: "Girish Ghosh, don't worry. People will be amazed at your transformation."

From my early childhood it had been my nature to do the very thing that I was forbidden to do. But Sri Ramakrishna was a unique teacher. Never for one moment did he restrict me, and that in itself worked a miracle in my life. Whenever any lustful thought would arise in my mind, it would quickly fade. My head would bow low before Brahman and Shakti, and Sri Ramakrishna would appear in my mental vision. Behind the degenerate words and actions of worldly people, I felt the eternal play of God. Again, it was my habit to tell occasional lies. Though Sri Ramakrishna was very strict with regard to truthfulness and would not allow anyone to tell an untruth even in fun, when I approached him to confess my guilt, he replied: "You need not worry. Like myself, you are above truth and falsehood." Yet afterwards, when even a thought of telling a lie arose in my mind, the mental image of Ramakrishna would again appear before me, and no untruth could escape my lips.

Sri Ramakrishna has taken full possession of my heart and bound it with his love. But such a love cannot be measured by any earthly standard. If I have acquired any virtues, it is not through my own efforts, but solely due to his grace. He literally accepted my sins and left my soul free. If any of his devotees would speak of sin and sinfulness, he would rebuke him saying: "Stop that. Why talk of sin? He who repeatedly says, 'I am a worm, I am a worm,' becomes a worm. He who thinks, 'I am free, I am free,' becomes free. Always have that positive attitude that you are free, and no sin will cling to you."

The significance of the word *guru* has dawned on me gradually. It was a slow process, but its effect was deeply penetrating. Now I have realized that the guru is everything. He is my all in all. Through him my life has been blessed. To this redeemer of my soul I have paid little homage. In a drunken state I have abused him. When given the opportunity to serve him, I have ignored it. But I have no regrets. In my attempts to escape all discipline I found myself disciplined without knowing it. Such is my guru's grace — an infinite ocean of mercy, not conferred because of merit, nor withheld because of sin, but lavished on saint and sinner alike. With a love transcending reason, he has given me sanctuary, and I have no fear. Hail Sri Ramakrishna!

[From: *Vedanta and the West* (Hollywood: Vedanta Press), March-April 1953]

Vaikuntha Nath Sanyal in Calcutta

20

Vaikuntha Nath Sanyal

Vaikuntha Nath Sanyal (1856-1936) was a householder disciple of Sri Ramakrishna and was very devoted to the Master and the monastic disciples. He wrote Sri Sri Ramakrishna Lilamrita, *a Bengali biography of Sri Ramakrishna.*

I shall record here what little I have understood of Sri Ramakrishna. My objective is twofold: We shall purify ourselves by singing the praises of the Lord, and we shall learn how to mould our lives after the great ideal of the saints.

It would be difficult to give an idea of the peace and bliss I obtained from Sri Ramakrishna without first describing the state of my mind before I met him. I was born a Hindu and had from my boyhood a yearning for religion. Whenever I chanced to meet any preacher of religion I would have talks and discussions with him, but the longing in my heart was never satisfied. Rather, the more I searched, the more I found confusion and deceit. I then met teachers of different sects, but found to my disappointment that they taught one thing and acted in quite a different way. Days and months were spent this way, and I was left with as much doubt and disillusionment as ever. Religion seemed to be empty words and was meant merely to hoodwink the ignorant. A sort of opportunism and a formal adherence to moral rules were implied to be the only course left.

At this juncture I met a Vedanta teacher, a relative of mine. We had a long discussion, and with great love he said to me: "My boy, we are not real teachers of religion, nor do we lead a religious life. We are mere traders in religion, that is all. And like other traders, we deal out a few set phrases of religion to people and make our living. Like you, I too went through a period of search and struggle for religion. I searched in many places from Calcutta to Kurukshetra, but nowhere did I come across a saint or sage. It seems that no one can have access to a real teacher until the right time comes, when the guru can be found at one's very door. I do not know if there is some law operating in this matter, but I am inclined to believe so, for I was about to be drowned in worldliness — just as you are — when I had the good fortune to meet a great saint who lives near Calcutta, in the Kali temple of Rani Rasmani at Dakshineswar. Ramakrishna Paramahamsa is his name. With the little understanding I have, I think him almost as great as an avatar. If you want to know what religion is, or wish to realize it, go to that saint and your desire will be fulfilled."

I listened to his words, but at first I did not have the inclination to go to Dakshineswar, for I feared this might be just another case of humbug. After inquiry, however, I found that there were others who felt the same about this man, and I decided to visit him. One day I accompanied a favourite disciple of Sri Ramakrishna's [later known as Swami Premananda] to see him at Dakshineswar. I never dreamed that this meeting with the Master would transform my life the way it did.

I saw a wonderful man who, though aged, was childlike in behaviour. His lips were expressive and beautiful, and his eyes were swimming with devotion. His face was radiant, as if he were the very embodiment of bliss. It made a deep impression on me, immediately bringing the idea of divinity to my mind.

"What is this?" I thought. "Is he so immersed in the thought of God as to lose his identity and sport in an ocean of bliss? What superhuman power of the mind is this in a mortal frame? He is in the world but not of it." Seeing his unique expression and deportment, all my egotism was shattered and my whole soul was in raptures. I felt him to be my nearest and dearest, and my scepticism vanished altogether. As a moth is charmed by the dazzle of the flame and madly embraces it, my mind suffered a similar fate, and instantly my proud head bent low before his blessed feet. Before I knew what I was doing I had bowed before him, and the Master very cordially asked me to sit near him.

I took my seat, and as I gazed at his remarkable features, I wondered why he was so kind to me. I was a sceptic. How could I deserve his ethereal love? Or did he fathom the secrets of my heart and know I had been thirsting in vain for a haven of peace? Was it this that made him so compassionate towards me? I thought: "Every incident has its cause, and there must be some cause for the manifestation of this embodiment of light and love. Was it that he was born to deliver erring souls like me from a wilderness of doubt and despair and hold up an ideal of religion before humanity?" Thoughts like these arose in my mind, and the more I listened to his words, the more I became attracted to him. I scarcely noticed how the day passed. I returned home with loving thoughts about him and his extraordinary behaviour. I was overjoyed that he had asked me to visit him again.

I have already said that from the very first sight I considered him to be very near me — as if I were an intimate relative of his. This feeling gradually deepened. I began to visit him whenever I had the opportunity, but the more I became acquainted with him, the more I considered him to be ever-new, and his tenderness to me took on newer and newer aspects each day. None knew as he how to make others his own. He opened himself to me as to an intimate acquaintance, and I too, moved by his love, poured out my heart to him without the least reserve. Before I had become aware of it, I was a prisoner of his love. And no wonder, for no one who beheld that matchless combination of manly austerity and feminine softness, that firmness and grace, that gravity and lightness, could ever hold himself aloof. I have had the experience of family love and affection, but such selfless love as his I have met with nowhere else. Compared to the Master's love, all other love pales to insignificance. Nobody ever saw or heard of such love. It was inexpressible, known only to the person who enjoyed it. When we went to him, he would be delighted beyond measure. His very manner of caressing, talking, feeding, and joking with us indicated that. I had read in the Bible: God is love and love is God. These words now stood explained in the light of Sri Ramakrishna's love. Whoever visited him must have felt this attraction.

I remember that it was not so much to listen to his teachings as to be with him and see him that I would visit him. Those who were content to hear his teachings instead of being in his presence seemed to me to have missed the mark. I thought, "Words might fade from memory but his form would leave an indelible mark on the heart." Who, for instance, could forget his beautiful dancing? I observed with mute wonder his superhuman renunciation. He was so thoroughly imbued with the idea of renunciation that, far from touching coins, he could not even bear the touch of brass utensils — and his fingers would become stiff if they came in contact with them. Even in sleep, the slightest touch of metal would cause his hands to stiffen.

I also observed his passion for truth. The world has not seen another example of truthfulness like his. I had read in the Ramayana that Sri Ramachandra had gone to the forest to fulfill his father's promise. It seemed remarkable. But it fell short of what I actually witnessed. Many times I noticed how Sri Ramakrishna, in the course of his meals, would say something like, "I won't take anymore food," after which his hand would actually become stiff. It would not go to his mouth, try as he might. He had therefore to stop eating, and consequently would be very hungry in a short time.

He was so active. No one could work as incessantly as he. From early in the morning till ten o'clock at night he would be engaged in teaching, making pleasantries, chanting the Lord's name, or dancing in ecstasy, and so forth, for the welfare of those assembled. On some days he barely had time to eat, and he would gulp down a meal in five minutes and again begin talking and singing without a moment's rest.

The Master's samadhi was another unique phenomenon. He would frequently lose himself in the course of devotional talks. At such times his mind would be withdrawn from the external world and no bodily consciousness would remain. Then his body would become motionless like a statue, with no activity, and sometimes even without respiration or heartbeat. Such deep samadhi would occur whenever he was wholly concentrated upon something. One day during such a state he came in contact with a piece of live charcoal, a part of which burned his body, but he knew nothing of it at the time. A doctor had to be called in to extract it, and it left a permanent scar on the right side of his back.

How can I describe the boundless devotion of the Master, at whose touch many a scoffer turned into a devotee? The uncommon traits which are mentioned in the Vaishnava scriptures as indicative of *mahabhava*, the highest state of ecstasy, were constantly noticeable in him. And what can I say about his knowledge? Only this much I can say: that he had not that penny's worth of knowledge that we ordinary mortals have. Through his knowledge he looked upon all beings as part of himself, and he saw the manifestation of the One in all. His mercy transformed many ordinary people into great knowers of Brahman. This may serve as a hint.

One day I boldly asked the Master: "Sir, what is meant by *tapas* [austerity], or *sadhana*? And why did you undergo so much of it?" He answered: "Tapas, or sadhana, is the concentrated effort of the mind to gain some desired end. One undergoing it has not the least concern for the body or sense pleasures. For example, an angler is fishing and a fish is nibbling at the bait. Meanwhile, it is raining hard and a man is asking the angler a question, but the angler pays no heed to anything but the fish. It is only after the fish has been hooked that he spreads his umbrella and answers the question. Without tapas and hard practice, no one can attain Brahman. How much labour is needed to pass an examination, the goal of which is to earn a little money! One has to read day and night, scarcely paying heed to meals and the like. Then one becomes successful. Just imagine then how much more effort is needed for the realization of Brahman.

"Tapas is the source of all strength. The scriptures say that even God performs austerities for the creation, preservation, and dissolution of the world. How much more then do we need it! A twelve-year-long tempest of tapas swept over me. Heat and cold and rain would pass over my body. I used to sit on an uneven area of ground losing all outward consciousness. My eyes would not blink and I would be absorbed in God. Someone used to strike my back with a stick to bring back a little consciousness so he could feed me, but I would become senseless in the very act of eating. Sometimes I would laugh heartily, blessed with a vision of the Divine Mother. At other times I would cry bitterly for not having her vision. I have heard that people would throng around to look at me. Sometimes again the body would become stiff with no sign of life. I used to meditate, and people say birds would sit on my head, mistaking it for lifeless matter. I had no idea of the world and things of that sort. At first I used to meditate on the Lord, thinking he was the object of worship and I was the worshipper. Then all distinctions disappeared, and a state of perfect identity was the result.

"The scriptures say that if one remains for three weeks in this state, the body falls off. But as I said, a man used to force food down my throat after bringing me to consciousness by beating me. That preserved the body. After about six months that state passed. I then had a desire to realize the Mother in diverse forms. I had heard that Hanuman was an exemplar in worshipping God with the attitude of servant to master and had thus realized Sri Rama. I too remained in that attitude for some time and had a vision of Sita and Rama. Practising the attitude of a gopi, or milkmaid of Vrindaban, I realized Radha and Krishna. I also called upon the Divinity as a child does his mother and I saw Mother Kali, the source of all Energy. In three days I attained nirvikalpa samadhi and realized Brahman while meditating in an attitude free from all emotion. My guru Tota Puri, the naked one, was amazed and said: 'What a divine phenomenon! In three days he has attained the knowledge of Brahman, which I achieved after forty years of intense struggle!' I meditated on Allah and was blessed with his vision, and I saw Jesus also. Furthermore, I have practised sixty-four branches of tantric disciplines."

I said to the Master: "Sir, I have heard the story of your sadhana. What was the need for so many different kinds of practice?" Immediately, like a child, his tearful eyes quivered with emotion and he replied: "My boy, I did everything for all of you. Otherwise I personally had no need of them." Saying this, he went into samadhi. Upon returning from samadhi he spoke with faltering accents half-audibly: "O man, I have done so much for you. You do a minute fraction for me." Afterwards he said with a smile: "My boy, do you think everyone has got to cook for himself? The mother has cooked everything. Have faith. Partake of the meal and be blessed." In the Master I saw the sign of God which the scriptures mention as the "boundless, unmotivated ocean of mercy." Otherwise why did he suffer so much for others?

Again the Master solemnly said: "Look. Such practices are needed in order to set an example. I have gone through all sixteen parts. You do one part." I asked: "Sir, while talking about and listening to divine topics, you become quite stiff and unconscious, but your face beams with a joyous smile and your body too becomes radiant. Why is that? What do you experience in that state?" He smiled and replied: "Well, it is called samadhi, the culmination of meditation. I borrow one-sixteenth part of the mind from the Divine Mother and talk and laugh with you, but the remaining portion rests with the Mother, meditating on her real essence as Existence-Knowledge-Bliss Absolute. When I talk or hear about the Mother, the whole mind goes to the Absolute and samadhi immediately ensues.

"Do you know what samadhi really is? It is complete absorption in Brahman. Do you know how I feel at that time? Suppose there is a basin of water on the seashore and a fish is confined in it. If the basin is accidentally broken, the fish finds its way to the unfathomable ocean. It then frolics in the height of joy, doesn't it? Similarly, during samadhi my mind leaps out of this body, as it were, and plunges into Existence-Knowledge-Bliss Absolute. Hence the body appears like that. In other words, there is no body-consciousness, and the soul merges in the higher Self — the Paramatman — in the thousand-petalled lotus of the head and experiences unspeakable bliss. That experience sends a wave of divine bliss to the face, and the body becomes radiant. This very self then becomes Shiva, the Absolute."

I shall briefly refer to one or two of the wonderful manifestations of spiritual power that I observed in the Master. Sometimes arguments and doubts would come to my mind. I would mull over them for a week or so and finally decide to ask the Master to resolve them. But then I would find him raising those very topics in conversation with someone else and thus solve them! Once a devotee carried a tray of sweets to the Master and mentally offered four of them to him. The rest of the sweets were to be for the devotees. I saw that the Master accepted his share and rejected the rest. I also saw him convert unbelievers and atheists into great devotees by a mere wish or blessing or touch. Whenever out of his grace he touched someone, a distinctive joy would come over that person's mind and body that would remain for three or four days. Words defy description. It was known only to those who witnessed or experienced it.

One day I was extremely hungry, and the Master, as if aware of the fact, quickly took two sweetmeats from the shelf in his room. I thought he knew I was hungry and was going to give them to me, but he did just the opposite. He took them himself. He then asked me to give him a glass of water, which he drank. Then, with evident signs of satiety, he said: "Oh, how relieved I am! I am satisfied." And strange to say, his satisfaction removed my hunger and thirst. I was reminded of the story in the Mahabharata of how Sri Krishna took a particle of spinach from the cooking pot of Draupadi and appeased the hunger of the sage Durvasa and his party. The same phenomenon revealed itself to me on that day.

Unlike us, Sri Ramakrishna would not announce a meeting for a lecture. He used to say, "Mother, if you have kept this body for doing your work, bring people yourself and make my mouth utter whatever you like." He would say: "Lust and gold are the two things that have kept the world spellbound. These are the obstacles to the realization of God. I have discarded them both as if they were poison. But there is a funny thing about them: If you always look upon a woman as your mother, instead of hindering you in the spiritual path, she will be helpful to you. I therefore look upon all women as manifestations of the Divine Mother. And gold too will not be so harmful if you use it in the service of God or his devotees."

Again the Master would say: "Look. The best austerity for realizing God is truthfulness. Unite the mind and speech. You must speak only what you think at heart. Otherwise, where there is deceit, God will never manifest himself. The more the mind becomes pure through spiritual practices, the clearer it will reflect God. As a dusty mirror does not clearly reflect the face, so an impure mind fails to adequately catch God's reflection. Therefore I say, weep in the name of the Lord, and when the heart's impurities are washed away with tears, you will see the Lord. Otherwise, mere dancing and jumping will do nothing. Devotional practices are necessary as long as tears do not trickle down from one's eyes.

"Another means of attaining God is renunciation. What is meant by this? When there is deep love for God, all other things drop off by themselves, as when one advances to the north the south is left further and further behind. Therefore I ask you to love the Lord intensely. You must have as much longing for God as the wife feels for her husband, the child for its mother, and the miser for his wealth. Another thing: Whatever you do with your body, mind, and speech, you must always think that it is the Lord's work. He is the Master and you are the servant. Still another method of discipline is to always discriminate between what is real and what is unreal. Keep the mind in a state of perfect equanimity and try to see the manifestation of the Lord in all beings. My boy, what name of the Lord you choose and what religious faith you follow does not make any difference. Every religious faith is a path to God. All names are his. Hold on wholeheartedly to one doctrine or one name. This is called steadfast devotion to the Ideal.

"And do you know what yoga is? It is uniting the mind with God. One may attain this union by all three paths — work, devotion, and knowledge. What is work? Karma yoga consists in disinterestedly serving the Lord's children, offering the fruits of one's actions to him, and constantly remembering him. Karma yoga removes the bondage of maya and unites a person with God. And why not? When a person thinks day and night of the Lord while doing his duties, the Lord is sure to manifest himself in that person.

"Devotion and knowledge are identical in the end. People do not understand them well and mistakenly think that they are different. What is bhakti [devotion]? Love for God and playing with him in various ways. The devotee says: 'Thou art the Master and I am thy servant. Thou art all, and all is thine.' Knowledge also means absolute love. That love is so intense that the jnani [the man of knowledge] never wants to be separated from God. He wants to become one with him. Hence he says: 'I am He. I am Shiva, the Absolute.' Hanuman, the prince of devotees, said to Sri Ramachandra: 'Lord, when I have consciousness of the body, then thou art the Master and I am thy servant. When I consider myself as a jiva, or individual soul, then thou art the whole and I am thy part. And when I think I am the Atman, that is, in the samadhi state, I feel thou art I and I am thou. There is no difference.'

"But there is a gradation of spiritual experiences. A mother has five children, and all have not the same digestive power. She knows this and gives them different kinds of food to suit their stomachs. Otherwise they will not be able to digest the food. And how will a person get strength from something he cannot digest? Similarly, the guru does not instruct all disciples in the same manner. He chooses his instructions to suit the varying needs of the disciples, and this does them good. But if anyone rashly attempts to take up another sadhana, he lags behind and cannot live up to the ideal.

"In this present age, the path of bhakti according to Narada — that is, chanting the Lord's name — is best for ordinary people, because their minds are scattered in different directions. How and when will they find time to practise discrimination, japam, or meditation? It is not good for a devotee, a jnani, or a worker, to be one-sided or dogmatic. I do not like that at all. God is Existence-Knowledge-Bliss Absolute. He, though one, has become many. He is the sum total of all ideals and paths. I worship him in various ways, such as knowledge, devotion, work, worship, kirtan [singing], japam, and meditation. Do you think that only a particular aspect which appeals to you or me is found in God, while all other aspects are to be counted as nothing? I am not in favour of such exclusiveness. This dogmatic view limits God. Remember: Neither God nor his aspects have any end. The Vedas say, 'Not this, not this.'

"Some people believe God is with form, while others believe he is formless. This also limits God. I say God is with form, without form, and again beyond both. Take for example the sound of a bell — *dhong*. The first letter represents the aspect with form, the nasal portion his formless aspect, and the impression the word leaves in the mind after the whole has been pronounced stands for the Absolute aspect. Furthermore, God has many forms and many names. For instance, a confectioner takes fresh cheese and sugar and makes a preparation over fire, which he then forms into various shapes, giving them different names. But the real substance is the same, no matter what shape or name is given. Similarly, whatever names and forms you see or hear are all made by combining Purusha [Spirit] and Prakriti [matter] aspects of Satchidananda Brahman. It is due to distance that God looks small or variously coloured, but when you go near him, you will find he is omnipresent and self-luminous.

"Would you like to know what Brahman and Shakti are? It is a subject that can neither be described nor comprehended. How can I describe that which is beyond mind and speech, and how can you understand? Let me therefore give an idea through a simile. Brahman and Shakti are identical: He who is Brahman is also Shakti, as fire and its burning power are identical. The fire represents Brahman, and the burning power his Shakti. Or there is the example of the snake moving and the snake at rest: When it is at rest it may be likened to Brahman, and when it is active it represents Shakti."

*　　　*　　　*

The supreme principles of religion are eternal, only new clothing is put on them in different ages according to the tastes and capacities of the people and the needs of the times. This is especially true in India, where religion is the nation's backbone. India has never given up religion, nor has religion ever given up India. Therefore it seems that after a shining galaxy of epoch-making prophets, Sri Ramakrishna, the apostle of the harmony of all religions, was born.

Sri Ramakrishna's new interpretation of the eternal religion surpassed the previous religions of the age by its catholicity and depth. The innate power of this new religion has been felt in Europe and America, where it reverberated soon after its inception. It is needless to say anything about its originality. While almost every one of the foregoing teachers and avatars declared that the particular set of doctrines which he preached was the only path for the progress and well-being of humanity, Sri Ramakrishna held that all doctrines are equally true, each of them being a path leading to the highest and indivisible Truth. Previous teachers said, "Man, have pity on your fellow beings," but Sri Ramakrishna said, "O man, look upon every human being as the veritable form of God and serve him with all your might." The preceding teachers abhorred or avoided women as obstacles, but Sri Ramakrishna declared: "Every woman is the Divine Mother herself in another form. Give her special reverence and serve her without the least taint of carnality. Then the Divine Mother will be pleased with your worship and open gates for your prosperity and liberation." Past teachers said, "Kill your passions and you will attain religion," whereas Sri Ramakrishna said, "Turn those passions Godward and they will be your greatest assets for realizing the Truth." Previous teachers said, "Unless you read various scriptures, your eye of illumination will never open," but Sri Ramakrishna boldly declared through example and precept, "O man, if you give up all pride and egotism and are as eager as a child for the blissful companionship of the Mother of the Universe, then full realization will be within your easy reach, even if you are illiterate."

It is not for me to describe the infinite facets of Sri Ramakrishna, the embodiment and synthesis of all religions, the unfathomable ocean in which an infinite number of ideals, like so many streams, are engulfed. Let us now all prostrate ourselves before Sri Ramakrishna, and, fired with new life and inspiration through his power, let us loudly declare: "Glory to all religions — Hinduism, Buddhism, Islam, Christianity, and all. Glory to the Vedas, the Puranas, the Koran, the Bible, and all other scriptures of the world. Glory to the four great paths — jnana, karma, bhakti, and yoga. Glory to the prophets of all countries and all ages. Glory to Sri Ramakrishna, the embodiment of all religions, of all ideals, of all avatars."

[From: *Prabuddha Bharata* (Mayavati: Advaita Ashrama), April 1919]

21

Yogin-ma
(Yogindra Mohini Biswas)

Yogin-ma (1851-1924) met Sri Ramakrishna in 1882 at Balaram Basu's house and often stayed at Dakshineswar with Holy Mother in order to serve her and the Master. After the Master's passing away Yogin-ma became one of Holy Mother's main attendants.

Balaram Babu was related to me, being my husband's maternal uncle. He had many excellent qualities. For example, whenever he decided to visit Sri Ramakrishna at Dakshineswar, he would hire a boat, and early in the morning he would go from door to door inviting the Master's devotees to accompany him. Such humility! It was his wish that they share with him the bliss that he enjoyed in the Master's presence.

One day Sri Ramakrishna came to Balaram Babu's house and we went to see him. It was the first time I saw him. The Master was standing at one side of the hall in deep samadhi. He had no outer consciousness. Since no one dared touch him, people bowed down to him from a distance. We also did the same. At that time I had no idea what samadhi was. I at first thought that he was a drunken devotee of Kali. I could not understand the Master at my first meeting. Moreover, it immediately came to my mind that my married life had been ruined by a drunken husband, and again should I undo my spiritual life through the influence of this seemingly drunken person? But gradually I became acquainted with the Master.

At first we went to Dakshineswar with Balaram Babu, but later, my mother and I, together with Balaram Babu's wife and other women devotees, would go by ourselves. Gradually I began to feel an attraction for the Master. Just the thought of visiting him would make my mind dance with joy. On the day that I planned to go there I would get up early and finish my household duties as quickly as possible. My longing

351

Yogin-ma (Yogindra Mohini Biswas), a woman devotee
of Sri Ramakrishna

to see him knew no bounds. After arriving at his room I would forget everything, sitting in his presence. The Master used to experience samadhi off and on, and at that time we would look at his face with wonder. He was so compassionate! Whenever I brought him some ordinary preparations he would relish them like a young boy, saying joyfully, "Very tasty! Delicious!" And always at the time of our departure he would say, "Come back again."

When I returned home after my visit with the Master, I would spend the whole week in an intoxicated mood. This established a strong relationship. I cannot express the joy I felt. Even while I was engaged in cooking or other household activities, my mind was with the Master. After some days, when I would feel my intoxication diminishing, my mind would again long to see him.

Some time after my first visit, Holy Mother left for her country home. I stood on the bank of the Ganga and watched her departure, waiting until the boat was no longer visible. After that I returned to the nahabat and wept bitterly. The Master, on his way back from the Panchavati, noticed me crying, and after returning to his room he sent for me. "Her leaving caused a great deal of pain for you," he said tenderly. He then began to console me by recounting the marvellous spiritual experiences he had had during his days of tantric sadhana. When Holy Mother returned after about a year and a half, he told her: "That girl with nice large eyes, who comes here frequently, loves you very much. She wept profusely at the nahabat when you left for home." Mother replied: "Yes, I know her very well. Her name is Yogin."

My maternal uncle's house was at Kumartuli in West Calcutta. The Smashaneshwara Shiva temple belonged to his family. My grandmother was the first in my family to see the Master. During the 1870s the people of Calcutta learned about Sri Ramakrishna by reading Keshab Chandra Sen's newspaper and magazine articles. My grandmother read about the Master and went to Dakshineswar to meet him. Strangely enough, on arriving there the first person she encountered was Sri Ramakrishna. She did not know who he was, since there was nothing unusual about his dress or appearance. Addressing the Master, she asked, "Can you tell me where Ramakrishna Paramahamsa is and how I can see him?" The Master replied: "What do I know about him? Some people call him 'Paramahamsa,' some call him 'Young Priest,' and others call him 'Gadadhar Chatterjee.' Please ask someone else to help you find him." Unfortunately my grandmother did not press the matter further and returned home.

One day the Master told me: "Look. Your Chosen Deity is in this place [*pointing to his body*]. If you think of me, that will bring recollectedness of your Chosen Deity." Now, whenever I sit for meditation, I feel the Master's presence.

He also taught me how to practise japam, showing how the four fingers of the right hand must be kept tightly together. "The result of japam goes away," said the Master, "if there is any gap between the fingers." Another time he told me, "In this kali yuga a Gopala mantram [a name of baby Krishna] or a Kali mantram produces quick results."

Several times I noticed that whenever a question arose in my mind, someone else would ask the Master the same question. Thus, in answering that person's question, the Master would remove the doubts in my mind also. He was all-knowing.

Holy Mother used to live in the nahabat like a shy bride. She wore a cloth with a broad red border and vermilion on her forehead, and her hair was black, thick, and long. She also wore a necklace, a nose ring, earrings, and bracelets. [*These bracelets were given by Mathur Babu to the Master while he was practising the spiritual discipline of madhura bhava.*] Her company gave me immense joy. She liked very much the way I braided her hair, and I was delighted to do it for her.

One day she said to me: "Yogin, the Master awakens God-consciousness in so many people, but you know I have not gotten anything. Would you please tell him about this?" I was so simple-minded that I did not understand her. I went straight to the Master and reported to him what she had said, but he did not reply. When I went back to the nahabat, I saw that the Mother was performing worship and was in an ecstatic mood. One moment she was laughing, another moment she was crying, and again another moment she was sitting motionless. I was amazed to witness this divine play. When Holy Mother came down to the normal plane of consciousness, I asked her, "You complained that you do not experience samadhi, but what is all this?" She smiled.

Whatever I learned was through the Master's grace. He asked me to read devotional scriptures, although normally he did not approve of much reading unless it was accompanied by the practise of spiritual disciplines. "What will you gain," he would say, "by reading a lot of books?"

One day I asked him, "What will happen to us?"

"What more do you want?" he replied. "You have seen me, fed me, and served me. What else do you need? Don't worry. The thousand-petalled lotus of your seventh plane [i.e., the sahasrara] will bloom at the time of your death." He further said: "At the last moment of the devotees, I shall have to appear before them. Otherwise, how will they get liberation?"

Once the Master said about the Mother: "Do you think she is an ordinary woman? She is a part of Saraswati — the goddess of learning — and very intelligent. So she loves to dress herself nicely, since Saraswati is the embodiment of beauty. She is not a common woman — she is my Power."

[From: *Ramakrishna-Saradamrita*, by Swami Nirlepananda (Calcutta: Karuna Prakashani), 1968; *Sri Sri Mayer Katha* (Calcutta: Udbodhan Office), vol. I, 1969]

Sri Ramakrishna in samadhi in front of the Krishna temple
at Dakshineswar, October 1883

22

A Woman Devotee

To us [women devotees] Sri Ramakrishna did not usually seem to be a man at all. It seemed that he was one of us. That is why we did not feel the slightest shyness or hesitation in his presence, as we normally do in the presence of men. If, however, such a feeling came on rare occasions, we forgot it immediately and would express to him our thoughts without any hesitation whatever.

As we knew the Master liked sar [a sweet made from thick boiled milk], one day we bought a large piece for him from the shop of Bhola, the famous sweet maker of Calcutta. Five of us then together hired a boat and arrived at Dakshineswar without notice. But we were informed that the Master had gone to Calcutta. We were at a loss, not knowing what to do. Brother Ramlal was there. Asked where in Calcutta the Master had gone, he said that he had gone to the house of M. [Mahendra Nath Gupta] at Kambuliatola [in Shyampukur]. Hearing this, A.'s mother said: "I know that house. It is near my father's. Will you go? Come, let us go. What is the good of waiting here?" All agreed. We handed over the sweet to Brother Ramlal and left, saying, "Please give it to the Master when he comes."

We had already sent the boat away, so we started on foot. But such was the Master's grace that hardly had we covered the short distance to Alambazar when an empty carriage returning to Calcutta was available. We hired the carriage and reached Shyampukur. There, fresh trouble awaited us. A.'s mother could not find the house. After taking us from place to place she stopped the carriage in front of her father's house and called a servant. He came with us and pointed out the house. Thus we succeeded at last in reaching M.'s house. And how can we blame A.'s mother? She was three or four years younger than us. She was about twenty-six or twenty-seven then. A mere daughter-in-law, she never came out alone to a road. Moreover the house was in a narrow lane and how could she recognize it?

Finally, with great difficulty, we reached the house. We were not then acquainted with M.'s family. Entering the house, we saw the Master sitting on a small wooden cot in a small room. There was no one near him. As soon as he saw us he laughed and said affectionately, "Ah, how could you come here?" We saluted him and told him the whole story. He was very happy. Then he asked us to sit down, and he began to talk on various subjects. Nowadays many people say he did not allow women to touch him or even to approach him. We laugh to hear it and think, "We are not dead yet." Who will know how kind he was? He had the same loving attitude towards women as towards men. But it is true that if women stayed near him long he would say, "Please go now and pay reverence to the presiding deities of the temples." We have heard him ask men also to do likewise.

However that may be, we were sitting and speaking with him. The two of us who were elderly sat very near the door and the other three sat in a corner in the room. In the meantime Prankrishna Mukhopadhyay, whom the Master called "the fat brahmin," came quite unexpectedly. There was no chance to get out from that small room.[1] Moreover, where could we go? There was a window near the door. The two elderly ones took their seats there, and the rest, the three of us, made our way under the cot on which the Master was seated and lay there. Each one of us had her whole body swollen on account of mosquito bites. What could we do? There was no possibility of movement. We lay there without moving. The brahmin talked for about an hour with the Master and left. We then came out laughing.

The Master was taken to the inner apartment for some light refreshment, and we accompanied him. Afterwards he got into a carriage to go to Dakshineswar, and we walked back home. It was about 9 o'clock at night.

The next day we went to Dakshineswar again. As soon as we arrived the Master came to us and said: "Ah! I took almost all of your sweet. There was only a little left over. But there was no illness or anything of the kind. Only the stomach was just a little heavy." I was surprised to hear that he had taken a whole piece of sar because I knew that rich food did not suit his delicate stomach. Then I heard that he had taken it while in a state of divine semi-consciousness. I was told that the Master had taken his food at the house of M. and came to Dakshineswar at 10:30 P.M. Shortly after his arrival he went into ecstasy and said to Ramlal: "I am very hungry. Give me whatever there is in the room." Immediately

---

[1] At that time young married women were very bashful. They wore veils over their faces or hid themselves from unknown gentlemen.

Brother Ramlal brought the piece of sar and placed it before the Master. He ate almost all of it. Then we remembered what we had heard from Holy Mother and Sister Lakshmi about his taking an abnormal quantity of food sometimes in an ecstatic mood and digesting it. Ah! So much grace we had from him! It cannot be expressed in words what that compassion was. And what attraction! Even we ourselves do not know or understand how we used to go to him and do all those things. Why, we cannot go now in that manner on foot anywhere to unknown people's houses without informing anybody, to see a holy man or listen to words on spirituality. Such things have ended with him by whose power we acted that way. We do not know why we still live though we have lost him.

One day the Master began to show in our presence the gestures that women make when they see men — that pulling of the veil, removing of the tresses near the ear, pulling of the cloth over the breast, speaking various unnecessary and meaningless words. The imitation was perfectly accurate. We saw it and began to laugh, but we felt ashamed and hurt, thinking that the Master was thus looking down upon women. We thought, "Why, are all women like that?" After all we were women. We naturally felt pained to see women caricatured like that. Ah, the Master immediately understood our thoughts and said affectionately: "Well, I don't mean you. You are not of a worldly nature. It is women of that nature only who behave that way. . . . I know the nature of a person by a mere look. I know who is good and who is bad, who is of noble descent and who is not, who is a man of knowledge and who is one of devotion, who will realize God and who will not. All these things I know, but I do not express it lest they should feel pained."

[From: *Sri Ramakrishna, The Great Master,* by Swami Saradananda (Madras: Sri Ramakrishna Math) vol. I, 1978]

Nistarini Ghosh, a woman devotee of Sri Ramakrishna

23

Nistarini Ghosh

Nistarini Ghosh (?-1932) was the wife of Navagopal Ghosh. Both of them were very devoted to Sri Ramakrishna, and one of their sons later became a monk of the Ramakrishna Order. About Nistarini, Sri Ramakrishna said: "She is a great soul. She is a partial incarnation of one of the ten forms of the Divine Mother."

For a long time my husband had been searching for a sadhu [holy man] who could tell him how to realize God. He had begun to follow the instructions of one, when a friend said: "Why do you waste your time on this man? Go to Dakshineswar. There you will find a paramahamsa [an illumined soul] who will be able to clear all your doubts." So one Sunday my husband and I went to Dakshineswar and saw Sri Ramakrishna. He received us most kindly, and at once I felt that he was divine.

For three years we did not return. My husband was practising certain sadhanas [spiritual disciplines], and he felt that he must finish them before he went to another teacher. Suddenly one day the Master said to a visitor at the temple: "About three years ago a man by the name of Navagopal Ghosh came to see me with his wife. He has never been back since. Tell him I would like to see him." After all those three years he recalled the name. And it was just at the moment when my husband had finished the sadhanas that he sent for us.

We went to him the following Sunday, and from that time on we went regularly every Sunday, going at ten in the morning and staying until ten at night.

When I would come he would send all the gentlemen out and remain talking with me alone. Once he asked me why I came, what I found in him to draw me so often to Dakshineswar. I replied: "I cannot say. All I know is that which made Prahlada forget his father, and Dhruva and others forget their parents, that I find here."

A friend had told me I should chant Haribol [repeat the name of the Lord] and I did so. But it caused great perplexity in my mind. "Here I am calling upon Hari" [a name of the Lord], I said to myself, "and yet I am told that one should seek salvation through the guru alone." I went to Dakshineswar to see Sri Ramakrishna, but before I could explain my trouble he said to me, "The guru and Hari are one."

One day he was coming to our house and a number of devotees had gathered to see him. When he arrived, he came straight upstairs and remained for some time talking with me. At that time I had a picture of Sri Krishna in my shrine, and I told him I was anxious to have a vision of Krishna. He went downstairs where all the devotees were singing sankirtan [holy songs]. They put a heavy garland around his neck which reached his feet. At once he went into samadhi and assumed the exact posture of Sri Krishna. All the devotees also went into a higher state of consciousness on seeing him. Later he asked me if I was now satisfied. I said I would like to see Radha by Sri Krishna's side. He smiled and replied, "Oh, you will have to wait awhile for that."

At another time when he came to our house, he dressed himself in a sari [woman's cloth] and put on bangles and jewels. As he sat down to eat the fruits and sweets prepared for him, he talked and acted just like a young wife begging her husband for more jewels. He kept up the play for an hour or more. His power of mimicry was remarkable.

One Sunday we were all at Dakshineswar. A poor woman came with four rasagollas [sweet, juicy cheeseballs] for the Master, but his room was so full of devotees that she dared not enter and offer them to him. She came over to Holy Mother's verandah [at the nahabat] and began to weep bitterly that she had come so far and now she must go away without seeing the Master. We knew too that to bring even these four rasagollas meant a great sacrifice for her. Suddenly while she was thus weeping, Sri Ramakrishna appeared on the round verandah overlooking the river. He stood for a few minutes gazing at the Ganga, and then he came down the steps and walked quickly towards Mother's house. When he entered the verandah, he looked hither and thither as if searching for someone. Then seeing the poor woman, he went to her and said: "I am feeling very hungry. Can you give me something to eat?" The woman in great joy offered him her rasagollas. He ate all the four with evident relish and returned to his room, while she went home with her heart full of happiness.

Even animals found tender shelter with him. Once a cat took refuge in Sri Ramakrishna's room at Dakshineswar with her three little kittens. The mother cat would sometimes sleep on his bed near his feet, and if he reached down and touched her with his hand, at once she would get up and seem almost to make a *pranam* [salute him]. It greatly troubled the Master to know what to do with the cat and her kittens, for he felt that they did not get proper food at the temple. So one day when I came to see him, he asked me, "Will you do something for me?" I clasped my hands before him and said, "Whatever it is, that I must do." But again he asked and I replied as before. Then he told me of the cats and asked me to take them. "Remember," he said, "that they have taken refuge with me, so see that they get the best of care."

I took them home and whenever I went to the temple he would question me in every detail about the cats: Were they getting proper food? Had the kittens grown? What did I mean to do with them? He was much concerned lest I might give them away to someone who would not treat them kindly, and again he would remind me, "Remember, they took refuge with me." The mother cat never had another family. At the end of a year she was suddenly taken ill and died. As she was dying I poured Ganga water into her mouth and repeated Sri Ramakrishna's name.

At Cossipore garden he asked me again why I came to him. "You have children. You have jewels and furniture. Why then do you want to come to me?" I replied: "I do not want all these things. I come because I love you, because I want you. I want your blessing." At once he went into samadhi, and as he came out of it he put his hand on my head and blessed me.

Once I carried some sweets to Sri Ramakrishna at Cossipore. As I stood hesitatingly before him, he asked, "What do you want?" "I want to give you some sweets," I said. "Very well!" and he let me put some in his mouth. Still I stood before him. "Are you satisfied?" he asked. "No? Then what do you want?" I clasped my hands and answered, "I want to give you more sweets." He let me put a little more in his mouth, and seeing me still unsatisfied, he asked the question a third time. When again I asked to feed him, he said: "No, no more now. Wait. In my *sukshma sharira* [subtle body] I shall take all the sweets you and everyone can offer me."

Once I went to Cossipore garden, but I found so many visitors there that I could not go upstairs. I waited for sometime and then Sri Ramakrishna sent down one of his photographs, saying, "Tell her to be content with looking at this today." Later he told me, referring to the picture, that it "would travel in railway carriages and on ocean steamers and by bearers. And people would carry it in their pockets and even on their watch chains."

[From: *Sri Ramakrishna and His Disciples* and *Days In An Indian Monastery*, by Sister Devamata (La Crescenta: Ananda Ashrama), 1928 & 1927]

Sri Ramakrishna's parental home at Kamarpukur

24

Kedar Nath Bandyopadhyay

Kedar Nath Bandyopadhyay (1863-1949) was a devotee of Sri Rama-krishna. These reminiscences were written more than sixty years after Kedar Nath's meeting with the Master. In some places Kedar has used quotation marks, and in others he has expressed the Master's ideas in his own words.

My family home was in Dakshineswar, very near the Ganga. On the way to bathe, or just passing by in the evening, my friends used to come to our festival hall and play indoor games or sit around and chat. It was a Sunday or a holiday in 1881 or perhaps 1882 that my neighbour, Haridas Chatterjee, who was studying for his B.A. degree, stopped in to see me and said: "One of my fellow students in Calcutta has come [to Dakshineswar], and I would like to introduce him to you. Come with me."

I went with him, and on the way I asked: "Is there some special reason for this invitation? If there is, please tell me before I meet your friend."

Smiling, Haridas replied: "Nothing special. Just as you are the best talker and conversationalist in our group here, full of knowledge, humour, and wit, so is he in our circle at college. Everybody seeks his company. Seldom will you find such a lovable and fascinating speaker."

Hearing this I was a little uneasy, as though I were going to appear for an examination. But there was no time to think before we had arrived at the place where I was to meet Haridas's friend. As soon as his friend saw me, he put a handful of puffed rice into his mouth and said, "Welcome, my mighty friend!" And pushing the tray of puffed rice towards me, he said, "Please take some."

Haridas introduced us: "This is my college friend, Narendra Nath Datta of Calcutta, and his knowledge is so vast that I can't think of anything in this world that he does not know."

Narendra interrupted: "What about mathematics? Ishwar Chandra Vidyasagar is still alive. Have you not read in his primary book, 'Always speak the truth'?"

Then Haridas introduced me, "This is my village friend, Kedar Nath Bandyopadhyay."

Narendra was not only very handsome, he was also a fine speaker. Everyone was overwhelmed by his charming personality. His satirical remarks were most amusing, and at the same time his ideas were deep, meaningful, and vivacious. People were astounded to see such vast knowledge in one so young. That was my first meeting with Narendra, and in all my life, before or since, I have never seen such a man.

In the afternoon we all went at Narendra's request to visit the Kali temple built by Rani Rasmani. He said: "Let us go and see that unlettered brahmin, who was previously a worshipper of Mother Kali and is now a perfected soul. It is very common in our country for people to pay money to see magic, but here, I understand, no charge is made. I have been there once before and, although this man has nothing to say to me that I want to hear, I would like to see him again." As far as I can remember, Narendra spoke in this way.

He asked me if I knew Sri Ramakrishna. In reply, I asked, "Is he the yogi of Dakshineswar about whom Keshab Chandra Sen has written in his *Sunday Mirror*?"

"Yes, yes. He is that great soul. Then you know him?"

"No," I replied. "My elder brother who lives in Meerut wanted me to see this holy man and write about him, but, I am sorry to say, I forgot all about it."

"All right. Then let us go," said Narendra.

When we reached the temple garden we sat on the embankment and Narendra started to sing. Presently a man came and said, "Sri Ramakrishna is calling you." Narendra got up and said, "Come, let us go," and we followed him.

Sri Ramakrishna's room was in the northwest corner of the temple courtyard. We entered and saluted him with folded hands. He was seated on a cot wearing a cloth with a small border. There was a smile on his face. Some other visitors were seated on the floor. Looking at Narendra he said: "Why do you not come? Don't you know I have been waiting for you? The last time you came you left quickly to go for a walk around the temple." Then he asked Narendra to sing a song.

What an unusual young man Narendra was! As soon as he was asked, he started to sing without any hesitation or fear. While he was singing, Sri Ramakrishna all of a sudden stood up and went into samadhi. He was about to fall when two or three of the devotees caught him and put him on the cot again. Narendra was watching all this intently. This was the first time in my life that I had witnessed samadhi.

A devotee said: "The Master loves to hear someone sing, but he seldom enjoys the whole song. He goes into samadhi."

What I saw that day was unique. It would be inaccurate to say that I only saw — I actually got something. When I looked at Narendra, he smiled and said, "Well, now you can write four pages to your brother about the Master."

Sri Ramakrishna said to Narendra, "Come to see me now and then."

Narendra: "I am now going to college and I have to study."

Master: "That is all right. Enjoy this spiritual life also. What is the harm in hearing spiritual talks?"

Narendra: "Sir, I understand that you have had no education and that whatever you say you must have heard from someone else. I know all that stuff."

I was startled at Narendra's words, but the Master smiled at him and said: "That is fine. Then I will not have to talk much. If you come once in a while it will not do you any harm. Besides, I like to see you. All right, you may go now, but please come again."

Narendra: "I shall try."

As we took leave of Sri Ramakrishna, I felt uncomfortable. When we had left his room, Narendra said to me, "Do you think I was rude to him?"

"You know it very well," I replied.

"Next time I shall come alone." Saying this, Narendra left.

Afterwards, on my way home, I forgot all about Sri Ramakrishna, for my mind was occupied with thoughts of Narendra. Although he was my peer, he was really exceptional. He was fearless and full of wisdom. He was born to be a leader — a commander-in-chief, not a soldier. And I could see that Sri Ramakrishna wanted him for some special reason. It was a glorious day in my life when I saw them together on that occasion.

That was my first meeting with Sri Ramakrishna. Since we had many family deities at home I often went to pick flowers from the temple garden to offer them. So I may have seen the Master many times after that, but there is nothing of any special interest to recall about those occasions. He lived like an ordinary man, wearing neither an ochre cloth [the garb of a monk] nor any religious marks. His attire was simply a white cloth with a small red border.

* * *

Who can describe Sri Ramakrishna? Sometimes I went to the Kali temple to hear him, and on these occasions there were always two or three carriages outside and throngs of devotees from Calcutta in his room. I would sit down near the door and listen while the devotees "swallowed," as it were, his inspired talks, leaving a little share for me. Since they were all householders (I too had married), most of his advice was directed towards them.

Here are some examples of what the Master would say to us: Never forget that the goal of human life is to realize God. Remember this first and then do your household duties. Why are you so afraid of hearing about bhakti? Bhakti is love for God. One can attain God by love. Love conquers all. People shed a jugful of tears for wife and children, but who weeps for God? Weep, weep, weep for him.

Once somebody said, "God is formless and so nobody can see him." The Master replied: "God is with form and also formless. Look all around. He is in everything and every being. You know how difficult it is to meet a rich man. You will have to get past the gatekeepers and secretaries, and finally you will have to spend a handsome sum for a presentation gift. In addition, you may have to wait from morning to evening. And you want to see God without doing anything? Is it possible? How much trouble you must undergo to see a rich man, and you want to see the Lord of the Universe without any effort? In the beginning work hard. Have faith in him. Have longing for God."

I used to see a number of young boys with the Master, who were junior to me but very bright and jolly. I did not know all of them. Gradually their number increased to seventeen or eighteen. They did not all come at the same time, nor did they come with the older people. The Master's conversation with these boys was fascinating. He spoke to them in a lighter, more humourous vein, cutting jokes with them and testing them by asking some of them to go home and to marry. And he reminded them that anybody who relieves a poor man by marrying his daughter attains some virtue. Sometimes he would ask them to stay away for some days, saying, "Be careful, lest I get a scolding from your parents because you come here."

Among this group of youngsters, two were known to me. One was Yogin Roychoudhury [later, Swami Yogananda], who came from a rich family of Dakshineswar. Polite, calm, and sparing of words, he was one year senior to me in Baranagore High School.

The second boy, who was my classmate at Dakshineswar School, was Brahmapada of Ariadaha. Both Yogin and Brahmapada wanted to become intimate disciples of Sri Ramakrishna. It is possible that the Master told Brahmapada to get permission from his parents and that they refused to give it. At any rate, one day I heard that Brahmapada had committed suicide and that there was a great turmoil in the village. The Master was deeply shocked and expressed great sympathy for him.

Immediately after this Yogin's parents planned to trap him in the life of a householder, and they found a beautiful young girl in Ariadaha for him to marry. Yogin vehemently protested and fervently begged his parents not to force him into marriage, but it was of no avail. Even great wealth and a young wife could not divert his mind from God. Yogin left home.

All Sri Ramakrishna's conversations centred around two sayings: "Brahman is real and the world is unreal," and "First realize God and then do whatever you like." I heard these words again and again from the Master. He spoke in such a simple way that everybody could understand.

Rasik was a sweeper of the Kali temple, who lived in Dakshineswar. One day I heard the Master talking with him in the latter's courtyard. They were talking very intimately, as though they were close friends. The Master smiled at him and said, "Don't drink too much." Rasik was drunk and rolling on the ground. "Master," he replied, "I can't afford to drink. Luckily, Natabar Panja's mother died and so I got some extra money for doing some cleaning. But whose mother is going to die every day?"

I heard that the Master met Keshab Chandra Sen at the garden house of Belgharia, where they had an interesting talk. Keshab Babu was a wonderful orator, commanding great respect from all, and the young students flocked to him. Although Keshab Babu's followers considered the Master to be crazy, Keshab Babu listened to him with great attention. I myself saw Keshab Babu sitting cross-legged on the floor of the Master's room, listening attentively to the Master's words, and never, at least in my presence, uttering a single word himself.

Many young students would come from Calcutta to ask Sri Ramakrishna difficult questions about religion and philosophy — about Dualism, Qualified Monism, and Monism. Some of them came to test his knowledge. The Master would laugh and say: "Well, such subtle divisions of philosophy can be understood by practising more and more spiritual disciplines. Have you practised anything?" At this, they all kept quiet. The younger generation was then hungry for religion, and they thronged to Keshab Babu to hear about the different religions of the world. But their hunger only increased more and more. At last they came to Sri Ramakrishna to find the essence, because the Master was the custodian of religion.

One day I started for my office and crossed the Ganga by boat, but due to some family trouble, my mind was very disturbed. It occurred to me that it would be better to go to the Master than to the office, so I took another boat and landed at the temple ghat of Rani Rasmani.

The Master was standing on the western verandah of his room, looking at the Ganga. As I walked up to him, he said: "What! You ran away from your office? That is not good. Live in this world like a crocodile. It lives under water, but sometimes it raises its snout above water, takes a deep breath, and again dives below the surface. People are submerged in their worldly life, and they come here only when they are suffocating at home. Does anybody tread the path of religion without first undergoing sorrows and sufferings? Misery has a great value. It helps a person find the path to God."

He continued: "I know you are married. Do you have a mother?" "Yes, my mother is still alive," I replied. He was silent for some time, and then he said: "All right, now stay at home. A little misery is good. It helps one to make progress in spiritual life. If there were no misery, would anyone chant the Lord's name?"

He went on talking in this way, but it seemed to me that he was tired. Indeed, the cancer in his throat was developing day by day. I said to him: "Sir, please take a little rest. You have just finished your lunch and I am disturbing you."

"It is true," he said, "the pain is there. But if you wish to know anything, you may ask." Smiling, I replied, "We want to know so many things, but where is our capacity for understanding?"

The Master said: "Know God. Make some effort and you will find him. He is ever present. Develop a deep longing for God."

I then implored him, "Sir, please bless me." In reply he said: "Longing does not come through blessings. It depends upon self-effort. Increase your love for God." He was ready to answer my questions, but I could not think of any. After returning with him inside his room, I left for home.

The Master came to awaken God-consciousness in us. We are fortunate to have had him in our midst. Now the more I think of him the more my heart yearns for him and tears flow from my eyes.

After the Master's passing away, one day, quite unconsciously I said, "If only the Master were alive today." Then and there I actually experienced his presence. I have no words to describe his grace.

[From: *Udbodhan* (Calcutta: Udbodhan Office), vol. 50, nos. 1-2, 1947]

25

Manmatha Nath Ghosh

Manmatha Nath Ghosh was a devotee of Sri Ramakrishna.

My family lived in Calcutta on Beadon Street. In those days small concert groups of instrumental music were in vogue. Being just a youth, I had no inclination for study, but I did have an aptitude for music, so I joined a neighbourhood concert group of which many of my friends were members.

One morning our concert party started for Panihati by boat on the Ganga, singing as we went along. Presently we came to the Kali temple of Rani Rasmani, and we asked the boatman to stop there. When the boat reached the landing ghat, one of my friends said: "I am very hungry. I have heard that there is a paramahamsa at this temple who will give food to whoever goes to him."

A discussion then began as to who would represent our group. At last I said: "Why are you hesitating so much about going to the paramahamsa? I will go and bring back some food." I stepped out of the boat onto the ghat, and, after finding out where Sri Ramakrishna lived, soon reached his room.

When he saw me he asked with a smile, "Hello, what do you want?"

I simply said: "Our concert group is from Calcutta and we are on our way to Panihati. We left home early this morning without any food, so we are hungry. Please give us something to eat."

The Master looked at me intently. Then he rose from his seat and gave me some fruits and sweets on a leaf plate. "What shall I do with this little amount?" I asked. "There are about a dozen people in our group. This small quantity is only enough for me. Sir, you have plenty in your basket. Give us more."

At this, the Master covered the basket with his hand like a small boy, lest I should forcibly take it away from him. Then he said indignantly: "Go away, go away! Be satisfied with what I have given you. 'He who has nothing to spare must not even keep a dog.' You are hungry, so you eat. Why are you demanding food for your whole group?"

"Sir," I said, "I don't care to eat without my friends. Please take back your food." Having said this, I was about to leave.

Then he called me back sweetly and said, "Take more, my child, but don't be greedy." And he gave me some more food.

"But, sir, this is still not sufficient. We are all terribly hungry. You have plenty and you are purposely not giving us enough!"

Hearing this, the Master laughed. "Well," he said, "why should I give to all of them? Can't they come here? Who has asked you to plead for them?"

I replied, "Sir, if you don't believe me, please come to our boat and see whether we are a dozen or not. If we weren't hungry, then why should we have come to you?"

The Master then called someone and asked him to give me a basket full of fruits and sweets. I carried the basket back to my friends and told them, "Look, you didn't come with me, but I have brought all these things for you." This was my first visit to Sri Ramakrishna.

Later I used to visit Dakshineswar now and then. The very sight of Sri Ramakrishna would captivate my mind. I would see him surrounded by well-known visitors like Keshab Sen, Vijay Krishna Goswami, and many other scholars, so I did not dare talk to him. Whenever he saw me, he would say to his attendant: "Give that boy some good food. He is very hungry." And I would feel ashamed.

After I was married I could not visit the Master, as I had to go here and there looking for a job. At last I secured a position with Rally Brothers, but my monthly salary was so small that I could not afford to hire a carriage to go to the office. I had to walk back and forth from our house on Beadon Street to the office in Dharmatala via Geratala.

One evening as I was passing by the Geratala mosque, I heard the loud prayer of a Muslim fakir [holy man]: "O my Beloved, please come! Please come, O my Beloved!" He was repeating this prayer with love and longing as tears rolled down his cheeks.

Suddenly I saw Sri Ramakrishna climb down from a hired carriage and rush up to the fakir. The two embraced each other. This incident happened when the Master was returning from Kalighat after visiting the Divine Mother there. What a wonderful sight it was! Two other people were in the carriage. One of them was Ramlal, a nephew of Sri Ramakrishna, who used to give me prasad at the Master's command at Dakshineswar.

That picture of the Master still lives vividly in my memory. At that time very few people knew the Master, and how many even tried to know him? Now, in my old age, I regret that, although I met the merciful Lord, I could not understand him. There is the element of time. Now I lament that I lost a precious thing because of youthful attractions.

[From: *Udbodhan* (Calcutta: Udbodhan Office), vol. 57, no. 11, 1955]

The temple garden of Dakshineswar, where Sri Ramakrishna lived for thirty years

26

Bepin Behari Sen

Bepin Behari Sen was a nephew of Adhar Lal Sen, a householder disciple of Sri Ramakrishna. His father's name was Dayal Chandra Sen. Bepin later became a cashier of the Calcutta Custom House.

Adhar Lal Sen, my uncle, was a great devotee of Sri Ramakrishna. He was my father's brother, and our two families lived together. During the years 1883-84 the Master visited our home almost every Saturday. Thus it was that I had the great good fortune of coming in contact with Sri Ramakrishna at the age of twelve. Whenever the Master came, the devotees would assemble and there would be kirtan [devotional singing]. Our living room would be full, with many people standing in the courtyard and even in the street. Bankim Chandra Chatterjee, Girish Chandra Ghosh, and many other prominent people visited our house at those times.

At the time of kirtan, and especially when Vaishnav Charan sang, the Master would dance in ecstasy and sometimes go into samadhi. What a wonderful sight! It would appear to us that Sri Chaitanya had descended again on earth. After coming back to normal consciousness he would talk to the devotees, always with a smiling face, and would answer their questions. One day the Master asked Swami Vivekananda, "Naren, please play the violin a little." Swamiji then played a sweet melody for some time. After that Kali Babu of the Star Theatre sang this song: *Keshava kuru karuna dine* [O Krishna, bestow mercy on the lowly].

Once Sri Ramakrishna came to our house at the time of the Durga Puja to attend the worship of the Divine Mother. Master Mahashay [M.] and Rakhal Maharaj [Swami Brahmananda] were with him. Sri Ramakrishna stood before the image with folded hands and went into samadhi. After returning to normal consciousness he said, "I have never before seen such a smiling image." Because of his presence our house was crowded and overflowing with joy. My uncle was so absorbed in serving the

Master that he could not think of anything else. After an hour Sri Ramakrishna ate something and then left. Although the worship was still going on, all of us felt an air of sadness in the house after his leaving.

I was still quite young and had to carry out the orders of my seniors. Consequently, at their request I carried drinking water to the Master many times. He greatly enjoyed drinking iced water from a big glass, and he was also fond of sweet mangoes.

Almost every day after returning home from his office my uncle would bathe, eat something, and then go to Dakshineswar. At that time there were no automobiles, so he had to go by a hired carriage, returning home about midnight. Sometimes his young daughter and I would accompany him to Dakshineswar, and on those occasions he would return a little earlier.

One day we were present at the time of the arati [vesper service] at Dakshineswar. Sri Ramakrishna stood before the Divine Mother with folded hands, looking at her intently. I noticed that his lips were moving. When the arati was over a conch was blown. The Master then took in his hand that part of his cloth which was draped over his shoulder and touched the Mother's feet with it. Touching the cloth to his head, he returned to his room. In order that the Mother might not suffer any discomfort or pain from his hand he had touched her feet very carefully. His constantly moving lips indicated that as long as he was in the temple, he was chanting hymns to the Mother.

Probably it was on 8 January 1885 that my uncle fell from a horse, fracturing his left arm and incurring the fatal injuries from which he passed away eight days later. Once during these last days Sri Ramakrishna came to see him. The Master looked very pale that day. He stroked my uncle's body and wept. By then my uncle had almost lost his voice, but when he saw the Master, tears rolled down his cheeks. The Master talked to him a little, but since I was so young I could not follow what was being said. I did observe, though, that my uncle's face beamed with joy when he saw the Master. After a while the Master ate something and then left with a heavy heart.

A year after the death of my uncle, I went to visit the Master at Dakshineswar with another uncle. I took the dust of the Master's feet and sat in his room, which was filled with devotees. The Master noticed me and said, "I have seen this boy before somewhere." Rakhal Maharaj said, "Yes. He is Bepin, a nephew of Adhar." The Master raised his hand and said, "That is good." Then he talked to my uncle and asked about the welfare of our family.

Many devotees of Sri Ramakrishna still visit our house and salute the floor that was touched by the Master's blessed feet.

[From: Udbodhan (Calcutta: Udbodhan Office), vol. 40, no. 9, 1938]

27

Manindra Krishna Gupta

Manindra Krishna Gupta (1870-1939) was a grandson of Ishwar Chandra Gupta, a famous poet of Bengal. Manindra was an artist and a playwright. He met Sri Ramakrishna when he was quite young and was blessed by him. Swami Saradananda requested him to write these reminiscences.

After Sri Ramakrishna's meeting with Keshab Chandra Sen, his name began to spread among the members of the Brahmo Samaj. Keshab's followers, as well as members of other groups, flocked to hear the Master's sublime teachings. During the summer vacation or on any holiday, Brahmabandhav Upadhyay (Bhavani Charan Bandyopadhyay), an evangelist, used to visit Sri Ramakrishna at Dakshineswar with his friends. Since he was a leader of a group of young boys, he never missed an opportunity to invite me and other youngsters along. And this is how I first went to Dakshineswar — not for any religious reasons.

I was then about eleven or twelve years old. I remember that we used to go on a big boat and that the trip on the Ganga was very pleasant. When we had landed at Dakshineswar, we bathed either in the Ganga or in the pond. We swam, splashed, and had lots of fun. Afterwards we would assemble on the northern verandah of Sri Ramakrishna's room. The Master would put out an assortment of offered sweets, fruits, sugar candy syrup, and other delicacies, and he himself would invite us to eat them. Thus I saw him several times, but all I remember is his sweet and affectionate manner.

After eating the prasad, the seniors would listen to the Master while we youngsters would play in the temple garden or rest in the Panchavati.

One day, out of curiosity, I peeped through the eastern door of the Master's room. He was seated on his small cot, and I can still remember that he had a small bag containing cinnamon, cloves, and other spices. Now and then as he talked he would take a few of them and put them

Manindra Krishna Gupta

in his mouth. I don't remember what he was talking about, but one thing I do remember: Pointing to the audience in his room, he said, "Look, here is a gathering of bright jewels." I was so impressed with his beautiful, loving face, that I could not turn to look in any other direction. I stood there for some time, forgetting everything. When my companions left his room, I followed them and we went back to Calcutta.

Due to a change in my father's place of work, my family moved to Bhagalpur and I did not see the Master for three years. One afternoon after we had returned to Calcutta, an acquaintance, Sarada Babu, asked me, "Would you like to go with me to visit a place?" Now and then, when school was over for the day, I would go with him for a walk in the countryside. So I said, "All right, let us go." Sarada Babu understood what was in my mind, and he said: "But today I am not going for a walk. Sri Ramakrishna is now living in a house at Shyampukur. Let us go and see him." "That will be very nice. I'll put on my shirt," I replied. I then entered my room, dressed, and we started out.

Luckily there were no strangers in Sri Ramakrishna's room when we arrived at the house. As far as I can remember, only Mahendra Nath Gupta [recorder of *The Gospel of Sri Ramakrishna*] and Narendra Nath [Swami Vivekananda] were present. The Master was lying on his bed, facing north. As soon as we entered and he saw us, he got up. We saluted him. Looking at me for a moment, he touched his eyes with his fingers and turned his head towards M. and Swamiji. Then, it seemed to me, he asked them, by pointing one of his fingers, to look at my eyes. After that, he turned the finger around and made a sound by rubbing his middle finger and thumb against each other. I did not understand the meaning of it all.

He then beckoned me to come near him. I was a little embarrassed because, although Sarada Babu and I had come together, he was calling only for me. I moved slowly towards him. Smiling a little, he whispered to me: "Come alone tomorrow. Don't come with him." He said this in such a way that Sarada Babu could not hear.

On our way home Sarada Babu, out of curiosity, asked me, "What did he say to you?" I was hesitant to tell him that the Master had asked me to come without him the next time, so I said, "Well, he asked me to visit him another day." "My boy, your luck is good," Sarada Babu said in a sad voice. "He did not talk to me at all." All the way home I felt an irresistible attraction pulling my mind back to Shyampukur, but I did not talk about it to Sarada Babu.

It was evening when I reached home. I felt that strange, compelling attraction more and more, and I was absorbed in deep thought. All around me I kept seeing the smiling face of the Master, and his voice kept ringing in my ears, saying, "Come alone tomorrow." "What has happened to me?" I wondered. "Am I crazy?" I decided to have an early supper and go to bed. I thought perhaps a good sleep would cool my brain. But even when under the mosquito net of my bed, I saw there also the smiling face of the Master.

Some may think that because I was then just a teenager, my description is somewhat exaggerated. But please remember that, just as truth does not change with the passing of time, neither does one's experience. The joy of seeing the moon when one is young is the same as the joy of seeing it when one is old. At any rate, I remember vividly that I had to struggle for sleep the whole night, and it was not until the early hours of the morning that I finally fell asleep.

The next afternoon I again went to Shyampukur. When I arrived, I saw Mahendra Babu and some other devotees in the Master's room. Most of the disciples of Sri Ramakrishna were unknown to me except Mahendra Babu, who was a relative (my sister's husband was his wife's brother), and Swamiji, whom I had known before seeing him with the Master. As a matter of fact, it might not be out of place to explain, at this point, how I had first seen Swamiji.

Beni Adhikari, a famous singer, was our neighbour, and Swamiji used to come to his home every morning for a singing lesson. On his way, he would stop at Ambu Babu's gymnasium, which was also near our home, for exercise and wrestling.

Just across our lane there were some lawns with two Shiva temples. On winter mornings the youngsters of the neighbourhood (myself included) would sun themselves there and play around the Shiva temples.

Every day I noticed a man going along the lane. He wore a short cloth, reaching just below his knees, and he had a grey shawl wrapped around his body. His cheap slippers were half worn out so that his heels partly scraped the ground. He walked straight ahead, looking neither left nor right. His face was calm and so attractive that it held my eyes with a power I could not resist. Finally I asked about him and was told who he was. Thus, I recognized Swamiji when I saw him that first day in the Master's room.

On this second day, as I entered the Master's room, it appeared to me that the Master knew of my coming and was waiting to receive me. Before I could sit down, he asked everyone to go away and beckoned me to come and sit near him. "Where have you been for so long?" he asked. Saying this, the Master burst into tears. He talked to me as if I were a near and dear relative. Then he touched me, and I noticed a slight smile on his face. Suddenly his body became stiff like a corpse. I remained motionless. What was this? Never having seen samadhi before, I was quite at a loss. I checked his breathing but could detect no sign of it. His eyes were half-closed and his eyelids motionless. After fifteen minutes I saw that he was gradually returning to normal consciousness. Then, touching my chest, he muttered something and asked me in a deep voice, "What do you want?"

The way in which he asked this left me with the conviction that he was prepared to give me anything I wished. But there is a saying, "If a husking machine goes to heaven, it continues to husk there." That was the state of my mind, and I missed the glorious opportunity of asking for the highest. Without considering the pros and cons, I simply said: "I want to express my ideas about the beauty of the world and of human character. That is my desire."[1] "That is fine," said the Master with a smile. "But if you realize God, you will achieve everything."

One day when I went to visit him, the Master was returning from the bathroom to his room, which was across the verandah. I was waiting for him on the northern verandah, and I followed him. I noticed that Ram Chandra Datta and some other devotees entered the Master's room. Seeing Ram, the Master said: "Hello, Ram. Just now I had a vision of a monk with a well-built body who was wearing an ochre loin cloth. I have never seen him before."

Ram replied with a smile: "Sir, what do we know? You see so many things in heaven and earth. How can we comprehend them all?" "Really I have seen a monk," said the Master. "But I don't know who he is." My memory of that simple, childlike statement is still vivid. Then the subject was dropped. Slowly the Master sat down on his bed. Ram and other devotees sat in front of him. I sat in the room adjacent to the Master's, which was near the steps. About an hour later I saw a man come upstairs. He wore a black shirt and a black cap. It seemed to me that he was a native of Bihar. He asked me: "Sir, does Ramakrishna Paramahamsa live here? I have come to see him. Could I see him right away?" "Of course," I replied. "Please follow me." I took him to the Master's room.

After sitting there quietly for a while, he said to the Master: "Sir, I am a Christian, and for a long time I have meditated in solitude on Christ. Though I am a Christian and my Chosen Deity is Christ, my mode of worship is like the Hindus, and I believe in their yoga scriptures. Once I had a desire to find someone who had attained the highest spiritual realization while still in the world. One day in meditation I saw two persons. I had the strong feeling that one of them had attained the highest and that the other one, seated at his feet, though he had not yet reached the highest, was not an ordinary person.

---

[1] The writer of these reminiscences became an artist and a writer.

"After this vision I felt certain that such great souls must exist, but where were they, and how could I find them? I travelled to many places, especially in the western part of India, seeking the two I had seen in my vision. At last I heard of Pavhari Baba of Ghazipur, and I went to see him. But when I met him, I was greatly disappointed because he bore no resemblance whatever to either of the two men I was seeking. To my astonishment, however, I saw a picture of one of them hanging on the wall in his room. When I asked Pavhari Baba about it, he said it was a picture of Ramakrishna Paramahamsa. Eagerly I asked, 'Where can I find him?' Then Pavhari Baba told me that for many years he had lived at Dakshineswar, but was now very ill and his devotees had moved him to Calcutta for treatment. So I am here, having come to Calcutta at Pavhari Baba's suggestion."

Then the man went on to say: "These clothes that I am wearing are not my usual dress." And as he spoke he stood up and removed his outer garments, revealing an ochre cloth. Instantly the Master also stood up and went into samadhi, raising his hand, as it is seen in the picture of Christ. At this, the monk knelt down before him with folded hands and looked intently at Sri Ramakrishna. The monk was shedding tears and was shivering.

We were all amazed to see the spiritual moods of both. And as my gaze again fell on his ochre cloth, I wondered: "Is this the holy man in ochre dress whom the Master saw in his vision?"

After some time the Master came back to normal consciousness and sat on his bed. The monk looked at us, his face beaming with joy, and exclaimed: "Today I am blessed." Then he continued more calmly: "As you see, this inner cloth is my regular dress, and it is also my favourite dress because it is worn by the yogis of India. I was born in a brahmin family, and even though I am a Christian, why should I give up the traditions of my ancestors? I have great faith in our Indian manners and customs."

Then we took him to an adjacent room, where Swami Vivekananda offered him prasad and food. Finally, we asked the monk[2] to tell us the cause of his ecstasy. "Well," he replied, "today I saw the one on whom I have meditated for so many years. I saw Lord Jesus in him." Sri Ramakrishna was Jesus himself — this was the conviction that the monk expressed to us.

[From: *Udbodhan* (Calcutta: Udbodhan Office), vols. 38-41, 1935-39]

---

[2] The monk's name was Prabhudayal Mishra. His birthplace was in the western part of India, and he belonged to the Quaker sect of Christianity.

III
Brahmo Devotees
and Admirers

Pratap Chandra Majumdar, a Brahmo leader

28

Pratap Chandra Majumdar

Pratap Chandra Majumdar (1840-1905) was a follower of Keshab Chandra Sen and met Sri Ramakrishna through him. He was a writer and orator, and he represented the religion of the Brahmo Samaj at the Parliament of Religions, Chicago, in 1893.

My mind is still floating in the luminous atmosphere which that wonderful man [Sri Ramakrishna] diffuses around him whenever and wherever he goes. My mind is not yet disenchanted of the mysterious and indefinable pathos which he pours into it whenever he meets me. What is there in common between him and me? I, a Europeanized, civilized, self-centred, semi-sceptical, so-called educated reasoner, and he, a poor, illiterate, unpolished, half-idolatrous, friendless Hindu devotee. Why should I sit long hours to attend to him — I who have listened to Disraeli and Fawcett, Stanley and Max Müller, and a whole host of European scholars and divines? I who am an ardent disciple and follower of Christ, a friend and admirer of liberal-minded Christian missionaries and preachers, a devoted adherent and worker of the rationalistic Brahmo Samaj — why should I be spellbound to hear him?

And it is not I only, but dozens like me who are the same. He has been interviewed and examined by many. Crowds pour in to visit and talk with him. Some of our clever, intellectual fools have found nothing in him. Some of the contemptuous Christian missionaries would call him an imposter or a self-deluded enthusiast. I have weighed their objections well, and what I write now I write deliberately.

The Hindu saint is a man under forty. He is a brahmin by caste; he is well-formed in body naturally, but the dreadful austerities through which his character has developed appear to have disordered his system. Yet, in the midst of this emaciation, his face retains a fullness, a childlike tenderness, a profound, visible humbleness, and unspeakable sweetness of expression, and a smile that I have seen on no other face that I can remember. A Hindu saint is always particular about his externals. He wears the ochre cloth, eats according to strict rules, refuses to associate with men, and is a rigid observer of caste. He is always proud and professes secret wisdom. He is always *guruji*, a universal counsellor and a dispenser of charms. But this man is singularly devoid of such claims. His dress and diet do not differ from those of other men except in the general negligence he shows towards both, and as to caste, he openly breaks it every day. He most vehemently repudiates the title of *guru*, or teacher. He shows impatient displeasure at any exceptional honour which people try to pay to him and emphatically disclaims the knowledge of secrets and mysteries. He protests against being lionized and openly shows his strong dislike to be visited and praised by the curious. The society of the worldly-minded and carnally-inclined he carefully shuns. He has nothing extraordinary about him. His religion is his only recommendation. And what is his religion? It is orthodox Hinduism, but Hinduism of a strange type.

Ramakrishna Paramahamsa (for that is the name of this saint) is the worshipper of no particular Hindu god. He is not a Shaiva; he is not a Shakta; he is not a Vaishnava; he is not a Vedantist. Yet he is *all these*. He worships Shiva; he worships Kali; he worships Rama; he worships Krishna; and is a confirmed advocate of Vedanta doctrines. He accepts all the doctrines, all the embodiments, usages, and devotional practices of every religious cult. Each in turn is infallible to him. He is an idolater, yet is a faithful and most devoted meditator on the perfections of the one formless, infinite Deity whom he terms *Akhanda Satchidananda* (Indivisible Existence-Knowledge-Bliss). His religion, unlike the religion of ordinary Hindu monks, does not mean too much dogma or controversial proficiency or outward worship with flowers, sandalwood, incense, and offerings. His religion means ecstasy; his worship means transcendental insight. His whole nature burns day and night with the permanent fire and fever of a strange faith and feeling. His conversation is a ceaseless breaking forth of this inward fire and lasts long hours. While his interlocutors are weary, he, though outwardly feeble, is as fresh as ever. He merges into rapturous ecstasy and outward unconsciousness often during the day — most often in conversation when he speaks of his favourite spiritual experiences or hears any striking response to them. But how is it possible that he has such a fervent regard for all the Hindu deities together? What is the secret of his singular eclecticism? To him each of these deities is a force, an incarnated principle, tending to reveal the supreme relation of the soul to that eternal and formless Being who is unchangeable in his blessedness and the Light of Wisdom.

Take for instance Shiva. The saint views and realizes Shiva as the Incarnation of contemplativeness and yoga. Forgetful of all worldly care and concern, merged and absorbed in samadhi, in the meditation on the ineffable perfections of the supreme Brahman, insensible to pain and privation, toil and loneliness, ever joyful in the blessedness of Divine communion, calm, silent, serene, immovable like the Himalayas where his abode is, Mahadeva is the ideal of all contemplative and self-absorbed men. The venomous serpents of evil and worldliness coil around his beatified form but cannot hurt him. The presence of death surrounds him in various forms of dread and danger but cannot daunt him. Shiva takes upon himself the burdens and cares of all the world, and swallows the deadliest poison to confer immortality upon others. Shiva renounces all wealth and enjoyment for the benefit of others, makes his faithful wife the companion of his austerities and solitude, and takes the ashes and the tiger skin as his only ornaments. Shiva is the god of the yogis. And this good man, while expatiating on the attributes of Shiva, would be immersed in the sublimity of his ideal, and become entranced and remain unconscious for a long time.

Then, perhaps, he would talk of Krishna, whom he realizes as the Incarnation of love. "Behold," he says, "the countenance of Krishna as represented popularly. Does it resemble a man's face or a woman's? Is there a shadow of sensuality in it? Is there a hair of masculine coarseness? It is a tender female face that Krishna has. In it is the fullness of boyish delicacy and girlish grace. By his affection, many-sided and multiform, he won the hearts of men and women to the religion of bhakti, or devotion." To prove that divine love can take the form of every sanctified human relation is the great mission of Krishna. As a loving child monopolizing all the fondness of the hearts of aged parents; as a loving companion and friend attracting the profoundest loyalty and affection of men and brethren; as an admired and adored master, the sweetness and tenderness of whose teaching and whose affectionate persuasions converted girls and women to the self-consecration of a heartfelt piety, Krishna, the beauty and depth of whose character still remain beyond the reach of men's appreciation, introduced the religion of love into India. Then the good man would say how for long years he dressed himself as a cowherd or a milkmaid to be able to realize the experiences of that form of piety in which the human soul was like a faithful wife and a loyal friend to the loving Spirit, who is our Lord and only friend. Krishna is the Incarnation of bhakti. Then in the intensity of that burning love of God, which is in his simple heart, the devotee's form and features suddenly grow stiff and motionless, unconsciousness overtakes him, his eyes lose their sight, and tears trickle down his fixed, pale, but smiling face. There is a transcendent sense and meaning in that unconsciousness. What he perceives and enjoys in his soul when he has lost all outward perception, who can say? Who will fathom the depth of that insensibility which the love of God produces? But that he sees something, hears, and enjoys when he is dead to all the outward world, there is no doubt. If not, why should he, in the midst of that unconsciousness, burst into floods of tears and break out into prayers, songs, and utterances, the force and pathos of which pierce through the hardest heart and bring tears to eyes that never before wept under the influence of religion?

Anon he would begin to talk of Kali, whom he addresses as his mother. She is the Incarnation of the Shakti, or power of God as displayed in the character and influence of woman. Kali is the female principle in the nature of the Deity. She tyrannizes over all tyrants. She brings her husband down low upon the ground and places her foot upon his bosom. She charms and conquers all beings. Yet she is the Mother of Creation. Her tremendous power is a guarantee that she can save and protect her children, those that come to her as their mother and ask the shelter of her feet. Her motherly solicitude excites the tenderest filial affection in the hearts of her devotees, and the inspiration of Ramaprasad Sen, which expressed itself in the most wonderful songs of filial piety ever sung, bears strange testimony to the reality and effectiveness of the worship of Kali. The adoration of Shakti (which literally means "Force") is, according to our saint, a childlike, whole-souled, rapturous self-consecration to the motherhood of God as represented by the power and influence of woman. Woman, therefore, has long been renounced by our friend in every material and carnal relation. He has a wife but has never associated with her. Woman, he says, is unconquerable by man except by him who looks up to her as a son. Lust fascinates and keeps the whole world from the love of God. The highest and holiest saints have been brought back to carnality and sin by the power of lust. The absolute conquest of lust has been his lifelong ambition. For many years, therefore, he says he made the utmost efforts to be delivered from the influence of woman. His heartrending supplications and prayers for such deliverance, sometimes uttered aloud in his retreat on the riverside, brought crowds of people who bitterly cried when he cried and could not help blessing him and wishing him success with their whole hearts.

He has successfully escaped the evil of carnality which he dreaded. His Mother to whom he prayed — that is, the goddess Kali — made him recognize every woman as her Incarnation, so that he now honours each member of the other sex as his mother. He bows his head to the ground before women and before little girls; he has insisted upon worshipping not a few of them as a son might worship his mother. The purity of his thoughts and relations towards women is most unique and instructive. It is the opposite of the European idea. It is an attitude essentially, traditionally, gloriously national. Yes, a Hindu *can* honour woman.

The other sin which he spent his life to be free from is the love of money. The sight of money fills him with strange dread. His avoidance of women and wealth is the whole secret of his matchless moral character. For a long time he practised a singular discipline. He took in one hand a piece of gold and in the other a lump of earth. He would then look at both, repeatedly calling the gold *earth*, and the earth *gold*, and then shuffling the contents of one hand into the other, he would keep up the process until he lost all sense of the difference between the gold and the earth.

"My father," says the Paramahamsa, "was a worshipper of Rama. I too have accepted the Ramayat covenant. When I think of the piety of my father, the flowers with which he used to worship his favourite god bloom again in my heart and fill it with divine fragrance." Rama, the truthful and dutiful son, the good and faithful husband, the just and fatherly king, the staunch and affectionate friend, is regarded by him with the love and profound loyalty of a devoted servant. As a master, the privilege of whose service is sufficient reward to the favoured, faithful servant; as a master in whose dear and matchless service the laying down of life is a delightful duty; as a master who has wholly enslaved the body and soul of his adoring slave, the contemplation of whose holy and glorious worth transcends every thought of remuneration and return, is Rama viewed by Ramakrishna. Hanuman, the renowned follower of Rama, is to him a model of a faithful servitor, a being who was devoted to his master's cause, inspired by such unworldly love and honour, such superhuman faithfulness as scorned alike death and danger or hope of reward.

His ideal of service is absolute unworldliness and freedom from the desire of gain. He loves and serves Rama because Rama is the best and most loving master. The service of the true saint is the service of the purest affection and most unselfish loyalty. Some of the songs he sings, expressive of this touching devotedness, are exceedingly pathetic, and show how very negligent we often are.

Nor is this reverence confined within Hinduism. For long days he subjected himself to various disciplines to realize the Muslim idea of an all-powerful Allah. He let his beard grow; he fed himself on Muslim diet; he continually repeated sentences from the Koran. His reverence for Christ is deep and genuine. He bows his head at the name of Jesus, honours the doctrine of his sonship, and we believe he once or twice attended Christian places of worship. These ideas, at all events, show the catholic religious culture of this great Hindu saint.

Each form of worship that we have tried to indicate above is to the Paramahamsa a living and most enthusiastic principle of personal religion, and the accounts of discipline and exercise through which he has arrived at his present state of devotional eclecticism are most wonderful, although they cannot be published. He never writes anything, seldom argues; he never attempts to instruct; he is continually pouring out his soul in a rhapsody of spiritual utterances; he sings wonderfully, and makes observations of singular wisdom. He unconsciously throws a flood of marvellous light upon the obscurest passages of the Pauranic shastras [mythological scriptures] and brings out the fundamental principles of the popular Hindu faith with a philosophical clearness that strangely contrasts itself with his simple and illiterate life. These Incarnations, he says, are but the forces (*Shakti*) and dispensations (*Lila*) of the eternally wise and blessed *Akhanda Satchidananda* [Brahman], who never can be changed or formulated, who is one endless and everlasting ocean of light, truth, and joy.

If all his utterances could be recorded they would form a volume of strange and wonderful wisdom. If all his observations on men and things could be reproduced, people might think that the days of prophecy, of primeval, unlearned wisdom had returned. But it is most difficult to render his sayings in English.

This good and holy man is living evidence of the depth and sweetness of the Hindu religion. He has wholly controlled his flesh. It is full of soul, full of the reality of religion, full of joy, full of blessed purity. As a *siddha* [perfect] Hindu ascetic, he is a witness of the falsehood and emptiness of the world. His testimony appeals to the profoundest heart of every Hindu. He has no other thought, no other occupation, no other relation, no other friend in his humble life than his God. That God is more than sufficient for him. His spotless holiness, his deep, unspeakable blessedness, his unstudied, endless wisdom, his childlike peacefulness and affection towards all men, his consuming, all-absorbing love for God are his only reward. And may he long continue to enjoy that reward! Our own ideal of religious life is different, but as long as he is spared to us, gladly shall we sit at his feet to learn from him the sublime precepts of purity, unworldliness, spirituality, and inebriation in the love of God.

[From: *Theistic Quarterly Review*, October 1879]

29

Shivanath Shastri

Shivanath Shastri (1847-1919) was a preacher in the Sadharan Brahmo Samaj. When he first met Sri Ramakrishna, Shivanath was very fond of the Master. But later he stopped seeing Sri Ramakrishna because the latter helped some drunkards and actors and actresses. Moreover, some of the Master's disciples began to proclaim that Sri Ramakrishna was an Incarnation of God. Shivanath even considered Sri Ramakrishna's sama-dhi to be a derangement of the brain. When the Master heard this he told Shivananth, "How can one become unconscious by thinking of Consciousness?"

Shivanath wrote several books, including History of the Brahmo Samaj *and* Men I Have Seen. *For readability, this article has been thoroughly edited. Although some parts of it are controversial, it has some historical value. The article shows how some of the Brahmos regarded Sri Ramakrishna.*

My personal acquaintance with Ramakrishna Paramahamsa began in 1875. I was then employed as Headmaster in the South Suburban School of Bhowanipore, Calcutta. While working there I became friends with a teacher from the London Missionary Society's Institution. He had been married at Dakshineswar, a village in the northern suburbs, where Ramakrishna Paramahamsa lived. After his visits to Dakshineswar, my friend would come and relate the sayings and doings of a Hindu mendicant who lived at the Kali temple there. Some of these sayings seemed so remarkable to me that one day I accompanied my friend to see him. Ramakrishna Paramahamsa was not well known then. Later, his fame spread when Keshab Chandra Sen began to publish accounts of his visits with him in his paper.

I have not kept any notes of our meetings. Consequently I am not able to record things in chronological order. But I shall narrate certain events as they linger in my memory without any special reference to time.

Shivanath Shastri, a Brahmo leader

I do not remember what he said during our first interview, but I vividly recall that he received me very warmly, perhaps because my friend had previously mentioned my name to him. Addressing me again and again in his open-hearted, simple, and childlike manner, he said: "I am so delighted to see you. Will you come here now and then?" From the little of his personal history that I could gather from persons living there, I learned that he was an unlettered, poor brahmin who was formerly employed as a priest in the Kali temple. As a result of his extraordinary penances and austerities he had attained a state of perfection seldom seen.

Our friendship became closer after repeated visits, and he began to reveal his experiences to me. When acting as a priest in the temple he came in contact with many Hindu monks, saints, sages, and mendicants who, on their way to and from Puri, or Jagannath, would visit the Kali temple and often stay there for a while. Personal contact with these men brought about a revolution in the life of Ramakrishna. His hunger and thirst for spiritual truth, which was naturally great, was further strengthened. As a result, he devoted himself to the religious exercises many of them taught, and he practised austerities that were very severe.

I recollect some of them as related by the saint. What struck him most, and had an abiding influence on his mind, was the devastating effect of *kamini kanchan*, or "lust and greed." He emphasized that the most effective way to ensure spiritual detachment was to avoid "lust and greed" like poison. The means that he adopted for this purpose were unique. For instance, with a quantity of dust in one hand and some coins in the other, he would sit by the side of the river and compose himself into a state of meditation, trying to realize the equal worthlessness of both dust and coins. He would repeat, "Dust is money; money is dust. Dust is money; money is dust," and so on until the realization of that truth was complete. Then he would throw them both into the river. . . . I was personally present on an occasion when a few coins were placed in his hand by an inquiring visitor as an experiment. The saint fell into his usual ecstatic state and did not come back to consciousness until the coins were removed from his hand.

. . . Ramakrishna had earnestly resolved to practise what the visiting mendicants had taught him. For instance, one sage told him that the best way to acquire perfect obedience to the divine will was to cultivate the spirit of Hanuman, the famous monkey-servant of Rama, as delineated in the Ramayana. In order to cultivate that spirit, Ramakrishna shut himself in a room for a number of days and meditated on the virtues of Hanuman. He jumped about in the room saying, "Lord, Lord, I am thy devoted servant."

... Added to all these [spiritual exercises] were strict regulations on diet and sleep. He fasted for days and denied himself rest during the nights. One can easily imagine that these severe austerities told upon his constitution, which seems to have been naturally frail. The first result was that his health completely broke down and he got throat cancer, which eventually caused his death. The other result was ... whenever there was any strong emotion or excitement, he would lose consciousness for the time being and his whole countenance would assume a radiant glow.

This seems to be unique to religious persons. It is said of Chaitanya, the famous prophet of Bengal, that under strong emotion his figure would assume such an ethereal glow that men would be struck with wonder and many would kiss his whole frame. It is also said of Muhammad that under deep religious emotion he would fall into an ecstatic state, and that many of his utterances given soon after such a state have been recorded in the Koran. Cases have also been known of Christian saints, both men and women, who went into ecstasy under strong religious emotion. To us Hindus of Bengal, both in the Brahmo Samaj and in the Vaishnava community, it is a fact of repeated experience that men and women become ecstatic during rapturous singing of sankirtan [devotional singing]. What the latter achieved occasionally, men like Ramakrishna, Chaitanya, and Muhammad experienced habitually. Ramakrishna personally told me that he had such ecstasy as a result of the austerities mentioned above. Upon my expressing regret for their weakening his health, he said: "Yes, my friend, that will kill me. I have these ecstasies as a result of literally carrying out the injunctions of the monks who visited this temple."

... The impression left in my mind from my association with him was that I had seldom come across any other man in whom the hunger and thirst for spiritual life was so great and who had undergone so many privations and sufferings for the practice of religion. Secondly, I was convinced that he was no longer a sadhak [spiritual aspirant], but was a siddha-purusha [perfected soul], or one who had attained the direct vision of spiritual truth. He had direct spiritual visions of the Divine Mother, and from her flowed a fountain of noble impulses in his soul. He loved to speak of God as his Mother. The thought of the Divine Mother would rouse all his emotions, and he would go into ecstasy when singing of the Mother's love. Yet his concept of motherhood stretched far beyond any idol or image to a sense of the Infinite. When he spoke or sang about the Mother, his thoughts far surpassed the limits of the four-handed goddess Kali. One of his favourite songs was, "Oh Mother, dance, once commingling thy smiles and thy flute" — i.e., commingling

Kali and Krishna. He would often say that only fools make the distinction between Kali and Krishna. They are the manifestations of the same Power.

Speaking of Ramakrishna's spirituality and catholicity, one incident comes to my mind. A Christian preacher of Bhowanipore, who was my personal friend, once accompanied me on a visit to Ramakrishna. When I introduced him to Ramakrishna, I said, "Today I bring a Christian preacher, who, having heard of you from me, was very eager to see you." The saint bowed his head to the ground and said, "I bow again and again at the feet of Jesus." Then the following conversation took place:

My Christian friend: "How is it, sir, that you bow at the feet of Christ? What do you think of him?"

Ramakrishna: "Why, I look upon him as an Incarnation of God."

My friend: "Incarnation of God! Kindly explain what you mean by that."

Ramakrishna: "An Incarnation like our Rama or Krishna. Don't you know there is a passage in the Bhagavat that says the Incarnations of Vishnu, or the Supreme Being, are innumerable?"

My friend: "Please explain further. I do not quite understand."

Ramakrishna: "Just take the case of the ocean. It is a wide and almost infinite expanse of water, but owing to certain circumstances some parts of this wide sea become solidified into ice. When transformed into ice it can be easily manipulated and applied to special use. An Incarnation is something like that. Like that infinite expanse of water, there is the Infinite Power immanent in matter and mind. But for some special purposes, in special regions, a portion of that Infinite Power assumes, as it were, a tangible shape in history. That is what you call a great man, but actually he is a local manifestation of the all-pervading Divine Power — in other words, an Incarnation of God. The greatness of great men is essentially the manifestation of Divine Energy."

My friend: "I understand your position, though we do not quite agree with it. [*Then, turning to me*] I would like to know what my Brahmo friends say to this."

Ramakrishna: "Don't talk to those fools [*meaning, members of the Brahmo Samaj*]. They have no eyes to see such things."

Myself [*addressing Ramakrishna*]: "Sir, who told you we don't believe that the greatness of the great teachers of humanity was divinely communicated and in that sense they were Incarnations of a Divine Idea?"

Ramakrishna: "Is that what you really believe? I did not know that."

Afterwards there was a conversation during which the saint illustrated, in his well-known, homey way, many spiritual truths which struck my Christian friend as being very noteworthy.

After this I visited the saint whenever I had the leisure. Many were the meetings and many were the utterances. I do not remember all of them, but the following incident still lingers in my mind.

On one occasion I was in his room along with a few others who, during the saint's temporary absence, began to discuss the feasibility of certain divine attributes. I was getting tired of the discussion when the saint returned. While entering the room, he caught some words of the discussion and also observed the heated nature of it. At once he put a stop to the discussion by saying: "Stop, stop! What is the good of discussing the feasibility of divine attributes? These attributes are acquired by prayerfully waiting and thinking. For instance, you say God is good. Can you convince me of his goodness by reasoning? Take that terrible flood that recently occurred at Dakhin Sabazpore as a result of a storm at sea. We hear thousands of men, women, and children were carried away and drowned. How can you prove to me that a good God, a beneficent Deity, ordered all that? Perhaps you will answer by pointing out the good that resulted from the flood — how it carried away the filth, how it fertilized the soil, and so on. But my question is this: Could not a good God do all that without carrying off hundreds of thousands of innocent men, women, and children?" At this point one in the audience interrupted Ramakrishna by saying, "Are we then to believe that God was cruel?" Ramakrishna responded: "You fool! Who tells you to believe that? Join your hands in reverential humility and say: 'Oh God, we are too weak and too incompetent to know thy nature and thy doings. Do thou enlighten our understanding.'"

Then he illustrated this truth with the following parable: "Take the case of two men who, while travelling on a certain road, take shelter in a mango grove. It is the season for mangoes. One of them sits with pencil and paper in hand and begins to calculate. He counts the number of mango trees in the garden, the number of branches on each tree, and the average number of mangoes on each branch. Then he tries to imagine how many cartloads of mangoes the garden will supply and then again, taking each cartload to be worth so many rupees, how much money the garden will fetch in the market.

"While this man is counting up the probable income from the garden, the other is engaged in plucking ripe mangoes and eating them. Which one do you consider wiser?" "The second one was wiser," said a visitor, "for it is certainly wiser to eat the fruits than to count up the probable income from the garden." Then the saint smiled and remarked: "Likewise, it is wiser to pray to God and cultivate communion with him rather than to argue about the reasonableness of his attributes. Pray and open your hearts to him and the light will come to you."

On another occasion I was seated with Ramakrishna when a number of men arrived, one of whom asked whether it was necessary for a man to place himself under the guidance of a guru, or spiritual preceptor, for the purpose of spiritual improvement. Ramakrishna replied: "Certainly it is an advantage and a great, good fortune if a man can find a worthy director of his spiritual life. Such a person would help him. Not that he cannot attain true spiritual progress by his own self-exertions, but such a director would certainly facilitate it." Then, turning to the river flowing nearby, he pointed to a passing steamer and asked his questioner, "When do you think that steamer will reach Chinsurah?" The man said, "By five or six in the evening." The saint said: "Attach a boat by a rope to the stern of the steamer. With the help of the steamer that boat also will arrive at Chinsurah by that time. But suppose that boat is released from the steamer and has to ply unaided. When do you think it will reach Chinsurah?" The questioner replied, "Most likely not before the next morning." The saint concluded: "Exactly like that, a man may go on unaided in his spiritual life through his weaknesses and blunders — it only takes time. But if he has the companionship and help of an advanced spirit, he can accomplish the journey of ten or twelve hours in four."

On another occasion one of the visitors asked, "Of jnana, or knowledge of God, and bhakti, or ardent love of God, which is better?" In his reply, Ramakrishna took advantage of the gender of the Sanskrit words, calling jnana male and bhakti female. Through his ignorance of Sanskrit grammar, however, he committed a mistake, for jnana is neuter. Nevertheless, his application of Sanskrit grammar in this instance was quite striking. After describing one as masculine and the other feminine, he then referred to the Indian custom of confining women to their inner living quarters. He said, "Jnana, being male, is obliged to stand and wait at the outer court of the Divine Mother's house, whereas bhakti, being female, is able to go directly to the inner quarters, to the very presence of the Mother."

In another instance, one of the visitors asked, "Living in the world as we do, surrounded by our daily cares and duties, how can we concentrate our attention on the Divine?" The saint replied: "Have you ever seen women making cheerah [flattened rice]? The husking machine has a big pestle which moves up and down in a measured movement. A woman generally takes her seat near a small pit made in the ground where the grain is to be threshed. As the large pestle rises and falls over the grain, she quickly gathers up the threshed grain and spreads it out under the sun. In gathering up the grain, she has to be very careful or the pestle will come down on her hand and crush her fingers. Now take the case of a woman thus employed. With her left hand she is removing the threshed grain from the pit and at the same time she is also feeding a baby on her lap and talking to a neighbour about the price of some cheerah. Where do you think that woman's primary attention is directed? Certainly it is to her hand in the pit, lest it be crushed by the pestle. Similarly, in this world be occupied with many concerns and be attentive to many duties, but primarily attend to your spiritual interests. Take care that these are not crushed."

On another occasion the conversation turned to the usefulness of counting beads and repeating the names of gods or goddesses. The saint said: "The mere repetition of a name in itself is nothing unless it is accompanied by a corresponding spiritual emotion. Take, for instance, the case of a parrot. Its master has taught it the names of his own deities. Accordingly the parrot repeats, in season and out of season, the names of Radha and Krishna. 'Radha Krishna, Radha Krishna,' the parrot repeats morning and evening, and he seems to be quite in love with them. One day, however, a wily cat pounces upon it from behind and tries to kill it. What do you hear then? Perhaps you observe that 'Radha Krishna' has vanished from its throat and now you hear the terror-stricken bird's natural cry, 'Kan, Kan, Kan.' Likewise, your bead-counting man, when tempted, perhaps forgets the name he repeats. Your professed lover of God forgets his God's name and falls into his natural mood of disbelief and lack of resignation. A faith that cannot stand the trials of life is no faith at all."

Let me now relate some incidents which show the saint's personal affection for me. At one time he had been sending repeated messages asking me to come and see him. But being detained by Brahmo Samaj work, I was unable to go. Then one day he turned up at my house, perhaps on his way to another engagement. The following conversation took place:

Ramakrishna: "How is it that you have not seen me for such a long time, even after repeated requests and your repeated promises?"

Myself: "The work of the Brahmo Samaj detains me. I am very busy now."

Ramakrishna: "Perish your Brahmo Samaj if it denies you liberty to see your friends!"

Then, looking at my face, he smiled and said, "As I was coming to see you, the fellows [*meaning, his new disciples*] said: 'Why should you visit a Brahmo? He is not worthy of it.' Do you know what I told them?"

Myself: "What did you tell them?"

Ramakrishna: "I told them: 'Now look here! One who has publicly registered her name goes to all, whoever seeks her [*referring to the custom then prevalent of all public women registering their names before commencing their profession*]. I am at the service of all.'"

Another incident occurred as I was approaching the temple of Dakshineswar after a long absence. I found the saint, in his simple and childlike fashion, trying to drive crows away from the trees with a bow and arrow. This sight surprised me. "What is this? Have you turned into an archer?" I exclaimed. He seemed to be equally surprised to see me after so long and, throwing down the bow and arrow, he ran to embrace me. So great was his delight that he fell into ecstasy. Slowly I took him to his room, laid him on his bed, and waited for him to regain consciousness. When he was able to speak again he suggested I accompany him to the Zoological Gardens where some of his disciples wanted to take him to see the lions. The manner in which he expressed his joy at the thought of seeing the lions was charming in its simplicity. Repeatedly he asked if I would like to see the lions, the celebrated riding beasts of the goddess Durga. I smiled and said, "I have seen the lions several times." To which he replied, "Wouldn't it be a pleasure to go with me to see them once more?" I said: "Yes, it would be a great pleasure, no doubt, but unfortunately I have another engagement. However, I shall accompany you to Sukeas Street in Calcutta and then shall send for Naren (subsequently known as Vivekananda) and he will take you to the Zoological Gardens."

So it was arranged, and a carriage was brought by a young disciple, who, as far as I remember, became our fellow-passenger in the carriage. . . . As we rode along, Ramakrishna fell into an ecstatic state, and then I witnessed a scene that I shall never forget. His whole countenance was aglow with a strange spiritual light, and before he became fully unconscious he began to pray incoherently in the following fashion: "Oh Mother, my beloved Mother, do not make me unconscious. Oh Mother! I am going to see the lions in the Zoological Gardens. Oh Mother, I may have a fall from the carriage. Do, do let me be all right until the journey is finished." At this point he became thoroughly unconscious, leaning on my arm for a few minutes. After consciousness returned he once again began conversing in his usual, childlike, simple manner until we reached Sukeas Street and Naren was sent for. As far as I remember, Naren came at once, took my place in the carriage, and went with his Master to the Gardens.

During the last few years of the saint's life my visits became less frequent. There were two reasons: First, due to his childlike simplicity Sri Ramakrishna was drawn away by some of his new disciples into friendship with many objectionable characters such as the actors of the Indian theatres. I did not like to be associated with such men. Second, during the last days of his life some of his new disciples were proclaiming him to be an Incarnation of God. I was afraid my meeting with such men would give rise to unpleasant discussions, so I kept away.

But when I received the news of his rapidly declining health, I left all work and went to Dakshineswar. I found him very low. That was before he moved to the Cossipore garden house. Ramakrishna took me to task for neglecting him. I pleaded guilty to the charge and made a clean breast of it by letting him know the exact causes. I smiled and said, "As there are many editions of a book, so there have been many editions of God, and your disciples are about to make you a new one." He too smiled and said: "Just fancy, God Almighty dying of throat cancer. What great fools these fellows must be!" That was my last interview with him, after which he left Dakshineswar, was placed under the treatment of the most distinguished physicians in town, and was devotedly nursed by his disciples. But nothing could stay the progress of his disease, and he passed away leaving behind him a memory that is now spiritually feeding hundreds of earnest souls. My acquaintance with him, though short, was fruitful and strengthened many a spiritual thought in me. I owe him a debt of gratitude for the sincere affection he bore towards me. He was certainly one of the remarkable personalities I have come across in my life.

[From: *The Modern Review*, November 1910]

30

Girish Chandra Sen

Girish Chandra Sen (1835-1910), a devoted follower of Keshab Chandra Sen, was a well-known writer and an esteemed editor of Brahmo journals. He knew six languages — Bengali, Sanskrit, English, Parsi, Arabic, and Urdu — and translated the Koran into Bengali. Because of his knowledge of and writings on Islam he was known as "Maulavi" in the New Dispensation Church. He collected 184 sayings of Sri Ramakrishna and published them in 1878 under the title Sri Ramakrishna Paramahamser Ukti.

Our respected Sri Ramakrishna Paramahamsa was born in 1836 at Kamarpukur, Hooghly, and passed away in 1886 from throat cancer at Cossipore. From his childhood he was spiritually inclined. Whenever he met any mendicants, he would associate with them; and like them, he would wear a loin cloth, even if it meant tearing up his own cloth. He had very little school education, but he knew many stories from the Puranas, which he had heard from scholars. He had a tremendous memory and was very intelligent. Whatever he heard once, he remembered.

His elder brother [Ramkumar] was a great scholar who taught in Calcutta, and Sri Ramakrishna went there and lived with him for some time. Later, Sri Ramakrishna moved with him to Dakshineswar, where the brother officiated as a priest at the dedication ceremony of Rani Rasmani's Kali temple. Sri Ramakrishna was then eighteen years old. Mathur, Rasmani's son-in-law, was impressed with Sri Ramakrishna's spiritual nature and engaged him as a priest of the Kali temple.

Sri Ramakrishna began his spiritual journey in the Panchavati grove of Dakshineswar on the bank of the Ganga. For eight years he practised severe austerities, such as fasting, staying awake at night, and meditation, and as a result his body became like a skeleton. He did not follow the prescribed disciplines of the yoga scriptures. Being led by intense

401

Keshab Chandra Sen and his followers

Sitting from left to right: Gourgovinda Roy, Kedarnath De, Banga Chandra Roy, Pratap Chandra Majumdar, Aghorenath Gupta, Girish Chandra Sen, Mahendra Nath Bose, Keshab Chandra Sen, Ramchandra Sinha, Prasanna Kumar Sen, Amritalal Bose, Dinananth Majumdar, Trailokya Nath Sanyal, Umanath Gupta
Standing from left to right: Peary Mohan Chowdhury, Kanty Chandra Mittra

longing for God-realization, he adopted various methods for controlling passion and increasing renunciation. He also practised various sadhanas for purification of the mind and for God-vision. Seeing the setting sun, he would cry, "Mother, another day is gone and still I have not seen you!" Once somebody asked him, "What is the way to realize God?" "Yearning," he replied. "But without the grace of God, yearning does not come. I was once carried away by the tempest of longing."

Even at the beginning of his spiritual quest he knew that lust and gold are the two great obstacles to God-realization, so he underwent hard austerities and conquered them. He used to bow down to women, seeing the Divine Mother in them. When he married, his wife was seven [*actually, five*] years old, and he never had any physical relationship with her. She later lived with him, but he remained a self-controlled yogi. Once during his sadhana Sri Ramakrishna threw money into the Ganga, saying, "Money is clay and clay is money." Later, his hand would become numb if he even touched money inadvertently. He never thought about his daily needs nor did he save anything for the future. He had a dispassionate attitude towards the world and had little faith in worldly-minded people. He cared neither for the wealthy nor the learned. At times he told them unpleasant truths, which made them upset.

While talking about God or singing the Lord's name, Sri Ramakrishna would go into ecstasy. Sometimes he would laugh and sometimes he would cry. Sometimes he would behave like a drunkard and sometimes like a child. Again, sometimes he would be in deep samadhi, motionless like a statue. Truly, just by seeing his divine ecstasy, one could be spiritually benefitted. The scepticism of the sceptics and the sin of the sinners would be wiped away. Coming in contact with Sri Ramakrishna, many drunkards and debauchees were transformed. He was an unlettered man, yet many highly educated people were influenced by his pure life and became his disciples. He expressed profound spiritual truths in simple village language with common day-to-day examples. His conversations were so sweet and captivating that even a grief-stricken person would forget his grief and pain within a few moments. People became enchanted, seeing his smiling face, his childlike simplicity, his exuberant devotion for the Divine Mother, and his absorption in samadhi.

When he went into samadhi his eyes would be fixed without blinking, tears of ecstasy would flow down his cheeks, and a sweet smile would spread over his face. He then had no outer consciousness, and his body would be stiff and motionless like a statue. He would return to his normal plane of consciousness only after someone had chanted "Om" repeatedly near his ears.

He was above all social customs and manners. He always talked about God and spiritual life, and never indulged in worldly talk. He had a tremendous sense of humour and remarkable presence of mind. His Chosen Deity was both with form and without form. While talking about Kali the Mother, he would cry and become ecstatic. Someone once asked him about Kali and he replied: "I do not worship Kali made of clay and straw. My Mother is the conscious principle. My Mother is pure Satchidananda — Existence-Knowledge-Bliss Absolute. That which is infinite and deep is always dark-coloured. The extensive sky is dark-coloured and so is the deep sea. My Kali is infinite, all-pervading, and consciousness itself."

Sri Ramakrishna was not an idol-worshipper. One day he was passing through a street and saw a man cutting a tree with an axe. Immediately he burst into tears, saying, "My Mother is present in this tree, and the axe is striking her." He was as much a Shakta as he was a Vaishnava and a Vedantin. Yoga and bhakti were wonderfully harmonized in him. While chanting God's name he would become intoxicated and dance like Chaitanya used to do. At that time, in an ecstatic state, the cloth would fall from his body and he would pass into samadhi. Childlike simplicity, devotion, and knowledge were all seen in him. Even at the beginning of his spiritual journey Sri Ramakrishna was the embodiment of the harmony of religions, and he foreshadowed the New Dispensation. If he had not been endowed with catholic views, he could not have repeated the name of Allah and eaten Muslim food. A picture of Jesus hung on the wall in his room along with pictures of Chaitanya, Nityananda, and others.

In March 1875 Sri Ramakrishna arrived with his nephew Hriday at the Belgharia garden house of Jay Gopal Sen. At that time Keshab Chandra Sen was conducting a retreat there with his ministers. He was practising self-control, renunciation, and other austerities such as cooking and eating food under a tree. When Sri Ramakrishna arrived Keshab and his followers [including this writer] were seated on the ghat of the pond, preparing themselves for bathing. Hriday got down from the carriage, went to Keshab, and said to him: "My uncle loves to hear about God, and sometimes out of exuberant devotion he passes into samadhi. He has come to hear you talk about God."

Keshab consented to the visit, and Hriday helped Sri Ramakrishna get down from the carriage and brought him to us. Sri Ramakrishna was wearing a red-bordered cloth, without a shirt or chadar. One end of his lower cloth was thrown over his shoulder. His body was lean and weak. Seeing this, the ministers took him to be an ordinary person. Sri Ramakrishna approached us and said, "I hear that you have had visions of

God, so I have come to hear about it." Thus the religious conversation began. Afterwards Sri Ramakrishna sang a song by Ramprasad, and while singing he went into samadhi. No one considered this samadhi to be a high state of spiritual consciousness; rather they thought he was feigning. Immediately Hriday began to chant "Om" loudly and requested others to do the same, which they did. After a while Sri Ramakrishna came back to the normal plane and smiled. Then he began to talk about profound spiritual truths, and the ministers were amazed. They now realized that Sri Ramakrishna was a divine being and not an ordinary person. All were deeply moved by his company, and they forgot about their usual routine. It was late that day when they finished their bath and prayers.

On this occasion Sri Ramakrishna said: "If any other kind of animal comes to a herd of cattle, they turn on it and gore it with their horns. But if a cow joins the herd, they lick its body and welcome it as one of themselves. . . . That's what has happened to us here today." Then, addressing Keshab, he added, "Your tail has dropped off." He went on to explain: "As long as the tadpole has its tail it can only live in the water, but when the tail drops off, it can live on land as well as in the water. As long as a man wears the tail of ignorance he can only live in the world, but when the tail drops off he can live either in the knowledge of God or in the world, whichever he pleases. Your mind, Keshab, has reached that state now. You can live in the world and still be aware of God." A holy man can recognize another holy man. After this visit Sri Ramakrishna and Keshab became close to each other.

From time to time Keshab would visit Sri Ramakrishna at Dakshineswar with his followers, and Sri Ramakrishna also would come to Keshab's house at Calcutta with Hriday. On such occasions Keshab's neighbours and relations would assemble at his house to meet and listen to Sri Ramakrishna. These spiritual discourses continued for five to seven hours at a time. What a joyful and festive occasion it always was! Every year after the annual festival of the New Dispensation, Keshab would visit Sri Ramakrishna at Dakshineswar, travelling by steamer or boat with his Brahmo followers. Sometimes he would go to his Belgharia retreat and send a carriage to take Sri Ramakrishna there. To have Sri Ramakrishna's holy company was a part of the festival. Keshab's life was very much influenced by Sri Ramakrishna, and Sri Ramakrishna's by Keshab. It was due to the influence of Sri Ramakrishna that the concept of the Motherhood of God was enkindled to a great extent in the Brahmo Samaj. Keshab learned from Sri Ramakrishna how to call on God as Mother and how to pray to and make demands on her. For, in spite of the devotional aspect in it, the Brahmo religion was more a religion of faith and rationalism. However, Sri Ramakrishna's influence added more sweetness and fervour to it. With Keshab's help Sri Ramakrishna also advanced more towards the formless God,[1] acquired a catholic religious attitude, and learned to some extent the etiquette of social life.

After Keshab began writing articles for the *Indian Mirror* and *Dharmatattwa* about Sri Ramakrishna's pure life and lofty teachings, people came to know about him. A small pamphlet, *Paramahamser Ukti* (Sayings of Sri Ramakrishna), was also published and distributed. Besides the Brahmos, men and women of other classes now began going to Sri Ramakrishna for spiritual guidance. It was not the aim of Sri Ramakrishna to start a new religion, to preach, or to form a sect. If anybody asked for advice, he would say: "Go to Keshab. He is meant for that." Later, Sri Ramakrishna gave spiritual instructions to many people, and many educated young men became his devoted disciples.

Sri Ramakrishna had wonderful insight by which he could recognize the inner nature of a person. Seeing someone's face or hearing a few words from him, he could at once know what kind of person he was. Sri Ramakrishna once said: "Many years ago I went one Wednesday to the Brahmo Samaj at Jorasanko. I saw at that time young Keshab meditating at the pulpit and other worshippers seated on both sides of him. I studied Keshab intently and observed that his mind was absorbed in Brahman, that his float had sunk. From that time my mind was drawn to him. The rest of the congregation, I noticed, were seated with weapons, as if ready to fight. Observing their faces I realized that their minds were full of passion, ego, greed, and attachment to sense objects." Ever since then Sri Ramakrishna was fond of Keshab, but the latter did not know anything about it. Many years later they met at Belgharia. It was necessary for the Brahmos at that time to have contact with Sri Ramakrishna. We have to accept it as Divine Providence.

We do not accept all the religious views of Sri Ramakrishna, and some of them are not approved of by the Brahmo religion, but we have no doubt that his exalted life, endowed with yoga and devotion, was utilized by Providence for the betterment of the New Dispensation. Keshab — the great religious leader and world famous scholar — would sit next to the unlettered Sri Ramakrishna like a disciple or younger brother. He listened to Sri Ramakrishna with love and respect, and he never argued with him. Keshab absorbed the spiritual treasures of Sri

---

[1] Sri Ramakrishna had realized Brahman, the Impersonal God as early as 1866 under the guidance of Tota Puri, and for six months he had been constantly in that state. This was nearly ten years before he met Keshab Chandra Sen. He had also realized, before meeting Keshab, the Islam and the Christian ideals of the Godhead: formless but with attributes. Regarding catholicity, it has been mentioned previously by the writer.

Ramakrishna in his own life. He demonstrated how to respect a holy person and how to imbibe holiness.

Whenever we visited Dakshineswar, Sri Ramakrishna always served some refreshments. And when he went to Keshab's house he was also served with luchis and vegetable curries. He was very fond of ice cream. Keshab would always try to get some ice cream for him, and sometimes he would send it to Dakshineswar. Sri Ramakrishna was also fond of jilipis [a sweet]. Once after dinner someone asked him to eat some more. He said, "My stomach is full, but if you give me a jilipi I shall eat it." Then he explained: "During the fair the roads are jammed and over-crowded. At that time it is difficult for a man to pass through the street. But if the Viceroy's carriage comes along, all other carriages make room for his to pass. Similarly, the stomach makes room for jilipis."

One day Sri Ramakrishna went to a Brahmo temple with a Brahmo minister. When he heard that three hundred people were worshipping there and chanting God's name, he went into ecstasy. He never attended the service in the temple, for how could he do so? Even before the service had begun he was in ecstasy.

Sri Ramakrishna went to see Keshab during his last illness, and they talked about profound spiritual topics. When Sri Ramakrishna later received word of Keshab's death, he was overwhelmed with grief. He said: "Keshab's death has taken half my life away. He was like a great banyan tree, giving comfort and shelter to thousands of people. Where will you get another such tree? We are like betel-nut and palm trees, incapable of sheltering a single soul."

Sri Ramakrishna's humility was marvellous. As soon as he met a person he would salute him before the other could do so. He never cared for his teachings to be published, or that publicity be given about him in the papers, or that his photograph be taken. It was impossible to take his photograph except when he was in samadhi and had lost all outer consciousness. During samadhi he neither fell on the ground uncon-scious nor stepped on anybody around him. At that time he would either sit or stand motionless. Such a great soul is a living example of divine grace. His life is a beacon light of hope to people whose lifeboats are almost sinking in the ocean of relative existence, covered with dark ignorance.

We read about Chaitanya and other great souls of the world, but we were blessed to have seen the divine life of Sri Ramakrishna with our own eyes. He never cared for the present-day civilization, he never attended any meetings or gave any lectures, nor did he read books or newspapers. He demonstrated to the world how one can attain a high spiritual state through divine grace and one's earnestness alone, without help from anyone. As a swan takes only the milk and rejects the water, so Sri Ramakrishna took only the essence of Hinduism and rejected the nonessentials.

He was like a simple child. The examples he used in his teachings he wanted to see with his own eyes. For that reason he expressed a desire to ride a steamer. Once Keshab picked Sri Ramakrishna up from Dakshineswar in a steamer. Some Brahmo followers were with them. Sri Ramakrishna was pleased to hear the *jhak-jhak* sound of the steamer. One of our friends requested him to look through the telescope of the steamer, but he replied: "My mind is now attached to God. How can I withdraw it from him and put it on this telescope?"

Sri Ramakrishna passed away on August 16, 1886. His body was placed on a cot and decorated with flowers, garlands, and ochre cloths. The disciples and friends of Sri Ramakrishna took the dust of his feet and then carried the cot to the Cossipore cremation ground. Nearly one hundred and fifty people followed the procession, and a group of Vaishnavites led it, singing kirtan with drums and cymbals. Some Brahmo devotees and four ministers from the New Dispensation — Amritalal Basu, Trailokya Nath Sanyal, Prankrishna Datta, and I — joined Sri Ramakrishna's funeral service. Banners imprinted with the symbols of different religions — the Trident and Om of Hinduism, the Spud of Buddhism, the Crescent of Islam, and the Cross of Christianity — were carried at the head of the procession.

After reaching the cremation ground, the devotees sang kirtan, encircling Sri Ramakrishna's body. Then at the devotees' request Trailokya Nath Sanyal sang three or four songs befitting the occasion. Sri Ramakrishna had been very fond of his melodious singing. Finally Sri Ramakrishna's body was placed on the funeral pyre, and the devotees again bowed down to him. His eyes were slightly open, and his face had a sweet smile. He had left his body in samadhi. I heard that before he entered into mahasamadhi the previous night, he had uttered thrice, "Kali." By evening Sri Ramakrishna's pure body was consumed by fire.

[From: *Adi Kathamrita* by Girish Chandra Sen. Ed. by Shyamal Basu. (Calcutta: Ananya Prakashan), 1983; *Prabuddha Bharata*, February 1936]

31

Krishna Kumar Mittra

Krishna Kumar Mittra (1851-1936) was born at Tangayal (Mymensingh) in Bangladesh. He joined the Brahmo Samaj in 1874 and later became one of its leaders. In 1908 he was banished from India, along with Aswini Kumar Datta and Pulin Chandra Das, because of his work in the Indian National Movement, of which he was a pioneer.

I came to Calcutta in 1871. At that time I knew nothing about Sri Ramakrishna, and it was only after some years that I even heard about him. I first saw him in 1881 at the home of Nepal Chandra and Gopal Chandra Mallik in Sinduriapati, Calcutta. They were members of the Brahmo Samaj, and a religious service was held once a week in their home. Sri Ramakrishna was very fond of Nepal Babu and Gopal Babu and sometimes attended their religious service. On this occasion, when I first met Sri Ramakrishna, Pandit Shivanath Shastri conducted the worship (*upasana*) and Vijay Krishna Goswami lectured. The closing song was: "O Mother, what love you have for your children! When we think of it, tears stream from our eyes."

Sri Ramakrishna had been sitting calmly until he heard the line, "What love you have for your children." These words moved him deeply, and he stood up. His body shivered in ecstasy, and within a moment or two he lost consciousness. His nephew, who was always by his side, began to chant "Om, Om" in his ear. After some time Sri Ramakrishna regained outer consciousness and sat down. He said: "Please forgive me. I am sorry to disturb your service." But we were very impressed to see his wonderful ecstasy.

Another day he suddenly came to the temple of the Sadharan Brahmo Samaj. His nephew was with him. Pandit Shivanath Shastri was conducting the service and Narendra Nath Datta [later, Swami Vivekananda] sang. I don't remember the song, but again, while listening to the singing, Sri Ramakrishna lost consciousness, and again his nephew chanted "Om, Om" until he became normal.

The third time I met Sri Ramakrishna was at the garden house of Benimadhav Pal in Sinthi, North Calcutta. Beni Babu had a shop at Radhabazar in Calcutta. Every year he arranged a Brahmo festival in his garden and sumptuously fed his guests, and every year Sri Ramakrishna attended this festival. I saw him there three or four times. He would come early in the morning and stay till evening. And here, as he did at other festivals and services, he would merge into samadhi at the time of worship.

Beni Babu always arranged a grand feast. While eating, Sri Rama-krishna used to tell many stories. And even after the meal was finished the same spiritual talk continued.

Once this question arose: "Is it possible for a person to know the infinite God?" Sri Ramakrishna replied, "As one feels the touch of air, so do I feel the touch of God."

I still remember those unforgettable words.

[From: *Udbodhan*, vol. 38, no. 2, 1935]

32

Upadhyay Brahmabandhav

Bhavani Charan Banerjee, better known as Upadhyay Brahmabandhav, was at first a staunch Brahmo and a follower of Keshab Chandra Sen. As a speaker, leader, and editor of the Bengali daily Sandhya, *he was well known. Later he left Keshab's New Dispensation and joined the Anglican Church, and after that, the Roman Catholic church.*

Who is Ramakrishna? Well, that I do not know. But this much I can say, that in the firmament of Bengal no other moon of such sweetness has risen since Lord Gauranga. I have compared him with the moon. Even the moon is not spotless, but this moon of Ramakrishna is absolutely free from spots. Ah, his divine body was pure and bright like fire itself. Never was it contaminated by the slightest touch of sex. When he was married, his wife was only six. Ten years after his marriage he met for the second time this woman, who was chastity personified. Ramakrishna worshipped her when she was sixteen as the Divine Mother. He followed all the details of Hindu rituals and then offered his rosary at her feet [*i.e., the result of his sadhana*]. After this consecration Ramakrishna shone in his fullest splendour, like the full moon with its bright halo. What a beautiful life! It is unique in human history. Many saints and prophets renounced their wives for God, but Ramakrishna's renunciation was not of an ordinary type. It was the highest acceptance. The light of the moon cannot be separate from the moon. And neither did this woman, the incarnation of chastity, live apart from Sri Ramakrishna. Ever since that unique worship she was always by Sri Ramakrishna's side as his Shakti [power]. Go once and sit for a while at the blessed feet of this woman, so reverentially worshipped by Sri Ramakrishna. Through her grace you will be able to understand and realize the greatness of Sri Ramakrishna. You will be blessed indeed![1]

---

[1] When this article was written, Sri Sarada Devi was alive.

Who is this Ramakrishna? He was a knower of Brahman. Sri Ramakrishna once said: "What Brahman is cannot be described. All scriptures in the world — the Vedas, the Puranas — have been defiled, like food that has been touched by the tongue, for they have been uttered by the tongue. Only one thing has not been defiled in this way, and that is Brahman. It is like a dream of a dumb person, who is unable to express what he saw in his dream.

Who is this Ramakrishna? He is the prince of sadhakas [spiritual aspirants]. He practised the main spiritual disciplines of various religious sects of the world with great sincerity, intensity, and love, and thus he realized God in many ways. He attained samadhi by following the path of yoga, tasted divine love by following the path of the gopis, and saw the Divine Mother by following the path of Tantra. He also practised sadhana according to Islam and Christianity. Thus Sri Ramakrishna's life depicts the harmony of all religions. Fully established in his consciousness of the immutable Brahman and keeping intact the continuity of the Eternal Religion of the Aryans, Sri Ramakrishna welcomed with open arms all the diversities of spiritual life and enriched India by incorporating in it all the new spiritual forces and directing all of them to Advaita [Oneness].

Salutations to Sri Ramakrishna, conqueror of lust and gold, knower of Brahman, king among the devotees, saviour of mankind, and a deep ocean where the rivers of all religions merged.

[From: *Prabuddha Bharata*, February 1936]

33

Sarada Sundari Devi

Sarada Sundari Devi was the mother of Keshab Chandra Sen, the well-known Brahmo leader.

Sri Ramakrishna once went to visit the Adi Brahmo Samaj and saw three persons meditating there. Afterwards he said, "One [Keshab Chandra Sen] among these three has experienced the truth." He later became acquainted with Keshab. Sri Ramakrishna visited our house quite often, and I first met him in our hall on the third floor.

Once during the winter festival of the Brahmo Samaj, he came to the Lily Cottage [Keshab's home]. When the kirtan [singing] was over I said to him, "Sir, please have some refreshments." He thought a while and said, "Yes, the Divine Mother told me to eat a jilipi [a sweet] at Keshab's house." I gave him a jilipi, which he took in his hand and ate. Then while leaving, he said to Keshab, "The Divine Mother also told me to eat an ice cream cone at Keshab's house." Keshab was wondering where he could get an ice cream cone, as there was no shop nearby. Just then, however, an ice cream vendor came by. Keshab bought an ice cream cone, and Sri Ramakrishna ate it joyfully.

Sri Ramakrishna and Keshab danced that day, holding each other's hands during the kirtan. When the function was over he said to me: "Blessed is the womb that gave birth to such a wonderful son! In the future many people of the world will be delighted to have Keshab's company."

I was very fond of Sri Ramakrishna, and I used to visit Dakshineswar off and on. Now I don't remember all his wonderful, inspiring teachings except one thing he said: "God laughs when two brothers divide their land with a string, saying to each other, 'This side is mine and that side is yours.' He laughs and says to himself, 'The whole universe belongs to me, but they say they own this portion or that portion.'" Sri Ramakrishna used to tell many wonderful stories, but now I don't remember them all.

[From: *Samasamayik Drishtite Sri Ramakrishna Paramahamsa*, by Brajendra Nath Bandyopadhyay & Sajani Kanta Das (Calcutta: General Printers & Publ. Pvt. Ltd.), 1968]

34

Trailokya Nath Sanyal

Trailokya Nath Sanyal was a staunch follower of Keshab Chandra Sen and was known as the singing apostle of the New Dispensation Church. He is famous for his devotional compositions and is the author of Keshab Charit, *the life of Keshab in Bengali.*

It is necessary to mention something about Keshab's relationship with Sri Ramakrishna Paramahamsa of Dakshineswar. Keshab first met Sri Ramakrishna at the garden house of Belgharia, and from that first meeting they became very close to each other. Holy men alone bring to light other holy men who are forgotten or unknown to the world. In this present age Keshab not only introduced Jesus, Moses, Chaitanya, Buddha, Socrates, and Muhammad to the modern, educated spiritual aspirants and created a respect for religious personalities, but he also made Sri Ramakrishna known to these aspirants.

The Brahmo Samaj added much to its devotional aspect from an exchange of religious ideas between these two great souls. It was Keshab's nature to assimilate whatever good there was in anybody. His was not an exact imitation, but he would give a new form to whatever he learned from others. What he learned he could develop tenfold. Sri Ramakrishna's humility, childlike simplicity, faith, and devotion influenced Keshab's yoga-sadhana, renunciation, devotion, ethics, and longing for God. The manifestation of the devotional aspect and the idea of the Motherhood of God which are seen nowadays in the Brahmo Samaj are mainly due to Sri Ramakrishna. As Sri Ramakrishna talked like a child with his blissful Mother and sang and danced in ecstasy during kirtan [singing], Keshab also followed this same sadhana in his last days. Many know that the worship of God as Mother and the use of simple and colloquial language in worship and prayer, which Keshab later introduced, were the result of his coming in contact with this great soul. But how many, other than Keshab, were able to assimilate these ideas?

At the same time Keshab's influence expanded Sri Ramakrishna's religious outlook. Sri Ramakrishna had previously not recognized free will or the possibility of householders acquiring devotion and renunciation. When the topic of preaching religion would arise, he would motion to Keshab, saying, "He is meant for that."

Sri Ramakrishna once said: "Many years ago I went to the Adi Brahmo Samaj where I saw everyone sitting silent with eyes closed. It appeared to me that internally they were all fighting. But seeing Keshab I found that his float had sunk." Sri Ramakrishna meant that the fish was nibbling at Keshab's bait, i.e., he was near to God-realization. He had also heard from the Divine Mother that her work would be done by this person [i.e., Keshab]. At present, Sri Ramakrishna's influence is helping the cause of the Brahmo Samaj in a nonsectarian spirit. The religious world has gained much in many ways by the meeting of these two great souls. All those lofty religious ideals to be found in the various sects and subsects of Hinduism have found a place in the Brahmo Samaj through the followers of the New Dispensation. What was at one time a very dry, puritanical religion has thus become simple and sweet. What an ocean of difference between the dry discussions on Vedantic knowledge and the conversations with the Divine Mother like a child!

[From: *Samasamayik Drishtite Sri Ramakrishna Paramahamsa,* by Brajendra Nath Bandyopadhyay & Sajani Kanta Das (Calcutta: General Printers & Publ. Pvt. Ltd.), 1968]

35

Priyanath Mallik

Priyanath Mallik was a devoted follower of Keshab Chandra Sen and a minister of the New Dispensation Church.

I have had the blessed privilege of seeing Sri Ramakrishna and of coming in contact with him. Moreover, I prayed, sang, and danced with him. I cannot recall now the exact date that I first saw him, but as far as I remember I was present at four or five meetings between Keshab and Ramakrishna during the years 1880 and 1883. I also visited him at other times with my young friends.

Whenever I came to see him, Sri Ramakrishna would notice me first, and before I could nod to him, he would nod to me. He conversed and chatted with us and spoke in parables, and he explained religious truths by means of simple, homely illustrations. He also told us the stories of his sadhana — how he was driven by a "storm of earnestness" and how he sought the company of the seekers of God from different religious denominations.

In relating the story of his first meeting with Keshab at the Adi Brahmo Samaj, he said: "I did not know Keshab then. I saw three Acharyas [ministers] sitting on the dais. The middle one struck me as the one whose fishing line float had sunk." He meant by this that Keshab's soul was immersed in God. After that he was eager to become acquainted with Keshab.

In 1875 Sri Ramakrishna went to Keshab's house at Coolootola, and not finding him at home went to the Belgharia garden house where Keshab was practising sadhana [spiritual disciplines] with his followers. Keshab named this garden "tapovana" [a hermitage].

Once we went with Keshab by steamer to visit Sri Ramakrishna at Dakshineswar. Sri Ramakrishna went into samadhi holding Keshab. Afterwards they both danced, clasping each other's hands and singing, "The Mother is ours and we are the Mother's." It was a heavenly scene.

On another occasion Sri Ramakrishna came to Keshab's "Lily Cottage," where he talked, sang, and danced. At such meetings Sri Ramakrishna almost monopolized the conversation. Keshab hardly said anything. He only expressed his appreciation by smiling and nodding his head. In the midst of the meeting, when a tray of fruits and sweets was brought, Sri Ramakrishna said: "I shall take only two jilipis. They make room in the stomach, just like when the Viceroy's carriage drives by, the road is cleared of all traffic."

Sri Ramakrishna came to see Keshab during his last illness, but I was not present then. After Keshab passed away Sri Ramakrishna cried like a little child. He met Keshab's mother and consoled her saying: "Blessed is the womb that gave birth to such a wonderful son! Several generations will be benefitted from his life."

Sri Ramakrishna was a veritable child — a guileless, saintly soul who was intoxicated with the spirit of God. Narendra [Swami Vivekananda] was a close friend of mine. We held prayer meetings at 1, Nanda Kumar Choudhuri Lane, Calcutta, where Rajmohan Basu lived. I used to conduct the services and Naren was our hymn singer. One evening when we were having our service, Sri Ramakrishna came with his disciple Ram Chandra Datta. I did not know that he was there. After the service Sri Ramakrishna began to sing a devotional song in his sweet voice. I at once recognized him, and we then enjoyed a spiritual feast. Addressing me as "Acharya," he asked me to visit him more often. He particularly requested Naren to see him [at Dakshineswar], and he told him, "I am deeply impressed with your singing."

Sri Ramakrishna was an image worshipper in his early life, but he was later lifted out of the grossness of such worship to have a clear vision of God without form. Thus I believe that it was to show people the way to evolve from image worship to Spirit worship that Sri Ramakrishna was sent by God.

Keshab loved and honoured Sri Ramakrishna as a God-intoxicated devotee of the Hindu school of culture and a renouncer of lust and gold. Sri Ramakrishna was strongly averse to forming a sect, and he discouraged any false show of piety, such as wearing an ochre cloth. Not only did he vehemently denounce attachment for lust and gold, but he had no physical relationship with his wife, and he did not touch any money.

The last rites of Sri Ramakrishna were performed by his disciples and our friends. I was one of the party who carried the sacred relics of the saint in a procession to Ram Datta's Yogodyana at Kankurgachi, Calcutta.

[From: *Prabuddha Bharata*, February 1936]

36

Kshirod Chandra Sen

Kshirod Chandra Sen, a follower of Keshab Chandra Sen, became well known as the author of Sidelights on Western Civilization.

I have been trying to recall the great events of my life that took place in 1879. I was then in my second year at the General Assembly's College, Calcutta. At the end of that year I passed the I.A. [Intermediate of Arts] examination. But the most important event that comes to my mind is my meeting with Sri Ramakrishna at Dakshineswar. This opened a new world, a new current of thought with a new orientation concerning the problems of life as conceived by my immature, youthful mind. Not that it changed the course of my life at once. Indeed my ideas were vague and hazy, and it took many years for them to develop a definite shape. But I deeply felt that there was something higher to pursue in life than a graduate's diploma or a comfortable post in the public service. Both of these achievements came to me and subsequently proved to be hollow.

More than half a century has passed since that memorable day, but I still feel proud that I gathered something on that occasion which helps me to live cheerfully even now. I cannot clearly describe what I got. It works invisibly, but its reality is unmistakable.

One morning in October 1879, ten students from two boarding houses met together and decided that they would spend the evening at the beautiful temple garden of Dakshineswar, where a holy man named Sri Ramakrishna lived. He was then known by only a few, but to those he was reverentially referred to as "Paramahamsa" [an illumined soul — literally, a great swan]. The title was puzzling to my uncultivated mind. I instinctively tried to associate it with an amphibious bird.

The oldest of the group, whom I shall indicate by the initials C.K., told me the plan and asked if I would like to join the party. He said that the excursion would cost about three annas for passage money and other incidental expenses. And he added that the visit would enable me to meet a great holy man who had already been interviewed several times by Keshab Chandra Sen and Pratap Chandra Majumdar. These were both leaders of the Brahmo Samaj, for whom I had great reverence and who I considered to be men of knowledge and devotion.

Keshab was a distinguished speaker, a profound thinker, a great man, who was honoured by Queen Victoria and the British public. To me he was the founder of the true religion for humanity, the latest prophet in the history of the world. If such a person thought the holy man of Dakshineswar worthy of successive visits, I would be disrespectful if I failed to avail myself of this opportunity to visit my guru's guru. To be perfectly honest, I had no idea that we were going not merely to meet Sri Ramakrishna, but also to hear him speak and to receive instructions from him on spirituality and ideal morality.

We arrived at the landing ghat of the Kali temple at 4:30 P.M. There seemed to be no one else at the place. We walked around looking in all the doors in expectation of seeing the holy man somewhere. At last we saw him in a small, narrow room in the northwestern corner of the temple complex. He was in deep meditation. The front door of his room was open, and the afternoon sun was falling on his face. We looked in through another door. A second man, who seemed to be an attendant, with a prominent sacred thread on his shoulder, warned us against entering the room and politely told us to wait outside. He then suggested that we walk in the garden until Sri Ramakrishna was comfortable enough to see us. Strictly following the instructions of the attendant, we left and walked around the garden, looking at several buildings in the compound.

At sunset we made a desperate attempt to meet Sri Ramakrishna as he was slowly walking in an open area to the north of his room. There was a cluster of large trees, and under one of them two Hindustani monks, whose bodies were smeared with ashes, were lighting a fire and arranging materials for cooking a simple meal. Sri Ramakrishna approached them and said something which I either did not hear or do not remember. One of them said by way of a reply, "You are a *Mahatma* [a great soul]." Sri Ramakrishna smiled and walked slowly away. I cannot say why he smiled. Any other man would have either politely acknowledged the compliment or denied its truth. It seems that evasiveness in personal matters is a common trait of prophets. Christ shared it. Other prophets also had it. Keshab alone was explicit. In a speech delivered at the Town Hall, he told the audience that he was not a prophet but only an exceptional man.

When an earthen lamp was lighted in Sri Ramakrishna's bedroom we were invited to come in. We sat on a mat on the floor in front of a bed where he was seated. He talked on various topics and gave no indication that he was anything but an ordinary man living in ordinary surroundings. His knowledge of men and manners seemed limited, and though his wit at times lapsed into vulgarity, there was no malice in it.

He spoke about Keshab with affection and an easy air of personal superiority which we associate with seniority in age and intimacy of relationship. I tried to feel offended but was checked by a sense of reverence creeping into my heart. He spoke of Keshab as a good young man in need of spiritual help to guide him in life. It now seems to me that if Keshab had been a young man at the time and if he had not been the acknowledged leader of a reforming church, he would have taken the place that Vivekananda subsequently occupied in Sri Ramakrishna's heart.

Sri Ramakrishna said, "Keshab came to me one day, and, as he was still living a married life, I told him that it was high time he practised celibacy." He also told us: "One evening I went at Keshab's request to visit his group. [*He meant that he attended the service at the New Dispensation Church at Mechuabazar Street in Calcutta.*] There was a fairly large gathering of men, but the whole show seemed to me like a meeting of monkeys who sometimes sit down together as if they are plunged in deep meditation, and then suddenly disperse in all directions to carry on their privileged and predatory profession in the orchards and vegetable gardens of the neighbourhood."

Sri Ramakrishna's earlier remark on Keshab's personal life had been excusable, but this reference to the general misbehaviour of his followers seemed highly offensive. The reference was too sweeping, and it was indirectly a reflection on me and most of my companions, for we were Keshab's followers in the pursuit of a higher life.

Sri Ramakrishna's attendant then called us to have supper, which consisted of a few luchis [bread] fried in rancid ghee [clarified butter], and a vegetable curry. After supper a common mat was spread for us on the verandah so we could sleep. I was restless the whole night. Sri Ramakrishna's face was not handsome, as every impartial observer knows, and his words so far had not been inspiring. I almost thought it was disappointing. Even my body did not escape. There were bugs in the mat and mosquitoes in the air.

The next morning I suggested that we return to Calcutta at the first opportunity that presented itself. My companions evidently felt the same way and immediately agreed that we should leave, except for C.K., who yielded after a little demurring. It was decided that we should take the first train at Bally. C.K. suggested that we wait until we were in a position to salute Sri Ramakrishna and take leave of him. We were strolling around when C.K. saw Sri Ramakrishna walking with his attendant in the temple garden. We hurried towards him. One of us told him that we wanted to cross the river to Bally and take the train to Howrah. The attendant said that that was not an easy way to travel. But Sri Ramakrishna smiled and said to the attendant: "You are an ignorant fellow. In pursuit of pleasure a person will gladly suffer pain. The railway journey will be a pleasant variation for these young men."

We bowed, but in accepting our salute, Sri Ramakrishna expressed wonder as to what we had come there for. C.K. promptly replied, "We came for instructions, but unfortunately there was something wrong in our choice of time." Sri Ramakrishna smiled and said: "What instructions do you want, my children? Sit down and I shall hear what you want." We sat down, and Sri Ramakrishna sat near us. C.K. then asked questions and Sri Ramakrishna answered. But before stating those questions and answers I shall digress a little to describe in my own way the manner in which Sri Ramakrishna spoke, for the manner seemed even more impressive than the matter, which, of course, was charming, particularly to my youthful mind.

His sentences were terse, usually consisting of three or four words each. They were seldom grammatically complete, but were pregnant with meaning. Certainly his thoughts were coherent, but his sentences sometimes seemed discontinuous. It took time to logically connect consecutive sentences. But Sri Ramakrishna spoke slowly. He paused perceptibly at the end of each sentence, and this enabled us to connect his thoughts. He easily and artistically arranged flowers of thoughts, but seldom strung them together. He did not care to use thread and needle. But he spoke with the confidence of a prophet. He seemed to be an organized personification of inspiration and expression.

If brevity is the soul of wit, it is the soul of wisdom also. Sri Ramakrishna possessed all three at once and possessed them to an exceptional degree. The only parallel that suggests itself is Nietzsche. The one lived in the unseen world and the other dwelt on mundane experiences. The one worshipped the God of Love; the other, the God of Power. The one said, "Thy will be done"; the other insisted on the power of the human will. The sentences were discontinuous and unstrung in both cases. They were hard to grasp. But Nietzsche's sentences were long and Sri Ramakrishna's were short. Nietzsche wrote and Sri Ramakrishna spoke.

I shall now give some of the questions which C.K. asked and their answers:

Q: "Why is Krishna painted dark?"

A: "People suffer from the illusion of remoteness. The sky surrounds you. The sky is in the firmament. They are identical. The one is bright.

The other looks blue. Take a close look at Krishna. Look at him fully in the face. He is bright."

Q: "Is submission to a guru absolutely necessary for salvation?"

A: "You wish to go to Hooghly. You may walk. You may hire a boat. You may get a passage on a steamer. The question is one of speed only. If you are earnest, you will arrive at Hooghly. You may stop the boat at Srerampore and return. You may halt there. You may jump into the river and die. Be earnest. Have no fear."

Q: "Which is better: to be a monk or a householder?"

A: "You have no choice. Your will is not free. A few men become monks. The majority live as householders. Both ways of life are difficult. People suppose the life of the householder is natural. Diversity is a divine law. Shukadeva was a true monk. He was naked. Women bathing in the tank were not ashamed to look at him. But they hid themselves in the water when his old father appeared. King Janaka played with two swords, one in each hand. He reconciled the two kinds of life. In essence they are not conflicting. The great thing is to escape contamination — undue attachment to worldly interests. The mud fish lives in the mud. It is never soiled by it. A human being is not a mere fish. He is surrounded by dirt, mud, venom, etc. How to live untouched by them? Milk poured into water loses its sweetness. It loses its power of nourishment. Water cannot saturate butter. Butter must be churned early in the morning. It is vain to churn milk for butter at midday. Grown-up trees are not spoiled by the cow. She chews on the young saplings. They must be fenced. Make up your minds, my children, accordingly. Acidity is persistent. The sight of tamarind [*which is very sour and causes acidity*] has a charm for one who suffers from it. A man may resolve to avoid tamarind, but his resolution must be strong.

"The green coconut is filled with water. Shake it. (He brought his hands together against his left ear, as if he were shaking a coconut.) You hear no sound. The water, the shell, and the fibres all seem to be one and the same thing. Then shake the ripe coconut. The water makes a sound. When completely dry, there is no water in the shell, and the kernel is separated from the shell. Shake it. The kernel gives a sound of its own. It says: 'I live in the fibrous cover, but that cover does not contaminate me. I have freed myself from attachment.'"

Sri Ramakrishna continued talking like this for quite a long time. I do not remember all that he said. That was more than half a century ago, and I was young and not accustomed to hearing lessons on the value of detachment, complete or partial. Perhaps I did not understand all that I heard. But what I did understand struck a vital chord in my youthful heart. I have never forgotten the music of it. There have, no doubt, been variations in tune and pitch, but it has always been musical, never a jumble of discordant notes. I was then eighteen and I am now seventy-one. Detachment has been the dominant note of my life. I have tried to live like the mud fish, unsoiled by the surrounding mud. I cannot say I have succeeded, but I am convinced that detachment is more congenial to me than attachment. If there is any good in the kind of life I am living, it is largely due to Sri Ramakrishna's discourse on attachment and detachment.

Sri Ramakrishna was then not a famous man. Fame came to him three or four years later, when he began to gather apostles for a new mission. He was successful, for his apostles have undoubtedly made some noise in the world, and the noise has been largely musical. Sri Ramakrishna's mission forms one out of many, but it is not an inconsiderable one. The world is now suffering from cyclonic weather, and nobody knows whether it is going towards a harmonious union or a noisy dispersion. One thing is certain: If disruption comes, nobody will be able to throw any of the blame on Sri Ramakrishna's mission. There is no separation, no malice, no jealousy or spite in it. It wants to unite mankind and to find salvation for all in its own humble way.

[From: *Prabuddha Bharata*, December 1932]

37

Kamakhya Nath Bandyopadhyay

Kamakhya Nath Bandyopadhyay was a Brahmo and a follower of Keshab Chundra Sen.

Sri Ramakrishna first saw Keshab Chandra Sen when Keshab was meditating on the dais of the Adi Brahmo Samaj at Jorasanko, Calcutta. Seeing Keshab, Sri Ramakrishna said: "Of all who are meditating here, this young man's 'float' alone has sunk under water. The 'fish' is biting at the hook." In other words, Sri Ramakrishna saw Keshab's face and realized that his mind was immersed in Brahman.

Sometime after this Sri Ramakrishna went with his nephew Hriday to meet Keshab at his Coolootola residence, but he was told that Keshab had gone to a garden house at Belgharia with his Brahmo followers to conduct a retreat. Sri Ramakrishna immediately went to Belgharia and met Keshab there. They talked about spiritual life for three or four hours, and a strong spiritual relationship was established between the two. After this meeting Keshab wrote in his journals about Sri Ramakrishna's spiritual greatness, steadfast devotion, and longing for God, and thus the public came to know about him. I was attracted to Sri Ramakrishna by reading Keshab's articles and listening to the Brahmos who had witnessed Sri Ramakrishna's ecstasy. Many educated people became interested in knowing him, and I became anxious to meet him. As far as I remember I met Sri Ramakrishna five times and listened to him each time for four or five hours. Sometimes I asked him questions. I don't remember all those conversations in detail, but some important things I do remember.

On my first visit Sri Ramakrishna talked about his first meeting with Keshab at Jorasanko, and on my second visit he narrated how he met Keshab at the retreat house in Belgharia. He said: "When I arrived in

425

Belgharia Keshab had just finished his prayer and meditation. He received me cordially and asked the reason for my visit. I said, 'I hear that you have seen God, so I have come here to hear about it.' Keshab described his experience. Listening to him I understood that Keshab was a very special person, and I went into ecstasy. His words touched my heart. At first Keshab talked and I listened, and then I talked and Keshab listened. Thus we spent four or five hours."

Sri Ramakrishna quite often visited Keshab's Lily Cottage, and I met him there also. Once he said to the Brahmo devotees: "A person who does not speak the truth cannot make any progress in spiritual life. God cannot be realized through deception." Whenever Sri Ramakrishna visited Keshab, the latter fed him various sweets and delicacies. Sri Ramakrishna was fond of jilipis [a sweet].

I shall tell one incident that will make people understand how Sri Ramakrishna was true to his word. One day I went to Dakshineswar with some of my friends. After talking some time he said: "Look, if I say that from today I shall go to answer the call of nature twice, then in the evening, even if I have no urge, I go to the bathroom for the sake of truth."

Sri Ramakrishna was truly an honest person. He never hesitated to speak even a harsh truth. He abhorred hypocrisy in the name of religion and did not care for any external show, such as the ochre cloth, a rosary around the neck, or religious marks on the forehead.

Sri Ramakrishna had steadfast devotion as well as tremendous longing for God. Once he decided to realize God according to the Islamic path. He began to pray five times a day, and he ate Muslim food and wore Muslim dress. As a result of this sadhana he had a vision within a few days of a radiant person with a long beard and Muslim dress.

Undoubtedly Keshab was a spiritual companion of Sri Ramakrishna's. At the time of the winter festival of the Brahmo Samaj, Sri Ramakrishna would come to the Lily Cottage and sing and dance holding Keshab's hand. Keshab was also delighted to have his company. As Keshab was influenced by Sri Ramakrishna, so also Sri Ramakrishna was influenced by Keshab. During Keshab's last illness Sri Ramakrishna came to see him at the Lily Cottage. He said to Keshab, "Keshab, if you leave, with whom shall I talk?" After Keshab's passing away, Sri Ramakrishna was shocked. As a magnet attracts iron, these two great personalities attracted each other.

[From: *Samasamayik Drishtite Sri Ramakrishna Paramahamsa*, by Brajendra Nath Bandyopadhyay & Sajani Kanta Das (Calcutta: General Printers & Publ. Pvt. Ltd.), 1968]

38

Nagendra Nath Gupta

Nagendra Nath Gupta (1861-1940) went to school with Swami Viveka-
nanda. Many years later, when Nagendra was living in Lahore and
Swami Vivekananda had returned to India after his first trip to the West,
Swamiji stayed at Nagendra's home for a few days. He was an editor of
the Lahore Tribune.

In 1881 Keshab Chandra Sen, accompanied by a fairly large party, went on board a steam yacht belonging to his son-in-law, Maharaja Nripendra Narayan Bhup of Cooch Bihar, to Dakshineswar to meet Ramakrishna Paramahamsa. I had the good fortune to be included in that party. We did not land, but Ramakrishna, accompanied by his nephew Hriday, who brought a basket of puffed rice and some sandesh [an Indian sweet] for us, boarded the steamer which steamed up the river towards Somra. Ramakrishna was wearing a red-bordered dhoti and a shirt which was not buttoned. We all stood up as he came on board, and Keshab took Ramakrishna by the hand and made him sit close to him. Keshab then beckoned to me to come and sit near them, and I sat down almost touching their feet.

Ramakrishna was dark complexioned, kept a beard, and his eyes never opened very wide and were introspective. He was of medium height, slender almost to leanness and very frail-looking. As a matter of fact, he had an exceptionally nervous temperament, and was extremely sensitive to the slightest physical pain. He spoke with a slight but charming stammer in very plain Bengali, mixing the two "yous" [formal and informal address] frequently. Practically all the talking was done by Ramakrishna, and the rest, including Keshab himself, were respectful and eager listeners. It is now more than forty-five years ago that this happened and yet almost everything that he said is indelibly impressed on my memory. Ramakrishna stayed in the boat for about eight hours, and except for the few minutes during which he remained in samadhi he never ceased speaking. I have never heard any other man speak as he did. It was an unbroken flow of profound spiritual truths and experiences welling up from the perennial spring of his own devotion and wisdom. The similes and metaphors, the apt illustrations, were as striking as they were original. At times as he spoke he would draw a little closer to Keshab until part of his body was unconsciously resting in Keshab's lap, but Keshab sat perfectly still and made no movement to withdraw himself.

After he had sat down Ramakrishna glanced around him and expressed his approval of the company sitting nearby, saying: "Good, good. They all have good large eyes." Then he peered at a young man wearing English clothes, sitting at a distance on a capstan. "Who is that? He looks like a sahib." Keshab smilingly explained that he was a young Bengali who had just returned from England. Ramakrishna laughed: "That's right. One feels afraid of a sahib." (The young man was Kumar Gajendra Narayan of Cooch Bihar, who shortly afterwards married Keshab's second daughter.) The next moment he lost all interest in the people present and began to speak of the various ways in which he used to perform his spiritual practices: "Sometimes I would fancy myself to be a brahminy duck calling for its mate." There is a poetic tradition in Sanskrit that the male and female of a brace of brahminy ducks spend the night on the opposite shores of a river and keep calling to each other. Again, "I would be the kitten calling for the mother cat and there would be the response of the mother." After speaking in this way for some time he suddenly pulled himself up and said with the smile of a child, "Everything about secret spiritual disciplines should not be told." He explained that it was impossible to express in language the ecstasy of divine communion when the human soul loses itself in the contemplation of the deity.

Then he looked at some of the faces around him and spoke at length on the indications of character by physiognomy. Every feature of the human face was expressive of some particular trait of character. The eyes were the most important, but all other features, the forehead, the ears, the nose, the lips, and the teeth were helpful in the reading of character. And so the marvellous monologue went on until Ramakrishna began to speak of the *nirakara* [formless] Brahman. "The manifestation of the Formless has to be realized." He repeated the word *nirakara* two or three times, and then quietly passed into samadhi, as a diver slips into the fathomless deep. While he was unconscious, Keshab Chandra Sen explained that recently there had been some conversation between Ramakrishna and him about the nirakara Brahman, and Ramakrishna had appeared to be profoundly moved.

We intently watched Ramakrishna Paramahamsa in samadhi. The whole body relaxed and then became slightly rigid. There was no twitching of the muscles or nerves, no movement of any limb. Both his hands lay in his lap with the fingers lightly interlocked. The sitting posture of the body was easy but absolutely motionless. The face was slightly tilted up and in repose. The eyes were nearly but not wholly closed. The eyeballs were not turned up or otherwise deflected, but they were fixed and conveyed no message of outer objects to the brain. The lips were parted in a beatific and indescribable smile, disclosing the gleam of the white teeth. There was something in that wonderful smile which no photograph was ever able to reproduce.

We gazed in silence for several minutes at Ramakrishna's motionless form, and then Trailokya Nath Sanyal, the singing apostle of Keshab Chandra Sen's church, sang a hymn to the accompaniment of a drum and cymbals. As the music swelled in volume, Ramakrishna opened his eyes and looked around him as if he were in a strange place. The music stopped. He looked at us and said, "Who are these people?" And then he vigorously slapped the top of his head several times and cried out, "Go down, go down!"[1] No one made any mention of the ecstasy. Ramakrishna became fully conscious and sang in a pleasant voice, "What a wonderful machine Kali the Mother has made!" After the song he gave a luminous exposition as to how the voice should be trained for singing and the characteristics of a good voice.

It was fairly late in the evening when we returned to Calcutta after leaving Ramakrishna at Dakshineswar.

Ramakrishna paid several visits to Keshab at the latter's house, called the Lily Cottage, on the Upper Circular Road in Calcutta. In connection with these visits there was a beautiful little incident which has not been hitherto recorded. On one occasion when Ramakrishna arrived at Keshab's house, he was met at the entrance gate by some Brahmo missionaries. The first thing that Ramakrishna did was to touch the gate reverently with his forehead. Asked as to what he was doing, he replied: "I am saluting Keshab's mother. When the avatar Narasimha [the man-lion] tore open the body of the wicked giant Hiranyakashipu with his claws, he entwined the intestines round his head, saying, 'These are part of the body out of which Prahlada was born.' Before meeting Keshab I am doing reverence to the mother who bore him."

---

[1] When the kundalini power reaches the crown, i.e., the seventh plane of consciousness, one enters into samadhi. Then it is not possible for a person to talk or move. Sri Ramakrishna's unusual behaviour indicates that he was forcing his mind down to a lower plane so that he could talk to those people about God.

I had seen and heard Ramakrishna in the company of Keshab Chandra Sen. Soon after, I had to go away to the other end of India. The next time I saw him was when he was lying in the peace and silence and supreme majesty of death, surrounded by his disciples and a few others. The unseen angel of Death, his mission accomplished, stood by with folded wings. Nothing could be more serene or more tranquil than the calm countenance upon which we gazed. Ramakrishna's appointed work had been finished, and he had passed away into the peace and rapture of eternal communion.

Ramakrishna Paramahamsa's place is secure among the avatars. He is recognized and worshipped as such by many Hindus all over India. He is revered by members of other communities in India and a number of men and women in the West. Blessed are the eyes that saw him! Blessed are the ears that heard him!

[From: *Vedanta and the West* (Hollywood: Vedanta Press), no. 143, May-June 1960; *Ramakrishna-Vivekananda*, by Nagendra Nath Gupta (Bombay: Sri Ramakrishna Math), 1933]

39

Dr. Abdul Wajij

Dr. Abdul Wajij was a Muslim devotee of Sri Ramakrishna. Originally from East Bengal (now Bangladesh), he studied medicine in Calcutta and later worked at Noakhali Municipality as a doctor. He met the Master in 1885 through Ram Chandra Datta. On Sunday, August 7, 1898, Dr. Wajij came to see Ram Chandra Datta at the Kankurgachi Yogodyana. Ram was delighted to see his old friend after such a long time. The devotees received him cordially. Before going to the shrine, the Muslim doctor removed his shoes and socks, and then he bowed down three times to Sri Ramakrishna. The memory of the Master brought tears to his eyes, which he wiped with a handkerchief. He was a vegetarian and had a calm, sweet nature. At the devotees' request Dr. Wajij told his reminiscences of Sri Ramakrishna.

I was born at Satkhira in the Khulna district of East Bengal. After finishing school I worked for some time at Chuadanga and then moved to Calcutta. I studied homeopathy under Dr. Mahendralal Sarkar and worked as a physician in his charitable dispensary. There I heard about Sri Ramakrishna, the great saint of Dakshineswar, who accepted all religions to be true, and I learned that Ram Babu was his main disciple.

I had believed all along that the truth exists in all religions and that it was important to read all the scriptures of the world. Though I am a Muslim and Islam is my religion, I have no animosity towards people of other faiths. I wanted to visit Sri Ramakrishna, but I decided to make an appointment with Ram Babu first and go with him.

I was then living in Beliaghata (in the eastern part of Calcutta). Just at that time I got dysentery and was unable to go to work for four or five days. I decided that as soon as I felt better I would meet Ram Babu and go to Dakshineswar.

I usually slept late in the morning, but one day I got up very early and heard the whistle of a nearby jute mill. It was 4:30 in the morning and there was a light rain. As it was a Sunday, I decided that I would go to Dakshineswar that day with Ram Babu. My stomach was also better. My friend Abbas Ali (who is now the deputy magistrate at Pheni Bazar in Shyllet) came with me, and after a long search we located Ram Babu's house. As soon as we informed Ram Babu of our intention, he expressed his happiness and we left for Dakshineswar.

When we arrived, Sri Ramakrishna was not in his room. He had gone to the pine grove to answer the call of nature. We waited for him at the Panchavati. When Sri Ramakrishna came there Ram Babu bowed down to him. We decided not to bow down as, according to our religious tradition, we are not supposed to bow down to anyone other than Allah. We were, however, willing to pay proper respect to him. But as soon as he came near he bowed down to us. We were puzzled and were compelled to bow down to him.

Sri Ramakrishna then took us to his room and spread a carpet for us to sit on. He sat on another carpet and began talking to us. While sitting there I started thinking: "We heard that he is a holy man. Then why has he kept us at a distance? Has he given us a separate carpet because we are Muslims and he a Hindu brahmin?" This doubt did not last long, however. While talking about God, Sri Ramakrishna became so intoxicated that he gradually came closer and closer until at last he was sitting on our carpet. This holy man's loving behaviour gave us immense joy.

While coming to Dakshineswar, I had thought of three questions to ask him. But I was amazed to find that there was no need of asking him those questions. He answered all three of them in a convincing manner during his conversation. One of the questions was: "Is it possible to practise yoga while living as a householder?" In the course of conversation he said: "If one enters the family life after practising spiritual disciplines, there is less chance for one to fall from the spiritual path. But it is extremely difficult to make spiritual progress while entangled in family life. If you live in a room full of soot, your body will be a little soiled, however clever you may be. Similarly, if you practise spiritual disciplines while living a householder life, a little attachment will remain somewhere."

We had heard from Ram Babu earlier that Sri Ramakrishna had a pain in his throat, so we did not want to disturb him with too many questions. But he talked of his own accord in such an ecstatic mood that it removed all doubts from our minds and filled our hearts with joy. When Sri Ramakrishna had finished speaking, Ram Babu introduced me to him as a doctor. Sri Ramakrishna looked at me and said: "Very well. Why don't you cure me of the pain in my throat?" I replied: "Sir, if you give me the power I can try. Otherwise I would not be capable of curing the disease of someone like you."

Sri Ramakrishna fed us some sweets. As we said good-bye, he told me, "Come here three more times." But we could not make any more trips to Dakshineswar to see him. We were afraid that if we had too much inclination towards spiritual life we would have to renounce the world.

Our holy Koran mentions some signs of a prophet. We noticed those signs in Sri Ramakrishna. After seeing and listening to him we believed that he was a prophet. I still had some attachment to lust and gold, so I did not dare visit him again at Dakshineswar.

I did meet Sri Ramakrishna once more, however — this time at Ram Babu's house. Amrita, Doctor Sarkar's son, accompanied me there. When we arrived we saw Sri Ramakrishna dancing and singing kirtan with a group of people. As he danced, he went into samadhi. I had never before seen such a thing. I asked Amrita what was going on, and he explained about samadhi.

When the kirtan was over we bowed down to Sri Ramakrishna. He smiled at us and inquired about our welfare. Then he asked me: "Why didn't you visit me again? Try to come now and then." Spiritual talk went on for awhile, and there was also more devotional singing. After that we enjoyed a nice feast at Ram Babu's house and then went home. I never met Sri Ramakrishna again, as I had to move to different cities to earn money.

[From *Yogodyana Mahatmya*, by Jnanendra Nath Biswas (Calcutta: Navabhava Library), 1941]

Aswini Kumar Datta

40

Aswini Kumar Datta

Aswini Kumar Datta (1856-1923) was known as a great educationist, patriot, and lover of God. Through the Brajamohan Institute, which was founded and conducted by him, he inspired and trained many young students. He also led boycott movements and wrote several books on love of God, including Bhaktiyoga, *which is still widely read today.*

It was probably during the autumn holidays of 1881 that I met Sri Ramakrishna the first time. I arrived at Dakshineswar in a country boat and, going up the steps of the landing-ghat, asked someone where the Paramahamsa was.

"There is the Paramahamsa," was the reply. A man was pointed out on the north verandah, which faces the garden. He was sitting reclining against a bolster. He wore a black-bordered cloth. At the sight of the bolster and the black-bordered cloth I said to myself, "What kind of paramahamsa is this?"[1]

Going nearer, I found him half leaning against the bolster with his hands clasped around his drawn-up knees. Then I thought: "Evidently he is not used to pillows as gentlemen are. So perhaps he is the Paramahamsa." At his right, very near the pillow, sat a gentleman whose name, I came to know, was Rajendra Lal Mittra, later an Assistant Secretary to the Government of Bengal. A little farther off sat some others.

After a few moments the Master said to Rajendra Babu, "See whether Keshab is coming." Evidently Keshab Sen was expected that day.

Someone walked away a few steps and, coming back, said, "No, he isn't."

---

[1] A cloth with black borders, bolster, and so forth, regarded as articles of luxury, are used by householders. A paramahamsa, on the other hand, is an all-renouncing monk.

After a brief interval, hearing a sound outside, he said, "Please look once more."

Again someone went out and came back with the same reply.

Then Sri Ramakrishna laughed and said, quoting a popular saying, "The leaves rustle outside, and Radha says, 'Oh, here comes my Sweetheart!'" Continuing, he said: "You see, Keshab always tantalizes me like this. It is his way."

At dusk Keshab came with his party. Keshab bowed low before the Master, touching the ground with his forehead. The Master returned his salutation in the same manner.

Shortly afterwards Sri Ramakrishna said, in a state of partial consciousness: "Look! He has brought the whole Calcutta crowd. I am supposed to deliver a lecture. I won't do anything of the sort. Do it yourself if you like. Lecturing is none of my business."

Still in the ecstatic mood, he said with a divine smile: "I shall eat, drink, and be merry. I shall play and sleep. But I can't give lectures."

As Keshab Babu watched him, he became overpowered with divine emotion. Every now and then he said, "Ah me! Ah me!"

I too watched the Master and said to myself, "Can this be pretence?" I had never seen anything like it before.

Coming back from samadhi, the Master said to Keshab: "Keshab, once I went to your temple. In the course of your preaching I heard you say, 'We shall dive into the river of devotion and go straight to the Ocean of Satchidananda.' At once I looked up [at the gallery where Keshab's wife and the other ladies were sitting] and thought, 'Then what will become of these ladies?' You see, Keshab, you are householders. How can you reach the Ocean of Satchidananda all at once? You are like a mongoose with a brick tied to its tail. When something frightens it, it runs up the wall and sits in a niche. But how can it stay there any length of time? The brick pulls it down and it falls to the floor with a thud. You may practise a little meditation, but the weight of wife and children will pull you down. You may dive into the river of devotion, but you must come up again. You will alternately dive and come up. How can you dive and disappear once for all?"

Keshab Babu said: "Can't a householder ever succeed? What about Maharshi Devendra Nath Tagore?"

Twice or thrice the Master repeated softly, "Devendra Nath Tagore — Devendra — Devendra" and bowed to him several times.

Then he said: "Let me tell you a story. A man used to celebrate the Durga Puja at his house with great pomp. Goats were sacrificed from sunrise to sunset. But after a few years the sacrifice was not so imposing. Then someone said to him, 'How is it, sir, that the sacrifice at your place has become such a tame affair?' 'Don't you see?' he said. 'My teeth are gone now.' Devendra is now devoted to meditation and contemplation. It is only natural that he should be, at his advanced age. But no doubt he is a great man.

"You see, as long as a man is under maya's spell, he is like a green coconut. When you scoop out the soft kernel from a green coconut, you cannot help scraping a little of the shell at the same time. But in the case of a ripe and dry coconut, the shell and kernel are separated from each other. When you shake the fruit you can feel the kernel rattling inside. The man who is freed from maya is like a ripe and dry coconut. He feels the soul to be separated from the body. They are no longer connected with each other.

"It is the 'I' that creates all the trouble. Won't this wretched ego ever leave a person? You see a peepal tree growing from the rubbish of a tumbledown house. You cut it down today, but tomorrow you find a new sprout shooting up. It is the same with the ego. You may wash seven times a cup that onions have been kept in, but the wretched smell never leaves it."

In the course of the conversation he said to Keshab: "Well, Keshab, I understand that your Calcutta babus say that God does not exist. Is that true? A Calcutta babu wants to climb the stairs. He takes one step, but before taking the next he cries out: 'Oh, my side! My side!' and drops down unconscious. His relatives raise a hue and cry and send for a doctor, but before the doctor arrives the man is very likely dead. And people of such stamina say, 'There is no God'!"

After an hour or so the kirtan began. What I saw then I shall never forget either in this life or in the lives to come. Everybody danced, Keshab included. The Master was in the centre. All danced around him in a circle. During the dancing Sri Ramakrishna suddenly stood motionless, transfixed in samadhi. A long time passed this way. After hearing his words and seeing all this, I said to myself, "Yes, a paramahamsa indeed!"

Another day, probably in 1883, I visited the Master with a few young men from Srerampore. Looking at them, he asked, "Why have they come here?"

Myself: "To see you."

Master: "What's there to see in me? Why don't they look at the buildings and temples?"

Myself: "Sir, they haven't come to see those things. They have come to see you."

Master: "Ah! Then they must be flints. There is fire in them. You may keep a flint under water a thousand years, but the moment you strike it, sparks come out. They must be of that type. But it will be useless to try to strike fire out of me!"

At this last remark we all laughed. I do not recall now what other things he said to us that day. But it seems to me he told us about the renunciation of "woman and gold" and the impossibility of getting rid of the ego.

I visited him another day. When I bowed down to him and took a seat, he said, "Can you bring me some of that stuff — a little sour, a little sweet — that begins to fizz when you push down the cork?"

Myself: "Lemonade?"

Master: "Why don't you bring a bottle for me?"

I think I brought him a bottle. So far as I remember, I was alone with him that day. I asked him a few questions.

Myself: "Do you observe caste?"

Master: "How can I say yes? I ate curry at Keshab Sen's house. Let me tell you what once happened to me. A man with a long beard[2] brought some ice here, but I didn't feel like eating it. A little later someone brought me a piece of ice from the same man, and I ate it with great relish. You see, caste restrictions fall away of themselves. As coconut and palm trees grow up, the branches drop off of themselves. Caste conventions drop off like that. But don't tear them off as those fools do [meaning the Brahmos]."

Myself: "What do you think of Keshab Babu?"

Master: "Oh, he is a saintly man."

Myself: "And Trailokya Babu?"

Master: "A fine man. He sings very well."

Myself: "Shivanath Babu?"

Master: ". . . A very good man. But he argues."

Myself: "What is the difference between a Hindu and a Brahmo?"

Master: "There is not much difference. In the serenade we have here, one flutist plays a single note right along, while another plays various melodies. The Brahmos play one note, as it were; they hold to the formless aspect of God. But the Hindus bring out different melodies; that is to say, they enjoy God in his various aspects.

"The formless Deity and God with form may be likened to water and ice. The water freezes into ice. The ice melts into water through the heat of jnana [knowledge]. Water takes the form of ice through the cooling influence of bhakti [devotion].

"The Reality is one. People give It various names. Take the case of a lake with four landing-ghats on its four banks. People who draw water

_____
[2] Perhaps the Master meant a Muslim.

at one ghat call it 'jal,' and those who draw it at the second ghat call it 'pani.' At the third ghat they call it 'water,' and at the fourth, 'aqua.' But it is one and the same thing: water."

I told the Master that I had met Achalananda Tirthavadhuta of Barisal.

Master: "Isn't that Ramkumar of Kotrang?"

Myself: "Yes, sir."

Master: "How did you like him?"

Myself: "Very much."

Master: "Well, whom do you like better — him or me?"

Myself: "Oh, can there be any comparison between you two? He is a scholar, an erudite person; but are you one?"

Sri Ramakrishna was a little puzzled at my reply and became silent. A moment later I said: "He may be a scholar, but you are full of fun! There is great fun in your company."

At this the Master laughed and said: "Well said! Well said! Right you are!"

He asked me, "Have you seen my Panchavati?"

Myself: "Yes, sir."

He told me a little of what he had practised there — his various religious austerities. He also told me about Nangta [Tota Puri].

Then I asked him, "How can I realize God?"

Master: "You see, he is constantly attracting us, as a magnet attracts iron. But the iron cannot come to the magnet if it is covered with dirt. When the dirt is washed away, the iron is instantly drawn to the magnet. Weep for God and the tears will wash away the dirt from your mind."

As I was writing down his words, he remarked: "Look here. Only repeating the word *siddhi* will not produce intoxication. You must actually get some hemp, rub it in water, and then drink the solution. . . ."

Later he said: "Since you are going to lead a householder's life, create a roseate intoxication in your mind with the thought of God. You will be doing your duties, but let that pleasant intoxication remain with you. You cannot, of course, like Shukadeva, be so inebriated with the thought of God that you will lie naked and unconscious. As long as you have to live in the world, give God the power of attorney. Make over all your responsibilities to him. Let him do as he likes. Live in the world like a maidservant in a rich man's house. She bathes her master's children, washes them, feeds them, and takes affectionate care of them in many ways, as if they were her own children, but in her heart she knows very well that they do not belong to her. No sooner is she dismissed than all is over. She has no more relationship with the children.

"Before breaking open the jackfruit you should rub your hands with oil in order to protect them from the sticky juice. Likewise, protect yourself with the oil of devotion. Then the world will not cling to you and you will not be affected by it."

All this time Sri Ramakrishna was seated on the floor. Now he got up and stretched himself on his cot.

He said to me, "Fan me a little."

I began to fan him and he was silent.

After a while he said: "Oh, it's so hot! Why don't you dip the fan in water?"

"Ah!" I said. "You have your fancies, too!"

The Master smiled and drawled out, "And — why — not?"

"Very well!" I said. "Have your full measure of them."

I cannot express in words how immensely I enjoyed his company that day.

The last time I visited him I had with me the headmaster of our school, who had just then graduated. As soon as Sri Ramakrishna saw him, he asked me: "Where did you pick him up? He's a fine fellow!"

Then he continued: "You are a lawyer. You are very clever. Can you give me a little of your cleverness? The other day your father came here and stayed three days."

Myself: "How did you find him?"

Master: "A nice man. But now and then he talks nonsense."

Myself: "Please help him get over it when you see him next."

At this Sri Ramakrishna smiled a little.

Myself: "Please give us a few instructions."

Master: "Do you know Hriday?"

Myself: "Your nephew? I know him only by name."

Master: "Hriday used to say to me: 'Uncle, please don't give out your stock of instructions all at once. Why should you repeat the same things over and over again?' I would reply: 'You fool, what's that to you? These are my words and if I like I shall repeat them a hundred thousand times. You keep quiet!'"

Myself (smiling): "Exactly so!"

A little later he sat up on the bed. He repeated "Om" several times and began to sing a song whose first line is: "Dive deep, O mind, dive deep in the Ocean of God's Beauty."

Hardly had he sung one or two lines when he himself dived deep and was lost in samadhi.

When the samadhi was over, he began to pace the room and with both hands pulled up the cloth he was wearing till it reached his waist. One end of it was trailing on the floor and the other was hanging loose.

Nudging my companion, I whispered, "See how nicely he wears his cloth!"

A moment later he threw away the cloth, with the words: "Ugh! What a nuisance! Off with it!"

He began to pace up and down the room naked. From the northern end of the room he brought an umbrella and a stick, and asked us, "Are these yours?"

Scarcely had I replied no when he said: "I knew it. I can judge a man by his stick and umbrella. They must belong to that man who was here some time ago and swallowed a lot of my words without understanding them."

A few minutes later he sat down, still naked, on the northern end of his cot, facing the west, and asked me, "Well, do you consider me ungentlemanly?"

Myself: "Of course not. You are a perfect gentleman. But why do you ask me that?"

Master: "You see, Shivanath and others don't think I am a gentleman. When they come I have to wrap a cloth or something around me. Do you know Girish Ghosh?"

Myself: "Which Girish Ghosh? The one who is in the theatre?"

Master: "Yes."

Myself: "I have never seen him. But I know him by reputation."

Master: "A good man."

Myself: "They say he drinks."

Master: "Let him! Let him! How long will he continue that? Do you know Narendra?"

Myself: "No, sir."

Master: "I wish very much that you could meet him. He has passed the B. A. examination and is unmarried."

Myself: "Very well, sir. I shall meet him."

Master: "Today there will be a kirtan at Ram Datta's house. You may meet him there. Please go there this evening."

Myself: "All right."

Master: "Yes, do. Don't forget."

Myself: "It is your command. Shall I not obey it? Surely I will go."

He showed us the pictures in his room and asked me whether a picture of Buddha could be had.

Myself: "Very likely."

Master: "Please get one for me."

Myself: "Very well. I'll bring one when I come again."

But alas, I never returned to Dakshineswar.

That evening I went to Ram Babu's house and met Narendra. In one of the rooms the Master sat reclining against a pillow. Narendra sat at his right, and I in front.

He asked Narendra to talk with me. But Narendra said: "I have a bad headache today. I don't feel like talking."

I replied, "Then let us put it off until another day."

And that came to pass in May or June of 1897, at Almora. The will of the Master had to be fulfilled, and it was fulfilled after twelve years. Ah, how happily I spent those few days with Swami Vivekananda at Almora! Sometimes at his house, sometimes at mine, and one day on the top of a hill with nobody accompanying us. I never met him after that. It was as if to fulfill the Master's wish that we saw each other at Almora.

I saw the Master not more than four or five times, but in that short time we became so intimate that I felt as if we had been classmates. How much liberty I took while speaking with him! But no sooner had I left his presence than it flashed on me: "Goodness gracious! Think where I have been!" What I saw and received in those few days has sweetened my whole life. That Elysian smile of his, laden with nectar, I have locked up in the secret closet of my memory. That is the unending treasure of a hapless person like myself. A thrill of joy passes through my heart when I think how a grain of the bliss shed from that laughter has been sweetening the lives of millions, even in distant America.

[From: *The Gospel of Sri Ramakrishna*, tr. by Swami Nikhilananda (New York: Ramakrishna-Vivekananda Center), 1969]

IV
Appendix

A group of Sri Ramakrishna's devotees

Front row: Tarak Datta, Akshay Sen, Girish Ghosh, Swami Adbhutananda, M. (Mahendra Nath Gupta)
Middle row: Kalipada Ghosh, Devendra Majumdar, Swami Advaitananda
Back row: Devendra Chakrabarty, unknown, unknown, Abinash Mukhopadhyay, Mahendra Kaviraj, Vijay Majumdar

41

Sri Ramakrishna: Some New Findings

Swami Saradananda

Swami Saradananda had planned to write a sixth part for Sri Sri
Ramakrishna Lilaprasanga *(Sri Ramakrishna, The Great Master).*
With that in mind, he kept two small notebooks in which he jotted down
information gathered from various people as they reminisced about the
Master, as well as ideas that came to him from time to time. It was in one
of these notebooks that he made a note of his plan for a sixth part of the
Lilaprasanga, *called "Sri Ramakrishna in Cossipore."*

Swami Saradananda's plan never materialized, but he did write three
further articles, based on his notes, which were incorporated in the fifth
part of the Lilaprasanga. *The unused portions of Swami Saradananda's*
notebooks have been published by Swami Nirlepananda (a grandson of
Yogin-ma) in a small book, Bhagavan Sri Sri Ramakrishnadeva, *and*
the following is translated from that work.

From Yogin-ma

When Holy Mother was living in Dakshineswar, Sri Ramakrishna
would often ask her opinion on various matters. Mother would always
reply: "Please excuse me. I would rather not answer right now. I shall
give you my opinion later."

"Why not now? With whom are you going to consult?" the Master
would insist.

But the Mother's reply would invariably be: "Oh no. Let me think a
little and then I shall talk with you about it."

Returning to the nahabat, the Mother would pray fervently to the
Divine Mother: "Please tell me, Mother, what to say."

As a result of her prayers, Holy Mother would get an answer to the Master's question, which she would then tell him.

*   *   *

When Sri Ramakrishna was gravely ill at the Cossipore garden house, Holy Mother was stricken with grief. One day she had a vision: A black girl with long hair appeared and sat near her. Realizing that it was Mother Kali, she exclaimed: "Oh, you have come!"

"Yes, I have come from Dakshineswar."

After further conversation, Holy Mother observed that the girl's neck was bent to one side. She asked: "What has happened to your neck?"

Mother Kali: "Well, I have a sore throat."

Holy Mother: "My goodness! The Master has a sore throat and you also have it?"

Mother Kali: "That is true."

Thus, Holy Mother was made to understand that the Divine Mother and Sri Ramakrishna were one and the same.

*   *   *

On another day in Cossipore Holy Mother carried the Master's food to his room, which was on the upper floor. The Master asked her, "Do you know how to play *asta-kaste*?" [*This is a game similar to English "ludo" or American "parcheesi."*]

Holy Mother: "No."

Master: "If one can pair two checkers, the opponent cannot take them. Likewise, one should unite oneself with the Chosen Deity and thus be rid of fear. Otherwise, a ripe checker [that is, one which is near the goal], if it is still single can be turned back. If a person can move in this world with his Chosen Deity like a pair of checkers, he will be saved."

As Holy Mother listened she continued with a small household task in which she had been engaged. Suddenly the Master said jokingly, "Are you listening to me or not?" Holy Mother was embarrassed.

*   *   *

One day Yogin-ma went to Dakshineswar with Balaram's wife, taking some kshir-kamala [rice pudding with orange] that she had made for the Master. While there, Yogin-ma heard that Balaram would be returning from Vrindaban the following morning. She went again the next afternoon, and the Master told her that he had saved some of her delicious pudding for Rakhal and Balaram and had fed them.

*   *   *

Usually either Ramdayal [Balaram Babu's priest] or Master Mahashay arranged for kirtan at Dakshineswar. Once the Master sent Haripada to invite Yogin-ma, Bhavini, and some other Calcutta devotees for one of these occasions. When they arrived, the Master asked them to sit on a blanket on the northern verandah. The kirtan that day was dull. The singer made so many gestures with his hands that he appeared to be quarrelling with someone. The Master at no time was ecstatic. He spent his time chatting with others.

When the kirtan was over, the Master said: "Ram, you people did not dance during the kirtan. Why not?"

"Do monkeys dance of their own accord?" Ram Babu replied. "Sir, you did not dance, so how could we?"

Then the Master asked Yogin-ma and the women devotees to visit Mother Kali. When they returned to the Master's room they found him clad in a green shirt, dancing with the devotees and singing this song:

> Is Kali, my Mother, really black?
> The Naked One, of blackest hue,
> Lights the Lotus of the Heart . . .

Yogin-ma and the others entered the room and stood to one side. By nine o'clock that evening the Master still had not come down from ecstasy.

Yogin-ma was anxious to return home because Bhavini's mother would make a fuss if they were too late. They were about to leave accompanied by Haripada when all were astonished to hear the Master suddenly shout in ecstasy. He then came down to the normal plane and asked, "Who is leaving without taking any prasad?"

Haripada replied, "We are leaving, sir."

The Master gave prasad to Haripada, Yogin-ma, and the other women devotees. After that they left, arriving home at midnight.

*   *   *

The Master called Bhavini "the cook of Vaikuntha [heaven] — perfect in preparing sukta [a vegetable soup made with bitter squash]."

Once the Master went with Yogin-ma and some others to visit Jadu Mallik's garden house, where he sang and gave the devotees advice.

On another occasion he went to the Beadon garden [in Calcutta] to see some Masonic symbols along with Golap-ma and others. It was nine o'clock in the morning and all were hungry and thirsty. One of the devotees bought two pice worth of rasamundi [sweets] and offered them to the Master, who ate them all and then drank a glass of water. This satisfied the hunger and thirst of everyone. Golap-ma had hoped that the Master would give her some prasad, but she now discovered that she was full to her heart's content. The Master's satisfaction gave satisfaction to all. They were amazed and finally told the Master about it.

*   *   *

Once when Yogin-ma was in a disturbed state of mind, she decided to go to the Master and tell him about her problems. Early one morning she left for Dakshineswar on foot, and on arrival she discovered that Gopal's mother [Aghoremani Devi] was also there.

The Master was standing on the northern verandah, leaning against the wall and as soon as she saw him, Yogin-ma forgot all her worries. She had plucked some flowers from the garden and tied them in the corner of her cloth. "What are you carrying?" the Master asked.

Yogin-ma showed him the flowers and offered them at his feet. In ecstasy the Master touched one foot to her head. Gopal's mother told her to hold the Master's foot to her chest, which she did.

After the passing away of the Master, Yogin-ma was practising japam one day when she heard a voice say, "The imprint of the lotus feet of Gadadhar [an epithet of Vishnu as well as the boyhood name of Sri Ramakrishna] is on your chest."

*   *   *

Another day Yogin-ma went to Dakshineswar along with Gauri-ma. That day Tarak's [Swami Shivananda's] father was there. The Master was very pleased to see him and touched his chest and head. Yogin-ma was reluctant to leave the Master, but the boat was waiting for her, so she saluted him and left. Two days later Yogin-ma and Gauri-ma came back to Dakshineswar from Sukhchar (Khardah) via Panihati. They had bought some sandesh [sweets] for the Master, but Gauri-ma secretly withheld some for Nityagopal, and so the Master could not eat them. No one could understand why he refused them. The mystery was solved later.[1]

*   *   *

It was the month of Jaishtha [May-June] 1885 — the last Panihati festival attended by the Master. The Master had asked Yogin-ma to cook for the devotees who were supposed to go with him. Golap-ma assisted her. While the Master was having his meal, a number of devotees arrived, and still more came late. In any event all the food was consumed and there was nothing left for the women devotees. Holy Mother then hurriedly cooked rice and a vegetable curry with some ripe eggplants, green plantains, etc., and it was delicious. Yogin-ma, along with several others, went in the same boat with the Master.

*   *   *

One day early in the morning Yogin-ma and Golap-ma arrived at Cossipore. They had brought some food for the Master, which they sent to him. When he learned of their arrival, he asked that they wait down-

---

[1] Sri Ramakrishna could not touch food that had not been offered to the Divine Mother, and since a portion had been set aside for someone, the food could not be offered, even mentally, to her.

stairs. After a while he sent for them, saying: "These are my children. Ask them to come here." The room was full of his men devotees to whom he had been telling the story of a salt doll that went to measure the depth of the ocean.

The Master blessed Yogin-ma and Golap-ma, touching their heads, and then asked them to go downstairs again. Rakhal Maharaj was seated on the Master's right and said to him, "Yogin-ma wants to salute you by touching your feet." The Master then extended his feet, and she touched them with her head and left the room.

One night in the Cossipore garden house the Master had a terrible hemorrhage. The next morning Yogin-ma went to see the Master and say good-bye before leaving for Vrindaban. The Master asked her to take a picture of Mother Yashoda from the wall. He worshipped it with flowers and then pointed to his own feet. For a moment Yogin-ma did not understand. Then she realized what it was that the Master was indicating, and she worshipped his feet with flowers.

In the past, whenever Yogin-ma would say as she took leave of the Master, "Permit me to go," he would say, "Come back again." But this time he said nothing in reply, because he knew that she would not see him again.

From Golap-ma

On 11 March 1885 the Master had supper at Girish's house and stayed that night at the home of Balaram. Golap-ma did not eat anything at Girish's house, for which the Master scolded her. Later she asked Girish for a luchi [fried bread] and she ate that.

*   *   *

Once at midnight Golap-ma saw the Master in a high spiritual mood, strolling in the temple garden at Dakshineswar. It seemed to Golap-ma as though Mother Kali herself were strolling there, and her hair stood on end.

Gopal-dada [Swami Advaitananda] was sent one day to do some shopping. He spent half a rupee and tied his purchases up tightly in a piece of cloth. Golap-ma reported to the Master that the knot was so tight she could not untie it. On seeing so many groceries the Master was upset and said to Holy Mother, "Why did you ask Gopal to buy so many things?"

Holy Mother: "But there are a lot of devotees here."

Master: "You know that here at the Kali temple there is an arrangement to feed devotees and yet you have spent so much! Moreover, the heat from the fire will make you ill if you cook twice a day and in such large quantities. You don't have to cook so much, and anyway I am not going to eat all those things." He did not touch any of the food, and consequently it was all sent to the temple kitchens.

Holy Mother was hurt and she wept.

The Master then consoled her: "You know it is too great a burden for you. I spoke like that because I was concerned for your health. I have decided that henceforth I won't ask you to cook a particular dish for me. 'Eat what chance brings you' — I shall follow that method. If you have a desire to cook for me, please do, but don't ask me what I would like."

From Rakhal Maharaj

It was Swamiji [Vivekananda] who first took the Master to the house of Shashadhar Pandit. Swamiji had heard Shashadhar lecture and he was acquainted with Bhudhar, so he would go occasionally to see the pandit for the pleasure of arguing with him. Later Shashadhar gave a lecture at Alambazar and from there went to Dakshineswar to visit the Master.

From Shashi Maharaj

Niranjan presented a beautiful mosquito curtain to Gopal's mother, but she spent a sleepless night worrying that the curtain would be torn by mice. The next morning she came to the monastery [Baranagore] and returned the curtain.

Another day Gopal's mother had cooked rice and was trying to empty it onto her leaf plate, but because of the wind her leaf plate was skittering about and she could not manage it. Suddenly a small boy appeared and held the leaf plate steady while she emptied out her food. When she had finished, she thought to herself, "Who is this boy?" But no one was there.

From Kishori Mohan Roy (Abdul)

I had an agreement with my wife whereby both of us would be initiated by the same guru. One day when I was in my office I received a letter from my wife, who was at her father's house, asking me to send her some money as she had decided to be initiated with her mother by another guru. I was very upset and left for the Cossipore garden house to see the Master.

That day X— was the gatekeeper and he would not allow me to see the Master. Moreover, he scolded me as I approached the steps. At this my anguish became unbearable, and my eyes filled with tears. As I was leaving, Swamiji stopped me and asked, "Why do you look so awful today?" I told him everything. Swamiji said: "There is something wrong today. The Master has not yet (3:00 P.M.) taken his lunch. Some unwanted visitors went without warning to the Master's room and disturbed him. But that gatekeeper is a dumbbell. He could have told you frankly about the incident. All right, would you like to see the Master? Perhaps seeing you the Master will be happy and ask for some food from you. You know how the Master loves the devotees!"

I was not inclined to go, but Swamiji forced me. He scolded the gatekeeper and pushed me to the steps. Climbing the steps I reached the door of the Master's room. I saluted him from there and was about to leave when the Master beckoned me to come near him. I said, "Sir, your gatekeeper will scold me." He showed his thumb [a gesture of disdain] and asked me to come in. Then he showed me his throat. I said, "Sir, today you look so thin. Perhaps you have not eaten anything. Shall I bring you some food?" Farina pudding was ready in his room. He asked me to warm it up. After finishing his food, he said: "Is any amlaki [a fruit] available? Can you bring some?" Then he asked me to go with Gopal-dada to bring some amlaki from Sil's garden. While eating, the Master had asked Gopal-dada to tell me the story about the initiation of Suresh Mittra's wife. I was dumbfounded.

Gopal-dada said to me: "You see, Suresh Babu's wife wanted to take initiation from a particular guru, but Suresh Babu would not consent. As a result there was misunderstanding between them, and gradually the Master learned of it. The Master said to Suresh Babu, 'Suresh, what would you do if your wife wanted to be wicked?' Suresh, 'Well, how could I stop her?' Master: 'Why then are you opposing her wish to take initiation? After all she is trying to do something good.'"

I learned my lesson.

From Tejachandra Mittra

Tejachandra's first visit to the Master was in the summer of 1883 with Hari [Swami Turiyananda]. Hari had said, "Let us go and see a holy man." Tejachandra replied, "All right." It was a Sunday. Balaram Babu and Master Mahashay were present at Dakshineswar. The Master asked Tejachandra his name and said: "Very good. Come now and then." Later he questioned Hari Maharaj about Tejachandra.

On the first day the Master asked Tejachandra, "Are you married?" "Yes, sir," replied Tejachandra. Master, "All right, all right." Another day the Master asked, "Can I meet your wife?" "How is it possible, sir?" replied Tejachandra. Master: "All right, have your wife meet Hari one day. That will do." (Later the Master learned from Hari that her signs were good — i.e., she was a *vidyashakti*, who would help her husband realize God.)

The second visit was related by Tejachandra:

I did not find Hari at his house, so I went alone to Dakshineswar. The Master was pleased to see me. I don't remember who was present there that day. It was Saturday. The Master took me to the southern verandah and put his finger on my chest and tongue.

Master: "Whom do you like as your Chosen Deity?"

I did not respond.

Master: "Oh, you don't like to mention it. All right — [pointing to Kali] you like this deity — isn't that true?"

I nodded my head and the Master gave me the mantram. Later I said to the Master, "Sir, you have initiated me, but if my family guru is upset, will it not be harmful to me?"

Master: "Why? Take a mantram from him also. Or if you don't want to take a mantram from him, then give him his usual fee."

The Master fed me well, and I returned home after spending the whole day at Dakshineswar.

*   *   *

It was the Phalaharini Kali Puja day of 1884. Either Hari or Narayan was with me. When we reached Dakshineswar, the Master asked me to spend the night there. I was in a fix because on the one hand there was the Master's invitation, and on the other I had never stayed out overnight. I said to the Master: "Sir, I can stay but where shall I eat?" Master: "You will not have to think about that. I shall feed you." So I stayed and sent a message home through either Hari or Narayan. At midnight the Master took me to the Kali temple and then fed me at one o'clock in the morning.

We returned to his room and he asked me, "What do you want?" It came to my mind to ask for money, but I kept quiet. The Master said: "All right, all right. I understand what you want."

The next morning I returned home on foot.

From Atul Chandra Ghosh
[Brother of Girish Chandra Ghosh]

Sri Ramakrishna visited the house of Dinu Babu [in North Calcutta] one day, and my older brother, Girish, went to see him. When he returned I asked him, "What is this man like?"

"A hypocrite," he replied.

Thus I was dissuaded from making any further inquiries about the Master. But my brother soon became a frequent visitor to Dakshineswar, and I began to observe that Deven Babu and my brother were always whispering about him, keeping everything secret from me.

One day, probably in March 1885, I came home to find Deven Babu and Haripada with my brother, and when I entered the room they began whispering as usual. "What are you whispering about?" I asked. "Is it about the Paramahamsa? Your Master is not a paramahamsa, he is a rajahamsa.[2] He wears a red-bordered cloth, beautiful shirts, polished slippers, and sleeps on a comfortable bed."

I was talking this way when Sri Ramakrishna entered the room, accompanied by Narayan, saying, "Girish, it is by the grace of God that I have come to you." The Master had crossed the courtyard and climbed the steps to the first floor without any of us being aware of his presence until we heard his voice.

My brother and the others saluted him by lying full length on the floor, and since it was our family tradition that "a brahmin should be respected," I too saluted him with folded hands. The Master then took a seat. My brother sat in front of him while the rest of us sat in a circle around him.

My brother, Girish, introduced me saying, "This is my younger brother, but he has just been criticizing you." Then he looked at me and said: "Why are you silent now? Are you charmed by his presence?"

I was somewhat embarrassed, but not at all fearful or intimidated by the Master. So I said to him: "Sir, you are not a paramahamsa. You are a rajahamsa — that is what I was saying when you arrived."

The Master then said to my brother: "But this is not a criticism. When milk and water are mixed together, the swan separates them and drinks only the milk. Moreover, if you go to Varanasi you will find innumerable paramahamsas all over the place, and he has made me their king. It has been well said."

I could see that the Master was very intelligent and was not to be caught by my comments. I wanted to test his ego, so I asked, "Sir, what is your name?"

Caressing my back, the Master replied: "Do we have names? 'Hey,' 'Hello' — in this way one can call me and I will know who is being called."

"What is this?" I thought to myself. "Is he reading my mind?" I knew a little about thought-reading and had practised it for some time.

The Master continued: "Before today I was a little frightened of you. The other day I was passing by your house. Knowing that Girish was not at home, Narayan, who was with me, pointed out to me that you were seated on the verandah and asked whether he should speak to you as to the whereabouts of Girish. I forbade him and we went on to

---

[2] *Parama*=great, *hamsa*=swan. *Paramahamsa* signifies an illumined soul who lives in the world without being contaminated by worldliness, as a swan lives on water without being wetted by it. *Raja*=king, *hamsa*=swan. *Rajahamsa* means a majestic or regal-looking swan. Actually there is a species of swan called *rajahamsa*.

Balaram's. Seeing your long beard I was frightened of you, but now it is all gone."

"Sir," I replied, "how do I know the cause of your fear and why it has gone away today? I am the same man with the same beard."

About that time, M., Paltu, and the younger Naren entered. The Master said to M.: "Welcome, O three-and-a-half degree holder. Come in." They saluted the Master, smiling at him, and took their seats.

The conversation got underway with a discussion as to whether God is formless or with form. Then came the question of knowledge and devotion — which was the higher way.

The Master: "Both are ways, and one can attain God through both of them. The path of knowledge and the path of devotion both lead to the same goal, and after arriving there one understands that pure knowledge and pure devotion are one and the same." The conversation continued in this way for a while and then all left.

As time passed I learned that many of the devotees always took something to the Master when they visited him. I rarely presented anything to him. One day, sitting near the Master at Cossipore, I was thinking to myself that it would give me so much pleasure if he would ask me to bring him something.

Just then the Master said: "My stock of barley has run out. Rakhal, would you check the can?" Rakhal opened the can and found it empty.

Then the Master asked me: "Could you buy a can of barley for me and bring it tomorrow?" I hesitated, since it would not be possible for me to bring it the next day. Immediately he said: "Please buy the barley tomorrow morning and send it to Balaram. Inform him that I have no barley and that it must reach me without delay. He will make the necessary arrangements."

[From: *Vedanta Kesari* (Madras: Sri Ramakrishna Math), October-November 1975]

42

The Photographs of Sri Ramakrishna

Swami Vidyatmananda

Swami Vidyatmananda is a monk of the Ramakrishna Order and is well known for his writing ability.

Since the death of Sri Ramakrishna on August 16, 1886, two major biographies of the Master by Westerners have been published. The first is *Ramakrishna: His Life and Sayings,* by the famous Oxford orientalist Max Müller. Written in English, this book was brought out in 1898. The second is *The Life of Ramakrishna,* by the celebrated French author Romain Rolland. This work was published in 1929 in French. The English translation came out a year or so later. After a long lapse of time, in 1965, a new major biography of Sri Ramakrishna by a Westerner came out. Authored by Christopher Isherwood, it is entitled *Ramakrishna and His Disciples.*

Ramakrishna and His Disciples is well illustrated. The book contains a frontispiece and a sixteen-page portfolio containing thirty-two pictures. Since I was in India in 1963-64, Mr. Isherwood asked me to assist in assembling this picture collection and in writing descriptive notes concerning each of the illustrations. This proved to be a challenging assignment.

One aspect interested me deeply — namely, a study of the photographic portraits of Sri Ramakrishna. I discovered that knowledge concerning the photographs of the Master was fragmentary and scattered. There did not seem to exist in any one place definitive information about the circumstances of the Master's pictures, or even very much about his physical appearance. It seemed most important to have on hand any and

all information about the likenesses of the Master — not only for publication in the new biography, but so that general knowledge on the
subject should be as complete as possible.

Hence I did considerable research on the matter of Ramakrishna's
portraits, consulting available references and interviewing seniors of the
Ramakrishna Order. I was able to gather facts concerning the pictures
of Sri Ramakrishna which, so far as I know, have never before been
brought together in one place. I also discovered that there is a great deal
about Ramakrishna's appearance and pictures which is not known with
any degree of certainty.

It was desirable that the picture section in *Ramakrishna and His Disciples* should include all the photos that had been taken of Sri Ramakrishna. But to determine exactly what pictures had been taken of the
Master was not easy. There are in existence today a great number of
likenesses, similar, but varying from one to another in certain particulars. I found out, after study, that three pictures were taken of Sri
Ramakrishna during his lifetime. There is Picture 1, which shows Sri
Ramakrishna standing at Keshab Sen's house. Picture 2 is the studio
portrait of Ramakrishna, in which he is shown standing with his hand
on a column. Picture 3 is the famous "worshipped" pose, in which
Ramakrishna is seated in samadhi at Dakshineswar. Authentic copies of
the originals of these photos are not available. The many published
variations — including a famous painted portrait by the Czech artist
Frank Dvorak — were made by retouching or reworking the originals
or using originals as guides for new imaginary portraits.

In due course I learned that, in addition, two photos were taken of Sri
Ramakrishna's body on the afternoon of his death. These would be
counted Pictures 4 and 5. The two are similar; it is not known in which
order the exposures were taken and consequently which should be
numbered 4 and which 5.

Finally, Swami Nirvanananda, a vice-president of the Ramakrishna
Order, reported that he heard from Swami Akhandananda, a direct
disciple of Sri Ramakrishna, that Ram Chandra Datta had a photograph
taken of the Master. On seeing the print the Master remarked: "Who is
this? Am I such an angry man?" Ram Chandra gave no reply. He
understood that the photo did not meet the approval of the Master. So
Ram Chandra took the print, along with the negative, and threw them
in the Ganga. Devotees of today must applaud Ram Chandra's obedience to his guru's attitude, while at the same time regretting they will
for all time be denied knowing what the photograph looked like.

This would mean that altogether, as far as is known, Ramakrishna
was photographed six times, five of the photos being extant.

Hence four portraits of Ramakrishna appear in the new biography — Pictures 1, 2, 3, and either 4 or 5 — all of them now identified insofar as possible as to time, place, and other relevant circumstances.

It seemed to me that the information I gathered concerning Ramakrishna's pictures, in doing the assignment for *Ramakrishna and His Disciples*, was important. These findings are interesting and valuable. For this reason I have written down for publication all that I learned — the established facts as well as the points of mystery — so that it may be known to others and may be preserved. I am sorry I could not proceed farther, running down every clue, investigating every area of doubt. In any case, this is the proper work for an Indian research scholar, who knows Bengali. I hope such a person will come forward to carry on the small start I have made.

The reader will find it useful, when reading this article, to have prints of the pictures before him. Pictures 1, 2, and 3 are to be found in many publications; but so far as I know, neither Picture 4 nor 5 has been published anywhere in recent years except in *Ramakrishna and His Disciples*.

The information which I gathered, summarized in the pages which follow, came principally from four sources: *The Gospel of Sri Ramakrishna*, compiled by M., known in Bengali as the *Sri Sri Ramakrishna Kathamrita*; a book called *Sri Sarada Devi: the Holy Mother*, by Swami Tapasyananda and Swami Nikhilananda, which includes Holy Mother's conversations and is known in Bengali as *Mayer Katha*; seniors of the Ramakrishna Order, principally Swami Nirvanananda; and some articles authored by a Calcutta teacher, Mr. Surendra Nath Chakrabarty, which appeared in the early 1960s in the Bengali magazine of the Ramakrishna Mission, the *Udbodhan* [vol. 63, no. 9; vol. 64, no. 9-10]. A few other books besides the *Gospel* and *Holy Mother* provided material. Swami Nirvanananda referred not only to his memory but to one or two published Bengali works. Chakrabarty's articles were based on accounts in certain Bengali books, as well as on personal investigations which he made and on statements heard firsthand from seniors of the Ramakrishna Order and others.

The scheme of this article is as follows: First some general information about Sri Ramakrishna's physical appearance and his portrait is given. Then each of the photographs of the Master is considered one by one, as to what the photograph actually shows and what facts are known about the likeness, with authorities listed. Speculation and possibilities concerning each portrait are also given, clearly labeled as such.

A few general facts about Ramakrishna's appearance are known.

Ramakrishna's weight and height were not recorded. Swami Nir-vanananda, however, in providing guidance to a sculptor who was preparing the marble figure of Sri Ramakrishna installed early in the 1950s at Ramakrishna's birthplace, Kamarpukur, calculated that the Master was 5 feet 9 1/4 inches tall. The swami made this calculation on the basis of the length of a coat of Sri Ramakrishna, now at the Cossipore garden house. This is the coat the Master wore in Picture 2. By measuring the coat and calculating the relation of the coat to the figure, Swami Nirvanananda established Ramakrishna's height.

In her conversations published in *Sri Sarada Devi: the Holy Mother*, Holy Mother had the following to say about Sri Ramakrishna's appear-ance (fourth edition, p. 343):

"His complexion was like the colour of gold. . . . His complexion blended with the colour of the golden amulet he wore on his arm. When I used to rub him with oil, I could clearly see a lustre coming out of his entire body. . . . When he would come out of his room in the temple, people used to stand in line and say to one another, 'Ah, there he goes!' He was fairly stout. Mathur Babu gave him a low stool to sit on. It was a rather wide stool, but it was not quite big enough to hold him comfort-ably when he would sit cross-legged to take his meals. People would look at him wonderstruck when he went with slow, steady steps to the Ganga to take his bath.

"I never saw the Master sad. He was joyous in the company of everyone, were he a boy of five or a man of ripe old age."

In the *Gospel*, March 11, 1883, M. gives the following description:

"When it was time for his noon meal, Sri Ramakrishna put on a new yellow cloth and sat on the small couch. His golden complexion, blend-ing with his yellow cloth, enchanted the eyes of the devotees."

Pratap Chandra Majumdar was a contemporary of Sri Ramakrishna. In an article published in 1879 Majumdar gave the following firsthand description of the Master:

"The Hindu saint . . . is well formed naturally. . . . His face retains a fullness, a childlike tenderness, a profound visible humbleness, and unspeakable sweetness of expression, and a smile that I have seen on no other face that I can remember."

Swami Nirvanananda remembers an incident which gives some in-formation on certain of Ramakrishna's physical features. Swami Nir-vanananda's account follows:

"The following happened probably in the winter of 1918 when Swami Brahmananda was staying at Balaram Basu's house in Calcutta. I was present, as Maharaj's attendant.

"At that time a devoted lady of the Bhowanipore section of Calcutta, who was the wife of Achal Kumar Maitra, a solicitor, and an initiated disciple of Maharaj, occasionally used to come to visit Maharaj at Balaram Basu's house. From there she would usually go to Holy Mother's at the Udbodhan Office. Swami Saradananda, who lived at the Udbodhan Office, had great affection for the devoted lady. In due course the woman conceived the idea of having a marble statue of Sri Ramakrishna made for herself. She sought the advice of Swami Saradananda about the matter. Swami Saradananda encouraged the woman. At that time a well-known Maharashtrian sculptor was working in the Jhautala section of Calcutta. The woman went to the studio of this sculptor and placed an order for the statue. She asked the sculptor to make the statue as promptly as possible.

"After that the woman occasionally went to the Udbodhan Office to report on the progress of the statue.

"When the clay model was ready, the lady went to the Udbodhan Office and asked Swami Saradananda to please go to the studio and approve the model.

"Shortly after this conversation, Swami Saradananda, one morning, appeared at Balaram Basu's house to tell Maharaj the whole story of the statue. He appealed to Maharaj to go to the studio and approve the model.

"On hearing about the statue from Swami Saradananda, Maharaj kept silent for a while and then asked: 'Sharat, which figure of the Master should I approve? Even on the same day I saw the Master in many forms. Sometimes one would find him lean and emaciated, sitting silently in a corner. Again, after some time one would notice him singing kirtans, all the time clapping his hands, totally forgetful of his body and dress. Sometimes he would be lost in deep samadhi; then there would be a wonderful expression in his face, which beamed with celestial bliss, while his body radiated a divine light. At times he would be found to possess a stature much taller and stronger than the usual one and move from one end of the southern portico to the other with big, long steps.'

"Swami Saradananda replied humbly: 'Maharaj, I mean that particular figure of the Master which he himself said would be worshipped in every house. You are to approve the model of that form.'

"Maharaj, with a smiling face, replied, 'All right, I shall go.'

"That very afternoon arrangements were made for Maharaj to go to the studio. Swami Saradananda, Swami Shivananda, and many other monks accompanied Maharaj on that occasion. Golap-ma and Yogin-ma also went.

"Maharaj scrutinized the model minutely. Then he pointed out to the sculptor, 'You see, you have the Master bending forward a bit.'

"'Yes,' replied the sculptor. 'You see, sir, if anyone sits in that posture, with his hands clasped in front of the legs, he is bound to have to bend forward a little.'

"Maharaj replied: 'We never saw the Master sitting like that. What you say is applicable to ordinary individuals but was not true in the case of the Master. He had very long arms. His hands reached to his knees.'

"Further, Maharaj pointed out to the sculptor something about the Master's ears. 'You see, generally the ears of people begin above the eyebrows and you have modelled the ears of the Master in the same way. But the Master's ears began from below the line of his eyes.'

"The people present were extremely interested to hear these detailed facts about Ramakrishna's appearance. The sculptor agreed to correct the model according to Maharaj's instructions. He said, 'Please come after a week and I will have completed the model by that time.'

"After one week Maharaj and his party went to the studio again. Looking at the corrected model, Maharaj expressed deep satisfaction with the remark, 'Now it is quite exact.'

"The model was so vivid that everybody who accompanied Maharaj on that day felt the living presence of the Master in that model. In due course the marble statue was finished and delivered to the devotee, and it represented the Master's appearance faithfully; except that black spots appeared in the marble, changing the expression and making it seem advisable to cover the stone figure with paint. After the death of the devotee the statue found its way to the shrine of the Advaita Ashrama at Varanasi, where it is today, and has been for many years worshipped daily."

We learn from this account that Ramakrishna's arms were unusually long and that his ears were set unusually low on his head. Both of these attributes can be seen clearly in Picture 3. In Picture 1, if one looks carefully, one can see that the extended arm indeed looks very long. In Picture 2, the fact that the Master's ears are low is noticeable.

Chakrabarty quotes the Holy Mother as having said in the *Mayer Katha* (Second series of Conversations) that the men and women of the present day are very clever indeed. Incarnations of God have appeared on earth again and again, but only the people of the present age have been intelligent enough to invent a device for recording and preserving their likenesses — the camera.

Photography came into general use in the latter half of the nineteenth century. Ramakrishna lived from 1836 to 1886. He was the first avatar [Divine Incarnation] in history to be photographed. In the case of all previous Incarnations, it has been necessary, to gain the idea of their appearance, to depend upon descriptions handed down from ancient times or given by mystics to whom the avatars appeared in visions. Painters and sculptors did their best to give concrete form to such descriptions. Not so concerning the physical aspects of Sri Ramakrishna. Photographic portraits were taken which show him as he was.

The Holy Mother said something else of interest on this subject (*Sri Sarada Devi: the Holy Mother*, pp. 345-46). She stated that the Master's photograph not only represents him; to the devotee the photo is Sri Ramakrishna. "The body and the shadow are the same. And what is his picture but a shadow? If you pray to him constantly before his picture, then he manifests himself through the picture."

It appears that Sri Ramakrishna never sought to have his picture taken — did not, in fact, exactly agree to being photographed. Indeed, in his normal physical consciousness he seems to have discouraged efforts by those who wished to photograph him. Swami Abhedananda, a direct disciple of Sri Ramakrishna, stated in *Man O Manush* that Ramakrishna never allowed anyone to take his photograph.

Pratap Chandra Majumdar is quoted by Chakrabarty as follows, the quotation coming from the Bengali *Sri Ramakrishna Dev* by Shashi Bhushan Ghosh: "Sri Ramakrishna did not like to have his photograph taken by anybody. His photograph could not be taken unless he was in samadhi — hence not conscious of what was being done." Ramakrishna was in samadhi in Pictures 1, 2, and 3 as will be shown later.

Despite these statements we may speculate that Sri Ramakrishna was not opposed to being photographed. Nothing is unknown to the avatar, nor can anything be done against his will. If a picture was taken of Sri Ramakrishna we must assume it was taken with his consent. Speculation suggests that absence of ego resulted in Sri Ramakrishna's not caring to pose for a picture, while his love for mankind caused him to permit a tangible record of his form and appearance to be made.

Picture 1: Ramakrishna at Keshab's House[1]

This photo shows the following: Ramakrishna is seen standing, with his right arm extended, his left hand against his breast. The face is beaming; the eyes are nearly closed. A man is supporting the Master. Ramakrishna is dressed in the clothes of a Bengali gentleman: white cotton dhoti with a small border; long-sleeved white cotton punjabi or shirt; and an upper cloth or chadar. The chadar is tied around the waist. Several men are sitting on the floor. The window of a room and a slatted

---

[1] See p. 2.

sun screen are to be seen behind the men. There are sheets of cloth and a bolster on the floor, and a small rug at Ramakrishna's feet.

According to the Appendix of the *Kathamrita* (5/1/3, p. 11), the facts of Picture 1 are as follows: The photograph was taken on Sunday, September 21, 1879, at Keshab Chandra Sen's house, the Lily Cottage, located on Upper Circular Road, Calcutta, on the occasion of a Brahmo festival. Ramakrishna was in samadhi. His nephew, Hriday, is shown supporting him. The well-known singer and Brahmo devotee, Trailokya Nath Sanyal, was present.

Ramakrishna and Keshab became friends in March 1875. Keshab was an important figure in India at that time. He was a noted preacher and a leader in a reformed type of Hinduism known as the Brahmo movement. He had been to England where he had met Queen Victoria. But within the next few years after meeting Ramakrishna until his death in 1884, Keshab became a devoted follower of Ramakrishna, slowly changing his own ideas of religion and accepting those of the Master.

By September 1879 Keshab had known Ramakrishna for more than four years. He had become devoted to him. Having himself been photographed, Keshab, it can be assumed, felt a photo should be taken of Ramakrishna. Perhaps he simply wanted a photo made because he wished to possess a likeness for his own use. I was not able to discover anything as to how Keshab arranged for a photographer to be present at his house on September 21 or who the photographer was. An old print of his photo in the possession of the Vedanta Society of Southern California carries the following notation stamped on the back: "The Bengal Photographers. Est. 1862. 19/8, Bow Bazar Street, Calcutta." This suggests, but does not prove, that Keshab called in a photographer from this firm. I visited the Bow Bazar address in 1963. There is no trace of the Bengal Photographers; and inquiries made in Calcutta failed to reveal the fate of this organization or of any plates that may once have been in its possession.

What happened to the original negative is not known. Nor is it known how many prints were made or where they went. Only two prints can be accounted for. One print of Picture 1 was certainly obtained by Keshab and placed in his home. (It must have been this pose, for Picture 2 was not taken until later in the afternoon of December 10, 1881, after the conversation occurred which is reproduced below.) The following appears in the *Gospel* (Appendix, Saturday, December 10, 1881):

On the wall of Keshab's room hung a picture of Sri Ramakrishna absorbed in samadhi.

Rajendra (*to Keshab*): "Many people say that he [*pointing to the picture*] is an incarnation of Chaitanya."

Keshab (*looking at the picture*): "One doesn't see such samadhi. Only men like Christ, Muhammad, and Chaitanya experienced it."

The disposition of a second print of Picture 1 can be accounted for as follows: In the official *Life of Swami Vivekananda* published by the Advaita Ashrama, (vol. II, p. 84 of the three-volume edition) the statement is made that "Keshab Chandra Sen, in searching throughout India for mahapurushas [great souls], heard of this yogi (Pavhari Baba) as possessed of most exalted wisdom, and visited him." Chakrabarty says that Keshab presented a copy of Picture 1 to Pavhari Baba, citing as his authority a statement to this effect made by Swami Vishuddhananda, the seventh president of the Ramakrishna Math and Mission. It is known that Pavhari Baba — who lived in a cave at Ghazipur near Varanasi — possessed a picture of Ramakrishna on the basis of the following passage from the *Gospel* (October 27, 1882):

Another Brahmo devotee said to the Master: "Sir, these gentlemen visited Pavhari Baba. He lives in Ghazipur. He is a holy man like yourself." The Master could hardly talk. He only smiled. The devotee continued, "Sir, Pavhari Baba keeps your photograph in his room." Pointing to his body the Master said with a smile, "Just a pillowcase."

Chakrabarty gives the following account of what occurred at Keshab's September 21st festival, the source of his information being Swami Raghavananda, a disciple of Swami Brahmananda, who died in 1957. The devotional music threw Sri Ramakrishna into ecstasy. He uttered the word "Om" and stood up, raising his right hand. His outer senses left him and he went into samadhi. Fearing that the unconscious body would fall to the ground, Ramakrishna's nephew and attendant, Hriday, supported Sri Ramakrishna. Ramakrishna had probably been wearing his chadar either over his shoulders, or hanging folded from his left shoulder, as is the custom. But when Ramakrishna rose, the chadar fell to the ground. Hriday picked it up and tied it around Ramakrishna's waist for safekeeping. At this point Keshab had the picture taken.

Trailokya Sanyal was identified by Chakrabarty as the man sitting on the floor immediately to Ramakrishna's right. So far as I know, the others in the picture have not been identified.

Is there a meaning in the particular position of Ramakrishna's hands and the gesture of his fingers — that is, is he making a mudra? Swami Nirvanananda reports that Swami Premananda, a direct disciple of Sri Ramakrishna, speculated that the meaning is this: "Everything is there (up, right hand) not here in this world (left hand)."

The following comments can be made about the room in which the picture was taken. The floor appears to have been carpeted, and the carpet covered with sheets. This is a normal way to furnish a living room in India. Guests leave their shoes outside. Coming into the room, they sit on the sheet-covered floor, possibly reclining against bolsters. Nothing can be said about the window except that it appears to be large. The screen was apparently a movable sunscreen capable of being placed in openings to keep out the sun, while letting in the air. Apparently the picture was taken by strong natural light coming from the right.

There are two possibilities as to the exact spot where the picture was taken. It may have been taken in the drawing room on the second floor of the large two-storied Lily Cottage. It may have been taken in the ground-floor garden house, containing one large room and a verandah, in Keshab's yard. Swami Nirvanananda, Mr. Chakrabarty, and a knowledgeable native resident of Calcutta, Dr. B. P. Roy, think it logical that a festival should have been held in the garden room if, as there was at Keshab's house, such a room was available. With its cemented floor and separation from the domestic quarter, such a room makes a practical place for a group of men to meet, sing, and dance.

The Lily Cottage property has now been incorporated into the grounds of a school known as the Victoria Institution. A two-storied section of the original house, containing a bedroom in which Keshab died, has been preserved, the balance of the house has been torn down. The garden room in its entirety remains to this day, to the east of the main house, behind a monument marking the place of Keshab's cremation. The large windows of the garden room allow much natural light to enter the room.

A picture, taken in 1963, of the south facade of Keshab's garden room and the verandah on which it opens, has also been printed in the present issue [*Vedanta and the West*, March-April, 1965].

Picture 2: Studio Portrait of Ramakrishna[2]

This picture shows the following: Ramakrishna is standing with his right hand resting on a column. The column appears to be a "stage property" of a photographic studio. The fingers of the right hand appear to be somewhat rigid. The left hand, as in Picture 1, is against the breast. The position of the hands in Picture 2 is basically the same as in Picture 1 except that the right arm is not raised. Ramakrishna is dressed in a dhoti, a long-sleeved punjabi, and a dark coat. He is wearing "scuffs" — slippers with toes but no heels. There is a backdrop behind the figure and a small piece of carpeting lies on the floor. Ramakrishna's eyes are half-closed. He is smiling.

---

[2] See p. 12.

The following is known from the *Gospel* (Appendix, December 10, 1881): About 3:00 P.M. on Saturday, December 10, 1881, Ramakrishna arrived at the house of Manomohan Mittra in Calcutta. He rested there awhile and had some refreshments. Surendra Nath Mittra took the Master in a carriage to the studio of the Bengal Photographers in the Radhabazar section of Calcutta. The art of photography was explained to Ramakrishna, and he was shown how glass covered with silver nitrate takes an image. As the Master was being photographed he went into samadhi.

Ramakrishna referred to the experience in the following words (*Gospel*, Appendix, Saturday, December 10, 1881):

Master (*with a smile*): "Today I enjoyed very much the machine by which a man's picture is taken. One thing I noticed was that the impression doesn't stay on a bare piece of glass, but it remains when the glass is stained with a black solution. In the same way, mere hearing of spiritual talk doesn't leave any impression. People forget it soon afterwards. But they can retain spiritual instruction if they are stained inside with earnestness and devotion."

Ramakrishna also later spoke of his having been photographed in these words (*Gospel*, Sunday, February 24, 1884):

"I was taken to Radhabazar to be photographed. It had been arranged that I should go to Rajendra Mittra's house that day. I heard that Keshab would be there. I planned to tell him certain things, but I forgot it when I went to Radhabazar."

Ramakrishna referred to his knowledge of photography (*Gospel*, December 14, 1882):

"A man with 'green' bhakti cannot assimilate spiritual talk and instructions, but one with 'ripe' bhakti can. The image that falls on a photographic plate covered with black film is retained. On the other hand, thousands of images may be reflected on a bare piece of glass, but not one of them is retained. As the object moves away, the glass becomes the same as it was before. One cannot assimilate spiritual instruction unless one has already developed love of God."

It is speculated that what happened at the studio of the Bengal Photographers was the result of some advance planning on the part of Surendra. Ramakrishna had a lively interest in the things of the day. It is known that he went to a balloon ascension in the Calcutta Maidan, to a circus, to the zoo, to the theatre on several occasions, to the British fort at Calcutta, Fort William, and to a museum maintained by the Asiatic Society at its premises at 1, Park Street. It does not seem out of character that Ramakrishna should like to go to a photographic studio and learn about the workings of a camera. The *Gospel* account says he inquired into the processes. It can be speculated that Surendra had alerted the photographer in advance. And when the spiritual implications of the photographic process elevated Ramakrishna's mind so that he was not physically conscious, the photographer seized the opportunity to take his picture.

From poor prints it may look as though Ramakrishna is wearing high shoes. More detailed prints show that this is not true. The legs below the dhoti are in shadow, hence look dark. The scuffs are clearly discernible.

I was not able to discover any facts concerning the negative or the disposition of any of the original prints.

Shortly after the Studio Portrait was taken, Ramakrishna's figure was copied from it and (with the position of the arms reversed) inserted in an oil painting illustrative of the harmony of religions. This painting, on the basis of the following circumstantial evidence, was almost certainly made between December 10, 1881, and October 27, 1882. The studio pose, which is used in the painting, was taken on the first day and there is a reference in the *Gospel* to the completed painting on the second date. According to the Bengali *Life of Manomohan Mittra*, by Gauri Mohan Mittra, Ram Chandra Datta and Manomohan Mittra conceived an idea for a picture symbolizing the harmony of religions. Surendra arranged to have the picture painted. The painting shows a Christian church, a mosque, and a Shiva temple. In front of these places of worship are ranged a Shakta, a Vaishnava, a Shaiva, a Christian, a Muslim, and a Buddhist. Christ is dancing with Sri Chaitanya, their hands nearly touching, while three or four devotees look on. In the left corner stands Ramakrishna in a modification of the studio pose drawing Keshab's attention to the scene. This painting[3] also is reproduced in the present issue.

Ramakrishna saw the original painting at least once. The following is from the *Gospel*, October 27, 1882:

"The carriage arrived at the house of Suresh Mittra, who was a great devotee of the Master and whom he addressed affectionately as Surendra. He was not at home. The members of the household opened a room on the ground floor for the Master and his party. . . . Ramakrishna and the devotees were invited to the drawing room upstairs. The floor of the room was covered with a carpet and a white sheet. A few cushions were lying about. On the wall hung an oil painting especially painted for Surendra, in which Ramakrishna was pointing out to Keshab the harmony of Christianity, Islam, Buddhism, Hinduism, and other religions.

---

[3] See p. 486.

On seeing the picture Keshab had once said, 'Blessed is the man who conceived the idea.'"

Keshab's quotation is actually from a letter in Bengali which Keshab addressed to Surendra after seeing the painting. The letter is quoted in the *Life of Manomohan Mittra*.

It is known that a reproduction of the original painting existed, which the Master saw at least once, in the house of Nanda Bose. The following appears in the *Gospel* (Tuesday, July 28, 1885):

"Nanda Bose and his brother, Pashupati, saluted Ramakrishna. The devotees of the Master also arrived. Girish's brother, Atul, came, and Prasanna's father, who was a frequent visitor at Nanda's house, was there.

"A picture of Keshab's Navavidhan hung on the wall. Suresh Mittra, a beloved householder disciple of the Master, had had it painted. In this picture Sri Ramakrishna was pointing out to Keshab that people of different religions proceed to the same goal by different paths.

"Master: 'That was painted for Surendra.'

"Prasanna's father (*smiling*): 'You too are in that picture.'

"Master (*smiling*): 'Yes, it contains everything. That is the ideal of modern times.'"

I was not able to discover who painted the original. There is a blurred signature visible in a negative of the photograph of this picture in the possession of the Advaita Ashrama. The signature appears to be "Vily." I could not find out where the original is or how many copies were made and where they may be.

Picture 3: Ramakrishna at Dakshineswar[4]

It is, as the "worshipped" pose, probably the most important of the portraits. Yet facts about it are even less well established than about the other portraits.

The picture shows the following: Ramakrishna is seated on a small carpet or asana on the floor, his hands lightly clasped in front of him. He wears only a white cloth, covering his waist and thighs. Below the thighs the legs are not covered. One end of the cloth is thrown over the left shoulder. Part of his left foot is visible. The right foot is tucked inside. The right leg is placed over the sole of the left foot. All the fingers except the little fingers can be seen. The thumbs of both hands are touching each other, and the other fingers are interlocked. The figure is not sitting quite straight; that is, it is a little slumped to one side, making the head more to the left than to the right. The eyes are nearly closed; the sight seems

---

[4] See p. 356.

to be indrawn. The lips are parted, with the centre teeth of the upper jaw showing. In some prints the left arm looks a little flat and twisted.

Picture 3 was taken on the verandah of the Radhakanta temple at Dakshineswar. Ramakrishna was seated on the western side of the Radhakanta temple, facing across the courtyard towards the northern group of Shiva temples. The most authentic account of the circumstances of this photo comes from Swami Nirvanananda, who published the following small report in Bengali in the Udbodhan [vol. 64, no. 12] in 1963:

At Belur one day, Swami Akhandananda asked us in the course of conversation: "Well, do you know anything about the photo of Sri Ramakrishna that is worshipped these days?" On being told by us that we knew nothing that is really important, he related the following:

Bhavanath Chatterjee, the Master's devotee from Baranagore, wanted to take a photograph of the Master. One day he requested him very strongly to give his consent, and on the afternoon of the next day brought a photographer along with him from Baranagore. He could not make the Master agree. The Master just went away near the Radhakanta temple.

In the meantime Narendra arrived on the scene and heard everything. He said, "Wait a bit. I shall put everything straight." Saying this, he went to the verandah to the north of the Radhakanta temple where Sri Ramakrishna was sitting and started a religious conversation with him. The Master went into samadhi. Swamiji went and called the others and ordered them to get ready quickly to take the picture.

In the state of samadhi the Master's body was bent on one side and therefore the cameraman went to make him sit erect by softly adjusting his chin. But as soon as he touched his chin the whole body of the Master came up like a piece of paper — so light it was!

Swamiji then told him: "Oh, what are you doing? Be quick. Get the camera ready." The cameraman took the exposure as hurriedly as possible. The Master was completely unaware of this incident.

After some days, when Bhavanath brought the printed copy of the photo, the Master remarked: "This represents a high yogic state. This form will be worshipped in every home as time goes on."

It is interesting to note that Holy Mother said that Ramakrishna had said that he would have many devotees among white people.

I asked Swami Nirvanananda if it was normal for a person in samadhi to be weightless. The swami replied that he had heard that people experiencing samadhi of a certain type or depth generally do become light.

Chakrabarty gives a somewhat different and much more detailed account of the circumstances of Picture 3. This account is summarized in the paragraphs which follow. In the opinion of Swami Nirvanananda the account leaves something to be desired in the way of authentification as to certain particulars.

Picture 3 was taken through the efforts of Ramakrishna's devotee, Bhavanath Chatterjee, on the raised verandah outside the Radhakanta temple at Dakshineswar. The photographer was Abinash Chandra Dahn, who like Bhavanath lived in Baranagore, a northern suburb of Calcutta near the Dakshineswar temple and the Cossipore garden house. According to Chakrabarty the photo was taken on a Sunday in October 1883, at about 9:30 A.M. Chakrabarty quotes Swami Raghavananda as having said that the picture was taken with the Master seated on the western verandah of the Radhakanta temple. Chakrabarty lists the following sources for the fact that Abinash Chandra Dahn was the photographer: Swami Abhedananda said so in *Man O Manush*. Vaikuntha Sanyal said so in the Bengali *Lilamrita*. And Devendra Nath Majumdar said so in the Bengali *Mahatma Devendra Nath*. In the latter book Ramakrishna himself is quoted as having said to Devendra that Dahn took the picture.

The date and time of the picture were established by Chakrabarty in the following way: Dahn took the photograph on a Sunday two days before a son was born to him. Dahn's son was named Manmatha. The widow of Manmatha told Chakrabarty that she heard it from her father-in-law that it was on a Sunday two days before the birth of Manmatha that he had taken the picture, and she gave a Tuesday in October 1883 as Manmatha's birth date. The horoscope of Manmatha Dahn is not available, and the date of his birth is a matter of the memory of this widow. Swami Nirvanananda does not believe Picture 3 was taken in 1883. He thinks it was taken some time after February 2, 1884, because of the following reason. In the *Gospel* (February 2, 1884) we read that Sri Ramakrishna had just recently broken his left arm. Swami Nirvananananda is under the impression that the arm was never set properly and that it thereafter had a somewhat flattened and twisted appearance. He gained this impression from statements made to him by Swami Ambikananda, a disciple of Swami Brahmananda, who died in 1954. Swami Ambikananda was an artist. In painting Ramakrishna's figure he had come to the conclusion that the left arm as shown in prints of Picture 3, revealed a break which had never been set properly. A twisted, flattened appearance in the left arm is visible if one studies Picture 3. If this is the case, Picture 3 must have been taken after February 2, 1884. Finally, as to the time 9:30 A.M., this time was given by Sushil Kumar Banerjee in his Bengali book *Premer Thakur*. Swami Nirvanananda questions this, not only because Swami Akhandananda told him the picture had been taken in the afternoon, but because also it is known that the Banerjee's book in many particulars is not reliable.

Swami Abhedananda said in *Man O Manush* that when Abinash Dahn was removing the glass negative after having photographed the Master he accidentally dropped it and cracked one upper corner. Swami Abhedananda further reports that, due to this, Dahn cut off a portion of the upper part in the shape of a semicircle to disguise the fault. Swami Nirvanananda questions this because in some prints the crack can still be seen. He thinks Dahn gave the portrait an arched top merely to make it attractive. Many pictures of the Victorian period were arched at the top.

In any case, Dahn developed a few prints which he gave to Bhavanath.

Chakrabarty reports that Swami Vishuddhananda stated that when Ramakrishna saw the photo he went into ecstasy and, touching the photo to his head several times, said: "The photo is very nicely taken. This mood is very high — fully merged in Him. Here the Lord is fully depicted in his own nature."

We find from the *Gospel* (Sunday, March 1, 1885) that a portrait of himself hung in Ramakrishna's own room at Dakshineswar. Swami Nirvanananda feels sure it was Picture 3:

Sri Ramakrishna returned to his room accompanied by M. and another devotee carrying a tray of red powder. He offered a little of it to all the pictures of gods and goddesses in his room, but not to those of Jesus Christ and himself.

I was not able to determine what happened to the original negative of Picture 3. There is, however, some knowledge as to the disposition of the original prints. Swami Madhavananda, president of the Ramakrishna Math and Mission, said that he definitely knows there had been six originals. The following is a quotation from *Sri Sarada Devi: the Holy Mother*, page 342, and accounts for one of the prints.

Disciple: Mother, that photograph of Sri Ramakrishna which you have with you is a very good one. One feels it when one sees the picture. Well, is that a good likeness of the Master?

Mother: Yes, that picture is very, very good. It originally belonged to a brahmin cook. Several prints were made of his first photograph. The brahmin took one of them. The picture was at first very dark, just like the image of Kali. Therefore it was given to the brahmin. When he left Dakshineswar for some place — I do not remember where — he gave it to me. I kept the photograph with the pictures of other gods and goddesses and worshipped it. At one time I lived on the ground floor of the nahabat. One day the Master came there, and at the sight of the picture he said, "Hello, what is all this?" Lakshmi and I had been cooking under the staircase. Then I saw the Master take in his hand the bel leaves and flowers kept there for worship and offer them to the photograph. He worshipped the picture. This is the same picture. That brahmin never returned, so the picture remained with me.

This picture which Ramakrishna worshipped is now at the Udbodhan Office in Calcutta. It is on the shrine, worshipped daily. This fact is authenticated by Swami Madhavananda, Swami Vireswarananda, and Swami Nirvanananda. Chakrabarty reports that Swami Atmabodhananda, who was the head of Udbodhan for many years until his death in 1959, told him the Udbodhan print was the one Ramakrishna worshipped at the nahabat.

According to Swami Vireswarananda, Gopaler-ma [Aghoremani Devi], a direct woman disciple of Sri Ramakrishna, obtained one of the original prints from Bhavanath. Further, Swami Vireswarananda states that Gopaler-ma died in Sister Nivedita's house in Baghbazar, and the picture was left with Holy Mother. When Mother's belongings were brought to Belur Math after her death, this picture was brought with them. This picture is now on the altar of Holy Mother's temple at Belur Math, where it is worshipped daily. That this is one of the originals was confirmed by Swami Madhavananda and Swami Nirvanananda.

A third original is upstairs in the so-called bedroom of Ramakrishna in the main temple at Belur Math. This print was originally in the Baranagore Math. When Belur Math was established Swami Vivekananda installed the photo in the original Belur Math shrine. It remained there for many years until removed to its present position in about 1938. This account of the third original was given by Swami Vireswarananda and Swami Nirvanananda. Swami Nirvanananda believes this was the print which originally hung in Ramakrishna's room at Dakshineswar, as it is known that when Ramakrishna was moved from Dakshineswar in 1885 his monastic disciples moved the Master's possessions with him, and when he died they took charge of them.

A fourth original was given by Swamiji to Pramadadas Mittra of Varanasi before he, Swamiji, went to America. Years later, perhaps about 1929, when the other originals had become so dim that it was difficult to make good negatives and prints from them, this print was discovered among the pages of a volume of the Encyclopedia Britannica, where it had remained for many years. It was unfaded. Hence it could be used for making new negatives. Swami Sankarananda, the sixth president of the Ramakrishna Math and Mission, saw the print in Varanasi, acquired it, and gave it to the Advaita Ashrama. Perhaps a majority of the prints now in existence are descended from this copy. I was not able to discover where this print is now. This account of the fourth original was given by Swamis Vireswarananda and Nirvanananda.

Pictures 4 and 5: Sri Ramakrishna After Death[5]

The pictures show the following: Ramakrishna's body is lying some-what on the left side on a decorated cot. The face looks very thin. The eyes are half-closed and the arms lie against the body. The right leg is above the left leg. Sandal paste has been placed on the forehead and garlands hung around the neck.

The cot is covered with flowers and garlands. There are at the four corners of the cot upright members for supporting a mosquito curtain. The top and bottom uprights of the cot's left side are tied with garlands. Part of the Cossipore garden house is shown behind. A pile of bedding (possibly bedding used by Ramakrishna, set out to sun) can be seen on the left. More than fifty people — devotees and friends — are seen in the picture, ranged behind the cot. About half of these people have been identified.

Balaram Basu is seen holding a staff with a symbol on the top of it. Chakrabarty identifies this as a symbol of the harmony of religions. In the symbol the trident of the Shaivites, the Om of the Advaitists, the kanthi (a hand holding a necklace of tulsi beads) of the Vaishnavas, the half-moon of the Muslims, and the cross of the Christians are seen.

The two photos are similar except that some of the devotees have changed their positions; and in one Narendra is wearing a chadar over the upper part of his body, while in the other he is bare from the waist up.

Readers of this article are likely to have seen a part of Picture 4 or 5. The upper portion, showing the devotees only, has been printed very often in books about Sri Ramakrishna. But in books sponsored by the Ramakrishna Order it has been traditional to omit the lower portion of the photo, in which Sri Ramakrishna's figure is shown — the reason being that devotees will find it too painful to see the emaciated condition of the body. And to the devotee it is inconceivable to think of Sri Ramakrishna as being dead.

The following is summarized from the *Life of Sri Ramakrishna*, pub-lished by the Advaita Ashrama: Ramakrishna died at the Cossipore garden house on August 16, 1886. At 1:02 A.M. he entered into maha-samadhi, a state of total absorption from which the mind does not return. By morning the news had spread all over Calcutta and people came in large numbers to have a last look at the Master's form. It was hoped by some that the Master was not dead but only in an unusually deep samadhi. At about noon Dr. Mahendralal Sarkar, who had been

---

[5] See facing page.

Two group pictures taken after Sri Ramakrishna's death at
the Cossipore garden house, August 16, 1886

attending Sri Ramakrishna, arrived. He examined the body and said that life had departed only half an hour before. Dr. Sarkar's opinion was accepted as final, and arrangements were made for the funeral.

A handwritten diary of Dr. Sarkar's is in the possession of Swami Advayananda of the Advaita Ashrama. I copied the following excerpt from the diary:

> Monday, August 16, 1886.
> to Paramahamsa whom I found, dead — he died last night at 1:00 A.M. He was lying on the left side with legs drawn up, eyes open, mouth partly open. His disciples, some at least, were under the impression that he was in samadhi, not dead. I dispelled this impression. I asked them to have his photograph taken and gave them Rs. 10/- as my contribution.

The Life account continues: At about five o'clock the body was brought downstairs and laid on a cot. It was dressed in an ochre cloth and decorated with sandal paste and flowers. The photograph was taken. An hour later the body was carried to the burning ghat at Cossipore, to the accompaniment of devotional music. Spectators wept as they saw the procession pass. The body was placed on the funeral pyre. Trailokya Sanyal sang some suitable songs. Within a couple of hours everything was finished.

The Cossipore burning ghat, on the bank of the Ganga almost directly across from the Belur Math, is still in daily use. A monument marks the place of Ramakrishna's cremation.

Referring to the Master, Holy Mother once told a devotee: "Really and truly he was God himself. He assumed this human body to remove the sorrows and sufferings of others. He moved about in disguise as a king walks through his city. He disappeared the moment he became known."

Disappeared? No, he was captured and kept on earth for the good of mankind. Captured and retained, that is, on film. To the devotee the photos of Ramakrishna are relics left by the living God. Indeed, they are more than that; as Holy Mother said, they are the tangible face and form of the Divine.

[From: *Vedanta and the West* (Hollywood: Vedanta Press), no. 172, March-April 1965]

43

The Temple Garden of Dakshineswar

(A Short Description)

M. (Mahendra Nath Gupta)

For thirty years (1855-1885) Sri Ramakrishna enacted his divine drama at the temple garden of Dakshineswar, so to the devotees of the Master every spot of this ground is holy. The tiled courtyard which Sri Rama-krishna crossed so many times, the porch where Swami Vivekananda had his famous first interview with the Master, the Kali temple where the Mother still stands just as she did when Sri Ramakrishna saw her come to life, the Panchavati where the Master practised his sadhana, the room where he lived and talked about God — these are well known to the devotees. They bring back vivid thoughts of their beloved Master, and they feel his presence.

In the eyes of the devotees Sri Ramakrishna is still in Dakshineswar and Dakshineswar is still as it was in the 1880s. Of course, due to the passing of time some minor changes have taken place in the temple garden. The temples have deteriorated, most of the trees growing during the Master's time are now dead, and pilgrims have turned the solitary temple garden into a crowded place. Such changes are inevitable. But until we can see the Master and the temple garden truly as they were and always will be, we are thankful to M. (Mahendra Nath Gupta, the recorder of The Gospel of Sri Ramakrishna*) for the following vivid account and description.*

1. Sri Ramakrishna in the Temple Garden

It is Sunday. The devotees have the day off, so they come in large numbers to the temple garden to visit Sri Ramakrishna. His door is open

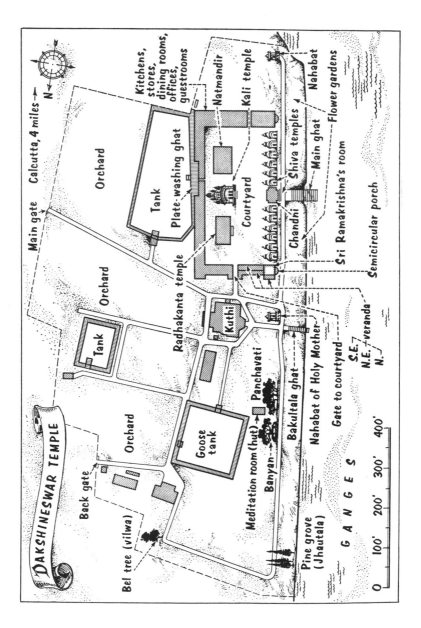

Map of the Dakshineswar temple garden

to everybody, and he talks freely with all, irrespective of caste or creed, sect or age. His visitors are monks, paramahamsas [illumined souls], Hindus, Christians, Brahmos, the followers of Shakti and Vishnu, men and women. Blessed was Rani Rasmani! She, out of her religious disposition, built this beautiful temple garden and brought Sri Ramakrishna, the embodiment of divinity, to this place. She made it possible for people to see and worship this God-man.

2. The Chandni [Porch] and Twelve Shiva Temples

The Kali temple of Dakshineswar is situated about five miles north of Calcutta on the bank of the holy river Ganga. One can go there by boat and land on the broad brick steps of the ghat leading to the temple. Sri Ramakrishna used to bathe at this ghat. East of the landing is the chandni, or porch. The roof of this building resembles an awning and is supported by pillars. The chandni is used mainly at night by the temple guards on duty. Their camp cots, wooden boxes, and water pots are often found lying around. The gentlemen of the neighbourhood come here regularly and sit awhile before bathing in the holy water. They gossip as they rub themselves with oil. Many holy men and women belonging to various Hindu sects come to the temple for prasad [consecrated food] and wait at the chandni till the bell is rung. Sometimes one can see an ochre-robed Bhairavi [a nun of the tantric sect] seated there holding a trident, which is the symbol of her Order. She is also welcome to have her noon meal at the guesthouse. The chandni is located at the centre of twelve Shiva temples — six of them on the north and six on the south. Seeing the twelve temples from a distance, passengers in boats on the Ganga point out to one another: "Look! There is the temple garden of Rani Rasmani."

3. Radhakanta Temple and the Courtyard

East of the chandni and twelve temples is a large tiled courtyard. There are two temples in the middle of the courtyard — the Radhakanta [Krishna] temple on the north side and the Kali [Divine Mother] temple on the south side. In the Radhakanta temple there are two images on the altar — Radha and Krishna — standing and facing west. Steps lead from the courtyard into the sanctuary. The floor of this temple is paved with marble. Chandeliers hang from the ceiling of the verandah. They are usually covered with red linen and used only during festive occasions. In front of the verandah is a row of columns. A guard sits at the entrance to the passage between two of these columns. In the afternoons the direct rays of the setting sun find their way into the sanctuary, so canvas screens have been placed between the columns. In the southeast corner of the verandah is a big jar containing holy water from the Ganga. Close to the threshold of the door leading into the sanctuary is a small brass vessel containing the sanctified water [charanamrita]. The devotees come, bow down to the deities, receive some drops of this sacred water in their right hand, and drink it with great reverence. Sri Ramakrishna's first appointment as a priest was in this temple.

4. Kali Temple

South of the Krishna temple is the Kali temple. The beautiful image of the Divine Mother is made out of black stone and her name is "Bhavatarini," or the Saviour of the World. The floor of this temple is paved with white and black marble. A high altar, with steps to the south, is also made out of stone . Above this is a thousand-petalled lotus made out of silver, on which Lord Shiva is lying, with his head to the south and feet to the north. The image of Shiva is made of white marble. On his chest stands the beautiful three-eyed image of Mother Kali, wearing a Varanasi silk sari and various ornaments.

The Mother's feet are adorned with several kinds of anklets called *nupur, gujari, pancham, panjeb,* and *chutki.* The women of western India wear panjebs. As Sri Ramakrishna had a wish that the Mother should wear panjebs, Mathur, the son-in-law of Rani Rasmani, bought them for her. The Mother's feet are also covered with scarlet hibiscus and fresh bel leaves touched with perfumed sandal paste. Her arms are adorned with various ornaments made of gold and set with jewels. On her lower arms are bracelets known as "coconut flowers," *paincha, bauti,* and *bala,* and on her upper arms are armlets called *tarr, baju,* and *tabiz,* the last one having an attached pendant. Around her neck there is a gold *cheke,* a pearl necklace of seven strings, a gold necklace of thirty-two strings, a chain of stars, and a gold garland of human skulls. There is a gold crown on her head, and her ears are adorned with *kanbala, kanpash, phul-jhumko* [a type of earring that looks like flowers], *chaudani,* and golden fish. Her aquiline nose is adorned with a beautiful gold ring with a pearl-drop attached.

The Divine Mother has three eyes, the third one representing divine vision. And she has four arms. A sword is in her upper left hand and a human head is in her lower left hand. With her upper right hand she indicates to her devotees "do not fear," and with her lower right hand she offers boons. [*Thus the symbol of Kali reconciles both the terrible aspect and the benign aspect of life. The Divine Mother is everything — both good and evil. She also represents energy, which can be both constructive or destructive.*] Around her waist there is a girdle of sculptured human arms as well as gold waist-chains called *neem fruit* and *komarpata.*

In the northeast corner of the shrine is a bed on which the Mother takes her rest. A *chamar* [the white bushy tail of the chamari cow] hangs on the wall. Sri Ramakrishna fanned the Divine Mother with that chamar many times. On the step of the altar is a silver glass full of drinking water for the Mother. To the west of the lotus altar is a lion made of eight metals, and to the east, a trident and an image of an iguana. Southeast of the altar stands an image of a she-fox, to the south an image of a bull made of black stone, and to the northeast a swan. There is an emblem of Narayana [Vishnu] on a small silver throne placed on the step of the front altar. On one side of the altar there is an image of Ramlala [the child Ramachandra], made of eight metals, which Sri Ramakrishna received from a monk, plus a small image of Baneshwara Shiva and images of other deities. The Divine Mother stands facing the south.

The sacred pitcher has been installed in front of the Divine Mother [at the south of the altar]. This pitcher is filled with water and is decorated with vermillion, flowers, and a garland. It is the symbol of the All-Auspicious Mother. Near the north wall there is a copper vessel filled with holy water of the Ganga, which the Mother uses to wash her face. Above the image of the Mother is a beautiful canopy, and behind her is a piece of Varanasi silk embroidered with flowers of many colours. Around the four corners of the holy image are twelve silver columns on the dais. The elegant canopy adds greatly to the beauty of the image.

This is a medium-sized temple. The entrances to the shrine are protected by strong, heavy doors, and a guard sits near one of them. At the threshold there is a small brass vessel containing sanctified water, which has been offered at the time of worship. The roof of the temple is adorned with nine pinnacles — four at the lower level, four at the middle, and one at the top. Sri Ramakrishna worshipped in this temple.

5. Natmandir (Theatre Hall)

In front of the Kali temple and just to the south is the spacious natmandir. It is rectangular and the terrace is supported by both inner and outer rows of columns. Theatrical performances take place here on special occasions, especially during the night of Kali Puja. On the front side of the roof of the natmandir there are images of Shiva and his followers, Nandi and Bhringi. Sri Ramakrishna used to salute Lord Shiva with folded hands before entering the Mother's temple, as if he were seeking his permission to enter the temple.

6. The Sacrificial Place

To the south of the natmandir is the place of sacrifice. A goat is sacrificed every new moon night.

7. Storeroom, Kitchen, and Guesthouse

West of the courtyard is the row of twelve Shiva temples, and on the three other sides are rooms with connecting corridors. The rooms to the east are the storeroom, the room for preserving sweets and fruits, the room for preparing food offerings, the vegetarian kitchen for Krishna, the nonvegetarian kitchen for Kali, and the long corridor that is used as a dining hall. At noon, after the food has been offered to the deities, the prasad is distributed among the guests, beggars, and mendicants at the guesthouse. They all eat on leaf plates. If any guest or monk does not want cooked food, he can go to the temple manager and ask for rice, lentils, and other things. The manager then instructs the storekeeper to give him what he wants.

The manager has his meals in his room. The owners of the Kali temple, who are descendants of Rani Rasmani, occasionally come to Dakshineswar and live in the kuthi [mansion], and they are served their meals there.

8. Office Quarters

On the south side of the courtyard is a row of rooms which are for the temple officers. The manager and cashier are always there. The storekeepers, servants, maidservants, priests, cooks, guards, and visitors are also to be seen moving around the office area. Some of these rooms are kept locked. They are storage places for sacred utensils, furniture, carpets, the canopy for the courtyard, and so on. A few of them were used as storerooms on the occasion of the birth anniversary festival held in honour of Sri Ramakrishna. The cooking for this great festival was done on the adjoining yard south of the office rooms.

On the north side of the courtyard there is a series of rooms, and the main entrance to the courtyard is in the middle. As at the chandni, guards are stationed here. People take off their shoes before entering the inner temple compound.

9. Sri Ramakrishna's Room

In the northwest corner of the courtyard and immediately to the north of the row of twelve Shiva temples is the well-known room where [for 14 years] Sri Ramakrishna passed his days in communion with God. To the west of this room is a semicircular verandah. Standing here facing west, Sri Ramakrishna would watch the holy river Ganga flow by. In front of the verandah is a narrow garden path running from north to south. On the other side of this path is the flower garden and then the embankment. From here, one can hear the sweet, melodious murmuring of the Ganga.

10. Nahabat (The Music Tower) and Bakul-tala

To the north of Sri Ramakrishna's room is a rectangular verandah, and next to that is a garden path running from east to west. North of this path is a flower garden, and on the other side of that the nahabat. Sri Ramakrishna's mother lived in the lower room [in another version, the upper room] of the nahabat, and later Holy Mother, Sri Sarada Devi, lived there. West of the nahabat are a bakul tree and a bathing ghat. The women of the neighbourhood bathe at this ghat. In 1877 Sri Ramakrishna's aged mother passed away there. Following the Hindu custom, the Master's dying mother was taken to this ghat and the lower half of her body was immersed in the holy water of the Ganga. She breathed her last in the presence of her weeping son.

There is a second nahabat [music tower] in the southwest corner of the temple garden, next to the office rooms.

11. Panchavati

A little north of the bakul tree is the Panchavati. This is a grove of five trees — banyan, pipal, ashoka, amlaki, and bel — which were planted under Sri Ramakrishna's supervision. After returning from his pilgrimage [in 1868] he spread the holy dust of Vrindaban around this place. The Master practised various kinds of sadhana [disciplines] in the Panchavati grove, sometimes going there alone at night. Later he often accompanied the devotees as they walked around the holy spot. East of the Panchavati is a thatched hut [now, a brick room], in which Sri Ramakrishna practised meditation and austerities [Advaita sadhana under Tota Puri].

Next to the Panchavati is an old banyan tree which has grown around a pipal tree, both looking as if they were one tree. The banyan is an ancient tree, and as a result there are many holes in it which are the homes of birds and other animals. Around this tree is a circular brick platform with steps on two sides — north and south. The platform is used by people who visit the temple garden and especially by those who wish to sit in solitude and meditate on God with the holy Ganga flowing before them. Sri Ramakrishna used to sit on the northwest corner of the platform and practise various kinds of spiritual disciplines. He would cry to the Divine Mother with a longing heart, as the cow longs for her calf.

Recently a branch of the pipal tree fell on this holy platform, though the branch had not been completely severed from the main tree. It seems that no other great soul has yet been born to sit there. Is that why nature is guarding this spot with the broken branch?

12. Jhau-tala [Pine grove] and Bel-tala

Going a little north of the Panchavati one reaches a fence of iron wire. North of this fence is the pine grove — a collection of four pine trees. Sri Ramakrishna and the devotees would use this place to answer the call of nature.

East of the pine grove is the bel-tala. Sitting under this bel tree, Sri Ramakrishna practised many difficult disciplines [especially tantric sadhanas under the guidance of Bhairavi Brahmani]. To the north of the pine grove and bel tree is the high boundary wall of the temple garden, and on the other side of the wall is a government magazine.

13. Kuthi [Mansion]

Coming out of the temple courtyard through the northern portico, one comes across a two-storied mansion called the kuthi. Whenever Rani Rasmani or her son-in-law Mathur and other relatives came to visit Dakshineswar, they stayed in this kuthi. During their lifetime Sri Rama-krishna lived [for 16 years] in a room on the west side of the ground floor of this mansion. From this room one can go to the bakul-tala ghat and have a very good view of the Ganga.

14. Gazi-tala and the Main Gate of the Temple Garden

There is a path running east to west between the northern portico of the courtyard and the kuthi. While walking east, one can see a beautiful pond with a concrete ghat on the right side. There is another ghat for this pond on the eastern side of the Kali temple, which is used to clean the sacred utensils and dishes. A pipal tree is next to the northern ghat. This place is called Gazi-tala. Long ago an old Muslim saint lived here, passing his days in the contemplation of God. His departed spirit is worshipped even today by Hindus and Muslims who live near the temple. [At Gazi-tala Sri Ramakrishna practised Islamic sadhana under the guidance of a Sufi named Govinda Roy.]

The main gate of the temple garden is a little east of the Gazi-tala. People who come from Alambazar or Calcutta enter the temple compound through this gate, and the people of Dakshineswar come through the northeastern gate, which is a little north of the main gate. A guard protects the main gate. When the Master would return late from Calcutta by carriage, sometimes even at midnight, the guard at the main gate would unlock the gate for him. Then the Master would invite the guard to his room and feed him fried bread and sweets which had been sent as prasad.

15. Goose Pond, Cowshed, and the Back Gate

There is another pond, called the goose pond, east of the Panchavati, and northeast of this are the stables and the cowshed. East of the cowshed is the back gate, or the northeastern gate, used by the people of Dakshineswar and by workers of the temple who live in the village with their families. Those without families live in quarters within the temple compound.

16. Flower Gardens

There is a narrow path running from the southern extremity of the temple garden straight north to the Panchavati. This path runs along the bank of the Ganga and has flowering plants on both sides. Another garden path runs from the west to the main gate on the east, between the temple complex and the kuthi. This path also is lined on both sides with flowering plants.

A third garden path begins at the Gazi-tala on the south and runs to the cowshed on the north. It is situated east of the kuthi and goose pond. The garden to the east of this path contains many flowering plants and fruit trees as well as a pond.

Early in the morning, before the eastern horizon becomes red, the morning service [*mangala-arati*] to the Divine Mother begins with the sweet sound of temple bells. In the nahabat, morning melodies are then played on the flageolet to the accompaniment of drums and cymbals. These are welcome sounds of love and joy to all, for the Mother of the Universe has awakened to bless her beloved children. Gardeners also start picking flowers for the worship of the deities at this time.

On the bank of the Ganga and just to the west of the Panchavati are a bel tree and a sweet-scented, milk-white *gulchi* flower tree. Sri Rama-krishna was very fond of *mallika* [a type of jasmine], *madhavi*, and *gulchi*. He brought a *madhavi* plant [a flowering creeper which Radha liked] from Vrindaban and planted it in the Panchavati. East of the goose pond and the kuthi is another pond around which are many flowering plants such as the *champak*, the five-faced hibiscus, the pendant hibiscus [resembling earrings], roses, and the *kanchan* [gold]. On a fence there is an *aparajita* [a blue flower used in the worship of the Divine Mother], and nearby are jasmine and *shefalika*.

West of the twelve Shiva temples, there are many flowering trees such as the white oleander, red oleander, rose, jasmine, and double-petalled jasmine. Also growing there are *dhutura* flowers, which are used for the worship of Shiva. Tulsi [basil] plants grow in brick vases between these flowering trees.

South of the nahabat are more double-petalled jasmine as well as other varieties of jasmine, gardenias, and roses. Two more flowering trees grow near the chandni ghat: the lotus oleander and the *kokilaksha*, or cuckoo-eyed flower. The colour of the latter resembles that of the eyes of a cuckoo. West of the Master's room there are quite a few plants: *Krishna-chura*, double-petalled jasmine, jasmine, gardenia, *mallika*, roses, hibiscus, white oleander, red oleander, five-faced hibiscus, china-rose, and so on.

Formerly Sri Ramakrishna picked flowers for worship. One day when he was plucking bel leaves from a bel tree near the Panchavati, a layer of bark came off the tree. At that moment he experienced that God, who dwells in every being and everything, must have felt pain at this. He never again picked bel leaves for worship. Another day while picking flowers he had a vision: He saw that the flowers of each tree formed a bouquet and all those bouquets hung around the neck of the cosmic form of Shiva. Thus he experienced that the worship of God is going on day and night. After that experience he could no longer pick flowers.

17. The Two Verandahs Adjacent to Sri Ramakrishna's Room

East of Sri Ramakrishna's room there is a verandah facing the temple courtyard. The Master used to sit here with the devotees and talk to them about God or sing kirtan. Another verandah is opposite this one, facing the north. Here the devotees used to celebrate the Master's birthday. They would sing devotional songs in chorus and eat prasad with him. Keshab Chandra Sen and his followers often met with the Master here to talk about God. Afterwards the Master would feed them puffed rice, coconut, fried bread [luchi], and sweets. On this same spot Sri Ramakrishna, seeing Narendra [Swami Vivekananda], went into samadhi.

18. The Abode of Bliss

The temple garden of Dakshineswar has become an abode of bliss. Daily worship with food offerings is done to the presiding deities of the temple garden — Bhavatarini Kali, Shiva, and Radha-Krishna. Guests and mendicants are well taken care of. On the west side one can have a view of the holy Ganga, and on the other side a view of the flower garden — full of various colours and sweet fragrances. In the midst of these surroundings lived an illumined person, absorbed in divine ecstasy day and night.

The Blissful Mother's endless festival is going on in this temple garden. Various kinds of melodies that are played in the nahabat reverberate through the garden, beginning early in the morning at mangala-arati. The music resumes at 9:00 A.M. when the worship begins, again at 12 noon during the food offering to the deities, at 4:00 P.M. when the temples are opened after the noon rest, then during the vesper service, and at last at 9:00 P.M. during the evening food offering. After this the priests put the deities to bed. The sacred music reminds us day and night that our Mother not only has created us but is constantly looking after us.

[From: *Sri Sri Ramakrishna Kathamrita*, by M. (Mahendra Nath Gupta) (Calcutta: Kathamrita Bhavan), vol. I, 1961]

A painting on the harmony of religions

Surendra Nath Mittra, a devotee of Sri Ramakrishna, had it painted. In this picture Sri Ramakrishna was shown pointing out to Keshab that people of different religions proceed to the same goal by different paths. Sri Ramakrishna: "That was painted for Surendra." Prasanna's father (*smiling*): "You too are in the picture." Sri Ramakrishna (*smiling*): "Yes, it contains everything. This is the ideal of modern times."

Index

(Brackets [ ] indicate chapters; RK = Ramakrishna)

Works by Swami Satprakashananda

The Goal and the Way: The Vedantic Approach to Life's Problems

The Universe, God, and God-Realization: From the viewpoint of Vedanta

Methods of Knowledge: Perceptual, Non-Perceptual, and Transcendental: According to Advaita Vedanta

Meditation: Its Process, Practice and Culmination

Hinduism and Christianity: Jesus Christ and His Teachings in the Light of Vedanta

Sri Ramakrishna's Life and Message in the Present Age; With the Author's Reminiscences of Holy Mother and Some Direct Disciples

Swami Vivekananda's Contribution to the Present Age

Pamphlets: Ethics and Religion; How is a Man Reborn?; The Use of Symbols in Religion; World Peace — How?

Works by Swami Chetanananda

Ramakrishna: A Biography in Pictures
(Biographical Introduction by Swami Smaranananda)

They Lived with God

Ramakrishna as We Saw Him

Sarada Devi: A Biography in Pictures
(Biographical Introduction by Swami Smaranananda)

Vedanta: Voice of Freedom

Meditation and Its Methods

A Guide to Spiritual Life

Swami Adbhutananda: Teachings and Reminiscences

Avadhuta Gita — The Song of the Ever-Free

Audio Tapes *(Sanskrit Chants with English translation)*: Echoes of the Eternal: Peace, Bliss, and Harmony *(3 tapes)*; Breath of the Eternal: Awakening, Reflection, and Illumination *(3 tapes)*

Video Tapes: Ramakrishna *(A Documentary)*; The Parables of Ramakrishna *(40 Parables of Ramakrishna)*; Vivekananda as We Saw Him *(A Documentary)*

Ramakrishna, Vivekananda, Vedanta, and other religious literature.
Call or write for more information:

Vedanta Bookshop
205 South Skinker Boulevard
St. Louis, Missouri 63105 U.S.A. (314)721-5118